Praise for *Family Interventions in Domestic Violence*

"This book makes significant advances in the field of domestic violence research. With its offerings of contemporary theoretical perspectives and original empirical findings, it is poised to be a valuable resource for researchers, clinicians, and policy makers alike." -- **Jamila Bookwala**, PhD, Associate Professor, Department of Psychology, Lafayette College

"... an eye opening book that offers pragmatic and innovative solutions on the prevention and treatment of intimate partner violence in the 21st century. As the founder of a gender-inclusive nationwide domestic violence victim's organization I implore public policy makers, law enforcement personnel, and those who work in the domestic violence and mental health fields to read this book! As well it should be a required text for college students going into those fields. As Dr. Straus so aptly states in chapter 3 of the book, 'It is time to make the effort be one that is aimed at ending all partner violence, not just violence against women. Only then will women, as well as all other human beings, be safe in their own homes.' I absolutely concur!" -- **Jan Brown**, Founder and Executive Director, Domestic Abuse Helpline for Men and Women

"For nearly four decades, intimate violence research, policy, and treatment have been intertwined with feminist theory, in general, and patriarchy theory, in particular. While this conceptual marriage has served the political agenda of advocates and eased the communication of the causes and consequences of intimate violence, this limited theoretical frame focuses our attention of partner assault as a woman's issue, and not a human issue. With the present anthology, researchers, clinicians, policymakers, and advocates have a compilation of articles that examines the gender-intimate violence relationship. The authors do not assume a male-female difference in the forms or consequences of intimate violence; rather they critically evaluate the literature and carefully draw their conclusions based on this evidence. All gender-based assumptions are open to questioning ... There are no simple answers; these chapters offer the reader insights into the complexity of intimate violence. They represent a step-forward in the understanding and treatment of a problem that characterizes so many relationships. Perhaps, most importantly, these chapters push the debate to the next level ... As clinicians and policymakers, the "one-model-fits-all" needs replacing. We have to appreciate intimate violence's diversity and tailor our interventions and policies. This book shows the reader where we have been and where we must go if we wish to confront adequately this social problem." -- **David B. Sugarman**, PhD, Chair & Professor of Psychology, Rhode Island College

Family Interventions in Domestic Violence

John Hamel, LCSW, a graduate of the University of California, Los Angeles, has been a court-certified Batterer Intervention Provider since 1992, headquartered in the Greater San Francisco Bay Area. His clinical services included family violence assessments and treatment programs for abusive men, women and families. Mr. Hamel has provided consultation and training to mental health professionals, batterer intervention providers, victim advocates, attorneys and law enforcement, and has served as an expert court witness in criminal and family law courts. His articles on partner violence have appeared in the *Family Violence & Sexual Assault Bulletin* and *International Journal of Men's Health*. Mr. Hamel is also the author of *Gender-Inclusive Treatment of Intimate Partner Abuse: A Comprehensive Approach* (Springer, 2005). His web site is www.JohnHamel.net.

Tonia L. Nicholls, PhD, obtained a doctorate in Law and Forensic Psychology from Simon Fraser University in 2002. The Social Sciences and Humanities Research Council of Canada and the Michael Smith Foundation for Health Research funded her three-year postdoctoral fellowship in the department of psychiatry, University of British Columbia and the BC Institute Against Family Violence. Currently, she is Senior Research Fellow, Forensic Psychiatric Services Commission, BC Mental Health and Addictions Services and Adjunct Professor of Psychology, Simon Fraser University. Her scholarly work has earned her "Brain Star" awards from the Institute of Neurosciences Mental Health, and Addictions, Canadian Institutes of Health Research, the Canadian Psychological Association President's New Researcher Award, and the American Psychological Association Award for Distinguished Professional Contribution by a Graduate Student.

Family Interventions in Domestic Violence

*A Handbook of Gender-Inclusive
Theory and Treatment*

John Hamel, LCSW
Tonia L. Nicholls, PhD
Editors

SPRINGER PUBLISHING COMPANY
New York

HV
6626.2
.F345
2007

Springer Publishing Company, LLC
11 West 42nd Street
New York, NY 10036

Acquisitions Editor: Sheri W. Sussman and Lauren Dockett
Production Editor: Emily Johnston
Cover design by Mimi Flow
Typeset by Apex Publishing, LLC

07 08 09 10/ 5 4 3 2 1

Library of Congress Cataloging-in-Publication Data

Family interventions in domestic violence : a handbook of gender-inclusive theory and treatment / John Hamel & Tonia Nicholls.
    p. cm.
  Includes index.
  ISBN 0–8261–0245–x
  1. Family violence—United States. 2. Family violence—United States—Prevention. 3. Family violence—Treatment—United States. I. Hamel, John. II. Nicholls, Tonia.
HV6626.2.F345 2006
362.82'92—dc22   2006018587

Printed in the United States of America by Edwards Brothers

To Judi—for your kindness and patience. And thank you,
Aviva and Jacob, for making me smile, and for reminding me
every day of the things that really matter.

J.H.

To my daughters, Samara and Aly—may you find as much
love, happiness, and peace as you have brought into my life.
Love, Mom.

T.N.

Contents

About the Authors   xix

Foreword   xxxv

    Linda G. Mills, New York University

Acknowledgments   xxxvii

Introduction   xxxix

    John Hamel and Tonia L. Nicholls

PART I. RESEARCH AND THEORY

1   **Domestic Violence: A Gender-Inclusive Conception**   3

        John Hamel

        Interventions Should Be Based on a Thorough,
Unbiased Assessment

        All Treatment Modalities and Options
Should Be Considered, Based on the Facts
of the Individual Case

        Both Men and Women Can Be Victims and/or
Perpetrators, and Everyone Is Responsible for
His or Her Behavior

        The Causes of Partner Abuse Are Varied but Similar
Across Genders

        Victim/Perpetrator Distinctions Are Overstated,
and Much Partner Abuse Is Mutual

        Both Genders Are Physically and Emotionally
Impacted By Abuse

"Gender Inclusive" Does Not Mean "Gender
Neutral" or "Gender Equal"

The Gender-Inclusive Approach Is a *Feminist*
Approach

Regardless of Perpetrator Gender, Child Witnesses
to Partner Abuse Are Adversely Affected and Are
at Risk for Perpetrating Partner Abuse and Becoming
Victimized as Adults

Family Violence Is a Complex Phenomenon, With
Reciprocal Interactions Between the Individual
Members

Conclusion

2   **Thinking Outside the Box: Gender and
Court-Mandated Therapy**   **27**

     Donald G. Dutton

The Therapeutic Problem With the Duluth
Model

The Theoretical Problem With the Duluth
Model

Anger and Violence

Subtypes of Perpetrators

Treatment Outcome Studies of the Duluth Model

Expanded Targets for Perpetrator Treatment

Treatment of Female Batterers

Couple Violence and Treatment

Interactional Studies

Couples Therapy

3   **Risk Factors for Physical Violence Between
Dating Partners: Implications for Gender-
Inclusive Prevention and Treatment of Family
Violence**   **59**

     Rose A. Medeiros and Murray A. Straus

Relevance of Information on Dating Partners

Previous Research on Gender Differences
in Risk Factors

Method

Results

Discussion

4   **Power and Control in Relationship Aggression**   **87**

   Nicola Graham-Kevan

Terminology

Consequences of Controlling Behavior

Theories of Controlling Behavior

Empirical Research on Controlling Behaviors and
Partner Violence: Women's Shelter and Batterer
Intervention Studies

Scales That Measure Controlling Behaviors:
A Selected Review

Implications of the Controlling Behavior Literature

5   **Intimate Stalking and Partner Violence**   **109**

   *Stacey L. Williams, Irene Hanson Frieze, and
   H. Colleen Sinclair*

Stalking Defined

Stalking in the Context of Breakup

Courtship Stalking and Its Link to Breakup Stalking

Issues of Gender in Stalking and Partner Violence

Clinical Implications of Stalking

6   **Couple Violence: A New Look at
Some Old Fallacies**   **125**

   Patricia Noller and Laurance Robillard

Women and Violence

The Levels-of-Analysis Issue

Male Potential for Abuse

7   **Partner Violence Typologies**   **145**

   Nicola Graham-Kevan

Theories of Partner Violence

Typology Theory and Research

8   The Impact of Domestic Violence on
     Children's Development   165

         Patrick T. Davies and Melissa L. Sturge-Apple

     Child Adaptation to Domestic Violence:
     The Context of Interparental Interactions

     Mediating Mechanisms Underlying the Risk of
     Domestic Violence

     Moderating Conditions Underlying the Risk of
     Domestic Violence

     Bidirectional Processes Underlying the Risk of
     Domestic Violence

     Summary and Implications

9   Family Lessons in Attachment and Aggression:
     The Impact of Interparental Violence on
     Adolescent Adjustment   191

         Marlene M. Moretti, Stephanie Penney,
         Ingrid Obsuth, and Candice Odgers

     Developmental Pathways to Aggression
     and Violence

     Exposure to Family Violence: Implications for Youth
     Aggression

     Lessons Learned From Interparental Violence

     Do the Effects of Maternal Versus Paternal IPV on
     Daughters and Sons Differ?

     Implications for Future Research

     From Research to Prevention and Intervention

10   The Evolution of Battering Interventions:
     From the Dark Ages Into the Scientific Age   215

         Julia C. Babcock, Brittany E. Canady,
         Katherine Graham, and Leslie Schart

     What We Know About Psychotherapy in General
     May Inform Batterers' Interventions

     Grassroots Movement

     Why Doesn't the Feminist Psychoeducational Model
     Work Better?

     Is the Duluth Model Set Up to Fail?

On the Road Toward the Scientific Era

Where Do We Go From Here?

Different Formats for Interventions

Who Should Be Targeted in Interventions for
Domestic Violence?

Interventions for Situational Violence

Interventions for Characterological Violence

Tailoring for Specific Cultural Groups

Women Arrested for Domestic Violence

Conclusions

PART II. ASSESSMENT AND TREATMENT

11　Gender-Inclusive Family Interventions in
Domestic Violence: An Overview　　　247

　　　John Hamel

The Evolution of Family Interventions

The Gender-Inclusive Approach

Case Examples

12　Violence Risk Assessments With Perpetrators
of Intimate Partner Abuse　　　275

　　　Tonia L. Nicholls, Sarah L. Desmarais,
　　　Kevin S. Douglas, and P. Randall Kropp

Pitfalls to Avoid in Conducting Risk Assessments:
Judgment Errors in Human Decision Making and
Cognitive Simplification Strategies That Can Backfire

Methods for Reducing Reliance on Heuristics and
Biases to Improving Decision-Making Accuracy

General Approaches to Violence Risk Assessment:
An Overview of Leading Methods

Assessing Men and Women for Risk of Perpetrating
Abuse in Intimate Relationships

The Value of Violence Risk Assessment Instruments
Developed to Assess General Offending

Conclusions and Implications

13   **Male Victims of Domestic Violence**   303

        David L. Fontes

        Addressing the Problem of Male Victims of Domestic
        Violence

        Obstacle 1: Men and Patriarchy

        Obstacle 2: Feminism

        Obstacle 3: Gender Politics

        Treating the Male Victim of Domestic Violence

14   **Domestic Violence in Ethnocultural Minority
        Groups**   319

                *Kathleen Malley-Morrison, Denise A. Hines,
                Doe West, Jesse J. Tauriac, and Mizuho Arai*

        North American Native American Communities

        African American Communities

        Hispanic/Latino Communities

        Asian American Communities

        Conclusions

15   **Systems Considerations in Working With
        Court-Ordered Domestic Violence Offenders**   341

                Lonnie Hazlewood

        A Developing Clinical Perspective

        The Criminal Justice Response

        Treatment Approaches to Domestic Violence

        Group Treatment

        Case Example 1

        Case Example 2

16   **Treatment of Psychological and Physical
        Aggression in a Couple Context**   363

                K. Daniel O'Leary and Shiri Cohen

        Who Are Appropriate Candidates for Treating
        Aggression Conjointly?

        What Evidence Supports a Couple-Based Approach?

        Arguments for Treating Psychological and Physical
        Aggression in a Couple Context

Screening Appropriate Clients for Couple Treatment

A Dyadic Treatment Model

Overview of Treatment Program

Initial Stages of Treatment

Midstages of Treatment

Follow-Up

17   Couple Violence and Couple Safety: A Systemic and Attachment-Oriented Approach to Working With Complexity and Uncertainty   381

Arlene Vetere and Jan Cooper

Building a Safe Context for Practice

Complexity and Uncertainty: Working With Jane and John

18   Dangerous Dances: Treatment of Domestic Violence in Same-Sex Couples   397

Vallerie E. Coleman

Overview of Violence in Lesbian and Gay Couples

Assessment

Treatment

Case Example: Joel and Martin

Summary

19   Treatment of Family Violence: A Systemic Perspective   417

Michael Thomas

Why We Commit Violence Against the People We Love

Our Splintered Response to Family Violence

A Family-Systems Approach

How Does Attachment Theory Help Us Treat Family Violence?

What About the Children?

Balancing Safety and Family Therapy

The Advantages of Family Therapy

The Therapist's Stance

Treating "Perpetrators" and "Victims"

Calming Our Own Anxiety

20   **Anger, Aggression, Domestic Violence,
and Substance Abuse**   437

    Ronald T. Potter-Efron

Common Themes, Situations, and Messages
for Families in Which Both Family Violence and
Substance Abuse Are Co-Occurring Problems

The Challenge to Core Paradigms in Both Fields

Possible Relationships Between Alcoholism/
Substance Abuse and Anger/Aggression/Domestic
Abuse

Research Correlations Between Substance Abuse
and Domestic Violence

Types of Domestic Abusers and Substance Abuse

Assessment Questions

Case Study: An Angry Man Who Becomes
Dangerous to His Wife When He Drinks

Case Study of an Angry and Violent "Needy"
Woman

Case Study of a Family With Violence and
Substance Abuse Issues: "Who Gets to Throw
the Turkey This Year?"

Summary

21   **Therapy With Clients Accused of Domestic
Violence in Disputed Child Custody Cases**   457

    Michael Carolla

One Size Doesn't Fit All

Case Examples

Conclusion

22   **Family Therapy and Interpersonal Violence:
Targeting At-Risk Adolescent Mothers**   477

    *Jennifer Langhinrichsen-Rohling, Lisa A. Turner,
and Marilyn McGowan*

Parenting Interventions With Adolescent Mothers

Intimate Partner Relationship Interventions With
Adolescent Mothers

The Building a Lasting Love Relationship
Intervention

Future Directions

23 **Family Group Therapy: A Domestic Violence
Program for Youth and Parents** 499

Nancy Carole Rybski

Background and Justification

Neidig and Friedman's Domestic Violence
Program

Research Design

Results

Discussion

Discussion of Differences

Directions for Future Research

24 **Family Violence Parent Groups** 519

L. Darlene Pratt and Tom Chapman

John Hamel & Associates

Peace Creations

25 **Healing Child Victims and Their Parents in the
Aftermath of Family Violence** 541

Christina M. Dalpiaz

Popular Terminology: The Buzzwords

Changing the Impact Abuse Has on
Parent–Child Relationships

Generating Plans to Meet Children's Goals

26 **Gender-Inclusive Work With Victims and
Their Children in a Coed Shelter** 561

Carol Ensign and Patricia Jones

The Shelter Movement

The Valley Oasis Shelter: Origins

The Coed Model

Cooperation With Law Enforcement and Batterer
Intervention Programs

Responses From the Domestic Violence Community

Responses From Victims and Their Families

Services

Addressing Safety Concerns

Clinical Services

Case Examples

Postdischarge Services

The Future

27   **Justice Is in the Design: Creating a Restorative
Justice Treatment Model for Domestic Violence**   579

*Peggy Grauwiler, Nicole Pezold, and
Linda G. Mills*

An Alternative Theory of Justice

The Problem of Safety in Treating Intimate Abuse

Construyendo Circulos de Paz: A New
Restorative Model

28   **Domestic Violence: New Visions, New Solutions**   601

*Cathy Young, Philip Cook, Sheila Smith,
Jack Turteltaub, and Lonnie Hazlewood*

Arrest and Prosecution

Restraining Orders

Batterer Intervention and Victim Counseling

Family Violence: New Visions, New Solutions

Conclusion

Index   621

About the Authors

Mizuho Arai, PhD, is an assistant professor in the Behavioral Science Department at Bunker Hill Community College, Boston, Massachusetts. She has presented a series of research papers on family violence from a cross-cultural perspective at meetings of professional associations such as the American Psychological Association and the Eastern Psychological Association. Her chapter on Japanese orientations to family roles and family violence was published in *International Perspectives on Family Violence* (2004). She has also authored a chapter, "The Impact of Culture on Women's Meanings and Experiences of Work: Asian American and Asian Immigrant Women," in *Psychotherapy with Women* (2005). Her recent article on issues of elder abuse in Japan was published in *Educational Gerontology* in January 2006.

Julia C. Babcock, PhD, is an associate professor of psychology at the University of Houston. Her areas of interest include marriage and marital therapy, intimate partner violence, psychopathy, and borderline personality disorder. She is a member of Division 12 (Clinical Psychology) of the American Psychology Association, the Association for the Advancement of Behavior Therapy, and the Society for Psychophysiological Research. Her research on the psychophysiological correlates of borderline personality and psychopathy was funded by the National Institute of Mental Health. She coauthored the first meta-analysis on batterers' interventions, published in *Clinical Psychology Review* (Babcock, Green, & Robie, 2004). Dr. Babcock serves as a consulting editor for *Psychology of Women Quarterly,* and as a reviewer for many psychology journals, including *Journal of Abnormal Psychology* and *Journal of Family Psychology.*

Brittany E. Canady, MA, is a clinical psychology graduate student at the University of Houston. She obtained her BS degree in 2000 from Virginia

Tech, and her masters in 2002 from Marshall University. Her areas of interest are intimate relationships and health. She has presented papers on domestic violence at the International Family Research Conference in New Hampshire, and cowrote with Julia Babcock, "Applying the Transtheoretical Model to Female and Male Perpetrators of Intimate Partner Violence: Gender Differences in Stages and Processes of Change," which appeared in a 2005 issue of *Violence and Victims*.

Michael Carolla, MFT, is executive director for Touchstone Counseling Services in Pleasant Hill, California. In addition to his anger management and domestic violence treatment programs, he is currently developing, with his staff, a "families in divorce" counseling and mediation system. This program is intended to help individuals and families in high conflict divorce situations to establish new functional family systems in the changing family structure.

Tom Chapman, MBA, MA, is executive director and founder of Peace Creations, headquartered in San Ramon, California. Peace Creations is one of the largest California Probation Certified Anger Management and Domestic Violence agencies in Alameda and Contra Costa Counties. Tom has led spiritual growth seminars for 20 years, both in the community and in prisons. He helped bring Kairos Prison Ministry into California in 1985 and served as Chair for six years, coordinating efforts in three federal and five state institutions. Tom developed QUEST as a result of the anger management program in Oakland and tested the program at California State Prison, Sacramento (New Folsom), a maximum security prison.

Tom and his wife, Jo, have been married 35 years and have led marriage encounter seminars and are working together with youth and prison programs. Both Tom and Jo have developed and presented mentoring programs for youthful offenders, mentoring programs for children of the incarcerated, jail-based parenting programs, and training for foster and kinship care. They are adjunct faculty at Las Positas College in Livermore, California.

Shiri Cohen, MA, is currently completing her PhD in clinical psychology at Stony Brook University. Shiri's research focuses primarily on the bidirectional relationship between marital/relationship functioning and individual psychopathology such as depression. More specifically, she is interested in various aspects of relationship functioning including marital discord, negative marital events, and partner aggression, particularly as they relate to each partner's individual mental health. Shiri has published work on the link between separation/divorce and subsequent outcomes in major depression such as relapse and recovery, and has developed a new measure of risk for partner aggression, the Fear of Partner Scale. Currently, Shiri is conducting her doctoral research, which is aimed at developing a brief, couples-based psychoeducational intervention for depressed women and their partners, for which she was awarded a two-year National Research Service Award Predoctoral Fellowship from the National Institutes of Mental Health.

Vallerie E. Coleman, PhD, is a clinical psychologist and psychoanalyst in private practice in Santa Monica, California, and she is on the faculty at the Newport Psychoanalytic Institute and Loyola Marymount University. Although her work with individuals and couples draws on a variety of psychoanalytic perspectives, it is largely informed by an integration of object relations theory, attachment theory, and psychoneurobiology. In addition to her clinical and academic work, Dr. Coleman has provided expert witness testimony on lesbian battering and led numerous workshops on same-sex domestic violence.

Philip Cook is an award-winning journalist, and the author of *Abused Men: The Hidden Side of Domestic Violence* (1997). "I highly recommend him as a speaker and the research he has done for your organization," James J. Londis, PhD, Director of Ethics and Values Integration, Kettering Medical Center; "Explains the many aspects of domestic violence . . . a wealth of material that could be helpful to professionals," "Dear Abby" Abigail Van Buren. Mr. Cook has appeared on CNN, MSNBC, "The O'Reilly Factor," "The Sally Jesse Raphael Show," "The Montel Williams Show," and more than 50 radio talk shows. His articles have appeared in *Employee Assistance Professional "Exchange" Magazine, The Oregonian,* and with coauthors in the academic publication *The Journal of Human Behavior in the Social Environment,* as well as several college supplemental textbooks.

Jan Cooper, CQSW, MSc, is a UKCP Registered Family Therapist. She is codirector with Dr. Arlene Vetere of Reading Safer Families. She also works as an independent practitioner combining clinical work, supervision, and training. Jan and Arlene have written a number of articles on systemic therapy for domestic violence, which have appeared in several publications, including the *Journal of Family Therapy.* They have recently published *Domestic Violence and Family Safety: A Systemic Approach to Working with Violence in Families* (2005). In addition, they regularly teach about their approach to domestic violence and family safety in a number of European countries.

Christina M. Dalpiaz, PhD, founder of CHANCE (Changing How Adults Nurture Children's Egos), provides parenting strategies to families and others struggling with discipline. She also educates society on how family violence impacts child development. She has helped produce training videos and has written extensively on this very sensitive issue. Ms. Dalpiaz speaks regularly at conferences, educational facilities, legal establishments, corporations, and other nonprofit agencies. She was "The Above and Beyond Child Advocate of the Year," an honor bestowed by the Aurora Family Violence Response Team; assisted in the production of a documentary for television titled "The Truth about Teen Violence"; and coordinated a conference titled "A CHANCE for a Healthy and Violence-free Childhood." Her mission is to make family violence socially unacceptable for the sake of the children.

Patrick T. Davies, PhD, is professor of psychology in the Department of Clinical and Social Sciences in Psychology at the University of Rochester. His interests include understanding the interplay between family adversity, interparental discord, and developmental child psychopathology. Recipient of the APA Boyd McCandless Early Career Award for Significant Contributions to Developmental Psychology, Davies is a codeveloper of the emotional security theory, principal investigator on NIMH-funded projects concerned with relations between family process and child adjustment, and coauthor of several books and research publications. Davies received an undergraduate teaching award and has sponsored federal training fellowships for predoctoral and postdoctoral students. He is an associate editor of *Development and Psychopathology* and a member of other editorial journal boards and review panels for NIMH.

Sarah L. Desmarais, PhD, is a post doctoral Candidate in Psychology with a specialization in Law and Forensic Psychology at Simon Fraser University, where she obtained her Master's in 2005. Sarah is also a Research Officer for the British Columbia Mental Health and Addictions services. Her research interests include intimate partner abuse perpetration and victimization and the implications of victim interviews. She is also conducting research assessing risks in psychiatric patients and examining jury decision making. With the coauthors of the chapter, she is involved in the development and validation of the *Decision Making in Abusive Relationships Interview* (DIARI), professional guidelines for risk/needs assessments with victims of intimate partner abuse.

Kevin S. Douglas, PhD, currently is on faculty at Simon Fraser University, in the Law and Forensic Psychology Area of the Department of Psychology. He has a doctorate in clinical (forensic) psychology, as well as a law degree. He has published more than 50 articles, chapters, and books within the area of forensic assessment, most of which focus on violence risk assessment and related topics such as psychopathy. In addition, he is a coauthor of the HCR-20 violence risk assessment scheme. His research has been funded by grants from the National Science Foundation, the Social Sciences and Humanities Research Council of Canada, and the Michael Smith Foundation for Health Research as a Career Scholar Award recipient.

Donald G. Dutton, PhD, received his doctorate in psychology from the University of Toronto in 1970. After receiving training as a group therapist at Cold Mountain Institute, he cofounded the Assaultive Husbands Project in 1979, a court-mandated treatment program for men convicted of wife assault. He has published more than 100 papers and 3 books, including the *Domestic Assault of Women* (1995), *The Batterer: A Psychological Profile* (1995), and *The Abusive Personality* (2002). *The Batterer* has been translated into French, Spanish, Dutch, Japanese, and Polish. Dutton has frequently served as an expert witness in civil trials involving domestic abuse and in criminal trials involving family violence. He is currently professor of psychology at the University of British Columbia. His latest work, *Rethinking Domestic Violence* (2005), includes an examination of how the gender paradigm developed in domestic violence research and policy. His other recent books include a review of recent research on personality disorder, developmental neuroscience, and intimate abusiveness (*The Abusive Personality*, 3rd ed., 2006), and an explanation for the psychology of genocide and military massacres (*Transformations to Evil: State Initiated Violence* [2007]).

Carol Ensign, LCSW, has worked with victims of crime for more than 21 years. Ms. Ensign has been the executive director of the Antelope Valley Domestic Violence Council for nine years. She is a strong advocate for male victims of domestic violence and has appeared on "The Montel Williams Show," was in the documentary *Hidden Victims: Children of Domestic Violence,* has been interviewed on CNN, NBC, and many other television shows, as well as addressed many groups and organizations on the subject of domestic violence. She was Woman of the Year in 2000 in L.A. County and Citizen of the Year in 2004 in the Antelope Valley.

David L. Fontes, PhD, is the Employee Assistance Program (EAP) manager for the California Department of Social Services (CDSS). He has been the EAP manager since January 1990, providing a confidential resource to assist any of the 4,500 CDSS state employees resolve their personal or work-related problems. He is also a licensed clinical psychologist in private practice at Creekside Counseling Associates in Elk Grove, California. Dr. Fontes received his bachelor's degree from the University of California at Davis, his master's degree in Counseling from California State University at Sacramento, and his doctoral degree in clinical psychology from The Professional School of Psychology in Sacramento in 1998. His doctoral dissertation was on the topic of male victims of domestic violence, titled "Domestic Violence Against Men: Development of a Comprehensive Partner Conflict Survey."

Irene Hanson Frieze, PhD, is a professor of psychology and women's studies at the Unversity of Pittsburgh. Her book, *Hurting the One You Love: Violence in Relationships,* was published in 2005 by Thompson/Wadsworth. She has published a number of articles and book chapters on the topic of violence in relationships. Her work on battered women began in the 1970s, and since then she has also researched dating violence and stalking.

Katherine Graham, MA, is a PhD student in the counseling psychology program at the University of Houston. She is a member of the American Psychology Association, the Association for Behavioral and Cognitive Therapies, and the Texas Psychological Association. Her research interests are communication patterns in couples with male intimate partner violence and issues surrounding clinical supervision. She has coauthored an article on typologies of men engaging in intimate partner violence published in the *Journal of Family Psychology.* She coauthored a poster at the 2005 Association for Behavioral and Cognitive Therapies on communication patterns of men who engage in intimate partner violence, and copresented a workshop titled "Ethical and Legal Pitfalls in Clinical Supervision" at the Texas Psychological Association 2005 annual convention.

Nicola Graham-Kevan, BSc, PhD, is a senior lecturer in psychology at the University of Central Lancashire, United Kingdom. Her area of expertise is relationship aggression. She has coauthored several articles on aggression including: "Physical Aggression and Control in Heterosexual Relationships: The Effect of Sampling" (*Violence and Victims,* 2003, 181–198); "Patriarchal Terrorism and Common Couple Violence: A Test of Johnson's Predictions in Four British Samples" (*Journal of Interpersonal Violence,* 2003, 1247–1270); and "Investigating Three Explanations of Women's Relationship Aggression" (*Psychology of Women Quarterly,* 2005, 270–277). She regularly presents her work at European and U.S. conferences and to clinicians in the United Kingdom. Nicola is a fellow of the International Society for Research on Aggression and the British Psychological Society with chartered psychology status. Additionally Nicola is acting editor for a special issue of men's domestic violence and victimization for the *International Journal of Men's Health* and has engaged in national government-led consultations on violence and human trafficking.

Peggy Grauwiler, LCSW, has dedicated the past 12 years to developing domestic violence programs for victims and their children within the criminal justice and child welfare systems. Her work includes the creation of the New York Domestic Violence Court Model, which continues to be replicated statewide. She has provided group and individual treatment to battered women, consulted on the development of statewide standards for batterer intervention programs in New York, and provided domestic violence training nationally for court personnel, judges, and victim advocates. She is the coauthor of several articles on restorative justice and intimate abuse, which have appeared in publications such as the *Journal of Sociology and Social Welfare* and *Public Health Reports*. She is currently a doctoral candidate in clinical social work at New York University.

Lonnie Hazlewood, MSHP, LCDC, CCCJS, is a licensed chemical dependency counselor in the state of Texas and a certified clinical criminal justice specialist. He has 30 years experience in the substance abuse field and for the past 25 years has also worked in the domestic violence field. He has worked on community task forces on domestic violence, helped to develop criminal justice interventions and policies, directed the Family Violence Diversion Network (1982–1987), developed a number of violence prevention programs, and conducted research on both substance abuse and family violence. He is the director of the Domestic Violence, Threat Containment Intensive Treatment Program for the most serious domestic violence offenders, has coauthored two books on domestic violence; *Violent Men, Violent Couples* (1987) and *The Violent Couple* (1992), and collaborated on several articles on this population. Much of this work was to determine the effectiveness of treatment interventions. He has consulted with the Bastrop Federal Correctional Facility and presented training on anger management and risk assessment to Texas Community Supervision Officers and others dealing with domestic violence. He also served on a National Consensus Panel to develop a Treatment Improvement Protocol for the Center for Substance Abuse Treatment (TIP #25, Substance Abuse and Domestic Violence).

Denise A. Hines, PhD, is a visiting assistant professor in the Department of Criminal Justice at the University of Massachusetts, Lowell, and a research associate at the Family Research Laboratory and Crimes Against Children Research Center at the University of New Hampshire, where she did her postdoctoral training with Murray Straus and David Finkelhor. She received her PhD in 2003 from Boston University. Her dissertation, a behavioral genetic study of aggression in intimate relationships, was supported by an individual National Research Service Award from the National Institute of Mental Health. She has several publications related to family violence, including two books coauthored with Kathleen Malley-Morrison: *Family Violence in the United States* and *Family Violence in a Cultural Perspective.*

Patricia Jones, MS, joined the staff of the Antelope Valley Domestic Violence Council/Valley Oasis Shelter in 1999 after enjoying five years as a stay-at-home mom. This position brought her back to her first professional love, victim assistance. Patricia holds a bachelor's degree in sociology from Eastern Connecticut State University and Applied Social Relations with a focus in Criminal Justice as well as a master's degree in Criminal Justice/Corrections from the American University, Washington, DC, where she graduated with distinction. Patricia passionately advocates for all victims of domestic violence, both male and female, while drawing inspiration from the determination of the victims and their children to succeed despite the obstacles they face.

P. Randall Kropp, PhD, is a clinical and forensic psychologist specializing in the assessment and management of violent offenders. He works for the Forensic Psychiatric Services Commission of British Columbia, Canada, and is adjunct professor of psychology at Simon Fraser University. He has conducted workshops on psycholegal issues and risk assessment in 15 countries on 5 continents. He has frequently consulted with provincial, state, and federal governments on matters related to violence against women and children. He has published numerous journal articles, book chapters, and research reports, and he is coauthor of several works on risk assessment, including the *Manual for the Spousal Assault Risk Assessment Guide,* the *Manual for the Sexual Violence Risk—20,* and the *Risk for Sexual Violence Protocol (RSVP).*

Jennifer Langhinrichsen-Rohling, PhD, is a clinical psychologist and psychology professor at the University of South Alabama. Langhinrichsen-Rohling received her undergraduate degree in psychology from Brown University, her doctorate in psychology from the University of Oregon, and was a National Institute of Mental Health postdoctoral fellow studying marital violence at SUNY, Stony Brook. Langhinrichsen-Rohling's clinical work includes both battered women and abusive couples. She has published more than 70 articles and book chapters on topics related to intimate partner violence, the intergenerational transmission of abuse, or at-risk adolescent behavior. Her scholarship and teaching have garnered her several awards; she has received more than a million dollars in grant funding; and she sits on the editorial advisory boards of three journals. She currently serves as Youth Violence Research Scholar for the University of South Alabama.

Kathleen Malley-Morrison, PhD, is professor of psychology in the Program in Human Development, Boston University. Since completing a post-doctoral fellowship in family violence at Children's Hospital in Boston, she has focused primarily on issues in family violence, particularly in cross-cultural and international contexts. She is coauthor (with Anne P. Copeland) of *Studying Families* (1991), coauthor (with Denise A. Hines) of *Family Violence in a Cultural Perspective* (2004), and coauthor (with Denise A. Hines) of *Family Violence in the United States: Defining, Understanding, and Combating Abuse* (2004). She also edited *International Perspectives on Family Violence and Abuse* (2004). She has authored or coauthored many journal articles and conference papers related to family violence. She is increasingly focusing on issues of war and peace.

Rose A. Medeiros, PhD, is a doctoral candidate in sociology at the University of New Hampshire. Her professional interests include research methods and statistics, partner assault, corporal punishment of children, gender roles in relationships, and relationship dynamics in same-sex couples. She is coauthor of the forthcoming book, *The Primordial Violence: Corporal Punishment by Parents, Cognitive Development, and Crime.*

Marilyn McGowan, PhD, is an instructor in the Department of Leadership and Teacher Education at the University of South Alabama (USA). She teaches classes in the area of special education teacher preparation and is currently a doctoral candidate in instructional design and development at USA. Her research interests include mentoring relationships with adolescent mothers and the integration of instructional design principles in the development of intervention programs for at-risk youth. She served as a special education teacher in numerous districts in Alabama and Mississippi. From 2002 to 2005 she served as the program coordinator for two programs: a parent intervention, which included a mentoring component, and a relationship intervention aimed at preventing interpersonal violence with adolescent mothers.

Linda G. Mills, PhD, LCSW, JD, is professor of social work, law, and public policy at New York University, where she also serves as Vice Provost for Undergraduate Education and University Life. In 2004, she founded the Center on Violence and Recovery to promote alternative healing approaches to intimate abuse and other violent or traumatic events. She is currently overseeing a study, funded by the National Science Foundation, to compare a batterer intervention program with a restorative justice treatment for domestic violence offenders in Nogales, Arizona. She is the author of numerous articles and books on trauma and intimate abuse, including the 1999 *Harvard Law Review* article, "Killing Her Softly: Intimate Abuse and the Violence of State Interventions" and *Insult to Injury: Rethinking Our Responses to Intimate Abuse* (2003).

Marlene M. Moretti, PhD, has focused her research on the importance of parent-child attachment as a determinant of health development. She is particularly interested in the transition to adolescence and the development of self-regulatory competence. Her work spans from identification of risk and protective factors to the development and evaluation of innovative programs to promote well-being in youth at high-risk. Moretti is a full professor of psychology at Simon Fraser University and past director of the Clinical Psychology Program and the Clinical Psychology Centre. She currently leads a multisite Canadian Institutes of Health Research New Emerging Team Grant on gender and aggression and has published extensively in the fields of developmental psychopathology, social-clinical psychology, and intervention. Moretti has served as a member of several government committees working to promote the use of evidence-based intervention. She is a coauthor of the book, *Girls and Aggression: Contributing Factors and Intervention Principles* (2004), and cowrote the chapter, "Parental Attachment and the Self from a Systemic Perspective," included in *Clinical Applications of Attachment Theory* (2003).

Patricia Noller, PhD, FASSA, is currently Emeritus Professor of Psychology at the University of Queensland. For seven years, she was director of the University of Queensland Family Centre. She has published extensively in the area of marital and family relationships, including 12 books and more than 100 journal articles and book chapters. She is a Fellow of the Academy of the Social Sciences in Australia and of the National Council on Family Relationships (USA). She has served on a number of editorial boards and was appointed as foundation editor of *Personal Relationships: Journal of the International Society for the Study of Personal Relationships* (International Association for Relationship Research), which was a position she held from 1993 to 1997. She was then president of that society from 1998 to 2000.

Ingrid Obsuth, MA, is a doctoral student in child clinical psychology at Simon Fraser University. She completed her MA degree in clinical psychology at Charles University, Prague, Czech Republic. Her research and clinical interests are in adolescent mental health, family dynamics, attachment, emotion regulation, and family violence. She is funded through the Human Early Learning Partnership and has published a number of papers on psychosocial factors related to adolescent mental health.

Candice Odgers, PhD, is a Social Sciences and Humanities Research Council Postdoctoral Fellow and Michael Smith Foundation for Health Research Trainee. Odgers received her doctorate in psychology from the University of Virginia (2005) and is currently a coinvestigator on a Canadian Institutes of Health Research multisite study of gender and aggression. Recently, Odgers was awarded the Alice Wilson Medal by the Royal Society of Canada for her research related to female aggression. Her current program of work focuses on mapping the developmental course of antisocial behavior, among normative and high-risk populations, using advanced longitudinal methods for the study of growth and change. Her articles on adolescent offenders have appeared in several journals, including *Law and Human Behavior* and *Canadian Academy of Child and Adolescent Psychiatry Review.*

K. Daniel O'Leary, PhD, is a Distinguished Professor of Psychology at Stony Brook University. O'Leary was among the top 100 cited psychologists in the English-speaking world (*American Psychologist*, December, 1978). He received the Distinguished Scientist Award from the clinical division of the American Psychological Association in 1985, and he was appointed the National Academies of Practice in Psychology in 1986. He is the author or coauthor of 10 books. The most recent include: *The Couples Psychotherapy Treatment Planner* (with R. E. Heyman and A. E. Jongsma, 1998) and *Psychological Abuse in Violent Domestic Relations* (with R. D. Maiuro, 2001). His research focuses on the etiology and treatment of partner aggression, and the marital discord/depression link.

Stephanie Penney, MA, focuses her research on gender-specific risk factors for juvenile aggression, as well as the role of affect regulation in aggression and violence among youths. She has carried out research investigating the roles of psychopathic and narcissistic personality features in youth, and how these features may moderate risk for aggression and violence among adolescents. Ms. Penney is currently a doctoral student in the clinical-forensic psychology program at Simon Fraser University. She has received awards from the Social Sciences and Humanities Research Council as well as the Michael Smith Foundation for Health Research to carry out her doctoral research on affect regulation, and is currently involved in a large scale research initiative on gender and aggression funded by the Canadian Institutes of Health Research. She has been published in the *International Journal of Forensic Mental Health* and is coauthor of "The Relation of Psychopathy with Concurrent Aggression and Antisocial Behavior in High-Risk Adolescent Girls and Boys" (in press).

Nicole Pezold is a writer in New York City and communications director for New York University's Center on Violence and Recovery. She has written both popular and academic articles on subjects ranging from domestic violence among newly arrived immigrants to the hidden meanings of museum installations. She previously served as a Peace Corps volunteer in Mali, West Africa, where she worked with women's associations and youth. She is also books editor for InTheFray.com and an associate editor at *NYU Alumni Magazine*.

L. Darlene Pratt, MFT, is a marriage and family therapist and certified domestic violence counselor in Pleasant Hill and Berkeley, California. She works with individuals and couples who are struggling with anger and communication difficulties. With John Hamel and Associates, she facilitates batterer intervention groups for both males and females as well as a 52-week high conflict/family violence parenting program. As an anger management specialist, she conducts assessments for Family Court Services, Children and Family Services, and Alameda County adoption agencies. She is on the faculty at Diablo Valley College in Pleasant Hill in the Addictions Studies Department. Ms. Pratt also works with families dealing with the issue of sexual addiction, and she is an EMDR practitioner. A member of the Family Violence Treatment and Education Association, she has conducted professional trainings in Family Violence Assessment and Treatment.

Ronald T. Potter-Efron, MSW, PhD, is a clinical psychotherapist at First Things First Counseling Center in Eau Claire, Wisconsin. He is the author of the *Handbook of Anger Management* (2005), *Angry All The Time* (2004), and several other books for professionals and the general public.

Laurance Robillard, BS, is a registered psychologist. She has a bachelor of psychology with First Class Honours from Griffith University, Gold Coast Campus in Queensland. She is currently undertaking a clinical PhD in psychology at the University of Queensland, under the supervision of Professor Patricia Noller and Associate Professor Judith Feeney. Her area of research focuses on the influence of various personality traits such as rejection sensitivity on couple violence and couple communication, using a standard content methodology.

Nancy Carole Rybski, PhD, MBA, has worked with families in crisis since 1983, beginning her career by providing services in women's domestic violence shelters. Her clinical areas of expertise are in juvenile delinquency and adult sexual offending; she has also served as executive director at a shelter for pregnant teens. Rybski is a licensed marriage and family therapist in both Arizona and Illinois. She completed her doctorate at the University of Arizona in 1998, and an earned an executive MBA at San Diego State University in 2004. She has been teaching at the University of Phoenix since 2000. In 2004, she created Family Business Dynamics, LLC, a consulting firm for family-owned businesses. Rybski also has a private counseling practice in Tucson, Arizona.

Leslie Schart, MA, is a doctoral student in the University of Houston Clinical Psychology Program. Her areas of interest include marriage and marital therapy, intimate partner sexual abuse, and sexual disorders. She is also involved in the Anxiety Disorder Clinic at the University of Houston, where she conducts assessments and coleads anxiety groups. She previously worked in an animal behavior lab, where she was trained to section, stain, and analyze rat brains.

H. Colleen Sinclair, PhD, is an assistant professor in the Department of Psychology at Mississippi State University. She has a doctorate in social psychology from the University of Minnesota, with minors in interpersonal relationships research, law and quantitative methods. Her research focuses on psychology and the law and the obstacles that individuals face in pursuing interpersonal relationships. These interests combine in her work on relationship violence (stalking, acquaintance rape, and dating violence).

Sheila Smith, LCSW, is a 1985 graduate of Portland State University's School of Social Work. Sheila is in private practice and has provided services and assessments for the chronically mentally ill and the corrections population. She testifies in a variety of cases for child welfare agencies, the courts, medical boards, county mental health agencies, and consults, both privately and with law enforcement, in sex crimes and homicide cases. As an adjunct professor at Portland State University, she taught courses in criminal profiling, homicide, sex crimes, infanticide, juvenile violence, and psychopathy. Smith is a member of the Academy of Behavioral Profiling and the Forensic Science Society. Her company, Deducere Limited Inc., provides training in the area of crime investigation and analysis. As an authority on crime, she has appeared on KOIN TV, KATU TV, and as a guest on local radio. Sheila serves as a board member of SAFE (Stop Abuse for Everyone), an international human rights organization dedicated to serving minority victims of domestic violence.

Murray A. Straus, PhD, is professor of sociology and founder and codirector of the Family Research Laboratory at the University of New

Hampshire. He has been president of the National Council on Family Relations, the Society for the Study of Social Problems, and the Eastern Sociological Society. He is the author or coauthor of more than 200 articles on the family, research methods, and South Asia, and 15 books, including *Corporal Punishment by Parents in Theoretical Perspective* (Yale, 2006); *Physical Violence in American Families: Risk Factors and Adaptations to Violence in 8,145 Families* (Transaction, 1990); *Stress, Culture, and Aggression* (Yale, 1995); and *Beating the Devil Out of Them: Corporal Punishment in American Families* (Transaction, 2001).

Melissa L. Sturge-Apple, PhD, holds a BA from the University of Rochester, a Med from Harvard University, and a doctorate in developmental psychology from the University of Notre Dame. She was awarded an NIMH postdoctoral fellowship to examine the role of gender in relations between interparental conflict and parenting in 2002–2005 under the direction of Patrick Davies. Currently, she is a visiting assistant professor in the department of clinical and social sciences at the University of Rochester. Sturge-Apple's research interests concentrate on examining the interrelatedness among family subsystems from a process-oriented perspective with a primary focus on understanding associations between marital and parenting domains as well as the implications for children's adjustment trajectories. She has coauthored several recent journal articles on the topic, which have appeared in *Child Development, Journal of Family Psychology, Parenting: Science and Practice and Development,* and *Psychopathology.*

Jesse J. Tauriac, MA, is a doctoral candidate in the clinical psychology program at the University of Massachusetts, Boston. His research interests include academic success and academic adjustment of African American males, resilience, family violence among African Americans, and racial and ethnic identity. He has coauthored journal articles on issues related to family violence and culturally competent clinical training.

Michael Thomas, MA, LMFT, is in private practice in Bellevue, Washington. He is a clinical member of the American Association of Marriage and Family Therapists, and a Washington State licensed marriage and family therapist. He has worked with family violence, particularly sexual abuse, at a number of different settings since 1985. He also trains professionals, locally and nationally, to recognize and treat family violence from a gender-inclusive, systemic framework. Mr. Thomas is currently working on a book about female sex abuse of boys (including mother-son incest).

Lisa A. Turner, PhD, is an associate professor of psychology at the University of South Alabama. Ms. Turner received her PhD in experimental psychology from the University of Alabama. Her current research focuses on the risk and protective factors that contribute to the cognitive and emotional development of adolescent mothers and their children.

Jack Turteltaub, PhD, is a licensed clinical psychologist who lives in Portland, Oregon. He completed his bachelor's degree at the University of Washington in 1983. He completed his PhD in clinical psychology from Wayne State University in 1993 with a dissertation on alcohol expectancies. He is licensed to practice in Utah and Oregon. Turteltaub worked for almost four years from 1991 to 1994 at Cornerstone Counseling Center in Salt Lake City as a domestic violence therapist. Turteltaub was a full-time staff psychologist at the Oregon State Hospital (Portland campus) for eight years from 1995 to 2003. Since 2003, he has been in part-time private practice doing psychotherapy with individuals and couples, adult assessment, and coaching. Turteltaub has been a member of the board of SAFE (Stop Abuse for Everyone) since 2004.

Arlene Vetere, PhD, is deputy programme director for the Clinical Psychology Doctorate at Surrey University, United Kingdom. She is a chartered consultant clinical psychologist and a UKCP registered systemic psychotherapist. Arlene is president of the European Family Therapy Association, and an Academician of the Academy of the Learned Societies in the Social Sciences. She codirects, with Jan Cooper Reading Safer Families, a domestic violence service based in Reading, England. They have recently published *Domestic Violence and Family Safety: A Systemic Approach to Working with Violence in Families*. In addition, they regularly teach about their approach to domestic violence and family safety in a number of European countries.

Doe West, BA, BS, MS, MDiv, PhD, has been a social justice activist throughout her adult life within disability, Native American, and women's rights movements. In addition to clinical work as a psychotherapist, West is currently a National Institute of Health Fellow with Columbia University as a researcher in epidemiology. Her current grant is for the study of the genetics of idiopathic epilepsy. This will be worked in tandem with a special area of working within sleep medicine and the interplay of parasomnias in children. She also teaches part time at Boston University and other colleges and universities in the Boston area. She has been published in the areas of disability issues, family violence, and bioethics in texts, articles, and instructional materials.

Stacey L. Williams, PhD, a social and health psychologist, is currently completing an NIMH-funded postdoctoral fellowship in social environment and health at the Institute for Social Research. Her research focuses on: (1) intimate partner violence and other traumas, and (2) stigma and identity. Within both of these areas Stacey studies how these social issues are linked with social interactions, self-related cognitions, and mental health-related processes. Taking a contextual approach to her work, she also considers how sociocontextual factors of gender, social status, and race and ethnicity might moderate people's experiences. Among her accomplishments, Stacey has contributed articles to issues of *Psychology of Women Quarterly* and *Sex Roles,* which focused on intimate partner violence and gender. She is actively involved in the Society for the Psychological Study of Social Issues.

Cathy Young is a journalist whose columns regularly appear in the *Boston Globe.* She has written numerous articles on the subject of domestic violence, and is the author of *Ceasefire: Why Women and Men Must Join Forces to Achieve True Equality.*

Foreword: Movement Forward

In 1996, I attended a forum sponsored by the UCLA School of Law debating the importance of mandatory arrest and prosecution as a strategy for addressing domestic violence, later chronicled in the 1997 spring/summer volume of the *UCLA Women's Law Journal*. As I now recall, it seems that I was the only person at the forum presenting an alternative point of view, proposing that mandatory interventions are worth reexamining. This position sparked an explosive response from some present. One comment, in particular, has stuck in my mind these past 10 years. A Los Angeles prosecutor argued vehemently that domestic violence must be fought with a weapon—a big stick—that is larger than the batterer's. And, of course, the batterers she referenced were uniquely male. "It's the 'stick' of putting him in jail," she said, "that gives me the power to counteract him, and nothing you can say will persuade me to give that up."

Freudian implications aside, this female prosecutor wanted to match aggression with aggression, his stick with hers, because she believed this would somehow overcome or supersede his violence and, ultimately, solve the problem. This brings to mind Jim Gilligan's observations from his book *Violence,* published that same year: "[T]he moral and legal way of thinking about and responding to violence (by calling it evil, forbidding it—'just say no'—and punishing it) will prevent violence (or at least bring it under control)—has been singularly unsuccessful in reducing the level of violence" (p. 94).

For far too long, the theory, research, and practice in the field of intimate and family violence have been stifled by a punishment paradigm that focuses on only part of the problem: heterosexual male violence caused by gender imbalance. This paradigm has limited the creativity of scholars and practitioners, as I saw in 1996, to address this seemingly intractable problem and has shut out women and whole families from playing a meaningful role in treatment. Having questioned the salience of such assumptions myself, I have found that in recent years many theorists, researchers, and practitioners have been caught up in the politics of domestic violence, as several of the authors in this volume acknowledge. Painfully, this tunnel vision has caused many key thinkers to lose sight of the importance of asking fresh questions that may give rise to new solutions.

In 1996, I did not respond to the prosecutor. I listened attentively, as I often have when my presentations are met with anger. Ten years later, I would feel more confident responding to her narrow prognosis amidst the renewed flow of discourse in domestic violence, which this important volume, skillfully edited by John Hamel and Tonia Nicholls, thoughtfully captures. The introduction by Hamel and Nicholls and the first chapters of the book provide a comprehensive road map for navigating this new conversation, to which scholars and practitioners from around the world have contributed in theory and research and in assessment and treatment.

The uniting theme of this work is treating men, women, and children "where they are"—a basic tenet of good clinical practice that has long been missing from the field of domestic violence. Instead, past interventions have often judged clients for the violence in their lives without providing them with the tools they need to address it. We now know—and the research and interventions described in this volume affirm—that treatment must encompass a wide range of gender dynamics, including violence perpetrated by heterosexual females or between same-sex partners, as well as the fact that abuse can deeply penetrate family systems and cross generations.

"Proof" that the theories and practices that make up this volume are indeed comprehensive enough remains an open question. Nonetheless, we can thankfully observe that this field is far from stagnant today, with scores of skilled scholars and practitioners responding specifically to the gender-inclusive treatment demands of families affected by domestic violence.

What this work reveals—and what I sensed even 10 years ago— is that alternative voices have long been a part of the struggle to address intimate and family violence—and now they are finally being heard.

Linda G. Mills, PhD, LCSW, JD

Acknowledgments

Thanks to the "mavericks" who came before us, from Peter Neidig and Erin Pizzey to Terri Moffitt and John Archer, and all the remarkable men and women who contributed to this book. We especially acknowledge Murray Straus, Richard Gelles, and Suzanne Steinmetz. Their brave and scientifically grounded pioneering work on family violence, particularly female aggression, has had a tremendous influence on our work and paved the way for many others like us to challenge engrained sociopolitical perspectives on the causes and consequences of violence in intimate relationships. The domestic violence field is forever indebted to them for their persistence and dedication to the scientific enterprise, despite the unpopularity of their findings.

Introduction

John Hamel and Tonia L. Nicholls

A Revolution is taking place in the field of domestic violence.

Quietly, without fanfare, a growing body of research is challenging some of the most cherished, long-established assumptions guiding policy and intervention (e.g., Dutton & Nicholls, 2005; Felson, 2002; Hines & Malley-Morrison, 2005; Kelly, 2003). Under investigation is the role that female-perpetrated abuse (verbal, emotional, and physical) plays in the dynamics of intimate partner relationships, the systemic nature of partner abuse in couples and families, and the limits of ideologically driven, "one-size-fits-all" treatment approaches.

TRADITIONAL VIEWS

Public information brochures disseminated by battered women's shelters and victim advocacy organizations, as well as papers from most established academic researchers, have traditionally framed intimate partner violence as a gender issue, and assert that men are overwhelmingly the perpetrators and women overwhelmingly the victims. For years, it has been claimed that male-perpetrated domestic violence accounts for 95% of intimate partner abuse (e.g., Hamberger & Potente, 1995). When more comparable rates between the genders are acknowledged, the significance and impact of female-perpetrated abuse is minimized and understood as either defensive or situational in nature, an isolated expression of frustration in communicating with an unsympathetic partner, in contrast to the presumably intentional, pervasive, and generally controlling behaviors exhibited by men (Henning, Jones, & Holdford, 2003; Johnson & Leone, 2005). In the most extreme manifestations of this sentiment (Dobash, Dobash, Wilson, & Daly, 1992; Walker, 1983; Yllo, 1993), men are presumed to weld greater power simply by virtue of their gender:

The willingness to use force is coupled with a set of beliefs and standards regarding the appropriate hierarchical relationship between men and women in the family and rightful authority of husbands over wives. Thus, all men see themselves as controllers of women, and because they are socialized into the use of violence they are potential aggressors against their wives. (Dobash & Dobash, 1979, p. 24)

Reflective of these views, public policies have targeted predominantly male offenders for arrest and have mandated same-sex batterer education programs. Women are presumed to be victims, even when they admit to having initiated violence against partners and children (Laframboise, 1998; Stacey, Hazlewood, & Shupe, 1994), although some advocates are now willing to acknowledge (e.g., Pence, 1999) "the possibility that a 'battered woman' might have morally contaminating personal characteristics independent of her victimization" (Loseke, 1992, p. 162). Alternative treatment modalities, including couples or family therapy, are expressly forbidden (Austin & Dankwort, 1999). Initially, these laws made some sense. When domestic violence first began to be taken seriously in the 1970s and 1980s, perpetrators who came to the attention of law enforcement did so because the seriousness of their assaults could no longer be ignored. Many of these cases were not amenable to couples or family therapy. Furthermore, because clinicians in the mental health community lacked appropriate assessment tools (for a discussion of risk assessment for partner abuse, see Nicholls, Desmarais, Douglas, and Kropp, chapter 12 in this volume) and a sufficient understanding of domestic violence dynamics (Aldarondo & Straus, 1994), victims would feel blamed, and their safety was compromised (Bograd, 1984).

THE PARADIGM SHIFT

Since the introduction of mandatory arrest laws in the 1990s, an increasing proportion of offenders are presenting with less pathology and less extensive histories and consequences of abuse (Apsler, Cummins, & Carl, 2002; Hamel, 2005a). This, along with the failure of batterer intervention programs (especially those based in feminist sociopolitical ideology) in reducing recidivism among court-mandated clients (Jackson et al., 2003; Saunders & Hamill, 2003), the emerging literature on systemic factors in partner abuse, and the demand by victims to have a greater say in intervention alternatives, including help with their own anger (Mills, 2003; Shupe, Stacey, & Hazlewood, 1987), makes it clear that current policies are anachronistic and in dire need of revision.

Contrary to the popular notion that abuse in intimate relationships generally reflects patriarchal male privilege, evidence that the bulk of domestic violence involves abuse by both parties has been amassing for at least two and a half decades. The polarization of the field into the "Gender Camp" (i.e., guided by the belief that men are the vastly predominant perpetrators and women make up the considerable majority of victims and that patriarchy and male privilege drive domestic violence) (Dobash et al., 1992; Walker, 1983; Yllo, 1993) and the "Conflict Tactics Camp" (i.e., guided by the belief that men and women are perpetrators and victims and that abuse in intimate relationships reflects diverse causes that frequently interact) has a lengthy infamous history considered at length in many previous relevant publications and is beyond the scope of this chapter (e.g., Dutton & Nicholls, 2005; Shupe et al., 1987; Steinmetz, 1977–1978; Straus, 1999).

Research from the Conflict Tactics Camp was often met with disbelief, fear, and disregard. Several prominent figures in the field who published the controversial findings were confronted with threats to their physical safety (see Cook, 1997; Shupe et al., 1987; see also Medeiros and Straus, chapter 3 in this volume), and others neglected to examine or report the data. For example, Kennedy and Dutton (1989) reported the incidence of male-perpetrated intimate abuse, and Dutton and Nicholls (2005) noted that it was not until two female colleagues pushed for the publication of all the data that they found that the women perpetrated more abuse than they suffered (Kwong, Bartholomew, & Dutton, 1999). Data on abusive women has been ignored or deliberately suppressed by mainstream academic journals and by such organizations as the Ontario, Canada government and the Kentucky Commission on Women (see Fontes, 2002; see also Medeiros and Straus, chapter 3 in this volume).

Building on this well-established history and the continuously expanding extant literature, the breakthrough book by Linda Mills of New York University, *Insult to Injury: Rethinking Our Responses to Intimate Abuse* (2003), calls for major changes in public policy. At the same time, organizations such as Stop Abuse for Everyone (http://www.safe4all.org), the Domestic Abuse Helpline for Men and Women (Hines, Brown, & Dunning, in press), and the Family Violence Treatment and Education Association (http://www.FAVTEA.com) have emerged. These organizations are anchored in principles of gender inclusiveness and evidence-based practice; individuals at every level of intervention are beginning to question the status quo and to become increasingly open to innovation and new ideas (Adams, 2002; Kilzer, 2005). Perhaps nothing presses this movement forward more than the dismal evidence for the efficacy of current intervention strategies (Babcock, Green, & Robie, 2004).

The voices in this book join together in a swelling chorus, advocating for a widening scope of research and the implementation of alternative intervention policies. Clearly and unequivocally, these scholars and practitioners assert that *finding effective ways to reduce domestic violence in our communities is more important than adhering to what is politically correct.* This book is intended for anyone who works with victims or perpetrators of intimate partner abuse, whether primarily court-referred cases or self-referred clients in private practice or agency settings. It also will be relevant to researchers and policymakers interested in evidence-based practice. Its gender-inclusive approach to assessment and intervention represents a significant departure from traditional paradigms, and the combination of theory, research, and policy and practice should serve to cross these essential pillars.

OUTLINE OF CHAPTERS

Part 1: Theory and Research

The chapters in part 1 provide a firm foundation for the policy and practice recommendations that follow in part 2. The first four chapters in this volume offer extensive reviews of the literature and provide new research findings that serve to challenge traditional approaches to investigating and preventing abuse in intimate relationships. In the opening chapter to this section of the book, John Hamel articulates the core principles of the emerging gender-inclusive conception of domestic violence and summarizes key research findings. "Gender-inclusive," he points out, does not mean "gender neutral," and he shows how this new conception is, at its core, empirically based yet faithful to traditional feminist principles.

In chapter 2, Donald Dutton challenges readers to "think outside the box" about gender and court-mandated therapy. His chapter confronts traditional feminist paradigms head-on and dismantles the outdated Duluth model of treatment, piece by piece. Dutton closes with recommendations for gender-inclusive therapeutic interventions for partner abuse to replace the Duluth model. Rose Medeiros and Murray Straus then provide a comprehensive overview of risk factors for dating violence and further add to the scant literature on risk factors for female-perpetrated aggression in dating relationships. Their chapter uses empirical evidence to critically and objectively examine the long-standing assertion that women's violence is unique from men's violence in relationships. Graham-Kevan's first chapter in this volume, "Power and Control in Relationship Aggression," suggests that the etiology of abuse in intimate relationships in the general population is mostly parallel for men and women. Graham-Kevan articulates the terminology and consequences of controlling behaviors, setting controlling behavior firmly along the continuum of partner violence. She reminds the reader that the psychological vulnerability of individuals subjected to severe control (independent of physical abuse) often surpasses the psychopathology associated with physical violence. The chapter provides a comprehensive overview of theories of controlling behavior, empirical studies of women's and men's use of control in selected and nonselected samples, and scales for measuring control in romantic relationships. Graham-Kevan concludes that the implications of controlling behavior can be severe and that, unlike physical aggression, controlling behavior does not appear to diminish in longitudinal research. Independently and in combination, these four chapters (as do many of the chapters in the book) unequivocally contradict the prevailing assumption that *male* dominance is the key variable to successfully end domestic violence.

Stalking can be found in either of the extreme ends of the continuum of abuse in intimate relationships. At the one extreme, stalking reflects the perpetrator's attempts to *initiate* a relationship, and at the other extreme it reflects attempts to *prevent the termination* of a relationship (intimate or otherwise). Research demonstrates that one of the most dangerous periods in many abusive intimate relationships is the point at which one partner attempts to end the relationship. Williams, Frieze, and Sinclair provide a comprehensive overview of stalking in intimate relationships, focusing on stalking in the context of relationship breakups. Their chapter introduces the reader to empirical data on courtship stalking and demonstrates the theoretical and empirical link between seemingly benign behaviors during courtship that may be key indicators of abusive behaviors occurring during a relationship and when a couple separates. Williams and her colleagues provide a comprehensive overview of the sparse research literature examining gender differences and similarities in stalking. The chapter closes with an overview of the clinical implications of stalking for men and women.

Noller and Robillard revisit three firmly entrenched urban myths about domestic violence. First, they assert that violence by women, in addition to violence against women, should be considered a pressing social and public health issue. Second, they propose that we cannot truly appreciate the *dynamics* of couple violence until we extend our unit of analysis beyond a singular explanation (i.e., partriarchy). Finally, they challenge the notion that *all* men are potentially violent.

Nicola Graham-Kevan's chapter "Partner Violence Typologies" discounts traditional explanations of partner abuse (e.g., biological sex or patriarchal society) and offers the reader alternative explanations (e.g., psychopathology) supported by a comprehensive review of the literature. Of particular interest, Graham-Kevan empirically documents the considerable overlap between the characteristics of male and female perpetrators. She concludes that partner violence interventions need to be evidence based and that appropriate treatment must be made available to both female and male victims as well as female and male perpetrators. Given that her evaluation of the research demonstrates that partner abuse is not a unitary phenomenon, she asserts that interventions must similarly be multidimensional, taking into consideration developmental and psychological variables as well as couple interaction styles.

The next two chapters are essential contributions to a text intended to elucidate the reciprocal relationship between intimate partner abuse and the family system. Davies and Sturge-Apple reflect on the accomplishments of the first generation of research into the risk of psychopathology among children exposed to interparental violence. In an effort to propel the field to address remaining gaps in the literature and expedite a new generation of research that will move beyond the first generation's focus on delineating the degree and scope of vulnerability imposed on children as a result of interparental violence, these authors address the processes and the principal variables that might mediate or moderate the risk that domestic violence has for child development and future maladjustment. They elucidate the multiple pathways through which parental violence can result in undermining child development and delineate the transactional processes or bidirectional interactions between the child and the violent adults. Their chapter provides a firm theoretical foundation and empirical evidence for understanding the heightened vulnerability of some children (i.e., while many children remain symptom free) to interparental violence.

Moving through the family and the life span, in the next chapter, Moretti, Penney, Obsuth, and Odgers reflect on adolescence as a "sensitive" period for learning about relationships. These authors assert that families offer a point of reference for adolescents to begin to explore romantic relationships. As discussed previously, considerable effort has been expended to investigate the influence that fathers' aggression has for their children's subsequent risk for aggression and violence in close relationships. Moretti and her colleagues present much-needed new research evidence examining the influence of mothers' aggression for the intergenerational transmission of intimate aggression. Their findings suggest that aggression and violence perpetrated by mothers may have a comparable—or perhaps even more deleterious—effect on their children's future romantic relationships. These two chapters on the broader family system remind us that there is often more than one victim of domestic violence and that the perils that children who witness domestic violence face represent a major public health concern that extends far beyond the individual family system (i.e., the intergenerational transmission of aggression).

Babcock, Canady, Graham, and Schart take us from the "Dark Ages" to the "Scientific Age" of evidence-based policy and practice. These authors track the history of the failures of traditional/current interventions for domestic violence and offer theoretical and empirical insights into why the Duluth model is destined to fail. They assert that advances in other areas of psychotherapy can be used to advance treatment with batterers and make the claim that the field of domestic violence is as much as a decade behind the developments accomplished in other, related areas of scholarly investigation. Acknowledging that it is easy to criticize existing intervention approaches but a much more difficult task to replace them with something superior, Babcock and her colleagues provide templates for "what works."

Part 2: Assessment and Treatment

In part 1 of this book, an impressive body of research that exposes the shortcomings of current intervention polices—both on theoretical grounds and outcome studies—and convincing case for why we ought to adopt models with a more gender-inclusive, family systems orientation are presented by some of the most respected scholars in the field of domestic violence. In part 2, we build on this foundation of formal academic theory and research and provide the reader with practical guidance for evidence-based clinical interventions. This is, after all, a book geared primarily toward practitioners. Although many of these chapters, too, explore the relevant research literature, the emphasis here is on the "nuts and bolts" of treatment. Wherever possible, case examples are presented to make the information clearer and more meaningful.

The opening chapter, by Hamel, describes how the gender-inclusive, family systems conception evolved out of and in response to established and evolving models, such as the patriarchal, conflict-tactics, and typologies/asymmetry conceptions. The treatment models advanced in this volume indeed have roots deep in the research literature among such early pioneers as Straus, Gelles, Steinmetz, and Neidig and derives their impetus both from the "mavericks" in the research community and from public policy changes, including the arrest of less serious offenders, gays, lesbians, and heterosexual women and the gender-inclusive language incorporated into the new, reauthorized Violence Against Women Act. Following this historical overview, Hamel offers guidelines for assessing the entire family system, discusses issues of victim safety, and gives a preview of the treatment possibilities explored in the remainder of the book.

One of the most immediate considerations in assessment is determining a perpetrator's dangerousness and lethality potential. The chapter by Nicholls and her colleagues identifies the cognitive and heuristic problems inherent in assessment, including the pervasive perception that only women can be victims of partner abuse, and suggests how such problems can be minimized. In addition, the features of the more reliable, validated domestic violence assessment instruments are delineated (e.g., Spousal Assault Risk Assessment Guide [Kropp, Hart, Webster, & Eaves, 1999] and Danger Assessment [Campbell, 1986, 2006]). In the next chapter, Fontes explains the psychological and cultural reasons for why men are rarely perceived as victims and proposes ways in which mental health providers, policy-makers and male victims themselves can better overcome this pervasive bias. Following this, Malley-Morrison and her colleagues review the existing literature on family violence among Native American, Latino, African American, and Asian American communities. The authors correct common misperceptions regarding these ethnominority groups (e.g., assumptions of within-group homogeneity) and suggest culturally relevant treatment interventions, including systemic work with the nuclear and extended family.

Among the "pioneers" of domestic violence research and intervention, there have been few as significant as the Austin, Texas, team of Anson Shupe, William Stacey, and Lonnie Hazlewood, who in the 1980s began to publish research on offender treatment, quite radical for its time, acknowledging mutual violence and high levels of power and control tactics exhibited by both the arrested perpetrator and the victim. In his chapter, Hazlewood offers suggestions for batterer intervention providers on ways to increase the effectiveness of this inherently limited treatment modality by eliciting the cooperation of victims and other family members and addressing common treatment dilemmas, such as taking time-outs without one's partner feeling abandoned or controlled and coping with victim retribution following a cessation of violence. Hazlewood explains how the group facilitator can hold clients fully responsible for their behavior while avoiding the counterproductive, shaming tactics employed by traditional models such as Duluth.

Conducting couples therapy for domestically violent partners is the subject of the next three chapters, by O'Leary and Cohen, by the British team of Vetere and Cooper, and finally by Valerie Coleman. After a review of the relevant research literature that finds couples counseling at least as effective and safe as traditional group approaches, O'Leary and Cohen articulate the benefits of this modality and then describe the program they developed at the State University of New York at Stony Brook. This program, intended for "first phase" work (Hamel, 2005b), places a great deal of emphasis on a proper screening, to ensure safety. Treatment consists of between 15 and 20 one-hour conjoint sessions and unfolds as a sequence of stages in which the therapist forms a therapeutic bond with the clients and assists them in examining the origins of their interactive styles, developing treatment goals, and building anger management and positive communication skills. Cooper and Vetere, although equally concerned about safety, describe procedures for doing more in-depth work around the couple's underlying issues, including interaction and attachment styles and patterns established in their families of origin. Adherents to the feminist model developed by Virginia Goldner, the authors present a case example that, in the end, leads to a refreshingly honest reappraisal of their theoretical assumptions. Coleman then explores similar clinical terrain in her chapter on abusive gay and lesbian relationships, elucidating how childhood issues, attachment styles, and merger phenomena, together with internalized homophobia and fear of being "outed," perpetuate abuse dynamics among same-sex partners. Through an extended, thoughtful case example involving a gay male couple, she demonstrates how clinicians can foster a climate of safety while challenging clients to overcome their fears and establish a peaceful, loving relationship.

At this point, the book both expands and narrows its focus to include work with children and adolescents within various family therapy configurations. Thomas, a private practitioner in Seattle, describes a family systems approach that focuses as much or more on direct child abuse as on the interparental violence with which it is so often associated. Thomas rightly criticizes the current fragmentation of services, in which interventions in partner abuse, child physical abuse, and child sexual abuse are typically conducted by separate and often conflicting agencies. He articulates, through vivid case examples, the benefits of a systemic approach to family violence. Potter-Efron, too, works with the entire family system, and his chapter offers practical suggestions on how to handle cases involving both family violence and substance abuse. Following this chapter, Michael Carolla addresses domestic violence assessment and treatment issues within the context of disputed child custody cases. The "good news" is that family courts have finally begun to take interparental abuse seriously. The "bad news" is that mediators, evaluators, and judges are being trained in traditional, outdated models that hyperemphasize the victimization of women and make few distinctions between true battering and high-conflict relationships. According to Carolla, replacement of the "tender years" doctrine by "best interests of the child" guidelines has encouraged contentious parents to make exaggerated and sometimes fabricated abuse charges against the other parent. Whether the charges are true, false, or only partly true, clinicians must match the appropriate intervention for each particular case. Carolla rightly eschews reflexive, "one-size-fits-all" solutions (e.g., batterer intervention program [BIP] treatment for everyone), outlining instead a number of sensible, innovative treatment options, including coparenting counseling, therapeutic supervised visitation, and parent–child reconciliation work.

Family violence can be successfully addressed through group work, as described in the next three chapters. Taking an intergenerational, systemic perspective on family violence, Langhinrichsen-Rohling and her colleagues at the University of South Alabama describe a group treatment program for at-risk adolescent mothers. The program addresses both physical child abuse and violence against partners and teaches anger management, self-care, and interpersonal communication skills, integrating several established curricula, among them Neidig and Friedman's manual for partner abuse. Rybski adopts this latter curriculum for her own group therapy model, consisting of five sessions that bring adolescent offenders of both genders together along with their mothers. Follow-up research has demonstrated preliminary support for the effectiveness of this program in reducing adolescent and parent aggression (verbal and physical) and increasing parental authority and adolescent social and school functioning. The next chapter then outlines two similar programs, a High Conflict Family Violence Parent Group (Pratt) and Chapman's Anger Management Parenting Group. In contrast to BIPs, these programs accept both men and women and allow the participation of couples when the risk level is considered low and manageable. Informed by research and clinical experience that finds high correlations between partner violence and child abuse, as well as evidence for the intergenerational transmission of dysfunction and abuse, these programs expand the narrow focus from partner abuse to all forms of family violence.

Although mutual abuse and high-conflict forms of violence are far more prevalent than any other, some relationships are nonetheless dominated by one perpetrator whose level of emotional and/or physical abuse has a severe impact on his or her victims. Dalpiaz, a victim advocate from Boulder, Colorado, offers detailed, thoughtful, and practical suggestions for helping children and their victimized parents heal in the aftermath of severe family violence with insights that can come only from someone who has experienced these problems firsthand. When victims require more intensive services than can be found in an outpatient agency setting, they may benefit from the help that a shelter can provide. In their chapter, two remarkable women, Carol Ensign and Patricia Jones, write about the Antelope Valley Oasis Shelter in Lancaster, California, one of only three shelters in the United States that accept male residents. Having courageously withstood the initial (and sometimes continuing) backlash from doctrinaire feminists, the shelter staff has since forged a successful alliance with law enforcement, BIPs, and other victim advocates and is a beacon for progressive, gender-inclusive victim advocates everywhere. Clients with children especially benefit from the unique coed environment and find that interactions with abused individuals of the opposite gender can be a healing, learning experience.

Following this chapter, Grauwiler, Pezold, and Mills describe a truly revolutionary intervention approach currently used with individuals arrested for spousal abuse in Nogales, Arizona. In contrast to traditional criminal justice approaches, the program, Construyendo Circulos de Paz, is based on a restorative justice model of intervention. Like many of the other intervention models proposed in this volume, it recognizes: (a) that victims who choose to stay typically don't want their partners incarcerated but rather want them to obtain help to change their behavior, and (b) that patriarchal and other unidimensional explanations for violence are limited and ignore the reality of mutual abuse and the complexity of couples dynamics. The program, according to the authors, brings "family and supportive friends of the offender and the victim, together with a facilitator and relevant child welfare and criminal justice professionals, in a structured setting to hold the offender accountable for the harm done, ensure victim safety, facilitate open dialogue about the violence, and develop a plan to rectify the problem."

Coauthored by a group of victim advocates, mental health professionals, a journalist, and a batterer intervention provider, the final chapter draws on much of the research presented in this book and offers a critical review of gender-biased polices in arrest, the use of restraining orders, and court-mandated intervention. In Chapter 28 "Domestic Violence: New Visions, New Solutions," the authors heed Dutton's call for "outside of the box" thinking and outline a sensible, much-needed set of recommendations for gender-inclusive research, assessment, offender intervention, and delivery of victim service. These and the other suggestions put forth elsewhere in this book provide us with a blueprint for action, a way for us to finally move out of what Babcock calls the "Dark Ages" of intervention to the "Scientific Age." And as we do so, deliberating on the validity of one study versus another or the value of this intervention as opposed to that one, let us not forget our one common purpose—to reduce family violence in our communities.

REFERENCES

Adams, S. (2002). Women who are violent: Attitudes and beliefs of professionals working in the field of domestic violence. *Military Medicine, 167*(6), 445–453.

Aldarondo, E., & Straus, M. (1994). Screening for physical violence in marital therapy. *Family Process, 33,* 425–439.

Apsler, R., Cummins, M., & Carl, S. (2002). Fear and expectations: Differences among female victims of domestic violence who come to the attention of the police. *Violence and Victims, 17*(4), 445–453.

Austin, J., & Dankwort, J. (1999). Standards for batterer programs. *Journal of Interpersonal Violence, 14*(2), 152–168.

Babcock, J. C., Green, C. E., & Robie, C. (2004). Does batterer's treatment work? A meta-analytic review of domestic violence treatment. *Clinical Psychology Review, 23,* 1023–1053.

Bograd, M. (1984). Family systems approaches to wife battering: A feminist critique. *American Journal of Orthopsychiatry, 54,* 558–568.

Campbell, J. (1986). Nursing assessment of risk of homicide for battered women. *Advances in Nursing Science, 3,* 67–85.

Campbell, J. (2006). *The Danger Assessment.* Retrieved January 4, 2006, from http://www. dangerassessment.com/WebApplication1/pages/product.aspx.

Cook, P. (1997). *Abused men: The hidden side of domestic violence.* Westport, CT: Praeger.

Dobash, R. P., & Dobash, R. E. (1979). *Violence against wives: A case against the patriarchy.* New York: Free Press.

Dobash, R. P., Dobash, R. E., Wilson, M., & Daly, M. (1992). The myth of sexual symmetry in marital violence. *Social Problems, 39,* 71–91.

Dutton, D. G., & Nicholls, T. L. (2005). A critical review of the gender paradigm in domestic violence research and theory: Part I—Theory and data. *Aggression and Violent Behavior, 10,* 680–714.

Felson, R. (2002). *Violence and gender reexamined.* Washington, DC: American Psychological Association.

Fontes, D. (2002). *Violent touch: Breaking through the stereotype.* Stop Abuse for Everyone. Retrieved April 10, 2003, from http://www.safe4all.org.

Hamberger, L., & Potente, T. (1994). Counseling heterosexual women arrested for domestic violence: Implications for theory and practice. *Violence and Victims, 9*(2), 125–137.

Hamel, J. (2005a). Fixing only part of the problem: Public policy and batterer intervention. *Family Violence and Sexual Assault Bulletin, 21*(2/3), 18–31.

Hamel, J. (2005b). *Gender inclusive treatment of intimate partner abuse: A comprehensive approach.* New York: Springer.

Henning, K., Jones, A., & Holdford, R. (2003). Treatment needs of women arrested for domestic violence: A comparison with male offenders. *Journal of Interpersonal Violence, 18*(8), 839–856.

Hines, D., Brown, J., & Dunning, E. (in press) Characteristics of callers to the domestic abuse helpline for men. *Journal of Family Violence.*

Hines, D., & Malley-Morrison, K. (2005). *Family violence in the United States: Defining, understanding, and combating abuse.* Thousand Oaks, CA: Sage.

Jackson, S., Feder, L., Forde, D., Davis, R., Maxwell, C., & Taylor, B. (2003). *Batterer intervention programs: Where do we go from here?* (NCJ 195079). Washington, DC: U.S. Department of Justice.

Johnson, M., & Leone, J. (2005). The differential effects of intimate terrorism and situational couple violence: Findings from the National Violence Against Women Survey. *Journal of Family Issues, 26*(3), 322–349.

Kelly, L. (2003). Disabusing the definition of domestic abuse: How women batter men and the role of the feminist state. *Florida State University Law Review, 30,* 791–855.

Kennedy, L. W., & Dutton, D. G. (1989). The incidence of wife assault in Alberta. *Canadian Journal of Behavioural Science, 21,* 40–53.

Kilzer, L. (2005, April 29). *Prosecutors seek change in treatment for batterers.* Rocky Mountain News. Retrieved May 12, 2005, from http://www.rockymountainnews. com/drmn/local/article/0, 1299, DRMN_15_3687637,00.html.

Kropp, P. R., Hart, S. D., Webster, C. D., & Eaves, D. (1999). *Manual for the Spousal Assault Risk Assessment Guide* (3rd ed.). Toronto, Ontario, Canada: Multi-Health Systems.

Kwong, M. J., Bartholomew, K., & Dutton, D. G. (1999). Gender differences in patterns of relationship violence in Alberta. *Canadian Journal of Behavioral Science, 31,* 150–160.

Laframboise, D. (1998; November 23). *Sheltered from reality.* National Post Online. Retrieved March 1, 2002 from http://www.nationalpost.com/artslife.asp?f = 981123/2041765.html.

Loseke, D. (1992). *The battered woman and shelters: The social construction of wife abuse.* Albany: State University of New York Press.

Mills, L. (2003). *Insult to injury: Rethinking our responses to intimate abuse.* Princeton, NJ: Princeton University Press.

Pence, E. (1999). Some thoughts on philosophy. In M. Shepard & E. Pence (Eds.), *Coordinating community responses to domestic violence* (pp. 25–40). Thousand Oaks, CA: Sage.

Saunders, D., & Hamill, R. (2003). *Violence against women: Synthesis of research on offender interventions* (NCJ 201222). Washington, DC: U.S. Department of Justice.

Shupe, A., Stacey, W., & Hazlewood, L. (1987). *Violent men, violent couples: The dynamics of domestic violence.* New York: John Wiley & Sons.

Stacey, W., Hazlewood, L., & Shupe, A. (1994). *The violent couple.* Westport, CT: Praeger.

Steinmetz, S. (1977–1978). The battered husband syndrome. *Victimology: An International Journal, 2,* 499–509.

Straus, M. (1999). The controversy over domestic violence by women. In X. Arriaga & S. Oskamp (Eds.), *Violence in intimate relationships* (pp. 17–44). Thousand Oaks, CA: Sage Publications.

Walker, L. (1983). *The battered woman syndrome.* New York: Springer.

Yllo, K. (1993). Through a feminist lens: Gender power and violence. In R. Gelles & D. Loseke (Eds.), *Current controversies in family violence* (pp. 47–62). Newbury Park, CA: Sage Publications.

PART I

Research and Theory

Domestic Violence: A Gender-Inclusive Conception

John Hamel

Domestic violence, also known as intimate partner violence or IPV, is being increasingly perceived as a human problem rather than a gender problem. Having for years debated *whether* women are as abusive as men, researchers are now seeking to determine *how* and *to what extent.* Similarly, studies investigating the impact of interparental abuse on children no longer depend on samples of battered women in shelters and are drawing on more representative clinical and community samples to examine the role of violence by mothers. The focus has expanded from an exclusive concern with father-perpetrated abuse to a gender-inclusive conception of partner and family violence that eschews simplistic causal explanations and takes into account systemic principles and the complex, interactive nature of family relationships. The gender-inclusive conception can be summarized as a set of ten interrelated principles and research findings as described here.

INTERVENTIONS SHOULD BE BASED ON A THOROUGH, UNBIASED ASSESSMENT

Under the "one-size-fits-all" same-sex group intervention model mandated in most jurisdictions in the United States, clients are subjected to a cursory intake procedure, often by individuals lacking professional training, that is designed primarily to orient the individual to the group process and to sign documents related to legal requirements and victim safety. Other than to obtain the most basic demographic information and screen for the most obvious signs of substance abuse and mental illness, the purpose of these procedures is not really to assess as much as to "enroll." There is little connection, if any, between the intake findings and the treatment offered.

Clinicians in private practice settings or mental health clinics may not be so constrained, but given the pervasiveness of traditional models of assessment and treatment, clinicians are predisposed to focus on a narrow range of domestic phenomena, such as severe, unilateral, male-perpetrated battering. In fact, there are different types of domestic violence, characterized by varying degrees of physical and emotional abuse and psychopathology, as well as extent of mutuality (Dutton, 1998; Hamel, 2005; Holtzworth-Munroe & Stuart, 1994; Johnson & Leone, 2005; Johnston & Campbell, 1993). Clinicians should be aware of these distinctions (see also chapter 12 in this volume).

ALL TREATMENT MODALITIES AND OPTIONS SHOULD BE CONSIDERED, BASED ON THE FACTS OF THE INDIVIDUAL CASE

Clinicians should be free to intervene at all points in the relationship and family system as necessary. "Family therapy," of course, need not involve all members of the family in the same session or even in the overall course of treatment. Rather, interventions are made on the basis of the relationships among the family members, the type of abuse, how each member is affected, and their role in maintaining the dysfunction. Outcome studies have convincingly demonstrated that couples counseling can be an appropriate treatment choice (Greene & Bogo, 2002; Ziegler & Hiller, 2002), safe and effective, especially when conducted in a structured multifamily group format (Brannen & Rubin, 1996; Dunford, 2000; Fals-Stewart, Kashdan, O'Farrell, & Birchler, 2002; Heyman & Schlee, 2003; O'Leary, Heyman, & Neidig, 1999; Stith, Rosen, & McCollum, 2004). Recent studies suggest that relatively novel approaches such as restorative justice might also have utility in certain circumstances (Strang & Braithwaite, 2002; chapter 27 in this volume).

BOTH MEN AND WOMEN CAN BE VICTIMS AND/OR PERPETRATORS, AND EVERYONE IS RESPONSIBLE FOR HIS OR HER BEHAVIOR

Purported rates of 85% to 95% for male-perpetrated assaults have their basis in samples of battered women or in crime surveys that inhibit respondents, particularly males, from fully disclosing their victimization (Straus, 1999; see also Dutton & Nicholls, 2005). More reliable surveys using the Conflict Tactics Scales (CTS2; Straus, Hamby, Boney-McCoy, & Sugarman, 1996) indicate comparable rates of verbal and physical abuse in intimate relationships regardless of gender (Archer, 2000; Fiebert, 1997; Straus & Gelles, 1990). Critics assert that surveys in which violence is framed as a possible conflict resolution tactic are not credible because men aggress primarily to dominate their partners (DeKeseredy, 2002; Kimmel, 2002). However, research indicates that these questionnaires facilitate disclosure and thus *increase* reported rates of violence (Archer, 1999). "There is no evidence," Hines and Malley-Morrison (2001) pointed out, "that either men or women will refrain from reporting a slap, punch, or beating, merely because it seemed to come out of nowhere" (p. 4). One wonders how candid a response might be elicited from a survey respondent or client undergoing assessment when subjected to an alternative line of questioning, such as "How often did you punch your partner when exercising your male privilege to dominate?" Inquiries regarding motive, including those of power and control, are better pursued *after* the initial CTS2 interview (Hamel, 2005).

THE CAUSES OF PARTNER ABUSE ARE VARIED BUT SIMILAR ACROSS GENDERS

Given that we continue to live in a patriarchal society, patriarchal explanations for abuse are certainly not irrelevant, but they are insufficient and often lead to superficial assessments and inappropriate treatment, thus reducing rather than increasing the odds of treatment success. The large number of equalitarian relationships in our society and the correlation between violence and relationship domination by both females and males (Coleman & Straus, 1990; Medeiros & Straus, this volume); the fact that most men are neither physically abusive nor prone to engage in power and control tactics (Cook, 1997; Dutton, 1994); the high rates of female-on-female abuse in lesbian relationships (McClellen, Summers, & Daley, 2002; Renzetti, 1992; West, 1998), and research indicating that violent men in fact display *less* traditional masculine characteristics than their nonviolent counterparts (Felson, 2002; Neidig, Friedman, & Collins, 1986; Sugarman & Frankel, 1996) negate simplistic explanations along culture and gender lines.

Men do not "naturally" and universally dominate women; economic scarcity and other ecological factors determine whether they assume positions of power and are likely to abuse that power. Anthropological data from around the world (Sanday, 1981) fix the number of strictly male-dominated societies at approximately one-third of the total, with equalitarian societies making up another third and the rest composed of those in which men have "mythical" rather than absolute dominance over women. In other words, the greater structural power enjoyed by men in patriarchal societies does not necessarily translate to dyadic relationships (Glick & Fiske, 1999). An extensive review of the literature by Hotaling and Sugarman (1986) found no differences in sex role inequality between violent and nonviolent couples. Felson (2002) wrote,

> In sum, I have suggested that the relative power of husbands and wives depends on their personal situation, and that power is specific to relationships. The fact that the U.S. Senate is run by men is largely irrelevant to the private conflicts of individuals. Even a senator who has power does not necessarily have power over his wife. If he is smitten, she has power over him. In general, the economic power of the average man and woman in society and the fact that our political leaders are male are not likely to be significant factors in violent spousal conflicts. From this perspective, dyadic power has much stronger effects on how spouses treat each other than structural power. It would not be too much of an exaggeration to say that "all conflict is local." (p. 61)

Certainly, there continue to exist in our society cultural norms approving of public displays of aggression by men and disapproving of those by women (Eagly & Steffen, 1986), and there is ample cross-cultural evidence of much higher rates of physical aggression and somewhat higher rates of verbal aggression by men (Archer, 2004). This is not, however, because women are less angry or hostile than men—gender differences are, in fact, negligible or nonexistent (Archer, 2004; Averill, 1983). Females of all ages engage in indirect aggression against peers, coworkers, and others (Bjorkqvist, 1994; Frieze, 2005), and adolescent girls use indirect forms of aggression at significantly higher rates than boys (Archer, 2004). Furthermore, when given the opportunity to engage in direct aggression, women will do so when they feel justified or can do so anonymously (Frodi, Macaulay, & Thome, 1977; Richardson, 2005).

Even among lower animals, the males are typically no more dominant or aggressive than the females, except in displays of interspecies conflict, which tend to be those most often studied and filmed. "There is no support," writes psychologist David Adams (1992), "for the myth that humans have inherited a general mammalian tendency for males to be more aggressive than females" (p. 23).

In contradistinction to aggression outside the home, societal norms actually *support* rather than inhibit female aggression in the home (Johnson & Ferraro, 2000; Straus, Kaufman-Kantor, & Moore, 1997), where a wife and mother will be driven to defend her interests (Straus, 1999).

In intimate relationships, men and women express anger and emotionally abuse and engage in most forms of power and control tactics at about the same rate, and this includes stalking when broadly defined (Averill, 1983; Coker, Davis, Arias, Desai, Sanderson, et al., 2002; Davis & Frieze, 2000; Graham-Kevan & Archer, 2005; Hammock & O'Hearn, 2002; Kasian & Painter, 1992; Straus, Gelles, & Steinmetz, 1980). Male and female survey respondents alike endorse control, retribution, and a need to get a partner's attention as motives for engaging in partner violence (Babcock, Miller, & Siard, 2003; Carrado, George, Loxam, Jones, & Templar, 1996; Cascardi & Vivian, 1995; Fiebert & Gonzalez, 1997; Follingstad, Wright, Lloyd, & Sebastian, 1991; Harned, 2001; Makepeace, 1986).

So, if patriarchy is a poor explanation for partner violence, what *is* its etiology? Risk factors for female-perpetrated violence include the stress of low income and unemployment (Magdol, Moffitt, Caspi, Fagan, & Silva, 1997), being in a dating or cohabitating relationship or being under 30 years of age (Morse, 1995; Sommer, 1994; Straus et al., 1980), childhood abuse (Babcock et al., 2003; Conradi, 2004), and pro-violent attitudes (Follingstad et al., 1991; Simmons, Lehmann, & Cobb, 2004). Certain personality features have also been identified, among them dependency and jealousy, common among both heterosexual and lesbian offenders (Coleman, 1994; Shupe, Stacey, & Hazlewood, 1987), as well as those that either meet the criterion for a personality disorder, such as borderline, antisocial, or narcissistic (Henning, Jones, & Holdford, 2003; Johnston & Campbell, 1993; Kalichman, 1988; Simmons, et al., 2004), or characterized by a generally aggressive personality (Ehrensaft, Moffitt, & Caspi, 2004; Felson, 2002; Follingstad, Bradley, Helff, & Laughlin, 2002; O'Leary, 1988; Sommer, 1994). These same factors have been found in the etiology of male-perpetrated violence (Dutton, 1998; Hamberger & Hastings, 1986; Holtzworth-Munroe & Stuart, 1994). Of course, alcohol and drug abuse are also implicated in violent relationships among both victims and perpetrators (Anderson, 2002; Leonard & Roberts, 1998; Magdol et al., 1997; Straus et al., 1980).

VICTIM/PERPETRATOR DISTINCTIONS ARE OVERSTATED, AND MUCH PARTNER ABUSE IS MUTUAL

The factors that cause and perpetuate partner abuse are found not only in the respective individuals but in the conflict itself—in the dynamics found in those relationships characterized by, for instance, poor communication and conflict resolution skills and situational stressors (Babcock, Waltz, Jacobsen, & Gottman, 1993; Burman, John, & Margolin, 1992; Cordova, Jacobsen, Gottman, Rushe, & Cox, 1993; Moffitt, Robins, & Caspi, 2001; Ridley & Feldman, 2003; Telch & Lindquist, 1984). Research also indicates that the pairing of individuals with particular attachment styles, such as someone who fears intimacy and someone who fears abandonment, increases the likelihood of physical abuse (Bartholomew, Henderson, & Dutton, 2001; Bookwala, 2002; Roberts & Noller, 1998).

A dynamic, however dysfunctional, does not automatically implicate both parties as willful contributors to the abuse. Accounts of battered women (e.g., Pagelow, 1984; Walker, 1979) and men (Cook, 1997; Migliaccio, 2002; Pearson, 1997) indicate that in many relationships one partner is clearly the dominant abuser and the other the victim. An analysis of the National Family Violence Surveys, using the women's reports (Straus, 1993), found that unilateral violence by one partner occurred at rates of about 25% for men and women. It also found that in approximately half the households, both partners had physically assaulted each other in the past year and that the women had initiated the violence in the majority of the cases. Other large surveys, longitudinal studies, and research on dating populations reveal high levels of mutual violence, some well above 50%, and initiated at roughly equal rates by both genders (Anderson, 2002; Bookwala, Frieze, Smith, & Ryan, 1992; Deal & Wampler, 1986; DeMaris, 1992; Langhinrichsen-Rohling, Neidig, & Thorn, 1995; Moffitt & Caspi, 1999; Morse, 1995; Nicholls & Duttton, 2001; O'Leary, Barling, Arias, Rosenbaum, Malone, & Tyree, 1989; Williams & Frieze, 2005). Remarkably, in Gondolf's (1996) multisite study of men's batterer intervention programs, the female victims reported to have initiated the violence in 40% of the cases during a treatment follow-up period.

Thus, despite claims by victim advocates to the contrary (Hamberger & Potente, 1994; Henning et al., 2003), self-defense is not the predominant motive for assaults by either gender. Reports of self-defense by women range from as low as 5% in clinic samples (Cascardi & Vivian, 1995) up to 40% among women residing in shelters (Saunders, 1986). General population surveys and studies of dating populations (Follingstad et al., 1991; Sommer, 1994) fix the rates of self-defense at only between 10% and 20% for men and women, respectively. The extent to which men or women engage in genuine self-defense is unclear because of the difficulty in distinguishing it from retaliation. In a large representative English sample (Carrado et al., 1996), 21% of the women and 27% of the men who had been violent reported that their motive was "getting back at him/her for some physical action she/he had used against me."

What percentage of these figures represents self-defense was not determined by the researchers. In the often-cited Saunders (1986) study, 30% of the women indicated that they were "fighting back," a phenomenon the researchers regarded as a distinct construct, but the terms are often used interchangeably (e.g., Hamberger & Potente, 1994) and are further confused with the concept "dominant aggressor."

Determining the dominant aggressor requires an investigation both into the pattern of physical assaults and the use of controlling and emotionally abusive behaviors. Research with women court-ordered to participate in a batterer intervention program has found comparable or greater numbers of dominant aggressors among the male partners (Henning & Feder, 2004; Swan & Snow, 2002). In Conradi's (2004) study of female perpetrators, only 9% were deemed to be dominant aggressors. However, these studies had serious methodological flaws, such as failing to consider power and control tactics used by women and relying solely on the women offenders' reports and records of previous domestic violence calls to the police, which are far more often made by women and do not always indicate who is the actual or primary victim. Similar research bias has marred Johnson's otherwise excellent attempt to typologize partner abuse (Johnson & Leone, 2005). A study comparing women arrested for spousal abuse and women in shelters (Abel, 2001) found significantly higher trauma symptomology in the latter group. Moreover, studies with male offenders (Shupe et al., 1987) have also found comparable rates of violence, emotional abuse, and power and control tactics between the partners.

Labeling individuals as "victims," "perpetrators," or "dominant aggressors" is standard procedure in determining legal culpability and may help clinical assessments by delineating treatment options (Hamel, 2005), but it is rarely clear-cut, and it may confuse rather than elucidate. Many perpetrators have been victims of abuse in their current relationship, in previous relationships, or in their childhoods of origin (Coker et al., 2002; Dutton, 1998). Are we to consider all such individuals "victims," or do we draw a line at some point in time and inform the offender that "it's been too long since your last victimization, so now you are officially a perpetrator"? Obviously, preemptive assaults by victims of severe intimate terrorism who have been so traumatized that they literally fear for their lives ought to be regarded differently than most other cases, in which the retaliation merely adds to the escalating violence and guarantees further victimization for both parties.

And what about relationships in which one partner is solely responsible for the physical violence but the other engages in high levels of emotionally abusive and controlling behaviors? It is for these reasons that consideration of systemic factors is crucial to successful intervention in intimate partner abuse. In fact, as amply demonstrated throughout this book, even cases involving clear "victims" and "perpetrators" require a systemic approach because untreated victims who escape their abuser tend to reinvolve themselves in abusive relationships, subjecting themselves and their children to further trauma and increasing the probability of abuse in the next generation. A systemic approach makes no a priori assumptions about culpability; rather, it is a means of understanding, a way of obtaining information and determining the particular elements and modalities of intervention.

BOTH GENDERS ARE PHYSICALLY AND EMOTIONALLY IMPACTED BY ABUSE

Let us suppose that there were an outbreak of a deadly and widespread new virus and that the victims were 95% male. Treatment was available but dependent on early detection and screening. Would cash-strapped health organizations be faulted if they concentrated their outreach resources on men—for instance, advertising in men's magazines or disseminating information specifically to men's advocacy groups, say, father's rights organizations? What if those virus victims were 85% male? One can easily imagine the outrage if women were ignored at rates any lower than this. As previously discussed, men and women are equally victims of assaults in intimate relationship. Furthermore, men are the victims in fully a quarter of intimate partner homicides (Department of Justice, 2002). The National Violence Against Women Survey found that 41% of female victims had suffered any physical injury in the past year, compared to 19% of the male respondents (Tjaden & Thoennes, 2000), and in the meta-analytic review by Archer (2000), men were found to have suffered 38% of physical injuries. Clearly, this is a reason for concern and a major reason for the gender-inclusive position taken in this volume.

With some exceptions (e.g., Callahan, Tolman, & Saunders, 2003), in the majority of studies conducted on the effects of physical abuse, females report higher levels of anxiety, fear, depression, posttraumatic stress, health problems, substance abuse, and lost wages due to days missed on the job than males (e.g., Anderson, 2002; Straus & Gelles, 1990; Vivian & Langhinrichsen-Rohling, 1994; Williams & Frieze, 2005; for an excellent review of research on the effects of female-perpetrated abuse, see Hines & Malley-Morrison, 2001). However, the effects of general *abuse,* including verbal put-downs, jealousy-fueled isolation behaviors, and other control tactics, would seem to be comparable between genders, according to the National Violence Against Women Survey (Pimlott-

Kubiak & Cortina, 2003). This is not surprising in light of research indicating the more profound impact of emotional abuse on victims of both genders, particularly verbal abuse (Arias & Pape, 1999; Cook, 1997; Frieze, 2005; Harned, 2001; O'Leary, 1999; Simonelli & Ingram, 1998). Many clinicians, unfortunately, are unaware of these findings and focus primarily or solely on the effects of men's abuse (Dutton & Nicholls, 2005; Follingstad, DeHart, & Green, 2004).

"GENDER INCLUSIVE" DOES NOT MEAN "GENDER NEUTRAL" OR "GENDER EQUAL"

As discussed previously, women suffer the greater share of physical injuries, especially severe injuries. A female colleague with many years experience conducting batterer intervention programs for men once told this author (Hamel) that she had "never known a man who'd gotten the snot beat out of him." In fact, men are indeed far more likely than women to beat up their partners with their fists (Archer, 2002; Straus et al., 1990); and, as discussed above, women suffer the greater share of physical injuries, especially severe injuries. Because of their typically larger size, men can more effectively use physical intimidation as a way to dominate their partners with or without the use of violence. Men, who can better protect themselves and gain physical control over their partner (Johnston & Campbell, 1993), will often dismiss women's violence as inconsequential or even amusing (Hamberger & Guse, 2002). Women, at rates three times higher than men, express fear of physical danger from their abusive partners (Follingstad et al., 1991; Morse, 1995). When they kill their partners, women are more likely than men to do so in response to previous physical attacks (Felson & Messner, 1998).

Furthermore, although women engage in high degrees of unwanted sexual behavior toward men, some of it coercive (Frieze, 2000; Krahe, Waizenhofer, & Moller, 2003), men perpetrate the overwhelming number of rapes in intimate partner relationships (Tjaden & Thoennes, 2000). Here is one victim's account:

> He would tie me whenever we had sex to a bed or a chair or whatever. Sometimes he would force me to suck him and would stick his penis in my mouth all the time. Sometimes he would tie me and turn me around facing the other way and would have anal sex with me. He ripped my rectum so many times that the doctors in the emergency room used to laugh when I'd walk in . . . he would stick all kinds of things in my vagina, like the crucifix with the picture of Jesus on it. (Walker, 1979, p. 121)

These findings have led some researchers (e.g., Jacobsen & Gottman, 1998) to claim that, while women may physically assault men and cause physical injuries, only men can be said to "batter" their partners. "Battering," a term sometimes used synonymously with "intimate terrorism" (Johnson & Leone, 2005; for a discussion, see chapters 2 and 10 in this volume), is thought to occur only when a perpetrator combines emotional abuse and power and control tactics with physical violence, usually severe violence. Research showing that women use abuse/control tactics at rates comparable to men are overlooked, as is the fact that they make up for their lesser strength by using objects and weapons and carrying out assaults when their partners are asleep, drunk, or not paying attention (Cook, 1997; Mann, 1988; McCleod, 1984; Shupe et al., 1987; Steinmetz & Lucca, 1988). Here is one man's account, courtesy of Cook (1997):

> She would lose her temper and throw things at me. The first time, I was walking down the hall . . . and a set of keys hit me in the back of the head. . . . A lot of times, I would be working on some papers and there would be a coffee cup there, and she would intentionally spill the coffee; she went from that to throwing the coffee, and then throwing the cup and the coffee. She would throw hot scalding coffee in my face . . .
>
> She would hit me with things. One time we had an argument, and I decided to let her go into the bedroom and let her settle down, so I went to sleep on the couch. About an hour later, I was awakened with a terrible pain on my forehead. She had taken one of my cowboy boots and, with the heel, whacked me on the forehead. (p. 39)

Indeed, men may not have the snot "beat" out of them nearly as often as females, but it is certainly shot, knifed, burned, or dislodged out of them with objects (Straus & Gelles, 1990). However, because of prevailing cultural norms that require men to be strong and in control and that minimize the significance of female-perpetrated abuse (Mooney, 2000; Straus et al., 1997; Simon, Anderson, Thompson, Crosby, Shelley & Sacks, 2001; Sorenson & Taylor, 2005), men are reluctant to admit fear of their female partners (Dutton & Nicholls, 2005; Fontes, 2002). Some men clearly are afraid of their partners, but when they contact law enforcement, they are not taken as seriously as female victims (Buzawa & Austin, 1993; Watkins, 2005). Much like battered women, they will disclose their fears only when they feel safe enough to do so (Hines, Brown, & Dunning, in press).

In short, if we define "battering" or "intimate terrorism" as the perpetration of emotionally abusive/controlling behaviors in combination with physical abuse, there are as many female intimate terrorists as male intimate terrorists (Graham-Kevan & Archer, 2005). When we narrow our definitions to take into account the higher physical injuries suffered by women and men's greater ability to engender fear of *physical* harm, we find that men clearly perpetrate the majority of this violence. We ought not, however, discount fear of *emotional* harm. In light of the generally greater effects of emotional abuse, it would seem reasonable to take seriously *all* types of "abuse" regardless of how we define that term. One is pressed to determine what is the greater fear—of being shoved by your spouse across the room next time he or she has a bad day or of being called a "loser" in front of your children or having your sexual performance ridiculed.

Treatment of domestic violence must also take into account differences between the genders in biology, personality, communication, and social roles, and clinicians who conduct intervention groups for female perpetrators (e.g., Koonin, Cabarcas, & Geffner, 2002; Leisring, Dowd, & Rosenbaum, 2003; Petracek, 2004) structure their programs accordingly, including time for such topics as premenstrual syndrome and its role in self-care and anger management. Women generally put a higher value on relationship intimacy and are more emotive, whereas men value autonomy and have a more linear, problem-solving orientation (Tannen, 1990). According to Farrell (1988), men are conditioned to view women as sex objects, but women, who have traditionally favored economic stability, often regard men as *success* objects. Men may become frustrated and escalate their anger when sexually unsatisfied or when their partners do not behave in a stereotypically female "nurturing" manner, while some women may absolve themselves of financial responsibility and expect to secure custody of the children in the event of a divorce. Because a great part of their self-esteem comes from being providers, men are more prone to experience work stress, whereas the tasks associated with child care and homemaking are what typically cause stress in women—even more so in dual-income families, where they still carry the greater domestic burden (Allen & Hawkins, 1999; Cascardi & Vivian, 1995).

In assuming these roles and invoking male privilege, some men seek to dominate their partners (Pence & Paymar, 1993), whereas domination and control by women is often based on *female privilege*—the assumption that in matters of child care and homemaking, they know better and should not be questioned (Allen & Hawkins, 1999). Indeed, traditional gender roles, especially when they are forced rather than agreed on, do have an impact on couples' conflict and the escalation of aggression for both men and women (Coleman & Straus, 1990; Stith, Rosen, Middleton, Busch, Lundeberg, et al., 2000). Such communication and gender role disparities, unless properly understood and managed, may easily fuel relationship conflict. Thus, to the extent that there exists "gendered" violence, such violence cannot be said to be perpetrated only by men.

THE GENDER-INCLUSIVE APPROACH IS
A *FEMINIST* APPROACH

The research to be found in this volume, together with the authors' suggestions for treatment and policy, honor the pioneering efforts of victim advocates and the shelter movement in finally getting domestic abuse to be taken seriously and are meant to build on this work. No one wishes to return to a time when violence between intimate partners was regarded as a "private matter" rather than the criminal offense that it is. Along the way, however, the movement has taken a strange turn, producing a rigid, exclusionary, and ideologically driven form of feminism remarkably unconcerned about its original principles of equality, truth, and social justice. This feminism, which has dominated research and been responsible for the intervention policies currently in existence, has been called *victim feminism* or, alternatively, *gender feminism* (Sommers, 1994) and has, ironically, much in common with the patriarchy it would overthrow. Corvo and Johnson (2003) write,

> Such a feminist epistemology was to ensure . . . the honoring of process, and of complex interpersonal systems. It was to encourage dialectical, "both/and" thinking, as opposed to the "either/or" dualism attributed to "patriarchal" mindsets. It was to foster an awareness that "the personal is the political," that individual psychology, motivations, and actions impact at cultural and sociopolitical levels. It was to avoid the projection of our own unacceptable fears and thoughts onto those perceived as somehow "other than" ourselves; it was to eschew the wholesale objectification and dismissal of entire classes of people . . .
>
> Those working in the field of domestic violence must be allowed to make good on feminist claims as to the purported value of examining the full range of the problem as it manifests along a variety of dimensions, of recognizing complex and multifactorial etiological processes at work in the perpetuation of the problem, and in rejecting stereotypical characterizations of males as well as females, without either their feminist loyalties or compassion credentials being called into question. (pp. 268–269)

The gender-inclusive approach is an attempt to make good on those early promises of feminism. An *equity feminism* seeks to protect all members of the family system and holds perpetrators of both genders accountable for their behavior. As yet, scholars have not adequately explained how it can be that women are a priori powerless in intimate relationships yet possess the physical strength, stamina, mental toughness, and drive to become police officers, firefighters, and business executives. "As long as women subscribe to the notion of universal victimization," writes Reena Sommer (1995), "they will never experience the freedom that goes along with having control over their lives" (p. 3). And, we hasten to add, our common goal of eliminating domestic violence from our communities will remain compromised.

REGARDLESS OF PERPETRATOR GENDER, CHILD WITNESSES TO PARTNER ABUSE ARE ADVERSELY AFFECTED AND ARE AT RISK FOR PERPETRATING PARTNER ABUSE AND BECOMING VICTIMIZED AS ADULTS

A recent meta-analytic review of the literature (Kitzmann, Gaylord, Holt, & Kenny, 2003) found that 63% of children who had witnessed marital violence exhibited lower overall functioning than other children. Among the symptoms identified in this study and previously by other investigators (e.g., Wolak & Finkelhor, 1998) were poor self-esteem, anxiety and trauma symptoms, depression, aggression, disrupted peer relations, and poor academic performance. Child symptomology has also been linked to witnessing marital conflict and verbal abuse (Cummings & Davies, 2002; Repetti, Taylor, & Seeman, 2002; Straus & Smith, 1990; Wolak & Finklehor, 1998).

Whether because of sampling limitations from an overdependence on shelter samples, because of an "evolutionary process," or reflecting a more pervasive bias within the research community (Corvo & Johnson, 2003; Dutton, 2005; Dutton & Nicholls, 2005), researchers investigating the impact of partner abuse on children have focused almost exclusively on violence by the father on the mother. In the rare exceptions when mothers' violence is investigated, similar internalizing and externalizing symptomology have been found in children (English, Marshall, & Stewart, 2003; Johnston & Roseby, 1997) as well as in adolescents (Fergusson & Horwood, 1998; Mahoney, Donnelly, Boxer, & Lewis, 2003; see also chapter 9 in this volume). These findings are significant because of the correlations found between children witnessing marital abuse by either parent and a host of adult psychosocial problems, including perpetration of intimate partner abuse (Langhinrichsen-Rohling et al., 1995; Straus, 1992). In fact, these studies by Langhinrichsen-Rohling et al. as well as by Straus revealed *higher* rates of violence among adult perpetrators who had seen the mother assault the father compared to father assaulting mother. More recently, research with 112 delinquent juveniles found correlations between previous exposure to interparental aggression by the mother but not by the father and perpetration of dating violence by both girls and boys (Moretti, Obsuth, Odgers, & Reebye, in press). A college dating population survey (Kaura & Allen, 2004) additionally found that abusive women were more likely to have lived with a violent father, whereas violent men typically grew up with a violent mother. In contrast, a study by Sommer (1995), using a large community sample, found evidence for same-sex modeling, as did a study involving 1,576 college students (Jankowski, Leitenberg, Henning, & Coffey 1999).

FAMILY VIOLENCE IS A COMPLEX PHENOMENON, WITH RECIPROCAL INTERACTIONS BETWEEN THE INDIVIDUAL MEMBERS

Interventions in intimate partner abuse must take into account the family system (see chapters 8 and 9 in this volume) because human beings are relational creatures and because the effect of one person's behavior has repercussions for the larger group. In cases where couples have no children, the dyadic relationship *is* the system. When working with a childless perpetrator whose victim has left, the clinician should still be mindful of the possibility that the client has a history of abuse in his or her family of origin and of the effects it may continue to have in the present.

Severe intimate violence (e.g., punching, kicking, and choking) between parents occurs at rates of approximately four to five per hundred couples, a rate half as high as severe physical child abuse or severe abuse perpetrated by a child on a parent (Straus & Gelles, 1990). Sibling abuse represents the highest rates of family violence (Caffaro & Con-Caffaro, 1998) and is more prevalent than abuse from peers in Family (Finkelhor, Ormrod, Turner, & Hamby, 2005).

Family violence researchers have well documented the relationship between marital abuse and physical child abuse. A number of commonalities have been identified, including major risk factors (Daro, Edleson, & Pinderhughes, 2004; Merrill, Crouch, Thomsen, & Guimond, 2004). The focus has been almost exclusively on abuse perpetrated by fathers. When mothers are found to have perpetrated child abuse, it is typically explained as a consequence of the stress and trauma from their victimization by their partners (e.g., Wolak & Finkelhor, 1998). In fact, research indicates that women who hit their children are more often perpetrators rather than victims of partner abuse (English et al., 2003) and that, regardless of their perpetrator or victim status, fathers and mothers involved in intimate partner abuse are equally at risk of hitting children (Appel & Holden, 1998; Margolin & Gordis, 2003; Straus & Smith, 1990). Analyzing the results of their well-designed study on family violence, Mahoney et al. (2003) concluded that "mothers' and fathers' aggression in the marital and parent-child subsystems cannot be easily disentangled; neither parent clearly emerges as the primary perpetrator or victim of aggression in the family system" (p. 16). A major new study involving 453 couples with young children (Slep and O'Leary, 2005) found that bidirectional partner aggression occurred in 65% of the families and that 51% of couples engaged in both partner and child abuse "Battering dad" patterns (severe violence by dad on mom accompanied by severe abuse of the child by either parent) accounted for only 2% of families with severe violence.

We know from a recent meta-analysis (Kitzmann et al., 2003) that partner and child abuse have roughly equal effects on children, although the greatest impact may be from the verbal abuse directed by parents against the children (English et al., 2003; Moore & Pepler, 1998). We also know that the effects of marital violence on the family system extend beyond the discrete internalizing and externalizing symptomology in children to include shifts in alliances and the blurring of boundaries between subsystems (Johnston & Roseby, 1997). Many children learn through observation to become violent toward siblings or the parents (Ullman & Straus, 2003). According to English et al. (2003),

> A direct link between DV directed at the primary caregiver and subsequent child outcomes may be difficult to find because domestic violence as measured here reflects a *family* use of violence, *involving the female caregiver as perpetrator twice as often as victim*. A picture emerges of households with a general atmosphere of negative, hostile and aggressive behavior occurring between all "family" members. (p. 54)

Research is revealing the central role of stress in family violence (Margolin & Gordis, 2003; Salzinger, Feldman, Ing-mak, Majica, Stockhammer, et al., 2002) and is beginning to elucidate some of the causal pathways in which the victim of one person's abuse may reciprocate that abuse (as in mutually abusive adult partner relationships) and may also be the perpetrator to another person in the same family system. As can be gleaned from studies showing child behavior problems causing high levels of parental stress prior to and independently of marital violence (Lynch & Cicchetti, 1998), the "top down" or "trickle effect" mechanisms in which partner abuse leads to child abuse offer only a partial explanation for a much more complex picture. Potter-Efron (2005) writes,

> Although by no means inevitable, physical violence may be a serious problem in chronically angry families. Negative verbal interactions within these families can easily spiral toward violence over time. Grumbling turns into shouting and then shouting converts to threatening, threatening changes into shoving, shoving becomes slapping, and

slapping finally yields to hitting. Although not necessarily everyone in the family becomes physically violent, everybody is deeply affected by the aggression. Adults who become violent often feel guilty and not in control of themselves or the family. Nonviolent spouses often feel frightened and helpless. Children can be traumatized when witnessing parental violence or when they themselves have become the recipients of harm. They can also learn in this manner that violence is an acceptable form of communication, something they can do either right away or when they grown up and have their own partners and children . . .

Members of chronically angry families seldom take responsibility for their actions. Instead, they blame other family members, essentially playing a game of "It's not my fault.". . . Each person will need to make a personal commitment to contain his or her own anger and anger-provoking behaviors before the family as a whole can change. (pp. 166–167)

CONCLUSION

There is now a substantial, rapidly growing body of evidence pointing to serious shortcomings in the paradigms that currently drive domestic violence research, intervention, and policy. The gender-inclusive approach seeks to correct for these shortcomings while retaining the original feminist values of fairness and social justice as well as the twin priorities of victim safety and perpetrator accountability that advocates have championed for years. Rather than simply present a new ideology, the gender-inclusive approach is, at its core, empirically based, guided by the data, and loyal only to interventions derived from them. Perhaps this approach is not so revolutionary; after all, the scientific study of family violence was pioneered by Straus, Gelles, and Steinmetz some 30 years ago, before many of today's researchers had entered college. They understood very well that abuse is not solely a matter of gender and that partner violence cannot be adequately understood outside the context of family. That the trails blazed by these pioneers are only now beginning to reach their destinations is due not to the failure of their vision but rather to fear, human nature, and the myopia of politics. In a sense, we have come "full circle," the new breed of researchers joining with the old. We are in good company, indeed.

REFERENCES

Abel, E. (2001). Comparing the social service utilization, exposure to violence, and trauma symptomology of domestic violence female "victims" and "batterers." *Journal of Family Violence, 16*(4), 401–420.

Adams, D. (1992). Biology does not make men more aggressive than women. In K. Bjorkqvist & P. Niemela (Eds.), *Of mice and women: Aspects of female aggression* (pp. 17–25). San Diego, CA: Academic Press.

Allen, S., & Hawkins, A. (1999). Maternal gatekeeping: Mother's beliefs and behaviors that inhibit greater father involvement in family work. *Journal of Marriage and the Family, 61,* 199–212.

Anderson, K. (2002). Perpetrator or victim? Relationships between intimate partner violence and well-being. *Journal of Marriage and the Family, 64,* 851–863.

Appel, A., & Holden, G. (1998). The co-occurrence of spouse and physical abuse: A review and appraisal. *Journal of Family Psychology,* 12(4), 578–599.

Archer, J. (1999). Assessment of the reliability of the Conflict Tactics Scale. *Journal of Interpersonal Violence,* 14(12), 1263–1289.

Archer, J. (2000). Sex differences in aggression between heterosexual partners: A meta-analytic review. *Psychological Bulletin,* 126(5), 651–680.

Archer, J. (2004). Sex differences in aggression in real-world settings: A meta-analytic review. *Review of General Psychology,* 8(4), 291–322.

Arias, I., & Pape, K. (1999). Psychological abuse: Implications for adjustment and commitment to leave violent partners. *Violence and Victims, 14,* 55–67.

Averill, J. (1983, November). Studies on anger and aggression: Implications for theories of emotion. *American Psychologist,* 1145–1160.

Babcock, J., Miller, S., & Siard, C. (2003). Toward a typology of abusive women: Differences between partner-only and generally violent women in the use of violence. *Psychology of Women Quarterly, 13,* 46–59.

Babcock, J., Waltz, J., Jacobsen, N., & Gottman, J. (1993). Power and violence: The relation between communication patterns, power discrepancies, and domestic violence. *Journal of Consulting and Clinical Psychology,* 61(1), 40–50.

Bartholomew, K., Henderson, A., & Dutton, D. (2001). Insecure attachment and abusive intimate relationships. In C. Culow (Ed.), *Adult attachment and couple psychotherapy* (pp. 43–61). New York: Brunner-Routledge.

Bjorkqvist, K. (1994). Sex differences in physical, verbal and indirect aggression: A review of recent research. *Sex Roles,* 30(3/4), 177–188.

Bookwala, J. (2002). Adult attachment styles and aggressive behaviors in dating relationships. *Journal of Social and Personal Relationships, 15,* 175–190.

Bookwala, J., Frieze, I., Smith, C., & Ryan, K. (1992). Predictors of dating violence: A multivariate analysis. *Violence and Victims, 7,* 297–311.

Brannen, S., & Rubin, A. (1996). Comparing the effectiveness of gender-specific and couples groups in a court-mandated spouse abuse treatment program. *Research on Social Work Practice,* 6(4), 405–424.

Burman, B., John, R., & Margolin, G. (1992). Observed patterns of conflict in violent, nonviolent, and nondistressed couples. *Behavioral Assessment, 14,* 15–37.

Buzawa, E., & Austin, T. (1993). Determining police response to domestic violence victims: The role of victim preference. *American Behavioral Scientist,* 36(5), 610–623.

Caffaro, J., & Conn-Caffaro, A. (1998). *Sibling abuse trauma: Assessment and intervention strategies for children, families and adults.* Binghamton, NY: Haworth Maltreatment & Trauma Press.

Callahan, M., Tolman, R., & Saunders, D. (2003). Adolescent dating violence victimization and well-being. *Journal of Adolescent Research,* 18(6), 664–681.

Carrado, M., George, M., Loxam, F., Jones, L., & Templar, D. (1996). Aggression in British heterosexual relationships: A descriptive analysis. *Aggressive Behavior, 22,* 401–415.

Cascardi, M., & Vivian, D. (1995). Context for specific episodes of marital violence: Gender and severity of violence differences. *Journal of Family Violence, 10,* 265–293.

Coker, A, Davis, K., Arias, I., Desai, S., Sanderson, M., Brandt, H., & Smith, P. (2002). Physical and mental health effects of intimate partner violence for men and women. *American Journal of Preventive Medicine, 23*(4), 260–268.

Coleman, D., & Straus, M. (1990). Marital power, conflict and violence in a nationally representative sample of American couples. In M. Straus & R. Gelles (Eds.), *Physical violence in American families* (pp. 287–300). New Brunswick, NJ: Transaction Publishers.

Coleman, V. (1994). Lesbian battering: The relationship between personality and perpetration of violence. *Violence and Victims, 9*(2), 139–152.

Conradi, L. (2004, September 18). *An exploratory study of heterosexual females as dominant aggressors of physical violence in their intimate relationships*. Paper presented at the FVSAI 9th International Conference on Family Violence, San Diego, CA.

Cook, P. (1997). *Abused men: The hidden side of domestic violence*. Westport, CT: Praeger.

Cordova, J., Jacobsen, N., Gottman, J., Rushe, R., & Cox, G. (1993). Negative reciprocity and communication in couples with a violent husband. *Journal of Abnormal Psychology, 102*(4), 559–564.

Corvo, K., & Johnson, P. (2003). Vilification of the "batterer": How blame shapes domestic violence policy and interventions. *Aggression and Violent Behavior, 8*, 259–281.

Cummings, E., & Davies, P. (2002). Effects of marital conflict on children: Recent advances and emerging themes in process-oriented research. *Journal of Child Psychology and Psychiatry, 43*(1), 31–63.

Daro, D., Edleson, J., & Pinderhughes, H. (2004). Finding common ground in the study of child maltreatment, youth violence, and adult domestic violence. *Journal of Interpersonal Violence, 19*(3), 282–298.

Davis, K., & Frieze, I. (2000). Research on stalking: What do we know and where do we go? *Violence and Victims, 15*(4), 473–487.

Deal, J., & Wampler, K. (1986). Dating violence: The primacy of previous experience. *Journal of Social and Personal Relationships, 3*, 457–471.

DeKeseredy, W. (2002). *Measuring the extent of woman abuse in intimate relationships: A critique of the Conflict Tactics Scale*. Retrieved June 1, 2005, from http://www.vawnet.org.

DeMaris, A. (1992). Male versus female initiation of aggression: The case of courtship violence. In E. Viano (Ed.), *Intimate violence: Interdisciplinary perspectives* (pp. 111–120). Washington, DC: Taylor & Francis.

Department of Justice. (2002). *Crime in the United States, 2001*. Uniform Crime Reports. Washington, DC: Federal Bureau of Investigation.

Dunford, F. (2000). The San Diego navy experiment: An assessment of interventions for men who assault their wives. *Journal of Consulting and Clinical Psychology, 68*(3), 468–476.

Dutton, D. (1994). Patriarchy and wife assault: The ecological fallacy. *Violence and Victims, 9*(2), 167–182.

Dutton, D. (1998). *The abusive personality*. New York: Guilford Press.

Dutton, D. (2005). The domestic abuse paradigm in child custody assessments. *Journal of Child Custody, 2*(4), 23–42.

Dutton, D., & Nicholls, T. (2005). A critical review of the gender paradigm in domestic violence research and theory: Part I—Theory and data. *Aggression and Violent Behavior, 10*, 680–714.

Eagly, A., & Steffen, V. (1986). Gender and aggressive behavior: A meta-analytic review of the social psychological literature. *Psychological Bulletin, 100*(3), 309–330.

Ehrensaft, M., Moffitt, T., & Caspi, A. (2004). Clinically abusive relationships in an unselected birth cohort: Men's and women's participation and developmental antecedents. *Journal of Abnormal Psychology, 113*(2), 258–270.

English, D., Marshall, D., & Stewart, A. (2003). Effects of family violence on child behavior and health during early childhood. *Journal of Family Violence, 18*(1), 43–57.

Fals-Stewart, W., Kashdan, M., O'Farrell, T., & Birchler, G. (2002). Behavioral couples therapy for drug-abusing patients: Effects on partner violence. *Journal of Substance Abuse Treatment, 22,* 87–96.

Farrell, W. (1988). *Why men are the way they are.* New York: Berkeley Books.

Felson, R. (2002). *Violence and gender reexamined.* Washington, DC: American Psychological Association.

Felson, R., & Messner, S. (1998). Disentangling the effects of gender and intimacy on victim precipitation in homicide. *Criminology, 36*(2), 405–424.

Fergusson, D., & Horwood, J. (1998). Exposure to interparental violence childhood and psychosocial adjustment in young adulthood. *Child Abuse and Neglect, 22*(5), 339–357.

Fiebert, M. (1997). Annotated bibliography: References examining assaults by women on their spouses/partners. In B. M. Dank & R. Refinette (Eds.), *Sexual harassment and sexual consent* (Vol. 1, pp. 273–286). New Brunswick, NJ: Transaction Publishers.

Fiebert, M., & Gonzalez, D. (1997). Women who initiate assaults: The reasons offered for such behavior. *Psychological Reports, 80,* 583–590.

Finkelhor, D., Ormrod, R., Turner, H., & Hamby, S. (2005). The victimization of children and youth: A comprehensive national survey. *Child Maltreatment, 10*(1), 5–25.

Follingstad, D., Bradley, R., Helff, C., & Laughlin, J. (2002). A model for predicting dating violence: Anxious attachment, angry temperament and a need for relationship control. *Violence and Victims, 17*(1), 35–47.

Follingstad, D., DeHart, D., & Green, E. (2004). Psychologists' judgments of psychologically aggressive actions when perpetrated by a husband versus a wife. *Violence and Victims, 19*(4), 435–452.

Follingstad, D., Wright, S., Lloyd, S., & Sebastian, J. (1991). Sex differences in motivations and effects in dating relationships. *Family Relations, 40,* 51–57.

Fontes, D. (2002). *Violent touch: Breaking through the stereotype.* Stop Abuse for Everyone. Retrieved April 10, 2003, from www.safe4all.org.

Frieze, I. (2000). Violence in close relationships—Development of a research area: Comment on Archer (2000). *Psychological Bulletin, 126,* 681–684.

Frieze, I. (2005). *Hurting the one you love: Violence in relationships.* Belmont, CA: Wadsworth.

Frodi, A., Macaulay, J., & Thome, P. (1977). Are women always less aggressive than men? A review of the experimental literature. *Psychological Bulletin, 84*(4), 634–660.

Glick, P., & Fiske, S. (1999). Gender, power dynamics, and social interaction. In M. M. Ferree, J. Lorber, & B. Hess (Eds.), *Revisioning gender* (pp. 365–398). Thousand Oaks, CA: Sage.

Gondolf, E. (1996). *Characteristics of batterers in a multi-site evaluation of batterer intervention systems.* Retrieved March 4, 2004, from http://www.mincava.umn.edu/documents/gondolf/ batchar.html.

Graham-Kevan, N. & Archer, J. (2005). Using Johnson's domestic violence typology to classify men and women in a non-selected sample. *9th International Family Violence Research Conference,* New Hampshire.

zHamberger, L., & Guse, C. (2002). Men's and women's use of intimate partner violence in clinical samples. *Violence Against Women, 8,* 1301–1331.

Hamberger, L., & Hastings, J. (1986). Personality correlates of men who abuse their partners. *Journal of Family Violence, 1*(4), 323–341.

Hamberger, L., & Potente, T. (1994). Counseling heterosexual women arrested for domestic violence: Implications for theory and practice. *Violence and Victims, 9*(2), 125–137.

Hamel, J. (2005). *Gender-inclusive treatment of intimate partner abuse: A comprehensive approach.* New York: Springer.

Hammock, G., & O'Hearn, R. (2002). Psychological aggression in dating relationships: Predictive models for male and females. *Violence and Victims, 17,* 525–540.

Harned, M. (2001). Abused women or abused men? An examination of the context and outcomes of dating violence. *Violence and Victims, 16,* 269–285.

Henning, K., & Feder, L. (2004). A comparison of men and women arrested for domestic violence: Who presents the greater threat? *Journal of Family Violence, 19*(2), 69–80.

Henning, K., Jones, A., & Holdford, R. (2003). Treatment needs of women arrested for domestic violence: A comparison with male offenders. *Journal of Interpersonal Violence, 18*(8), 839–856.

Heyman, R., & Schlee, K. (2003). Stopping wife abuse via physical aggression couples treatment. In D. Dutton & D. Sonkin (Eds.), *Intimate violence: Contemporary treatment innovations* (pp. 135-157). New York: Haworth Maltreatment & Trauma Press.

Hines, D., Brown, J., & Dunning, E. (in press). Characteristics of callers to the domestic abuse helpline for men. *Journal of Family Violence.*

Hines, D., & Malley-Morrison, K. (2001). Psychological effects of partner abuse against men: A neglected research area. *Psychology of Men and Masculinity, 2*(2), 75–85.

Holtzworth-Munroe, A., & Stuart, G. (1994). Typologies of male batterers. *Psychological Bulletin, 116*(3), 476–497.

Hotaling, G., & Sugarman, D. (1986). An analysis of risk markers in husband to wife violence: The current state of knowledge. *Violence and Victims, 1,* 101–124.

Jacobsen, N., & Gottman, J. (1998). *When men batter women.* New York: Simon & Schuster.

Jankowski, M. K., Leitenberg, H., Henning, K., & Coffey, P. (1999). Intergenerational transmission of dating aggression as a function of witnessing only same sex parents vs. opposite sex parents vs. both parents as perpetrators of domestic violence. *Journal of Family Violence, 14,* 267–279.

Johnson, M., & Ferraro, K. (2000). Research on domestic violence in the 1990s: Making distinctions. *Journal of Marriage and the Family, 62,* 948–963.

Johnson, M., & Leone, J. (2005). The differential effects of intimate terrorism and situational couple violence: Findings from the National Violence Against Women Survey. *Journal of Family Issues, 26*(3), 322–349.

Johnston, J., & Campbell, L. (1993). A clinical typology of interpersonal violence in disputed-custody cases. *American Journal of Orthopsychiatry, 63*(2), 190–199.

Johnston, J., & Roseby, V. (1997). *In the name of the child.* New York: Free Press.

Kalichman, S. (1988). MMPI profiles of women and men convicted of domestic homicide. *Journal of Clinical Psychology, 44*(6), 847–853.

Kasian, M., & Painter, S. (1992). Frequency and severity of psychological abuse in a dating population. *Journal of Interpersonal Violence, 7*(3), 350–364.

Kaura, S., & Allen, C. (2004). Dissatisfaction with relationship power and dating violence perpetration by men and women. *Journal of Interpersonal Violence, 19*(5), 576–588.

Kimmel, M. (2002). "Gender symmetry" in domestic violence: A substantive and methodological research review. *Violence Against Women, 8*(11), 1332–1363.

Kitzmann, K., Gaylord, N., Holt, A., & Kenny, E. (2003). Child witnesses to domestic violence: A meta-analytic review. *Journal of Consulting and Clinical Psychology, 71*(2), 339–352.

Koonin, M., Cabarcas, A., & Geffner, R. (2002). *Treatment of women arrested for domestic violence: Women ending abusive/violent episodes respectfully.* San Diego, CA: Family Violence & Sexual Assault Institute.

Krahe, B., Waizenhofer, E., & Moller, I. (2003). Women's sexual aggression against men: Prevalence and predictors. *Sex Roles, 49*(5/6), 219–232.

Langhinrichsen-Rohling, J., Neidig, P., & Thorn, G. (1995). Violent marriages: Gender differences in levels of current violence and past abuse. *Journal of Family Violence, 10*(2), 159–175.

Leisring, P., Dowd, L., & Rosenbaum, A. (2003). Treatment of partner aggressive women. In D. Dutton and D. Sonkin (Eds.), *Intimate violence: Contemporary treatment innovations* (pp. 257–277). New York: Haworth Maltreatment & Trauma Press.

Leonard, K. E., & Roberts, L. J. (1998). The effects of alcohol on the marital interactions of aggressive and nonaggressive husbands and their wives. *Journal of Abnormal Psychology, 107*(4), 602–615.

Lynch, M., & Ciccheti, D. (1998). An ecological-transactional analysis of children and contexts. *Developmental Psychopathology, 10,* 235–257.

Magdol, L., Moffitt, T., Caspi, A., Fagan, J., & Silva, P. (1997). Gender differences in partner violence in a birth cohort of 21 year olds: Bridging the gap between clinical and epidemiological approaches. *Journal of Consulting and Clinical Psychology, 65,* 68–78.

Mahoney, A., Donnelly, W., Boxer, P., & Lewis, T. (2003). Marital and severe parent-to-adolescent physical aggression in clinic-referred families: Mother and adolescent reports on co-occurrence and links to child behavior problems. *Journal of Family Psychology, 17*(1), 3–19.

Makepeace, J. (1986, July). Gender differences in courtship violence victimization. *Family Relations, 35,* 383–388.

Mann, C. (1988). Getting even? *Justice Quarterly, 5,* 33–51.

Margolin, G., & Gordis, E. (2003). Co-occurrence between marital aggression and parents' child abuse potential: The impact of cumulative stress. *Violence and Victims, 18*(3), 243–258.

McClellen, J., Summers, A., & Daley, J. (2002). The lesbian partner abuse scale. *Research on Social Work Practice, 12,* 277–292.

McLeod, M. (1984). Women against men: An examination of domestic violence based on an analysis of official data and national victimization data. *Justice Quarterly, 1,* 171–193.

Merrill, L., Crouch, J., Thomsen, G., & Guimond, J. (2004). Risk for intimate partner violence and child physical abuse: Psychosocial characteristics of multirisk male and female navy recruits. *Child Maltreatment, 9*(1), 18–29.

Migliaccio, T. (2002). Abused husbands: A narrative analysis. *Journal of Family Issues, 23,* 26–52.

Moffitt, T., & Caspi, A. (1999, July). *Findings about partner violence from the Dunedin Multidisciplinary Health and Development Study* (NCJ 170018). Washington, DC: National Institute of Justice.

Moffitt, T., Robins, R., & Caspi, A. (2001). A couples analysis of partner abuse with implications for abuse-prevention policy. *Criminology and Public Policy, 1*(1), 5–36.

Mooney, J. (2000). *Gender, violence, and the social order.* New York: St. Martin's Press.

Moore, T., & Pepler, D. (1998). Correlates of adjustment in children at risk. In G. Holden, R. Geffner, & E. Jouriles (Eds.), *Children exposed to domestic violence* (pp. 157–184). Washington, DC: American Psychological Association.

Moretti, M. M., Obsuth, I., Odgers, C., & Reebye, P. (in press). Exposure to maternal versus paternal partner violence and aggression in adolescent girls and boys: The moderating role of PTSD. *Aggressive Behavior.*

Morse, B. (1995). Beyond the Conflict Tactics Scale: Assessing gender differences in partner violence. *Violence and Victims, 10*(4), 251–269.

Neidig, P., Friedman, D., & Collins, B. (1986). Attitudinal characteristics of males who have engaged in spouse abuse. *Journal of Family Violence, 1*(3), 223–233.

Nicholls, T., & Dutton, D. (2001). Abuse committed by women against male intimates. *Journal of Couples Therapy, 10,* 41–57.

O'Leary, K. D. (1988). Physical aggression in spouses: A social learning theory perspective. In R. Van Hasselt, R. Morrison, A. Bellack, & M. Hersen (Eds.), *Handbook of family violence* (pp. 31–55). New York: Plenum Press.

O'Leary, K. D. (1999). Psychological abuse: A variable deserving critical attention in domestic violence. *Violence and Victims, 14*(1), 3–23.

O'Leary, K., Barling, J., Arias, I., Rosenbaum, A., Malone, J., & Tyree, A. (1989). Prevalence and stability of physical aggression between spouses: A longitudinal analysis. *Journal of Consulting and Clinical Psychology, 57,* 263–268.

O'Leary, K. D., Heyman, R., & Neidig, P. (1999). Treatment of wife abuse: A comparison of gender-specific and conjoint approaches. *Behavior Therapy, 30,* 475–505.

Pagelow, M. (1984). *Family violence.* New York: Praeger.

Pearson, P. (1997). *When she was bad: Women and the myth of innocence.* New York: Penguin.

Pence, E., & Paymar, M. (1993). *Education groups for men who batter: The Duluth model.* New York: Springer Publishing.

Petracek, L. (2004). *The anger workbook for women.* Oakland, CA: New Harbinger.

Pimlott-Kubiak, S., & Cortina, M. (2003). Gender, victimization and outcomes: Reconceptualizing risk. *Journal of Consulting and Clinical Psychology, 71*(3), 528–539.

Potter-Efron, R. (2005). *Handbook of anger management: Individual, couple, family, and group approaches.* New York: Haworth Press.

Renzetti, C. (1992). *Violent betrayal: Partner abuse in lesbian relationships.* Newbury Park, CA: Sage.

Repetti, R., Taylor, S. E., & Seeman, T. E. (2002). Risky families: Family social environments and the mental and physical health of offspring. *Psychological Bulletin, 128*(2), 330–366.

Richardson, D. (2005). The myth of female passivity: Thirty years of revelations about female aggression. *Psychology of Women Quarterly, 29,* 238–247.

Ridley, C., & Feldman, C. (2003). Female domestic violence toward male partners: Exploring conflict responses and outcomes. *Journal of Family Violence, 18*(3), 157–171.

Roberts, N., & Noller, P. (1998). The association between adult attachment and couple violence. In J. Simpson & W. Rholes (Eds.), *Attachment theory and close relationships* (pp. 317–350). New York: Guilford Press.

Salzinger, S., Feldman, R., Ing-mak, D., Majica, E., Stockhammer, T., & Rosario, M. (2002). Effects of partner violence and physical child abuse on child behavior: A study of abused and comparison children. *Journal of Family Violence, 17*(1), 23–52.

Sanday, P. (1981). *Female power and male dominance: On the origins of sexual inequality.* New York: Cambridge University Press.

Saunders, D. (1986). When battered women use violence. *Violence and Victims, 1*(1), 47–60.

Shupe, A., Stacey, W., & Hazlewood, L. (1987). *Violent men, violent couples: The dynamics of domestic violence.* New York: John Wiley & Sons.

Simmons, C., Lehmann, P., & Cobb, N. (2004, September 18). *Personality profiles and attitudes toward violence of women arrested for domestic violence: How they differ from and are similar to men arrested for domestic violence.* Paper presented at the FVSAI 9th International Conference on Family Violence, San Diego, CA.

Simon, T., Anderson, M., Thompson, M., Crosby, A., Shelley, G., & Sacks, J. (2001). Attitudinal acceptance of intimate partner violence among U.S. adults. *Violence and Victims 16*(2), 115–126.

Simonelli, C., & Ingram, K. (1998). Psychological distress among men experiencing physical and emotional abuse in heterosexual dating relationships. *Journal of Interpersonal Violence, 13*(6), 667–681.

Slep, A., & O'Leary, S. (2005). Parent and partner violence in families with young children: Rates, patterns, and connections. *Journal of Consulting and Clinical Psychology, 73*(3), 435–444.

Sommer, R. (1994). *Male and female perpetrated partner abuse: Testing a diathesis stress model*. Winnipeg, Canada: University of Manitoba.

Sommer, R. (1995, October 14–15). *Controversy within family violence research*. Paper presented at the Women's Freedom Network Conference, Washington, DC. Retrieved December 15, 2001, from http://www.reenasommerassociates.mb.ca/a_wfn.html.

Sommers, C. (1994). *Who stole feminism? How women have betrayed women*. New York: Touchstone.

Sorenson, S., & Taylor, C. (2005). Female aggression toward male intimate partners: An examination of social norms in a community-based sample. *Psychology of Women Quarterly, 29*, 78–96.

Steinmetz, S., & Lucca, J. (1988). Husband battering. In V. Van Hasselt (Ed.), *Handbook of family violence* (pp. 233–246). New York: Plenum Press.

Stith, S., Rosen, K., & McCollum, E. (2004). Treating intimate partner violence within intact couple relationships: Outcomes of multi-couple versus individual couple therapy. *Journal of Marital and Family Therapy, 30*(6), 305–315.

Stith, S., Rosen, K., Middleton, K., Busch, A., Lundeberg, K., & Carlton, R. (2000). The intergenerational transmission of spouse abuse: A meta-analysis. *Journal of Marriage and the Family, 62*, 640–654.

Strang, H., & Braithwaite, J. (Eds.). (2002). *Restorative justice and family violence*. London: Cambridge University Press.

Straus, M. (1992, September). *Children as witnesses to marital violence: A risk factor for lifelong problems among a nationally representative sample of American men and women*. Report of the 23rd Ross Roundtable on Critical Approaches to Common Pediatric Problems (M5796). Columbus, OH: Ross Laboratories.

Straus, M. (1993). Physical assaults by wives: A major social problem. In R. Gelles & D. Loseky (Eds.), *Current controversies on family violence* (pp. 67–87). Newbury Park, CA: Sage.

Straus, M. (1999). The controversy over domestic violence by women. In X. Arriaga & S. Oskamp (Eds.), *Violence in intimate relationships* (pp. 17–44). Thousand Oaks, CA: Sage.

Straus, M., & Gelles, R. (1990). *Physical violence in American families*. New Brunswick, NJ: Transaction Publishers.

Straus, M., Gelles, R., & Steinmetz, S. (1980). *Behind closed doors: Violence in the American family*. Newbury Park, CA: Sage.

Straus, M., Hamby, S., Boney-McCoy, S., & Sugarman, D. (1996). The Revised Conflict Tactics Scales (CTS2): Development and preliminary psychometric data. *Journal of Family Issues, 17*(3), 283–316.

Straus, M., Kaufman-Kantor, G., & Moore, D. (1997). Change in cultural norms approving marital violence: From 1968 to 1994. In G. Kaufman-Kantor & J. Jasinski (Eds.), *Out of the darkness: Contemporary perspectives on family violence* (pp. 3–16). Thousand Oaks, CA: Sage.

Straus, M., & Smith, C. (1990). Family patterns and child abuse. In M. Straus & R. Gelles (Eds.), *Physical violence in American families* (pp. 245–262). New Brunswick, NJ: Transaction Publishers.

Sugarman, D., & Frankel, S. (1996). Patriarchal ideology and wife-assault: A meta-analytic review. *Journal of Family Violence, 11*(1), 13–39.

Swan, S., & Snow (2002). A typology of women's use of violence in intimate relationships. *Violence Against Women, 8*(3), 286–319.

Tannen, D. (1990). *You just don't understand*. New York: Ballantine.

Telch, C., & Lindquist, C. (1984). Violent vs. non-violent couples: A comparison of patterns. *Psychotherapy, 21*(2), 242–248.

Tjaden, P., & Thoennes, N. (2000). Extent, nature, and consequences of intimate partner violence: Findings from the National Violence Against Women Survey. NCJ 181867. Washington, DC: U.S. Department of Justice.

Ullman, A., & Straus, M. (2003). Violence by children against mothers in relation to violence between parents and corporal punishment by parents. *Journal of Comparative Family Studies, 34,* 41–60.

Vivian, D., & Langhinrichsen-Rohling, J. (1994). Are bi-directionally violent couples mutually victimized? A gender-sensitive comparison. *Violence and Victims, 9*(2), 107–124.

Walker L. (1979). *The battered woman*. New York: Harper & Row.

Watkins, P. (2005). Police perspective: Discovering hidden truths in domestic violence interventions. *Journal of Family Violence, 20*(1), 47–54.

West, C. (1998). Leaving a second closet: Outing partner violence in same-sex couples. In J. Jasinski & L. Williams (Eds.), *Partner violence: A comprehensive review of 20 years of research* (pp. 163–183). Thousand Oaks, CA: Sage.

Williams, S., & Frieze, I. (2005). Patterns of violent relationships, psychological distress, and marital satisfaction in a national sample of men and women. *Sex Roles, 52*(11/12), 771–785.

Wolak, J., & Finkelhor, D. (1998). Children exposed to partner violence. In J. Jasinski & L. Williams (Eds.), *Partner violence: A comprehensive review of 20 years of research* (pp. 184–209). Thousand Oaks, CA: Sage.

Ziegler, P., & Hiller, T. (2002, March/April). Good story/bad story: Collaborating with violent couples. *Psychotherapy Networker,* 63–68.

CHAPTER 2

Thinking Outside the Box: Gender and Court-Mandated Therapy

Donald G. Dutton

A major setback for the chances of performing effective court-mandated therapy with domestic violence offenders was the enforcement of "psycho-educational models" by several state and county commissions. Gelles (1996) saw these as a by-product of the feminist stereotype of all males as potentially violent and conservative courts as wishing to punish transgressors. It is, in many ways, a reprise of the "whipping-post legislation" proposed in the early part of the 20th century (Pleck, 1987), only now the punishment was for being male or part of an "oppressor group" or for using "male privilege." Of course, when one reads the demographics of arrested client populations, one finds that court-mandated clients are frequently working class, unemployed, African American, or Hispanic or a member of another cultural minority (Sherman et al., 1992). That was the case, too, when the whipping-post legislation was passed in three states. It was used disproportionately against African American men (Pleck, 1987, pp. 119–120).

The punishment aspect now takes the form of shaming the clients and getting them to repent their gender privilege rather than the corporal punishment described by Pleck. It generates short-term compliance with a set of gender-political beliefs while leaving the infrastructure of abuse untouched: a homeostatic system of emotions and cognitions that derive from them (Dutton, 2003). In other works (e.g., Dutton, 1994b; Dutton & Nicholls, 2005), I have criticized the feminist approach to "intervention." I have pointed out that the "Duluth model" of psychoeducational intervention

(Pence & Paymar, 1993) fails to establish a therapeutic bond and reshames clients who have, as part of their clinical problem, shaming (Dutton, 2003).

THE THERAPEUTIC PROBLEM
WITH THE DULUTH MODEL

The Duluth Domestic Abuse Intervention Project (DAIP) designed an intervention program to be applied to men who had assaulted their female partners but who were not going to receive jail time (Pence & Paymar, 1993). The objective of the program was to ensure safety of the women victims (protection from recidivist violence) by "holding the offenders accountable" and by placing the onus of intervention on the community to ensure the women's safety. The curriculum of the Duluth model was developed by a "small group of activists in the battered women's movement" (Pence & Paymar, 1993, p. xiii) and was designed to be used by "facilitators" in court-mandated groups. It is now one of the most commonly used court-sanctioned interventions for men convicted who have mandatory treatment conditions placed on their probation. This is true in many states and Canadian provinces. The curriculum of the model stresses that violence is used as a form of "power and control," and a "power and control wheel" has become a famous insignia of the program. In addition, power and control tactics are seen as being an exclusively male problem. As the authors put it, "They are socialized to be dominant and women to be subordinate" (p. 5). Hence, the "educational" aspect of the program deals with male privilege that exists in patriarchal structures such as North American countries. The DAIP view of female violence is that it is always self-defensive. "Women often kick, scratch and bite the men who beat them, but that does not constitute mutual battering" p. 5). Male battering stems from beliefs that are themselves the product of socialization. These include the belief that the man should be the boss in the family, that anger causes violence, that women are manipulative, that women think of men as paychecks, that if a man is hurt it is natural for him to hurt back, that smashing things is not abusive, that women's libbers hate men, that women want to be dominated by men, that men batter because they are insecure, that a man has the right to choose his partners' friends and associates, and that a man can't change if the woman won't change (pp. 7–13). According to the manual, the basis for these beliefs came from a sample of five battered women and four men who had completed the Duluth program. The authors do not comment on the obvious problems with the small sample size or lack of representativeness.

The Duluth perspective on psychological problems is outlined in their manual: "Most group members are participating not because of a personal problem or family dysfunction but rather because violence is a socialized option for men. To attach a clinical diagnosis to the batterers' use of violence provides a rationalization for behavior that may not be accurate" (Pence & Paymar, 1993, p. 23). In the rare case where "mental illness" is diagnosed, other treatment is recommended.

The Duluth model's focus on power and control has men keeping "control logs" and reviewing the socialization that leads to expectations of "male privilege." It "discusses how making women into sex objects and then defining sex objects as bad degrades women and lowers their self esteem. From there it goes on to discuss why men would want women to have low self-esteem" (Pence & Paymar, 1993, p. 41). It does not address any psychological issues or emotions that group members may have. "Negative feelings" are seen as caused by patriarchal beliefs (p. 48). Instead, it focuses on patriarchy, including drawing a pyramid on the board and asking "who is at the top?" and a "how did he get there?" (p. 43). *The facilitator is advised to use slavery or a colonial relationship as an example to "draw a picture of the consciousness of domination"* (p. 49). The Duluth model uses role plays to show male abusiveness (p. 61) and raises men's consciousness about trivializing women's anger (p. 62). Men are encouraged to "respond in a respectful way" (p. 63) when their female partner gets angry. Since only 9.6% of U.S. marriages are male dominant (Coleman & Straus, 1985) but 100% of master–slave relationships were (by definition) master dominant, the analogy seems somewhat stretched.

The objectives of the Duluth model, respectful and nonabusive relationships, are not different from other theoretical models of intervention for abusive men (such as cognitive-behavioral therapy [CBT] or even psychodynamic treatment). However, the means to the end differ significantly from psychological models that have been proven to be more effective than the pure Duluth Model (Babcock, Green, & Robie, 2004). Many of the processes and skills that the Duluth programs utilize are, in fact, similar to psychotherapeutic models of intervention (e.g., affect regulation, assertiveness skills, negotiation skills, and so on). The primary difference seems to be the unyielding adherence to their etiology of violence: the sociodemographic "oppressor model" of male domination with instrumental violence taken as a given and the emphasis on male control of women (to the exclusion of other factors contributing to abuse). The Duluth model avoids utilizing the term *therapy* because therapy implies that there is something wrong with clients, whereas, according to the Duluth philosophy, they are normal, simply following cultural dictates. My own position, based on the research data for interpersonal partner violence (IPV), is that psychological (individual and interpersonal), biological, and social/political causal factors are not inherently incongruent and that, if we truly want to develop effective models of intervention for domestic violence, we must consider all levels of explanation. This has been referred to as a "nested ecological model" (Dutton, 1995b).

The Duluth model psychoeducational groups were legislated as mandatory in many states, and state "domestic violence councils" were put in place to "oversee" that treatment groups adhered to the model, including making group leaders "accountable" to victim advocates (Maiuro, Hagar, Lin, & Olson, 2001; Tolman 2001). In California, the policy gave leeway to therapists to add on to the essential components of the Duluth model: That all abuse was a male-generated need for "power and control." In other locations, service providers became disenchanted with the Duluth program to the point that, when a recent treatment outcome study sought to compare Duluth with CBT models, only one "pure" Duluth model could be found. The others had reverted to using CBT techniques blended with Duluth perspectives in order to satisfy state requirements (Babcock et al., 2004). Dutton (2003) argued that Duluth models had a major flaw that was contraindicative of effective treatment in that "facilitators" were required to take a strong adversarial stance to clients, precluding the formation of a therapeutic bond with their clientele.

THE THEORETICAL PROBLEM WITH THE DULUTH MODEL

The theoretical problem with the Duluth model has been explored here and in other papers (Archer, 2000; Corvo & Johnson, 2003; Dutton, 1994b). Simply put, it is that the evidence for patriarchy as a "cause" of wife assault is scant and contradicted by several data sets, including data showing that male-dominant couples constitute only 9.6% of all couples (Coleman & Straus, 1985), women are at least as violent as men (Archer, 2000), women are more likely to use severe violence against nonviolent men than the converse (Stets & Straus, 1992b), powerlessness rather than power seems related to male violence, and there are no data supporting the idea that men in North America find violence against their wives acceptable (Dutton, 1994b). To the contrary, only 2.1% of U.S. men think it is acceptable for a man to strike a woman to "keep her in line" (Simon et al., 2001). Finally, abuse rates are higher in lesbian relationships than in heterosexual relationships (Lie, Schilit, Bush, Montague, & Reyes, 1991), suggesting that intimacy and psychological factors regulating intimacy are more important than sexism. Studies such as Archer's (2000) meta-analytic combination of numerous studies with a combined sample size of 60,000 found women to be more violent than men, especially as the age of the sample dropped (Archer, 2000). Other studies ruled out the rejoinder that this was all self-defensive violence (Dutton & Nicholls, 2005; Follingstad, Wright, Lloyd, & Sebastian, 1991). In fact, less than 3% of all males (and about one-third of males in court-mandated treatment) fit the stereotype of terrorist violence put forward by the Duluth model (Dutton, 2006a, 2006b, 2006-Manuscript under review; Dutton & Nicholls, 2005). Many males will be arrested who come from families where violence is dyadic, minor, or female per-petrated (Stets & Straus, 1992b). According to Duluth, all men must be treated as patriarchal terrorists regardless of differences in etiology.

The single most predictive factor for successful therapeutic outcome is the therapeutic relationship (e.g., Schore, 2003). However, it becomes extremely difficult to form a positive relationship when the therapist is required to disbelieve acts of violence by the partner, can lose their certi-fication with probation if they don't confront their clients enough, or are considered enabling or manipulated when they advocate for their clients' continued treatment.

One must balance confrontation with support, belief, and caring in order to develop a solid therapeutic alliance. Building a therapeutic alli-ance without colluding with dangerous acting-out behaviors is one of the greatest challenges facing domestic violence perpetrator treatment providers. Because so many of these individuals experienced abuse by authority figures, the process of building a trusting relationship is par-ticularly difficult (see also Mills, 1999).

According to Luborsky (1984), the therapeutic alliance may be defined as "that point in the therapeutic relationship when the client on one hand elevates the therapist to a position of authority, but on the other hand believes that this power and authority is shared between them, that there is a deep sense of collaboration and participation in the process. In this way a positive attachment develops between the client and the therapist" (p. 134).

Luborsky (1984) describes two types of therapeutic alliance: the type 1 therapeutic alliance, which is more evident at the beginning of therapy and where the alliance is based on the client's experiencing the therapist as supportive and helpful, and the type 2 therapeutic alliance, which is more typical of the later phases of treatment and where there is a joint struggle against what is impeding the client, a shared responsibility for working out treatment goals, and a sense of we-ness.

Luborsky (1984) makes several recommendations to therapists on how to develop this alliance:

1. Freud's suggestions, made almost 75 years ago, still hold true today. "A friendly, sympathetic attitude toward the client is ben-eficial for the initial development of the alliance."

2. Feeling and expressing empathy toward the client.
3. Helping clients feel invested in the tasks necessary to change (e.g., client-involved treatment planning).

These recommendations run counter to the Duluth model, which emphasizes confrontation and accountability. Given the inherent dangerousness of domestic violence situations, it is important for therapists to incorporate clear guidelines and structure in treatment to minimize acting out; however, without a positive relationship with the therapist, the client is not going to truly be invested in treatment and is likely to either fake it (comply) or drop out altogether, being labeled as "unmotivated" (not unlike the abused child who is viewed by teachers not as a victim but as a problem). Murphy and Baxter (1997) also cautioned against highly confrontational approaches, and the Michigan Governor's Task Force on adopted standards for IPV treatment specified that programs that use abusive or hostile confrontational techniques are contraindicated because such techniques may reinforce the use of abusive control at home (Tolman, 2001, p. 227).

Maiuro et al. (2001) surveyed the treatment modalities allowed in the state standards examined, finding that 90% of states dictated group therapy (mostly feminist psychoeducational approaches). Surprisingly, 55% of states allowed individual treatment, 55% allowed couples therapy, 65% specified gender-specific treatment, and 35% specified gender-specific treatment before couples therapy. No specific comparisons of individual versus group therapy existed, but Maiuro et al. listed the advantages of group treatment: group cohesiveness to maintain treatment, economy, and "shame detoxification" (Maiuro et al., 2001). Maiuro et al. caution that "although few would question the need for employing certain methods in order to protect the safety of victims, there is danger in prematurely dismissing potentially effective approaches. The risk is magnified by the fact that such generalizations may become officially codified in standards as a 'known' basis for practice" (p. 34). This premature "knowledge" of what works is a risk for treatment practice. Maiuro et al. call this "the greatest risk of stunting the development of new or alternative interventions for families afflicted with domestic violence. In this respect more work is needed to assure that the existing guidelines truly protect the well-being of victims without inadvertently impeding much needed program development" (p. 38).

Of greater concern was that, of the states surveyed, only 20% required a college degree for treatment providers and required only "specialized training in domestic violence" (i.e., socialization into the prevailing paradigm). This reflects, in my view, the antiprofessional perspective of feminist activists. Maiuro et al. (2001) recognize this and suggest: (a) that the lack of required research training may contribute to a lack of familiarity with research methods (contrary to the Boulder model of training for psychologists), and (b) that care must be taken to avoid a state standards committee made up exclusively of activists and treatment providers. They recommend an ethicist to ensure against conflicts of interest, including "secondary gain in the form of training contracts for a particular intervention approach or an agenda to put those competitors out of business who do not adopt a particular philosophy or offer a specific form of program" (p. 37). One method to ensure this is to have a rotating multidisciplinary board (including at least one researcher) with reappointments every two years. Maiuro et al. also suggest a national blue ribbon panel of experts to provide consultation to state boards. I believe that these are excellent recommendations.

ANGER AND VIOLENCE

One shibboleth of the Duluth philosophy is that anger does not cause violence (Pence & Paymar, 1993, pp. 9, 105). The Duluth perspective is rather critical of CBT, which it frequently mislabels as "anger management," although CBT has never focused primarily on anger and has, at minimum, approximately 16 treatment objectives. The Duluth model's view of abuse is that it is always an instrumental act and hence not a product of anger. Again, this view is not supported by the evidence. Maiuro, Cahn, Vitaliano, Wagner, and Zegree (1988) found that domestically violent men had significantly higher levels of both anger and hostility than controls. The authors concluded that their findings supported the "idea that anger *dyscontrol* is a key issue in the profile of domestically violent men" (Maiuro et al., 1988, p. 17) and noted that depression as well as anger were elevated in this group. Margolin, John, and Gleberman (1989) found that physically aggressive husbands reported significantly higher levels of anger than husbands in three control groups. Dutton and Browning (1988) showed videotaped husband–wife conflicts to wife assaulters and control males. The assaultive males reported significantly higher levels of anger than controls, especially in response to an "abandonment" scenario. Sonkin and Dutton's (2003) application of attachment theory to domestic violence also contradicts this notion. According to attachment theory, insecure attachment patterns are essentially maladaptive methods of regulating affect, particularly anger and other emotions stemming from loss.

Dutton and Starzomski (1994) found elevated anger scores for assaultive men as measured by the Multidimensional Anger Inventory (Siegel, 1986). They related the anger to certain personality disturbances, especially borderline personality disorder, antisocial personality disorder, aggressive-sadistic personality disorder, and passive-aggressive personality disorder, all of which have anger as a component of the personality disorder. Dutton, Starzomski, Saunders, and Bartholomew (1994) found elevated anger in assaultive males to be related to certain attachment disorders, especially an attachment style called "fearful" attachment that they relabeled "fearful-angry" attachment. Citing Bowlby's (1969) work on attachment that viewed anger as having a first function of reuniting with an attachment object and dysfunctional anger as further distancing the object, Dutton and his colleagues explored developmental origins of elevated anger in assaultive males, viewing it as being produced by paternal rejection, exposure to abuse, and a failure of protective attachment (Dutton, 1994a, 2006a; Dutton, Saunders, Starzomski, & Bartholomew, 1994). Failure to address these underlying issues therapeutically while focusing on symptomatic beliefs and "male privilege" would be counterindicative of treatment success.

Jacobson et al. (1994) recruited physically aggressive and maritally distressed nonviolent control couples to discuss "areas of disagreement" in a laboratory setting. Both maritally violent husbands and wives displayed significantly more anger than controls (although the study focused on husbands, 50% of the wives committed severe acts of abuse as well).

Eckhardt, Barbour, and Stuart (1997) and Eckhardt, Barbour, and Davis (1998) reviewed several anger measures and asserted that both anger and hostility were elevated in maritally violent men. Eckhardt et al. (1998) used an "articulated thoughts simulated situations" technique that found that maritally violent men articulated more anger-inducing irrational thoughts and cognitive biases than nonviolent controls. In short, numerous studies from several independent sources have found anger to be prominent in physically assaultive males. Clearly, the research evidence shows that anger and arousability are components of abuse that require treatment in managing, not neglect.

SUBTYPES OF PERPETRATORS

Despite the Duluth focus on "male oppression," men who are court mandated for treatment for wife assault come from couples varying in their violence patterns (Stets & Straus, 1992a, 1992b). Stets and Straus analyzed gender, relationship status (married, cohabiting, and dating), and level of violence used (none, minor, or severe) in data reported from the U.S. 1985 National Survey (Stets & Straus, 1992b; Straus & Gelles, 1985, 1992). The most common form of couple subtype was mutual violence, followed by female more severe (to nonviolent on less violent males), followed by male more severe. However, men who are arrested in dyadic violence couples (the most common form) and who report their wives as being violent are disbelieved in Duluth model groups. Their experience is invalidated and treated as rationalization and victim blaming. Furthermore, Duluth models in some areas (e.g., Arizona) preclude therapists from interviewing wives to make assessments of whether violence is dyadic or unilateral; hence, the therapist cannot know if clients are excusing their behavior or making veridical reports. Although men would be responsible for their own violence in either case, differential treatment strategies might be invoked given the information on the presence or the absence of dyadic violence. When a client reports victimization by his partner and is disbelieved or invalidated by his therapist, it only supports the attitude that many victims of child abuse experience—don't bother telling because no one will believe you. In addition, even if the man is a unilateral abuser, he may vary in terms of the personality structure that supports his use of violence, beliefs surrounding violence, and emotional response to intimate relationships (Dutton, 2002a; Hamberger & Hastings, 1986; Holtzworth-Munroe & Stuart, 1994; Saunders, 1993; Tweed & Dutton, 1998).

Sonkin and Dutton (2003) described an attachment theory conceptualization of domestic violence. Studies have indicated that batterers, like the general population, consist of individuals with differing attachment categories. These different categories stem from different parenting experiences in childhood. For example, some batterers have learned to deactivate attachment-related emotions (dismissing), whereas others have learned to hyperactivate attachment distress (preoccupied). Persons suffering from unresolved trauma or loss have developed extremely maladaptive mechanisms for regulating attachment distress (disorganized or fearful), such as dissociation or extreme aggression. By treating all batterers the same, the Duluth model misses the nuances that other models, such as attachment theory, capture and that provide useful information for intervention.

Duluth model treatment does not assess for and cannot treat personality disorders, disbelieves clients who claim that their partner is violent too, and does not have the flexibility to tailor therapy to fit individual needs of clients. It shames perpetrators, emphasizing their use of "power and control" and "male privilege" when the client may feel powerless in the world.

TREATMENT OUTCOME STUDIES
OF THE DULUTH MODEL

Because of the ever-present risk of confounds among quasi-experimental studies, results from randomized experiments are the "gold standard" for evaluation. In a treatment outcome study done on the Duluth model,

Shepard (1987, 1992) found a 40% recidivism rate in a 6-month follow-up of Duluth clients, higher than most control recidivism levels. Babcock et al. (2004) put recidivism rates at 35% for a 6- to 12-month follow-up according to wives and 21% for the same time period using criminal justice data (i.e., arrests).

Feder and Forde (1999) randomly assigned batterers on probation to either a feminist-psychoeducational program or no treatment in Broward County, Florida. In general, there were no statistically significant differences between the two groups on recidivism as measured by police records ($d = .04$) or by victim report ($d = -.02$). There was a small but significant effect on recidivism among the subset of men randomly assigned to group treatment who attended all 26 sessions. In this study, random assignment apparently failed, with an uneven number of men being assigned to the treatment and control condition (Feder & Forde, 1999). Moreover, this study suffered from a particularly high attrition rate of men from treatment (60%) and a low response rate from victims at follow-up (22%).

Davis, Taylor, and Maxwell (1998) compared a long (26-week) psychoeducational group to a brief (8-week) psychoeducational group and to a community service control (70 hours of clearing vacant lots, painting senior citizen centers, and so on) in Brooklyn, New York. They found a statistically significant reduction in recidivism and a small but respectable effect size of $d = .41$ based on criminal records among the long treatment group only; the 8-week group was indistinguishable from the community service control ($d = .02$). When based on victim report of recent offenses, neither the long nor the brief intervention had a statistically significant effect on reassault when compared to no treatment. Correspondingly, the effect size due to treatment based on partner report of subsequent violence was small ($d = .21$). It is important to note that, like in the Broward County experiment (Feder & Forde, 1999), random assignment may have been compromised. In the Brooklyn experiment (Davis, Taylor, & Maxwell, 2000), nearly 30% of initial assignments were subjected to "judicial overrides" (Gondolf, 2001); that is, judges reassigned defendants to different interventions.

Ford and Regoli (1993) designed a study that randomly assigned batterers into treatment as a pretrial diversion (i.e., defendants' criminal records would be cleared pending treatment completion) or treatment as a condition of probation postconviction versus alternative sentencing strategies (e.g., paying a fine or going to jail). Even though this study was designed to test different sentencing options rather than effects due to treatment, one can compare batterers sentenced to treatment versus batterers not sentenced to treatment (although the type of treatment and actual attendance rates were not specified). Again, there were no significant differences or effect sizes comparing recidivism rates based on victim report between men sentenced to treatment versus those who were not. Neither treatment as pretrial diversion ($d = .00$) nor treatment as a condition of probation postconviction ($d = -.22$) was found to be superior to purely legal interventions.

Conducting an experiment in which judicial discretion is sacrificed and criminals are randomly assigned to treatment or no treatment can be problematic on ethical as well as practical grounds (Dutton, Bodnarchuk, Kropp, Hart, & Ogloff, 1997). Adopting an experimental design does not *guarantee* a more rigorous evaluation than quasi-experimental designs afford (Gondolf, 2001). While it is true that experimental designs permit greater confidence in conclusions regarding causal relations, it is also the case that problems with differential attrition and failure of random assignment reduce internal validity of this design. It is recommended that researchers report both recidivism rates for all batterers who were assigned to treatment as well as those who actually completed treatment (few studies have done so).

Babcock et al. (2004) conducted a meta-analytic examination of 22 studies of treatment outcome. The d' for Duluth treatment was .19. Comparisons between CBT and Duluth were not significant, but "pure" Duluth models were hard to find. As the authors stated, "Modern batterer groups tend to mix different theoretical approaches to treatment, combining feminist theory of power and control as well as specific interventions that deal with anger control, stress management and improved communication skill" (p. 1045). It is hard to imagine a therapeutic case for a positive treatment result in groups where no therapeutic bond is developed.

The d' of .34 reported by Babcock et al. (2004) is less than optimal for most therapeutic outcomes. The average effect size in psychotherapy studies is $d' = .85$, but it is substantially lower for court-mandated treatment (Davis & Taylor, 1999). By standards of court-mandated client populations, however, this is an average result.

EXPANDED TARGETS FOR PERPETRATOR TREATMENT

There are several ways to increase the treatment success of same-sex-group court-mandated therapy. All rely on established CBT techniques used for other problem areas and simply recognize the relevance of these techniques for batterer treatment. A rich psychology of intimate violence perpetrators has developed since the first wave of treatment was developed. Essentially, this research has unearthed what emotions, cognitions, and situational interactions intermingle to generate and support abusive behavior. They constitute the infrastructure of abuse.

Borderline Personality Organization and Assaultiveness: The Theoretical Connection

Dutton has shown empirically a strong relationship between border-line traits in male perpetrators and intimate abusiveness (Dutton, 1998, 2002a, 2002b). In a series of studies, Dutton and his colleagues (for a review, see Dutton, 1995a, 1995c, 1998, 2002b) have examined person-ality profiles of assaultive males. The overall strategy of this work has been based on self-report scales filled out by abusive men as part of an assessment procedure for treatment and corroborated through the female partners' reports of the men's abusiveness. Men's self-reported self dis-turbances (of a borderline character) were similar to those for diagnosed borderlines and were significantly related to chronic anger, jealousy, wives' reports of clients' use of violence, and experiences of adult trauma symptoms in the wife assault group.

In effect, a constellation of personality features (borderline personal-ity organization, high anger, fearful attachment, chronic trauma symp-toms, and recollections of paternal rejection) accounted for reports of abusiveness by one's intimate partner in all these groups. Each of these features of abusiveness is a potential target for treatment. With minor variations, this constellation was replicated with blue-collar controls, college students, psychiatric outpatients, and gay male couples (Dutton, 1998, 2002b).

Attachment and Abusiveness

If early experiences influenced adult abusiveness, attachment theory might provide a valuable perspective in the etiology of abusiveness. Bowlby (1969) viewed interpersonal anger as arising from frustrated attachment needs and functioning as a form of "protest behavior" directed at regaining contact with an attachment figure. He viewed dys-functional anger as anger expressions that increased the distance from the attachment object.

In turn, chronic childhood frustration of attachment needs may lead to adult proneness to react with extreme anger ("intimacy-anger") when relevant attachment cues are present. Thus, attachment theory sug-gests that an assaultive male's violent outbursts may be a form of protest behavior directed at his attachment figure (in this case, a sexual part-ner) and precipitated by perceived threats of separation or abandonment. A "fearful" attachment pattern may be most strongly associated with intimacy-anger. Fearful individuals desire social contact and intimacy but experience pervasive interpersonal distrust and fear of rejection. This style manifests itself in hypersensitivity to rejection (rejection-sensitivity) and active avoidance of close relationships where vulnerability to rejection exists. While the fearful share anxiety over abandonment with another insecurely attached group (called "preoccupied"), their avoidance orientation may lead to more chronic frustration of attachment needs.

Dutton and colleagues assessed attachment styles in abusive men. Fearfully attached men experience high degrees of both chronic anxiety and anger (Dutton, Saunders et al., 1994). Fearful attachment alone accounted for significant proportions of variance in both emotional abuse criterion factors completed by female partners. Fearful attachment was also strongly correlated with borderline personality organization. Since both anxiety ($+0.42$) and anger ($+0.48$) are strongly associated with fearful attachment, one could argue that an emotional template of intimacy-anxiety/anger is the central affective feature of the fearful attachment pattern. Using a structured interview, Babcock, Jacobson, Gottman, and Yerington (2000) also found insecure attachment styles to be related to abusiveness. Mikulincer (1998) found, as had Dutton et al. (1995), that attachment style related to dysregulation of negative emotions in intimate relationships.

Early Trauma From Shaming and Exposure to Violence

In abused boys, a prominent sequela of abuse victimization is hyper-aggression. Carmen, Reiker, and Mills (1984) suggested that abused boys are more likely than abused girls to identify with the original aggressor and eventually to perpetuate the abuse on their spouse and children. In their view, an effect of physical maltreatment by a parent is to exaggerate sex role characteristics, possibly as a means of attempting to strengthen the damaged self. Van der Kolk (1987) noted that traumatized children (including physical abuse) had trouble modulating aggression and included being physically abused as a child as a trauma source.

Herman and van der Kolk (1987) noted how posttraumatic stress disorder (PTSD) included poor affect tolerance, heightened aggression, irritability, chronic dysphoric mood, emptiness, and recurrent depression and was "described in patients who have been subjected to repeated trauma over a considerable period of time" (p. 114). This profile also described spouse abusers. Hence, the possibility was presented that PTSD may be another link or mediating variable between childhood abuse victimization and adult perpetration of intimate abuse.

In order to test this notion, wife assaulters were compared to two groups of diagnosed PTSD men from independent studies (Dutton, 1995d). In the wife assault sample, 45% of all men met research criteria for PTSD, and assaultive men exhibited elevated levels of chronic trauma symptoms.

The source of trauma, as revealed in this work, was physical abuse combined with shaming by the father and with a lack of secure attachment to the mother. Consequently, the latter could not provide buffering against the former (Dutton, 1998, 2002b). Tangney, Wagner, Fletcher, and Gramzow (1992) have presented a more focused analysis of the potential role of shame as a mediator between the early experiences of assaultive men and their adult experience of anger and abusiveness. They describe shame proneness as a moral affective style that has to do with "global, painful, and devastating experience in which the self, not just behavior, is painfully scrutinized and negatively evaluated" (p. 599). In this sense, shame-inducing experiences, which generate a shame-prone style, may be viewed as attacks on the global self and should produce disturbances in self-identity. Shame-prone individuals have been found to demonstrate a limited empathic ability, a high propensity for anger, and self-reports of aggression (Wallace & Nosko, 2003). Dutton, van Ginkel, and Starzomski (1995) found recollections of shame-inducing experiences by parents of assaultive men to be significantly related to the men's self-reports of both anger and physical abuse and to their wives' reports of the men's use of dominance/isolation.

Dutton et al. (1995) found three recalled sources of shame in assaultive males. These were public scolding, random punishment, and generic criticism. All three were recalled as generating experiences of shame. These, in turn, were correlated with adult anger and tendencies to project blame. Not surprisingly, given these tendencies, abusive actions also correlated with recalled shame experiences. Partial correlations revealed that parental shaming still correlated significantly with measures of abusive personality after physical abuse by the parents had been partialed out. The converse, however, was not true. With parental shaming partialed out, physical abuse by parents did not correlate significantly with abusive personality measures. Hence, the experience of being shamed seemed to interact with exposure to violence to produce assaultiveness. It is for this reason, above all, that shaming clients in Duluth groups on the basis of their being male is contraindicated.

Surprisingly, until now these features of an abusive personality—insecure attachment, borderline traits, and trauma reactions—have not been a focus of CBT for spouse assault. Dutton (2006a) has outlined a "blended behavioral therapy" that has a multifocus on anger, attachment, shaming, trauma, and borderline personality traits.

TREATMENT OF FEMALE BATTERERS

Given that Stets and Straus (1992b) found that three times as many women as men used severe violence against a nonviolent partner, treatment for female batterers seems a necessity. Nevertheless, the dominant view of male perpetrator/female victim pervades female perpetrator treatment as well. Hamberger and Potente (1994) described their court-mandated sample as "battered women who have gotten caught up in pattern of violence, that most often, they did not initiate and do not control" (p. 127). What is interesting is the attention paid to the context of women's violence, whereas in "psychoeducational groups" all mention of partner violence is construed as victim blaming and failing to take responsibility for one's actions. While the male perpetrator who claims partner violence is viewed as being in denial, this problem is assumed and sought after as part of an "assessment" of female perpetrators. Hamberger and Potente claim that only 3 of 67 women were primary perpetrators. A question is raised about the apparent discrepancy between Hamberger and Potente's data showing so few female instigators and the data from the Moffitt, Caspi, Rutter, and Silva (2001) study and Archer's (2000) research showing female violence to be more frequent than male and just as severe. In the Moffitt et al. (2001) study, females were even more violent than males in a large community sample. Furthermore, the female violence in relationships was predictable by their antisocial behavior three years prior to entering the relationship. Hence, on the basis of current longitudinal studies of community groups (Ehrensaft et al., 2003; Moffitt et al., 2001), we would expect to see more females in court-mandated treatment and many of them being the instigator of aggression.

Busch and Rosenberg (2003) found that arrested female perpetrators were just as violent as males. This study uses criminal justice data to compare women and men arrested for domestic violence on their levels of violence, reported victimization, general criminality, and substance abuse. Participants were 45 women and 45 men convicted of domestic violence between 1996 and 1998. Results indicated that women were less likely than men to have a history of domestic violence offenses and nonviolent crimes. They were also more likely to report that they had been injured or victimized by their partner at the time of their arrest. However, in other ways, women and men were similar: They were equally likely to have used severe violence and inflicted severe injuries on their victims, to have previously committed violence against nonintimates, and to have been using drugs or alcohol at the time of their arrest.

Both Dowd (2001) and Renzetti (1992) call for a more thoughtful and complex analysis than the dominant feminist view, which has largely precluded treatment of aggressive women. Whether male or female clients are treated, a thorough assessment is necessary to evaluate seriousness and locus of instigation of any bidirectional violence. Renzetti (1992) found that substance abuse, dependency, and jealousy were clinically significant in battering lesbians. Similarly, Margolies and Leeder (1995) found dependency, jealousy, and black-and-white thinking clinically significant in lesbian batterers. These issues also all surfaced in male heterosexual perpetrators.

Leisring, Dowd, and Rosenbaum (2003) suggest an important clinical goal for female perpetrators is to stop their violence because it is a predictor of male violence. The University of Massachusetts treatment program for women (which they implemented) had some didactic components in common with men's treatment: anger recognition and control, personal responsibility, empathy, time-outs, communication training, reframing cognitions, and substance abuse. Leisring et al. emphasize personal safety for the woman client, attention to one's own needs, increased emphasis on PTSD in creating anger control problems, increased attention to conditions that undermine mood stability, and less emphasis on power and control. The authors argue, on the basis of the National Violence Against Women Survey data (Tjaden & Thoennes, 1998), that men fear their partners less than women do, so power and control issues are not as important for women. I will not revisit the reasons why crime victim surveys misrepresent the larger population. Suffice it to say that Follingstad et al. (1991) found power and control motivated female as well as male self-reported motives for IPV.

Henning and his colleagues compared female to male domestic violence offenders. Rising numbers of women arrested for domestic violence present many theoretical and practical challenges (Henning & Feder, 2004; Henning, Jones, & Holford, 2003). At the theoretical level, there is ongoing debate about whether women are equally aggressive as men (Pagelow, 1984). At the practical level, little research is available to guide how female cases are handled in the criminal justice system. In this study, data were obtained regarding demographic characteristics, mental health functioning, and childhood familial dysfunction for a large sample of male ($n = 2,254$) and female ($n = 281$) domestic violence offenders. The women were demographically similar to the men, and few differences were noted in their childhood experiences. Women were more likely than men to have previously attempted suicide, whereas more men had conduct problems in childhood and substance abuse in adulthood. Compared to the male offenders, women reported more symptoms of personality dysfunction and mood disorder. Ninety-five percent of the women offenders had one or more personality disorders above 75 on the Millon Clinical Multiaxial Inventory-3 compared to 70% of the male offenders. Females were six times more likely than men to have borderline scores above 75. These data suggest that the trauma model used for male perpetrators described here should also be useful for female perpetrators. Court-based treatment, whether of male or of female perpetrators, needs to include a focus on attachment, trauma, shame, and intimacy issues. It is indeed time to think "outside the box" created by a traditional feminist "one size fits all" paradigm of how intervention must be.

COUPLE VIOLENCE AND TREATMENT

Stets and Straus (1992b) found that couples using the sample level of violence (mild or severe) was the most common form of domestic violence. An ensuing controversy, touched off by a paper by Johnson (1995), focused on "common couple violence" versus "patriarchal terrorism," overlooking the fact that a female severe/male nonviolent pattern was three times as prevalent as "patriarchal terrorism." Suffice it to say that data do not support the feminist view that all female violence is self-defensive and not serious (Dutton & Nicholls, 2005). The implication of the feminist view was that couple violence was never applicable to domestic violence. In fact, it is not applicable to patriarchal terrorism. However, some studies have found couples treatment effective with violent couples (Heyman & Schlee, 2003; O'Leary, Heyman, & Neidig, 1999). Obviously, the form of treatment is dictated by an assessment of violence levels and danger, but to rule it out a priori, as the Duluth model does, operates against treatment efficacy.

INTERACTIONAL STUDIES

Gayla Margolin and her colleagues (1984, 1989, 1993) have contributed consistently to this line of study (see also Margolin & Burman, 1993). Margolin's work started with an examination of interaction patterns in four different types of couples called physically abusive (PA), verbally abusive (VA), withdrawn but nonabusive (WI), and nondistressed and nonabusive (ND) based on responses to the Conflict Tactics Scales (CTS) and the Dyadic Adjustment Scale . At that time, self-report questionnaires were used to assess interaction style (e.g., Communication Apprehension Inventory and Spouse Specific Assertivness Scale); later these would become more sophisticated techniques for videotaping and scoring marital interaction.

By 1988, Margolin et al. (1989) had moved to assessment of "in vivo" interactions. Typically, couples would sign in for the research, would undergo an initial screening/assessment, and then were asked to "discuss" two "problematic topics" (chosen from three offered in the screening self-reports of the couples). These discussions were videotaped for later coding. Experimenters observed the interaction through a one-way mirror (and later reviewed the videotapes).

As with her previous studies, Margolin and her colleagues examined PA couples, VA couples, WI, and ND couples. Again, these categories were based on self-report measures of CTS and the Dyadic Adjustment Scale by both members of the couple. The women in these studies did not perceive themselves as battered (even in the PA group) and, according to Margolin et al., ranged considerably in the extent to which they themselves had engaged in "physical violence" (p. 31). Margolin et al. (1989) found the chief differentiating factor between the PA group and other groups was in the behavior of the husbands; PA husbands exhibited more instances of negative voice and more overtly negative behaviors than husbands in the other groups. PA husbands also reported more sadness, fear, anger, and feeling attacked (and somewhat more physiological arousal) than the husbands in the other three groups.

Despite the controlled and semipublic nature of the discussions, PA husbands exhibited negative affect patterns that were indicative of non-constructive approaches to conflict and that could escalate into a more extreme expression of aggression. These included irate, angry, whining, yelling, sarcastic, nagging, lecturing, accusatory, mocking, and otherwise irritating voice tones. Negative behaviors included signs of dismissal, waving arms, pointing a finger at the other, threatening or mimicking gestures, and negative physical contact. They tended not to exhibit head hanging or leaning away and maintained eye contact.

PA wives showed a greater escalation of offensive negative behaviors than did VA or WI wives during the middle portions of the discussion period and then showed a greater deescalation in the final period. The authors concluded that "paradoxically, the wives' backing down may negatively reinforce the husbands' behaviors and may inadvertently strengthen his attack" (Margolin et al., 1989, p. 31). Of course, we do not know the outcome had the women continued to escalate. To draw that conclusion, we would have to follow a group of women who never deescalated and trace the outcome. What group were they in? It may be that, regardless of their response at this point, violence would occur. This view is more consistent with work on personality disorders in abusive men (e.g., Dutton, 1998). A borderline male batterer or an individual who has an "abusive personality" would proceed to the aggression phase of the conflict at this point on the basis of physiological arousal and misconstrual of the woman's actions.

Burman, Margolin, and John (1993) utilized sequential analysis of couple interactions from videos taken in the couples' homes. These were believed to be "more ecologically valid." The PA group was again comprised of bidirectionally violent couples. Couples were instructed to recall a typical serious conflict and how it began, who said what to whom, how the conflict progressed, and how it ended. Couples then reenacted these conflicts. These reenactments (which averaged 10 minutes in length) were videotaped and coded. Instead of coding 15-second intervals, this time "floor switches" (a statement of one person bounded on either side by a statement of the other) were used. This created a series of "lags" from one person's action to the reaction of the other and so on. PA couples were characterized in the data by exhibiting more hostile affect and by the number of contingent behavior patterns involving anger. Nondistressed couples can "exit these negative interaction cycles quite quickly" (Burman et al., 1993, p. 37). The authors concluded that "contrary to images of women in abusive relationships as passive and reticent, the women in the types of PA relationships presented here are angry with or contemptuous of husbands and are quick to respond to their husband's anger" (p. 37).

The University of Washington (UW) group (Babcock, Waltz, Jacobson, & Gottman, 1993; Babcock et al., 2000; Cordova, Jacobson, Gottman, Rushe, & Cox, 1993; Levenson & Gottman, 1983) also used sequential analysis for assessing three dimensions of marital interaction: positive–negative affect, reciprocity, and asymmetry. The UW lab focused these techniques on domestic violence, expanding techniques previously used to study marital satisfaction. Their finding was that parallel patterning of physiological responses was related to reported marital satisfaction. In the UW studies, these techniques would be used on DV couples in an "experimental apartment" created in the psychology lab. Couples would re-create their most serious conflicts in that environment, and physiological reactions would be measured.

In turning to the study of domestic violence, the UW lab recruited participants through newspaper ads. The criterion for the DV group was wives' reports of husbands' violence on the CTS. Wives' reports were used because "we assumed husbands might underreport their own violence" (Babcock et al., 1993, p. 42). The focus of the study was on husband violence and categories of violent husbands developed from a popular book on the research, classifying violent husbands as "pit bulls" (tenacious, emotional) or "cobras" (cool, instrumental). Couples were solicited as "couples experiencing conflict in their marriage." One has to read the method section then to discover that *"according to the wives themselves, almost half (28/57) would have qualified for the DV group if wife violence had been the criterion"* (Jacobson et al., 1994, p. 983). In other words, there were bilaterally violent couples in the mix, although the focus became entirely on the males. No measures were taken of the wives' use of violence, and all independent variables focused on male violence as though it were being produced unilaterally in all relationships (even though it clearly was not).

Babcock et al. (1993) assessed power discrepancies between husband and wife based on economic status, decision-making power, communication patterns, and communication skills. DV couples were more likely than nonviolent controls (maritally distressed/nonviolent and happily married nonviolent) to engage in withdrawal behaviors (wife withdrawal/husband demand). Husbands who had less power were more physically abusive to their wives. The authors' viewed this as "compensatory power." Feminist views have been confusing on this topic. Yllo and Straus (1990) argued that as male power increased, violence toward women should increase. Instead, they found, on a state-by-state analysis of male power, a curvilinear relationship. The states with high-power males and the states with the lowest-power males used the most violence. The "compensation" argument was used for the low-power states. It is hard to see how the feminist hypothesis could be disconfirmed. If high-power males use more violence, it is interpreted as domination. If low-power males use more violence, it is interpreted as compensation for a wish to dominate. What data set can disconfirm? I suppose no relationship between male power and violence.

One interesting unreported piece of data from the Babcock et al. (1993) study was that male socioeconomic power was unrelated to decision-making power at home or to communication skill advantages. Power, it seems, generates from several levels, many of which are inconsistent or unrelated.

Cordova et al. (1993) used a Marital Interaction Coding Scheme (MICS) applied to videos taken of couples arguing in the UW lab. The MICS required coders to initially code interactions into three broad schemes: aversive behaviors, facilitative behaviors, and neutral behaviors. Since the study focused on changes in aversive behavior over time, sequential analyses were examined. Negative reciprocity was defined as the occurrence of aversive behavior given the prior occurrence of aversive behavior by the other partner. Various lag times for this reciprocity were measured (immediate vs. delayed). As with Margolin et al.'s (1989) sample, DV husbands exhibited a higher proportion of aversive behavior than did their nonviolent counterparts. Similarly, the authors concluded that "the behavior of DV wives in this sample does not suggest passivity, docility or surrender. Rather, the women are continuing in conflict engagement, even though they have histories of being subjected to physical abuse. . . . Although these women were being beaten, they had not been beaten into submission. They were standing up to rather than surrendering to their battering husbands" (Margolin et al.,

1989, p. 563). Of course, this explanation overlooks the fact, reported in Jacobson et al. (1994) (on the same sample), that 28 of 57 wives would themselves have qualified for the DV group given the criteria used. Why then depict them as "reactive victim/heroines"? Because that fit the paradigm of male perpetrator/female victim so prevalent in the DV literature at the time. In fact, Cordova et al.'s (1993) data table (table 2, p. 562) reveal that the DV women used more aversive acts than did the DV men (18.2 vs. 15.8) in the time assessed (that was also true for women in the other two groups). Unlike Margolin et al., Cordova et al. did not find a decrease in negative reciprocity at the end of the interaction sequence.

Cordova et al. (1993) are clearly troubled that the wives in their sample used so many aversive acts. They say that "these results appear to be surprising in the light of descriptions such as Walker's (1984) of the battered woman syndrome" (p. 564) and then try to explain away the female violence (the women felt safer in the lab, the women were trying to put an end to "protracted tension," and so on). Not once do they state the obvious: These women were almost as violent as their male partners.

Jacobson et al. (1994) studied the "affect, psychophysiology and verbal content of arguments in couples with a violent husband" (p. 982). Again, the same taped 15-minute arguments from the same couples were examined, although the sample had now increased to 60 DV couples and 32 DNV couples. Arguments were coded for (a) affect: affect-positive/neutral, aggressive, and distress (fear or sadness) and (b) content-withdrawal, criticize, defend, demand, emotional abuse, physical aggression, positive/neutral, distress, and self-defense. The chief finding was that "only husband violence produces fear in the partner." The authors state that "this gender difference underscores one of the major differences between husband and wife violence: Only husband violence produces fear in the partner" (Jacobson et al., 1994, p. 986) This finding was cited extensively as showing a differential effect for male versus female abuse. Dutton, Webb, and Ryan (1994), in studying gender differences in affective reactions to conflict, found that women used affect scales differently, reporting higher scores even in baseline controls. Jacobson et al. (1994) admitted "the men were less likely to acknowledge there was anything wrong with them" (p. 987). The data also showed that DV wives were more belligerent than their husbands and showed more contempt. The husbands showed more defensiveness than the wives. Jacobson et al. justify this interpretation by arguing that "even DV husbands admit that wife violence is largely reactive to either physical or emotional abuse on their part" (p. 986). Were the wives asked these questions as well? This is not reported. At the end of the paper, the authors describe "the intense anger, combined with fear and sadness, [which] may be part of the helplessness reported by battered women" (p. 987). Of course, that conclusion overlooks the fact that half the women were themselves physically abusive and that women in general exhibited more belligerence on the experimental tapes.

Gottman et al. (1995) focused on the physiological reactions observed in the conflicts: cardiac interbeat interval, pulse transmission time, finger pulse amplitude, and skin conductance level. In addition, MCMI-2 data were obtained for husbands and wives, and the laboratory interactions were coded as described previously using the SPAFF. On the basis of physiological reactivity, the men were classified as type 1 (those who lowered their heart rate during marital interaction) and type 2 (those who increased their heart rate). All data were reported through the filter of comparing these two groups of men (e.g., type 1 men had significantly higher rates of antisocial personality disorder and aggressive sadistic personality disorder than did type 2 men). Type 1 men were more angry, belligerent, and contemptuous than type 2 men. Type 1 men were more generally violent outside marriage and had greater problems with drug dependency.

Leonard and Roberts (1998) performed an unusually well controlled study of the interactive mechanisms in operation. Sixty maritally aggressive and 75 nonaggressive men received either no alcohol, a placebo, or alcohol (vodka). The couples (who had been married less than two years) were asked to discuss an issue that was a chronic source of conflict for them. Then the interactions between the men and their wives were videotaped and coded in a "baseline interaction" (before the alcohol administration and involving their second-most-important disagreement) and an experimental interaction (after the alcohol or placebo; most important issue of disagreement). As with the Jacobson et al. (1994) and Margolin et al. (1984, 1989, 1993) studies, aggressive couples exhibited more negative behavior (criticism, disagreement, interruptions, disapproval, put-downs, and so on) and higher levels of negative reciprocity (these behaviors are reciprocated) in their baseline interaction than did nonaggressive couples. Alcohol increased the husbands' use of negativity. This was not a placebo effect. It was a pharmacological effect of alcohol. Since baseline negativity was higher in the abusive couples, alcohol raised negativity levels still higher. The authors conclude that "it may be that alcohol simply disrupts attempts at conflict resolution for both aggressive and non-aggressive husbands. These disruptions, in turn, may lead some husbands to behave aggressively, but may lead to different outcomes among other husbands (Leonard & Roberts, 1998, p. 613). Finally, they concluded that "alcohol is neither a necessary nor sufficient cause of violence but there is growing evidence that it may contribute to violent behavior" (p. 614). Alcohol seems to potentiate an already dys-functional interaction sequence that is indicative of abusive couples.

COUPLES THERAPY

Given the interactional aspect of couple violence described here, marital or couples therapy (sometimes called systems therapy) seems like a logi-cal way to proceed. Heyman and Schlee (2003) have written a good over-view of this approach in which they review the Stony Brook Treatment Project using a system called Physical Aggression Couples Treatment (PACT), which emphasizes the circular causality demonstrated in the research studies on couples described in this chapter. In this system, each partner is held responsible for his or her own behavior, but each takes a role in conflict escalation (or, conversely, its reduction). PACT is an extended version of the Domestic Conflict Containment Program (Neidig & Friedman, 1984). The rationale is as follows: Most acts of phys-ical aggression in intimate relationships occur in the context of an argu-ment between partners. Conflict escalates until one or both partners strike each other (called "circular causality"). Two of the working rules are that: (a) this system is not used when the woman is still at risk for physical violence, and that (b) the purpose of the system is not to teach women to be "nonconflictual" (i.e., acquiesce to whatever the partner wants). Rather, it is to become aware of reactions to conflictual responses from one's partner, take responsibility for them, and control them. Neidig and Friedman (1984) called the perpetrator/victim distinction a "therapeu-tic dead end" and believed that people needed to learn to use assertive/nonviolent communication in vivo.

Family systems approaches (Giles-Sims, 1983; Neidig & Friedman, 1984) view wife assault from an interactive (microsystem) rather than an intrapsychic perspective. The rules of the family system, which define what behavior is acceptable, the power imbalances of that system, and the personal resources of individual members that provide a basis for exchange, are viewed as major contributors to family violence. Giles-Sims (1983) acknowledges that "victims may inadvertently be reinforcing the violent behavior" (p. 33), a perspective supported in the child abuse liter-ature by the interactive studies of Patterson and his colleagues. Patterson, Cobb, and Ray (1972), for example, observed parents' reinforcement of the violence of their highly destructive boys (Patterson, 1979). These parents were not aware of reinforcements they provided, and Giles-Sims suggests that the same may be true for battered women.

Neidig and Friedman (1984) begin their description of their cou-ples' treatment program with the statement that "abusive behavior is a relationship issue but it is ultimately the responsibility of the male to control physical violence" (p. 4). Their view is that approaches that attribute total responsibility to either party lead to blaming, compounding the problem. It does so, according to these authors, by beginning a chain of retributional strategies by the victim and the aggressor whereby each tries to "get even" for the other's most recent transgression. A systems approach avoids blaming by getting couples to think of the causes of violence from a circular feedback perspective rather than a linear one. This leads to "constructive interventions in the escalating process" that permit each partner to accept a portion of the responsibility. Having said that, however, Neidig and Friedman assign "ultimate responsibility to the male for controlling violence" as a recognition that both parties are not equal in physical strength. The difference between "total responsibility" and "ultimate responsibility" may sound like splitting hairs. If a man is responsible for his violence, then why is he not to blame if he acts violently? One answer may be that his violence occurred in a state of high arousal when he perceived no alternatives to the actions he took and where his partner played her part as well. Therapeutically, a couple approach and an individual approach have a fundamental disagreement: The couple approach tries to reduce blame, and the individual approach tries to increase responsibility.

The decision of whether an individual or a couple approach is best may depend on the client. If a man has a history of violence in several relationships with women, he may be a conflict generator capable of creating the system pattern observed by the systems therapist in his current relationship. Certainly, the "abusive personality" profiled here requires extensive therapeutic work at an individual level before couple treatment seems viable. In addition, as some therapists have shown (Richter, 1974), single persons are capable of generating entire interaction patterns within families on the basis of their individual pathology. Richter describes how a paranoid personality who holds power in a family can generate a shared paranoia in the entire family system. I expect that men with abusive personalities are conflict generators in all intimate relationships, regardless of the personality or style of their female partner. Of course, such men may also pick women with their own backgrounds of abuse victimization and personality disorders. I recommend obtaining detailed social histories of clients and their partners prior to embarking on a systems approach, especially in view of the Kalmuss and Seltzer (1986) findings reported in this chapter. If a male batterer has a history of violence with women that pre-dates his current relationship or strong indicators of an abusive personality, couples treatment may not be advisable. Where the female feels threat from the man's violence potential or where violence is still recent, couples therapy might be delayed until the man has successfully completed an anger management program and is violence free for a lengthy period. In general, where the violence and conflict seem specific to the present relationship, couples treatment may be more useful after the man's or woman's anger treatment.

Cascardi and Vivian (1995) found that the majority of couple-clients seeking marital therapy both engaged in aggressive acts and the woman got the worst of it (Cascardi & Vivian, 1995). Vivian and Langhinrichsen-Rohling (1994) classified couples as follows: (a) mild bidirectional—about 50% report low-level aggression (pushes, slaps, and grabs) committed by both husband and wife, (b) moderate, and (c) severe wife victimization—30% to 40% report high levels of wife victimization and much lower levels of husband victimization. This leads to the question from the Stets and Straus (1992b) table. What happens to female-dominant violent couples? Obviously, they do not seek marital therapy. Interestingly, only a small percentage of women seeking marital therapy report physical violence as a problem. O'Leary, Vivian, and Malone (1992), and Ehrensaft and Vivian (1996) found 14%, despite CTS reports revealing higher levels of physical aggression in the marriages.

Heyman and Schlee (2003) assess for levels of aggression prior to their treatment program and found that very few couples reported severe levels of aggression (p. 145). When someone was injured or fearful or when the husband was in denial, the couple was screened out. They did not comment on wives in denial. Posttreatment assessment revealed significant drops in aggression and increases in rated marital adjustment by both parties. The reduction in aggression was still significantly lower than its pretreatment level 1 year after cessation of treatment. Complete cessation was found with 26% 1 year later. Reductions occurred in a substantial subgroup.

Stith, Rosen, McCollum, and Thomsen (2004) also found significant reductions in male violence recidivism 6 months after couples treatment cessation in a study of 42 couples (only 25% recidivated). This was in a couples' group therapy format. In an individual couples format, 43% recidivated. In a nontreated control, 66% recidivated. By comparison, in a treatment outcome study done on the Duluth model, Shepard (1987, 1992) found a 40% recidivism rate in a 6-month follow-up of Duluth clients, higher than most control recidivism levels. Dutton (1987) found a recidivism rate of 16% (or 84% complete cessation) based on wife's reports for a cognitive behavioral group treatment for men. This was for a court-mandated group. Stith, Rosen, and McCollum (2003) reviewed six outcome studies of couples treatment and concluded that they were at least as effective as "traditional treatment." The latter seemed to include both "psychoeducational" and cognitive-behavioral group therapy for males.

In conclusion, I present evidence here to argue that a premature foreclosure has occurred in treatment of intimate partner abuse. Because feminist activists have determined the intervention of choice in many states, Duluth models proliferate despite a poor outcome record. Other therapeutic strategies that may be more appropriate with certain couples have been banned or ruled out. I have included the case for treating female perpetrators and for couples work. I have also presented the case for an expanded focus of male perpetrator treatment to include associated features of abusiveness. I would argue that, although the evidence is still scant, these foci will be relevant in the treatment of female perpetrators as well.

REFERENCES

Archer, J. (2000). Sex differences in aggression between heterosexual partners: A meta-analytic review. *Psychological Bulletin, 126*(5), 651–680.

Babcock, J. C., Green, C. E., & Robie, C. (2004). Does batterers' treatment work? A meta-analytic review of domestic violence treatment outcome research. *Clinical Psychology Review, 23,* 1023–1053.

Babcock, J. C., Jacobson, N. C., Gottman, J. M., & Yerington, T. P. (2000). Attachment, emotional regulation, and the function of marital violence: Differences between secure, preoccupied, and dismissing violent and nonviolent husbands. *Journal of Family Violence, 15*(4), 391–409.

Babcock, J. C., Waltz, J., Jacobson, N. S., & Gottman, J. M. (1993). Power and violence: The relation between communication patterns, power discrepancies, and domestic violence. *Journal of Consulting and Clinical Psychology, 61*(1), 40–50.

Bowlby, J. (1969). *Attachment and loss: Attachment.* New York: Basic Books.

Burman, B., Margolin, G., & John, R. S. (1993). America's angriest home videos: Behavioral contingencies observed in home reenactments of marital conflict. *Journal of Consulting and Clinical Psychology, 61*(1), 28–39.

Busch, A., & Rosenberg, M. (2003). Comparing women and men arrested for domestic violence: A preliminary report. *Journal of Family Violence, 19*(1), 49–57.

Carmen, E. H., Reiker, P. P., & Mills, T. (1984). Victims of violence and psychiatric illness. *American Journal of Psychiatry, 141,* 378–379.

Cascardi, M., & Vivian, D. (1995). Context for specific episodes of marital violence: Gender and severity of violence differences. *Journal of Family Violence, 10,* 265–293.

Coleman, D. H., & Straus, M. A. (1985, November). *Marital power, conflict, and violence.* Paper presented at the meeting of the American Society Criminology, San Diego, CA.

Cordova, J. V., Jacobson, N. C., Gottman, J. M., Rushe, R., & Cox, G. (1993). Negative reciprocity and communication in couples with a violent husband. *Journal of Abnormal Psychology, 102*(4), 559–564.

Corvo, K., & Johnson, P. J. (2003). Vilification of the "batterer": How blame shapes domestic violence policy and interventions. *Aggression and Violent Behavior, 8*(3), 259–281.

Davis, R. C., & Taylor, B. G. (1999). Does batterer treatment reduce violence? A synthesis of the literature. *Women and Criminal Justice, 10,* 69–93.

Davis, R. C., Taylor, B. G., & Maxwell, C. D. (1998). Does batterer treatment reduce violence? A randomized experiment in Brooklyn. *Justice Quarterly, 18,* 171–201.

Davis, R. C., Taylor, B. G., & Maxwell, C. D. (2000). *Does batterer treatment reduce violence? A randomized experiment in Brooklyn.* Washington, DC: National Institute of Justice.

Dowd, L. (2001). Female perpetrators of partner aggression: Relevant issues and treatment. *Journal of Aggression, Maltreatment and Trauma, 5*(2), 73–104.

Dutton, D. G. (1987). The criminal justice response to wife assault. *Law and Human Behavior, 11*(3), 189–206.

Dutton, D. G. (1994a). The origin and structure of the abusive personality. *Journal of Personality Disorder, 8*(3), 181–191.

Dutton, D. G. (1994b). Patriarchy and wife assault: The ecological fallacy. *Violence and Victims, 9*(2), 125–140.

Dutton, D. G. (1995a). *The batterer: A psychological profile.* New York: Basic Books.

Dutton, (1995b). *The domestic assault of women.* Vancouver: University of British Columbia Press.

Dutton, D. G. (1995c). Intimate abusiveness. *Clinical Psychology: Science and Practice, 2*(3), 207–224.

Dutton, D. G. (1995d). Trauma symptoms and PTSD-like profiles in perpetrators of intimate abuse. *Journal of Traumatic Stress, 8*(2), 299–316.

Dutton, D. G. (1998). *The abusive personality: Violence and control in intimate relationships.* New York: Guilford Press.

Dutton, D. G. (2002a). *The abusive personality: Violence and control in intimate relationships.* New York: Guilford Press.

Dutton, D. G. (2002b). Psychiatric explanation of intimate abusiveness. *Journal of Psychiatric Practice, 8*(4), 216–228.

Dutton, D. G. (2003). Treatment of assaultiveness. In D. L. Sonkin & D. G. Dutton (Eds.), *Intimate violence: Contemporary treatment approaches* (pp. 7–28). New York: Haworth Press.

Dutton, D. G. (2006a). *The abusive personality* (3rd ed.). New York: Guilford Press.

Dutton, D. G. (2006b). *Rethinking domestic violence* (2nd ed.). Vancouver: University of British Columbia Press.

Dutton, D. G. (2006). *Personality profile of intimate terrorists.* Manuscript under review.

Dutton, D. G., Bodnarchuk, M., Kropp, R., Hart, S., & Ogloff, J. (1997). Client personality disorders affecting wife assault post treatment recidivism. *Violence and Victims, 12*(1), 37–50.

Dutton, D. G., & Browning, J. J. (1988). Concern for power, fear of intimacy, and aversive stimuli for wife assault. In G. J. Hotaling, D. Finkelhor, J. T. Kirkpatrick & M. A. Straus (Eds.), *Family abuse and its consequences: New directions in research* (pp. 163–175). Newbury Park, CA: Sage.

Dutton, D. G., & Nicholls, T. L. (2005). The gender paradigm in domestic violence research and theory: The conflict of theory and data. *Aggression and Violent Behavior, 10,* 680–714.

Dutton, D. G., Saunders, K., Starzomski, A., & Bartholomew, K. (1994). Intimacy anger and insecure attachment as precursors of abuse in intimate relationships. *Journal of Applied Social Psychology, 24*(15), 1367–1386.

Dutton, D. G., & Starzomski, A. (1994). Psychological differences between court-referred and self-referred wife assaulters. *Criminal Justice and Behavior: An International Journal, 21*(2), 203–222.

Dutton, D. G., Starzomski, A., Saunders, K., & Bartholomew, K. (1994). Intimacy-anger and insecure attachment as precursors of abuse in intimate relationships. *Journal of Applied Social Psychology, 24*(15), 1367–1386.

Dutton, D. G., van Ginkel, C., & Starzomski, A. (1995). The role of shame and guilt in the intergenerational transmission of abusiveness. *Violence and Victims, 10,* 121–131.

Dutton, D. G., Webb, A. N., & Ryan, L. (1994). Gender differences in affective reactions to intimate conflict. *Canadian Journal of Behavioural Science, 26*(3), 353–364.

Eckhardt, C. I., Barbour, K. A., & Davis, G. C. (1998). Articulated thoughts of maritally violent and nonviolent men during anger arousal. *Journal of Consulting and Clinical Psychology, 66*(2), 259–269.

Eckhardt, C. I., Barbour, K. A., & Stuart, G. L. (1997). Anger and hostility in maritally violent men: Conceptual distinctions, measurement issues and literature review. *Clinical Psychology Review, 17*(4), 333–358.

Ehrensaft, M., & Vivian, D. (1996). Spouses' reasons for not reporting existing physical aggression as a marital problem. *Journal of Family Psychology, 10*(4), 443–453.

Ehrensaft, M. K., Cohen, P., Brown, J., Smailes, E., Chen, H., & Johnson, J. G. (2003). Intergenerational transmission of partner violence: A 20-year prospective study. *Journal of Consulting and Clinical Psychology, 71*(4), 741–753.

Feder, L., & Forde, D. R. (1999, July). *A test of efficacy of court mandated counseling for convicted misdemeanor domestic violence offenders: Results from the Brouward experiment.* Paper presented at the International Family Violence Conference, Durham, NH.

Follingstad, D. R., Wright, S., Lloyd, S., & Sebastian, J. A. (1991). Sex differences in motivations and effects in dating violence. *Family Relations, 40,* 51–57.

Ford, D. A., & Regoli, M. J. (1993). The criminal prosecution of wife assaults: Process, problems, and effects. In N. Z. Hilton (Ed.), *Legal responses to wife assault: Current trends and evaluation* (pp. 127–164). Newbury Park, CA: Sage.

Gelles, R. J. (1996). Do arrests and restraining orders work? In E. S. Buzawa & C. G. Buzawa (Eds.), *Domestic violence: The changing criminal justice response* (pp. 30–42). Sage: Thousand Oaks, CA.

Giles-Sims, J. (1983). *Wife battering: A systems theory approach.* New York: Guilford Press.

Gondolf, E. W. (2001). Limitations of experimental evaluation of batterer programs. *Trauma, Violence and Abuse, 2*(1), 79–88.

Gottman, J. M., Jacobson, N. S., Rushe, R., Shortt, J. W., Babcock, J., La Taillade, J. J., et al. (1995). The relationship between heart rate reactivity, emotionally aggressive behavior and general violence in batterers. *Journal of Family Psychology, 9*(3), 227–248.

Hamberger, K., & Potente, T. (1994). Counseling heterosexual women arrested for domestic violence: Implications for theory and practice. *Violence and Victims, 9*(2), 125–137.

Hamberger, L. K., & Hastings, J. E. (1986). Personality correlated of men who abuse their partners: A cross-validation study. *Journal of Family Violence, 1,* 323–341.

Henning, K., & Feder, L. (2004). A comparison of men and women arrested for domestic violence: Who presents the greater risk? *Journal of Family Violence, 19*(2), 69–80.

Henning, K., Jones, A., & Holford, R. (2003). Treatment needs of women arrested for domestic violence: A comparison with male offenders. *Journal of Interpersonal Violence, 18*(8), 839–856.

Herman, J., & Van der Kolk, B. (1987). Traumatic antecedents of borderline personality disorder. In B. Van der Kolk (Ed.), *Psychological trauma* (pp. 111–126). Washington, DC: American Psychiatric Association Press.

Heyman, R., & Schlee, K. A. (2003). Stopping wife abuse via physical aggression couples treatment. In D. G. Dutton & D. L. Sonkin (Eds.), *Intimate violence: Contemporary treatment innovations.* New York: Haworth Press.

Holtzworth-Munroe, A., & Stuart, G. L. (1994). Typologies of male batterers: Three subtypes and the differences among them. *Psychological Bulletin, 116*(3), 476–497.

Jacobson, N. S., Gottman, J. M., Waltz, J., Rushe, R., Babcock, J., & Holtzworth-Munroe, A. (1994). Affect, verbal content, and psychophysiology in the arguments of couples with a violent husband. *Journal of Consulting and Clinical Psychology, 62*(5), 982–988.

Johnson, M. P. (1995). Patriarchal terrorism and common couple violence: Two forms of violence against women. *Journal of Marriage and the Family, 57,* 283–294.

Kalmuss, D. S., & Seltzer, J. A. (1986). Continuity of marital behavior in remarriage: The case of spouse abuse. *Journal of Marriage and the Family, 48,* 113–120.

Leisring, P., Dowd, L., & Rosenbaum, A. (2003). Treatment of partner aggressive women. In D. G. Dutton & D. L. Sonkin (Eds.), *Intimate violence: Contemporary treatment innovations.* New York: Haworth Press.

Leonard, K. E., & Roberts, L. J. (1998). The effects of alcohol on the marital interactions of aggressive and nonaggressive husbands and their wives. *Journal of Abnormal Psychology, 107*(4), 602–615.

Levenson, R. W., & Gottman, J. M. (1983). Marital interaction: Physiological linkage and affective exchange. *Journal of Personality and Social Psychology, 45*(3), 587–597.

Lie, G., Schilit, R., Bush, J., Montague, M., & Reyes, L. (1991). Lesbians in currently aggressive relationships: How frequently do they report aggressive past relationships? *Violence and Victims, 6*(2), 121–135.

Luborsky, L. (1984). *Principles of psychoanalytic therapy: A manual for supportive-expressive treatment.* New York: Basic Books.

Maiuro, R. D., Cahn, T. S., Vitaliano, P. P., Wagner, B. C., & Zegree, J. B. (1988). Anger, hostility and depression in domestically violent versus generally assaultive men and nonviolent control subjects. *Journal of Consulting and Clinical Psychology, 56,* 17–23.

Maiuro, R. D., Hagar, T. S., Lin, H., & Olson, N. (2001). Are current state standards for domestic violence perpetrator treatment adequately informed by research? A question of questions. *Journal of Aggression, Maltreatment and Trauma, 5*(2), 21–44.

Margolies, L., & Leeder, E. (1995). Violence at the door: Treatment of lesbian batterers. *Violence Against Women, 1*(2), 139–157.

Margolin, G. (1984, July). *Interpersonal and intrapersonal factors associated with marital violence.* Paper presented at the Second National Family Violence Research Conference, Durham, NH.

Margolin, G., & Burman, B. (1993). Wife abuse versus marital violence: Different terminologies, explanations, and solution. *Clinical Psychology Review, 13,* 59–73.

Margolin, G., John, R. S., & Glebermen, L. (1989). Affective responses to conflictual discussions in violent and non-violent couples. *Journal of Consulting and Clinical Psychology, 56*(1), 24–33.

Mikulincer, M. (1998). Adult attachment style and affect regulation: Strategic variations in self-appraisals. *Journal of Personal Social Psychology, 75,* 420–435.

Mills, L. (1999). Killing her softly: Intimate abuse and the violence of state intervention. *Harvard Law Review, 113*(2), 551–613.

Moffitt, T. E., Caspi, A., Rutter, M., & Silva, P. A. (2001). *Sex differences in antisocial behavior.* Cambridge, England: Cambridge University Press.

Murphy, C., & Baxter, V. A. (1997). Motivating batterers to change in the treatment context. *Journal of Interpersonal Violence, 12,* 607–619.

Neidig, P. H., & Friedman, D. H. (1984). *Spouse abuse: A treatment program for couples.* Champaign, IL: Research Press.

O'Leary, K. D., Heyman, R., & Neidig, P. H. (1999). Treatment of wife abuse: A comparison of gender-specific and couple approaches. *Behavior Assessment, 30,* 475–505.

O'Leary, K. D., Vivian, D., & Malone, J. (1992). Assessment of physical aggression in marriage: The need for a multimodal method. *Behavior Assessment, 14,* 5–14.

Pagelow, M. D. (1984). *Family violence.* New York: Praeger.

Patterson, G. R. (1979). A performance theory for coercive family interactions. In R. Cairns (Ed.), *Social interaction: Methods, analysis, and illustrations* (pp. 87–112). Hillsdale, NJ: Lawrence Erlbaum Associates.

Patterson. G.R., Cobb, J.A. & Ray, R.S. (1972). A social engineering technology for retraining families of aggressive boys. In H.E. Adams and P.J. Unikel (Eds). *Issues and trends in behavior therapy.* Springfield, IL: Charles C. Thomas.

Pence, E., & Paymar, M. (1993). *Education groups for men who batter: The Duluth model.* New York: Springer.

Pleck, E. (1987). *Domestic tyranny: The making of American social policy against family violence from colonial times to the present.* New York: Oxford University Press.

Renzetti, C. (1992). *Violent betrayal: Partner abuse in lesbian relationships.* Newbury Park, CA: Sage.

Richter, H. (1974). *The family as patient.* New York: Farrar, Straus and Giroux.

Saunders, D. G. (1993). Husbands who assault: Multiple profiles requiring multiple responses. In N. Z. Hilton (Ed.), *Legal responses to wife assault: Current trends and evaluation* (pp. 9–34). Newbury Park, CA: Sage.

Schore, A. N. (2003). *Affect regulation and the repair of the self.* New York: Norton.

Shepard, M. (1987, July). *Interventions with men who batter: An evaluation of a domestic abuse program.* Paper presented at the Third National Conference on Domestic Violence, Durham, NH.

Shepard, M. (1992). Predicting batterer recidivism five years after community intervention. *Journal of Family Violence, 7*(3), 167–178.

Sherman, L. W., Schmidt, J. D., Rogan, D. P., Smith, D. A., Gartin, P. R., Cohn, E. G., et al. (1992). The variable effects of arrest on criminal careers: The Milwaukee domestic violence experiment. *Journal of Criminal Law and Criminology, 83*(1), 137–169.

Siegel, J. M. (1986). The multidimensional anger inventory. *Journal of Personality and Social Psychology, 5*(1), 191–200.

Simon, T. R., Anderson, M., Thompson, M. P., Crosby, A. E., Shelley, G., & Sacks, J. J. (2001). Attitudinal acceptance of intimate partner violence among U.S. adults. *Violence and Victims, 16*(2), 115–126.

Sonkin, D. J., & Dutton, D. G. (2003). Treating assaultive men from an attachment perspective. In D. L. Sonkin & D. G. Dutton (Eds.), *Intimate violence: Contemporary treatment Approaches* (pp. 105–134). New York: Haworth Press.

Stets, J., & Straus, M. (1992a). Gender differences in reporting marital violence. In M. A. Straus & R. J. Gelles (Eds.), *Physical violence in American families* (pp. 151–166). New Brunswick, NJ: Transaction Publishers.

Stets, J., & Straus, M. (1992b). *The marriage license as a hitting license: Physical violence in American families.* New Brunswick, NJ: Transaction Publishers.

Stith, S. M., Rosen, K. H., & McCollum, E. E. (2003). Effectiveness of couples treatment for spouse abuse. *Journal of Marital and Family Therapy, 29,* 407–426.

Stith, S. M., Rosen, K. H., McCollum, E. E., & Thomsen, C. J. (2004). Treating intimate partner violence within intact couple relationships: Outcomes of multi-couple versus individual couple therapy. *Journal of Marital and Family Therapy, 30,* 305–318.

Straus, M. A., & Gelles, R. J. (1985, November). *Is family violence increasing? A comparison of 1975 and 1985 national survey rates.* Paper presented at the American Society of Criminology, San Diego, CA.

Straus, M. A., & Gelles, R. J. (1992). How violent are American families: Estimates from the National Family Violence Resurvey and other surveys. In M. A. Straus & R. J. Gelles (Eds.), *Physical violence in American families* (pp. 95–108). New Brunswick, NJ: Transaction Publishers.

Tangney, J. P., Wagner, P., Fletcher, C., & Gramzow, R. (1992). Shamed into anger? The relation of shame and guilt to anger and self-reported aggression. *Journal of Personality and Social Psychology, 62*(4), 669–675.

Tjaden, P., & Thoennes, N. (1998). *Prevalence, incidence and consequences of violence against women: Findings from the National Violence Against Women Survey.* Washington, DC: U.S. Department of Justice.

Tolman, R. M. (2001) An ecological analysis of batterer intervention program standards. *Journal of Aggression and Maltreatment and Trauma, 5*(10), 221–234.

Tweed, R., & Dutton, D. G. (1998). A comparison of instrumental and impulsive subgroups of batterers. *Violence and Victims, 13*(3), 217–230.

Van der Kolk, B. (1987). *Psychological trauma.* Washington, DC: American Psychiatric Press.

Vivian, D., & Langhinrichsen-Rohling, J. (1994). Are bi-directionally violent couples mutually victimized? A gender-sensitive comparisons. *Violence and Victims, 9,* 107–124.

Walker, L. (1984). *The battered woman syndrome.* New York: Springer.

Wallace, R., & Nosko, A. (2003). Shame in male spouse abusers and its treatment in group therapy. In D. G. Dutton & D. J. Sonkin (Eds.), *Intimate violence: Contemporary treatment innovations* (pp. 47–74). New York: Haworth Press.

Yllo, K., & Straus, M. (1990). Patriarchy and violence against wives: The impact of structural and normative factors. In M. Straus & R. Gelles (Eds.), *Physical violence in American families* (pp. 383–399). New Brunswick, NJ: Transaction Publishers.

CHAPTER 3

Risk Factors for Physical Violence Between Dating Partners: Implications for Gender-Inclusive Prevention and Treatment of Family Violence

Rose A. Medeiros and Murray A. Straus

A sometimes bitter debate has waged for more than 25 years over research indicating that women physically assault their male partners at about the same rate as men physically attack female partners. Yet the evidence from almost 200 studies is overwhelming (Archer, 2000; Moffitt, Caspi, Rutter, & Silva, 2001; Straus, 1999, 2005b). In recent years, the focus of the debate has shifted somewhat. Although still denying the overwhelming evidence of approximately equal rates of assault by men and women, those who believe that male dominance and male degradation of women is almost always at the root of partner violence now tend to focus on asserting or implying that, when women physically assault a partner, the causes or motives are different than when men attack their partners. Unfortunately, much of what has been written on differences in causes and motives is based on the beliefs and values of the authors rather than on empirical comparisons of men and women.

Revision of a presentation at the "Town Meeting" discussion of "Women's Use of Violence in Intimate Relationships" at the American Society of Criminology annual meeting, Chicago, Illinois, November 14, 2002. For other papers on this and related issues, log on to http://pubpages.unh.edu/~mas2. It is a pleasure to express appreciation to the members of the Family Research Laboratory Seminar for valuable comments and suggestions. The work has been supported by National Institute of Mental Health grant T32MH15161 and by the University of New Hampshire.

For example, Dobash, Dobash, Wilson, and Daly (1992) asserted that men's and women's motivations for violence differ. But the only evidence they referred to is the greater injury rate suffered by women. Although it is true that female victims are more often injured, injury is a consequence of assault, not a cause. Neither Dobash et al.'s research nor any of the studies they cited provided evidence on differences in motivation or risk factors.

Similarly, Hamberger and Guse (2002) asserted that "men in contrast [to women] appear to use violence to dominate and control," but even though the article cited about 80 studies, none provided empirical evidence on gender differences in dominance and control motivation, yet there are at least eight studies showing that dominance or control is related to violence against a partner by women as well as by men (Graham-Kevan & Archer, 2005; Kim & Clifton, 2003; Laroche, 2005; So-Kum Tang, 1999; Stets & Pirog-Good, 1990; Straus, Gelles, & Steinmetz, 1980; Straus & Members of the International Dating Violence Research Consortium, 2006; Sugihara & Warner, 2002).

Yet another example of this type of claim is the statement by Nazroo (1995). However, the evidence he presents concerns differences on anxiety and fear and the fact that male violence is more intimidating. These are extremely important dimensions, especially for victim services, but none of these are etiological factors, and all could follow from the greater average size and strength of men rather than from the implied but undemonstrated difference in motives. We believe that the unstated agenda of authors such as Dobash and Dobash and Nazroo is to excuse violence by women by implying that violence by women is morally courageous because it is assumed to be in self-defense, whereas violence by men is morally indefensible because it is assumed to be an act of domination rather than self-defense. Some violence by women is in self-defense, but, as will be shown in the review of previous research later in this chapter, the available studies find that this also applies to some violence by men. The same distortion of the scientific evidence by selective citation applies to discussion of dominance and control. Only studies showing male use of violence to coerce, dominate, and control are cited despite a number of studies showing that this also applies to violence by female partners (Dutton & Nicholls, 2005). We agree that violence by men against a partner is morally indefensible but that this also applies to partner violence by women.

Although there has been much research on partner violence, including risk factors, most of the studies of risk factors and motivations for partner violence provide data only on these variables for violence by men. The comprehensive set of articles reviewing risk factors for family violence by Heyman and colleagues (Heyman & Slep, 2001) is restricted to violence by men. When women are included in a study, men are not (Straus, in press). For example, in one of the relatively few studies that obtained data on motives by women offenders, Fiebert and Gonzales (1997) found that 46% of women reported that they had hit their partner because he "wasn't sensitive to my needs," 44% "to gain my partner's attention," 38% because they did not believe the hitting would hurt him, 38% because he was "being verbally abusive to me," and 43% because the partner "was not listening to me." However, the sample was entirely women so that no comparisons with men were possible. Notable exceptions include the Winnipeg, Canada, study by Sommer (1994), which found self-defense to be a motive for only 10% of female and 15% of male respondents who had engaged in intimate partner violence, and the British Survey by Carrado, George, Loxam, Jones, and Templar (1996), in which the predominant motives for assaulting a partner were "to get through," reported by 53% of women and 64% of men, and to retaliate, given by 52% of women and 53% of men.

Given the overwhelming evidence that women physically assault partners at about the same rate as men, it is important to determine the extent to which this violence has different roots for men and women. Whatever the answer, it can help provide a sounder theoretical understanding of the phenomenon of partner violence and can help in designing prevention and treatment programs. This chapter is intended to provide some of the needed information by presenting the results of an empirical study of gender differences in risk factors for partner assault. The analysis compares men and women on the degree to which 21 hypothesized risk factors were related to physically assaulting a dating partner. The risk factors examined fall into two broad categories. The first category refers to personal psychological characteristics that are hypothesized to increase the probability of domestic violence, such as antisocial personality and attitudes approving violence. The second category refers to characteristics of the relationship, such as dominance of one partner and communication problems.

A clear answer to the etiological issues that are the focus of this chapter requires longitudinal data. However, the data available to us, like the data in almost all previous studies, are cross sectional. Consequently, we use the term *risk factor* (Kleinbaum, Kupper, & Morgenstern, 1982) because it refers to variables that are associated with an increased probability of the dependent variable but are not necessarily direct causes. For example, inadequate anger management skills could be a cause of violence in relationships. But for some it might be an effect of relying on physical force and therefore never having to learn to effectively control anger. Longitudinal research is needed to trace out the causal sequence, and a randomized trial is needed to determine whether anger management training contributes to primary or secondary prevention of partner violence. However, an important first step is to determine whether inadequate ability to deal with anger is associated with partner violence by women as well as men.

RELEVANCE OF INFORMATION ON DATING PARTNERS

Research on violence between dating partners is important for understanding domestic violence and for designing prevention and treatment programs. At least 50 studies have found that the rate of violence between dating couples is two to three times greater than among married couples (Stets & Straus, 1989; Straus, 2004b; Sugarman & Hotaling, 1989). Moreover, the risk factors for dating violence are remarkably parallel to the risk factors for martial violence, and violent behavior in dating relationships often carries over into marriage (O'Leary, Malone, & Tyree, 1994; O'Leary et al., 1989). Conceptually, dating is a stage in the family life cycle. Because dating violence is a stage in domestic violence, the study of dating couples can help increase our understanding of violence in marriage. In addition, dating may be a stage in the family life cycle that is strategic for purposes of primary prevention (O'Leary & Sweet Jemmott, 1995).

PREVIOUS RESEARCH ON GENDER DIFFERENCES IN RISK FACTORS

There does not seem to have been a systematic review of empirical studies of differences between men and women in the etiology of domestic assault. None of the three textbooks we checked contained a section on this issue, and our search of *PsychLit* and *Sociological Abstracts* did not uncover a review article. This could be the result of an absence of comparative research to review, but it might be the result of a reluctance to evaluate gender differences in etiology on the basis of empirical evidence. Those who subscribe to the patriarchal dominance theory of partner violence find the very idea of an empirical test ridiculous, offensive, or both. Those who are not committed to that ideology may fear they will be ostracized and blacklisted, as has happened to one of us Straus (Straus, 1990c).

Our search of literature from 1970 to 2004 identified 51 studies that met the criteria of including information for both men and women (Medeiros & Straus, 2006). These 51 studies included comparisons of men and women in respect to 242 variables. Most studies contributed data for more than one of the gender comparisons. Despite the extensiveness of the search and the large amount of research located, there are likely to be a number of studies that were missed. Nevertheless, the volume of research that we were able to locate suggests that the absence of previous systematic comparative reviews may reflect inattention to this controversial issue rather than a lack of research on the issue. In fact, the number of results in these 51 studies is so extensive the it required 19 pages of tables to summarize the results. Because the many tables and the many pages of explanatory text are more than can be included in a chapter on empirical results from a new study, those tables and their discussion are presented in a separate article (Medeiros & Straus, 2006).

Percentage of Studies Finding Similar Results for Men and Women

We identified four types of studies based on the type of data reported. The type that most adequately addressed the issue of gender differences in risk factors were studies that performed statistical tests for differences in the relationship between various risk factors and partner assault for men and women. We located seven studies that examined the relationship of 25 variables to partner violence and provided data on whether there was a statistically significant gender difference in the relationship between a risk factor and partner assault (i.e., an interaction effect). Seventy-two percent of the relationships analyzed found no significant difference between the risk factors for assault and gender for men and women.

In the second type of study, we located and compared violent men and violent women on a total of 56 characteristics, such as educational level and score on a measure of anger. In 73% of these comparisons, no significant difference was found between men and women in the risk factors examined.

The third type of study is similar to the second type in that it also compared violent men and women. However, unlike the second type of study, the authors did not test the significance of the gender difference. We classified the results as different for men and women if the percentage for the gender with the larger percentage was at least 20% greater. Using this criterion, of the 28 variables in six studies, 43% of variables had similar results for men and women.

The fourth type of study examined the relationship between risk factors and partner assault for men and women separately but did not test for differences between men and women. We located 23 studies of this type. They reported results on gender differences in the relation of 147 risk factors for partner assault but did not test for interactions or test for the significance of the difference in the correlation for men and women. Sixty percent of the variables showed the same relationship for men and women (e.g., both nonsignificant, both positive and both significant, both negative and significant, and so on). Thirty-nine percent showed relationships with the dependent variable that was in the same direction for both men and women but was significant for one and not the other. One percent of variables in these studies showed opposite relationships for men and women (one positive and significant, the other negative and significant). These results can be interpreted as showing that there was a similar etiological pattern for 60% of the risk factors examined or for 99% if studies showing the same direction of effect are included.

Specific Gender Differences and Similarities

The specific gender differences and similarities found in the studies we reviewed are given in the tables in Medeiros and Straus (2006). Examples include the following:

- Eight out of 10 of the analyses found similar relationships between youthfulness and partner assault for both men and women.
- All four studies of the link between conflict in the relationship and partner assault found similar relationships for males and females.
- In five of seven studies, similar numbers of men and women cited self-defense as a reason for assaulting their partner.
- Dominance was linked to partner assault for both men and women in four of five studies.
- Three of four studies found a similar relationship between having an angry personality and assaulting a partner for men and women. All six studies that looked at anger or provocation as a reason for partner assault found a similar relationship for men and women.

Conclusions From Previous Research

The studies that used tests of significance for gender differences in the characteristics of male and female offenders found parallel results for males and females for 72%. Studies that examined differences in risk factors found parallel relationships for males and females in 73% of the comparisons. For the two groups of studies that did not apply tests of significance, the first found parallel results for 43% of the comparisons. The second of these two groups of studies found parallel results for 60% of the comparisons using one criterion for "parallel results" and for 99% of the comparisons using another criterion. Taking all four types of studies together suggests that the studies reviewed found parallel results for males and females. If one rules out measurement and sampling error as the explanation for the one-quarter of comparisons showing a difference in risk factors for males and females, our review suggests that although the predominant pattern is parallel etiology for males and females, there are many exceptions. It is important for both theoretical understanding of the etiology of partner violence and for prevention and treatment efforts to more clearly identify the differences and similarities between men's and women's partner violence. The research described in the following sections is intended to contribute to that end.

METHOD

Sample

The sample consists of 854 undergraduate students (312 men and 542 women) from two universities who were enrolled in sociology courses or introductory psychology in 1998, 1999, and 2000. The sample was restricted to those who were or had been in a heterosexual romantic relationship of a month or longer. The sample was also restricted to unmarried students.

Data Collection

The questionnaire booklet consisted of: (a) a cover sheet explaining the purpose of the study and the participant's rights and providing the name of a contact person and telephone number for those who might have questions after the test session was over, (b) the demographic questions, and (c) the instruments described in the measures section.

The data were gathered using procedures reviewed by and approved by the board for protection of human subjects at each university. The sociology class participants were tested during a classroom period. The purpose, task demands, and rights were explained orally as well as in printed form at the beginning of each test session. Participants were told that the test session would involve answering questions concerning attitudes, beliefs, and experiences they may have had, including questions on sex and other sensitive issues. They were assured of the anonymity and confidentiality of their responses, and they were told that the session would take about an hour. In practice, most students completed the survey in 40 to 45 minutes. The psychology class participants were tested in groups of 20 to 30. They were asked to sign written consent forms before completing their questionnaires. After receiving directions about using the machine-scored answer sheets, they worked at their own paces. A debriefing form was given to participants as they left the testing room. It explained the study in more detail and provided

TABLE 3.1   Characteristics of Respondents and Their Relationships

Characteristic	Total ($n = 854^a$)	Men ($n = 312^a$)	Women ($n = 542^a$)	Chi-square
Year in college				3.77
Freshman	46	46	47	
Sophomore	22	22	21	
Junior	20	18	21	
Senior	12	15	11	
Age in years				
Median category[b]	19	20	19	26.7**
Father's education				2.33
High school/less	42	41	43	
Some college	7	8	7	
College degree	29	28	30	
Graduate degree	22	23	21	
Mother's education				16.1*
High school/less	46	47	45	
Some college	9	6	11	
College degree	29	33	27	
Graduate degree	16	15	16	
Family income				
Median group	60,000–69,999	70,000–79,999	60,000–69,999	44.42**
Reporting on current relation				
Previous	45	52	42	7.8**

(Continued)

TABLE 3.1   (Continued)

Characteristic	Total ($n = 854^a$)	Men ($n = 312^a$)	Women ($n = 542^a$)	Chi-square
Relationship Type				0.62
Dating	97	97	97	
Engaged	4	3	3	
Relationship Length[c]				12.71*
1–11 months	33	37	32	
1 Year–1 Year, 11 months	40	41	40	
2 Years or more	27	23	29	
Sexually active	75	71	78	5.53*

[a] The n's vary slightly from question to question because of variation in missing data.

[b] The categories used for the logistic regression are 18, 19, 20, 21, 22–24, 25–29, 30–39, and 40–49.

[c] The categories used for the logistic regression are 2 = about 1 month, 3 = about 2 months, 4 = 3–5 months, 5 = 6–11 months, 6 = about 1 year, 7 = more than 1 year but less than 2 years, 8 = about 2 years, 9 = more than 2 years but less than 4 years, and 10 = 4 years or more.

* $= p < .05.$ ** $= p < .01.$

names and telephone numbers of area mental health services and community resources, such as services for battered women. Students from the psychology subject pool received two credits toward the fulfillment of their introductory psychology course research requirement for their participation.

Table 3.1 shows that 40% of the respondents were in their first year at the university. The median age was 19 years, but some older students were included. Their socioeconomic background was relatively high: about half their parents had had at least some college education, and the median income category was $60,000 to $69,999.

Relationship Characteristics

Almost all the students described a dating relationship (97%) as opposed to more committed relationships. However, sexual relations were reported to be part of the relationship by 75% of respondents. About half the sample had been in the relationship described for between 1 and 11 months. Slightly more than half the sample described a current relationship, and the remainder described a previous relationship.

Gender Differences in Characteristics of the Sample

The male and female students were similar in year in school, father's level of education, and type of relationship (dating vs. engaged). Males reported higher median age and family income. Females were more likely to report that sex was part of the relationship. The women had been in their relationships slightly longer than the men, and more were in the relationship they described at the time of testing. The fact that more women than men had relationships of a year or more and the fact that more of them reported on current relationships may affect both the nature and frequency of experiences and behavior reported and memory for events that took place between respondents and their partners. The differences between the male's and female's reports of their mother's education were statistically significant, but no clear pattern of differences emerged.

Measures

Partner Assault

The revised Conflict Tactics Scales, or CTS2 (Straus, Hamby, Boney-McCoy, & Sugarman, 1996), was used to measure physical assault by the respondent. The CTS has been used in more than 300 studies of both married and dating partners in the past 25 years, and there is extensive evidence of reliability and validity (Archer, 1999; Straus, 1990a, 2005b; Straus & Ramirez, in press). The Physical Assault scale of the CTS2 was used for this study. It includes subscales for "minor" and "severe" assaults. The Minor Assault scale includes acts such as slapping or throwing something at the partner. The Severe Assault scale includes acts such as punching and choking. The difference between the minor and severe subscales is analogous to the legal categories of simple assault and aggravated assault. (For a complete list of the CTS questions and for data on validity and reliability, see Straus, 2004a; Straus et al., 1996.)

Risk Factor Variables

The Personal and Relationships Profile (PRP) was used to obtain the data on risk factors. The PRP is a 21-scale instrument designed for research on partner assault. The variables measured by the PRP scales were selected on the basis of a review of the theoretical and empirical literature on the etiology of partner violence. Some of the scales in the PRP measure personal or intrapsychic characteristics of the respondent, and some measure characteristics of the relationship as reported by the respondent. The personal characteristics scales are Antisocial Personality, Borderline Personality, Criminal History, Depression, Gender Hostility, Neglect History, Posttraumatic Stress Disorder, Social Desirability, Social Integration, Substance Abuse, Stressful Conditions, Sexual Abuse History, and Violence Approval. The relationship characteristics scales are Anger Management, Communication Problems, Conflict, Dominance, Jealousy, Negative Attribution, Relationship Commitment, and Relationship Distress.

The steps used to develop the PRP, along with data on reliability and validity, are given in Straus, Hamby, Boney-McCoy, and Sugarman (1999) and Straus and Mouradian (1999). The specific items used to measure each of the 21 constructs are given in Straus et al. (1999). The instructions for the PRP ask the respondents to indicate whether they agree or disagree that the statement describes themselves, using the following response categories: Strongly Disagree = 1, Disagree = 2, Agree = 3, and Strongly Agree = 4.

Social Desirability Scale

Research that uses self-reports to obtain data on sensitive issues needs to take into account defensiveness or minimization of socially undesirable behavior. We did this by using the Social Desirability scale of the PRP. This is a 13-item version of the widely used Marlowe-Crowne Social Desirability Scale developed by Reynolds (Reynolds, 1982). The scale measures the degree to which respondents tend to avoid disclosing socially undesirable behavior, such as partner assault and other crime.

Socioeconomic Status

A scale to measure the socioeconomic status (SES) of the student's family was computed using the number of years of education completed by the student's father and mother and family income. Each of these three variables were transformed to z scores and summed. The sum was transformed to a z score. This approach to measuring SES provides a score that indicates the number of standard deviations above or below the mean of the families of all students at their university.

Data Analysis

The relationship between gender, the 21 PRP scales, and assault on a dating partner was examined using nested multinomial logistic regression analyses. For each PRP scale, two models were run. The first model regressed partner assault on the PRP scale, respondent's sex, family SES, and social desirability. The second model included all the variables in the first model plus a gender by PRP scale interaction. The dependent variable for all models was the four-category Severity Level measure of assaults in the past year (Straus & Douglas, 2004): no assaults in past year, minor assaults in the past year but no severe assaults, and any severe assaults in the past year.

RESULTS

Prevalence Rates

Many previous studies of dating relationships have found that between 25% and 45% of respondents assaulted their partner in the previous 12 months (Stets & Straus, 1989; Sugarman & Hotaling, 1989). The 23% rate for this sample is consistent with those studies. Most assaults against dating partners fall within the "minor violence" category, and that is also

TABLE 3.2   Logistic Regression Results for the Relation of 21 Risk Factors to Minor Assault[a]

	Model 1			Model 2		
	OR	SE[2b]	z	OR	SE[2b]	z
Anger management	0.21	0.36	−4.34***	0.19	0.60	−2.78***
x gender				1.12	0.71	0.16
Anti-social personality	1.97	0.33	2.03**	2.67	0.53	1.87*
x gender				0.62	0.62	−0.76
Borderline personality	1.78	0.25	2.31**	1.48	0.46	0.86
x gender				1.27	0.51	0.46
Criminal history	1.28	0.24	1.00	1.29	0.24	0.72
x gender				1.00	0.35	−0.01
Relationship conflict	1.72	0.54	2.15**	2.05	0.44	1.62
x gender				0.77	0.51	−0.50
Communication problems	2.30	0.32	2.59**	3.77	0.53	2.49***
x gender				0.48	0.62	−1.18
Depression	0.90	0.26	−0.42	1.16	0.44	0.34
x gender				0.69	0.52	−0.72

(Continued)

TABLE 3.2 (Continued)

	Model 1			Model 2		
	OR	SE[2b]	z	OR	SE[2b]	z
Dominance	2.24	0.34	2.40**	3.36	0.56	2.16**
x gender				0.53	0.69	−0.91
Gender hostility	1.00	0.23	−0.01	1.39	0.23	0.88
x gender				0.60	0.37	−1.14
Jealousy	1.19	0.21	0.82	1.25	0.39	0.57
x gender				0.94	0.45	−0.14
Negative attributions	1.55	0.21	2.05**	1.71	0.36	1.48
x gender				0.86	0.43	−0.36
Neglect history	0.74	0.29	−1.02	0.75	0.47	−0.60
x gender				0.97	0.60	−0.05
Posttraumatic stress disorder	1.13	0.21	0.59	1.37	0.46	0.69
x gender				0.79	0.50	−0.48
Commitment	0.84	0.20	−0.87	0.99	0.35	−0.02
x gender				0.79	0.42	−0.57
Relationship distress	1.18	0.18	0.91	1.09	0.34	0.26
x gender				1.11	0.39	0.26
Sexual abuse history	1.00	0.29	0.00	1.39	0.47	0.71
x gender				0.59	0.58	−0.90
Social integration	0.71	0.31	−1.13	1.00	0.52	0.00
x gender				0.60	0.61	−0.84
Stressful conditions	0.69	0.32	−1.14	1.29	0.54	0.47
x gender				0.41	0.63	−1.43
Substance abuse	1.77	0.21	2.73**	1.94	0.35	1.88*
x gender				0.87	0.43	−0.33
Violence approval	1.28	0.29	0.86	2.04	0.48	1.48
x gender				0.49	0.58	−1.22
Violence socialization	1.10	0.25	0.37	1.02	0.45	0.05
x gender				1.10	0.52	0.19

[a] For risk factor x gender interactions, male = 0, female = 1.
[b] Standard errors (SE) are for the coefficient (b), not the odds ratio.
* $p < .10.$ ** $p < .05.$ *** $p < .01.$

TABLE 3.3   Regression Results for the Relation of 21 Risk Factors to Severe Assault[a]

	Model 1			Model 2		
	OR	SE[2b]	z	OR	SE[2b]	z
Anger management	0.14	0.47	−4.21***	0.19	0.74	−2.26**
x gender				0.63	0.89	−0.52
Antisocial personality	7.39	0.43	4.64***	10.74	0.70	3.40***
x gender				0.56	0.83	−0.70
Borderline personality	1.73	0.32	1.71	2.93	0.57	1.88*
x gender				0.49	0.65	−1.10
Criminal history	2.29	0.29	2.90***	1.79	0.43	1.36
x gender				1.50	0.54	0.75
Relationship conflict	3.83	0.33	4.08***	9.88	0.61	3.73***
x gender				0.26	0.70	−1.91*
Communication problems	4.92	0.42	3.78***	4.60	0.66	2.33**
x gender				1.12	0.79	0.14
Depression	1.02	0.33	0.05	1.45	0.55	0.68
x gender				0.59	0.65	−0.81
Dominance	3.77	0.43	3.07***	5.32	0.70	2.38**
x gender				0.57	0.88	−0.63
Gender hostility	1.70	0.29	1.84	1.89	0.45	1.41
x gender				0.84	0.56	−0.32
Jealousy	2.00	0.28	2.50***	1.53	0.49	0.87
x gender				1.46	0.58	0.65
Negative attributions	2.44	0.27	3.32***	3.26	0.44	2.68**
x gender				0.64	0.54	−0.84
Neglect history	2.01	0.32	2.21**	2.17	0.51	1.52
x gender				0.89	0.64	−0.19
Posttraumatic stress disorder	1.27	0.27	0.87	3.32	0.58	2.06**
x gender				0.29	0.65	−1.89*
Commitment	0.96	0.26	−0.14	0.84	0.44	−0.39
x gender				1.23	0.54	0.38

(Continued)

TABLE 3.3   (Continued)

	Model 1			Model 2		
	OR	SE[2b]	z	OR	SE[2b]	z
Relationship distress	1.38	0.23	1.41	1.64	0.42	1.17
x gender				0.79	0.50	−0.48
Sexual abuse history	1.99	0.30	2.30**	4.15	0.46	3.10***
x gender				0.29	0.62	−2.02**
Social integration	0.59	0.40	−1.31	0.68	0.66	−0.59
x gender				0.81	0.79	−0.26
Stressful conditions	2.26	0.41	2.00**	3.89	0.66	2.05**
x gender				0.44	0.78	−1.05
Substance abuse	1.29	0.27	0.95	2.84	0.46	2.26**
x gender				0.29	0.57	−2.19**
Violence approval	2.76	0.37	2.77***	7.02	0.61	3.20***
x gender				0.23	0.75	−1.98***
Violence socialization	1.49	0.31	1.31	1.69	0.54	0.97
x gender				0.84	0.64	−0.28

[a] For risk factor × gender interactions, male = 0, female = 1.
[b] Standard errors (SE) are for the coefficient (b), not the odds ratio.
$^*p < .10.$ $^{**}p < .05.$ $^{***}p < .01.$

the case for this sample. Fifteen percent of the sample restricted their violence to minor assaults, and 8% engaged in one or more of the acts in the Severe Assault scale of the CTS2.

The rates for perpetration of partner violence by men and women are also consistent with many previous studies of violence in dating relationships in that the rates for men and women are about the same or somewhat higher for women (Archer, 2000; Stets & Straus, 1989; Straus & Ramirez, in press; Sugarman & Hotaling, 1989): For Minor Violence, the rates are 13% for men and 16% for women. For Severe Violence, the rates are 7% for men and 8% for women.

Risk Factors for Minor Assaults

Total Sample

The columns of Table 3.2 under the heading "Model 1" give the results of the multinomial logistic regression analyses using the total sample to test the relationship between each of the risk factors measured by the PRP to minor assault. The following eight PRP variables were found to be associated with an increased probability of using only minor violence: Anger Management, Antisocial Personality Traits, Borderline Personality Traits, Relationship Conflict, Communication Problems, Dominance, Negative Attributions About Partner, and Substance Use.

To illustrate how to interpret this table, the entry in the row for "Anger Management" under "OR" (odds ratio) of .21 indicates that each increase of 1 point on the 4-point Anger Management scale multiplies the odds of a minor assault occurring by .21. Because multiplying by a fraction reduces the size of the product, this means that there is a *decrease* of 79% in the probability of minor violence. In short, the ability to control anger is a protective factor that greatly reduces the chances of physically attacking a partner. On the other hand, in the row labeled "Anti-Social Personality," the odds ratio is 1.97. This indicates that each increase of 1 point on the 4-point Antisocial Personality scale multiplies the odds of a minor assault 1.97 times (i.e., that each increase of 1 point on the Antisocial Behavior scale almost doubles the probability of a minor assault).

Risk Factor by Gender Interactions

The columns of Table 3.2 headed "Model 2" give the results of the multinomial logistic regression analyses in pairs. The first row of each pair is the main effect when an interaction term is added to model 1. The lower row of each pair gives the results of the test for the interaction of each of the risk factors measured by the PRP with the gender of the student. None of the interaction terms are statistically significant. This indicates that the relationships between the risk factors and partner assault do not differ significantly for men and women.

Risk Factors for Severe Assaults

Total Sample

The columns in Table 3.3 headed "Model 1" give the results of the logistic regression analyses for severe assault for the total sample. The following 12 PRP variables were associated with an increased probability of using severe violence: Anger Management, Antisocial Personality, Criminal History, Conflict With Partner, Communication Problems, Dominance, Jealousy, Negative Attribution About the

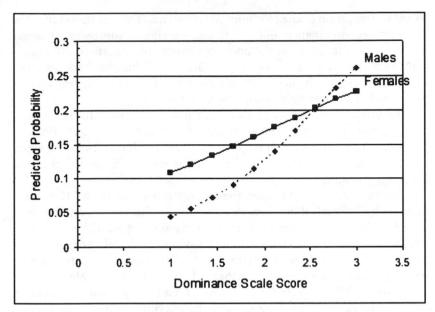

FIGURE 3.1   Relationship between Dominance scale score and probability of severe assault on a partner, by gender

Partner, Neglect History, Sexual Abuse History, Stressful Conditions, and Violence Approval.

Risk Factor by Gender Interactions

The columns of Table 3.3 headed "Model 2" give the results of the logistic regression analyses that included a test for the interaction of each risk factor with gender. Only 3 of the 21 risk factors had a significant interaction with gender at the $p < .05$ level, while two other risk factor $\times$ gender interactions approached significance ($p < .06$). Thus, for 16 of 21 risk factors examined, the relationship between the risk factor and severe partner assault is similar for men and women.

Because the presence or absence of an interaction with gender is the key issue of this chapter, Figure 3.1 illustrates the typical result (lack of a significant interaction). It shows that the more one partner dominates the relationship, the greater the probability of violence by the dominant partner, regardless of whether the dominant partner is male or female.

Visual examination of the plot lines for males and females shows that the link between dominance and severely assaulting is somewhat stronger for males than females but not enough stronger to be statistically significant. Even if it were significant, Figure 3.1 shows that, for both men and women, the greater the degree of dominance in a relationship, the greater the probability of severely assaulting a partner.

Three risk factors that had significant interactions with the respondent's gender are Sexual Abuse History, Substance Abuse, and Violence Approval. The differences in the effects of these risk factors for men and women, holding all other variables at their mean, are discussed in the following paragraphs.

For Sexual Abuse History, the interaction effect shows that for a man with a sexual abuse history score of 1 (the minimum), the predicted probability of assaulting a partner is about 4%, while for a man with a score of 4 (the maximum), the predicted probability of assaulting a partner is about 49%, an increase of 45 percentage points. Among women, a minimum score on the Sexual Abuse History scale is associated with an 8% predicted probability of assaulting a partner, holding all other variables at their mean, and the maximum score is associated with a 12% probability, a difference of only 4 percentage points. Thus, a history of sexual abuse victimization is a much greater risk factor for men to commit severe assaults on partners than for women.

For Substance Abuse, the significant interaction shows that men who reported the lowest score on the Substance Abuse scale had about a 3% predicted probability of assaulting a partner, while those with the highest score had a 21% probability of assaulting a partner, an increase of 18 percentage points. For women with the lowest score on the substance abuse scale, the probability of assaulting a partner is about 10%, while for women who use substances the most, the predicted probability of assaulting a partner is 9% (i.e., almost the same rate). Thus, substance abuse is a risk factor for severe partner assault by men but not by women.

For Violence Approval, the significant interaction shows that, for men with the minimum Violence Approval score, the predicted probability of assault is about 1%, while for men with the highest Violence Approval score, the predicted probability of assault is 44%, an increase of 43 percentage points. For women with the minimum Violence Approval score, the predicted probability of assaulting a partner is 6%, while for women with the maximum Violence Approval score, the predicted probability of assault is 30%, a difference of 24 percentage points. Thus, the significant interaction effect indicates that approval of violence is associated with an increased probability of actual violence for both men and women but less strongly for women.

In addition to the three significant interaction effects, there were two additional interaction effects that were marginally significant ($p < .06$): Posttraumatic Stress Symptoms and Relationship Conflict.

For Posttraumatic Stress Symptoms, the almost significant interaction shows that the predicted probability of severe partner assault is 2% for men with the lowest PTS scores, while for men with the maximum score, the predicted probability of severe partner assault is 32%, a difference of 30 percentage points. In contrast, for females, the predicted probability of partner assault remains the same.

For Relationship Conflict, the interaction shows that for men with the minimum Relationship Conflict score, the predicted probability of severely assaulting a partner is less than 1%, while for men with the highest scores, the predicted probability is 64%, a difference of 63 percentage points. For women with the lowest Relationship Conflict score, the predicted probability of a severe assault is 4%, while for women with the highest scores, the predicted probability of assault is 28%, a difference of 24 percentage points. Thus, increases in conflict are associated with partner assault by both males and females, but for males there is a substantially greater increase in the probability of assault than for females.

To summarize: Of the five significant and marginally significant interactions, two showed that the risk factor applied to both men and women but somewhat more strongly to men (Relationship Conflict and Violence Approval); one showed that the risk factor applied to both men and women but much more strongly for men (Sexual Abuse History); and only two showed that the risk factor applied only to men (Substance Abuse and Posttraumatic Stress Symptoms).

DISCUSSION

This chapter reported a study of 854 university students (312 men and 542 women) focused on the question of whether the risk factors for physically assaulting a dating partner were different for men and women. When the dependent variable was minor assaults, such as slapping and throwing things at a partner, 8 of the 21 risk factors were found to be related to the probability of assaulting a partner. For all eight, the relationship was parallel for male and female students:

Anger Management
Antisocial Personality Traits
Borderline Personality Traits
Relationship Conflict
Communication Problems

Dominance
Negative Attributions About the Partner
Substance Abuse

When the dependent variable was severely assaulting a partner, such as punching or choking, 12 risk factors were found to be associated with an increased probability of assaulting a partner:

Anger Management
Antisocial Personality
Conflict With Partner
Communication Problems
Criminal History
Dominance
Jealousy
Negative Attributions About the Partner
Neglect History
Sexual Abuse History
Stressful Conditions
Violence Approval

For 9 of the 12 risk factors (75%), the relationship of these risk factors to severely assaulting a partner was parallel for males and females. Only three had a significant interaction with gender, although two more approached significance. Sexual Abuse History was associated with an increase in the probability of assaulting a partner for both men and women, but the effect was far stronger for men than for women. Substance Abuse and Posttraumatic Stress Symptoms were associated with an increase in the probability of assaulting a partner for men but not for women. Relationship Conflict and Violence Approval were associated with an increase in the probability of assaulting a partner for both men and women, but the relationship was stronger for men.

Limitations

The fact that this study is based on a sample of university students rather than a "clinical" sample of men and women arrested for partner violence or men and women who are victims of partner violence is both a strength and an important limitation. It is a strength because population samples are needed to guide prevention efforts. What is true of a clinical population often does not necessarily apply to the general population (i.e., the target of primary prevention). To assume that it does apply has been called the "clinical fallacy." Conversely, what is true of the general population does not necessarily apply to clinical populations. To assume that it does has been called the "representative sample fallacy" (Straus, 1990b). A simple but important example is the widely held belief that once partner violence starts, it may escalate, but it will not cease. That is correct for samples of women in shelters for battered women. They would not be there if it had ceased. On the other hand, studies of the general population, such as Feld and Straus (1989), consistently find high rates of cessation. Thus, policies and practices based on the clinical group may not apply to the general population, just as advice based on the general population may not apply to clinical populations. Similarly, the results of this study concerning gender symmetry in perpetration and in etiology may not apply to severely assaulted and oppressed women, such as those who seek help from a shelter for battered women, or to women who are part of the less than 1% of violent couples who have had violence progress to the point of police intervention (Kaufman Kantor & Straus, 1990).

Caution is also needed because the results are based on cross-sectional data and may not reflect a cause-and-effect relationship between the risk factors studied and partner assault. However, the analyses controlled for a number of variables that could produce spurious results, such as confounding with socioeconomic status and social desirability response set.

Conclusion

With these limitations in mind, the results of this study suggest important conclusions about two widely held beliefs: that partner violence is an almost uniquely male crime and that when men hit their partners, it is primarily to dominate women, whereas partner violence by women is an act of self-defense or an act of desperation in response to male dominance and brutality. These beliefs were not supported by the results of this study. Instead, we found, as have many other studies, about equal rates of assaulting a dating partner by male and female students. Our investigation of risk factors also produced results that contradict the male dominance/female self-defense belief. The relationship to minor assaults of all 21 of the risk factors, including score on the Dominance scale, was parallel for men and women. For severe assaults, of the 12 risk factors found to be associated, we found no significant difference between men and women in nine of them, again including Dominance. Or, putting it the other way, around, 75% of the risk factors that were found to be associated with severely assaulting a dating partner were parallel for men and women. It may be more than a coincidence that our review of previous research also found that about 75% of the variables related to partner violence were related for both men and women.

In respect to the key variable of dominance in the relationship, the results showing a parallel relationship of score on the Dominance scale to assaulting a dating partner by either the male or the female partner are consistent with the eight studies mentioned in the introduction. Thus, it is the injustices and power struggles that are associated with inequality that give rise to violence, not just inequality in the form of male dominance. If male dominance is much more prevalent than female dominance (as is widely assumed), that aspect of inequality is extremely important for understanding, preventing, and treating family violence. However, the empirical research on American couples has found that equal power relationships are predominant. The percentage of male-dominant couples in three large surveys ranged from 9% (Coleman and Straus, 1986) to about 25% (Blood & Wolf, 1960; Blumstein & Schwartz, 1983). The percentage of female-dominant relationships is similar.

It is important for both a theoretical understanding of domestic violence and clinical practice to keep in mind that dominance is a "risk factor," not a one-to-one cause. For example, extremely male-dominant partners in the National Family Violence Survey had a 10 times greater *probability* of assaulting a partner than did equalitarian men, but that raised the rate from 2% to 20%, which means that 80% of extremely male-dominant partners did not assault their partner in the year covered by this study. These same principles apply to all risk factors such as binge drinking (Kaufman Kantor & Straus, 1987). Most binge drinkers are not violent to their partners, as can be seen from the fact that, despite the three times greater probability of partner violence (from 6% among non-drinkers to 22% for binge drinkers), more than three-quarters of binge drinkers in that study did not assault their partners in the year of the study.

These results do not indicate that there is no difference in the etiology of violence against partners by men and women. Our study in fact identified at least three such differences. If these results are confirmed by other studies, partner violence prevention or treatment programs need to be constructed in ways that are aware of both the ways in which the risk factors are similar for both men and women and the ways in which they are different.

Policy and Practice Implications

This study and those cited in chapter 1 in this volume have revealed an overwhelming body of evidence that mutual violence is the predominant pattern in the general population, and this study, along with a lesser but still large amount of evidence, suggests that the etiology of partner violence in the general population is mostly parallel for men and women. The fact that we found that dominance in the relationship is a risk factor for violence by women as well as by men is crucial because it contradicts the prevailing assumption that *male* dominance is the major element that needs to be changed to end domestic violence. Male dominance does need to be addressed, but so does female dominance and many other family system problems. In short, partner violence is more a gender-inclusive family system problem than a problem of a patriarchal social system that enforces male dominance by violence.

Unfortunately, the organization, funding, and staffing of current prevention and treatment efforts is wedded to the patriarchal dominance theory (Straus, in press). If researchers or service providers do not declare allegiance to these articles of faith, they risk being denied funding and ostracized (for two sets of personal experiences, see Holtzworth-Munroe, 2005; Straus, 1990c). For example, in December 2005, the National Institute of Justice published two "requests for proposals" for research on physical and sexual violence against partners. Both specified that applications that dealt with male victims would not be considered for funding. The set of nine articles that provided the most comprehensive available review of risk factors for family violence (Heyman & Slep, 2001) included an article on risk factors for male violence but nothing on violence by women. This omission was in response to the interest expressed by the funding agency.

The refusal to recognize the multicausal and family system nature of the problem has hampered the effort to end domestic violence. It has resulted in deliberately ignoring half of the perpetrators. Despite these obstacles, the situation is slowly changing. This book is an example of the process. Another example occurred when the Violence Against Women Act came up for renewal in late 2005. Men's rights groups were successful in having the act revised to include a paragraph permitting funding of services for male victims. These groups also recognize that, because of the ideological commitment and organizational structure of the funding agencies, legal permission to fund programs that address female violence and male victimization does not mean they will do so. Consequently, the groups that lobbied to have the act changed are now preparing for legal action to put that provision into effect. They are, of course, focusing on services for male victims. This will be an important start in recognizing the family system nature of most partner violence. However, much more is needed.

The domestic violence service system, including services for female victims, needs to replace the default assumption that partner violence is primarily the product of male dominance. Instead, the default assumption needs to be that partner violence is predominantly mutual violence and other kinds of mutual mistreatment and that the risk factors are mostly the same for males and females. At the same time, service providers need to remain alert to cases that do not fit the typical pattern, including cases that fit the classical image of an oppressed and battered spouse. Although there are men who fall in this category, it is more often women. In addition, the harmful effects of all levels of violence are greater for women, physically, psychologically, and economically. Consequently, although services for male victims are needed, the need for services for female victims will continue to be greater.

In addition to services for male victims, many important changes can follow from the predominance of mutual violence and the predominance of parallel etiology of violence by male and female partners. We believe that ignoring these facts hampers prevention and treatment efforts and that the needed changes in prevention and offender treatment programs include the following:

- Replace the single causal factor "patriarchal dominance" model with a multicausal model.
- Replace male dominance as the major risk factor in need of change with dominance by either party but only as one of many risk factors that need attention.
- Give equal attention to developing prevention programs targeted to violence by women and girls.
- Secondary prevention efforts need to be open to a variety of new approaches, of which one of the most promising is restorative justice (Strang & Braithwaite, 2002; see also chapter 27 in this volume).

We believe that these changes in policy and practice, rather than weakening efforts to protect women, will enhance the protection of women because violence by women is a major factor contributing to the victimization of women. When women are violent, they are the partners most likely to be injured (Straus, 2005a, 2005b). Therefore, efforts to end partner violence by women will contribute to the protection of women. It is time to make the effort be one that is aimed at ending all partner violence, not just violence against women. Only then will women, as well as all other human beings, be safe in their own homes.

REFERENCES

Archer, J. (1999). Assessment of the reliability of the Conflict Tactics Scales: A meta-analytic review. *Journal of Interpersonal Violence, 14*(12), 1263–1289.

Archer, J. (2000). Sex differences in aggression between heterosexual partners: A meta-analytic review. *Psychological Bulletin, 126*(5), 651–680.

Blood, R. O., & Wolfe, D. M. (1960). *Husbands & wives: The dynamics of married living.* New York: Free Press.

Blumstein, P., & Schwartz, P. (1983). *American couples.* New York: William Morrow and Company,

Coleman, D. H., & Straus, M. A. (1986). Marital power, conflict, and violence in a nationally representative sample of American couples. *Violence and Victims, 1*(2), 141-157. Also in (1996). M. A. Straus and R. J. Gelles (Eds.), *Physical Violence in American Families: Risk factors and adaptations to violence in 148,145 families.* (pp. 1289–1304). New Brunswick, NJ: Transaction Publishers.

Carrado, M., George, M., Loxam, F., Jones, L., & Templar, D. (1996). Aggression in British heterosexual relationships: A descriptive analysis. *Aggressive Behavior, 22,* 401–415.

Dobash, R. P., Dobash, E. R., Wilson, M., & Daly, M. (1992). The myth of sexual symmetry in marital violence. *Social Problems, 39*(1), 71–91.

Dutton, D. G., & Nicholls, T. L. (2005). The gender paradigm in domestic violence research and theory: The conflict of theory and data. *Aggression and Violent Behavior, 10,* 680–714.

Feld, S. L., & Straus, M. A. (1989). Escalation and desistance of wife assault in marriage. *Criminology, 27*(1), 141–161.

Fiebert, M. S., & Gonzalez, D. M. (1997). College women who initiate assaults on their male partners and the reasons offered for such behavior. *Psychological Reports, 80,* 583–590.

Graham-Kevan, N., & Archer, J. (2005). Investigating three explanations of women's relationship aggression. *Psychology of Women Quarterly, 29*(3), 270–277.

Hamberger, L. K., & Guse, C. E. (2002). Men's and women's use of intimate partner violence in clinical samples. *Violence Against Women, 8*(11), 1301–1331.

Heyman, R. E., & Slep, A. M. S. (2001). Risk factors for family violence: Introduction to the special series. *Aggression and Violent Behavior, 6,* 115–119.

Holtzworth-Munroe, A. (2005). Female perpetration of physical aggression against an intimate partner: A controversial new topic of study. *Violence and Victims, 20*(2), 251–259.

Kaufman Kantor, G., & Straus, M. A. (1987). The "drunken bum" theory of wife beating. *Social Problems, 34*(3), 213–230.

Kaufman Kantor, G., & Straus, M. A. (1990). Response of victims and the police to assaults on wives. In M. A. Straus & R. J. Gelles (Eds.), *Physical violence in American families: Risk factors and adaptations to violence in 8,145 families* (pp. 473–487). New Brunswick, NJ: Transaction Publishers.

Kim, J.-Y., & Clifton, E. (2003). Marital power, conflict, norm consensus, and marital violence in a nationally representative sample of Korean couples. *Journal of Interpersonal Violence, 18*(2), 197–219.

Kleinbaum, D. G., Kupper, L. L., & Morgenstern, H. (1982). *Epidemiologic research: Principles and quantitative methods.* Belmont, CA: Wadsworth.

LaRoche, D. (2005). *Aspects of the context and consequences of domestic violence-situational couple violence and intimate terrorism in Canada in 1999.* Quebec City, Quebec, Canada: Government of Quebec.

Medeiros, R. A., & Straus, M. A. (2006). *Gender differences in risk factors for physical violence between partners in marital and dating relationships.* Durham, NH: Family Research Laboratory, University of New Hampshire. Retrieved from http://pubpages.uhh.edu/mas2.

Moffitt, T. E., Caspi, A., Rutter, M., & Silva, P. A. (2001). *Sex differences in antisocial behavior.* Cambridge, England: Cambridge University Press.

Nazroo, J. (1995). Uncovering gender differences in the use of marital violence: The effect of methodology. *Sociology, 29,* 475–494.

O'Leary, A., & Sweet Jemmott, L. (Eds.). (1995). *Women at risk: Issues in the primary prevention of AIDS.* New York: Plenum Press.

O'Leary, K. D., Barling, J., Arias, I., Rosenbaum, A., Malone, J., & Tyree, A. (1989). Prevalence and stability of physical aggression. *Journal of Consulting and Clinical Psychology, 57*(2), 263–268.

O'Leary, K. D., Malone, J., & Tyree, A. (1994). Physical aggression in early marriage: Prerelationship and relationship effects. *Journal of Consulting and Clinical Psychology, 62*(3), 594–602.

Reynolds, W. M. (1982). Development of reliable and valid short forms of the Marlowe-Crowne Social Desirability Scale. *Journal of Clinical Psychology, 38*(1), 119–125.

So-Kum Tang, C. (1999). Marital power and aggression in a community sample of Hong Kong Chinese families. *Journal of Interpersonal Violence, 14*(6), 586–595.

Sommer, R. (1994). Male- and female-perpetrated partner abuse: Testing a diathesis-stress model. *Dissertation Abstracts International,*(UMI No. AAT NN99064).

Stets, J. E., & Pirog-Good, M. A. (1990). Interpersonal control and courtship aggression. *Journal of Social and Personal Relationships, 7,* 371–394.

Stets, J. E., & Straus, M. A. (1989). The marriage license as a hitting license: A comparison of assaults in dating, cohabiting, and married couples. *Journal of Family Violence, 4*(2), 161–180.

Strang, H., & Braithwaite, J. (2002). *Restorative justice and family violence.* New York: Cambridge University Press.

Straus, M. A. (1990a). The Conflict Tactics Scales and its critics: An evaluation and new data on validity and reliability. In M. A. Straus & R. J. Gelles (Eds.), *Physical violence in American families: Risk factors and adaptations to violence in 8,145 families* (pp. 49–73). New Brunswick, NJ: Transaction Publishers.

Straus, M. A. (1990b). Injury, frequency, and the representative sample fallacy in measuring wife beating and child abuse. In M. A. Straus & R. J. Gelles (Eds.), *Physical violence in American families: Risk factors and adaptations to violence in 8,145 families* (pp. 75–89). New Brunswick, NJ: Transaction Publishers.

Straus, M. A. (1990c). The national family violence surveys. In M. A. Straus & R. J. Gelles (Eds.), *Physical violence in American families: Risk factors and adaptions to violence in 8,145 families* (pp. 3–16). New Brunswick, NJ: Transaction Publishers.

Straus, M. A. (1999). The controversy over domestic violence by women: A methodological, theoretical, and sociology of science analysis. In X. Arriaga & S. Oskamp (Eds.), *Violence in intimate relationships* (pp. 17–44). Thousand Oaks, CA: Sage.

Straus, M. A. (2004a). Cross-cultural reliability and validity of the Revised Conflict Tactics Scales: A study of university student dating couples in 17 nations. *Cross-Cultural Research, 38*(4), 407–432.

Straus, M. A. (2004b). Prevalence of violence against dating partners by male and female university students worldwide. *Violence Against Women, 10*(7), 790–811.

Straus, M. A. (2005a, July 10–13). *Gender and partner violence in world perspective: Some results from the International Dating Violence Study.* Paper presented at the 9th International Family Violence Research Conference, Portsmouth, NH.

Straus, M. A. (2005b). Women's violence toward men is a serious social problem. In D. R. Loseke, R. J. Gelles, & M. M. Cavanaugh (Eds.), *Current controversies on family violence* (2nd ed., pp. 55–77). Newbury Park, CA: Sage.

Straus, M. A. (in press). Future research on gender symmetry in physical assaults on partners. *Violence Against Women.*

Straus, M. A., & Douglas, E. M. (2004). A short form of the Revised Conflict Tactics Scales, and typologies for seventy and mutuality. *Violence and Victims, 19*(5), 507–520.

Straus, M. A., Gelles, R. J., & Steinmetz, S. K. (1980). *Behind closed doors: Violence in the American family.* New York: Doubleday/Anchor Books. (reissued with a new foreword and a postscript chapter by Transaction Publishers, 2006)

Straus, M. A., Hamby, S. L., Boney-McCoy, S., & Sugarman, D. B. (1996). The Revised Conflict Tactics Scales (CTS2): Development and preliminary psychometric data. *Journal of Family Issues, 17*(3), 283–316.

Straus, M. A., Hamby, S. L., Boney-McCoy, S., & Sugarman, D. (1999). The Personal and Relationships Profile (PRP). Durham, NH: University of New Hampshire, Family Research Laboratory. Retrieved from http://pubpages.unh.edu/-mas2.

Straus, M. A., & Members of the International Dating Violence Research Consortium. (2006). *Unpublished data from the International Dating Violence Study.* Durham, NH: Research Laboratory, University of New Hampshire.

Straus, M. A., & Mouradian, V. E. (1999, November 19). *Preliminary psychometric data for the Personal and Relationships Profile (PRP): A multi-scale tool for clinical screening and research on partner violence.* Paper presented at the American Society of Criminology, Toronto, ON.

Straus, M. A., & Ramirez, I. L. (in press). Gender symmetry in prevalence, severity, and chronicity of physical aggression against dating partners by university students in Mexico and USA. *Aggressive Behavior.* Retrieved from http://pubpages.unh.edu/-mas2.

Sugarman, D. B., & Hotaling, G. T. (1989). Dating violence: Prevalence, context, and risk markers. In A. A. Pirog-Good & J. E. Stets (Eds.), *Violence in dating relationships: Emerging social issues* (pp. 3–31). New York: Praeger.

Sugihara, Y., & Warner, J. A. (2002). Dominance and domestic abuse among Mexican Americans: Gender differences in the etiology of violence in intimate relationships. *Journal of Family Violence, 17,* 315–339.

CHAPTER 4

Power and Control in Relationship Aggression

Nicola Graham-Kevan

TERMINOLOGY

Psychologically manipulating behaviors have been referred to by many different terms, including psychological abuse, psychological maltreatment, psychological aggression or violence, emotional abuse, emotional maltreatment, and verbal aggression. These terms for coercive behaviors are often used interchangeably within the literature. They are, however, subtly different. For example, O'Hagan (1995) defines emotional abuse of children as "the sustained, repetitive, inappropriate emotional response to the [target's] experience of emotion and its accompanying expressive behavior," whereas psychological abuse is defined as the "sustained, repetitive, inappropriate behavior which damages or substantially reduces the creative, . . . and mental faculties and processes" (p. 458). Such distinctions are rarely made in the partner violence literature.

O'Leary and Maiuro (2001) identified four dimensions of what they referred to as "psychological abuse." The first was "denigrating damage to a partner's self-esteem" and included shouting and swearing at a partner; insulting their appearance, personality, or intelligence; and invalidating or projecting feelings. The second dimension was "passive-aggressive," which included withholding of affection, ignoring the partner, and being emotionally distant. The third dimension was "threatening behavior" and included overt threats to harm the partner, their children, or others and threats of abandonment and infidelity. The final dimension was "restricting personal territory" and included social isolation, violation of personal privacy, and financial and physical control. As O'Leary and Maiuro stated, these dimensions are defined using a combination of behavioral, motivational, and consequential aspects.

Feminist researchers such as Pence and Paymar (1986, 1993) have placed behaviors such as those described by O'Leary and Maiuro (2001) under the umbrella term *controlling behaviors*. The term *controlling behaviors* places the emphasis on the perpetrator's motivation rather than the impact such behaviors have on the victim, which is an improvement over terms that presuppose domineering/abusive perpetrator motivations or negative victim impact. For example, although monitoring a partner's whereabouts has been placed within a wider context of abusive behaviors (e.g., Tolman, 1989), the motivations for such behavior may be diverse, ranging from a concern for a partner's safety to a desire to dominate a partner's life. The term *controlling behaviors* has advantages over terms that require behaviors to be abusive. The term *abusive* is appropriate for some samples, such as shelter women, and for some behaviors, such as insulting or swearing at one's partner. Even in violent relationships, however, the blanket term *abusive* can be too arbitrary. Marshall (2001) found that couples used what would appear to be abusive behaviors in loving, gentle, or joking ways. Her sample included couples selected for the presence of domestically violent men. Further, the term *abusive* is often inappropriate for some of the behaviors included under this term in nonclinical samples. For example, jealousy is often a central component of scales that measure psychological/emotional abuse, but this fails to address the meaning of jealousy for individuals. Relationship research has found that jealousy is positively correlated with love, which may indicate that a certain amount of jealousy is not only "normal" but may even be seen as healthy for relationships. Indeed, a lack of jealousy could be seen as a lack of commitment to the other person (and in extreme cases could even be abusive in itself). The abusiveness of some behaviors may be dependent on their context and frequency. A partner's jealousy in response to an attractive colleague's flirtatious behavior has a different contextual meaning than a partner's jealousy in response to a casual hello from a neighbor. And although occasional jealousy is normal for many relationships and is often viewed positively by its recipients (Henton, Cate, Koval, Lloyd, & Christopher, 1983), constant jealousy is destructive for both parties.

Terms that encapsulate an element of aggression can also suffer from similar problems. Terms such as *verbal aggression* often include items that are not verbally aggressive, such as "sulked or refused to talk about it" and even "cried." Straus, Hamby, Boney-McCoy, and Sugarman (1996) recognized this when they revised the Conflict Tactics Scales (CTS), renaming the subscale "Psychological Abuse." Although such behaviors may not be particularly constructive means of conflict resolution, they are not inherently abusive (see the previous discussion). The term *controlling behaviors* is appropriate for abusive acts such as insulting or swearing at one's partner, where such behavior can be seen as motivated by a desire to undermine a partner's self-confidence. But it is also appropriate for acts such as sulking. These acts are used to influence another person's actions, to control or constrain their behaviors.

Controlling behaviors may be best understood as falling on a continuum of abusiveness. Bicehouse and Hawker (1993) identified degrees of control with the first degree being normative behaviors, such as sulking, jealousy, and declaring ultimatums. Second-degree controlling behaviors are less socially sanctioned and include threats of violence and intimidation. The third degree encompasses severe threats and intimidation and direct physical aggression. It would be expected that first-degree controllers would confine themselves to these normative behaviors, whereas second-degree controllers would use threats and intimidation as well as more normative means of control, and third-degree controllers would use all types of control, including severe threats and physical aggression. By putting controlling behavior within a relationship context, it is possible to see that identical behaviors can have very different impacts on the victim, depending on the level of control previously used. For example, sulking (a first-degree behavior) may be irritating to a woman whose partner has only used normative means of control but might be very threatening to a woman whose partner has previously used physical aggression, as such behavior carries with it the implicit message that physical violence may ensue. Bicehouse and Hawker (1993) suggest that the terms *controller, abuser,* and *batterer* be used to describe these different types of control to allow differentiation.

Controlling behaviors encapsulate the interpersonal—rather than a structural—level analysis of control. Behavioral acts of control are most frequently investigated, although some research has looked at the need for control (Petrik, Olson, & Subotnik, 1994). Controlling behaviors within this conceptualization include economic deprivation, jealous and possessive behaviors, insults and name-calling, and threats and intimidation. Such behaviors are more common in relationships that have regular sexual intimacy than those that do not (Rouse, Breen, & Howell, 1988) but are not confined to them (Van Dijk, Flight, Oppenhuis, & Duesmann, 1998). There is some evidence to suggest women may be more sensitive to their partners' attempts at psychological manipulation than are men (Ehrensaft & Vivian, 1999), or more willing to report such behaviors. Unlike physical aggression, which tends to decrease during the course of a relationship (Aldarondo, 2002; Feld & Straus, 1990; Timmons Fritz & O'Leary, 2004), there is evidence to suggest that controlling behavior does not (Timmons Fritz & O'Leary, 2004) diminish over time.

The reason for this is not clear, although it may be due to the more normative nature of nonviolent controlling behavior.

CONSEQUENCES OF CONTROLLING BEHAVIOR

Being subjected to controlling behavior is related to higher levels of depression (Baldry, 2003; Dutton, Goodman, & Bennett, 2001; Sackett & Saunders, 2001), lower levels of self-esteem, higher levels of fear (Baldry, 2003; Dutton et al., 2001), and more symptoms of posttraumatic stress disorder (Arias & Pape, 2001; Dutton et al., 2001), independent of rates of physical aggression. Indeed, women who have been subject to severe partner aggression report that controlling behaviors are more damaging psychologically than actual physical aggression (O'Leary & Jouriles, 1993; Tolman, 1989).

THEORIES OF CONTROLLING BEHAVIOR

Feminist Theories of Control and Partner Violence

Feminist analysis of domestic violence places female victims within a patriarchal family and societal structure. The research tools utilized tend to be qualitative and descriptive in nature. The context of relationship aggression against women was historically seen as crucial to understanding domestic violence (Dobash & Dobash, 1979). At the relationship level, physical aggression was placed within a general framework of power and control. Aggressors were reported to use a range of control tactics, such as intimidation, threats, isolating the victim from friends and family, and preventing their partner from having access to money (Pence & Paymar, 1993; Stets, 1988). The physical aggression within this context could be seen as an event among many events all of which lie on the same continuum of control. Victims of domestic violence "criticised theories that described battering as cyclical rather than as a constant force in their relationship; that attributed the violence to men's inability to cope with stress; and that failed to fully acknowledge the intention of batterers to gain control over their partners' actions, thoughts, and feelings" (Pence & Paymar, 1993, p. 2). Feminist theorists assert that phenomena such as family violence cannot be studied without applying a gendered lens (Yllo, 1994). It is believed that men and women live gendered lives, and therefore a failure to take into account their differentiated experiences would result in research that lacks ecological validity.

At the societal level, Dobash and Dobash (1979) commented that "although domestic chastisement of wives is no longer legal, most of the ideologies and social arrangements which formed the underpinnings of this violence still exist. . . . Wives may no longer be the legitimate victims of marital violence, but in social terms they are still the 'appropriate' victims" (p. 439). There have been difficulties in finding empirical support for statements such as these. Miller and Simpson (1991) found that costs and societal sanctions of using physical aggression were perceived as more severe for men who used partner violence than for women. They found that men perceived both informal and formal sanctions to be more problematic to their lives and that men reported to have been socialized to "not hit a girl." A meta-analysis of patriarchal ideology and wife assault found that only a man's attitude toward violence predicted wife assault, with no consistent support for any link with traditional gender attitudes or gender schema (Sugarman & Frankel, 1996). There is even some evidence to suggest that patriarchal values may actually inhibit aggression toward women. Kantor, Jasnski, and Aldarondo (1994) found that more traditional Mexican men, those who endorse machismo values of dominance, independence, and obedience of women and children, were less likely to use physical aggression against a partner than were Anglo-American or Americanized Mexican men. This may be due to the belief in "chivalry" (Felson, 2002).

Population studies have found that men tend to view partner violence toward women as unacceptable. Straus, Kantor, and Moore (1997) investigated changes in societal attitudes to partner violence in the United States from 1968 to 1994. Four survey data sets were used: the 1968 National Violence Survey ($n = 1,176$), the 1985 National Family Violence Survey ($n = 6,002$), the 1992 National Alcohol and Family Violence Survey ($n = 1,970$), and the 1994 Gallup Survey ($n = 524$). All four surveys asked the same questions regarding approval for a wife slapping a husband and a husband slapping a wife. Straus and colleagues found that approval of husbands slapping their wives dropped from 20% of the population in 1968 to 10% in 1994 (approval for a wife slapping her husband, however, remained constant at 20% between 1968 and 1994). This demonstrates that between 80% and 90% of men do not approve of using physical aggression against women.

The presence of partner violence in gay and lesbian relationships also poses a challenge to the patriarchal theory of partner control. Research has shown that these relationships also have levels of partner violence used in conjunction with controlling behavior (e.g., Letellier, 1994).

Developmental Theories of Control and Partner Violence

Dutton (2000) identified witnessing parental violence, direct physical abuse, and parental shaming as traumatic experiences that adversely shape a child's personality. Drawing on the work of Bowlby (1969), Dutton identified attachment styles in adult men who used partner violence that closely resembled insecure attachment styles found in children. Dutton proposed that disruptions in the child–parent bond brought about through emotionally distant, inconsistent, or unreliable parenting resulted in maladaptive internal models of relationships that in turn lead to anger, insecurity, and a lack of trust in intimate relationships in adult life. Adverse childhood experiences with their caregivers produce biochemical changes to the brain's limbic areas that modulate attachment behaviors in adulthood (Beech & Mitchell, 2004). Maladaptive emotional styles such as withdrawing, dismissiveness, aggressiveness, and belligerence develop, in turn leading to partner violence perpetration and victimization. Bartholomew, Henderson, and Dutton (2001) stated that "relationship abuse has been conceptualized as an exaggerated and dysfunctional form of protest behavior" (p. 7). The protest is directed toward the romantic partner and is an attempt to reengage with the partner or prevent abandonment. Downey and Feldman (1996, cited in Ehrensaft & Vivian, 1999) also suggested that controlling behaviors and physical aggression may be used by people who are sensitive to rejection to avoid abandonment by their partners. The protest behavior can take the form of direct physical aggression or controlling behavior. Physical aggression and nonaggressive controlling behavior are seen within this conceptualization as being on a continuum and being motivated by a need to control a partner for emotional availability.

Conflict Theories of Control and Partner Violence

Straus (1979) distinguished between "conflicts of interest" and "conflict tactics." Conflicts of interest are unavoidable where family members, although sharing many common goals, ultimately have individual needs that may not be compatible with the desires of other members of their family. Indeed, many such situations are "zero sum" in that if one person achieves an objective, it is at the expense of other members. For example, if a couple with young children have no babysitter, then it is not possible for both of them to attend a dinner party, and a zero-sum conflict of interest arises: If the husband goes out, the wife must remain at home and vice versa. The techniques used by each member of a family to forward their own self-interest are conflict tactics. These can range from calm discussion to severe assault: What identifies them as conflict tactics is not the behavior but the reason for the behavior, the desire to take control of a situation. Straus (1979) distinguishes between rational tactics, such as reasoning; verbally and symbolically aggressive acts such as shouting at the other; and physical force, such as pushing and kicking. Family conflict researchers have been very influential in the field of relationship aggression research. Their research has paralleled the growth of feminist literature. Controversially, much of it has indicated that women are as physically aggressive, if not more, than men (for a meta-analytic review, see Archer, 2000).

Evolutionary Theories of Control and Partner Violence

The use of controlling behavior and partner violence have been explained in sociobiology as mate-guarding behaviors. Mate guarding is a term used by evolutionary theorists to describe activities engaged in by one member of a reproductive dyad to control and restrict the potential mating opportunities available to a sexual partner. Mate guarding may take a variety of forms, including controlling behaviors, verbal aggression, and physical aggression (Flinn, 1988; Wilson & Daly, 1993). Evolutionary psychologists (e.g., Peters, Shackelford, & Buss, 2002; Wilson & Daly, 1993) view physical aggression as a result of male proprietary attitudes toward women whose function is to control their partner's sexuality. Therefore, physical aggression is viewed as a more extreme type of mate-guarding behavior. Mate guarding is found in species such as humans that have internal fertilization and require parental investment by the male. Men who guard their mates increase their paternity certainty, whereas women who guard their mates increase the resources available to them and their offspring. Therefore, both evolutionary and feminist theory agree that controlling behavior and physical aggression are used by men to control women; evolutionary theory also accepts that women can be controlling and physically aggressive toward their partners (Flinn, 1988).

Evolutionary theory also predicts that there are cues that precipitate or escalate the use of controlling behavior. Continual mate guarding would be extremely time consuming and seriously impede the guarder's ability to engage in other important behaviors, such as acquiring food. Therefore, one would expect humans to have evolved sensitivity to cues that indicate when a mate needs more or less frequent guarding. Such cues may be external to the relationship, such as the presence of rivals, or from within the relationship, such as women's fecundity and men's and women's mate value. Symons (1992) defined mate value as "the degree to which each [mate] would promote the reproductive success of [the other] who mated with them" (p. 87).

Research has generally supported the link between women's fecundity and men's use of controlling behavior and partner violence (Buss & Shackelford, 1997; Figueredo & McCloskey, 1993; Peters et al., 2002; Wilson & Daly, 1993). The association between mate value and controlling behavior is less clear, however. Buss and Shackelford (1997) found that husbands used more controlling behaviors when their wives had higher mate value. Figueredo and colleagues (2001) found that the higher a woman's mate value, the less abuse (verbal, physical, sexual, and escalation) her partner used, whereas Flinn (1988) found no relationship between mate value and men's controlling behavior.

EMPIRICAL RESEARCH ON CONTROLLING BEHAVIORS AND PARTNER VIOLENCE: WOMEN'S SHELTER AND BATTERER INTERVENTION STUDIES

Research that has studied men's use of controlling behaviors in selected samples has found that those relationships that report physical aggression also report high rates of controlling behaviors. Follingstad, Rutledge, Berg, Hause, and Polek (1990) found that almost all their sample of physically abused women (97%) reported that controlling behaviors were used by their assaultive partners. Similarly, in a sample of help-seeking gay and bisexual men, 92% reported that the abuser used isolating behaviors, 89% had experienced emotional control, and 65% stated that their partner employed threatening control (Merrill & Wolfe, 2000). Battered lesbians also report high levels of controlling behaviors being used by their aggressive partners (Renzetti, 1992).

Shepard and Campbell (1992) used the Abusive Behaviour Inventory to measure controlling behavior as well as physically aggressive behaviors used by men attending a chemical dependency unit. They found that those men identified as being physically aggressive toward their female partners used higher levels of controlling behaviors than did the nonassaultive men, with scores being on average 26% higher for known physically abusive men. This suggests that physically abusive men are more controlling than are nonabusive men in selected samples. Correlational studies have found a significant relationship between the use of physical aggression and controlling behavior. Baldry (2003) studied Italian and eastern European shelter women's reports about their partners' use of controlling behavior and physical aggression using the Psychological Maltreatment of Women Inventory (PMWI; Tolman, 1989) and found a strong ($r = .66$) relationship between them. Men are not the only perpetrators of controlling aggression however, even in populations drawn from female shelters and male batterer programs. Gottman and colleagues (1995) found evidence of women's use of physical aggression as a coercive tool both toward their male partners and toward unrelated people. In a sample of couples referred because of the man's partner violence, Stacey, Hazlewood, and Shupe (1994) found reported rates of controlling behaviors by both the men and their partners that were similar; in some cases, the women's rates were higher, but the effect sizes in all cases would be very small.

It is not only the presence or frequency of controlling behaviors that differentiates physically aggressive men from nonviolent ones (or men who use severe physical aggression from those who use more minor aggression); the breadth of different types of control has also been found to be important. Stacey et al. (1994) reported the diverse range of controlling behaviors used by a sample of male batterers. They reported that "isolation of the woman; control of her relationships, resources, and activities; and ghettoising her emotionally: were all frequent forms of male abuse toward female victims" (p. 53). These actions were seen as an important part of the physical violence and were often antecedent to a physical assault. Follingstad et al. (1990) also found that a range of controlling behaviors were used by abusive men, with 72% of their abused women sampled reporting being subjected to four or more types of control. Dutton and Starzomski (1997) used the PMWI (Tolman, 1989) to assess the relationship between controlling behavior, physical abuse, propensity for abusive behavior, and personality. They interviewed 120 men (both court ordered and self-referred) and 76 of their partners, and as controls they included a sample of 45 men who worked for a union. The PMWI was grouped into categories that corresponded to the power and control wheel (PCW; developed by Pence and Paymar 1986). Results indicated that "emotional abuse" (mean study men = 42.72; mean control men = 28.67), "minimize/deny" (mean study men = 11.26; mean control men = 6.28), and "using children" (mean study men = 3.44; mean control men = 6.50) all differed significantly between the study and control men (although note that control men attack their partners' parenting skills more than assaultive men). The pattern of intercorrelations was also investigated. For the study men, all the octants of the PCW were interrelated with an average effect size of $r = .44$; however, this pattern was not found for the control sample. For these men, only emotional, coercion (threats), intimidation, and economic control were significantly interrelated. This suggests that abusive men use a broad range of such behaviors together, and this may add support to the belief that physical aggression by these men represents an attempt to control the woman's life (Johnson, 1995).

Dutton and Starzomski (1997) also studied the relationship between controlling behavior categories and the propensity for abusiveness. The study men showed significant relationships for intimidation, emotional, and male privilege. For the control men, only minimize/deny was significantly related to abusiveness ($r = .55$). Bennett, Goodman, and Dutton (2000) assessed the levels of controlling behaviors by a sample of men arrested for partner violence. They found that level of controlling behaviors, particularly "dominance" as measured by the PMWI (Tolman, 1989), was the strongest predictor of dangerousness and recidivism. They found support for the notion that controlling behavior and physical aggression are part of an overall pattern of power and control, and therefore controlling behavior should be included as an outcome variable and a risk factor in research studying reabuse.

It is not only male batterers who are reported to use controlling behaviors. George (1994) provided some rare data on male victims' accounts of their victimization. He stated that two-thirds of his sample cited bullying and control as the most important reason for their wives' use of physical aggression. George also reported on data from Australia, Canada, the United Kingdom, and the United States that have found similar findings. Migliaccio (2002) found similar relationships with both emotional control and isolating behaviors being present in the narratives of abused men and that both were antecedents and consequences of physical aggression directed at these men by their spouses.

Research on Women's and Men's Use of Control and Physical Aggression in Nonselected Samples

Using nonselected samples, researchers investigating control and physical aggression have found that associations are apparent for both men's and women's perpetration and victimization. One of the earliest researchers to investigate interpersonal control used by both men and women was Stets. Using qualitative accounts of control from her previous work (Stets, 1988), she devised a six-item control scale. Stets and Pirog-Good (1990) investigated control and physical aggression in a U.S. sample of undergraduates. Stets found that control and minor physical aggression were related for both men and women but not related to severe aggression, suggesting a different causal pathway for minor and severe aggression, and this would be consistent with Johnson's (1995) proposed distinction between common couple violence and patriarchal terrorism (see also chapters 2 and 10 in this volume). Other researchers have also found that controlling behaviors are frequently reported in nonselected samples. Rouse (1990) found that 76% of her male and female undergraduate respondents reported that they had monitored their partners' time, discouraged their partners from having same-sex (16%) and opposite-sex (52%) friends; 37% had been rude to their partner's friends, 60% had been overtly critical, and 40% had ridiculed their partners in front of others. Further, the use of these behaviors was significantly related to using physical aggression against their partners. This relationship has also been found in U.S. adolescent couples (Molidor, 1995), community samples (Julian, McKenry, Gavazzi, & Law, 1999; Marshall, 2001), and gay and lesbian relationships (Landolt & Dutton, 1997; Toro-Alfonso & Rodriguez-Madera, 2004).

When comparing men's and women's use of controlling behaviors, research using nonselected samples has found that there are no differences in their overall use (e.g., Graham-Kevan, & Archer, 2003,, 2005; Hamby & Sugarman, 1999; Salgado, Suvak, King, & King, 2004; Statistics Canada, 2000; Stets, 1991) and that control is an important predictor of physical aggression for men and women in nonselected samples (e.g., Follingstad, Bradley, Helff, & Laughlin, 2002; Graham-Kevan & Archer, 2003). Indeed, White, Merrill, and Koss (2001) found that in their sample of U.S. Navy recruits, controlling behaviors explained three times as much variance as background factors (such as child abuse). The authors commented on the "remarkable similarity" of men's and women's models. Other researchers have asserted that control may be pivotal to the understanding of relationship aggression (Follingstad et al., 2002). Salgado et al. (2004) found that controlling behaviors were associated not only with using physical aggression against a partner but also with being a victim of partner aggression. This suggests that a perpetrator's use of controlling behavior increases the likeliness of their physical aggression perpetration *and* victimization.

Sex differences have been reported on different types of controlling behaviors used by men and women in nonselected samples. Hamby and Sugarman (1999) found that men more frequently called their partners fat or ugly, destroyed partner's property, and made fun of their ability to do things. Women more frequently insulted and swore at their partners, stomped off during a disagreement, and shouted or yelled at them. Statistics Canada (2000) found that women were more likely to report being subjected to emotional, threatening, intimidating, and economic control. The rates for isolating control (which constituted three out of the seven items) were similar for men and women. In her mixed-sex undergraduate sample, Harned (2001) found that men were more likely to be subjected to psychological victimization ($d = .21$), isolation ($d = .15$), intimidation/threats ($d = .26$), and/or economic abuse ($d = .35$) than were women. Kasian and Painter (1992) found no sex difference on "diminishment of self-esteem" but did find that men reported that their partners used more frequent control, jealousy, verbal abuse, and withdrawal than women reported their partners using. Sugihara and Warner (2002) studied dominance in a sample of Mexican Americans and found that men and women did not differ on power and possessiveness, although men were higher on the decision-making and devaluation scales than were women. Men and women also did not differ on their use of psychological aggression as measured using the Conflict Tactics Scales 2 (CTS2; Straus et al., 1996). The research reviewed suggests that there are no consistent sex differences in the use of controlling behavior and that even in samples selected for high rates of male aggression, women sometimes also report using comparative frequencies of controlling behavior.

SCALES THAT MEASURE CONTROLLING BEHAVIORS: A SELECTED REVIEW

What follows is a review of selected instruments intended to assist mental health professionals and advocates in measuring controlling behavior in abusive intimate relationships. There are a variety of scales that measure controlling behavior; however, the scales vary in the number of controlling behaviors included and the inclusiveness of the items for both heterosexual and homosexual relationships, male and female, and victims and perpetrators. The chapter provides an overview of the purpose and development of each measure, an introduction to the nature of the items, and a brief discussion of the empirical evidence demonstrating the instruments' psychometric properties. Recommendations are made regarding the strengths and limitations of each measure and its anticipated clinical utility in diverse populations.

The range of controlling behaviors measured has been found to be important in distinguishing clinically identified assaultive men from a control sample (Dutton & Starzomski, 1997; Graham-Kevan & Archer, 2006). Therefore, when selecting a scale to use with clients, it is important to ensure that the scale measures controlling behavior in such a way that it is appropriate for men and women, who may or may not co-reside, and may not have children. The items should be of specific acts of control rather than more general statements. The rationale for using specific acts is that controlling behaviors are defined by the researcher, not the respondent, and this aids validity; in addition, listing specific behaviors acts as a prompt to aid recollection, thus increasing reliability. Therefore, any scales that could be used for research and practice should include a broad range of specific acts of control that are applicable to both men and women dating and living together and with or without children. The scales available to measure controlling behaviors are discussed here and are evaluated in terms of the previously mentioned criteria.

Many researchers have focused on controlling behaviors used by men toward their female partners. Hoffman (1984) offered a checklist of types of psychological abuse suffered by women devised through interviews with 25 women who identified themselves as being victims. This checklist was used by Tolman to devise a scale of psychologically abusive behaviors. Tolman's (1989) measure, the PMWI, is probably the most extensive measure of psychological abuse of women. It is a 58-item scale developed through the modification of earlier scales (such as the verbal aggression scale of the CTS; Straus, 1979). Tolman excluded items that involved "a direct physical component," such as interrupting sleep, although it is not clear why. He also excluded items that carried an implicit or explicit threat, such as breaking objects, as he believed that these were part of the CTS physical aggression scales (which they are not) (Tolman, 1989). New items were also generated to encompass a range of behaviors conceptualized as psychologically abusive. The scale was administered to a sample of 407 men identified as batterers and 207 women identified as battered women. Each item was endorsed by at least 25% of both the male and female respondents. Following factor analysis, the scale was divided into two subscales: Dominance-Isolation (DI), containing 26 items, and Emotional-Verbal (EV), containing 23 items.

The PMWI appears to be a good measure of psychologically abusive behaviors used by men who cohabit and have children with their partners and who are known to use physical aggression in such a way that they come in contact with the justice system (Tolman, 1989). Its use for a nonselected sample of dating and cohabiting people where both men's and women's use of such behaviors is the focus of interest is not appropriate. Of the 26 items making up the DI subscale, six involve items on cohabiting and use of shared resources (such as the telephone), and on the EV subscale, one item relates to physical aggression. Other items are not necessarily abusive, such as, "stingy with money," "acted irresponsibly with money," and "used money without consultation," all of which are from the DI subscale and may have a different meaning to members of a relationship who are not living together. Some items are also ambiguous when taken within the context of a "normal" as opposed to battering relationship. For example, "told could not manage" and other items may be examples of emotional ineptitude rather than being abusive, such as "acted insensitive to feelings," "acted insensitive sexually," and "withholding feelings." Molidor (1995) modified the PMWI for use with 736 undergraduate men and women. He used 15 items, 14 from the original scale (an item was developed to measure economic abuse, as none of the PMWI items were suitable for a mixed-sex dating sample). He selected two or three items to represent the following categories: isolation, monopolization, degradation, rigid sex role expectations, psychological destabilization, and emotional or interpersonal withholding. Shepard and Campbell (1992) developed a measure of the psychological and physical abuse of women using a sample of 100 men and 78 women from a chemical dependency clinic. The resulting 30-item scale included 12 items of physical or sexual aggression, four items related to housework or children, three items of isolation, two items of threats, one item of intimidation, three items of emotional abuse, three items measuring economic abuse, one item that was difficult to classify ("ended discussion and made decision himself"), and the item "drove recklessly when you were in the car," which would not be applicable to all respondents. The scale did show good internal consistency (alpha coefficients .70–.92) and reasonable validity. Not all items labeled "psychological abuse" loaded onto this scale: Several items loaded onto the physical aggression scale; notably, there were sex differences in which items loaded in that manner. Follingstad, Hause, and Rutledge (1992) also developed a scale for measuring controlling behaviors used by men, using a sample of 240 undergraduate women reporting on their partner's behaviors. From an original total of 46 items, 13 were retained to form the control scale. This final scale consisted of one item of physical aggression, seven items of jealous or isolating behavior, one item of threats, two items of emotional abuse, and one item that related to gender roles (e.g., "insisted I do things because I was a woman").

Rodenburg and Fantuzzo (1993) developed the Measure of Wife Abuse with a sample of 164 abused women. Using factor analysis, two scales relating to psychological and verbal abuse were devised. The psychological abuse scale contains 15 items, many of which would be difficult to conceptualize, such as "turned off electricity" and "stole food or money." One item relates to children. The verbal abuse scale contains 14 items, of which four relate to threats (two of which involved children), and the remaining 10 assess emotionally abusive behaviors. Of the emotional items, three relate to name-calling (bitch, whore, and cunt) and could have been amalgamated into one item of emotional abuse.

Dobash, Dobash, Cavanagh, and Lewis (1998) devised a controlling behaviors index from their work with 122 domestically violent men and 144 female victims. The 21-item scale comprises three items relating to children and three items that may be ambiguous in a nonselected sample: "have a certain look/mood," "point at her," and "nag her." The remaining items are three referring to isolation, two to threats, one to intimidation, one economic, and seven emotional. One other was difficult to categorize ("try to provoke an argument").

Smith, Earp, and DeVellis (1995) developed the Women's Experience with Battering Scale using 22 battered women to generate the initial 40 items, which were then reduced to 10 after factor analysis of responses to the scale from 185 battered and 204 nonbattered women. The scale contains items that relate to the feelings of the victim and so is not appropriate for generating reports of both perpetration and victimization.

Laner (1985) studied "negative" behaviors in dating relationships from a conflict approach in a sample of 400 Mormons and non-Mormons. She created a scale using items from the Index of Spouse Abuse and the CTS. Eleven of the 32 items relate to physical or sexual aggression, and two items relate to alcohol consumption. The remaining ones are either a mixture of isolation (two items), threats (one), intimidation (six), emotional abuse (six), or difficult to categorize (e.g., "is not a kind person"). Rouse (1990) devised a scale to measure dominance-possessiveness and physical aggression. The 16-item scale contained 10 items related to physically or sexually aggressive behaviors or injuries resulting from these behaviors. Of the remaining items, three related to isolation and three to emotional control. Stets and Pirog-Good (1990; Stets, 1991, 1993) devised a control scale to use with mixed-sex dating samples. The nine-item scale consists of general statements about control—for example, "I keep him/her in line" and "I set the rules in my relationship with him/her"—as opposed to more specific behaviors.

Stacey et al. (1994) reported a range of behaviors used by men and women who were in contact with the criminal justice system because of the man's physical aggression toward his wife. There were 13 items of psychological abuse, of which five were jealousy or isolation, three were threats, three were emotional, and two were economic.

To establish the use of control tactics by each partner, Graham-Kevan and Archer (2003) developed a scale, the Controlling Behaviors Scale (CBS) and the Controlling Behaviors Scale-Revised (CBS-R), using literature from the Domestic Abuse Intervention Project (Pence & Paymar, 1993). All the items are behavioral acts based on the specific illustrative examples given in each of the PCW octants. The final scale consisted of 24 items: five economic, four threat, five intimidation, five emotional, and five isolation. All the items are appropriate for male and female victims and do not rely on respondents cohabiting or having children. The drawback to the CBS and most of the scales reviewed is that the items are derived from accounts of female victims and so may not fully encompass the types of behaviors more usually used by women perpetrators (Borjesson, Aarons, & Dunn, 2003). Hamel (2005) devised the Controlling and Abusive Tactics Questionnaire on the basis of previous scales and his own clinical experience. The scale has 50 items measuring threats and intimidation (four items), isolation and jealousy (seven items), economic control (five items), diminishment of self-esteem (13 items), general control (four items), obsessive relational intrusion (three items), passive-aggressive/withdrawal (five items), using children (four items), legal system abuse (two items), and sexual abuse (three items). The broad range of types of control included in this scale is impressive; however, the scale is new, and therefore there is a lack of information on population norms at present.

IMPLICATIONS OF THE CONTROLLING BEHAVIOR LITERATURE

From the literature reviewed here, it is clear that controlling behavior and physical aggression co-occur and that the use of controlling behavior is not a male or a heterosexual preserve. Longitudinal data suggests that controlling behavior may be a precursor to physical aggression (Murphy & O'Leary, 1989) and that, unlike physical aggression, it may not diminish over time. The negative consequences for victims of psychological victimization are severe and independent of physical victimization. Although feminist, family conflict, evolutionary, and trauma theories are in agreement that controlling behavior and physical aggression are motivated by similar needs, the actual needs are not agreed on. There are many scales that measure aspects of controlling behavior, although no single scale has yet reached dominance in the literature, and, as such, no one scale is validated and accepted for research and clinical use.

Research

The most pressing issue for researchers is to refine existing scales to create a scale that is inclusive so that it can be used with mixed-sex populations and within heterosexual and homosexual relationships. Such a scale must not presuppose cohabitation or the presence of children, although additional items for these purposes would be helpful. Controlling behavior scales should aim to encompass the broad spectrum of controlling behaviors. Any scale measuring controlling behavior should be sensitive enough to discriminate between nonviolent and violent relationships as well as relationships in which physical aggression is mutual or unidirectional or minor or severe.

Future research should aim to move away from single-sex population studies and instead measure the use of control by men and women. Further, scholars should endeavor to identify nonviolent correlates of controlling behavior to increase the understanding of why and when control is likely to be used. As all behaviors within a relationship are dyadic, it is important that future research studies not only measure victims' reports of perpetrators' behaviors but also investigate both partners' behaviors.

Clinicians

Clinical practice should address the use of controlling behavior by both partners. Discordant levels of controlling behavior between partners may require different treatment approaches than relationships where couples use similar levels of control. Relationships where levels of control are low for both partners may require anger management types of interventions, whereas high levels of control may be more indicative of childhood trauma and attachment problems (see chapter 9 in this volume) that may require psychotherapy (see chapter 2 in this volume). Intervention should include the reduction of controlling behavior as a treatment aim and take measurements of controlling behavior pre- and postintervention to assess the effectiveness of intervention strategies to reduce controlling behavior.

REFERENCES

Aldarondo, E. M. (2002). Programs for men who batter: Intervention and prevention strategies in a diverse society. *Civic Research Institute, 25*, I-14.

Archer, J. (2000). Sex differences in aggression between heterosexual partners: A meta-analytic review. *Psychological Bulletin, 126*, 651–680.

Arias, I., & Pape, K. T. (2001). Psychological abuse: Implications for adjustment and commitment to leave violent partners. In K. D. O'Leary & R. D. Maiuro (Eds.), *Psychological abuse in violent relations* (pp. 137–151). New York: Springer.

Baldry, A. C. (2003). Bullying in schools and exposure to domestic violence. *Child Abuse and Neglect, 27*, 713–732.

Bartholomew, K., Henderson, A. J. Z., & Dutton, D. G. (2001). Insecure attachment and abusive intimate relationships. In C. Clulow (Ed.), *Adult attachment and couple work: Applying the "secure base" concept in research and practice* (pp. 43–61). London: Routledge.

Beech, A. R., & Mitchell, I. J. (2004). A neurobiological perspective on attachment problems in sexual offenders and the role of selective serotonin re-uptake inhibitors in the treatment of such problems. *Clinical Psychology Review, 25*, 153–182.

Bennett, L., Goodman, L., & Dutton, M.A. (2000). Risk assessment among batterers arrested for domestic assault. *Violence Against Women, 16*, 1190–1203.

Bicehouse, T., & Hawker, L. (1993). Degrees of games: An application to the understanding of domestic violence. *Transactional Analysis Journal, 23*, 195–200.

Borjession, W. I., Aarons, G. A., & Dunn, M. E. (2003). Development and confirmatory factor analysis of the abuse within relationships scale. *Journal of Interpersonal Violence, 18*, 295–309.

Bowlby, J. (1969). *Attachment and loss. Vol 1: Attachment.* Harmondsworth, Middlesex: Penguin.

Buss, D. M., & Shackelford, T. K. (1997). From vigilance to violence: Mate retention tactics in married couples. *Journal of Personality and Social Psychology, 72*, 346–361.

Dobash, R. P., & Dobash, R. E. (1979). *Violence against wives: A case against patriarchy.* New York: Free Press.

Dobash, R.P., Dobash, R. E, Cavanagh, K., & Lewis, R. (1998). Separate and intersecting realities: A comparison of men and women's accounts of violence against women. *Violence Against Women, 4*, 382–414.

Dutton, D. G. (2000). Witnessing parental violence as a traumatic experience shaping the abusive personality. *Journal of Aggression and Maltreatment, 3*, 59–67.

Dutton, D. G., & Starzomski, A. J. (1997). Personality predictors of the Minnesota power and control wheel. *Journal of Interpersonal Violence, 12*, 70–82.

Dutton, M. A., Goodman, L. A., & Bennett, L. (2001). Court-involved battered women's responses to violence: The role of psychological, physical and sexual abuse. In K. D. O'Leary & R. D. Maiuro (Eds.), *Psychological abuse in violent relations* (pp.177–195). New York: Springer.

Ehrensaft, M. K., & Vivian, D. (1999). Is partner aggression related to appraisals of coercive control by a partner? *Journal of Family Violence, 14*, 251–266.

Feld, S. L., & Straus, M. A. (1990). Escalation and desistence from wife assault in marriage. In M. A. Straus & R. J. Gelles (Eds.), *Physical violence in American families* (pp. 489–505). New Brunswick, NJ: Transaction Publishers.

Felson, R. B. (2002). *Violence and gender reexamined.* Washington, DC: American Psychological Association.

Figueredo, A. J., Corral-Verdugo, V., Frias-Armenta, M., Bachar, K. J., White, J., McNeill, P. L., et al. (2001). Blood, solidarity, status, and honour: The sexual balance of power and spousal abuse in Sonora, Mexico. *Evolution and Human Behavior, 22*, 295–328.

Figueredo, A. J., & McCloskey, L. A. (1993). Sex, money and paternity: The evolutionary psychology of domestic violence. *Ethology and Sociobiology, 14*, 353–379.

Flinn, M. V. (1988). Mate guarding in a Caribbean village. *Ethology and Sociobiology, 9*, 1–28.

Follingstad, D. R., Bradley, R. G., Helff, C. M., & Laughlin, J. E. (2002). A model for predicting dating violence: Anxious attachment, angry temperament, and the need for relationship control. *Violence and Victims, 17*, 35–47.

Follingstad, D. R., Hause, E. S., & Rutledge, L. L. (1992). Effects of battered women's early responses on later abuse patterns. *Violence and Victims, 17*, 109–128.

Follingstad, D. R., Rutledge, L. L., Berg, B., Hause, E. S., & Polek, D. S. (1990). The role of emotional abuse in physically abusive relationships. *Journal of Family Violence, 5*, 107–120.

George, M. J. (1994). Riding the donkey backwards: Men as unacceptable victims of marital violence. *Journal of Men's Studies, 3*, 137–159.

Gottman, J. M., Jacobson, N. S., Rushe, R. H., Shortt, J. W., Babcock, J. C., LaTaillade, J. J., & Waltz, J. (1995). The relationship between heart rate reactivity, emotionally aggressive behavior, and general violence in batterers. *Journal of Family Psychology, 9*, 227–248.

Graham-Kevan, N., & Archer, J. (2003). Patriarchal terrorism and common couple violence: A test of Johnson's predictions in four British samples. *Journal of Interpersonal Violence, 18*, 1247–1270.

Graham-Kevan, N. & Archer, J. (2005). Investigating three explanations of women's relationship aggression. *Psychology of Women Quarterly, 29*, 270–277.

Graham-Kevan, N. & Archer J. (2006). Does controlling behaviour predict physical aggression and violence towards partners? Unpublished manuscript. University of Central Lancashire, United Kingdom.

Hamby, S. L., & Sugarman, D. B. (1999). Acts of psychological aggression against a partner and their relation to physical assault and gender. *Journal of Marriage and the Family, 61*, 959–970.

Hamel, J. (2005). *Gender inclusive treatment of intimate partner abuse: A comprehensive approach.* New York: Springer.

Harned, M. S. (2001). Abused women or abused men? An examination of the context and outcomes of dating violence. *Violence and Victims, 16*, 269–285.

Henton, J., Cate, R., Koval, J., Lloyd, S., & Christopher, S. (1983). Romance and violence in dating relationships. *Journal of Family Issues, 4,* 467–482.

Hoffman, P. (1984). Psychological abuse of women by spouses and live-in lovers. *Women & Therapy, 3,* 37–47.

Johnson, M. P. (1995). Patriarchal terrorism and common couple violence: Two forms of violence against women. *Journal of Marriage and the Family, 57,* 283–301.

Julian, T. W., McKenry, P. C., Gavazzi, S. M., & Law, J. C. (1999). Test of family of origin structural models of male verbal and physical aggression. *Journal of Family Issues, 20,* 397–423.

Kantor, K., Jasnski, J. L., & Aldarondo, E. (1994). Sociocultural status and incidence of marital violence in Hispanic families. *Violence and Victims, 9,* 207–222.

Kasian, M., & Painter, S. (1992). Frequency and severity of psychological abuse in a dating population. *Journal of Interpersonal Violence, 7,* 350–364.

Landolt, M. A., & Dutton, D. G. (1997). Power and personality: An analysis of gay male intimate abuse. *Sex Roles, 37,* 335–359.

Laner, M.R. (1985). Unpleasant, aggressive, and abusive activities in courtship: A comparison of Mormon and Nonmormon college students. *Deviant Behavior, 6,* 145–168.

Letellier, P. (1994). Gay and bisexual domestic violence victimization: Challenges to feminist theory and responses to violence. *Violence and Victims, 9,* 95–106.

Marshall, L. L. (2001). Effects of men's subtle and overt psychological abuse on low-income women. In K. D. O'Leary & R. D. Maiuro (Eds.), *Psychological abuse in violent domestic relations* (pp. 153–175). New York: Springer.

Merrill, G. S., & Wolfe, V. A. (2000). Battered gay men: An exploration of abuse, help seeking and why they stay. *Journal of Homosexuality, 39,* 1–30.

Migliaccio, T. A. (2002). Abused men: A narrative analysis. *Journal of Family Issues, 23*(1), 26–52.

Miller, S. L., & Simpson, S. S. (1991). Courtship violence and social control: Does gender matter? *Law and Society Review, 25*(2), 335–365.

Molidor, C. E. (1995). Gender differences of psychological abuse in high school dating relationships. *Child and Adolescent Social Work Journal, 12*(2), 119–134.

Murphy, C. M., & O'Leary, K. D. (1989). Psychological aggression predicts physical aggression in early marriage. *Journal of Consulting and Clinical Psychology, 57,* 579–582.

O'Hagan, K. (1995). Emotional and psychological abuse: Problems of definition. *Child Abuse & Neglect, 19,* 449–461.

O'Leary, K. D., & Jouriles, E. N. (1993). Psychological abuse between adult partners: Prevalence and effects on partners and children. In L. L. Abate (Ed.), *Handbook of developmental family psychology and psychopathology* (pp. 330–349). New York: John Wiley & Sons.

O'Leary, K. D., & Maiuro, R. D. (2001). *Psychological abuse in violent domestic relations.* New York: Springer.

Pence, E., & Paymar, M. (1986). *Power and control: Tactics of men who batter.* Duluth: Minnesota Program Development, Inc.

Pence, E., & Paymar, M. (1993). *Education groups of men who batter: The Duluth model.* New York: Springer.

Peters, J., Shackelford, T. K., & Buss, D. M. (2002). Understanding domestic violence against women: Using evolutionary psychology to extend the feminist functional analyses. *Violence and Victims, 17,* 255–264.

Petrik, N. D., Olson, R. E., & Subotnik, L. S. (1994). Powerlessness and the need to control: The male abuser's dilemma. *Journal of Interpersonal Violence, 9,* 278–285.

Renzetti, C. M. (1992). *Violent betrayal: Partner abuse in lesbian relationships.* Thousand Oaks, CA: Sage.

Rodenburg, F.A. & Fantuzzo, J.W. (1993).The measure of wife abuse: Steps toward the development of a comprehensive assessment technique. *Journal of Family Violence, 8,* 203–228.

Rouse, L.P. (1990). The dominance motive in abusive partners: Identifying couples at risk. *Journal of College Student Development, 31,* 330–335.

Rouse, L. P, Breen, R., & Howell, M. (1988). Abuse in intimate relationships: A comparison of married and dating college students. *Journal of Interpersonal Violence, 13,* 414–429.

Sackett, L. A., & Saunders, D. G. (2001). The impact of different forms of psychological abuse on battered women. In K. D. O'Leary & R. D. Maiuro (Eds.), *Psychological abuse in violent relations* (pp. 105–117). New York: Springer.

Salgado, D. M., Suvak, M. K., King, L. A., & King, D. W. (2004). Associations of gender and gender-role ideology with behavioral and attitudinal features of intimate partner aggression. *Psychology of Men and Masculinity, 5,* 91–102.

Shepard, M. F., & Campbell, J. A. (1992). The Abusive Behavior Inventory: A measure of psychological and physical abuse. *Journal of Interpersonal Violence, 7*(3), 291–305.

Smith, P. H., Earp, J. A., & DeVellis, R. (1995). Measuring battering: Development of the Women's Experience With Battering (WEB) Scale. *Women's Health: Research on Gender, Behavior, and Policy, 1,* 273–288.

Stacey, W. A., Hazlewood, L. R., & Shupe, A. (1994). *The violent couple.* New York: Praeger.

Statistics Canada. (2000). Family violence in Canada: A statistical profile (No. 85-224-XIE). Canadian Centre for Justice Statistics. Ottawa, Ontario.

Stets, J. E. (1988). *Domestic violence and control.* New York: Springer-Verlag.

Stets, J. E. (1991). Psychological aggression in dating relationship: The role of interpersonal control. *Journal of Family Violence, 6,* 97–114.

Stets, J.E. (1993). Control in dating relationships. *Journal of Marriage and the Family, 55,* 673–685.

Stets, J. E., & Pirog-Good, M. A. (1990). Interpersonal control and courtship aggression. *Journal of Social and Personal Relationships, 7,* 371–394.

Straus, M. A. (1979). Measuring intrafamily conflict and violence: The Conflicts Tactics (CT) scales. *Journal of Marriage and the Family, 41,* 75–88.

Straus, M. A., Hamby, S. L., Boney-McCoy, S., & Sugarman, D. B. (1996). The revised Conflict Tactics Scale (CTS2). *Journal of Family Issues, 17,* 283–316.

Straus, M. A., Kantor, G. K., & Moore, D. W. (1997). Change in cultural norms approving marital violence from 1968 to 1994. In G. K. Kantor & J. L. Jasinki (Eds.), *Out of the darkness* (pp. 3–16). Thousand Oaks, CA: Sage.

Sugarman, D. B., & Frankel, S. L. (1996). Patriarchal ideology and wife-assault: A meta-analytic review. *Journal of Family Violence, 11,* 13–40.

Sugihara, Y., & Warner, J. A. (2002). Dominance and domestic abuse among Mexican Americans: Gender differences in the etiology of violence in intimate relationships. *Journal of Family Violence, 17,* 315–340.

Symons, D. (1992). On the use and misuse of Darwinism in the study of human behavior. In J. H. Barkow & L. Cosmides (Eds.), *The adapted mind: Evolutionary psychology and the generation of culture* (pp. 137–159). New York: Oxford University Press.

Timmons Fritz, P. A. & O'Leary, K.D. (2004). Physical and psychological partner aggression across a decade: A growth curve analysis. *Violence and Victims, 19,* 3–16.

Tolman, R. M. (1989). The development of a measure of psychological maltreatment of women by their male partners. *Violence and Victims, 4,* 159–177.

Toro-Alfonso, J., & Rodriguez-Madera, S. (2004). Domestic violence in Puerto Rican gay male couples: Perceived prevalence, intergenerational violence, addictive behaviors, and conflict resolution skills. *Journal of Interpersonal Violence, 19,* 639–654.

Van Dijk, T., Flight, S., Oppenhuis, E., & Duesmann, B. (1998). Domestic violence: A national study of the nature, size and effects of domestic violence in the Netherlands. *European Journal on Criminal Policy and Research, 6,* 7–35.

White, J. W., Merrill, L. L., & Koss, M. P. (2001). Predictors of courtship violence in a Navy recruit sample. *Journal of Interpersonal Violence, 16*(9), 910–927.

Wilson, M., & Daly, M. (1993). An evolutionary psychological perspective on male sexual proprietariness and violence towards wives. *Violence and Victims, 8,* 191–214.

Yllo, K. A. (1994). Through a feminist lens: Gender, power, and violence. In R. J. Gelles & D. R. Loseke (Eds.), *Current controversies on family violence* (pp. 47–62). Thousand Oaks, CA: Sage.

CHAPTER 5

Intimate Stalking and Partner Violence

Stacey L. Williams, Irene Hanson
Frieze, and H. Colleen Sinclair

In this chapter, we provide an overview of existing literature identifying stalking as a form of intimate violence. Starting with a definition of what constitutes intimate stalking, we move to a discussion of the prevalence, antecedents, and consequences of intimate stalking victimization. We highlight important issues, such as social perceptions of stalking, risk factors for violence escalation, gender differences and similarities in victimization reports, and the lack of resources for stalking victims—concerns to which victim advocates should pay particular attention.

STALKING DEFINED

Stalking came into public awareness in the United States in 1990 with the advent of the first antistalking law in California following a number of high-profile stalking cases. In 1993, the National Institute of Justice (NIJ) formulated its model antistalking code to serve as a template for states to construct their own laws (NIJ, 1993). Since that time, all states have constructed some form of antistalking statutes of their own (Office for Victims of Crime [OVC], 2002; St. George, 2001). Despite the widespread availability of antistalking statutes there is neither a widespread application of statutes nor uniform definition of stalking (Sinclair,

Chan, & Borgida, 2003). The general generic definition provided by the OVC (2002) defines stalking as the "willful or intentional commission of a series of acts that would cause a reasonable person to fear death or serious bodily injury and that, in fact, does place the victim in fear of death or serious bodily injury" (p. 1). By this definition, there are an estimated 1.4 million victims of stalking in the United States each year, and these victims are predominantly women and often acquainted with their stalker (Tjaden & Thoennes, 1998).

Just as legal definitions vary across jurisdictions, definitions of stalking by researchers also lack uniformity (for a detailed analysis of various researcher definitions, see Davis & Frieze, 2002). Before the advent of stalking legislation, researchers and practitioners struggled to label the behaviors that make up what we now call stalking since there were no clear definitions (for review, see Lowney & Best, 1995). Today, because of this complex history, a wide variety of labels exist in the literature, and definitions of stalking range from a set of "persistent" courtship behaviors to more serious acts of physical aggression. For example, Spitzberg and Cupach (1998, 2000) referred to "obsessional relational intrusion," while Langhinrichsen-Rohling, Palarea, Cohen, and Rohling (2002) used the term "unwanted relational pursuit" to describe similar, stalking-type behavior(s). Meanwhile, domestic violence researchers often have used the phrase "separation abuse" to describe the increased harassment and violence that victims of battering suffer when attempting to leave their abusers (Campbell, 1992; Mahoney, 1991; Wilson & Daly, 1993). Recurring elements in definitions of stalking include that the behavior is unwanted, repeated, and, often, distressing. Intimate stalking behavior may best be understood as a continuum of behaviors, escalating from courtship persistence to threats of physical violence, wherein the pursuer repeatedly attempts to maintain unwanted contact, directly and indirectly, with a target, and this behavior, intentionally or unintentionally, causes the target discomfort and, in extreme cases, fear. Perpetrator and victim definitions of stalking also vary, and many of the events that are identified by researchers may not be classified as stalking by those directly involved (Frieze & Davis, 2000). Similar patterns have been seen in other types of intimate violence, such as rape, where many of those classified as rape "victims" by researchers do not define their own experiences in the same way (e.g., Kahn, Jackson, Kully, Badger, & Halvorsen, 2003).

Research on stalking has suggested that there are two basic types of intimate stalking. One occurs before a relationship has ever begun and involves attempts to get the attention of an individual one is attracted to (Sinclair & Frieze, 2002). We have labeled this "courtship stalking." The other form of stalking occurs during the breakup of a relationship (e.g., Tjaden & Thoennes, 1998) and has received considerably more research attention. We review some of what is known about courtship stalking but focus our attention on breakup stalking and its relation to other forms of relationship violence and related behaviors.

STALKING IN THE CONTEXT OF BREAKUP

The breakup of a relationship appears to be a ripe context for intimate stalking. In an attempt to win back the affection of the love interest, individuals may behave in ways that constitute what researchers have labeled stalking. This form of stalking can occur in response to the breakup of marriages or dating relationships (Langhinrichsen-Rohling et al., 2002; Logan, Leukefeld, & Walker, 2002; Mechanic, Weaver, & Resick, 2002). Research has shown that stalking behaviors during the breakup of a relationship are relatively common. Up to 62% of young adults have been victims of stalking-like behaviors after the breakup of intimate relationships (Davis & Frieze, 2002). The majority of those who stalk are ex-spouses or ex-lovers. In one study of 200 female stalking victims, results indicated that three-quarters of the victims' stalkers were ex-partners (Kamphuis & Emmelkamp, 2001). Using National Violence Against Women (NVAW) Survey data, Davis, Coker, and Sanderson (2002) found that 41% of women and 28% of men who had been stalked reported the perpetrator was an ex–intimate partner. Spitzberg (2002), in a meta-analysis of studies on stalking-related behaviors, concluded that the majority of stalking is enacted by a person known by the victim and that in most of those cases the perpetrator is a former romantic partner. These studies included situations in which men as well as women were being stalked. Further, the most *violent* forms of stalking behaviors occur in situations where there had once been an intimate relationship between the victim and the stalker. Kamphuis and Emmelkamp (2001) found that women experienced more threats of physical violence when they had a prior intimate relationship with their stalker. Similarly, in a sample of men and women, Palarea, Zona, Lane, and Langhinrichsen-Rohling (1999) found that violent forms of stalking are more likely to occur in the context of intimate than nonintimate stalking. Thus, intimate stalking, especially by former and estranged partners, may pose serious physical dangers to victims.

A theoretical explanation for why some people engage in stalking behaviors has been demonstrated in research indicating that such behaviors likely occur in situations where an attachment to another is threatened or at times when individuals feel they have lost control over partners (Davis, Ace, & Andra, 2002). In this way, one might consider the breakup of a relationship to be the ultimate unrequited love scenario, particularly in the case where the decision to end the relationship is not a mutual one. Indeed, specific features of the breakup, such as who initiated the breakup, are related to the degree of stalking behaviors performed (Davis et al., 2002). Additional research is needed to better understand some of the motivating factors for breakup stalking, but it appears that breakup stalking may stem from a history of similar types of behaviors during the ongoing relationship.

There is strong evidence connecting breakup stalking behavior and former partner abuse (e.g., Burgess et al., 1997; Coleman, 1997; Logan et al., 2002; Melton, 2000). For instance, stalking victims often reported having been controlled and emotionally abused within their intimate relationship, implicating stalking as a means by which abusers continue this control and abuse outside the relationship (Brewster, 2003). Extending this work to include men and women, Logan et al. (2002) found in a sample of college students that those who were stalked following breakup had experienced more psychological and more physical abuse earlier in their relationships than those who had not been stalked during breakup. Accordingly, Logan et al. labeled stalking as a variant of intimate partner violence. As these studies imply, physical and psychological abusiveness during the course of an intimate relationship is a risk factor for being stalked when the relationship ends.

This recent research linking stalking to partner abuse is consistent with literature on battering relationships. Before the term "stalking" came into the American lexicon, relationship violence researchers had used the label "separation assault" (Mahoney, 1991) to describe the heightened risk for violence, including serious levels of violence and even homicide (Walker & Meloy, 1998), during relationship separation or termination (Campbell, 1992; Wilson & Daly, 1993). This "separation assault" (Mahoney, 1991) is intended to keep the partner from separating either physically or emotionally from the abuser. The term also refers to the retaliation that would occur should the partner attempt to separate. A recent study on batterers illustrates the connection between relationship battering and breakup stalking. In this study, batterers (90% men) who were court-mandated to an assessment program were asked about their behaviors toward their partners since being convicted of battering. The behaviors clustered into two clear patterns: The first represented ambivalent contact (e.g., watching her while harboring conflicting feelings of love and hate) and the second predatory contact (e.g., threatening to or actually causing harm to her) (Burgess, Harner, Baker, Hartman, & Lole, 2001). As can be gathered from these two patterns of behaviors by batterers (albeit mostly male), the specific acts are conceptually similar to stalking. Thus, the breakup of abusive relationships can put individuals at risk for future violence, including stalking. In extreme cases, those who leave these abusive relationships are killed by their estranged partners (McFarlane, Campbell, & Watson, 2002).

Other research also supports a link between stalking and relationship violence. Many of the behaviors associated with stalking, such as surveillance, have often been associated with very violent relationships (Frieze, 2005). The display of very violent behavior toward a romantic partner has been labeled by some as intimate terrorism (Johnson & Ferraro, 2000). Many of these relationships appear to involve a man who is abusive toward his female partner, but women also engage in intimate terrorism (for reviews, see Dutton & Nicholls, 2005; Frieze, 2005). In these relationships, often the violent partners closely monitor the behavior of the nonviolent or less violent partners and use violence to ensure that they report their activities and do what they are told by the abusive partners. A recent review of the literature on the link between violence and stalking by Douglas and Dutton (2001) highlights several commonalities between stalkers and severely violent men. For instance, they postulated that some of the same explanations for why individuals are highly abusive toward their partners, such as borderline/cyclical personality disorder, might also explain stalking. Similar diagnoses (e.g., borderline and psychosis) have also been indicated among some women stalkers as well (Meloy & Boyd, 2003), although most individuals who stalk have not been so diagnosed. Much more research needs to be done on the relationship between partner abuse and stalking.

That stalking during the course of a breakup might be predicted from abusive behaviors earlier in the relationship gives rise to other questions, such as whether violence and stalking can be predicted from behaviors performed during the *earliest* points in the relationship or prerelationship. Next, we briefly introduce this second form of stalking, courtship stalking, and how it might relate to breakup stalking.

COURTSHIP STALKING AND ITS LINK
TO BREAKUP STALKING

Courtship stalking occurs when someone is interested romantically in another person who does not reciprocate that interest. Defining what does or does not constitute courtship stalking is difficult. As part of the normal courtship process, one may send notes; seek out the other person in social, school, or work situations; or look for information about that person. All these behaviors appear to be quite common and are done by both sexes. Yet these relatively common behaviors can be defined as forms of "stalking," depending on the context in which the behaviors occur (Sinclair & Frieze, 2002). For instance, if these behaviors are unwanted by their recipient or committed in high frequencies, they can be harassing. In addition, definitions may not be the same for the target of the actions and for the person engaging in the pursuing behavior(s)

(Sinclair & Frieze, 2005). Further, cultural ideals about what is acceptable pursuit behavior may blur the line between normal courtship persistence and stalking behavior (Sinclair, Borgida, & Collins, 2002). Often, ardent pursuers are seen as romantic (Dunn, 1993; Sinclair et al., 2003), and the targets of the pursuit are expected to be flattered by the attention (Hall, 1998). We propose that men in particular are socialized to be persistent in trying to get the attention of women to whom they are romantically attracted, but our empirical data do show that both sexes engage in courtship stalking (Sinclair & Frieze, 2002; Williams & Frieze, 2005a).

In one of the few studies on courtship stalking, Sinclair and Frieze (2002) asked college students about experiences with unrequited courtships and what types of actions they took in that situation to woo their love interest. Experiences with unrequited attractions were reported by a large majority of the sample of men as well as women. Behaviors ranged from doing favors to get the person's attention (men = 74%, women = 72%) to verbal aggression (men = 14%, women = 13%) and even (primarily mild) physical violence (men = 2%, women = 16%).

Although there are limited empirical data on courtship stalking, it does appear that it is more likely to occur in cases where the feelings of the person engaging in stalking behaviors can be characterized as a love style known as mania (Sinclair & Frieze, 2002). The mania love style involves strong feelings of sexual passion as well as high levels of jealousy and anxiety about whether the beloved person really cares about oneself (Bookwala, Frieze, & Grote, 1994). Courtship stalking is also associated with an eros love style, characterized by strong feelings of sexual passion as well as feelings of closeness toward the beloved and enjoyment. Not surprisingly, the eros love style is more closely associated with using approach behaviors such as seeking contact, while mania is most associated with aggressive forms of stalking. In addition, men's and women's beliefs that the sexes are adversarial (Burt, 1980), such as "A woman will only respect a man who will lay down the law to her," "Women play games with men's affections," or "Men can be nice during the courtship period, but once they are in a relationship they act like a different person," are most associated with stalking that involved surveillance or intimidation (Sinclair & Frieze, 2002).

The principal importance of understanding courtship stalking may lie in its ability to predict subsequent relationship violence and (escalating) stalking. Returning to the question of whether breakup stalking can be predicted from the earliest part of a relationship or prerelationship, we recently examined persistence behaviors performed by college men and women during courtship (Williams & Frieze, 2005a). In our research, we predicted that seemingly benign types of courtship behaviors or even mildly aggressive behaviors could be associated with various types of violence during and following the ensuing relationship. We (like others; e.g., Billingham, 1987) proposed that during the earliest stages of relationships, the level of acceptability for future violence is established. Minor acts of aggression may be viewed as acceptable or even normal in the early part of a relationship (Straus, Gelles, & Steinmetz, 1980) or may be seen as signs of caring (Billingham, 1987); therefore, such behaviors may lead to the use of similar behaviors at later points in the relationship. In a sample of 300 college students, we found that early behaviors do in fact relate to behaviors performed at breakup (Williams & Frieze, 2005a). We assessed the persistence or stalking-type behaviors (approach, surveillance, intimidation, and mild aggression) performed by male and female students during courtship, the violence they performed during the dating relationship (both mild and more severe), as well as the stalking behaviors performed once the dating relationship ended. We found that minor acts of aggression during courtship are related to mild and severe violence during the relationship. Moreover, we found that courtship persistence behaviors are linked to performing those same types of behaviors (approach, surveillance, and aggression) once the relationship ends. Thus, we found initial evidence that courtship behaviors might predict later aggressive behaviors.

That persistence and stalking-type behaviors during courtship are linked with relationship violence as well as stalking behaviors during breakup implies that full-fledged relationships develop despite the presence of these persistent and sometimes aggressive behaviors during courtship. Although we cannot confirm causal relations, it may be that some relationships develop *because* of the use of persistent courtship tactics. That is, at least some early courtship behaviors may be "successful" in that they lead to relationship development. Although it may be intuitive that targets of such behavior would respond negatively to attempts of the actor to establish a relationship, several commonly held cultural and relationship beliefs support the notion of successful courtship stalking-related behaviors (Dunn, 1993; Sinclair et al., 2002, 2003). For instance, dating scripts involve approach behaviors, persistence, and romantic ideation (Lloyd, 1991; Rose & Frieze, 1993; Sinclair & Frieze, 2002). Individuals on the receiving end of such romantic pursuit may not interpret persistence behaviors as inappropriate but instead may be flattered (Dunn, 1993) and, in turn, respond with affection. In our study of 300 college men and women (Williams & Frieze, 2005a), we found that relationships developed *despite* the presence of persistence behaviors, implying that persistence often may not be seen as threatening during the courtship stage when ardent pursuit tactics are normative and romanticized (Sinclair et al., 2002). It is not clear if the persistence behaviors were perceived in a positive way and actually enhanced relationship formation or if they were seen as negative and merely were tolerated, an interesting topic for future research.

ISSUES OF GENDER IN STALKING AND PARTNER VIOLENCE

Whereas research consistently has shown that stalking behaviors are present during courtship and breakup, there is less agreement about gender differences in the experience of stalking behavior. In particular, findings in the extant research regarding the gender of stalking perpetrator and victim are equivocal. Some have argued that stalking is a gendered phenomenon with men more often perpetrating and women more often victimized (White, Kowalski, Lyndon, & Valentine, 2002) and as such have labeled stalking a "women's issue" (for review, see Melton, 2000). Empirical evidence at least partially supports this assertion, showing that more women than men are victims of stalking. In their examination of the NVAW Survey, Tjaden and Thoennes (1998) reported a sizable gender difference in the rates of stalking victimization such that women were stalked more often than men (8% of women vs. 2% of men). In addition, Spitzberg (2002), in his meta-analysis of stalking studies, found a large gender difference in the victimization and perpetration of stalking behaviors. Across 43 studies, he found that 75% of victims were female. In addition, in the fewer number of studies on perpetration, Spitzberg concluded that nearly 80% of perpetrators were males.

However, it is difficult to draw firm conclusions from these two sources of information. For instance, the NVAW Survey was focused on violence against *women* specifically, which could have biased the response rate of male victims of violence. Further, these numbers might also be skewed, as the NVAW Survey was a survey of *victimization* experiences and the meta-analysis a compilation of findings across multiple studies that involved only victimized samples. Certainly there could be substantial differences between those who would consider themselves "victims" and those who do not. Men may be less likely to classify themselves as victims (Dutton & Nicholls, 2005), as men are certainly less likely to report crimes when they are victims (Greenfield et al., 1998). Supporting this idea is the fact that many legal definitions of stalking involve victim fear. It does appear that stalking-related behaviors done by a man are more likely to generate fear in a woman than similar behaviors done by a woman to a male victim. When fear is removed from the definition, the gender differences in stalking perpetration decline (Sinclair & Frieze, 2005). Further, although many of the studies in the meta-analysis involved both males and females, four times as many studies on women only were included than on men only. Thus, on the basis of this research, there is no clear conclusion on gender differences.

Moreover, some evidence based on single studies indicates similar frequencies of stalking in men and women. This is especially true when people are asked about specific behaviors that are often classified as "stalking," but there is no requirement that these behaviors generate fear in the victim. For instance, Spitzberg, Nicastro, and Cousins (1998) found virtually no gender difference in the prevalence of stalking victimization among male and female undergraduate students. Similarly, McFarlane, Willson, Malecha, and Lemmey (2000) found no gender difference in the severity or extent of partner violence or stalking in a sample of individuals filing assault charges against their partners even though the majority (90%) of those filing charges were women. Other studies have shown that gender differences may lie not in the presence or absence of stalking but rather in the specific stalking or persistence behaviors performed. For instance, both Langhinrichsen-Rohling and colleagues (2002) and Sinclair and Frieze (2002) found that women likely perform more indirect forms of pursuit behavior (e.g., unwanted phone calls), whereas men perform more direct forms, such as in-person contact. For example, 92% of women reported asking friends about someone they were interested in, while only 86% of men did this. More women (85%) reported making a point of being at an event where they knew the person they were interested in would be, while only 79% of men did this. But 72% of men asked out the woman they were interested in (vs. 39% of women), and 67% of men sent gifts compared to 51% of women. Attempting to manipulate or coerce the desired partner into a date was reported by 28% of men and 17% of women. In fact, it may be this difference that contributes further to the difference in victimization reports. Men may report being targeted by stalking behavior less because women stalkers are more likely to use indirect tactics that may be harder to detect. For example, if a woman shows up at an event, the man she is interested in may not even notice her.

Thus far, research on women stalkers is sparse. In clinical samples of female stalkers, it has been found that women may be more likely to engage in same-sex stalking and stranger stalking than men. But, overall, few differences between male and female stalkers have been found (Purcell, Pathé, & Mullen, 2001). In another study, the only differences were that women were more likely to stalk to establish intimacy (i.e., courtship stalk) and were more likely to follow up on threats of violence with actual attempted violence than their male peers (Meloy & Boyd, 2003). Otherwise, aspects of stalking (intimacy-seeking, emotional experiences associated with stalking, intimates as primary targets, and likelihood of stalking behavior to lead to subsequent escalations in violence) were the same regardless of gender.

More research that considers both men and women victims and perpetrators is clearly needed in order to better delineate the gender differences or similarities in stalking behavior. Although controversial, it is possible that researchers will find overall similarities in frequency of stalking behaviors but may note that women's stalking behaviors are perceived by men as less serious than men's and are less likely to involve injury threat. This pattern has been supported by research on intimate partner violence between men and women more generally (Archer, 2000; Makepeace, 1986). In addition, there may be gender-specific motivations for unwanted pursuit and stalking behaviors (Langhinrichsen-Rohling et al., 2002) even though equivalent frequencies of stalking exist in men and women.

CLINICAL IMPLICATIONS OF STALKING

Stalking can have multiple psychosocial implications for those experiencing it. Much stalking-related behavior does not involve physical violence, but there is some risk of death for those exposed to severe and violent stalking (McFarlane et al., 2002). Individuals who are stalked may experience a variety of other mental and physical health-related consequences. Studies of the impact of being a victim of stalking are extremely limited, but it is generally thought that stalking victims experience many of the same physical and psychological consequences as those who have been severely battered (Frieze, 2005). These manifestations can range from physical limitations and chronic health problems to psychological symptoms of distress, depression, and anxiety (Golding, 1999). Stalking may yield these types of symptoms at levels in line with those suffering from posttraumatic stress disorder (PTSD; Kamphuis & Emmelkamp, 2001). Research also has shown other consequences among those who are stalked, including intense fear, missed workdays, having to move to another community, lost income, and lost relationships with others (Sheridan, 2006; Tjaden & Thoennes, 1998).

Much of the empirical research on the psychological effects of being stalked has focused on female victims. In one such study, Mechanic, Uhlmansiek, Weaver, and Resick (2002) extended this work on psychological sequelae of stalking by comparing the mental health symptoms of abused women who were stalked relentlessly with abused women who had very low levels of stalking. They found that those with relentless forms of stalking had more severe symptoms of both PTSD and depressive symptoms. But PTSD-related impairment was extremely high for both groups of women victimized by stalking. Like those who experience severe battering, those who are exposed to stalking may fear future violence and stalking even after the behaviors have remitted (Bennett, Goodman, & Dutton, 1999). This fear may cause further repercussions for other biopsychosocial aspects of health functioning, such as individuals' social relationships and support, as well as their lifestyles in general. Victims are often compelled to give up social activities or even change their address (Mullen & Pathé, 1994).

Limited research has explored the psychological impact of stalking among men as well as women. For instance, using data from the NVAW Survey, Davis et al. (2002) examined men and women who were stalked (i.e., experiencing stalking behaviors on more than one occasion and at least somewhat fearful). They found that, regardless of gender, those who were stalked had similar negative mental health consequences (i.e., more depression, injury, and substance use). Clearly, gender differences in the vulnerability to the effects of stalking should be examined further. Certainly, like partner violence more generally, there may be gender differences in the risk for injury and other consequences (e.g., Williams & Frieze, 2005b). It may be that men and women have different physical and psychological reactions to experiencing persistent pursuit and stalking behaviors from others. Future research is needed on the multiple consequences of stalking as well as how to deal with those consequences. Further, there may be variability in how individuals interpret stalking behaviors as well as how they respond, with some being more sensitive than others. Specific aspects of stalking behaviors may make them meaningful for victims' mental health. And, like the finding that aggressive behaviors can be interpreted as a sign of caring during courtship, some individuals may continue to believe that to be true, whereas others may come to see the behaviors as unwanted and unhealthy.

Mental health–related symptoms of stalking have obvious clinical relevance. In addition, victims of stalking may have unmet support-related needs. People who experience stalking may not know where to turn. While there are rape crisis centers and National Domestic Violence hotlines, there are few stalking-specific resources available (for an exception, see the Survivors of Stalking Web site). Individuals may not classify themselves as victims of domestic violence if they are being stalked, and, indeed, many are not stalked within the context of abusive relationships. Thus, labeling issues may prevent stalking survivors from seeking related victim advocacy resources. In addition, although research has not yet examined the social consequences of stalking, those who are pursued by their former intimates may be reluctant to seek out their informal support network. These individuals may fear repercussions from their estranged partners toward their friends and family, or they may fear social rejection from their network members (Williams & Mickelson, in press). Individuals found in clinical settings may be in even more need of a variety of social support, including informational, instrumental, and emotional.

Risk of stalking and fear of future abuse also may enter the clinical relationship. Clinicians may need to be particularly sensitive to these risks as well as to the needs of those (particularly women) who are terminating relationships. It is likely that ex-partners may attempt behaviors that mirror the persistence or stalking-type behaviors used during courtship that in that context had been successful in attracting the partner. However, now in the context of a terminated relationship, these behaviors are unwanted and potentially dangerous. Thus, issues of stalking need direct attention and assessment by clinicians whose clients are in troubled intimate relationships.

REFERENCES

Archer, J. (2000). Sex differences in aggression between heterosexual partners: A meta-analytic review. *Psychological Bulletin, 126,* 651–680.

Bennett, L., Goodman, L., & Dutton, M. A. (1999). Systemic obstacles to the criminal prosecution of a battering partner. *Journal of Interpersonal Violence, 14,* 761–772.

Billingham, R. E. (1987). Courtship violence: The patterns of conflict resolution strategies across seven levels of emotional commitment. *Family Relations: Journal of Applied Family and Child Studies, 36,* 283–289.

Bookwala, J., Frieze, I. H., & Grote, N. K. (1994). Love, aggression and satisfaction in dating relationships. *Journal of Social and Personal Relationships, 11,* 625–632.

Brewster, M. P. (2003). Power and control dynamics in prestalking and stalking situations. *Journal of Family Violence, 18,* 207–217.

Burgess, A. W., Baker, T., Greening, D., Hartman, C. R., Burgess, A. G., Douglas, J. E., et al. (1997). Stalking behaviors within domestic violence. *Journal of Family Violence, 12,* 389–403.

Burgess, A. W., Harner, H., Baker, T., Hartman, C. R., & Lole, C. (2001). Batterers' stalking patterns. *Journal of Family Violence, 16,* 309–321.

Burt, M. R. (1980). Cultural myths and supports for rape. *Journal of Personality and Social Psychology, 38,* 217–230.

Campbell, J. C. (1992). "If I can't have you, no one can": Power and control in homicide of female partners. In J. Radford & D. H. Russell (Eds.), *Intimate femicide: The politics of woman killing* (pp. 99–113). New York: Twayne.

Coleman, F. L. (1997). Stalking behavior and the cycle of domestic violence. *Journal of Interpersonal Violence, 12,* 420–432.

Davis, K. E., Ace, A., & Andra, M. (2002). Stalking perpetrators and psychological maltreatment of partners: Anger-jealousy, attachment insecurity, need for control, and break-up context. In K. E. Davis & I. H. Frieze (Eds.), *Stalking: Perspectives on victims and perpetrators* (pp. 353–375). New York: Springer.

Davis, K. E., Coker, A. L., & Sanderson, M. (2002). Physical and mental health effects of being stalked for men and women. *Violence and Victims, 17,* 429–443.

Davis, K. E., & Frieze, I. H. (2002). Research on stalking: What do we know and where do we go? In K. E. Davis & I. H. Frieze (Eds.), *Stalking: Perspectives on victims and perpetrators* (pp. 353–375). New York: Springer.

Douglas, K. S., & Dutton, D. G. (2001). Assessing the link between stalking and domestic violence. *Aggression and Violent Behavior, 6,* 519–546.

Dunn, J. L. (1993). What love has to do with it? The cultural construction of emotion and sorority women's responses to forcible interaction. *Social Problems, 46,* 440–459.

Dutton, D. G., & Nicholls, T. L. (2005). A critical review of the gender paradigm in domestic violence research and theory: Part I—Theory and data. *Aggression and Violent Behavior, 10,* 680–714.

Frieze, I. H. (2005). *Hurting the one you love: Violence in relationships.* Pacific Grove, CA: Wadsworth.

Frieze, I. H., & Davis, K. (2000). Introduction to stalking and obsessive behaviors in everyday life: Assessments of victims and perpetrators. *Violence and Victims, 15,* 3–6.

Golding, J. M. (1999). Intimate partner violence as a risk factor for mental disorders: A meta-analysis. *Journal of Family Violence, 14,* 99–132.

Greenfield, L. A., Rand, M. R., Craven, D., Flaus, P. A., Perkins, C. A., Ringel, C., et al. (1998). *Violence by intimates: Analysis of data on crimes by current or former spouses, boyfriends, and girlfriends* (NCJ-167237). Washington, DC: Department of Justice, Bureau of Justice Statistics.

Hall, D. M. (1998). The victims of stalking. In J. R. Meloy (Ed.), *The psychology of stalking* (pp. 115–136). San Diego, CA: Academic Press.

Johnson, M. P., & Ferraro, K. J. (2000). Research on domestic violence in the 1990s: Making distinctions. *Journal of Marriage and the Family, 62,* 948–963.

Kahn, A. S., Jackson, J., Kully, C., Badger, K., & Halvorsen, J. (2003). Calling it rape: Differences in experiences of women who do and do not label their sexual assault as rape. *Psychology of Women Quarterly, 27,* 233–242.

Kamphuis, J. H., & Emmelkamp, P. M. G. (2001). Traumatic distress among support-seeking female victims of stalking. *American Journal of Psychiatry, 158,* 795–798.

Langhinrichsen-Rohling, J., Palarea, R. E., Cohen, J., & Rohling, M. L. (2002). Breaking up is hard to do: Unwanted pursuit behaviors following the dissolution of a romantic relationship. In K. E. Davis & I. H. Frieze (Eds.), *Stalking: Perspectives on victims and perpetrators* (pp. 212–236). New York: Springer.

Lloyd, S. A. (1991). The darkside of courtship: Violence and sexual exploitation. *Family Relations: Interdisciplinary Journal of Applied Family Studies, 40,* 14–20.

Logan, T. K., Leukefeld, C., & Walker, B. (2002). Stalking as a variant of intimate violence: Implications from a young adult sample. In K. E. Davis & I. H. Frieze (Eds.), *Stalking: Perspectives on victims and perpetrators* (pp. 265–291). New York: Springer.

Lowney, K. S., & Best, J. (1995). Stalking strangers and lovers: Changing media typifications of a new crime problem. In J. Best (Ed.), *Images of issues: Typifying contemporary social problems* (2nd ed., pp. 33–57). New York: Aldine de Gruyter.

Mahoney, M. R. (1991). Legal images of battered women: Redefining the issue of separation. *Michigan Law Review, 90,* 1–94.

Makepeace, J. M. (1986). Gender differences in courtship violence victimization. *Family Relations: Journal of Applied Family and Child Studies, 35,* 383–388.

McFarlane, J., Campbell, J. C., & Watson, K. (2002). Intimate partner stalking and femicide: Urgent implications for women's safety. *Behavioral Sciences and the Law, 20,* 51–68.

McFarlane, J., Willson, P., Malecha, A., & Lemmey, D. (2000). Intimate partner violence: A gender comparison. *Journal of Interpersonal Violence, 15,* 158–169.

Mechanic, M. B., Uhlmansiek, M. H., Weaver, T. L., & Resick, P. A. (2002). The impact of severe stalking experienced by acutely battered women: An examination of violence, psychological symptoms, and strategic responding. In K. E. Davis & I. H. Frieze (Eds.), *Stalking: Perspectives on victims and perpetrators* (pp. 89–111). New York: Springer.

Mechanic, M. B., Weaver, T. L., & Resick, P. A. (2002). Intimate partner violence and stalking behavior: Exploration of patterns and correlates in a sample of acutely battered women. In K. E. Davis & I. H. Frieze (Eds.), *Stalking: Perspectives on victims and perpetrators* (pp. 62–88). New York: Springer.

Meloy, J. R., & Boyd, C. (2003). Female stalkers and their victims. *Journal of the American Academy of Psychiatry and the Law, 31*, 211–219.

Melton, H. C. (2000). Stalking: A review of the literature and directions for the future. *Criminal Justice Review, 25*, 246–261.

Mullen, P. E., & Pathé, M. (1994). Stalking and pathologies of love. *Australian and New Zealand Journal of Psychiatry, 28*, 469–477.

National Institute of Justice. (1993). *Project to develop a model anti-stalking code for states* (National Criminal Justice Reference Service No. 144477). Washington, DC: Author.

Office for Victims of Crime. (2002). Strengthening anti-stalking statutes. *Legal Series Bulletin, 1*, 1–5.

Palarea, R. E., Zona, M. A., Lane, J. C., & Langhinrichsen-Rohling, J. (1999). The dangerous nature of intimate relationship stalking: Threats, violence, and associated risk factors. *Behavioral Sciences and the Law, 17*, 269–283.

Purcell, R., Pathé, M., & Mullen, P. E. (2001). A study of women who stalk. *American Journal of Psychiatry, 158*(12), 2056–2060.

Rose, S., & Frieze, I. H. (1993). Young singles' contemporary dating scripts. *Sex Roles, 28*, 499–509.

Sheridan, L. (2006, March). The cost of stalking. In H. C. Sinclair (Chair), *Advances in research on stalking*. Panel conducted at the meeting of the American Psychology-Law Society, St. Petersburg, FL.

Sinclair, H. C., Borgida, E., & Collins, W. A. (2002, June). Exploring the antecedents and consequences of courtship persistence. In K. Davis (Chair), *Stalking and courtship: Classifications and social-personality predictors*. Symposium conducted at the Society for the Psychological Study of Social Issues Conference, Toronto, Ontario.

Sinclair, H. C., Chan, A., & Borgida, E. (2003, March). The thin blue line between love and hate: Stalking myths, romanticism and legal outcomes. In K. Davis (Chair), *Stalking research*. Symposium conducted at the Southeastern Psychological Association conference, New Orleans, LA.

Sinclair, H. C., & Frieze, I. H. (2002). Initial courtship behavior and stalking: How should we draw the line? In K. E. Davis & I. H. Frieze (Eds.), *Stalking: Perspectives on victims and perpetrators* (pp. 186–211). New York: Springer.

Sinclair, H. C., & Frieze, I. H. (2005). When courtship persistence becomes intrusive pursuit: A comparison of rejecter and pursuer perspectives of unrequited attraction. *Sex Roles, 52*, 839–852.

Spitzberg, B. H. (2002). The tactical topography of stalking victimization and management. *Trauma, Violence, and Abuse, 3*, 261–288.

Spitzberg, B. H., & Cupach, W. R. (1998). *The dark side of close relationships*. Mahwah, NJ: Lawrence Erlbaum Associates.

Spitzberg, B. H., & Cupach, W. R. (2000). Obsessive relational intrusion: Incidence, perceived severity and coping. *Violence and Victims, 15*(4), 357–372.

Spitzberg, B. H., Nicastro, A.M., & Cousins, A. V. (1998). Exploring the interactional phenomenon of stalking and obsessive relational intrusion. *Communication Reports, 11*, 33–47.

St. George, R. (2001). *Mending the Scared Hoop: STOP Violence Against Indian Women*. Duluth, MN: Technical Assistance Project. Retrieved from http://www.vaw.umn.edu/FinalDocuments/stalking.htm

Straus, M. A., Gelles, R. J., & Steinmetz, S. K. (1980). *Behind closed doors: Violence in the American family.* New York: Anchor.

Tjaden, P., & Thoennes, N. (1998). *Stalking in America: Findings from the National Violence Against Women Survey.* Washington, DC: National Institute of Justice and Centers for Disease Control and Prevention.

Walker, L. E., & Meloy, J. R. (1998). Stalking and domestic violence. In J. R. Meloy (Ed.), *The psychology of stalking: Clinical and forensic perspectives* (pp. 139–161). San Diego, CA: Academic Press.

White, J., Kowalski, R. M., Lyndon, A., & Valentine, S. (2002). An integrative contextual developmental model of male stalking. In K. E. Davis & I. H. Frieze (Eds.), *Stalking: Perspectives on victims and perpetrators* (pp. 163–185). New York: Springer.

Williams, S. L., & Frieze, I. H. (2005a). Courtship behaviors, relationship violence, and breakup persistence in college men and women. *Psychology of Women Quarterly, 29,* 248–257.

Williams, S. L., & Frieze, I. H. (2005b). Patterns of violent relationships, psychosocial distress, and marital satisfaction in a national sample of men and women. *Sex Roles, 52,* 771–784.

Williams, S. L., & Mickelson, K. M. (in press). *A paradox of social support and social rejection among the stigmatized.*

Wilson, M., & Daly, M. (1993). Spousal homicide risk and estrangement. *Violence and Victims, 8,* 3–16.

CHAPTER 6

Couple Violence: A New Look at Some Old Fallacies

Patricia Noller and Laurance Robillard

In this chapter, we wish to focus on three issues that we see as key to understanding couple violence. They are all issues where we see the data as contradicting the claims of many feminist writers. The first issue is the focus on violence *against* women as the only violence of importance and the tendency to ignore or downplay violence perpetrated *by* women. The second issue involves the tendency to focus on a single explanation for violence, namely, patriarchy. We call this issue the levels-of-analysis issue and believe strongly that we cannot come to a full understanding of couple violence unless we take into account various levels of analysis (individual, couple, family, and society). The third issue involves the assumption of a universal potential for violence in men.

WOMEN AND VIOLENCE

Although feminists such as Walker (1989) acknowledge that women can be involved in the abuse of other family members, they do not believe that such abuse should be the concern of researchers and clinicians, who should instead focus their attention on "the underbelly of interpersonal violence . . . the socialized androcentric need for power" (p. 695), which they see as central to the presence of violence in the world.

As Bograd (1988) notes, the focus of feminists is at the societal level, with violence against women seen as the product of a patriarchal society: "The reality of domination at the social level is the most crucial factor contributing to and maintaining wife abuse at the personal level" (p. 14). One reason that feminist scholars argue that researchers and policymakers should pay little attention to violence perpetrated by females is that such violence is seen as a lifesaving reaction of women abused by their male partners (Dobash & Dobash, 1988; Walker, 1989). The data on which this proposition is based, however, generally come from shelter samples and involve interviews with battered women, with no data provided by male partners. Such data can be considered unrepresentative of the broader sample of couples involved in violent relationships. Kwong, Bartholomew, and Dutton (1999) found that a substantial amount of the female-perpetrated violence in their study was not self-defense and that women not only initiated violence but also were often the sole perpetrators. In fact, there is now considerable evidence that females can be as violent as men. For example, Stets and Straus (1990b) found that unidirectional female intimate violence was more common than male unidirectional violence. In addition, in a large community sample, Straus, Gelles, and Steinmetz (1980) showed that as many females as males were violent to their partners (for further discussion of this issue, see Dutton, 1994; Dutton & Nicholls, 2005).

In fact, there is now little doubt that women are involved in the perpetration of violence, for whatever reason (Fiebert & Gonzalez, 1997; Graham-Kevan & Archer, 2003; Kwong et al., 1999; O'Leary, 2000; O'Leary, Barling, Arias, & Rosenbaum, 1989; Straus, 1997, 1999; Sugarman & Hotaling, 1989). Straus (1999) claims that at that time there were more than 100 studies indicating that men and women engaged in similar rates of domestic violence. Of course, it is also important to acknowledge, as does Straus, that because of size and strength differences in males and females, there is a lower probability of injury for men assaulted by women than for women assaulted by men.

In the Kwong et al. (1999) study, for example, men and women reported similar rates of both participation and victimization. In addition, Sugarman and Hotaling (1989) showed that across 21 studies of dating violence, women were more likely to perpetrate violence than were men. In their study of 21-year-old members of a cohort assessed regularly from birth, Magdol, Moffitt, Caspi, Newman, Fagan, et al. (1997) found that many more women than men reported being violent with an intimate partner. Of course, it is not enough to know which sex is most likely to report being violent; there are also important questions about the seriousness of the violence, the extent to which violence is resorted to only for self-defense, and which sex is most likely to suffer injury. We discuss these issues further later in this chapter.

Johnson and Ferraro's Typology of Couple Violence

As other authors in this volume (e.g., Graham-Kevan, chapters 4 and 7) have pointed out, Johnson and Ferraro (2000) have produced a typology of violent behavior in couples. They distinguish, in particular, between common couple violence (now known as situational violence) and intimate terrorism (what is generally called battering). Johnson and Leone (2005) argue that intimate terrorism is "embedded in a general pattern of controlling behaviors indicating that the perpetrator is attempting to exert general control over his partner" (p. 322). Situational violence, on the other hand, is related to specific conflicts where the argument escalates into a violent incident. In these cases, there is no evidence of an overarching desire for control over the partner. They make the case that the two types of violence should be defined not in terms of their nature or frequency but solely in terms of the level of control maintained by the perpetrator over the partner. They argue that in intimate terrorism, even relatively innocuous aggressive behaviors (such as a "dirty" look) can be very controlling, particularly if there have been earlier instances of severe abuse.

Johnson and Ferraro (2000) argued that the reason that the findings of feminist researchers and family conflict researchers such as Straus and his colleagues (Straus, 1990; Gelles & Straus, 1988; Straus & Gelles, 1986) are so different is that the samples they use come from very different populations. They claimed that intimate terrorism or battering is perpetrated largely by males and found in shelter and crime data, whereas situational violence is much more likely to be mutual, with both partners engaging in violent behavior as the conflict escalates. Situational couple violence is more likely to be found in general community samples.

Similarly, Straus (1997) criticizes two fallacies: the clinical fallacy and the representative fallacy. The clinical fallacy involves the "unwarranted assumption by clinical researchers that the predominance of assaults by men [in their studies] applies to the population as a whole" (p. 216), and the representative fallacy "largely stems from survey researchers' assumptions that their findings on rates of partner assault by men and women apply to cases known to the police and to shelters" (p. 216). As O'Leary (2000) notes, it is important for researchers to specify the limited applicability of their research in terms of the populations to which they do or do not apply.

Johnson and Ferraro's (2000) claims have been supported by research from other research groups. For example, Graham-Kevan and Archer (2003) found clear evidence for the two distinct types of abuse and also were able to show that intimate terrorism occurred predominantly in the shelter sample and that situational (or common couple) violence occurred predominantly in the samples not selected for their violent behavior. In addition, they also found that violence was most likely to be perpetrated by males in the shelter sample and to be mutual or sex symmetric in the other samples. Using self-reports of aggression in a community sample, however, Graham-Kevan and Archer (in press) found that a larger proportion of women than men who were involved in physically aggressive relationships could be labeled as intimate terrorists and that men were more likely than women to report that they were victims of intimate terrorism.

Violence and Injury

As noted earlier, Kwong et al. (1999) found not only that men and women reported perpetrating similar levels of violence but also that women initiated violence and could even be the sole perpetrators. A number of other studies have found similar results, with several showing more violence perpetrated by women than by men (Bensley, MacDonald, Van Eenwyk, Simmons, & Ruggles, 2000; Douglas & Straus, 2003; Hines & Saudino, 2003; Magdol, Moffitt, Caspi, Newman, Fagan, et al., 1997). Nevertheless, there is evidence that women are generally more likely to be injured as a result of couple violence than are men (Straus, 1999; Stets & Straus, 1990a), although the main reason seems to be that men tend to be physically larger and stronger than women (Felson, 1996). For example, Kwong and Bartholomew (1998) asked men and women about the severity of their injuries and whether they still experienced pain on the day following the abuse. Women were more likely in that study to report severe injuries and more likely to report ongoing pain.

O'Leary (2000) highlights the evidence that women are more likely than men to sustain injury as a result of domestic violence across a range of samples, including dating couples (Foshee, 1996), community samples (Stets & Straus, 1990a), samples obtained through marital therapists (Cascardi, Langhinrichsen, & Vivian, 1992), and samples where treatment has been mandated by the courts. In a meta-analysis of a large number of studies, Archer (2000) also found that men were more likely to inflict injury on a partner than were women. As Straus (1997) argues, "Because of the greater physical, financial and emotional injury suffered by women, they are the predominant victims" (p. 219). Straus (1999) also makes the point that when women assault their partners in a relatively minor way, they may put themselves at risk of a more violent response from their male partners in retaliation.

Nevertheless, it is important to note that this issue is not entirely one-sided. For example, there is evidence in some studies that more women than men engage in severe violence (Magdol, Moffitt, Caspi, Newman, Fagan, et al., 1997). These authors found that for both minor and severe physical violence, the percentage of participants reporting perpetration of violence was higher for women regardless of whether reports were by self or partner and that the percentage of women perpetrating severe violence was three times the percentage of men. In fact, women have been found to engage in more severe violence and cause greater injury not only in New Zealand but also in Scotland and Singapore (Douglas & Straus, 2003).

In addition, Morse (1995) found that females were higher than males on the seriously violent items on the Conflict Tactics Scales (kick, hit or bite with fist, hit with object, threaten with knife or gun, and use knife or gun). These data suggest that men are highly likely to be injured. Perhaps some women are prepared to compensate for their lack of physical strength by using weapons of various types (Douglas & Straus, 2003). Nevertheless, as Goodyear-Smith and Laidlaw (1999) note, there may be little relationship between perpetrator intent and outcomes, with many physically aggressive acts that were meant to hurt not causing any serious damage and acts that were not really intended to damage the victim accidentally causing serious injury (e.g., if a push leads to a victim banging his or her head on a hard surface). Where weapons are used, however, it would seem highly likely that the intent is to injure.

Other data, particularly from the work of Ehrensaft and colleagues, compared nonclinically and clinically abusive relationships. Women in both types of relationships had aggressive personalities and were diagnosed with conduct disorder as adolescents.

Men in clinically abusive relationships, but not those in nonclinically abusive relationships, tended to have experienced mental health problems in childhood and adolescence, along with personality deviance.

This study provides evidence for psychopathology as a predictor of partner abuse. In terms of consequences, when men were involved in clinically abusive relationships, the helath consequences for their female partners tended to be serious.(Ehrensaft, Moffitt, & Caspi, 2004).

THE LEVELS-OF-ANALYSIS ISSUE

Mauricio and Gormley (2001) comment on the unidimensionality of many approaches to the origins of male violence against women. As these authors point out, the feminist position on violence against women has been criticized because it fails to explain why all men are not batterers and because it fails to take account of the "contribution of individual psychological level variables that have been found to differentiate batterers from nonabusive men" (p. 1067). We consider some of these differences later in this section.

Similarly, Dutton (1994) also argued against single-factor explanations, whether they focus on sociobiology (Daly, Wilson, & Weghorst, 1982), psychiatric disorders (Faulk, 1974), or patriarchy (Dobash &Dobash, 1979; Yllo, 1988). Dutton (1994) argued that "patriarchy must interact with psychological variables to account for the great variation in power-violence data" (p. 167). Dutton (1988) takes the position that no single-level explanation provides an adequate explanation for violence against women and argues for a nested ecological theory that proposes that such violence stems from the interactive effects of the broader culture, the particular subculture in which the couple is involved, as well as family and individual factors. In fact, Dutton (1994) goes further in claiming that feminist analysis has been "characterized by broad statements about male privilege and male dominance in the face of clear evidence for heterogeneous male behaviors in intimate relationships" (pp. 169–70). We now present research in support of the relevance of individual factors (such as personality and psychopathology) and dyadic factors such as communication to understanding couple violence. We also explore some of the data that argue against the feminist position that focuses on patriarchy as the prime cause of couple violence.

Individual-Level Issues

Although, as noted earlier, feminists tend to argue against a focus on individual factors because they are seen as exonerating abusive men of responsibility for their violent behavior (Bograd, 1988; Goldner, Penn, Sheinberg, & Walker, 1990), there is considerable evidence that individual differences play a part in the etiology of violent behavior (Holtzworth-Munroe, Bates, Smutzler, & Sandin, 1997). Holtzworth-Munroe et al. claim that research comparing violent and nonviolent men indicates quite clearly that psychological symptoms are more evident in violent men as a group than in nonviolent men. Researchers have explored individual differences in personality, psychopathology, and attachment security. In the next two sections, we focus on the individual factors that are correlated with partner violence. First, we will look at correlates for men and then at those for women, keeping in mind, as we discuss later, that some researchers (e.g., Magdol, Moffitt, Caspi, Newman, Fagan, et al., 1997) have found similar antecedents for men and women.

Types of Violent Men

A number of researchers have developed typologies of violent men (Gottman et al., 1995; Holtzworth-Munroe & Stuart, 1994; Tweed & Dutton, 1998). In general, three subtypes have been found and have been labeled overcontrolled-dependent, impulsive-borderline, and instrumental-antisocial (e.g., Holtzworth-Munroe & Stuart, 1994). Gottman and his colleagues focused on two groups who differed in their physiological reactivity. They labeled these two groups antisocial (type 1) and impulsive (type 2). The antisocial group tended to use violence in nonintimate relationships as well as with their wives and displayed suppressed physiological responding during arguments with their wives. They also scored higher in terms of sadistic aggression and lower on dependency than the type 2 men. The impulsive type were more reactive physiologically in arguments with their wives and were violent only with their wives.

Tweed and Dutton (1998) found personality, psychopathology, and attachment style differences between these two groups of abusive men and a control group. The antisocial abusers showed evidence of aggression, narcissism, antisocial behavior, and preoccupied attachment and were involved in more severe violence. The impulsive group showed evidence of being passive-aggressive and having borderline personality organization and high chronic anger and either preoccupied or fearful attachment. What these attachment findings suggest is that the antisocial men have a negative view of themselves and that the impulsive men have a negative view of both themselves and others (Bartholomew & Horowitz, 1991). We also know that those with a negative view of self tend to be more insecure about their relationships and more jealous, suggesting that these men may be using violence as a way of making sure that their partner does not leave the relationship (Bowlby, 1988).

Holtzworth-Munroe, Stuart, and Hutchinson (1997) compared violent distressed husbands with nonviolent distressed and nonviolent nondistressed husbands across two studies involving different measures. They also found evidence for differences in attachment, with the violent husbands more insecure and preoccupied than their nonviolent counterparts. In addition, they were more dependent on their wives and were more jealous and less trusting of their marriages.

Roberts and Noller (1998), in a sample of dating couples, found evidence for attachment style and specifically anxiety over abandonment as a predictor of violence in both men and women. Both men and women were more likely to use violence if they were insecure about their relationships and feared that their partners might abandon them. In an analysis to explore the interaction effects of partners' attachment on violence toward the partners, these researchers found that the association between individuals' anxiety over abandonment and their perpetration of couple violence was strengthened if the partner was uncomfortable with emotionally intimate relationships.

There is some evidence to suggest that hypersensitivity to rejection can set off violent behavior in men toward their partners (Downey, Feldman, & Ayduk, 2000). Downey and Feldman (1996) and Downey et al. (2000)

drew selectively on both attributional and attachment perspectives in proposing that rejection sensitivity, a cognitive-affective processing disposition (Mischel, 1999), explains why some men may respond violently to mundane situations of rejection, whereas other men do not. According to this model, rejection-sensitive individuals are conceptualized as those who tend to expect rejection to perceive it even when it's not intended, and to overreact both emotionally and behaviorally when they notice any sign of rejection (Downey & Feldman, 1996).

Downey and Feldman (1996) hypothesize that rejection sensitivity originates in childhood and is based on rejecting experiences from important others (e.g., parents and peers). In addition, cultural, familial, environmental, and gender-specific experiences may produce differences in the rejection-sensitive person's expectations (anxious vs. angry) and behavioral reactions (avoidance vs. intimacy seeking) to perceived rejection in social situations (Levy, Ayduk, & Downey, 2001). Furthermore, this model proposes that the rejection-sensitive person becomes hostile not in general but specifically in reaction to potential rejection from a significant or important other (Mischel, 1999). Hence, this disposition will be most noticeable in situations and contexts where rejection is possible.

Across a number of studies, this model has been linked to insecure attachment in adulthood; distressed and troubled romantic relationships that end in failure, jealousy, controlling behavior, and partner aggression (in adolescent men); and withdrawal of support, hostility, and vulnerability to depression (in adolescent women) (Downey & Feldman, 1996; Downey, Freitas, Michaelis, & Khouri, 1998; Downey, Khouri, & Feldman, 1997). There is also evidence that rejection-sensitive men with a stronger masculine gender identity are more angered by hypothetical scenarios of rejection by their partners than are rejection-sensitive men with a weaker masculine identity (Ayduk, Downey, Testa, Yen, & Shoda, 1999, cited in Downey et al., 2000).

These findings suggest that this subtype of rejection-sensitive men may be more prone to aggressive behavior when confronted with potential rejection (Ayduk et al., 1999). In addition, high levels of rejection sensitivity predict intimate violence in college men who are highly invested (or intimacy seeking) in romantic relationships (Downey et al., 2000). These findings are consistent with the marital violence literature in illustrating that physically aggressive men can become particularly reactive to perceived threats of rejection (Dutton & Browning, 1988; Holtzworth-Munroe & Hutchinson, 1993). Furthermore, the data support Levy et al.'s (2001) rejection sensitivity model in establishing a link between expectations of rejection and cognitive-affective and behavioral overreactions such as anger, hurt, and violent behavior.

We are currently running a study that will test whether the link between rejection sensitivity and aggressive behavior is mediated or moderated by the rejection-sensitive individual's readiness to perceive hostile intent in his or her partner's negative behaviors. Preliminary results have provided support for a mediational model whereby hostile attributions (as measured by two attribution measures: the Negative Intentions Questionnaire [Holtzworth-Munroe & Hutchinson, 1993] and the Relationship Attribution Measure [Fincham & Bradbury, 1992]) mediate the relationship between rejection sensitivity (as measured by an amended version of the Rejection Sensitivity Questionnaire [Downey & Feldman, 1996]) and physically aggressive behavior (as measured by the Conflict Tactics Scales [Straus, 1979]) in rejection-sensitive individuals. In other words, our initial results support a mediational model whereby rejection sensitivity can lead to an individual attributing hostile intentions to his or her partner, and these hostile attributions increase the likelihood of relationship violence.

Types of Violent Women

Schoffrel (2004) reported a study in which two therapists made observations of a group of 12 female perpetrators of domestic violence as well as of two groups of men. There were three ways in which female perpetrators were seen as different from male perpetrators. First, females tended to be involved in compulsive and premature disclosure in the group, whereas men disclosed much less and more slowly. Second, men tended to see themselves more clearly as either perpetrators or victims, whereas women had more ambivalent self-perceptions and saw themselves as both victims and perpetrators. Finally, the women tended to devalue themselves, whereas the men tended to devalue their partners. It is important to keep in mind here that in the study by Magdol, Moffitt, Caspi, and Silva (1997), perpetrators and victims were largely the same people, suggesting that a lot of violence in couples involves both partners as perpetrators and victims.

Abel (2001) compared women categorized as batterers and attending a batterer intervention program with women categorized as victims and receiving victim services in a shelter situation. They found that both groups of women reported high levels of trauma symptomatology. These women differed in terms of their depression levels and levels of anxiety, sleep disturbance, dissociation, and posttraumatic sexual abuse trauma, with women in the group labeled as victims having significantly higher levels of all the measures of trauma symptomatology than those women labeled as batterers. It is important to note that the women in the batterer group are experiencing higher levels of trauma than those identified as nonabused in other research (e.g., Briere & Runtz, 1989).

Babcock, Miller, and Siard (2003) categorized women perpetrators as either generally violent or violent only with their partners. They found clear differences between these two groups of women. Generally, violent women reported that they were more physically abusive and more psychologically abusive than the other women, and they reported engaging in more severely violent behaviors and injuring their partners more during the previous year. They also reported that they were more likely to be violent in order to control the partner or to "push the partner's buttons" than did the other women, indicating that men are not the only ones who use violence for power and control. These women were also more likely to externalize blame for their violence onto their partners or claim that they themselves were out of control. Both groups of women reported being more likely to be violent in situations of verbal abuse or jealousy.

Thus, it seems clear that there are a number of individual factors related to the perpetration of violence. Personality factors such as aggression, attachment style, and rejection sensitivity, and aspects of psychopathology such as borderline personality organization all can play a role in the perpetration of violence in couple relationships. It is also interesting to note that for both men and women, perpetrators can be divided into those who are violent in a range of situations and those who are violent only with their intimate partners.

Dyadic Factors

Communication patterns are among the most frequently studied correlates of couple violence at the dyadic level, and there is considerable evidence that communication patterns predict the likelihood of violence. Anglin and Holtzworth-Munroe (1997) compared the responses of maritally violent and nonviolent spouses to a set of hypothetical marital and nonmarital problems. Spouses were asked how they would respond to these situations: what they would say and what they would do. They found that violent spouses tended to produce less competent responses than nonviolent spouses for both types of situations, suggesting a global deficit in communication skills. Further, when first responses were compared across the groups, the violently distressed spouses seemed to have particular difficulty with the marital situations, and this was true for both husbands and wives.

Demand/Withdraw Communication

There is also considerable evidence for particular patterns of demand/ withdraw communication (Christensen, 1988) being associated with couple violence (for a review, see Eldridge & Christensen, 2002). In a self-report study, Babcock, Waltz, Jacobson, and Gottman (1993) showed that violent distressed married couples reported significantly higher levels of husband-demand/wife-withdraw than nonviolent distressed couples, but there were no differences between the groups for wife-demand/husband-withdraw. On the other hand, when they compared the distressed violent and nonviolent couples with the nondistressed couples, both types of demand/withdraw were reported more frequently by the distressed groups. In an observational study of the same couples, Babcock et al. found that the violent distressed husbands engaged in more demanding behavior than their nonviolent counterparts.

Holtzworth-Munroe, Smutzler, and Stuart (1998) carried out a similar study but included a nondistressed violent group as well as the other three groups. They replicated the findings of the Babcock et al. (1993) study but were able to add the finding that the nondistressed violent couples did not display high levels of husband-demand/wife-withdraw. They suggest that the husband-demand/wife-withdraw pattern may be particularly characteristic of batterers. A study by Berns, Jacobson, and Gottman (1999), however, found that batterers exhibited more withdrawing behavior than nonviolent husbands but that battered wives were less likely to withdraw in response to their husbands' demands than wives in nonviolent marriages.

Straus (1999) has argued that in situations where men withdraw continually, women may resort to violence in order to gain the attention of the withdrawing (or withdrawn) partner: "When faced with a man who withdraws and refuses to talk about a problem . . . women may resort to slapping, kicking and throwing things in an attempt to coerce the partner to attend to the issue." (p. 34). Nevertheless, women have to take responsibility for their decision to use violence to achieve a goal, just as men are expected to.

Conflict Behavior

Leonard and Roberts (1998) found that four measures of conflict behavior were associated with physical aggression in their study: Husband and wife anger expression were positively associated with aggression, husband problem solving was also positively associated with aggression, but wife problem solving was negatively associated with aggression. They suggest that the reason that husband problem solving was positively associated with aggression is that the measure used included both facilitative and demanding/controlling behaviors. It seems likely, given the evidence from other studies, that the husbands were being demanding and controlling. As we have seen earlier, however, women are also likely to use aggression to control their partners (Babcock et al., 2003), especially if they are violent in relationships other than the partner relationship.

In a study of married couples involving the sequential analysis of couple behaviors as well as measures of physiological responding, Noller and Roberts (2002) explored the association between one partner's behavior and the other partner's consequent arousal (within the next 30 seconds). We present here just a few significant findings from that study.

Overall, the temporal association between one individual's behavior and the partner's arousal was stronger for those in violent relationships. For example, those in violent relationships tended to be more reactive to the partner's invalidation (being insensitive and using criticisms and put-downs). These findings support Lloyd's (1990) contention that individuals in violent relationships may be hypersensitive to one another's negativity.

For males only, there was also an association between one partner's anxiety/arousal and own withdrawal. The degree of this linkage was marginally higher for males in violent relationships than for those in nonviolent relationships. This finding supports Gottman and Levenson's (1988) contention that men's withdrawal in conflict situations is related to their physiological arousal, although Gottman and Levenson did not explore this issue for those in violent relationships. It is also important to keep in mind, however, that work by Kiecolt-Glaser and colleagues (1996) failed to support Gottman and Levenson's finding.

Noller and Roberts (2002) also found evidence for women in nonviolent relationships being more likely than those in violent relationships to invalidate the partner following his withdrawal. Those in violent relationships, on the other hand, tended to reciprocate the partner's withdrawal, perhaps as a way of avoiding violence. Noller and Roberts suggested that the women in these relationships may even be relieved by the withdrawal of the violent partner. Given that the males in violent relationships tended to withdraw in response to their own anxiety, they may also be working at avoiding violence. In support of that conclusion, females in violent relationships also tended to withdraw in response to the partner's hostility.

It seems clear, then, that the behavior of the marital dyad is important in the etiology of violent behavior in couples. This is not to say that the perpetrator of the violence is not responsible. He or she makes the choice to become violent and must take responsibility for that behavior. The point we are trying to make here is that we cannot understand violent behavior by invoking single explanations, whether at the individual or at the societal level. We need a multilevel approach, and it is clear from the data presented in this section that the interaction of the couple is important to that understanding. In fact, Kwong et al. (1999) go so far as to suggest that, in dealing with couples where there is violence, efforts at improving the couple's communication may be more beneficial in the prevention of violence than focusing only on the violence.

The Societal Level

It is clear that feminists believe that the most crucial factor associated with violence against women is patriarchy, or male domination at the societal level. Dutton (1995) argues, however, that there are a number of empirical findings that are difficult to explain in terms of feminist theory. First, there is evidence that abuse is present at high levels in lesbian relationships (Lie & Gentlewarrier, 1991; Lie, Schilit, Bush, Montague, & Reyes, 1991; Renzetti, 1992). Lie et al. (1991) found that more than 50% of the large sample of lesbian women surveyed reported violence in their relationships. Lie et al. (1991) also found high levels of abuse in lesbian relationships, most of which was mutual. There is also evidence that rates of husband-to-wife abuse are lower in more patriarchal cultures (Sorenson & Telles, 1991), although this may be because these wives are more obedient and submissive. In addition, there is no linear correlation between male power in relationships and wife assault (Yllo & Straus, 1990). Finally, Dutton points to the heterogeneity of men's beliefs about women and how they should behave toward them (Yllo & Straus, 1990). (For further discussion of this point, see Dutton, 1995.)

MALE POTENTIAL FOR ABUSE

The feminist stance is generally anti-male since all men are seen as potential abusers with the goal of subordinating women and keeping them in an oppressed social position. As Walker (1989) notes, "The causes of men's violence against women include preservation of men's need for power and status" (p. 697). And, according to Bograd (1988), even those men who refrain from abusing their wives (most men according to the data) benefit from the subordination of women in the society.

It is interesting to note that Pagelow (1981) cites a description of abusive men based on the clinical work of Wayne Blackburn. According to this clinician, abusive men have very specific characteristics: They are aggressive on the outside but dependent on the inside; require rules that are clear and unambiguous; have very rigid ideas of masculinity, femininity, and gender roles; are authoritarian and patriarchal; use primitive defense mechanisms such as denial and projection; and generally come from violent backgrounds (p. 106). Men with these characteristics seem to be representative not of men in general but of a particular group of men.

The feminist stance is also antifamily, with marriage and family seen as promoting, maintaining, and supporting violence against women and wife abuse seen as "a predictable and common dimension of normal family life as it is currently structured in our society" (Bograd, 1988, p. 14). Although we have no problems with the feminist focus on validating the experience of women who suffer abuse from partners or on advocating for such victims, it does not seem appropriate to generalize from the experience of one group of families to all families (Straus, 1999) and to blame the institutions that have functioned in all societies for thousands of years rather than perversions of those institutions. After all, according to Straus (1999), the outmoded laws that allowed a man to use corporal punishment against his wife ceased to be recognized by courts in the 1870s. In addition, considerable gains have been made over more recent decades in terms of a greater emphasis on equality between partners in marriage and greater choices for women in terms of workforce participation, although it has to be said that not all the "changes" have been positive for all women or for all families.

Dobash and Dobash (1979) argue that "men who assault their wives are actually living up to cultural prescriptions that are cherished in Western society—aggressiveness, male dominance and female subordination—and they are using physical force as a means of enforcing that dominance" (p. 24). As Dutton (1995) comments, "Domination of women is viewed, from the feminist perspective, as a cultural prescription, and violence against women as a means to that end" (p. 568). Such claims bring us back to the point raised by Mauricio and Gormley (2001) and the question about why, if the feminist view is correct, all men do not batter.

Straus (1999) discusses community attitudes to violence against women. He argues that violence against women is seen as a crime when there is injury to the victim or when the perpetrator is an ex-partner rather than a current partner and therefore could be seen as having no right to inflict punishment. Such a finding suggests that there are some residual beliefs in the community that erring wives deserve punishment or at least that seeking to punish them is understandable, especially if they have been unfaithful. Straus sees this belief as left over from the common-law right of men to punish unfaithful wives. He also argues that society has become less tolerant of abuse by men but that there has been no change in attitudes to women abusing, with around 22%

believing that a wife slapping a husband can be appropriate. It may be that cultural norms are more tolerant of wives' violent behavior because they are seen as less likely to inflict injury or because women's violence is generally seen as defensive. Nevertheless, there does not seem to be a lot of evidence for strong cultural beliefs in support of couples being violent toward one another and especially in support of husbands abusing wives.

Conclusion

We conclude our discussion of couple violence with a discussion of the findings of the New Zealand longitudinal study of families recruited after the birth of a child. In this study, couple violence was reported by 8.5% of wives across a 6-year period. The important point we want to make about this study is that it showed that couple violence was predicted by a number of different variables at different levels of analysis: relational factors, some characteristics of the husband, and some characteristics of the wife (Fergusson, Horwood, Kershaw, & Shannon, 1986). In terms of the relational factors, couples involved in violence were more likely to be cohabiting than married (or married only a short time before the birth) and to have had an unplanned pregnancy. In terms of individual factors, they were also likely to be young (both under 20 at the time of the birth), to be low in terms of educational level and socioeconomic status, and to not attend church. These findings suggest that couple violence needs to be studied not just at the sociological level but also in terms of the characteristics of the couple and of the individual members of the dyad.

Magdol, Moffitt, Caspi, and Silva (1997) followed up the 21-year-old offspring of the families in the Fergusson et al. (1986) study. They showed that the risk factors for partner abuse were similar for males and females, often because victims and perpetrators were the same individuals, underlining the reciprocal nature of much couple violence. The antecedents of abuse included factors from four different domains: socioeconomic resources, family relationships, educational achievements, and problem behaviors. In addition, the predictors were similar for both perpetrators and victims. Attachment insecurity and conflicted parent–child relationships, growing up without both parents and with parents in low-status occupations, dropping out of school, and problem behaviors such as drug abuse, conduct problems, or aggressive delinquency were all related to partner abuse. Thus, these findings provide support for the proposition that individual factors of both the perpetrator and the victim are important in the prediction of violent behavior in couples and that a range of social factors are also relevant. On the other hand, they do not support the proposition that couple violence is perpetrated mainly by power-hungry male representatives of a patriarchal society.

In this chapter, we have sought to argue three major points: first, that violence by women, as well as violence against women, needs to be taken seriously by researchers; second, that we cannot understand the dynamics of couple violence in terms of a single level of analysis but need to focus on the individual, dyadic, and societal levels of analysis; and, third, that violent men are a particular group, and it is incorrect to argue that all men are potentially violent. We hope that our discussion of these issues has shed more light than heat on the current debate concerning couple violence.

REFERENCES

Abel, E. M. (2001). Comparing the social service utilization, exposure to violence and trauma symptomology of domestic violence female "victims" and female "batterers. *Journal of Family Violence, 16,* 401–420.

Anglin, K., & Holtzworth-Munroe, A. (1997). Comparing the responses of maritally violent and nonviolent spouses to problematic marital and nonmarital situations: Are the skills deficits of physically aggressive husbands and wives global? *Journal of Family Psychology, 11,* 301–313.

Archer, J. (2000). Sex differences in aggression between heterosexual partners: A meta-analytic review. *Psychological Bulletin, 126,* 651–676.

Ayduk, O., Downey, G., Testa, A., Yen, Y., & Shoda, Y. (1999). Does rejection elicit hostility in rejection sensitive women? *Social Cognition, 17,* 245–271.

Babcock, J. C., Miller, S. A., & Siard, C. (2003). Toward a typology of abusive women: Differences between partner-only and generally violent women in the use of violence. *Psychology of Women Quarterly, 27,* 153–161.

Babcock, J. C., Waltz, J., Jacobson, N., & Gottman, J. M. (1993). Power and violence: The relations between communication patterns, power discrepancies and domestic violence. *Journal of Consulting and Clinical Psychology, 61,* 40–50.

Bartholomew, K., & Horowitz, L. (1991). Attachment styles among young adults: A test of a four-category model. *Journal of Personality and Social Psychology, 61,* 226–244.

Bensley, L., MacDonald, S., Van Eenwyk, J., Simmons, K. W., & Ruggles, D. (2000, July). *Prevalence of intimate partner violence and injury—Washington, 1998.* Seattle: Washington State Department of Health.

Berns, S. B., Jacobson, N. S., & Gottman, J. M. (1999). Demand-withdraw interaction in couples with a violent husband. *Journal of Consulting and Clinical Psychology, 67,* 666–674.

Bograd, M. (1988). Feminist perspectives on wife abuse: An introduction. In K. Yllo & M. Bograd (Eds.), *Feminist perspectives on wife abuse* (pp. 11–26). Thousand Oaks, CA: Sage.

Bowlby, J. (1988). *A secure base: Parent-child attachment and healthy human development.* New York: Basic Books.

Briere, J., & Runtz, M. (1989). The Trauma Symptom Checklist (TSC-33): Early data on a new scale. *Journal of Interpersonal Violence, 4,* 151–163.

Cascardi, M., Langhinrichsen, J., & Vivian, D. (1992). Marital aggression: Impact, injury and health correlates for husbands and wives. *Archives of Internal Medicine, 152,* 1178–1184.

Christensen, A. (1988). Dysfunctional interaction patterns in couples. In P. Noller & M. A. Fitzpatrick (Eds.), *Perspectives on marital interaction* (pp. 31–52). Clevedon, England: Multilingual Matters.

Daly, M., Wilson, M., & Weghorst, S. J. (1982). Male sexual jealousy. *Ethology and Sociobiology, 3,* 11–27.

Dobash, R. E., & Dobash, R. P. (1979). *Violence against wives: A case against the patriarchy.* New York: Free Press.

Dobash, R. E., & Dobash, R. P. (1988). Research as social action: The struggle for battered women. In K. Yllo & M. Bograd (Eds.), *Feminist perspectives on wife abuse* (pp. 51–74). Thousand Oaks, CA: Sage.

Douglas, E. M., & Straus, M. A. (2003, August). *Corporal punishment experienced by university students in 17 countries and its relation to assault and injury of dating partners.* Paper presented at the European Society of Criminology, Helsinki, Finland.

Downey, G., & Feldman, S. (1996). Implications of rejection sensitivity for intimate relationships. *Journal of Personality and Social Psychology, 70,* 1327–1343.

Downey, G., Feldman, S., & Ayduk, O. (2000). Rejection sensitivity and male violence in romantic relationships. *Personal Relationships, 7,* 45–61.

Downey, G., Freitas, A. L., Michaelis, B., & Khouri, H. (1998). The self-fulfilling prophecy in close relationships: Rejection sensitivity and reaction by romantic partners. *Journal of Personality and Social Psychology, 75,* 545–560.

Downey, G., Khouri, H., & Feldman, S. (1997). Early interpersonal trauma and adult adjustment: The mediational role of rejection sensitivity. In D. Cicchetti & S. Toth (Eds.), *Rochester Symposium on Developmental Psychopathology, VIII: The effects of trauma on the developmental process* (pp. 85–114). Rochester, NY: University of Rochester Press.

Dutton, D. G. (1988). Concern for power, fear of intimacy and aversive stimuli for wife assault. In G. Hotaling, D. Finkelhor, J. T. Kirkpatrick, & M. A. Straus (Eds.), *Family abuse and its consequences: New directions in research* (pp. 113–121). Newbury Park, CA: Sage.

Dutton, D. G. (1994). Patriarchy and wife assault: The ecological fallacy. *Violence and Victims, 9,* 167–182.

Dutton, D. G. (1995). Male abusiveness in intimate relationships. *Clinical Psychology Review, 15,* 567–581.

Dutton, D. G., & Browning, J. J. (1988). Power struggles and intimacy anxieties as causative factors of violence in intimate relationships. In G. Russell (Ed.), *Violence in intimate relationships* (pp. 163–175). Costa Mesa, CA: PMA Publishing.

Dutton, D. G., & Nicholls, T. (2005). The gender paradigm in domestic violence and theory: Part 1—The conflict of theory and data. *Aggression and Violent Behavior, 10,* 680–714.

Ehrensaft, M. K., Moffitt, T. E., & Caspi, A. (2004). Clinically abusive relationships in an unselected birth cohort: Men's and women's participation and developmental antecedents. *Journal of Abnormal Psychology, 113,* 258–271.

Eldridge, K. A., & Christensen, A. (2002). Demand-withdraw communication during couple conflict: A review and analysis. In P. Noller & J. A. Feeney (Eds.), *Understanding marriage: Developments in the study of marital interaction* (pp. 289–322). New York: Cambridge University Press.

Faulk, M. (1974). Men who assault their wives. *Medicine, Science and Law, 14,* 180–183.

Felson, R. B. (1996). Big people hit little people: Sex differences in physical power and interpersonal violence. *Criminology, 34,* 433–452.

Fergusson, D. M., Horwood, L. J., Kershaw, K. L., & Shannon, F. T. (1986). Factors associated with reports of wife assault in New Zealand. *Journal of Marriage and the Family, 48*, 407–412.

Fiebert, M. S., & Gonzalez, D. M. (1997). College women who initiate assaults on their male partners and the reasons offered for such behavior. *Psychological Reports, 80*, 583–590.

Fincham, F. D., & Bradbury, T. N. (1992). Assessing attributions in marriage: The relationship attribution measure. *Journal of Personality and Social Psychology, 62*, 457–468.

Foshee, V. A. (1996). Gender differences in adolescent dating abuse: Prevalence, types and injuries. *Health Education Research: Theory and Practice, 11*, 275–286.

Gelles, R. J., & Straus, M. A. (1988). *Intimate violence.* New York: Simon & Schuster.

Goldner, V., Penn, P., Sheinberg, M., & Walker, G. (1990). Love and violence: Gender paradoxes in volatile attachments. *Family Process, 29*, 343–364.

Goodyear-Smith, F. A., & Laidlaw, T. M. (1999). Aggressive acts and assaults in intimate relationships: Towards an understanding of the literature. *Behavioral Sciences and the Law, 17*, 285–304.

Gottman, J. M., Jacobson, N. S., Rushe, R., Short, J. W., Babcock, J., La Taillade, J. J., et al. (1995). The relationship between heart rate reactivity, emotionally aggressive behavior and general violence in batterers. *Journal of Family Psychology, 9*, 1–41.

Gottman, J. M., & Levenson, R. W. (1988). The social psychophysiology of marriage. In P. Noller, & M. A. Fitzpatrick (Eds.), *Perspectives on marital interaction* (pp. 182–200). Clevedon, England: Multilingual Matters.

Graham-Kevan, N., & Archer, J. (2003). Intimate terrorism in common couple violence: A test of Johnson's predictions in four British samples. *Journal of Interpersonal Violence, 18*, 1247–1270.

Graham-Kevan, N., & Archer, J. (2005, July). *Using Johnson's domestic violence typology to classify men and women in a non-selected sample.* Paper presented at the 9th Annual Family Violence Research Conference, Portsmouth, New Hampshire.

Graham-Kevan, N., & Archer, J. (in press). Investigating three explanations of women's relationship aggression. *Psychology of Women Quarterly, 29*, 270–277.

Hines, D. A., & Saudino, K. J. (2003). Gender differences in psychological, physical and sexual aggression among college students using the revised Conflict Tactics Scales. *Violence and Victims, 18*, 197–217.

Holtzworth-Munroe, A., Bates, L., Smutzler, N., & Sandin, E. (1997). A brief review of the research on husband violence. Part 1: Maritally violent versus nonviolent men. *Aggression and Violent Behavior, 2*, 65–99.

Holtzworth-Munroe, A., & Hutchinson, G. (1993). Attributing negative intent to wife behavior: The attributions of maritally violent versus nonviolent men. *Journal of Abnormal Psychology, 102*, 206–211.

Holtzworth-Munroe, A., Smutzler, N., & Stuart, G. (1998). *Journal of Consulting and Clinical Psychology, 66*, 731–743.

Holtzworth-Munroe, A., & Stuart, G. (1994). Typologies of male batterers: Three subtypes and differences among them. *Psychological Bulletin, 116*, 476–497.

Holtzworth-Munroe, A., Stuart, G., & Hutchinson, G. (1997). Violent versus nonviolent husbands: Differences in attachment patterns, dependency and jealousy. *Journal of Family Psychology, 11*, 314–331.

Johnson, M. P., & Ferraro, K. J. (2000). Research on domestic violence in the 1990s: Making distinctions. *Journal of Marriage and the Family, 62*, 948–963.

Johnson, M. P., & Leone, J. L. (2005). The differential effects of intimate terrorism and situational couple violence: Findings from the National Violence Against Women Survey. *Journal of Family Issues, 26*, 322–349.

Kiecolt-Glaser, J. K., Newton, T., Cacioppo, J. T., MacCallum, R. C., Glaser, R., & Malarkey, W. B. (1996). Marital conflict and endocrine function: Are men really more physiologically affected than women? *Journal of Consulting and Clinical Psychology, 64,* 324–332.

Kwong, M. J., & Bartholomew, K. (1998, August). *Gender differences in domestic violence in the city of Vancouver.* Paper presented at the American Psychological Association Conference, San Francisco.

Kwong, M. J., Bartholomew, K., & Dutton, D. G. (1999). Gender differences in patterns of relationship violence in Alberta. *Canadian Journal of Behavioural Science, 31,* 150–160.

Leonard, K. E., & Roberts, L. J. (1998). Marital aggression, quality and stability in the first year of marriage: Findings from the Buffalo Newlywed Study. In T. N. Bradbury (Ed.), *The developmental course of marital dysfunction* (pp. 44–73). Cambridge, England: Cambridge University Press.

Levy, S. R., Ayduk, O., & Downey, G. (2001). The role of rejection sensitivity in people's relationships with significant others and valued social groups. In M. Leary (Ed.), *Interpersonal rejection* (pp. 251–289). New York: Oxford University Press.

Lie, G-Y., & Gentlewarrier, S. (1991). Intimate violence in lesbian relationships: Discussion of survey findings and practice implications. *Journal of Social Service Research, 15,* 41–59.

Lie, G-Y., Schilit, R., Bush, J., Montague, M., & Reyes, L. (1991). Lesbians in currently aggressive relationships: How frequently do they report aggressive past relationships? *Violence and Victims, 6,* 121–135.

Lloyd, S. A. (1990). Conflict types and strategies in violent marriages. *Journal of Family Violence, 5,* 269–284.

Magdol, L., Moffitt, T. E., Caspi, A., Newman, D. L., Fagan, J., & Silva, P. A. (1997). Gender differences in partner violence in a birth cohort of 21-year-olds: Bridging the gap between clinical and epidemiological approaches. *Journal of Consulting and Clinical Psychology, 65,* 68–78.

Magdol, L., Moffitt, T. E., Caspi, A., & Silva, P. A. (1997). Developmental antecedents of partner abuse: A prospective longitudinal study. *Journal of Abnormal Psychology, 107,* 375–389.

Mauricio, A. M., & Gormley, B. (2001). Male perpetration of physical violence against female partners. *Journal of Interpersonal Violence, 16,* 1066–1081.

Mischel, W. (1999). Personality coherence and dispositions in a cognitive-affective (CAPS) approach. In D. Cervone & Y. Shoda (Eds.), *The coherence of personality: Social-cognitive bases of consistency, variability and organization* (pp. 37–60). New York: Guilford Press.

Morse, B. J. (1995). Beyond the Conflict Tactics Scale: Assessing gender differences in partner violence. *Violence and Victims, 4,* 251–257.

Noller, P., & Roberts, N. D. (2002). The communication of couples in violent and nonviolent relationships: Temporal association with own and partners' anxiety/arousal and behavior. In P. Noller & J. A. Feeney (Eds.), *Understanding marriage: Developments in the study of marital interaction* (pp. 348–378). New York: Cambridge University Press.

O'Leary, K. D. (2000). Are women really more aggressive than men in intimate relationships? A comment on Archer (2000). *Psychological Bulletin, 126,* 685–689.

O'Leary, K. D., Barling, J., Arias, I., & Rosenbaum, A. (1989). Prevalence and stability of physical aggression between spouses: A longitudinal analysis. *Journal of Consulting and Clinical Psychology, 57,* 263–268.

Pagelow, M. D. (1981). *Woman battering: Victims and their experiences*. Beverly Hills, CA: Sage.

Renzetti, C. (1992). *Violent betrayal: Partner abuse in lesbian relationships*. Thousand Oaks, CA: Sage.

Roberts, N. D., & Noller, P. (1998). The association between adult attachment and couple violence: The role of communication patterns and relationship satisfaction. In J. A. Simpson & W. S. Rholes (Eds.), *Attachment theory and close relationships* (pp. 317–350). New York: Guilford Press.

Schoffrel, A. (2004). Characteristics of female perpetrators of domestic violence in group therapy. *Smith College Studies in Social Work, 74*, 505–524.

Sorenson, S. B., & Telles, C. A. (1991). Self-reports of spousal violence in a Mexican-American and non-Hispanic white population. *Violence and Victims, 6*, 3–15.

Stets, J. E., & Straus, M. A. (1990a). Gender differences in reporting of marital violence and its medical and psychological consequences. In M. A. Straus & R. J. Gelles (Eds.), *Physical violence in American families: Risk factors and adaptations to violence in 8,145 families* (pp. 151–165). New Brunswick, NJ: Transaction Publishers.

Stets, J. E., & Straus, M. A. (1990b). The marriage license as a hitting license. In M. A. Straus & R. J. Gelles (Eds.), *Physical violence in American families: Risk factors and adaptations to violence in 8,145 families* (pp. 227–244). New Brunswick, NJ: Transaction Publishers.

Straus, M. A. (1979). Measuring intrafamily conflict and violence: The Conflicts Tactics Scales. *Journal of Marriage and Family, 41*, 75–86.

Straus, M. A. (1990). The national family violence surveys. In M. A. Straus & R. J. Gelles (Eds.), *Physical violence in American families: Risk factors and adaptations to violence in 8,145 families* (pp. 3–16). New Brunswick, NJ: Transaction Publishers.

Straus, M. A. (1997). Physical assaults by women partners: A major social problem. In M. R. Walsh (Ed.), *Women, men and gender: Ongoing debates*. New Haven, CT: Yale University Press.

Straus, M. A. (1999). The controversy over domestic violence by women: A methodological, theoretical and sociology of science analysis. In X. Arriaga & S. Oskamp (Eds.), *Violence in intimate relationships* (pp. 210–221). Thousand Oaks, CA: Sage.

Straus, M. A., & Gelles, R. J. (1986). Societal change and change in family violence from 1975 to 1985 as revealed by two national surveys. *Journal of Marriage and the Family, 48*, 465–479.

Straus, M. A., Gelles, R. J., & Steinmetz, S. K. (1980). *Behind closed doors: Violence in the American family*. Newbury Park, CA: Sage.

Sugarman, D. B., & Hotaling, G. T. (1989). Dating violence: Prevalence, context, and risk markers. In A. A. Pirog-Good & J. E. Stets (Eds.), *Violence in dating relationships: Emerging social issues* (pp. 3–31). New York: Praeger.

Tweed, R. G., & Dutton, D. G. (1998). A comparison of impulsive and instrumental subgroups of batterers. *Violence and Victims, 13*, 217–230.

Walker, L. (1989). Psychology and violence against women. *American Psychologist, 44*, 695–702.

Yllo, K. (1988). Political and methodological debates in wife abuse research. In K. Yllo & M. Bograd (Eds.), *Feminist perspectives on wife abuse* (pp. 28–50). Beverly Hills, CA: Sage.

Yllo, K., & Straus, M. (1990). Patriarchy and violence against wives: The impact of structural and normative factors. In M. Straus & R. Gelles (Eds.), *Physical violence in American families: Risk factors and adaptations to violence in 8,145 families* (pp. 383–399). New Brunswick, NJ: Transaction Publishers.

CHAPTER 7

Partner Violence Typologies

Nicola Graham-Kevan

THEORIES OF PARTNER VIOLENCE

Unitary Theory and Research

Early research into relationship aggression adopted a dyadic approach and studied both the perpetrator and the victim (Snell, Rosenwald, & Robey, 1964). Feminist researchers, in contrast, sought to highlight the problems faced by women in abusive relationships and also to counteract the findings of nonfeminist research, which they felt were at odds with other areas of violence research, by concentrating on the attributes of the victim rather than the perpetrator. Concentrating on the victims was seen as removing responsibility from the attacker as "victim blaming." They questioned the very assumptions on which such research was based and attacked as misogynist the then four prominent concepts surrounding battered wives: these were given as "traditional sex role socialization," "the provocative wife," "learned helplessness," and "personal resource" theories (Finkelhor, Gelles, Hotaling, & Straus, 1983).

Research based on samples from battered women's services generally found that there were correlates of male violence, such as a relationship between intra- and interfamilial severe violence, exposure to violence as a child and both severity and prevalence of battering behavior, and lower age and education. The victims, however, were not found to share such homogeneity. These findings were seen as offering no support for studying battered women in isolation; instead, the reasons for abuse were firmly placed within the psychological and sociological makeup of the abuser (Holtzworth-Munroe & Stuart, 1994), with the most compelling evidence for this being the relationship between severe and/or prevalent domestic violence and violence outside the home (Finkelhor et al., 1983). Therefore, relationship aggression was conceptualized as a unitary phenomena, of men's physical aggression toward women (Henderson, 1986).

TYPOLOGY THEORY AND RESEARCH

Biological Sex

Typologies based on biological sex are typically endorsed by feminist advocates and researchers. This typology is based on feminist understanding of the patriarchal structure of society that expects men to be dominant and women to be submissive (Dasgupta, 1999; Lloyd & Emery, 1994; Saunders, 1988; Walker, 1984). This understanding leads to all men's partner aggression being labeled as "controlling" and "instrumental aggression." Women's partner aggression in contrast is seen as primarily defensive (e.g., Dobash, Dobash, Cavanagh, & Lewis, 1998). Henning, Jones, and Holdford (2003) state that "many, if not most women arrested for intimate partner violence are victims of abuse who may have been acting in self defence" (p. 841). Statements such as these, although common, lack empirical support; indeed, research has found that where one sex is the sole perpetrator and hence self-defense cannot be the explanation, this is more likely to be a woman than a man (DeMaris, 1987; Gray & Foshee, 1997; Morse, 1995; O'Leary, Barling, Arias, & Rosenbaum, 1989; Riggs, 1993; Roscoe & Callahan, 1985). Additionally, research that has asked women (and men) why they used physical aggression toward their partners has found that self-defense is cited by a minority of women only (Foo & Margolin, 1995; Sommer, 1994) with the prevalence of self-defense attributions being similar to men's (Carrado, George, Loxam, Jones, & Templar, 1996; Harned, 2001). Women reported using physical aggression toward their partners for a variety of reasons, including control, anger, jealousy, and to get through to their partner (Carrado et al., 1996; Dasgupta, 1999; Graham-Kevan & Archer, 2005; Harned, 2001). Further evidence against the biological typology of partner violence comes from the literature on beliefs about aggression. This has found that physical aggression is associated with instrumental beliefs in both men and women (Archer & Graham-Kevan, 2003; Archer & Haigh, 1997a, 1997b; Campbell, Muncer, & Odber, 1997) and that men and women do not differ in their instrumentality when the type of violence is partner violence (Archer & Haigh, 1999).

Placing a belief in a patriarchal society that supports men's partner violence as a starting position has led to a body of literature that is almost entirely based on studies of men's aggression only and that actively avoids studying women's behaviors for fear of "victim blaming." This has led to some interesting logical acrobatics. For example, to justify a female partner's violence, the reader is told that "it is clear that Paul had been battering her by ignoring her and working late, in order to move up the corporate ladder" (Walker, 1979, p. 67), an extremely broad definition of "battering." My personal favorite is d'Ardenne and Balakrishma's (2001) statement when discussing the prevalence rates of heterosexual, lesbian, and gay partner violence: "The picture emerges of men as the initiators in all relationships, whether against same-sex or opposite-sex partners" (p. 232). How men are supposed to be the initiators in female-only perpetrator relationships is not explained; neither is it explained when the relationship contains only women (i.e., lesbian). For further discussion on rates of initiation and self-defense and the role of patriarchy and other motives, see chapters 2 and 3 in this volume.

Using biological sex as the criterion for the label "perpetrator" or "victim" may not only distort research findings and obscure the meaning of women's use of aggression but also deter women who need assistance from seeking it (Hamby & Gray-Little, 2000) and deny a defense to victims of relationship aggression who fail to live up to the image of the passive, victimized woman. Stark (1995) criticizes such stereotypes for failing to represent many women who find themselves in contact with the criminal justice system. The need for female victims to appear to be "classic" victims, "respectable relatively passive and middle-class women" (Stark, 1995, p. 1019), may result in "rough" women being denied a legal defense to their own violence when they do not fit Walker's (1979) traditional "battered woman syndrome" profile. "Broad spectrum theories such as socio-biology and feminist sociology cannot account for differences in serially abusive, situationally abusive and non-abusive males" (Dutton, 2000, p. 60).

Psychopathology

Holtzworth-Munroe and Stuart (1994) developed a typology of male partner violence based on a narrative review of the typology literature.

They identified 15 studies and from those 15 derived a three-category multidimensional typology. The three subtypes were labeled "family only," "dysphoric/borderline," and "generally violent/antisocial." These subtypes were predicted to differ on the severity of violence, psychological aggression, and sexual aggression, with the family-only group having lower scores than the other two groups. The family-only group was predicted to be unlikely to use physical aggression outside of the home, whereas the dysphoric group was moderately likely and the generally violent (as the name suggests) very likely to be violent both within and outside the family. The generally violent group was also expected to have criminal records for offenses other than family violence. Psychologically, the family-only group was believed to have no personality disorder or passive/dependent personality disorder and not be impulsive, and they were expected to have low (in relation to the other groups) risks of having substance abuse problems and depression and moderately likely to have anger management problems. The dysphoric group was predicted to present with borderline or schizoidal personality disorder, to be moderately likely to abuse substances, and to be highly likely to suffer from depression and anger management problems. The antisocial group was predicted to present with antisocial personality disorder or psychopathy, was highly likely to have substance abuse problems and be impulsive and unlikely to suffer from depression, and would be moderately likely to have problems with anger. Developmentally, genetic influences were most strongly suggested for the antisocial group and least for the family only. The same pattern was predicted for exposure to parental violence and child maltreatment, hostile attitudes to women, and attitudes supportive of violence. The antisocial groups were unlikely to be dependent or empathic, the family-only group was moderately likely to be dependent or empathic, and the dysphoric group was expected to be high in dependency but low in empathy. Empirical support for Holtzworth-Munroe and Stuart's (1994) typology came from a study by Babcock, Jacobson, Gottman, and Yerington (2000) and a review of the literature from 1994 on by Dixon and Browne (2003). Dixon and Browne, however, criticized the typology for its failure to apply scientific profiling techniques and to include victim behaviors, context to the violent incidents, and triggers for such violence.

Typology research seeking to classify women abusers has found some support for Holtzworth-Munroe and Stuart's (1994) classification. Babcock, Miller, and Siard (2003) found that generally violent women (approximately 50% of the sample) arrested for partner violence were more instrumental in their use of violence, reported using more psychological and physical aggression, inflicted more injuries, and reported more traumatic symptomology than partner-only women arrested for partner violence. These results are consistent with "generally violent/antisocial" men (Holtzworth-Munroe & Stuart, 1994). Generally, violent women were also more likely to have witnessed their mother's physical aggression, suggesting a genetic and/or socialization explanation for their generally violent behavior. Henning and Feder (2004) used a large sample of women arrested for partner violence to investigate typologies. They found that women classified as using instrumental aggression were more likely to have suffered child abuse, witnessed parental violence, and had early conduct disorder problems, again consistent with "generally violent/antisocial" male offenders.

Simmons, Lehmann, and Cobb (2004) compared men and women arrested for partner violence and found that more than 80% of both men and women arrested for partner violence were the sole aggressor in the relationship. They reported that in comparison to a sample of male domestic violence offenders, women were more likely to have a personality disorder; to be diagnosed as histrionic, narcissistic, and/or compulsive; but less likely to be diagnosed as dependent. On most of the personality traits, men and women did not differ. The women in the sample were also more likely to have prior arrests and to endorse attitudes supportive of violence, although the men were more likely to have a restraining order against them. Men and women were similar on prior nondomestic violence convictions, prior domestic violence treatment, prior drug or alcohol treatment, history of domestic violence–related restraining orders, history of violation(s) of domestic violence restraining orders, weapon use in the commission of a crime, children present during the domestic violence incident, victim separated from the defendant within the past eight months, and defendant under any form of community supervision (e.g., probation) at the time of the offense. These findings suggest that Simmons et al.'s (2004) sample was predominantly "generally violent/antisocial" offenders; however, no attempt was made to classify the participants.

Monson and Langhinrichsen-Rohling (2002) extended Holtzworth-Munroe and Stuart's (1994) typology to include sexual aggression. As approximately 95% of women who experience sexual violence also experience nonsexual violence, Monson and Langhinrichsen-Rohling asserted that it is probable that most sexually violent partners are to be found within existing partner violence typologies. They proposed a four-category typology based on Holtzworth-Munroe and Stuart's (1994) subtypes. The "family only" type is expected to use only nonsexual violence (45% of partner violent offenders), the "dysphoric/borderline" (25%) and the "generally violent" (25%) types are expected to use both nonsexual and sexual violence, and an additional subtype in which only sexual violence is used makes up approximately 5% of domestic violence offender populations.

Biological Factors

Research on aggression has demonstrated a link between head injury and general aggressiveness (Coccaro, 1992). Rosenbaum and colleagues (Rosenbaum & Hoge, 1989; Rosenbaum et al., 1994) have also found that domestically violent men can be distinguished from nonviolent men using tests of frontal lobe function. Rosenbaum, Abend, and Gearan's (1997) study suggested that serotonergic deficits may explain this link. This research suggests that the use of selective serotonin reuptake inhibitors may be a useful addition to traditional batterer intervention programs.

On the basis of work carried out in the general violence literature on heart rate and violent offending (Raine, 1996), Gottman, Jacobson, and Rushe (1995) investigated heart rate reactivity in a sample of martially violent men. Two types of heart rate responses were identified: a lowered heart rate and a raised heart rate. Gottman et al. termed these two types "cobras" and "pit bulls," respectively. In comparing the two groups, Gottman et al. found that cobras had an antisocial or sadistic personality style, had higher levels of drug dependence, were more likely to have witnessed family violence as a child, were more generally violent, and used more severe physical aggression than pit bulls, who typically had dependent personality styles. Meehan, Holtzworth-Munroe, and Herron (2001) attempted to replicate Gottman et al.'s (1995) findings but did not find any consistent evidence that cobras or pit bulls differed significantly on these measures. This suggests that the research on the psychophysiological heart rate of intimate abusers is inconclusive and requires further study.

Behavioral Typologies

Behavioral typologies use overt behaviors as category descriptors and thus are reasonably easy to use, as information can be provided by either the perpetrator or his or her partner and no clinical training is required to classify offenders. These typologies usually classify on the mutuality of physical aggression and some also include controlling behaviors. Davies, Ralph, and Hawton (1995) found that in their sample of conciliation-counseling couples, the majority of couples reported that physical aggression and/or controlling behavior was used by both partners. Graham, Plant, and Plant (2004) investigated physical aggression in a sample of 2,027 U.K. adults. They found that of those who reported involvement in partner aggression, 52% reported mutual physical aggression (there were no significant differences in men and women reporting mutual aggression), 25% reported being a victim only (with men being significantly more likely to report this than women), and 24% reported being the sole perpetrator of physical aggression (with men being significantly less likely to report this than women). Similarly, Anderson (2002) used data from 7,395 married and cohabiting couples from wave 1 of the National Survey of Families and Households and found that 70% of couples reported mutual violence, 14% reported perpetration, and 16% reported victimization only. Of those couples who reported only unidirectional partner violence, women were twice as likely to be the sole perpetrator using either perpetrator or victim reports. Ehrensaft and Vivian (1999) found similar results in their sample of U.S. undergraduates. Landolt and Dutton (1997) demonstrated that mutually violent gay couples in their sample had higher levels of controlling behavior and physical aggression, borderline personality organization, and parental rejection than unidirectionally violent couples.

Johnson (1995) proposed a typology based on a narrative review that was consistent with both feminist research and general population findings. He argued that there were actually two distinct forms of aggressive relationships: "patriarchal terrorism" and "common couple violence." Common couple violence could be understood in that "the dynamic is one in which conflict occasionally gets 'out of hand,' leading to 'minor' forms of violence, and more rarely escalating into serious, sometimes life-threatening, forms of violence" (p. 283). Patriarchal terrorism was defined as "a product of patriarchal traditions of men's right to control 'their' women . . . a form of terroristic control of wives by their husbands that involves the systematic use of not only violence, but economic subordination, threats, isolation, and other control tactics" (p. 282). The heart of the distinction that Johnson sought to make was that patriarchal terrorism was not merely a more extreme form of common couple violence but instead a qualitatively different phenomenon. Patriarchal terrorism was believed to be evident in data from police and hospital records and from women's accounts of men's violence taken from shelters. These accounts converged to paint a picture of frequent male physical aggression toward women who in turn were at substantial risk of injury. Common couple violence was apparent in the responses obtained from nonselected samples, such as general population surveys and undergraduate populations. These respondents told of low-frequency aggression perpetrated by men and women but rarely resulting in injury.

These two types of relationship aggression differed on dimensions other than the frequency of physical aggression. Johnson (1995) identified escalation of physical aggression as an area of contention between family violence and feminist researchers. Walker (1989) encapsulated the feminist position on escalation when she wrote that "violence between intimate partners always gets worse" (p. 697). However, this is not consistent with family violence research, which finds no such pattern of escalation; indeed, there is some evidence from longitudinal studies that violence actually decreases over the course of a relationship (see, e.g., Morse, 1995; O'Leary et al., 1989). Another area that Johnson considered would discriminate between patriarchal terrorism and common couple violence was the use of controlling behaviors. Johnson (1995) stated, "It is important not to make the mistake of assuming that this pattern of general control [characteristic of patriarchal terrorism] can be indexed simply by high rates of violence" (p. 287). Johnson predicted that the patriarchal terrorist would use a combination of controlling behaviors, of which violence is but one tool, to control his partner. In contrast, partners in the common couple violence groups were not believed to use physical aggression within a general control framework. Therefore, Johnson argued that this type of physical aggression would not form part of a general pattern of control. Common couple violence was evident in survey samples that Johnson proposed were not as representative as many believed. He highlighted the "representative sample fallacy," which views all people as equally likely to be included. Johnson suggested that several biases could distort the nature of physical aggression within relationships. Nonresponders may systematically differ from responders, with patriarchal terrorists and their victims potentially being less likely to respond. Although it is clear why victims may be reluctant to take part (for fear of reprisals), it is not altogether clear why perpetrators would be. If these men's aggression is due to patriarchal ideology, as Johnson and feminist scholars contend, they would be more likely to view their aggression as justified and even sanctioned by society. Therefore, one could equally well argue that they would be more rather than less likely to take part in such surveys. Although not acknowledged by Johnson, shelter data also are likely to be subject to reporting bias. As shelters are run by advocate groups, there is likely to be demand characteristics inherent in reports from women hoping to be allowed to enter the shelter or residents who are subject to the Duluth curriculum.

Johnson (1995) does not address the latter point but does seek to provide evidence for the proposition that general population surveys frequently miss victims and perpetrators of patriarchal terrorism. He compared figures based on projections from U.S. shelters and the U.S. National Family Violence Survey (NFVS). By extrapolation, Johnson concluded that the survey data tap only one-sixth to one-third of patriarchal terrorist couples. However, Johnson may have inadvertently attributed methodological differences to sampling differences. Therefore, before further discussion of these figures, it is appropriate to mention that the shelter data consist of reports about a partner's behavior that are known to be consistently higher than self-reports (Barnett, Lee, & Thelen, 1997; Claes & Rosenthal, 1990; Dobash et al., 1998; Okun, 1986) by a factor of approximately three

(Heyman & Schlee, 1997). Therefore, as 50% of the NFVS is self-reported and 50% partner-reported, one would immediately expect a discrepancy.

Johnson (1995) bases his estimate not on the number of women who are in shelters and hence eligible to take part in research (from which such estimates of frequencies of assault of between 35 and 65 are derived) but on all those who contacted shelters and were either housed *or turned away*. Unless the chance of being turned away from a shelter is purely random, one would expect there to be differences between those who were admitted and those who were not. Although other research has identified selection on the basis of whether the victim represents the stereotypical passive victim (e.g., Pizzey, 1982), let us presume that the victims who are admitted are chosen at least partly because of their severe victimization. If this is the case, we would expect such victims to report higher frequencies of aggression than those turned away. Therefore, we would not expect all—or even most—of Johnson's 491,659 extrapolated victims to have suffered such high-frequency physical aggression. This in itself may not be seen as problematic until one remembers that the frequency of assaults has been used as the criterion for whether the NFVS adequately accessed severely aggressive couples. If the average number of assaults within this 491,659 is only 7 per year, the effect that this would have on the projected number of such people sampled via the NFVS may be dramatic and explain the apparent discrepancy.

There are further problems with Johnson's (1995) comparisons of those who have ever contacted a shelter as reported by the NFVS and reported by shelter providers. The NFVS asked respondents whether they had "used the services of a women's shelter," whereas the shelter providers tell us only the number of domestic violence contacts. This figure is likely to include many women who have repeatedly contacted these services because of the ongoing nature of relationship aggression or even contacted them on behalf of someone else. In addition, the term "used the services of a women's shelter" may be interpreted as meaning having actually resided in a shelter rather than just contacting one. These problems stem from trying to compare directly related but distinct phenomena. It highlights the need to use the same measures when attempting to compare across samples to avoid attributing measurement differences to sample differences.

In seeking to provide empirical support for his typology, Johnson (1999) presented analyses of data collected by Frieze in the 1970s (Frieze, 1983; Frieze & Browne, 1989; Frieze & McHugh, 1992). Frieze interviewed a sample of women known through contact with shelters or the justice system to be or to have been involved in a violent relationship. She then interviewed one neighbor of each violent couple. Therefore, the sample was known to contain both women from relationships representing shelter populations and those more representative of the general population. Johnson first classed respondents as high or low in their use of controlling behaviors and in terms of whether they used physical aggression. At this point, it became apparent that the distinction he had previously made related only to one member of a relationship and that he needed to be able to place different types of aggression within a dyadic context. He therefore classified people on the basis of their own and their partner's use of control and aggression. Common couple violence (CCV) occurred when one or both members of the relationship used noncontrolling physical aggression; patriarchal terrorism (renamed "intimate terrorism" [IT]) occurred when the respondents used controlling aggression and their partner used either no physical aggression or noncontrolling aggression. Two new categories, violent resistance (VR) and mutual violent control (MVC; essentially two intimate terrorists fighting for control), were created. VR occurred when a partner of an intimate terrorist used noncontrolling physical aggression.

Using cluster analysis, Johnson (1999) categorized relationships involving physical aggression as CCV (55% male, 45% female), IT (97% male, 3% female), VR (4% male, 96% female), or MVC (50% male, 50% female). These types of relationship aggression were then identified as belonging to either a general survey sample (90% CCV) or a shelter sample (74% IT/VR). Johnson then compared male IT and CCV samples on measures of escalation of violence, severity of male violence (as indexed by injuries sustained by female partners), mutuality of violence, and frequency of violence, all on the basis of female partners' reports. He found that relationships labeled IT were more likely than those labeled CCV to have involved escalated levels of aggression, more injurious aggression, and disproportionate levels of aggression between partners. Johnson did not, however, find that victims of IT were any less likely to aggress than were partners in CCV relationships.

Further analysis by Johnson and Leone (2000) was presented on the basis of data from the National Violence Against Women Survey (NVAWS; Tjaden & Thoennes, 1998), again using only women's reports. Using the same classification techniques as Johnson (1999), they classified IT- and CCV-only couples. They found a surprisingly high number of ITs, with 35% of husbands' violence being so classified, contrasting with 10% in the previous study. This high number was attributed to the way the questions were framed in the NVAWS, which was a survey emphasizing women's personal safety. They found that, on average, IT was significantly more frequent, more likely to escalate, and more severe than CCV. However, there was wide variation in scores. IT victims were significantly more likely to have suffered an injury and to have suffered posttraumatic stress disorder, depression, and disruption of daily activities and to have left their partner because of violence.

Graham-Kevan and Archer (2003b) used a stratified sample of women in domestic violence shelters, male and female students, and male prisoners. Using Johnson's (1999) classification techniques, those who were in a relationship that involved physical aggression were categorized as IT, CCV, VR, or MVC. Twenty-two percent of the sample were ITs, with 87% of these being male and 68% being identified through the shelter sample. CCV was gender neutral (45% men), with the majority being identified through nonselected samples. VR was predominantly female (90%), with 70% being found in the shelter sample. MVC was equally likely to be perpetrated by men or women and was most frequently identified through the male prison sample (31%). Analysis of IT and CCV provided further support for Johnson's typology. In comparison with CCV perpetrators, ITs showed a profile of significantly higher-frequency physical aggression that was more likely to result in injuries to their partners and to have escalated over the course of the relationship.

Previous research has therefore found support for the distinction between IT and CCV. These findings, however, cannot be generalized to a general population (Graham-Kevan & Archer, 2003a). The preceding research has used a sample that includes either known female victims of male violence (Graham-Kevan & Archer, 2003a; Johnson, 1999) or samples drawn from crime surveys of women's victimization (Johnson & Leone, 2000). These sampling methods may in themselves at least partially explain the previous findings. The populations sampled are likely to contain highly victimized women but unlikely to equally represent highly victimized men. Indeed, when Johnson's (1999) typology was investigated in a nonselected population, contrary to previous findings, it was found that IT and VR were essentially sex symmetrical and that nonviolent victims of IT (i.e., those who do not use any physical aggression toward a physically aggressive partner) were more likely to be men than women (Graham-Kevan & Archer, 2005). These findings suggest that research that has used single-sex samples to provide information on their own and opposite-sex partner's aggressive behaviors may have drawn conclusions about sex differences when in reality the effects were driven by self- versus partner-report bias. Johnson proposed and found evidence for the asymmetric nature of IT and VR (Johnson, 1999; Johnson & Leone, 2000), with men being perpetrators and women being victims of controlling physical aggression. However, all previous analysis conducted by these researchers used only reports from women about their own perpetration and victimization, even when reports from men were available (Johnson & Leone, 2000). Graham-Kevan and Archer's (2005) study's findings suggest that Johnson's (1999) typologies have some utility. However, his approach has been found to be sensitive to reporting and sampling effects. Future studies should refrain from using stratified sampling techniques to study sex differences unless such techniques include comparable samples for men and women.

Johnston and Campbell (1993) created a typology based on their sample of couples engaged in child custody disputes. They created a five-category classification based on in-depth interviews and a battery of psychological tests of the men, women, and their children. The first category was "ongoing or episodic male battering," which comprised approximately 14% of the sample and involved unilateral, frequent, and severe male violence perpetrated by men suffering from personality disorders who endorsed negative attitudes toward women. The second category, "female-initiated violence," was also approximately 14% of the sample and was similar (although less injurious) than the ongoing or episodic male batterers. "Male-controlled interactive violence" accounted for 19% of the cases, where the physical aggression was mutual and conflict oriented. The fourth category was "separation and postdivorce violence," which represented almost half of all couples (48%); here, the violence was equally likely to be used by either partner and was infrequent and not part of a previous pattern of behavior. The final category was the smallest (6%) and occurred when a psychotic episode followed separation. This final category is limited, however, as it does not apply to intact couples and may need to be investigated in ongoing relationships (Hamel, 2005).

If replicated in future studies, these findings have far-reaching implications. They provide support for researchers, such as Steinmetz (1978) and George (1994, 2003), who have claimed not only that men as well as women can be mutually victimized in intimate relationships but also that men can be victims of "battering" in the same way that women can be battered by men. These conclusions are in direct contrast with feminist analyses, which have discounted such claims by asserting that men use controlling aggression and women use no (or, more recently, self-defensive) aggression (Dobash & Dobash, 1979; Dobash et al., 1998; Giles-Sims, 1983; Okun, 1986; Pence & Paymar, 1986, 1993; Saunders, 1988; Walker, 1979; Yllo, 1994). However, the present findings are supported by research that has investigated men's victimizations (George, 2003; McLeod, 1984; Migliaccio, 2002; Statistics Canada, 2000).

The present dominance of the sociopolitical/pro-feminist approach to domestic violence intervention programs in the United States (White & Gondolf, 2000) and to a large extent other Western nations, such as the United Kingdom and the Netherlands, may need to be reconsidered. The large dropout and reassault rates for perpetrators in such programs may be due to treatment being tailored to the minority of perpetrators who fit the label of "patriarchal men," whereas the majority of perpetrators are failing to get their criminogenic needs met, thus bringing into question the appropriateness of a "one size fits all" philosophy, particularly with the increasing number of women being arrested for domestic assault (see chapter 2 in this volume). Recently, clinicians in the United States have shown an interest in Johnson's (1999) work (S. H. Dempsey, personal communication, October 10, 2003; E. Dunning, personal communication, August 3, 2002) and have sought research on his typologies. Therefore, research on Johnson's typologies is timely, as both the strengths and the limitations of Johnson's work need to be investigated. The implications for the diagnosis and treatment of domestic violence perpetrators are that there is clear evidence to suggest that partner aggression is not a unitary phenomenon and that the frequency of the use of controlling behaviors and the mutuality of physical aggression need to be assessed before embarking on a diagnosis and treatment plan. However, the assessment should be sensitive to reporting biases when only the victim or the perpetrator accounts are available. Further, more recent research on women's partner aggression suggests that the use of partner aggression may be a human problem rather than a male problem, so treatment plans should concentrate primarily on the nature of the physical aggression rather than the gender of the perpetrator and victim. Such an approach has been successfully adopted by clinicians. Hamel (2005) created a model using the severity of violence and extent of mutuality as continuous variables. He then devised treatment plans based on the behaviors of both members of the relationship dyad. This model may prove useful for clinicians, as it integrates much of the male typology literature and is consistent with the emerging female literature as well.

Generally, however, further studies with a wider array of measures that are not violence related are needed to assess the validity of the present typology research findings. The classification systems detailed in this chapter need to move away from purely aggression-related variables if they are to prove useful not only in classifying types of perpetrators but also in predicting such behavior before it has begun or escalated. Such analysis could include not only individual-level variables (such as attachment) but also family- and societal-level influences. All the measures that have been found to differ across Johnson's categories (Johnson, 1999; Johnson & Leone, 2000) are aggression related, as are Holtzworth-Munroe and Stuart's (1994), and therefore it is possible that the predictive ability of these classification systems are an artifact of their relationship with aggression.

Implications of Typology Research for Clinical Practice

There is clear evidence of typologies of relationships where physical aggression is used and that a variety of factors influence the use of partner violence. Babcock et al.'s (2000) research suggests that understanding the attachment style of domestically violent individuals may help predict when physical aggression is most likely to be used and whether it is expressive or instrumental. This could aid treatment matching interventions to address specific offending needs. Babcock et al. found that men with preoccupied attachment styles tended to become physically aggressive when their partner withdrew from them during conflict. Babcock et al. explain such a reaction as demonstrating abandonment anxiety and typified as expressive (angry) physical aggression. Individuals with dismissing attachment styles were found to be most likely to use physical aggression when their partner became defensive, and the physical aggression used was instrumental in nature. Preoccupied individuals used expressive aggression to reduce negative affect and engage with their partner, whereas dismissing individuals used aggression to gain compliance. Consistent with the use of instrumental physical aggression is the finding that dismissing individuals also tended to be violent outside the home.

Roberts and Noller (1998) found a similar pattern for both men and women where one partner (male or female) was preoccupied and the other dismissive in his or her attachment style. Physical aggression was most likely to be reported. This finding is consistent with the results of Bartholomew, Henderson, and Dutton (2001), who found that preoccupied attachment was associated with both perpetration and victimization for both men and women. Indeed, research suggests that men and women are similar in the associations between attachment and partner aggression. Henderson, Bartholomew, Trinke, and Kwong (2005) found that gender did not moderate the relationship between preoccupied attachment and partner aggression. Bookwala and Zdaniuk (1998) also found that in reciprocal dating violence, preoccupied (and fearful) attachment styles were associated for both men and women.

The typology research reviewed suggests that perpetrators of partner violence differ on the prevalence of personality disorders. In particular, the most violent subgroups are frequently found to contain individuals who exhibit more antisocial behavior, are more generally violent, and are generally more resistant to mental health intervention than others (Hare, 1993). Huss and Langhinrichsen-Rohling (2000) have identified a parallel literature that contains similar clinical descriptions of violent individuals who have been diagnosed as psychopaths. This literature can act as a bridge between the personality disorder typologies, the physiological typologies, and, to an extent, the gender-based typology in that this literature "describes the violence tendencies, physiological responses, cognitive impairments, interpersonal/affective characteristics, and treatment responsiveness of these individuals in much greater depth and breadth than the current domestic violence literature" (p. 1).

The implications for the diagnosis and treatment of domestic violence perpetrators are that there is clear evidence to suggest that partner aggression is not a unitary phenomenon and that typologies of partner violence need to adopt a dimensional dyadic approach. Partner violence interventions need to be informed by empirical research, including the general violence literature. This research suggests that interventions must address developmental, psychological, and couple interaction styles to adequately understand and successfully treat partner violence.

Finally, appropriate treatment should be available for male victims, and practitioners should be made aware of the existence of men as victims to prevent discrimination. At present, men are often denied help and are either ignored or accused of being perpetrators. Davies et al. (1995) found in their sample of conciliation-counseling couples that most men and nearly half the women reported mutual abuse. When discussing men's reports, however, they stated that "the attribution of joint responsibility is possibly a reflection of men's denial of their responsibility for abuse" (p. 334). When discussing women's reports, they stated that "this high level of joint attribution of responsibility is probably a result of self-blaming by abused women" (p. 334). This type of interpretation suggests that presently neither victim nor perpetrator reports are sufficient for many counselors and psychologists to actually accept that men can be victims of partner aggression and control, "against such reasoning there is no defence" (Roth, 1993, p. 54). Once it is accepted that both men and women use partner violence, intervention programs can be designed to address women's offending behavior rather than being a proxy self-help group for women as suggested by some, such as L. Dowd (2001), who stated that batterer intervention groups could be a way of empowering women.

REFERENCES

Anderson, K. L. (2002). Perpetrator or victim?: Relationships between intimate partner violence and well being. *Journal of Marriage and the Family, 64,* 851–863.

Archer, J., & Graham-Kevan, N. (2003). Do beliefs about aggression predict physical aggression to partners? *Aggressive Behavior, 29,* 41–54.

Archer, J., & Haigh, A. (1997a). Beliefs about aggression among male and female prisoners. *Aggressive Behavior, 23,* 405–415.

Archer, J., & Haigh, A. M. (1997b). Do beliefs about aggressive feelings and actions predict reported levels of aggression? *British Journal of Social Psychology, 36,* 83–105.

Archer, J., & Haigh, A. (1999). Sex differences in beliefs about aggression: Opponent's sex and the form of aggression. *British Journal of Social Psychology, 38,* 71–84.

Babcock, J. C., Jacobson, N. S., Gottman, J. M., & Yerington, P. (2000). Attachment, emotional regulation, and the function of marital violence: Differences between secure, preoccupied, and dismissing violent and non-violent husbands. *Journal of Family Violence, 15,* 391–409.

Babcock, J. C., Miller, S., & Siard, C. (2003). Toward a typology of abusive women: Differences between partner-only and generally violent women in the use of violence. *Psychology of Women Quarterly, 13,* 46–59.

Barnett, O. W., Lee, C. Y., & Thelen, R. E. (1997). Gender differences in attributions of self-defence and control in interpartner aggression. *Violence Against Women, 3*, 462–481.

Bartholomew, K., Henderson, A., & Dutton, D. (2001). Insecure attachment and abusive intimate relationships. In C. Culow (Ed.), *Adult attachment and couple psychotherapy* (pp. 43–61). New York: Brunner-Routledge,.

Bookwala, J., & Zdaniuk, B. (1998). Adult attachment styles and aggressive behavior within dating relationships. *Journal of Social and Personal Relationships, 15*, 175–190.

Campbell, A., Muncer, S., & Odber, J. (1997). Aggression and testosterone: Testing a bio-social model. *Aggressive Behavior, 23*, 229–238.

Carrado, M., George, M. J., Loxam, E., Jones, L., & Templar, D. (1996). Aggression in British heterosexual relationships: A descriptive analysis. *Aggressive Behavior, 22*, 401–415.

Claes, J. A., & Rosenthal, D. M. (1990). Men who batter women: A study in power. *Journal of Family Violence, 5*, 215–224.

Coccaro, E. F. (1992). Impulsive aggression and central serotonergic function in humans: An example of a dimensional brain-behavior relationship. *International Clinical Psychopharmacology, 7*, 3–12.

D'Ardenne, P., & Balakrishma, J. (2001). Domestic violence and intimacy: What the therapist needs to know. *Sexual and Relationship Therapy, 16*, 229–246.

Dasgupta, S.D. (1999). Just like men?: A critical view of violence by women. In M. E. Shephard & E.L. Pence (Eds.), *Coordinating community responses to domestic violence* (pp.195–222). Thousand Oaks, CA: Sage.

Davies, B., Ralph, S., & Hawton, M. (1995). A study of client satisfaction with family court counselling in cases involving domestic violence. *Family and Conciliation Courts Review, 33*, 324–341.

DeMaris, A. (1987). The efficacy of a spouse abuse model in accounting for courtship violence. *Journal of Family Issues, 8*, 291–305.

Dixon, L., & Browne, K. (2003). The heterogeneity of spouse abuse: a review. *Aggression and Violent Behavior, 8*, 107–130.

Dobash, R.P., & Dobash, R.E. (1979). *Violence against wives: A case against patriarchy.* New York: The Free Press.

Dobash, R. P., Dobash, R. E., Cavanagh, K., & Lewis, R. (1998). Separate and intersecting realities: A comparison of men and women's accounts of violence against women. *Violence Against Women, 4*, 382–414.

Dowd, L. (2001). Female perpetrators of partner aggression: Relevant issues and treatment. *Journal of Aggression and Maltreatment, 5*, 73–104.

Dutton, D. G. (2000). Witnessing parental violence as a traumatic experience shaping the abusive personality. *Journal of Aggression and Maltreatment, 3*, 59–67.

Ehrensaft, M. K., & Vivian, D. (1999). Is partner aggression related to appraisals of coercive control by a partner? *Journal of Family Violence, 14*, 251–266.

Finkelhor, D., Gelles, R. J., Hotaling, G. T., & Straus, M. A. (1983). *The dark side of families: Current family violence research.* Beverly Hills, CA: Sage.

Foo, L., & Margolin, G. (1995). A multivariate investigation of dating aggression. *Journal of Family Violence, 10*, 351–377.

Frieze, I. H. (1983). Investigating the causes and consequences of marital rape. *Signs, 8*, 532–553.

Frieze, I. H., & Browne, A. (1989). Violence in marriage. In L. Ohlin & M. Tonry (Eds.), *Family violence* (Vol. 11, pp. 163–218). Chicago: University of Chicago Press.

Frieze, I. H., & McHugh, M. C. (1992). Power and influence strategies in violent and non-violent marriages. *Psychology of Women Quarterly, 16*, 449–465.

George, M. J. (1994). Riding the donkey backwards: Men as victims of unacceptable victims of marital violence. *Journal of Men's Studies, 3*, 137–159.

George, M. J. (2003). Invisible touch. *Aggression and Violent Behavior, 8*, 23–60.

Giles-Sims, J. (1983). *Wife battering: A systems theory approach.* New York: Guilford Press.

Gottman, J. M., Jacobson, N. S., & Rushe, R. H. (1995). The relationship between heart rate reactivity, emotionally aggressive behavior, and general violence in batterers. *Journal of Family Psychology, 9*, 227–248.

Graham, K., Plant, M., & Plant, M. (2004). Alcohol, gender and partner aggression: A general population study of British adults. *Addiction Research and Theory, 12*, 385–401.

Graham-Kevan, N., & Archer, J. (2003a). Patriarchal terrorism and common couple violence: A test of Johnson's predictions in four British samples. *Journal of Interpersonal Violence, 18*, 1247–1270.

Graham-Kevan, N., & Archer, J. (2003b). Physical aggression and control in heterosexual relationships: The effect of sampling procedure. *Violence and Victims, 18*, 181–198.

Graham-Kevan, N., & Archer, J. (2005, July). *Using Johnson's domestic violence typology to classify men and women in a non-selected sample.* Paper presented at the 9th International Family Violence Research Conference, New Hampshire.

Gray, H. M., & Foshee, V. (1997). Adolescent dating violence: Differences between one-sided and mutually violent profiles. *Journal of Interpersonal Violence, 12*, 126–141.

Hamby, S. L., & Gray-Little, B. (2000). Labelling partner violence: When do victims differentiate among acts? *Violence and Victims, 15*, 173–186.

Hamel, J. (2005). *Gender inclusive treatment of intimate partner abuse: A comprehensive approach.* New York: Springer.

Hare, R.D. (1993). *Without conscience: The disturbing world of the psychopaths among us.* New York: Guildford Press.

Harned, M. S. (2001). Abused women or abused men? An examination of the context and outcomes of dating violence. *Violence and Victims, 16*, 269–285.

Henderson, A.J.Z., Bartholomew, K., Trinke, S., & Kwong, M.J. (2005). When loving means hurting: An exploration of attachment and intimate abuse in a community sample. *Journal of Family Violence, 20*, 219–230.

Henderson, M. (1986). An empirical typology of violent incidents reported by prison inmates with convictions for violence. *Aggressive Behavior, 12*, 21–32.

Henning, K., Jones, A., & Holdford, R. (2003). Treatment needs of women arrested for domestic violence: A comparison with male offenders. *Journal of Interpersonal Violence, 18*, 839–856.

Henning, K. & Feder, L. (2004). A comparison of men and women arrested for domestic violence: Who presents the greater threat? *Journal of Family Violence, 19*, 69–80.

Heyman, R. E., & Schlee, K. A. (1997). Toward a better estimate of the prevalence of partner abuse: Adjusting rates based on the sensitivity of the conflict tactics scale. *Journal of Family Psychology, 11*, 332–338.

Holtzworth-Munroe, A., & Stuart, G. L. (1994). Typologies of male batterers: Three subtypes and the differences among them. *Psychological Bulletin, 116*, 476–497.

Huss, M. T., & Langhinrichsen-Rohling, J. (2000). Identification of the psychopathic batterer: The clinical, legal, and policy implications. *Violent and Aggressive Behavior, 5*, 403–422.

Johnson, M. P. (1995). Patriarchal terrorism and common couple violence: Two forms of violence against women. *Journal of Marriage and the Family, 57*, 283–294.

Johnson, M. P. (1999, November). *Two types of violence against women in the American family: Identifying intimate terrorism and common couple violence.* Paper presented at the annual meetings of the National Council on Family Relations, Irvine, California.

Johnson, M. P., & Leone, J. M. (2000, June). *The differential effects of intimate terrorism and common couple violence: Findings from the National Violence Against Women Survey.* Paper presented at the Tenth International Conference on Personal Relationships, Brisbane, Australia.

Johnston, J. R., & Campbell, L. E. (1993). A clinical typology of interparental violence in disputed-custody divorces. *American Journal of Orthopsychiatry, 63,* 190–199.

Landolt, M. A. & Dutton, D. G. (1997). Power and personality: An analysis of gay male intimate abuse. *Sex Roles, 37,* 335–359.

Lloyd, S. A., & Emery, B. C. (1994). Physically aggressive conflict in romantic relationships. In D. D. Cahn (Ed.), *Conflict in personal relationships* (pp. 27–46). Mahwah, NJ: Lawrence Erlbaum Associates.

McLeod, M. (1984). Women against men: An estimation of domestic violence based on an analysis of official data and national victimization data. *Justice Quarterly, 1,* 171–193.

Meehan, J. C., Holtzworth-Munroe, A., & Herron, K. (2001). Maritally violent men's heart rate reactivity to marital interactions: A failure to replicate the Gottman et al. (1995) typology. *Journal of Family Psychology, 15,* 394–408.

Migliaccio, T. A. (2002). Abused men: A narrative analysis. *Journal of Family Issues, 23,* 26–52.

Monson, C. M., & Langhinrichsen-Rohling, J. (2002). Sexual and nonsexual dating violence perpetration: Testing an integrated perpetrator typology. *Violence and Victims, 17,* 403–428.

Morse, B. J. (1995). Beyond the conflict tactics scale: Assessing gender differences in partner violence. *Violence and Victims, 10,* 251–272.

Okun, L. (1986). *Woman abuse: Facts replacing myths.* Albany: State University of New York Press.

O'Leary, K. D, Barling, J., Arias, I., & Rosenbaum, A. (1989). Prevalence and stability of physical aggression between spouses: A longitudinal analysis. *Journal of Consulting and Clinical Psychology, 57,* 263–268.

Pence, E., & Paymar, M. (1986). *Power and control: Tactics of men who batter.* Duluth: Minnesota Program Development, Inc.

Pence, E., & Paymar, M. (1993). *Education groups of men who batter: The Duluth model.* New York: Springer.

Pizzey, E. (1982). *Prone to violence.* Retrieved May, 15, 2006, from http://www.bennett.com/ptv/index.shtml.

Raine, A. (1996). Autonomic nervous system activity and violence. In D. M. Stoff & R. B. Cairns, (Eds.), *Aggression and violence: Genetic, neurobiological, and biosocial perspectives* (pp. 145–168). Mahwah, NJ: Lawrence Erlbaum Associates.

Riggs, D. S. (1993). Relationship problems and dating aggression: A potential treatment target. *Journal of Interpersonal Violence, 8,* 18–35.

Roberts, N., & Noller, P. (1998). The association between adult attachment and couple violence. In J. Simpson & W. Rholes (Eds.), *Attachment theory and close relationships* (pp. 317–350). New York: Guilford Press.

Roscoe, B., & Callahan, J. E. (1985). Adolescent's self-reports of violence in families and dating relationships. *Adolescence, 79,* 545–553.

Rosenbaum, A., Abend, S. S., & Gearan, P. J. (1997). Serotonergic functioning in partner-abusive men. In A. Raine, P. A. Brennan, D. P. Farrington, P. David, & S. A. Mednick (Eds.), *Biosocial bases of violence* (pp. 329–332). New York: Plenum Press.

Rosenbaum, A., & Hoge, S. K. (1989). Head injury and marital aggression. *American Journal of Psychiatry, 146,* 1048–1051.

Rosenbaum, A., Hoge, S. K., Adelman, S. A., Warnken, W. J., Fletcher, K. E., & Kane, R. L. (1994). Head injury in partner-abusive men. *Journal of Consulting and Clinical Psychology, 62,* 1187–1193.

Roth, P. (1993). *Operation shylock: A confession.* London: Random House.

Saunders, D. G. (1988). Wife abuse, husband abuse or mutual combat? A feminist perspective on the empirical findings. In K. Yllo & M. Bograd (Eds.), *Feminist perspectives on wife abuse* (pp. 90–113). Newbury Park, CA: Sage.

Simmons, C., Lehmann, P., & Cobb, N. (2004, September 18). *Personality profiles and attitudes toward violence of women arrested for domestic violence: How they differ from and are similar to men arrested for domestic violence.* Paper presented at the FVSAI 9th International Conference on Family Violence, San Diego, California.

Snell, J. E., Rosenwald, R. J., & Robey, A. (1964). The wifebeater's wife: A study of family interaction. *Archives of General Psychiatry, 11,* 107–112.

Sommer, R. (1994). Male and female perpetrated partner abuse. *Dissertation Abstracts International.* Section B: The Sciences and Engineering, Vol 56(9-B), 5185.

Stark, E. (1995). Re-presenting woman battering: From battered woman syndrome to coercive control. *Albany Law Review, 58,* 973–1036.

Statistics Canada. (2000). Family violence in Canada: A statistical profile. *Canadian Centre for Justice Statistics, 85.*

Steinmetz, S. K. (1978). The battered husband syndrome. *Victimology: An International Journal, 2,* 499–509.

Tjaden, P., & Thoennes, N. (1998). *Prevalence, incidence and consequences of violence against women: Findings from the National Violence Against Women Survey.* Washington, DC: U.S. Department of Justice.

Walker, L. E. A. (1979). *The battered woman.* New York: Harper & Row.

Walker, L. E. A. (1984). *The battered woman syndrome.* New York: Springer.

Walker, L. E. A. (1989). Psychology and violence against women. *American Psychologist, 44,* 695–702.

White, R. J., & Gondolf, E. W. (2000). Implications of personality profiles for batterer treatment. *Journal of Interpersonal Violence, 15,* 467–486.

Yllo, K. A. (1994). Through a feminist lens: Gender, power, and violence. In R. J. Gelles & D. R. Loseke (Eds.), *Current controversies on family violence* (pp. 47–62). Newbury Park, CA: Sage.

CHAPTER 8

The Impact of Domestic Violence on Children's Development

Patrick T. Davies and Melissa L. Sturge-Apple

Interparental violence, characterized by physical aggression between parents (Jouriles, Norwood, McDonald, & Peters, 2001), is a significant public health concern in the lives of children in the United States (Graham-Bermann & Edleson, 2001; Osofsky, 1999). Violence between parents is commonly regarded as a form of psychological maltreatment that poses a considerable risk to children's psychological and physical welfare (Barnett, Manly, & Cicchetti, 1993; Margolin & Gordis, 2000). As an extreme manifestation of interparental dysfunction, children from homes characterized by domestic violence are five to seven times more likely to experience significant psychological problems relative to children in the general population (Cummings & Davies, 1994; McDonald & Jouriles, 1991). Moreover, interparental physical aggression predicts a wide range of child psychological problems even when statistically controlling for general interparental discord, child maltreatment, and parent mental health (Fergusson & Horwood, 1998; McDonald, Jouriles, Norwood, Ware, & Ezell, 2000; Yates, Dodds, Sroufe, & Egeland, 2003). Yet the very same corpus of research that documents the substantial toll of witnessing domestic violence also underscores the considerable variability in the outcomes of child witnesses of violence between parents.

This research was supported by a National Institute of Mental Health grant (R01 MH071256).

For example, most children from violent homes (i.e., 35% to 45%) do not experience clinically significant levels of psychopathology at any one time (Hughes, Graham-Bermann, & Gruber, 2001).

As empirical documentation of risk for psychopathology and the variability in outcomes among children who witness domestic violence reaches a point of diminished returns (Grych, Jouriles, Swank, McDonald, & Norwood, 2000), the literature on domestic violence is now facing a critical transitional stage (Kitzmann, Gaylord, Holt, & Kenny, 2003). The first generation of research summarized previously aimed to delineate the degree and scope of vulnerability associated with exposure to domestic violence through tackling questions of whether or how much domestic violence predicts child adjustment problems. However, the analysis of associations between interparental violence and child functioning has typically occurred in isolation from the constellation of family and child characteristics associated with interparental violence (Jouriles, Spiller, Stephens, McDonald, & Swank, 2000; Jouriles et al., 2001). In rare instances in which family and child characteristics are included in analytic models, they are often treated as secondary, nuisance, or confounding variables (Fergusson & Horwood, 1998). As a result, this generation of research has yielded scant information on how, when, and why children exposed to domestic violence exhibit specific developmental outcomes over time. To address this gap, calls are increasing for a second generation of process-oriented research designed to address the processes that mediate or moderate associations between domestic violence and children's adjustment trajectories (Davies, Winter, & Cicchetti, in press; Kitzmann et al., 2003).

Toward this goal, the objective of this chapter is to address key parameters in the family system that may elucidate the processes and conditions that underlie the risk and variability of outcomes of children in homes characterized by interparental violence. Throughout the chapter, the main principles of developmental psychopathology will serve as a template for addressing important theoretical and research directions for characterizing associations between domestic violence and child functioning in the broader family system. Within the developmental psychopathology perspective, associations between domestic violence and child functioning are rough proxies for a vibrant undercurrent of evolving, bidirectional exchanges between the dynamic child in an ever-changing, multilayered constellation of biopsychosocial liabilities and resources in the family. Thus, in the developmental psychopathology approach, the developmental course of each child is to some degree unique because of the specific transactions between their prior and current experiences in family contexts and their own attributes, resources, and histories of adaptation. The derivative assumption, then, is that changes in children's adaptations and maladaptations can be lawfully predicted and explained

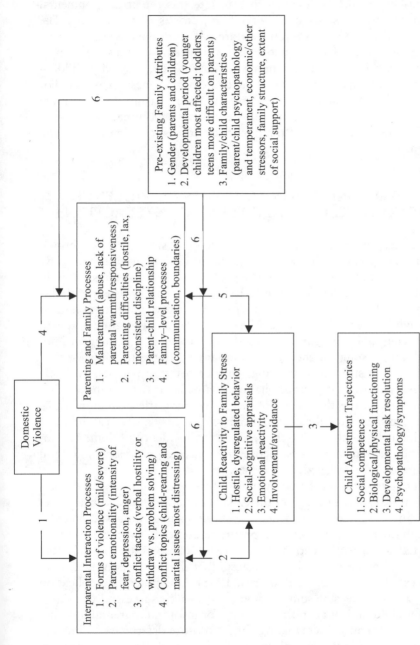

FIGURE 8.1   A family and developmental systems model for understanding the mediational processes and moderating conditions underlying the multiplicity of pathways between domestic violence exposure and child maladjustment

by elucidating the nature of transactions between the child and environment. Figure 8.1 is designed to translate this set of developmental assumptions to the study of children's trajectories of functioning. The figure specifically portrays a representative but not exhaustive overview of some of the key family factors that are worthy of consideration in further advancing an understanding of how, when, and why children develop psychological problems in the context of domestic violence. For the remainder of the chapter, this figure will serve as an organizational framework for addressing some of the central conceptual and empirical directions in the study of the impact of domestic violence on young children.

CHILD ADAPTATION TO DOMESTIC VIOLENCE: THE CONTEXT OF INTERPARENTAL INTERACTIONS

Many conceptual models of domestic violence share the assumption that witnessing violence between parents is a stressful event that directly undermines children's functioning (e.g., Davies et al., in press; Grych, Harold, & Miles, 2003; Johnston & Roseby, 1997). Consistent with this hypothesis, Milgram (1998) ranked witnessing acts of violence as moderate to high in adversity (i.e., 7 on a 9-point scale), a rating comparable to experiencing maltreatment, life-threatening illness, and permanent injuries. Although some of the risk accompanying domestic violence may result from the stress of witnessing violence between parents, domestic violence is part of a larger constellation of a wide array of forms of interparental interactions that in and of themselves may affect children. Thus, as path 1 in Figure 8.1 illustrates, progress in theory and research hinges on distinguishing more precisely between the incidence of domestic violence and accompanying destructive interparental processes and child exposure to these destructive processes.

A tacit assumption shared by much of the prior literature on domestic violence is that the general occurrence of domestic violence in a household is tantamount to the incidence of child exposure to domestic violence. Although the frequency of child exposure to domestic violence is, in fact, correlated consistently with the occurrence of domestic violence, the lack of a strong correspondence suggests that they are relatively distinct (Sternberg, Lamb, & Dawud-Nourisi, 1998). One potential implication is that parents, at least in some families, may be able successfully to shield or buffer children from exposure to some or most interparental dysfunction. Thus, carefully disentangling child exposure destructive to interactions between parents from the general incidence of domestic violence is a priority for conceptual and measurement models.

Nested within distinctions between the general and witnessed incidents of violence is also the importance of discriminating among multiple properties of domestic violence and associated forms of interparental dysfunction. Violence, itself, can assume multiple expressions that may have distinct implications for child adjustment. Although few studies have examined the unique risk posed by different forms of violence, the available evidence lends support to the notion that extreme forms of physical aggression (e.g., using knives or guns) predict child problems even after statistically controlling for other forms of domestic violence (e.g., Jouriles et al., 1998).

Violence between parents may also signify other patterns of interparental dysfunction that might play their own unique roles in the developmental course of child adjustment. Research has specifically shown that violence in the interparental relationship is associated with a greater incidence of other forms of destructive interactions between parents, such as verbal aggression and threats, hostility, escalating anger, poor resolution, child-rearing disputes, and disengagement between parents (Jouriles et al., 2001). Because the incidence of witnessing many of these "nonviolent" forms of interparental conflict is likely to be substantially higher than exposure to specific bouts of physical aggression, even in the most violent homes, these more rampant types of conflict may have a unique, insidious impact on children's adaptation. An unfortunate product of the primacy of physical aggression in studies of children's functioning in violent homes is the paucity of research on the developmental implications of exposure to these other forms of interparental difficulties. Conceptualizations of destructive interparental relations in the marital conflict literature may serve as useful blueprints as domestic violence researchers strive to address this knowledge gap.

In identifying the specific sources of risk associated with exposure to interparental conflict, Cummings and his colleagues have drawn distinctions between three classes of properties of interactions: parental emotionality, conflict tactics or behaviors, and conflict topics (Cummings, 1998; Cummings, Goeke-Morey, & Papp, 2004). Using diverse methodologies (e.g., diaries, analogue simulations of different conflict tactics, quasi-experimental designs), studies have indicated that children's distress and behavior dysregulation following exposure to conflict varies as a function of the type and intensity of parental negative emotionality (anger, sadness, and fear; Cummings, Goeke-Morey, Papp, & Dukewich, 2002; Cummings et al., 2004; Goeke-Morey, Cummings, Harold, & Shelton, 2003). Likewise, various conflict behaviors or tactics ranging from disengagement and withdrawal to threatening verbalizations have been shown to predict a wide array of children's immediate distress and coping responses to conflict and their long-term psychological (e.g., internalizing, externalizing) symptoms (Davies, Sturge-Apple, Winter, Cummings, & Farrell, 2006; Katz & Woodin, 2002). Emerging evidence also suggests that children's coping with interparental discord may hinge, in part, on the topic or substance of the interparental conflict. For example, some studies have indicated that disagreements revolving around child-rearing and marital issues carry greater risks for children than general exposure to interparental discord or conflicts about social and work issues (e.g., Cummings et al., 2004; Grych, 1998; Grych & Fincham, 1993; Jouriles et al., 1991).

Exclusively focusing on identifying interparental characteristics that undermine child development runs the risk of overpathologizing these home environments. If the majority of children from violent homes do not experience significant psychopathology at any particular time point, then other characteristics of the interparental relationship may be operating to offset or mitigate the risk associated with exposure to the destructive properties of the interparental subsystem. Thus, although constructive aspects of the interparental relationship diminish substantially as interparental violence increases (Jouriles et al., 2001), a primary assumption of resilience frameworks in developmental psychopathology is that some salubrious processes may still be present even in highly adverse or risky developmental contexts (Davies & Cummings, 2006). Research in the interparental discord literature has identified several dimensions of handling interparental conflict and interactions that have constructive or benign implications for the welfare of children, including parental resolution (e.g., Cummings, Ballard, El-Sheikh, & Lake, 1991; Kerig, 1996), problem-solving and supportive behaviors (e.g., Cummings, Goeke-Morey, & Papp, 2003), and positive emotionality (e.g., Cummings et al., 2002).

Despite these promising findings, research on the operation of these constructive characteristics of the interparental subsystem in families experiencing domestic violence is virtually nonexistent. Although it is possible that considerable risk associated with the high prevalence of destructive conflict processes may override or supersede any psychological benefits of witnessing violent parents engage in constructive forms of interparental conflict resolution, a plausible hypothesis is that constructive interparental conflict may mitigate the vulnerability associated with exposure to destructive conflict in violent homes through two channels. On the one hand, specific characteristics of the interparental subsystem that *directly* reduce or offset risk of exposure to domestic violence in their role as moderators of the transmission of distress in violent homes would signify the operation of *protective* factors in the interparental subsystem. On the other hand, constructive interparental parameters may *indirectly* affect the risk of exposure to domestic violence as *compensatory* factors that are broadly associated with heightened well-being in children, regardless of whether they face considerable adversity or risk

(Davies & Cummings, 2006). Thus, rather than affecting the relationship between domestic violence and child adjustment problems in their role as moderators, compensatory factors may play a unique role in the prediction of child adjustment even after taking into account destructive conflict properties and, in the process, reduce the incidence of child psychopathology.

Although the identification of constructive forms of interparental conflict has focused primarily on searching for inherently positive relational features of the interparental subsystem (e.g., positive emotions, support, resolution), adverse or stressful factors can also have protective effects in high-risk contexts. Following the assumption that growth results from adversity, challenge models in developmental psychopathology specify that stressful conditions, especially in small or moderate doses, may actually have "steeling effects" that serve to enhance coping and adjustment and inoculate individuals against subsequent psychological insult (Garmezy, Masten, & Tellegen, 1984). Thus, some inherently negative features of the interparental relationships (e.g., negative affect) may trigger children to develop effective ways of coping and adapting to adversity if they occur relatively infrequently.

MEDIATING MECHANISMS UNDERLYING THE RISK OF DOMESTIC VIOLENCE

Understanding children's adaptations in the multidimensional constellation of destructive and constructive properties in the interparental subsystem is a key step toward the broader goal of explaining why domestic violence and accompanying interparental processes are associated with child adjustment problems. In illustrating the utility of integrating interparental conflict and domestic violence literatures, theories of interparental conflict may provide useful guides in identifying the processes by which children in violent homes develop psychological problems. Theories of interparental conflict that may be particularly useful in identifying the mechanisms that mediate associations between domestic violence and child adjustment can be broadly classified into two classes: interparental process models and parenting process models.

Interparental Process Models

In interparental process theories, the stressfulness of witnessing destructive properties of the interparental relationship, including violence, increase child risk for psychopathology by directly undermining their adaptational abilities in the context of subsequent interparental and family difficulties. Originally distilled from models of developmental psychopathology (Cowan, Cowan, & Schulz, 1996), these theories draw distinctions between *risk factors, risk processes, and outcomes. Risk factors* in these models comprise pathogenic dimensions of the interparental relationship that increase the likelihood of children experiencing negative *outcomes* characterized by patterns of maladaptation that are manifested in relatively consistent ways across time and context (e.g., psychopathology, poor competence). As illustrated by path 2 in Figure 8.1 (interparental process models), repeated exposure to interparental risk factors (e.g., violence, emotionality, conflict tactics) is specifically theorized to result in the dynamic emergence of *risk processes* characterized by regularity in child response patterns in interparental and family contexts. In connoting the second component of the mediational process, interparental process models further postulate that these responses or coping patterns developed within the family system broaden, intensify, and crystallize over time into negative outcomes that evidence some degree of temporal and contextual consistency (e.g., psychopathology, poor competence; see path 3 in Figure 8.1). Numerous conceptual models postulate that interparental conflict directly sets in motion processes within children that increase their vulnerability to psychopathology, including but not limited to social learning theory (Cox, Paley, & Harter, 2001; Margolin, Oliver, & Medina, 2001), the cognitive-contextual framework (Grych & Fincham, 1990; Grych & Cardoza-Fernandes, 2001), and the emotional security theory (Davies & Cummings, 1994; Davies, Harold, Goeke-Morey, & Cummings, 2002).

Social learning theory specifies that children learn aggressive, dysregulated patterns of behavior through observational modeling of parents' destructive ways of managing disputes and negative reinforcement contingencies that operate during and in the aftermath of interparental disputes (Cox et al., 2001; Emery, 1989). In turn, patterns of hostility and dysregulation emerging within the interparental subsystem are theorized to intensify and generalize to extrafamilial settings and, in the process, crystallize into psychological problems. Although social learning theory is consistently invoked to explain associations between destructive interparental relations and child psychopathology (e.g., Crockenberg & Langrock, 2001; Graham-Bermann, 1998; Johnson & O'Leary, 1987), social learning explanations are typically provided post hoc. Thus, applying tenets of social learning theory to understanding why domestic violence and interparental dysfunction directly affect children will require greater precision in translating the broad theoretical principles into empirically testable hypotheses.

Rooted within social cognitive and stress and coping theories, a defining premise of the cognitive-contextual framework is that cognitive appraisals of the interpersonal meaning of interparental conflict partially mediate or account for associations between destructive interparental conflict and child adjustment problems (Grych & Fincham, 1990). As part of the distal component of the cognitive-contextual framework, past experiences with destructive interparental interactions are conceptualized as fostering greater negative appraisals and attributions about the consequences (e.g., threats to self) and sources of the dispute (e.g., blaming self). Appraisals of threat and self-blame in contexts of interparental difficulties, in turn, are proposed to increase children's vulnerability to mental health problems. In contrast to social learning theory formulations, Grych and colleagues have increasingly utilized the cognitive-contextual framework to test *a priori* predictions about the putative mediating processes underlying exposure to domestic violence (e.g., Grych, Fincham, Jouriles, & McDonald, 2000; Grych, Jouriles et al., 2000; also see Grych, 1998). Testifying to the value of the cognitive-contextual framework, the findings from these studies support the role of children's appraisals as intermediary mechanisms of exposure to domestic violence. For example, Grych, Fincham, and colleagues (2000) reported that perceived threat and self-blame were mediators in the associations between exposure to destructive properties of interparental conflict and their internalizing symptoms for children who experienced domestic violence.

Despite its promise, as with any mid-level theory designed to account for a portion of the risk associated with interparental discord, future tests of the cognitive-contextual framework with children exposed to domestic violence may present some formidable challenges. For example, because social-cognitive processes (e.g., self-blame, perceived threat) assessed in prior studies of the cognitive-contextual framework require children to possess advanced information-processing capacities and conscious, verbal articulation of interpersonal appraisals, the theory has yet to identify how affective and behavioral processes may also account for why interparental violence may pose a risk to the adjustment of children. Elaboration of the other components of the framework may help increase the efficacy of the theory by incorporating broader behavioral and emotional response patterns. For example, the cognitive-contextual framework conceptualizes appraisals as part of a more complex pattern of unfolding processes across multiple domains of functioning, including negative emotional arousal and emotion-focused (e.g., avoidance) and problem-focused (e.g., intervention in conflict) coping strategies.

Complementing the focus on social-cognitive mechanisms in the cognitive-contextual framework, the emotional security theory posits that emotions play a central role in understanding children's adaptations to destructive interparental conflict (Davies & Cummings, 1994; Davies et al., 2002). In the interparental process component of the theory, preserving security in the interparental subsystem is a significant goal for children in the family that serves to mediate the impact of interparental discord and violence on children (Davies et al., in press). Threats to the goal of preserving security are reflected in three observable classes of response processes, including: (a) emotional reactivity, characterized by proneness to intense, prolonged, and dysregulated experiences of fear and distress in response to interparental difficulties; (b) regulation of exposure to parent affect, evidenced by prolonged attempts to become involved in and avoid problems between parents; and (c) internal representations of interparental relations that are manifested in children's negative evaluations of the potential consequences that interparental difficulties have for their well-being. Although this constellation of negative reaction patterns to interparental conflict may hold some temporary adaptive value in attaining the goal of security by alerting children to potential dangers and energizing their psychological and physical resources to cope with threat, these difficulties in obtaining security are postulated to increase children's risk for developing psychological problems (e.g., depression, aggression, anxiety, conduct problems).

In comparison to many other theories of interparental conflict, the emotional security theory provides a detailed account of why difficulties in preserving security increase the likelihood of child mental illness (i.e., path 3, Figure 8.1). Illustrating one set of these putative processes, patterns of responding to interparental difficulties emerging from difficulties in achieving security may serve as guides for simplifying, interpreting, and coping with the complexity of subsequent challenging (i.e., stressful, novel) contexts. In this process, children from domestically violent homes may draw on their affective and sensory analogues (e.g., high vigilance, negative representations, avoidance or intervention) as "scripts" or alarm systems for scanning new or stressful social settings for old threats that originally stemmed from exposure to interparental conflict (Davies et al., in press; Johnston & Roseby, 1997). In another proposed pathway, difficulties in preserving security are assumed to require considerable expenditure of biopsychological resources that deplete children of resources necessary to maintain homeostasis and efficient allocation of psychobiological resources to important organismic challenges. Thus, in accordance with the concept of allostatic load (McEwen & Stellar, 1993; Repetti, Taylor, & Seeman, 2002), insecurity in family relationships may result in physiological dysregulation and accompanying problems maintaining homeostasis and mounting effective physiological responses to stress in several biological systems, including sympathetic-adrenomedullary, hypothalamic-pituitary-adrenocortical, and neuropsychological (e.g., attention focusing and shifting) functioning. In a related developmental pathway, distribution of considerable biopsychosocial capital toward security goals is thought to increase child psychopathology by undermining the ability of children to pursue and resolve significant developmental tasks or, more specifically, challenges that become prominent at a given developmental period (Davies et al., in press).

An advantage of the emotional security theory in informing models of domestic violence is that it has the potential to be applicable to broad developmental periods. For example, even young children, with limited social-cognitive and verbal capacities, are assumed to exhibit difficulties in preserving security in the face of family discord through rudimentary coping patterns and representational capacities rooted in sensorimotor schemes (e.g., Davies et al., in press; Johnston & Roseby, 1997). However, although children's concerns about security are likely to be salient in domestically violent homes as they contend with interparental aggression, proliferation of hostility to the parent–child relationship, and potential family dissolution, researchers have not examined whether the emotional security theory can inform an understanding of the functioning of children exposed to domestic violence.

In summary, numerous theoretical accounts are now available to explain why destructive properties of interparental conflict directly undermine children's adaptations. Nevertheless, significant gaps remain in utilizing these theories to elucidate the mechanisms that mediate associations between domestic violence and children's developmental outcomes. Thus, applying these theories to advance an understanding of interparental violence is a critical step in the next generation of research on domestic violence.

Parenting Process Models

As illustrated by paths 4 and 5 in Figure 8.1, parenting process models of interparental conflict also underscore that domestic violence may affect child functioning through its association with adversity in the broader family system. Within the domestic violence literature, the occurrence of physical abuse and other forms of maltreatment (e.g., neglect) have been theorized to account, at least in part, for the heightened vulnerability of children exposed to domestic violence (e.g., Edleson, 2001). At its most extreme, domestic violence is associated with substantial increases in child maltreatment. For example, recent reviews indicate that the median co-occurrence rate of interparental violence and child physical abuse is approximately 40% (e.g., Appel & Holden, 1998). Living with a violent partner is also a robust predictor of the incidence of child abuse even after taking into account over a dozen other potential risk factors, including childhood abuse history of the caregiver, maternal mental illness, child disabilities and illness, and the caregiver's perceptions of their children (Dixon, Browne, & Hamilton-Giachritsis, 2005). Maltreatment, in turn, has been associated with a wide array of psychological problems and difficulties in resolving developmental tasks (Cicchetti & Toth, 1995).

Although much of the theory and research has addressed the role of maltreatment in families experiencing domestic violence, aggression between parents may also be a cause, correlate, or sequelae of more subtle but still developmentally powerful forms of child-rearing difficulties. Violence in the interparental relationship has been specifically associated with low levels of parental warmth and responsiveness and the use of hostile, inconsistent, and lax disciplinary practices (Holden & Ritchie, 1991; Levendosky & Graham-Bermann, 2000; Margolin, Christensen, & John, 1996; Margolin & John, 1997). Consistent with the second link in the mediational chain, studies show that these more common forms of parenting difficulties predict child maladaptation in domestically violent homes (e.g., Holden & Ritchie, 1991; Levendosky, Huth-Bocks, Shapiro, & Semel, 2003; Margolin et al., 1996).

Because the vast majority of research on domestic violence study links between domestic violence and parenting or parenting and child outcomes in isolation from each other, they do not definitively test the mediational requirement that the putative risk process (i.e., parenting) accounts for substantial variance between the risk factor (i.e., domestic violence) and the outcome (i.e., child functioning). Increasing the urgency of empirically testing the mediational role of parenting, recent empirical delineations of parenting process pathways linking domestic violence, parenting difficulties, and child outcomes have yielded complex and sometimes counterintuitive results. For example, although a recent study did not explicitly test child physical abuse and neglect as mediators of interparental violence, domestic violence emerged as a more consistent predictor of child psychological problems than child abuse and neglect in a series of regression models containing an array of child, ecological, and family risks factors (Yates et al., 2003). In another study that incorporated multiple risk factors in a path-analytic model, Levendosky and colleagues (2003) found that domestic violence was actually associated with more effective parenting practices, which, in turn, was associated with greater child adjustment. Still other studies lend support for the mediational role of parenting disturbances in associations between interparental aggression and child psychological problems (e.g., Margolin & John, 1997).

Although future research may well support the hypothesis that disruptions in parenting partially explain the vulnerability of children exposed to domestic violence, achieving a comprehensive understanding of the unfolding sequence of processes outlined in a parenting process model demands increases in conceptual and methodological rigor. In the context of the predominant use of cross-sectional designs in domestic violence research, simply demonstrating that parenting accounts for substantial variance in the association between domestic violence and children's functioning does not necessarily establish the sequential chain of events in a mediational model. Definitive tests of mediation eventually will require documenting that interparental difficulties subsequently undermine child-rearing abilities, which in turn, prospectively increase child vulnerability to psychopathology. First, the notion that strife and discord between parents engenders parenting disturbances is one of many potential interpretations of the co-occurrence between interparental and parent–child problems (Appel & Holden, 1998). Linkages between parenting and interparental relations may be the product of the operation of additional variables such as parental antisocial attributes, parental developmental history, or the strain faced by a family's experience living with a disruptive child(ren) (Tajima, 2000). Thus, as research progresses, longitudinal analyses that model change over time will be needed to test the directionality of associations between family processes and child adjustment in parenting path models in relation to alternative models.

If future research supports the parenting process model, another important step in testing the viability of the model will be to explore how domestic violence increases child vulnerability by compromising parenting abilities. In addressing the first link in the model of parenting, theoretical perspectives on marriage and parenting place differential emphasis on specific processes that result from interparental dysfunction and that subsequently disrupt parenting (Sturge-Apple, Davies, Boker, & Cummings, 2004). Although relationship perturbations, coping processes, negative affect, and personality attributes have been variously discussed as possible mechanisms underlying domestic violence (Appel & Holden, 1998; Levendosky & Graham-Bermann, 2000), little attention has been devoted to developing precise conceptual and operational definitions of these constructs and testing the different mediating mechanisms (for exceptions, see Levendosky et al., 2003; Mahoney, Donnelly, Boxer, & Lewis, 2003; McGuigan, Vuchinich, & Pratt, 2000). In addressing the second link, identifying the processes that account for why parenting problems in violent homes increase child vulnerability to psychological difficulties would also further the next generation of research. As illustrated by path 5 in Figure 8.1, exposure to various parenting difficulties may set in motion multiple processes within children (e.g., affective-motivational, social learning, social information processing) that ultimately serve as more proximal causes of their psychopathology (Cummings, Davies, & Campbell, 2000). For example, the parenting path component of the emotional security theory proposes that parenting difficulties accompanying destructive interparental conflict engender child psychopathology by undermining children's security in the parent–child relationship (i.e., their confidence in parents as sources of protection and support) (Davies et al., 2002). Thus, evolving child response and coping patterns in parent–child and family contexts may help explain why parenting processes mediate associations between domestic violence and child maladjustment.

Parenting practices constitute only one class of family processes that may potentially mediate domestic violence in parenting process models. Thus, as illustrated in Figure 8.1, parent–child relationship dynamics and broader properties of the family system may explain a portion of variance in psychopathology experienced by children of domestic violence. Guided by attachment theory, one possibility is that elevated difficulties in responding to children's bids for support, comfort, and protection experienced by parents coping with domestic violence may undermine children's abilities to use the parents as a secure base. The resulting insecurity in the attachment relationship, in turn, may increase the probability of failures to successfully cope with and resolve important developmental challenges and, in the process, set the stage for developmental trajectories of maladaptation and psychopathology. Another possibility, consistent with interparental process pathways, is that witnessing frightening or frightened behaviors displayed by violent or hostile parents in interparental interactions directly undermines children's attachment security or their ability to utilize the caregivers as support figures. Although various empirical tests assessing destructive interparental conflict in community samples have yielded support for these pathways (Davies et al., 2002; Frosch, Mangelsdorf, & McHale, 2000; Owen & Cox, 1997), systematic analysis of the operation of attachment in the highly adverse context of domestic violence has yet to be undertaken. Attesting to the value of conducting future research in this area, the studies testing various elements of these models have, in aggregate, yielded inconsistent findings (e.g., Grych, Wachsmuth-Schlaefer, & Klockow, 2002; Levendosky et al., 2003).

Family systems theory may also serve as a useful heuristic for integrating the study of domestic violence in the broader family context. According to the principle of holism in family systems theory, the meaning of any perturbation in a specific family relationship or subsystem cannot be fully deciphered without an understanding of the relationship structures, boundaries, power distributions, and communication patterns of the other family subsystems and the whole family unit (Davies & Cicchetti, 2004). Thus, interparental conflict may exert an impact on children's functioning through its association with a broader pattern of communication, expressiveness, and boundary maintenance difficulties (i.e., ways of exchanging resources and materials across family members) in the family system. For example, Katz and Low (2004) reported that disturbances in the coparenting relationship or ability for parents to support each other in their child-rearing responsibilities partially mediated associations between marital violence and children's internalizing symptoms. In another study, Davies, Cummings, and Winter (2004) demonstrated that elevated interparental discord was the common denominator in two types of higher-order profiles of relationship functioning across interparental, coparental, and parent–child subsystems. More specifically, disengaged families experienced overly rigid, inflexible, and distant relationship boundaries that were manifested in high levels of family discord, hostility, and detachment across family subsystems, whereas enmeshed families exhibited weak boundaries across family subsystems and, as a result, display high levels of conflict, hostility, and psychological control. In comparison to children from cohesive families who experienced warmth, affection, and flexible well-defined boundaries in family relationships, children from disengaged families showed greater signs of insecurity in the interparental relationship and higher levels of concurrent and subsequent internalizing and externalizing symptoms. Although these findings in the context of the extant literature raise the possibility that broader family relationship patterns may partially account for associations between domestic violence and child adjustment difficulties (e.g., Belsky & Fearon, 2004; Kerig, 1995), direct empirical tests of this putative parenting pathway have yet to be conducted.

MODERATING CONDITIONS UNDERLYING THE RISK OF DOMESTIC VIOLENCE

Open systems conceptualizations of family and child functioning in developmental psychopathology and family systems approaches also highlight the importance of examining other family characteristics that may provoke reorganizations in family functioning and serve as architects of interdependencies (Davies & Cicchetti, 2004; Margolin et al., 2001). Thus, as path 6 of Figure 8.1 illustrates, the form and magnitude of interparental and parenting process pathways of domestic violence may vary, depending on preexisting attributes in the family system. Stated in statistical terminology, these other properties of the family system may specifically act as moderators that alter the strength and substance of developmental pathways underlying domestic violence and child functioning. By way of illustration, the following sections selectively address three potential moderators of domestic violence: gender, age and developmental period, and family characteristics.

Gender

Associations between domestic violence, interparental (e.g., child emotional reactivity to interparental difficulties) and parenting risk processes, and child vulnerability may depend on the gender of the parents and children. Data on the moderating role of parent gender are inconclusive at this early stage of the research process, particularly in the domestic violence literature. For example, given the greater size and strength of men, some models of domestic violence postulate that even a morphologically identical act of abuse (e.g., hitting) is likely to have more serious consequences for women, families, and children if the perpetrator is the male partner (Holtzworth-Munroe, Smutzler, & Sandin, 1997; Jouriles et al., 2001). Consistent with this interpretation, some studies have shown that male-initiated violence in intimate relationships is a predictor of a wider range of child adjustment problems than mother-initiated violence (e.g., Fergusson & Horwood, 1998). Major obstacles remain in identifying the role of parent gender in models of domestic violence. For example, the predominant emphasis on the assessment of male violence in samples of battered women and children (Jouriles et al., 2001) and the small corpus of research analyzing both male and female domestic violence preclude the analysis of whether associations between domestic violence and family or child problems vary significantly as a function of the parent's gender. In reflecting the complexity of disentangling process relations among domestic violence parameters and child adjustment, domestic violence is a robust risk factor for children regardless of the gender of the perpetrator. When gender differences are reported, the effects are often relatively weak and qualified by other family processes (e.g., Dutton, in press; Dutton & Nicholls, 2005). Broader inquiries into the impact of parameters of interparental conflict on children provide a glimpse of this complexity (see review by Davies & Lindsay, 2001). For example, even if male violence is a stronger predictor of child difficulties than female violence, other destructive forms of conflict may have a stronger impact on children if the mother is the primary initiator of the conflict. In a recent study of children's reactions to adult conflict tactics, children viewed physical aggression as the most destructive form of male-initiated conflict and threats to the intactness of the family as the most destructive form of female-initiated conflict (Goeke-Morey et al., 2003).

Any comprehensive, gender-inclusive model of domestic violence must also consider the possible role of child gender as a moderator of domestic violence processes. Although many large sample studies and meta-analyses of domestic violence have yielded complex and null results on the moderating role of child and parent gender (e.g., Herrera & McCloskey, 2001; Kitzmann et al. 2003; Yates et al., 2003), the inconclusive findings may result largely from the tendency for researchers to relegate gender to a secondary status in models of domestic violence. Whereas some studies ignore gender issues by pooling boys and girls together in primary analyses, other research considers boys and girls in isolation from each other or treats gender as a covariate in models. None of these approaches, however, examined the moderating role of child gender by directly testing whether the risk associated with domestic violence or the accompanying family processes differ for boys and girls.

Age and Developmental Period

Although age is increasingly acknowledged as a potential moderator in models of domestic violence and discord (Kitzmann et al., 2003), it is difficult to draw any conclusions about whether exposure to aggression between parents carries a disproportionate risk for children within any specific developmental period (Margolin, 1998). Meta-analytic findings provide some qualified evidence to suggest that preschoolers may exhibit greater vulnerability to domestic violence than older children (Kitzmann et al., 2003). If this finding is replicated, delineating the mechanisms underlying the moderating role of child age will be an important task for future research. For example, younger children may be more apt to exhibit vulnerability than older children by virtue of their disproportionately higher exposure to domestic violence (Fantuzzo, Boruch, Beriama, Atkins, & Marcus, 1997), greater reliance on the violent parents as attachment figures (e.g., Margolin, 1998), or low levels of perceived competence (Grych, 1998).

The most conclusive finding from the quantitative review by Kitzmann and colleagues (2003) was the documentation of a consistent association between domestic violence and child maladjustment across preschool, middle childhood, and adolescent periods. Thus, simply searching for the one age-group that is most vulnerable to domestic violence may not be the most fruitful developmental strategy. Rather, a more promising research direction may involve delineating the common and distinct processes that may underlie the interparental and parenting process pathways of domestic violence across developmental periods. For example, Jouriles and colleagues (2000) reported that appraisals of self-blame more strongly predicted internalizing symptoms for 10- to 12-year-old children than 8- to 9-year-old children. As another example, age-related vulnerability to marital conflict may vary, depending on the specific domain of child functioning. Stage-salient frameworks in developmental psychopathology conceptualize development as a series of challenges that assume prominence during a particular developmental period and remain salient throughout the life span (Cicchetti, 1993; Cummings et al., 2000). For example, the toddler and preschool years usher in developmental challenges such as exploration, autonomy, self-control, internal stage language, and internalization of moral standards. Because these tasks are demanding in and of themselves, signs of vulnerability resulting from exposure to domestic violence may be particularly evident in how children approach these challenges.

Family Characteristics

Path 6 in Figure 8.1 also underscores the possibility that family character-istics could modify the interparental and parenting pathways of domestic violence in their role as protective or potentiating factors (Davies et al., in press). According to the emotional security theory (Davies et al., 2002), the implications of destructive interparental interactions may depend on the configuration of risk and protective characteristics in the broader fam-ily system. On the one hand, when interparental difficulties take place in a distressed or unstable family unit, children may be especially likely to regard exposure to domestic violence and its associated interparental and parenting disturbances as threats to their security and welfare. Thus, any indices that reflect vulnerability in the family (e.g., parent psychopathol-ogy, family disengagement or enmeshment) may potentiate or amplify the deleterious impact of domestic violence on children's coping and adapta-tional capacities. On the other hand, domestic violence may assume a less pernicious meaning for children who have access to some psychosocial resources in the family (e.g., easy child temperament, family social sup-port, positive relationship with an adult). For example, although levels of psychosocial support in violent families are substantially lower than nonviolent families, violent families still experience considerable vari-ability in access to relational and psychological resources (e.g., cohesion; Katz & Low, 2004; McCloskey, Figueredo, & Koss, 1995). However, even in the face of calls for examining child and family attributes as moderators of interparental conflict (Davies & Cummings, 1994; Grych & Fincham, 1990), the empirical identification of family charac-teristics that modulate risk processes in high-risk, violent homes has been largely ignored (e.g., for an exception, see Grych, 1998).

BIDIRECTIONAL PROCESSES UNDERLYING THE RISK OF DOMESTIC VIOLENCE

Despite the well-established pitfalls and problems of drawing conclusions about directionality of effects without the use of longitudinal or experimen-tal designs, a prevailing conclusion from the largely concurrent associations among domestic violence and child functioning is that domestic violence and its accompanying destructive family processes undermine children's functioning. According to the principle of interdependency in family sys-tems theory, the functioning of any one individual or relationship in the family is regulated by the characteristics of other individuals or relationships in the family (Davies & Cicchetti, 2004). Stated differently, the interplay among family relationships and child development is assumed to be reciprocal in nature. Consistent with this principle, numerous formulations within the interparental conflict literature postulate that the impact of children's behavior on the family system may also account for both the risk and heterogeneity of outcomes experienced by children exposed to high levels of conflict (e.g., Davies & Cummings, 1994; Emery, 1989). Thus, translating these conceptualizations to the study of domestic violence may help elucidate the processes underlying the multiple pathways in our model.

Supporting the value of delineating transactional processes between child and family processes in violent homes, paths 2 and 5 of Figure 8.1 depict bidirectional paths running between family processes and dimensions of children's functioning. For example, individual differences in children's behavior problems may place strain on the quality of the relationship between parents, particularly given the preexisting relationship vulnerabilities exhibited by adults in homes characterized by domestic violence. In accordance with this hypothesis, not only has marital conflict been found to be a predictor of increases in children's psychological problems over time, but children's externalizing symptoms also predicted greater marital conflict over a 2-year period (Jenkins, Dunn, O'Connor, Rasbash, & Simpson, 2005). Testifying to the potential robustness of bidirectional processes in high-risk families, the power of child behavior problems in the prediction of marital difficulties was particularly strong in more complex, problematic family contexts containing stepparents (Jenkins et al., 2005; O'Connor & Insabella, 1999).

Signifying another type of bidirectional process, children's patterns of responding to interparental problems may also affect the nature and course of interparental problems. In his behavioral conceptualization of family violence, Emery (1989) proposed a transactional cycle of effects between children and the interparental subsystem. In the initial series of unfolding processes, children respond to witnessing violence with higher levels of distress that, in turn, precipitate specific attempts on the part of the children to alleviate their distress through disruptive (e.g., aggression, yelling) behaviors. At the subsequent phases of this reciprocal cycle, children's misbehavior broadens and intensifies in subsequent conflicts because it serves a negative reinforcement function of distracting parents from engagement in the aversive ongoing conflict. From a different theoretical perspective, the emotional security theory has postulated that children's intervention strategies (e.g., mediation) in interparental conflicts may help them to attain a sense of security by interrupting the course of escalating conflicts before they substantially threaten the family system (Davies & Cummings, 1994).

Although misbehavior, distress, and intervention strategies may temporarily disrupt parents from ongoing conflict, there is considerable disagreement about the long-term impact of children's patterns of responding to the interparental relationship. Some conceptualizations underscore that children's reactivity to adult problems may increase their salience as targets of family hostility and amplify the proliferation of violence across family subsystems, whereas other models suggest that child reactivity to conflict may alert parents to their children's distress and motivate them to resolve their differences (Schermerhorn, Cummings, & Davies, 2005). A recent study suggests that the viability of these models may depend on the specific type of reactivity exhibited by children. Whereas children's dysregulated behavioral reactions to parental conflicts (e.g., aggressive responses) predicted increases in marital conflict over a 1-year period, children's attempts to mediate (e.g., comfort or stop conflict) the conflict were associated with subsequent decreases in marital conflict over the same period (Schermerhorn, Cummings, DeCarlo, & Davies, in press). Because the nature and magnitude of child effects on the interparental relationship may differ in the context of the more volatile and vulnerable relationships in domestically violent homes, delineating the bidirectional effects between children and the interparental subsystem should be a priority in domestic violence research.

SUMMARY AND IMPLICATIONS

In summary, progress in generating and disseminating knowledge on the perils children face in witnessing domestic violence has already resulted in greater awareness of this public health problem in the community (Graham-Bermann & Edleson, 2001; Jaffe, Baker, & Cunningham, 2004). However, the scant scientific resources devoted to identifying the multiple pathways involved in understanding how and why domestic violence poses a risk for children's adjustment has hindered the generation of policy, legislation, and services for children and families experiencing domestic violence (Davies et al., in press). Thus, the purpose of this chapter was to provide a heuristic for a new generation of research aimed at identifying the mediating processes and moderating conditions that help elucidate the multiplicity of pathways underlying associations between domestic violence and child maladjustment. As this new generation of research progresses, resulting advances in scientific knowledge may specifically inform public policy and treatment initiatives by: (a) improving our ability to identify children and families most in need of treatment, (b) increasing our precision in specifying targets or goals of policy and treatment programs, and (c) assisting in the development of specific treatment or therapeutic tools (for more details about translational implications, see Davies et al., in press).

REFERENCES

Appel, A. E., & Holden, G. W. (1998). The co-occurrence of spouse and physical child abuse: A review and appraisal. *Journal of Family Psychology, 12,* 578–599.

Barnett, D., Manly, J. T., & Cicchetti, D. (1993). Defining child maltreatment: The interface between policy and research. In D. Cicchetti & S. L. Toth (Eds.), *Child abuse, child development, and social policy* (pp. 7–74). Norwood, NJ: Ablex.

Belsky, J., & Fearon, R. M. P. (2004). Exploring marriage-parenting typologies: Their contextual antecedents and developmental sequelae. *Development and Psychopathology, 16,* 501–523.

Cicchetti, D. (1993). Developmental psychopathology: Reactions, reflections, projections. *Developmental Review, 13,* 471–502.

Cicchetti, D., & Toth, S. L. (1995). A developmental psychopathology perspective on child abuse and neglect. *Journal of the American Academy of Child and Adolescent Psychiatry, 34,* 541–565.

Cowan, P. A., Cowan, C. P., & Schulz, M. S. (1996). Thinking about risk and resilience in families. In E. M. Hetherington & E. A. Blechman (Eds.), *Stress, coping, and resiliency in children and families. Family research consortium: Advances in family research* (pp. 1–38). Hillsdale, NJ: Lawrence Erlbaum Associates.

Cox, M. J., Paley, B., & Harter, K. (2001). Interparental conflict and parent-child relationships. In J. Grych & F. Fincham (Eds.), *Child development and interparental conflict* (pp. 249–272). New York: Cambridge University Press.

Crockenberg, S., & Langrock, A. (2001). The role of specific emotions in children's responses to interparental conflict: A test of the model. *Journal of Family Psychology, 15,* 163–182.

Cummings, E. M. (1998). Children exposed to marital conflict and violence: Conceptual and theoretical directions. In G. W. Holden, R. Geffner, & E. N. Jouriles (Eds.), *Children exposed to marital violence: Theory, research, and applied issues* (pp. 55–93). Washington, DC: American Psychological Association.

Cummings, E. M., Ballard, M., El-Sheikh, M., & Lake, M. (1991). Resolution and children's responses to interadult anger. *Developmental Psychology, 27,* 462–470.

Cummings, E. M., & Cummings, J. S. (1988). A process-oriented approach to children's coping with adults' angry behavior. *Developmental Review, 3,* 296–321.

Cummings, E. M., & Davies, P. T. (1994). Maternal depression and child development. *Journal of Child Psychology and Psychiatry, 35,* 73–112.

Cummings, E. M., Davies, P. T., & Campbell, S. B. (2000). *Developmental psychopathology and family process: Theory, research, and clinical implications.* New York: Guilford Press.

Cummings, E. M., Goeke-Morey, M., & Papp, L. (2003). Children's responses to everyday marital conflict tactics in the home. *Child Development, 74,* 1918–1929.

Cummings, E. M., Goeke-Morey, M. C., & Papp, L. M. (2004). Everyday marital conflict and child aggression. *Journal of Abnormal Child Psychology, 32,* 191–202.

Cummings, E. M., Goeke-Morey, M. C., Papp, L. M., & Dukewich, T. L. (2002). Children's responses to mothers' and fathers' emotionality and conflict tactics during marital conflict in the home. *Journal of Family Psychology, 16,* 478–492.

Davies, P. T., & Cicchetti, D. (2004). Editorial: Toward an integration of family systems and developmental psychopathology approaches. *Development and Psychopathology, 16,* 477–481.

Davies, P. T., & Cummings, E. M. (1994). Marital conflict and child adjustment: An emotional security hypothesis. *Psychological Bulletin, 116,* 387–411.

Davies, P. T., & Cummings, E. M. (2006). Interparental discord, family process, and developmental psychopathology. In D. Cicchetti & D. J. Cohen (Eds.), *Developmental psychopathology: Vol. 3. Risk, disorder, and adaptation* (2nd ed., pp. 86–128). New York: John Wiley & Sons.

Davies, P. T., Cummings, E. M., & Winter, M. A. (2004). Pathways between profiles of family functioning, child security in the interparental subsystem, and child psychological problems. *Development and Psychopathology, 16,* 525–550.

Davies, P. T., Harold, G. T., Goeke-Morey, M. C., & Cummings, E. M. (2002). Child emotional security and interparental conflict. *Monographs of the Society for Research in Child Development, 67,* 1–115.

Davies, P. T., & Lindsay, L. (2001). Does gender moderate the effects of conflict on children? In J. Grych & F. Fincham (Eds.), *Child development and interparental conflict* (pp. 64–97). New York: Cambridge University Press.

Davies, P. T., Sturge-Apple, M. L., Winter, M. A., Cummings, E. M., & Farrell, D. (2006). Child adaptational development in contexts of interparental conflict over time. *Child Development, 77,* 218–233.

Davies, P. T., Winter, M. A., Cicchetti, D. (in press). The implications of emotional security theory for understanding and treating childhood psychopathology. *Development and Psychopathology.*

Dixon, L., Browne, K., & Hamilton-Giachritsis, C. (2005). Risk factors of parents abused as children: A mediational analysis of the intergenerational continuity of child maltreatment (part I). *Journal of Child Psychology and Psychiatry, 46,* 47–57.

Dutton, D. G. (in press). Domestic abuse assessment in child custody disputes: Beware the domestic violence research paradigm. *Journal of Child Custody.*

Dutton, D. G., & Nicholls, T. L. (2005). The gender paradigm in domestic violence research and theory: Part 1—The conflict of theory and data. *Aggression and Violent Behavior, 10,* 680–714.

Edleson, J. L. (2001). Studying the co-occurrence of child maltreatment and domestic violence in families. In S. A. Graham-Bermann & J. L. Edleson (Eds.), *Domestic violence in the lives of children* (pp. 91–110). Washington, DC: American Psychological Association.

Emery, R. E. (1989). Family violence. *American Psychologist, 44,* 321–328.

Fantuzzo, J. W., Boruch, R., Beriama, A., Atkins, M., & Marcus, S. (1997). Domestic violence and children: Prevalence and risk in five major U.S. cities. *Journal of the American Academy of Child and Adolescent Psychiatry, 36,* 116–122.

Fergusson, D. M., & Horwood, L. J. (1998). Exposure to interparental violence in childhood and psychosocial adjustment in young adulthood. *Child Abuse and Neglect, 22,* 339–357.

Frosch, C. A., Mangelsdorf, S. C., & McHale, J. L. (2000). Marital behavior and the security of preschooler-parent attachment relationships. *Journal of Family Psychology, 14,* 144–161.

Garmezy, N., Masten, A. S., & Tellegen, A. (1984). The study of stress and competence in children: A building block for developmental psychopathology. *Child Development, 55,* 97–111.

Goeke-Morey, M. C., Cummings, E. M., Harold, G. T., & Shelton, K. H. (2003). Categories and continua of destructive and constructive marital conflict tactics from the perspective of U.S. and Welsh children. *Journal of Family Psychology, 17,* 327–338.

Graham-Bermann, S. A. (1998). The impact of woman abuse on children's social development: Research and theoretical perspectives. In G. W. Holden, R. Geffner, & E. N. Jouriles (Eds.), *Children exposed to marital violence: Theory, research, and applied issues* (pp. 21–54). Washington, DC: American Psychological Association.

Graham-Bermann, S. A., & Edleson, J. L. (2001). Introduction. In S. A. Graham-Bermann & J. L. Edleson (Eds.), *Domestic violence in the lives of children: The future of research, intervention, and social policy* (pp. 3–10). Washington, DC: American Psychological Association.

Grych, J. H. (1998). Children's appraisals of interparental conflict: Situational and contextual influences. *Journal of Family Psychology, 12,* 437–453.

Grych, J. H., & Cardoza-Fernandes, S. (2001). Understanding the impact of interparental conflict on children: The role of social cognitive processes. In J. Grych & F. Fincham (Eds.), *Child development and interparental conflict* (pp. 157–187). New York: Cambridge University Press.

Grych, J. H., & Fincham, F. D. (1990). Marital conflict and children's adjustment: A cognitive-contextual framework. *Psychological Bulletin, 108,* 267–290.

Grych, J. H., & Fincham, F. D. (1993). Children's appraisals of marital conflict: Initial investigations of the cognitive-contextual framework. *Child Development, 64,* 215–230.

Grych, J. H., Fincham, F. D., Jouriles, E. N., & McDonald, R. (2000). Interparental conflict and child adjustment: Testing the mediational role of appraisals in the cognitive-contextual framework. *Child Development, 71,* 1648–1661.

Grych, J. H., Harold, G. T., & Miles, C. J. (2003). A prospective investigation of appraisals as mediators of the link between interparental conflict and child adjustment. *Child Development, 74,* 1176–1193.

Grych, J. H., Jouriles, E. N., Swank, P. R., McDonald, R., & Norwood, W. D. (2000). Patterns of adjustment among children of battered women. *Journal of Consulting and Clinical Psychology, 68,* 84–94.

Grych, J. H., Wachsmuth-Schlaefer, T., & Klockow, L. L. (2002). Interparental aggression and young children's representations of family relationships. *Journal of Family Psychology, 16,* 259–272.

Herrera, V. M., & McCloskey, L. A. (2001). Gender differences in the risk for delinquency among youth exposed to family violence. *Child Abuse and Neglect, 25,* 1037–1051.

Holden, G. W., & Ritchie, K. L. (1991). Linking extreme marital discord, child rearing, and child behavior problems: Evidence from battered women. *Child Development, 62,* 311–327.

Holtzworth-Monroe, A., Smutzler, N., & Sandin, E. (1997). A brief review of the research on husband violence: Part II: The psychological effects of husband violence on battered women and their children. *Aggression and Violent Behavior, 2,* 179–213.

Hughes, H. M., Graham-Bermann, S. A., & Gruber, G. (2001). Resilience in children exposed to domestic violence. In S. A. Graham-Bermann & J. L. Edleson (Eds.), *Domestic violence in the lives of children: The future of research, intervention, and social policy* (pp. 67–90). Washington, DC: American Psychological Association.

Jaffe, P. G., Baker, L. L., & Cunningham, A. J. (2004). Purpose and overview. In P. G. Jaffe, L. L. Baker, & A. J. Cunningham (Eds.), *Protecting children from domestic violence: Strategies for community intervention* (pp. 3–7). New York: Guilford Press.

Jenkins, J., Dunn, J., O'Connor, T. G., Rasbash, J., & Simpson, A. (2005). Mutual influence of marital conflict and children's behavior problems: Shared and nonshared family risks. *Child Development, 76,* 24–39.

Johnson, P. L., & O'Leary, K. D. (1987). Parental behavior patterns and conduct disorders in girls. *Journal of Abnormal Child Psychology, 15,* 573–581.

Johnston, J. R., & Roseby, V. (1997). *In the name of the child: A developmental approach to understanding and helping children of conflicted and violent divorce.* New York: Free Press.

Jouriles, E. N., McDonald, R. N., Norwood, W. D., Ware, H. S., Spiller, L. C., & Swank, P. R. (1998). Knives, guns, and interparental violence: Relations with child behavior problems. *Journal of Family Psychology, 12,* 178–194.

Jouriles, E. N., Murphy, C., Farris, A. M., Smith, D. A., Richters, J. E., & Waters, E. (1991). Marital adjustment, childrearing disagreements, and child behavior problems: Increasing the specificity of the marital assessment. *Child Development, 62,* 1424–1433.

Jouriles, E. N., Norwood, W. D., McDonald, R., & Peters, B. (2001). Domestic violence and child adjustment. In J. H. Grych & F. D. Fincham (Eds.), *Interparental conflict and child development: Theory, research, and applications.* (pp. 315–336). Cambridge, England: Cambridge University Press.

Jouriles, E. N., Spiller, L. C., Stephens, N., McDonald, R., & Swank, P. (2000). Variability in adjustment of children of battered women: The role of child appraisals of interparent conflict. *Cognitive Therapy and Research, 24,* 233–249.

Katz, L. F., & Low, S. M. (2004). Marital violence, co-parenting, and family-level processes in relation to children's adjustment. *Journal of Family Psychology, 18,* 372–382.

Katz, L. F., & Woodin, E. M. (2002). Hostility, hostile detachment, and conflict engagement in marriages: Effects on child and family functioning. *Child Development, 73,* 636–651.

Kerig, P. K. (1995). Triangles in the family circle: Effects of family structure on marriage, parenting, and child adjustment. *Journal of Family Psychology, 9,* 28–43.

Kerig, P. (1996). Assessing the links between interparental conflict and child adjustment: The Conflicts and Problem-Solving Scales. *Journal of Family Psychology, 10,* 454–473.

Kitzmann, K. M., Gaylord, N. K., Holt, A. R., & Kenny, E. D. (2003). Child witnesses to domestic violence: A meta-analytic review. *Journal of Consulting and Clinical Psychology, 71,* 339–352.

Levendosky, A. A., & Graham-Bermann, S. A. (2000). Behavioral observations of parenting in battered women. *Journal of Family Psychology, 14,* 80–94.

Levendosky, A. A., Huth-Bocks, A. C., Shapiro, D., L., & Semel, M. A. (2003). The impact of domestic violence on the maternal-child relationship and preschool-age children's functioning. *Journal of Family Psychology, 17,* 275–287.

Mahoney, A., Donnelly, W. O., Boxer, P., & Lewis, T. (2003). Marital and severe parent-to-adolescent physical aggression in clinic-referred families: Mother and adolescent reports on co-occurrence and links to child behavior problems. *Journal of Family Psychology, 17,* 3–19.

Margolin, G. (1998). Effects of domestic violence on children. In P. K. Trickett & C. J. Schellenbach (Eds.), *Violence against children in the family and the community* (pp. 57–101). Washington, DC: American Psychological Association.

Margolin, G., Christensen, A., & John, R. S. (1996). The continuance and spillover of everyday tensions in distressed and nondistressed families. *Journal of Family Psychology, 10,* 304–321.

Margolin, G., & Gordis, E. B. (2000). The effects of family and community violence on children. *Annual Review of Psychology, 51,* 445–479.

Margolin, G., & John, R. S. (1997). Children's exposure to marital aggression: Direct and mediated effects. In G. K. Kantor & J. L. Jasinski (Eds.), *Out of darkness: Contemporary perspectives on family violence* (pp. 90–104). Thousand Oaks, CA: Sage.

Margolin, G., Oliver, P., & Medina, A. (2001). Conceptual issues in understanding the relation between interparental conflict and child adjustment: Integrating developmental psychopathology and risk/resilience perspectives. In J. Grych & F. Fincham (Eds.), *Child development and interparental conflict* (pp. 9–38). New York: Cambridge University Press.

McCloskey, L. A., Figueredo, A. J., & Koss, M. K. (1995). The effects of systemic family violence on children's mental health. *Child Development, 66,* 1239–1261.

McDonald, R., & Jouriles, E. N. (1991). Marital aggression and child behavior problems: Research findings, mechanisms, and intervention strategies. *The Behavior Therapist, 14,* 189–192.

McDonald, R., Jouriles, E. N., Norwood, W., Ware, H. S., & Ezell, E. (2000). Husbands' marital violence and the adjustment problems of clinic-referred children. *Behavior Therapy, 31,* 649–665.

McEwen, B. S., & Stellar, E. (1993). Stress and the individual: Mechanisms leading to disease. *Archives of Internal Medicine, 153,* 2093–2101.

McGuigan, W. M., Vuchinich, S., & Pratt, C. C. (2000). Domestic violence, parents' view of their infant, and risk for child abuse. *Journal of Family Psychology, 14,* 613–624.

Milgram, N. A. (1998). Children under stress. In T. H. Ollendick & M. Hersen (Eds.), *Handbook of child psychopathology* (3rd ed., pp. 505–533). New York: Plenum Press.

O'Connor, T. G., & Insabella, G. (1999). Marital satisfaction, relationships, and roles. In E. M. Hetherington, S. Henderson, & D. Reiss (Eds.), Adolescent siblings in stepfamilies: Family functioning and adolescent adjustment. *Monographs of the Society for Research in Child Development, 64*(4, Serial No. 259).

Osofsky, J. D. (1999). The impact of violence on children. *Future of Children, 9,* 33–49.

Owen, M. T., & Cox, C. J. (1997). Marital conflict and the development of infant-parent attachment relationships. *Journal of Family Psychology, 11,* 152–164.

Repetti, R. L., Taylor, S. E., & Seeman, T. E. (2002). Risky families: Family social environments and the mental and physical health of offspring. *Psychological Bulletin, 128,* 330–366.

Schermerhorn, A. C., Cummings, E. M., & Davies, P. T. (2005). Children's perceived agency in the context of marital conflict: Relations with marital conflict over time. *Merrill-Palmer Quarterly, 51,* 121–144.

Schermerhorn, A. C., Cummings, E. M., DeCarlo, C. A., & Davies, P. T. (in press). Children's influence in the marital relationship. *Journal of Family Psychology.*

Sternberg, K. J., Lamb, M. E., & Dawud-Nourisi, S. (1998). Using multiple informants to understand domestic violence and its effects. In G. W. Holden, R. Geffner, & E. N. Jouriles (Eds.), *Children exposed to marital violence: Theory, research, and applied issues* (pp. 121–156). Washington, DC: American Psychological Association.

Sturge-Apple, M. L., Davies, P. T., Boker, S. M., & Cummings, E. M. (2004). Interparental discord and parenting: Testing the moderating role of parent and child gender. *Parenting: Science and Practice, 4,* 365–384.

Tajima, E. A. (2000). The relative importance of wife abuse as a risk factor for violence against children. *Child Abuse and Neglect, 24,* 1383–1398.

Yates, T. M., Dodds, M. F., Sroufe, L. A., & Egeland, B. (2003). Exposure to partner violence and child behavior problems: A prospective study controlling for child physical abuse and neglect, child cognitive ability, socioeconomic status, and life stress. *Development and Psychopathology, 15,* 199–218.

CHAPTER 9

Family Lessons in Attachment and Aggression: The Impact of Interparental Violence on Adolescent Adjustment

Marlene M. Moretti, Stephanie Penney,
Ingrid Obsuth, and Candice Odgers

Adolescence is a remarkable developmental period in which children are transformed neurologically, hormonally, cognitively, and socially as they prepare for adult roles and relationships. One of the most important changes to occur during adolescence is the expansion of close relationships beyond family members and friends to romantic partners. For the first time, adolescents begin to "try out" interpersonal strategies for negotiating intimacy outside the family. While friendships with peers grow in importance, early romantic relationships are much more affectively and sexually charged, thereby eliciting a stronger need for greater intimacy and forming the basis of pair bonding (Fraley, Brumbaugh, & Marks, 2005). Experiences in these early romantic exchanges come at a time when adolescents are forming the capacity to extract, represent, and act on core beliefs that are necessary to solidify expectations and responses in intimate relationships. In short, the confluence of social-cognitive and relationship changes that occur in adolescence result in a "sensitive" period for learning about relationships: Adolescents are "primed" to attend to information about intimacy, and they use their

We gratefully acknowledge funding provided by the Canadian Institutes of Health Research, New Emerging Team Grant (# 54020) directed by Dr. M. Moretti. Special thanks to the staff and families at the Maples Adolescent Treatment Centre, Burnaby, British Columbia.

experiences within their families as a point of reference to understand and negotiate new interpersonal experiences. The lessons that adolescents learn in their families about intimacy, conflict, and aggression go far beyond simply modeling the behavior of their parents; rather, depending on the types of interparental behaviors to which children are exposed, they may come to believe that conflict is highly threatening and that aggression and violence are functionally effective responses. The consolidation of interpersonal behavior patterns and implicit knowledge about intimate relationships sets the foundation for later romantic relationships. For some adolescents, this foundation supports the development of healthy relationships; for others, it propels them into relationships marked by interpersonal aggression and violence that replicates parental relationships they have observed.

In this chapter, we discuss how adolescents' experiences within families are related to risk for aggression and violence in close relationships. We begin with a brief discussion of developmental pathways to aggressive behavior in adolescents and young adults and then review research on the relation between exposure to family violence and the use of interpersonal aggression among adolescents. We argue that adolescence is a critical period during which youth integrate knowledge structures about intimate relationships to guide their interpersonal strategies for negotiating conflict within their own relationships. Although the vast majority of studies have focused on exposure to spousal violence perpetrated by fathers, we discuss new findings from our research that suggest that aggression and violence perpetrated by mothers may be equally, if not more, significant in determining sons' and daughters' tendency to use violence in their relationships. We assert that attachment representations are an important vehicle through which lessons learned in the context of family violence and interparental violence (IPV) become enacted as adolescents enter romantic relationships. Implications for research and intervention are discussed.

DEVELOPMENTAL PATHWAYS TO AGGRESSION AND VIOLENCE

Research on developmental pathways to aggressive behavior has typically focused on physical aggression. A consistent finding across studies is that the use of physical aggression is common in very young children; however, most children successfully learn to inhibit this behavior and use alternate negotiation strategies by the time they are 4 or 5 years of age (Tremblay, 2004). However, the appearance of desistance in the use of overt physical aggression can be misleading because children may learn to express aggression through different means as they mature. While most children become less physically aggressive as they move from early to middle childhood, they frequently develop other, less obvious but no less damaging forms of aggressive behavior. Relational aggression, for example, tends to rise as children become more competent in the strategic use of language (Bonica, Arnold, Fisher, Zeljo, & Yershova, 2003).

The rise of relational aggression coincides with the escalation of bullying, which is seen as children move into late childhood and early adolescence. Bullying behavior, defined as "negative physical or verbal actions that have hostile intent, cause distress to victims, are repeated over time, and involve a power differential between bullies and their victims" (Craig & Pepler, 2003, p. 577), peaks at about 15 or 16 years of age (Pellegrini & Bartini, 2000; Pepler, Craig, Yuile, & Connolly, 2004; Rigby, 1998). Research on peer victimization in schools has consistently shown that bullying is a widespread problem with significant adverse mental health effects for both perpetrators and victims (Hugh-Jones & Smith, 1999; Olweus, 1994; Pepler, Craig, & Connolly, 1997; Rigby, 1999). In a recent study, almost 20% of approximately 16,000 grade 6 to 10 students reported involvement in bullying either as perpetrators (13%) or as both perpetrators and victims (6%; Nansel et al., 2001). Similar findings have been reported for schools in Canada, Europe, and Asia (Ballard, Argus, & Remley, 1999; Craig & Pepler, 2003; Olweus, 1994; Pellegrini, 2002; Sourander, Helstela, Helenius, & Piha, 2000; Vail, 1999).

Importantly, the escalation of bullying behaviors among adolescents often tends to coincide with pubertal development and first-time sexual experiences. As adolescents who bully transition from same-sex peer relationships into romantic relationships, the form and function of bullying behaviors also appear to change to better suit this new interpersonal arena. Incidences of sexual harassment—a prime example of "bullying" in a sexual context—increase significantly during middle school (McMaster, Connolly, Pepler, & Craig, 2002) and have been shown to precede acts of more serious forms of dating violence (Wolfe, Wekerle, Reitzel-Jaffe, & Lefebvre, 1998). For example, Connolly and colleagues (Connolly, Pepler, Craig, & Tardash, 2000) showed that youth aged 12 to 14 who were more advanced in pubertal development also reported bullying others more frequently and engaging in higher levels of aggression within their romantic relationships, thereby further supporting the idea that bullying becomes embedded in a sexual context during mid-adolescence. These researchers, as well as others (e.g., O'Leary, Malone, & Tyree, 1994; Stein, 1995), point out that the use of power and control in early peer-to-peer bullying experiences often persists into romantic relationships, thereby playing a salient role in the emergence of intimate partner violence later on.

The large body of research documenting the rise and fall of various forms of aggression across development forces us to reconsider the argument that most children are socialized out of the use of aggressive behavior early in development. While it appears that the majority of young children learn early to inhibit acts of overt physical aggression, they may nonetheless go on to display other less obvious and even socially condoned aggressive behaviors. These findings illustrate how the manifestation of aggression is transformed over development and highlight the need to cast a broad net when mapping developmental trajectories of aggression and violence. In particular, the rise in acts of covert and relational forms of aggression across development, among both adolescent males and adolescent females, pushes us to consider models of development that move beyond assuming a global decline in aggression as children mature.

The consideration of multiple forms of aggression, as well as multiple targets, seems particularly critical when evaluating the effects of exposure to risk factors, such as IPV. If researchers only measure one form of aggression (e.g., physical aggression) or one target person (e.g., peers), studies may not detect, for example, results showing that early risk exposure increases aggression much later in development or that risk exposure has cumulative effects on youth. At the same time, an analysis that incorporates multiple targets and forms of aggression helps to appreciate that the *function* of aggression may not change over development even though aggression is expressed through different means. Despite the fact that some acts of aggression may serve purely instrumental goals (such as a child using force to take a desired toy or a teen assaulting a victim in the course of a robbery), the majority appear to occur within personally relevant contexts and serve what are best referred to as social or relational goals (such as establishing or defending social dominance or punishing or prohibiting social rejection or abandonment). It is particularly important to consider alternative forms and targets of aggression in the study of female aggression. Statistics show, for example, that violent crimes committed by females are almost exclusively directed toward romantic partners, family members, or children (Archer, 2000; Ehrensaft, Moffitt, & Caspi, 2004).

The idea that aggression and violence serve important interpersonal functions is certainly not new. Such a view is encapsulated in psychodynamic models (Freud, 1972; Snyder & Rogers, 2002), attachment theory (Allen, Marsh, & McFarland, 2002), and social learning theory (Bandura, 1973, 2001; Mischel, 1973). If we accept this view, it raises the question of where and how children learn about the strategic use of aggression and violence to negotiate interpersonal relationships. Families have long been recognized as the "training ground" for future violence within adult relationships (Straus, 1978), and parents undoubtedly play a significant role in shaping their child's subsequent use of aggressive behavior. As Tremblay and others note (Reid, Patterson, & Snyder, 2002; Tremblay, Masse, Pagani, & Vitaro, 1996), parents can influence their young child's use of physical aggression by actively curbing this behavior and teaching other socially appropriate means of conflict resolution. It is also likely that parents play an important role in determining whether their children become involved in bullying and relational aggression. Research shows, for example, that bullies are more likely to have authoritarian parents (Baldry & Farrington, 2000; Knafo, 2003). We believe, however, that the lessons children learn in their families go beyond what is communicated through their direct experiences of parental socialization and disciplinary practices; what children observe regarding the use of aggression and violence between family members carries a much more powerful message. Not surprisingly, family violence, including aggression and violence toward children and between parents, has been consistently linked with aggressive behavior in children and youth (e.g., Lichter & McCloskey, 2004; Slep & O'Leary, 2005).

   In sum, research findings suggest that it is necessary to map developmental changes in both the form and the target of aggressive behavior to truly capture developmental trajectories from childhood to adulthood. The use of physical aggression may decline for most children; however, other forms of aggression can emerge. The targets of aggression also change as children move from primary relationships within their families to peer and romantic relationships. Families provide a consummate training ground for children to learn implicit rules about the interpersonal use and misuse of aggression and violence. In the next section, we review research on the effects of exposure to IPV as a prelude to discussing what children and adolescents learn about the interpersonal use of aggression and violence.

EXPOSURE TO FAMILY VIOLENCE: IMPLICATIONS FOR YOUTH AGGRESSION

Each year, more than 10 million children in the United States witness physical aggression between their parents (Straus, 1992). In 2001, children's exposure to family violence accounted for 58% of all substantiated cases of emotional abuse in Canada (Trocmé, MacLaurin, & Fallon, 2001). Similarly, the more recent 2004 General Social Survey on Victimization (Statistics Canada, 2005) found that 33% of all victims of spousal abuse also reported that their children saw or heard the violence take place.

Not that long ago, child witnesses to IPV were labeled as "the forgotten victims" (Elbow, 1982), and the impact of witnessing violent acts among family members was largely discounted. Early studies confounded the effects of exposure to IPV with the effects of experiencing direct child abuse (Edleson, 2001). Since then, a substantial body of evidence has emerged that supports the specific linkage between IPV and child aggression; of note, these studies control for the relationships between other forms of maltreatment and child aggression, thereby isolating the effects of IPV on children's aggression (Kitzmann, Gaylord, Holt, & Kenney, 2003). Some investigators have shown that exposure to IPV can produce negative effects on par with those found for direct maltreatment, including physical and sexual abuse (e.g., Carroll, 1994; Kitzman et al., 2003). For example, Maxwell and Maxwell (2003) compared the effects of child physical abuse with observing family violence and found that the latter was the most significant predictor of adolescent aggression. Similarly, results from Kernic et al. (2003) suggested that, compared to nonmaltreated children, exposure to maternal IPV was significantly associated with child behavior problems in both the presence and the absence of co-occurring child maltreatment. In terms of the manifestation of aggression, Connor, Steingard, Cunningham, Anderson, and Melloni (2004) demonstrated that exposure to IPV was related to proactive aggression, whereas physical abuse predicted reactive aggression. Not only do these studies underscore the profound effects of exposure to IPV on child and youth aggressive behavior, but they have led some researchers to argue that exposure to IPV is potentially even more damaging than direct abuse or neglect alone (Somer & Braunstein, 1999). The strong effect of IPV may be due to the fact that it carries salient information about the use and meaning of aggression in close relationships, which, as we discuss later, has a profound effect on adolescents' emerging belief systems and interpersonal response patterns.

Does the type of IPV that adolescents observe, such as physical versus verbal IPV, matter? An interesting finding to emerge from the literature is that physical IPV may have more detrimental effects than other forms of IPV, such as verbal aggression between parents alone. A recent comprehensive review and meta-analytic evaluation of 118 studies by Kitzmann and colleagues (2003) observed that 63% of children and adolescents (up to the age of 19) exposed to *physical* IPV functioned worse in the domains of psychological well-being and social and academic functioning than those not exposed. This effect was similar in studies of clinical and nonclinical populations and was comparable to the effects found in children exposed to physical abuse alone. Exposure to interparental *verbal* aggression, on the other hand, was not found to be associated with negative consequences of the same magnitude.

One possibility is that visually modeled aggressive and violent behavior is more emotionally provocative than merely hearing parents demean and threaten each other. Of course, it is worthwhile to point out that physical IPV likely includes acts of verbal IPV and therefore represents a more severe variant of interparental aggression. At a minimum, once IPV has escalated to physical acts of aggression, it is more serious because of its potential to result in both physical and emotional harm to one or both parents and the child. This interpretation is supported by research showing that physical IPV produces a wide range of mental health problems apart from aggressive behavior: It is associated with a host of internalizing problems, health issues, and overall maladjustment (Kitzmann et al., 2003). A similar conclusion was reached by Wolfe and colleagues (Wolfe, Crooks, Lee, McIntyre-Smith, & Jaffe, 2003) based on their meta-analysis of 41 studies examining the effects of children's exposure to domestic violence.

These findings have prompted investigators to undertake more in-depth studies on the effects of physical IPV that address how exposure to physical IPV at different points of development impacts short- and long-term outcomes. In the short-term, exposure to IPV in childhood has been shown to be associated with social or relational aggression (e.g., Crick et al., 1999), physical aggression (e.g., Cummings & Davies, 1994), and bullying (e.g., Baldry, 2003). Investigations of the long-term effects of exposure to IPV have revealed that children who observed their parents aggress against each other are at greater risk for being victims or perpetrators of violence during adolescence in both peer and romantic relationships (e.g., Wolfe et al., 1998) and are at greater risk to engage in aggressive acts toward romantic partners as young adults (e.g., Bensley, Van Eenwyk, & Simmons, 2003; Ehrensaft et al., 2004).

In sum, research clearly shows that exposure to IPV is concurrently associated with increased risk for aggression and violence in childhood and adolescence. More important, findings from longitudinal studies show that the effects of IPV are carried with children as they move toward adulthood and shift from a primary focus on family and peer relationships to involvement in romantic relationships. These findings suggest that children acquire basic rules about the interpersonal use of aggression and violence that they generalize across relationships. Next, we consider what these basic rules might be and how they develop.

LESSONS LEARNED FROM INTERPARENTAL VIOLENCE

What are the implicit lessons that children and adolescents learn through exposure to IPV? Interparental and family violence more generally provide an important learning context for the acquisition of new behaviors. Social learning theory (Akers, 1973; Bandura, 1973, 2001; Mischel, 1973) is unquestionably the most well-known model designed to account for the effects of exposure to family violence on the development of aggression in children and adolescents. According to this perspective, exposure to aggression creates a learning context for children to acquire aggressive behaviors via imitation. Models of aggression are particularly salient when they are personally relevant, as in the case of parents, and when the context in which modeling occurs is emotionally provocative (Crockenberg & Langrock, 2001). Thus, almost by definition, IPV situations are a high-impact learning context.

What underlying processes account for the lessons that children and adolescents learn through exposure to IPV *beyond* the acquisition of aggressive behavior through modeling? To answer this question, we draw from findings from research on attachment and developmental psychopathology. At the heart of attachment theory is the assumption that experiences within the child–caregiver relationship gradually become organized into an internal representation that embodies rich and multifaceted relational information (Bowlby, 1980). This "internal working model" guides the child's attention, encoding, and interpretation of relational events; it also gives rise to affective experiences of comfort or anxiety and to behavioral sequences of approach or avoidance toward the primary caregiver. The foundations of the internal working model are based on early experiences within caregiving relationships that set the course for navigating close relationships in later life (Hamilton, 2000; Waters, Merrick, Treboux, Crowell, & Albersheim, 2000). However, research clearly shows that the attachment system both shapes and is shaped by interpersonal experiences over the life span (Waters et al., 2000). For example, security of attachment can be undermined through exposure to family adversity (such as parental loss or divorce); conversely, insecure attachment can be mitigated through improved quality of parenting practices (Weinfield, Sroufe, & Egeland, 2000). Comparable shifts have been documented in adults who experience loss of close relationships versus those who experience opportunities for openness and intimacy within a romantic relationship (Crowell, Treboux, & Waters, 2002).

A number of researchers have examined the parameters of internal working models, demonstrating that these cognitive-affective representational structures result in largely "automatic" processing of information. For example, below-threshold activation of attachment representations automatically influences the interpretation of neutral stimuli (Mikulincer, Hirschberger, Nachmias, & Gillath, 2001), and attachment representations increase the accessibility of congruent memories related to interpersonal experiences (Baldwin, Keelan, Fehr, Enns, & Koh-Rangarajoo,

1996). Like other representational structures, the influence of attachment representations on information processing and reactions to provocative stimuli are difficult to inhibit, particularly when mental resources needed to maintain suppression are stressed (Mikulincer, Dolev, & Shaver, 2004).

Attachment needs reign on par to other basic biological needs, and most theorists agree that the attachment system exerts influence on affect, cognition, and behavior regardless of how atypical the child–caregiver relationship may appear to observers (Cicchetti, Toth, & Lynch, 1995; Sroufe, Carlson, Levy, & Egeland, 1999). Children who experience only intermittent but highly emotionally charged interactions with their parents are no less likely to be influenced by them than are children who experience consistent and relatively benign interactions. In fact, because the attachment system is triggered by perceived threat, exposure to emotionally provocative interactions with caregivers, such as those often found in family violence, will almost certainly exert a strong influence on shaping attachment representations (Owen & Cox, 1997). In these cases, automatic processing of threat cues through activation of the attachment system is essential for survival: Children must detect early signs of impending threat, anticipate escalation, and efficiently use behavioral strategies to ensure maximum caregiver proximity and protection within a context that is emotionally provocative. This presents an insurmountable challenge to the child: He or she must contend with the fact that the well-being of one or both caregivers may be at risk, and as a result, the well-being of the child is also at risk, even if the child is not a direct target of aggression and violence. Moreover, because both parents are likely attachment figures for the child, the attack of one parent on the other or mutual violence between parents necessarily doubles the level of threat. Of equal importance is the erosion of trust that the child invests in each parent to respect the role of the other parent as a source of comfort and support to the child and to one another.

Although few studies have specifically examined the relationship between exposure to IPV and child attachment, it would not be surprising to find that children exposed to chronic IPV are at higher risk for insecure attachment than those not exposed. By definition, children exposed to IPV experience frightening parental behavior in a context where their needs are likely overshadowed or ignored. We also know that insecure attachment in children and adolescents is linked concurrently and prospectively with aggressive behavior (Doyle & Moretti, 2000; Moretti, DaSilva, & Holland, 2004; Moretti & Peled, 2004). Insecure attachment can take several forms and can be related to IPV in different ways: In some children, for instance, the attachment system becomes "overactivated," leading to excessive anxiety and heightened proximity seeking.

This pattern of anxious-ambivalent/preoccupied attachment develops in response to inadequate parental sensitivity and inconsistent responsivity; the child learns that the parent will provide comfort and protection if the attention of the caregiver can be elicited. These children, therefore, vigilantly monitor the availability of their parents and often display heightened overtures of need to provoke parental responsiveness. As a result, they appear clingy, protest separation, and are likely to be drawn into IPV rather than avoid it. Their preoccupation with the availability of their parents inhibits appropriate exploration of the world and increases their sensitivity to conflict as a potential threat to security.

It is not difficult to understand how IPV can contribute to anxious-ambivalent/preoccupied attachment in children. IPV reduces both the psychological and the physical availability of one or both caregivers, and it specifically does so in situations that are directly threatening to the child. Furthermore, the unpredictability that typically characterizes IPV increases anxiety among family members that is then experienced by the child. The fundamental lesson learned by children in this context is that others are insensitive and unresponsive to their needs for protection from physical or psychological danger and unwilling to respond. As a result, expressions of need may escalate and may be communicated through behaviors that include but are not limited to extreme anger, threats and acts of aggression, and violence. The link between anxious-ambivalent/preoccupied attachment and aggression has been supported in several studies using both normative and clinical adolescent samples (Allen et al., 2002; Moretti et al., 2004).

Not all children, however, respond to IPV with anxiety and overactivation of the attachment system. Some children withdraw and disengage from family relationships, particularly during IPV incidents. From an attachment perspective, these children are seen to "deactivate" the attachment system, mask the expression of attachment needs, engage in avoidance behaviors, and suppress anxiety. Despite their calm presentation, research shows that anxious-avoidant/fearful children experience heightened physiological arousal when separated from attachment figures (Dozier & Kobak, 1992). Their avoidant stance develops in response to parental insensitivity and consistent rejection and punishment for the expression of attachment needs. The fundamental lesson learned by children in this context is that attachment figures are not available to meet one's needs regardless of how they are expressed and that the failure to mask their expression will lead only to rejection and punishment. The perception of conflict triggers anxiety and avoidance rather than aggressive behavior toward others. However, Mayseless (1991) suggests that aggression may be expressed when these individuals feel pressed into intimacy because this generates anxiety about anticipated rejection.

These two forms of adaptation to IPV represent "organized" strategies to manage the challenges to attachment that are present in this situation. Research has shown, however, that exposure of children to extreme trauma, such as chronic and severe family violence, often results in the failure of the child to develop an organized strategy in response to attachment needs (Liotti, 2004). "Disorganized attachment" (Holmes, 2004) is a response to the fundamental view that the attachment relationship is not an effective source of care and protection. The child vacillates between coercing the caregiver into action and alternatively providing care for the caregiver; both approach and avoidance behaviors are expressed but with little predictability. The child seems unable to integrate experiences of fear, loss, and abandonment and thus fails to form a coherent mental representation of experiences within the attachment relationship (West & George, 1999). This increases vulnerability in a number of ways but most notably in the impaired capacity to use an integrated mental representation from past experiences to modulate affective arousal and intimacy within new relationships. In recent years, disorganized attachment has emerged as a key risk factor predicting externalizing behavior problems, poor social-emotional functioning, and deficits in behavior and affect regulation (Green & Goldwyn, 2002; Lyons-Ruth, Alpern, & Repacholi, 1993).

What happens as children growing up in the context of IPV enter adolescence? Among the host of developmental changes that occur in the transition to adolescence, two stand out as particularly relevant in understanding the impact of IPV on adjustment. First, adolescents undergo qualitative shifts in metacognitive and representational capacity from early to late adolescence (Case, 1985; Chalmers & Lawrence, 1993; Selman, 1980) and develop a more differentiated and complex view of self and others (Harter, 1999; Marsh, 1989; Moretti & Higgins, 1999a, 1999b). As a consequence, adolescents begin to form increasingly generalized and traitlike conceptualizations of themselves and others—adolescents now begin to think about people as having personality types and predictable behavior based on these generalizations. Adolescents also enter a new social-psychological phase of life. Time spent with parents drops sharply, while time spent with peers rises and adolescents increasingly turn to peers for intimacy and support (Furman & Buhrmester, 1992; Laursen & Williams, 1997; Levitt, Guacci-Franco, & Levitt, 1993). Dating relationships also begin in early adolescence—around age 13 for girls and 14 for boys (McCabe, 1984), and adolescents begin to explore romantic relationships as a new forum for attachment.

As a function of these changes, adolescents begin to move into a person-based world rich in relationships. How do these shifts in metacognitive and social functioning influence the meaning of lessons learned from exposure to IPV? Adolescents now begin to encode IPV not only in terms of its direct impact on them but also as illustrative "blueprints" for negotiating conflict in romantic relationships. The lessons learned about intimacy and conflict during adolescence combine with earlier attachment lessons learned in the context of IPV, forming a rich internal representation that guides adolescents' navigation of new romantic relationships, particularly with respect to the management of conflict. Representations now include cognitive-affective expectations about the relative sensitivity and responsiveness of attachment figures to one's distress plus information on the meaning of conflict in intimate relationships and how aggression and violence can be strategically deployed in this context. Hence, IPV now has the potential to shape the adolescent's cognitive and emotional understanding of the *psychological and interpersonal meaning* of conflict in new, romantic relationships—that is, as a situation that is threatening rather than an opportunity for growth, intimacy, and resolution. In addition, IPV likely shapes the adolescent's understanding of viable solutions for conflict, which in this case include aggression and violence.

The impact of parent–child attachment representations on romantic relationships has been demonstrated in a number of studies. In early studies, researchers demonstrated a concordance between individuals' attachment representations of their parents and their representations of relationships with romantic partners (Owens, Crowell, Pan, & Treboux, 1995)—in other words, individuals appeared to develop attachment representations with romantic partners that mirrored their relationships with their own parents. Subsequent longitudinal studies have shown that security of attachment with parents in late adolescence predicts relationship quality (e.g., shared positive affect, overall quality) with romantic partners in early adulthood (Roisman, Madsen, & Hennighausen, 2001). Research has also pinpointed the important link between attachment security and how adolescents manage conflict in romantic relationships. Specifically, adolescents with insecure attachment have been shown to use less adaptive strategies in managing conflict in romantic relationships, including more escalation, negativity, and withdrawal, and the tendency to experience more fear, anger, and anxiety (Creasey & Hesson-McInnis, 2001).

In sum, adolescents exposed to IPV enter into the world of romantic relationships with significant handicaps. They are more likely to have an insecure and possibly disorganized attachment style and as a result are not only prone to perceive their new partners as insufficiently available to meet their attachment needs but also likely to experience considerable anxiety and threat in response to relationship conflict. Through exposure to IPV, they have come to learn that aggression, conflict, and intimacy are linked. In addition, they have not been provided with adequate models or learning opportunities to develop alternative conflict resolution strategies. A number of processes that have been discussed in relation to attachment are likely involved in mediating the relationship between IPV and aggression of adolescents in close relationships. These include negative self–other beliefs, impaired affect regulation, and limited capacity for reflective thought and integration (Fonagy, 2003). There are other factors that may influence the effect of exposure to IPV on the interpersonal use of aggression and violence by adolescents. For example, it is quite possible that the effects of IPV perpetrated by mothers versus fathers differ in how strongly and in what relationship contexts they impact risk for adolescent aggression and violence. It is also conceivable that daughters and sons are influenced differently in maternal- versus paternal-perpetrated IPV. We consider these issues next.

DO THE EFFECTS OF MATERNAL VERSUS PATERNAL IPV ON DAUGHTERS AND SONS DIFFER?

While a number of studies have examined sex differences in the outcome of exposure to IPV (i.e., impact on sons versus daughters; for reviews, see Kitzmann et al., 2003; Wolfe et al., 2003), few have investigated whether there are different effects when IPV is perpetrated by mothers versus fathers. In part, this is due to the fact that the majority of studies have focused on the effects of IPV on child outcomes in samples of "battered women" where only father-perpetrated IPV is measured (e.g., Ronfeldt, Kimerling, & Arias, 1998). Results from this research generally show that exposure to IPV is more strongly related to sons' rather than daughters' use of aggression. For example, adolescent boys exposed to IPV have been found to hold beliefs that condone the use of aggression in romantic relationships and to engage in more aggressive acts toward their partners (e.g., Kinsfogel & Grych, 2004). Similarly, Chen and White (2004) found that parental fighting predicted engagement in intimate partner violence in young men but not young women. These findings are consistent with early research examining retrospective reports of adult males who batter their partners: Men exposed to physical aggression between their parents were found to be three times more likely to abuse their wives compared to men not exposed to IPV (Straus, Gelles, & Steinmetz, 1980). Although this early research actually found comparable effects for mother's violence (e.g., Straus, 1979), a disinclination at that time among domestic violence professionals to examine female-perpetrated IPV allowed for the impression that the effect of IPV on children typically occurs via transmission of risk from fathers to sons through modeling of aggressive behavior.

Only recently have researchers returned to direct examination of the differential effects of female- versus male-perpetrated IPV; findings have been equivocal. Some have found that, compared to paternal IPV, exposure to maternal IPV is equally likely to predict intimate partner violence (e.g., Jankowski, Leitenberg, Henning, & Coffey, 1999), whereas others concluded that exposure to maternal IPV is more strongly related to later partner violence (e.g., Foshee, Bauman, & Linder, 1999; Ulman & Straus, 2003). For example, Ulman and Straus (2003) found that children who observed *only their mothers* engaging in violence toward their fathers were more aggressive than were children who observed *only their fathers* engaging in violence toward their mothers.

Studies examining the impact of maternal versus paternal IPV on daughters versus sons provide evidence for same-sex modeling effects. For example, Jankowski et al. (1999) showed that children who observed only their parent of the same sex (i.e., mothers of daughters vs. fathers of sons) perpetrate IPV were at greater risk for later physical aggression against their romantic partners, while children who observed only their opposite-sex parent engage in physical aggression were not. Further evidence of same-sex modeling was recently provided by Kaura and Allen (2004), who found that father- but not mother-perpetrated IPV was predictive of dating violence in young adult men and that mother- but not father-perpetrated IPV was predictive of dating violence in young adult women.

In our research (Moretti, Obsuth, Odgers, & Reebye, in press), we examined the effects of exposure to physical IPV perpetrated by mothers versus fathers on sons' and daughters' use of aggression across multiple relationships (friends, romantic partners, and parents). Participants were adolescent girls and boys with clinically elevated levels of aggressive behavior. We statistically estimated unique effects for maternal versus paternal IPV and found that their impact varied depending on the sex of the child and the relationship under question. Same-sex modeling effects were found when examining the impact of exposure to maternal versus paternal IPV on adolescent girls' and boys' use of aggression toward friends: fathers' perpetration of physical IPV was associated with increased physical aggression toward friends by sons but not daughters; in contrast, mothers' perpetration of physical IPV was associated with increased physical aggression toward friends by daughters but not sons. Turning to adolescent aggression within their romantic relationships, findings showed that only mothers' perpetration of physical IPV was significantly related to the use of aggression by both boys *and* girls toward their romantic partners; in contrast, father IPV was unrelated. Adolescent aggression toward parents was accounted for by parental physical abuse rather than exposure to IPV. Importantly, other findings remained significant even when we controlled for the effects of parental physical abuse against the adolescents.

Same-sex modeling of aggression via exposure to parental IPV may be important in determining aggression in friendships because close friendships during adolescence are often same sex rather than opposite sex. Of more relevance to the current discussion, our findings on the relationship between maternal IPV and aggression toward romantic partners by daughters and sons are intriguing, as they suggest that maternal IPV may carry a special message to daughters and sons about the use of aggression and violence in intimate relationships. Why might mothers play a special role in shaping the use of aggression and violence by their sons and daughters in romantic relationships? First, mothers spend more time than fathers interacting with their children throughout childhood and adolescence, and their interactions are characterized by more caregiving (Collins, Madsen, & Susman-Stillman, 2002). Second, mothers hold a favored position as primary attachment figures compared to fathers: Even as adults, individuals rank their mothers as more important attachment figures than their fathers, and mothers are typically ranked second only to romantic partners (Doherty & Feeney, 2004; Trinke & Bartholomew, 1997). Thus, the primary attachment of children with their mothers, combined with mothers' interactions with their partner, serve as a powerful training ground for learning about how attachment relationships are navigated.

We are not suggesting, however, that children are unaffected by their relationships with their fathers or by paternal IPV. Research shows that attachment to fathers also plays an important role in determining child and adolescent adjustment (Rubin, Dwyer, & Booth-LaForce, 2004). In contrast to mothers, whose relationships with their children are characterized mostly by caregiving, fathers spend more time in playful activities with their children (Williams & Radin, 1999). Through these activities, children develop social skills and social competence (Feiring & Taska, 1996) that become increasingly important as they mature and move toward autonomy. In fact, Parke and Buriel (1998) suggest that while fathers play an important role in their children's development of autonomy (i.e., separateness or independence), mothers play a crucial role in children's and adolescents' ability to develop and maintain connections with others (i.e., intimacy, secure attachment, relationships). Thus, children's attachment relationships with their mothers and fathers are equally important for their development but appear specific in their impact. As such, observing how mothers negotiate their relationships with their partners and particularly how they manage conflict may be especially salient for adolescents as they learn to navigate new romantic relationships.

Clearly, further research is needed to better understand the complex factors that underlie the influence of mothers' versus fathers' IPV on adolescents' use of aggression in relationships. Yet we suggest, based on findings from our research and other studies, that mothers may play a more important role than previously assumed in determining the strategies that their sons and daughters employ to manage conflict in their own romantic relationships. In contrast, same-sex modeling of aggression by parents seems to determine the effects of IPV on sons' and daughters' peer-directed aggression.

IMPLICATIONS FOR FUTURE RESEARCH

Our review of the literature on the relationship between IPV and adolescent aggression and the intergenerational transmission of partner violence highlights four central points. First, children's developing attachment representations may provide a powerful framework for understanding the relationship between IPV and the use of aggression during adolescence. As the discussion in this chapter illustrates, exposure to both father- and mother-perpetrated IPV exerts powerful and potentially wide-ranging effects on the developing child: Attachment models may bring us closer to understanding the heterogeneity in these outcomes. Future work examining attachment is required in order to bring us closer to understanding the mechanisms and processes that underlie the impact of exposure to IPV on adolescent outcomes. With that said, there are undoubtedly other important consequences of witnessing chronic or severe IPV that need to be considered alongside the effects on child attachment. Most important, research has clearly established that IPV often produces trauma symptoms and syndromes in children and adolescents that impair functioning and bias the processing of emotionally provocative information (Margolin & Gordis, 2000). Research on the etiology of disorganized attachment has shed some light on the relationship between trauma and the development of attachment representations, but again further work is necessary to understand the specific consequences of exposure to maternal versus paternal IPV for daughters and sons.

Second, this review provides yet another reason to view early adolescence as a critical period of development. Although early experiences have precedence in determining the foundations of attachment representations and early patterns of aggressive behavior, it may be more productive to understand development as a series of "sensitive" periods where particular issues have ascendance. In this sense, adolescence can be seen as a unique developmental window in which children consolidate early experiences in attachment relationships with new observations and experiences in romantic relationships. Further research is needed to investigate how adolescents consolidate their beliefs and interpersonal strategies during this critical period to negotiate romantic relationships, including the use of aggression and violence.

Third, research to date on IPV is hampered by the tendency to cast partner aggression in terms of individuals rather than dyadic interactions. While it is important to recognize that maternal IPV is more significant than previously assumed, we believe it is even more important to be mindful of the fact that IPV is essentially dyadic in nature. New research paradigms and analytic strategies for investigating the dyadic nature of IPV and the impact of these interaction patterns on children and adolescents are emerging (Ferrer & Nesselroade, 2003) and should be applied in future research.

Finally, although we have intentionally focused on the effects of IPV on the development of child and adolescent aggression, it is important to situate this line of research within the broader literature on aggression. Exposure to IPV and other forms of maltreatment is not the only cause of child and adolescent aggression, nor does it always produce the same effects in all youth. Research clearly shows that children differ in their vulnerability to harmful environments based on a wide range of genetic and neurodevelopmental factors (Caspi et al, 2002; Jaffe, Caspi, & Moffitt, 2005). Thus, it is best to view IPV as one of many risk factors and to understand that risk is a dynamic term that represents the interaction between child vulnerability and social context (Reiss, Neiderhiser, Hetherington, & Plomin, 2000).

FROM RESEARCH TO PREVENTION AND INTERVENTION

In this chapter, we have focused on examining theory and research as it pertains to understanding the impact of IPV on adolescent aggression from an attachment framework. Issues of prevention and intervention are beyond the scope of our discussion and are discussed elsewhere in this volume (see, e.g., chapters 19, 22, and 23). Nonetheless, our review and analysis prompts a few brief observations. First, in light of the fact that adolescence marks a sensitive period for the consolidation of beliefs about intimacy and the initiation of romantic relationships, efforts are needed to plan, implement, and evaluate risk reduction programs for youth exposed to IPV. Education programs have been developed to inform adolescents about partner violence, and some show promising findings in the general population (Foshee et al., 2004). However, few programs have been developed specifically for at-risk youth, and their effectiveness is unknown. Furthermore, while education about partner violence is important to disseminate to all youth, it is equally important that programs target beliefs about intimacy and violence and promote adaptive strategies and skills to negotiate interpersonal conflict.

Second, the growing evidence that attachment plays a significant role in the etiology and transgenerational transmission of aggression toward intimate partners (Serbin & Karp, 2004) points to the importance of targeting these issues in intervention. Unfortunately, the majority of programs designed to reduce IPV are primarily behaviorally focused and tend not to address underlying attachment issues. New therapeutic models that integrate attachment concepts have shown promise in working with perpetrators of partner violence (Sonkin & Dutton, 2003) and families dealing with aggressive and violent behavior (Moretti, Holland, Moore, & McKay, 2004; Obsuth, Moretti, Holland, Braber, & Cross, 2006; for reviews of existing interventions and promising approaches, see chapters 2 and 10 in this volume). Continued development and evaluation of programs with a strong base in attachment theory and research will push the field forward in understanding the problem of interpersonal violence and responding with effective interventions.

REFERENCES

Akers, R. L. (1973). *Deviant behavior: A social learning approach.* Belmont, CA: Wadsworth.

Allen, J. P., Marsh, P., & McFarland, C. (2002). Attachment and autonomy as predictors of the development of social skills and delinquency during midadolescence. *Journal of Consulting and Clinical Psychology, 70*(1), 451–467.

Archer, J. (2000). Sex differences in aggression between heterosexual partners: A meta analytic review. *Psychological Bulletin, 126,* 651–680.

Baldry, A. C. (2003). Bullying in schools and exposure to domestic violence. *Child Abuse Neglect, 27,* 713–732.

Baldry, A. C., & Farrington, D. P. (2000). Bullies and delinquents: Personal characteristics and parental styles. *Journal of Community and Applied Social Psychology, 10*(1), 17–31.

Baldwin, M. W., Keelan, J. P., Fehr, B., & Enns, V., Koh-Rangarajoo, E. (1996). Social-cognitive conceptualization of attachment working models: Availability and accessibility effects. *Journal of Personality and Social Psychology, 71*(1), 94–109.

Ballard, M., Argus, T., & Remley, T. P. (1999, May). Bullying and school violence: A proposed prevention program. *NASSP Bulletin,* 39–47.

Bandura, A. (1973). *Aggression: A social learning analysis.* Englewood Cliffs, NJ: Prentice Hall.

Bandura, A. (2001). Social cognitive theory: An agentic perspective. *Annual Review of Psychology, 52,* 1–26.

Bensley, L., Van Eenwyk, J., & Simmons, K. W. (2003). Childhood family violence history and women's risk for intimate partner violence and poor health. *American Journal of Preventive Medicine, 25*(1), 38–44.

Bonica, C., Arnold, D. H., Fisher, P. H., Zeljo, A., & Yershova, K. (2003). Relational aggression, relational victimization, and language development in preschoolers. *Social Development, 12*, 551–562.

Bowlby, J. (1980). *Attachment and loss: Vol. 1. Attachment* (2nd ed.). New York: Basic Books.

Carroll, J. (1994). The protection of children exposed to marital violence. *Child Abuse Review, 3*(1), 6–14.

Case, R. (1985). *Intellectual development: Birth to adulthood.* New York: Academic Press.

Caspi, A., McClay, J., Moffitt, T. E., Mill, J., Martin, J., Craig, I. W., et al. (2002). Role of genotype in the cycle of violence in maltreated children. *Science, 2,* 297(5582), 851–854.

Chalmers, D., & Lawrence, J. A. (1993). Investigating the effects of planning aids on adults' and adolescents' organisation of a complex task. *International Journal of Behavioural Development, 16,* 191–214.

Chen, P. H., & White, H. R. (2004). Interparental conflict and adolescent dating relationships: Integrating cognitive, emotional, and peer influences. *Violence Against Women, 10,* 1283–1301.

Cicchetti, D., Toth, S. L., & Lynch, M. (1995). Bowlby's dream comes full circle: The application of attachment theory to risk and psychopathology. *Advances in Clinical Child Psychology, 17,* 1–75.

Collins, W. A., Madsen, S. D., & Susman-Stillman, A. (2002). Parenting during middle childhood. In M. H. Bornstein (Ed.), *Handbook of parenting: Vol. 1. Children and parenting* (2nd ed., pp. 73–101). Mahwah, NJ: Lawrence Erlbaum Associates.

Connolly, J., Pepler, D. J., Craig, W. M., & Tardash, A. (2000). Dating experiences and romantic relationships of bullies in early adolescence. *Journal of Maltreatment, 5,* 299–310.

Connor, D. F., Steingard, R. J., Cunningham, J. A., Anderson, J. J., & Melloni, R. H. (2004). Proactive and reactive aggression in referred children and adolescents. *American Journal of Orthopsychiatry, 74*(2), 129–136.

Craig, W., & Pepler, D. (2003). Identifying and targeting risk for involvement in bullying and victimization. *Canadian Journal of Psychiatry, 48,* 577–582.

Creasey, G., & Hesson-McInnis, M. (2001). Affective responses, cognitive appraisals, and conflict tactics in late adolescent romantic relationships: Associations with attachment orientations. *Journal of Counseling Psychology, 48*(1), 85–96.

Crick, N. R., Werner, N. E., Casas, J. F., O'Brien, K. M., Nelson, D. A., Grotpeter, J. K., et al. (1999). Childhood aggression and gender: A new look at an old problem. In D. Bernstein (Ed.), *Gender and motivation* (pp. 75–141). Lincoln: University of Nebraska Press.

Crockenberg, S., & Langrock, A. M. (2001). The role of specific emotions in children's responses to interparental conflict: A test of the model. *Journal of Family Psychology, 15,* 163–182.

Crowell, J. A., Treboux, D., & Waters, E. (2002). Stability of attachment representations: The transition to marriage. *Developmental Psychology, 38*(4), 467–479.

Cummings, E. M., & Davies, P. T. (1994). *Children and marital conflict: The impact of family dispute and resolution.* New York: Guilford Press.

Doherty, N. A., & Feeney, J. A. (2004). The composition of attachment networks throughout the adult years. *Personal Relationships, 1*(4), 469–488.

Dozier, M., & Kobak, R. (1992). Psychophysiology in attachment interviews: Converging evidence for deactivating strategies. *Child Development, 63,* 1473–1480.

Doyle, A. B., & Moretti, M. M. (2000). Attachment to parents and adjustment in adolescence: Literature review and policy implications (File No. 032ss.H5219–9-CYH7/001/SS). Ottawa, Ontario: Health Canada, Division of Childhood and Adolescence.

Edleson, J. L. (2001). Studying the co-occurrence of child maltreatment and domestic violence in families. In S. A. Graham-Bermann & J. L. Edleson (Eds.), *Domestic violence in the lives of children: The future of research, intervention, and social policy* (pp. 91–110). Washington, DC: American Psychological Association.

Ehrensaft, M., Moffitt, T. E., & Caspi, A. (2004). Clinically abusive relationships in an unselected birth cohort: Men's and women's participation and developmental antecedents. *Journal of Abnormal Psychology, 113,* 258–271.

Elbow, M. (1982, October). Children of violent marriages: The forgotten victims. *Social Casework,* 465–471.

Feiring, C., & Taska, L. S. (1996). Family self-concept: Ideas on its meaning. In B. A. Bracken (Ed.), *Handbook of self-concept: Developmental, social, and clinical considerations* (pp. 317–373). Oxford, England: John Wiley & Sons.

Ferrer, E., & Nesselroade, J. R. (2003). Modeling affective processes in dyadic relations via dynamic factor analysis. *Emotion, 3,* 344–360.

Fonagy, P. (2003). Towards a developmental understanding of violence. *British Journal of Psychiatry, 183*(3), 190–192.

Foshee, V. A., Bauman, K. E., Ennett, S. T., Linder, G. F., Benefield, T., & Suchindran, C. (2004). Assessing the long-term effects of the Safe Dates Program and a booster in preventing and reducing adolescent dating violence victimization and perpetration. *American Journal of Public Health, 94,* 619–624.

Foshee, V. A., Bauman, K. E., & Linder, G. F. (1999). Family violence and the preparation of adolescent dating violence: Examining social learning and social control processes. *Journal of Marriage and Family, 61*(2), 331–342.

Fraley, R. C., Brumbaugh, C. C., & Marks, M. J. (2005). The evolution and function of adult attachment: A comparative and phylogenetic analysis. *Journal of Personality and Social Psychology, 89*(5), 731–746.

Freud, S. (1972). *The ego and the id.* New York: Norton.

Furman, W., & Buhrmester, D. (1992). Age and sex differences in perceptions of networks of personal relationships. *Child Development, 63,* 103–115.

Green, J., & Goldwyn, R. (2002). Annotation: Attachment disorganisation and psychopathology: New findings in attachment research and their potential implications for developmental psychopathology in childhood. *Journal of Child Psychology and Psychiatry, 43*(7), 835–846.

Hamilton, C. E. (2000). Continuity and discontinuity of attachment from infancy through adolescence. *Child Development,* 71, 690–694.

Harter, S. (1999). *The construction of the self: A developmental perspective.* New York: Guilford Press.

Holmes, J. (2004). Disorganized attachment and borderline personality disorder: A clinical perspective. *Attachment and Human Development, 6*(2), 181–190.

Hugh-Jones, S., & Smith, P. K. (1999). Self-reports of short- and long-term effects of bullying on children who stammer. *British Journal of Educational Psychology, 69,* 141–158.

Jaffe, S. R., Caspi, A., & Moffitt, T. E. (2005). Nature × nurture: Genetic vulnerabilities interact with physical maltreatment to promote conduct problems. *Development and Psychopathology, 17*(1), 67–84.

Jankowski, M. K., Leitenberg, H., Henning, K., & Coffey, P. (1999). Intergenerational transmission of dating aggression as a function of witnessing only same sex parents vs. opposite sex parents vs. both parents as perpetrators of domestic violence. *Journal of Family Violence* 14, 267–279.

Kaura, S. A., & Allen, C. M. (2004). Dissatisfaction with relationship power and dating violence perpetration by men and women. *Journal of Interpersonal Violence, 19*(5), 576–588.

Kernic, M. A., Wolf, M. E., Holt, V. L., McKnight, B., Huebner, C. E., & Rivara, F. P. (2003). Behavioral problems among children whose mothers are abused by an intimate partner. *Child Abuse and Neglect, 27*(11), 1231–1246.

Kinsfogel, K. M., & Grych, J. H. (2004). Interparental conflict and adolescent dating relationships: Integrating cognitive, emotional, and peer influences. *Journal of Family Psychology, 18*, 505–515.

Kitzmann, K. M., Gaylord, N. K., Holt, A. R., & Kenny, E. D. (2003). Child witnesses to domestic violence: A meta-analytic review. *Journal Consulting and Clinical Psychology, 71*, 339–352.

Knafo, A. (2003). Authoritarians, the next generation: Values and bullying among adolescent children of authoritarian fathers. *Analyses of Social Issues and Public Policy (ASAP), 3*(1), 199–204.

Laursen, B., & Williams, V. A. (1997). Perceptions of interdependence and closeness in family and peer relationships among adolescents with and without romantic partners. In S. Shulman & W. A. Collins (Eds.), *Romantic relationships in adolescence: Developmental perspectives* (pp. 3–20). New Directions for Child Development No. 78. San Francisco: Jossey-Bass.

Levitt, M. J., Guacci-Franco, N., & Levitt, J. L. (1993). Convoys of social support in childhood and early adolescence: Structure and function. *Developmental Psychology, 29*, 811–818.

Lichter, E. L., & McCloskey, L. A. (2004). The effects of childhood exposure to marital violence on adolescent gender-role beliefs and dating violence. *Psychology of Women Quarterly, 28*(4), 344–357.

Liotti, G. (2004). Trauma, dissociation, and disorganized attachment: Three strands of a single braid. *Psychotherapy: Theory, Research, Practice, 41*(4), 472–486.

Lyons-Ruth, K., Alpern, L., & Repacholi, B. (1993). Disorganized infant attachment classification and maternal psychosocial problems as predictors of hostile-aggressive behaviour in the preschool classroom. *Child Development, 64*(2), 572–585.

Margolin, G., & Gordis, E. B. (2000). The effects of family and community violence on children. *Annual Review of Psychology, 51*, 445–479.

Marsh, H. W. (1989). Age and sex effects in multiple dimensions of self-concept: Preadolescence to early adulthood. *Journal of Educational Psychology, 81*, 417–430.

Maxwell, C. D., & Maxwell, S. R. (2003). Experiencing and witnessing familial aggression and their relationship to physically aggressive behaviors among Filipino adolescents. *Journal of Interpersonal Violence, 18*, 1432–1451.

Mayseless, O. (1991). Adult attachment patterns and courtship violence. *Family Relations: Journal of Applied Family and Child Studies, 40*(1), 21–28.

McCabe, M. P. (1984). Toward a theory of adolescent dating. *Adolescence, 19*, 159–170.

McMaster, L. E., Connolly, J., Pepler, D., & Craig, W. (2002). Peer to peer sexual harassment in early adolescence: A developmental perspective. *Development and Psychopathology, 14*(1), 91–105.

Mikulincer, M., Dolev, T., & Shaver, P. R. (2004). Attachment-related strategies during thought suppression: Ironic rebounds and vulnerable self-representations. *Journal of Personality and Social Psychology, 87*(6), 940–956.

Mikulincer, M., Hirschberger, G., Nachmias, O., & Gillath, O. (2001). The affective component of the secure base schema: Affective priming with representations of attachment security. *Journal of Personality and Social Psychology, 81*(2), 305–321.

Mischel, W. (1973). Toward a cognitive social learning reconceptualization of personality. *Psychological Review, 80*(4), 252–283.

Moretti, M. M., DaSilva, K., & Holland, R. (2004). Aggression from an attachment perspective: Gender issues and therapeutic implications. In M. M. Moretti, C. Odgers, & M. Jackson (Eds.), *Girls and aggression: Contributing factors and intervention principles* (pp. 41–56). American Psychological Law Society Series. New York: Kluwer Academic Press.

Moretti, M. M., & Higgins, E. T. (1999a). Internal representations of others in self-regulation: A new look at a classic issue. *Social Cognition, 17*(2), 186–208.

Moretti, M. M., & Higgins, E. T. (1999b). Own versus other standpoints in self-regulation: Developmental antecedents and functional consequences. *Review of General Psychology, 3*(3), 188–223.

Moretti, M. M., Holland, R., Moore, K., & McKay, S. (2004). An attachment based parenting program for caregivers of severely conduct disordered adolescents: Preliminary findings. *Journal of Child and Youth Care Work, 19,* 170–179.

Moretti, M. M., Obsuth, I., Odgers, C., & Reebye, P. (in press). Exposure to maternal versus paternal partner violence and aggression in adolescent girls and boys: The moderating role of PTSD. *Aggressive Behavior.*

Moretti, M. M., & Peled, M. (2004). Adolescent-parent attachment: Bonds that support healthy development. *Pediatrics and Child Health, 9*(8), 551–555.

Nansel, T. R., Overpeck, M., Pilla, R. S., Ruan, W. J., Simons-Morton, B., & Scheidt, P. (2001). Bullying behaviours among U.S. youth: Prevalence and association with psychosocial adjustment. *Journal of the American Medical Association, 285*(16), 2094–2100.

Obsuth, I., Moretti, M. M., Holland, R., Braber, K., & Cross, S. (2006). Conduct disorder: New directions in promoting effective parenting and strengthening parent-adolescent relationships. *Canadian Child and Adolescent Psychiatry Review, 15*(1), 6–15.

O'Leary, K. D., Malone, J., & Tyree, A. (1994). Physical aggression in early marriage: Prerelationship and relationship effects. *Journal of Consulting and Clinical Psychology, 62*(3), 594–602.

Olweus, D. (1994). Annotation: Bullying at school: Basic facts and effects of a school-based intervention program. *Journal of Child Psychology and Psychiatry and Allied Disciplines, 35,* 1171–1190.

Owen, M. T., & Cox, M. J. (1997). Marital conflict and the development of infant-parent attachment relationships. *Journal of Family Psychology, 11,* 152–164.

Owens, G., Crowell, J. A., Pan, H., & Treboux, D. (1995). The prototype hypothesis and the origins of attachment working models: Adult relationships with parents and romantic partners. *Monographs of the Society for Research in Child Development, 60*(2–3), 216–233.

Parke, R. D., & Buriel, R. (1998). Socialization in the family: Ethnic and ecological perspectives. In W. Damon & N. Eisenberg (Eds.), *Handbook of child psychology: Vol. 3. Social, emotional, and personality development* (5th ed., pp. 463–552). Hoboken, NJ: John Wiley & Sons.

Pellegrini, A. D. (2002). Affiliative and aggressive dimensions of dominance and possible functions during early adolescence. *Aggression and Violent Behavior, 7*(1), 21–31.

Pellegrini, A. D., & Bartini, M. (2000). A longitudinal study of bullying, victimization, and peer affiliation during the transition from primary school to middle school. *American Educational Research Journal, 37*(3), 699–725.

Pepler, D. J., Craig, W. M., & Connolly, J. (1997). *Bullying and victimization: The problems and solutions for school-aged children.* Fact sheet prepared for the National Crime Prevention Council of Canada, Ottawa, Ontario.

Pepler, D., Craig, W., Yuile, A., & Connolly, J. (2004). Girls who bully: A developmental and relational perspective. In M. Putallaz & K. L. Bierman (Eds.), *Aggression, antisocial behavior, and violence among girls: A developmental perspective* (pp. 90–109). New York: Guilford Press.

Reid, J. B., Patterson, G. R., & Snyder, J. (2002). *Antisocial behavior in children and adolescents: A developmental analysis and model for intervention.* Washington, DC: American Psychological Association.

Reiss, D., Neiderhiser, J. M., Hetherington, E. M., & Plomin, R. (2000). *The relationship code: Deciphering genetic and social influences on adolescent development.* Cambridge, MA: Harvard University Press.

Rigby, K. (1998). The relationship between reported health and involvement in bully/victim problems among male and female secondary school children. *Journal of Health Psychology, 3,* 465–476.

Roisman, G. I., Madsen, S. D., & Hennighausen, K. H. (2001). The coherence of dyadic behaviour across parent-child and romantic relationships as mediated by the internalized representation of experience. *Attachment and Human Development, 3*(2), 156–172.

Ronfeldt, H. M., Kimerling, R., & Arias, I. (1998). Satisfaction with relationship power and the perpetration of dating violence. *Journal of Marriage and the Family, 60*(1), 70–78.

Rubin, K. H., Dwyer, K. M., & Booth-LaForce, C. (2004). Attachment, friendship, and psychosocial functioning in early-adolescence. *Journal of Early Adolescence, 24*(4), 326–356.

Selman, R. L. (1980). *The growth of interpersonal understanding: Developmental and clinical analyses.* New York: Academic Press.

Serbin, L. A., & Karp, J. (2004). The intergenerational transfer of psychosocial risk: Mediators of vulnerability and resilience. *Annual Review of Psychology, 55,* 333–363.

Slep, A. M., & O'Leary, S. G. (2005). Parent and partner violence in families with young children: Rates, patterns, and connections. *Journal of Consulting and Clinical Psychology, 73*(3), 435–444.

Snyder, J., & Rogers, K. (2002). The violent adolescent: The urge to destroy versus the urge to feel alive. *American Journal of Psychoanalysis, 62*(3), 237–253.

Somer, E., & Braunstein, A. (1999). Are children exposed to interparental violence being psychological maltreated? *Aggression and Violent Behavior, 4*(4), 449–456.

Sonkin, D. J., & Dutton, D. (2003). Treating assaultive men from an attachment perspective. *Journal of Aggression, Maltreatment and Trauma, 7*(1–2), 105–133.

Sourander, A., Helstela, L., Helenius, H., & Piha, J. (2000). Persistence of bullying from childhood to adolescence—A longitudinal 8-year follow-up study. *Child Abuse and Neglect, 24,* 873–881.

Sroufe, L. A., Carlson, E. A., Levy, A. K., & Egeland, B. (1999). Implications of attachment theory for developmental psychopathology. *Development and Psychopathology, 11,* 1–13.

Statistics Canada. (2005). *Family violence in Canada: A statistical profile* (Catalog No. 85-224-XIE). Ottawa, Ontario: Author.

Stein, N. (1995). Sexual harassment in school: The public performance of gendered violence. *Harvard Educational Review, 65*(2), 145–162.

Straus, M. A. (1978). Wife beating: How common and why. *Victimology, 2,* 443–458.

Straus, M. A. (1979). Measuring intrafamily conflict and violence: The Conflict Tactics (CT) Scales. *Journal of Marriage and the Family, 41,* 75–88.

Straus, M. A. (1992). *Children as witnesses to marital violence: A risk factor.* Columbus, OH: Ross Laboratories.

Straus, M. A., Gelles, R. J., & Steinmetz, S. K. (1980). *Behind closed doors: Violence in the American family.* New York: Doubleday/Anchor.

Tremblay, R. E. (2004). Decade of behaviour distinguished lecture: Development of physical aggression during infancy. *Infant Mental Health Journal, 25*(5), 399–407.

Tremblay, R. E., Masse, L. C., Pagani, L., & Vitaro, F. (1996). From childhood physical aggression to adolescent maladjustment: The Montreal prevention experiment. In R. Peters & R. J. McMahon (Eds.), *Preventing childhood disorders, substance abuse, and delinquency* (pp. 268–298). Thousand Oaks, CA: Sage.

Trinke, S. J., & Bartholomew, K. (1997). Hierarchies of attachment relationships in young adulthood. *Journal of Social and Personal Relationships, 14,* 603–625.

Trocmé, N., MacLaurin, B., & Fallon, B. (2001). *Canadian incidence study of reported child abuse and neglect: Final report.* Ottawa, Ontario: Minister of Public Works and Government Services Canada.

Ulman, A., & Straus, M. A. (2003). Violence by children against mothers in relation to violence between parents and corporal punishment by parents. *Journal of Comparative Family Studies, 34,* 41–60.

Vail, K. R. (1999). Words that wound. *The American School Board Journal, 186,* 37–40.

Waters, E., Merrick, S., Treboux, D., Crowell, J., & Albersheim, L. (2000). Attachment security in infancy and early adulthood: A twenty-year longitudinal study. *Child Development, 71,* 684–689.

Weinfield, N. S., Sroufe, L. A., & Egeland, B. (2000). Attachment from infancy to adulthood in a high-risk sample: Continuity, discontinuity, and their correlates. *Child Development, 71*(3), 695–702.

West, M., & George, C. (1999). Abuse and violence in intimate adult relationships: New perspectives from attachment theory. *Attachment and Human Development, 1*(2), 137–156.

Williams, E., & Radin, N. (1999). Effect of father participation in child rearing: Twenty-year follow-up. *American Journal of Orthopsychiatry, 69*(3), 328–336.

Wolfe, D. A., Crooks, C. V., Lee, V., McIntyre-Smith, A., & Jaffe, P. G. (2003). The effects of children's exposure to domestic violence: A meta-analysis and critique. *Clinical Child and Family Psychology Review, 6,* 171–187.

Wolfe, D. A., Wekerle, C., Reitzel-Jaffe, D., & Lefebvre, L. (1998). Factors associated with abusive relationships among maltreated and nonmaltreated youth. *Development and Psychopathology, 10*(1), 61–85.

CHAPTER 10

The Evolution of Battering Interventions: From the Dark Ages Into the Scientific Age

Julia C. Babcock, Brittany E. Canady, Katherine Graham, and Leslie Schart

Intimate partner violence (IPV) is a public health epidemic in the United States and Canada. Each year, approximately 6 million American women experience "mild" aggression (e.g., pushing, grabbing, slapping) at the hands of their husbands or boyfriends, and approximately 2 million women experience severe intimate violence (e.g., being hit with a fist, choked, and so on) (Straus & Gelles, 1990). Lifetime prevalence data indicate that between 21% and 34% of women will be the victims of physical aggression by their husbands or intimate partners (Browne, 1993). Comparing incidence and prevalence rates, more people are directly affected by IPV than by breast cancer (American Cancer Society, 2004). Despite gender-specific federal projects (e.g., the Violence Against Women Act), men are also victims of IPV, a topic that until recently has been downplayed. As is the case with male victims of breast cancer, the problem of male victims of IPV is real, although it has not been perceived as a health epidemic among men as it has among women.

Both breast cancer and IPV have grown as topics of scientific inquiry and media focus. Unfortunately, whereas the breast cancer field has seen improvements in early detection and the development of effective treatments, IPV has not. A meta-analysis of the experimental outcome studies (Babcock, Green, & Robie, 2004) reveals that the effects due to treatment are small. Despite declarations that arrest followed by court-ordered treatment offers "great hope and potential for breaking the destructive cycle of violence" (U.S. Attorney General, 1994, p. 48), there is little evidence that our current interventions are very effective in stopping the recurrence of family violence (Babcock et al., 2004; Feder & Wilson, 2005). Currently, most communities around the country have implemented mandatory arrest policies for domestic violence and offer or mandate some sort of batterers' intervention program (Healey, Smith, & O'Sullivan, 1998). However, these policy and practice guidelines have been based more on ideologies regarding the causes and course of domestic violence than on empirical research.

Current interventions, when studied appropriately with rigorous experiments, appear to be relatively ineffective at stopping domestic violence. In our meta-analysis of five randomized clinical trials (Davis, Taylor, & Maxwell, 2001; Dunford, 2000; Feder & Dugan, 2002; Ford & Regoli, 1993; Palmer, Brown, & Barrera, 1992), the effect sizes (d) due to battering interventions are .09 and .12, based on victim report and police records, respectively (Babcock et al., 2004). This means that treatment is responsible for an approximately one-tenth of a standard deviation improvement in recidivism. The practical importance of an effect size of this magnitude is that with treatment there is a 5% increase in success rate attributable to treatment (Rosenthal, 1995; Rosnow & Rosenthal, 1988). Based on partner reports, treated batterers have a 40% chance of being successfully nonviolent, and without treatment, men have a 35% chance of maintaining nonviolence. To a clinician, this means that a woman is 5% less likely to be reassaulted by a man who was arrested, sanctioned, and went to a batterers' program than by a man who was simply arrested and sanctioned. Feder and Wilson's (2005) meta-analysis, which excluded the Ford and Regoli (1993) nonpeer-reviewed findings, report similar results: $d = .01$ based on victim report, and $d = .26$ based on police records.

Compared to psychotherapy in general, the average effect size across psychotherapy studies is much larger, approximately $d = .85$ (Smith, Glass, & Miller, 1980). In practical terms, psychotherapy leads to benefits in 70% of cases (Rosenthal, 1995). A recent meta-analysis of psychotherapy with children and adolescents reveals that the effect size for treatments of aggression was $d = .32$ (Weisz, Weiss, Han, Granger, & Morton, 1995), indicating a 16% improvement in success rate over no treatment. Correctional treatments with adult prisoners result in effect sizes averaging $d = .25$ (Loesel & Koeferl, 1987, cited in Lipsey & Wilson, 1993), approximating a 12% improvement rate. Dutton (1998) speculated that the effects of battering interventions fall midrange between the effects due to psychotherapy and the effects due to rehabilitation of offenders. Results from this meta-analysis reveal that even Dutton's (1998) rather modest claim appears to be overly optimistic. The effects due to battering intervention are even smaller than the average rehabilitation effects among prisoners.

WHAT WE KNOW ABOUT PSYCHOTHERAPY IN GENERAL MAY INFORM BATTERERS' INTERVENTIONS

The history of intervention for IPV roughly mirrors that of the general psychotherapy literature (Paul, in press), although one could argue that the domestic violence field is at least a decade behind. According to Paul (in press), psychotherapy practices evolved from the "prescientific era" prior to the 1920s into the "early scientific era" of the 1960s and into the "evidence-based practice movement" of the 1990s. Stuart (2005) said that the field of IPV is on the verge of a "paradigm shift." We agree, to an extent; however, the concept of a paradigm shift implies a radical, nonevolutionary shift in group-think (Kuhn, 1962). We will argue that the IPV field is stumbling along a somewhat predictable path toward evidence-based practice. Perhaps the good thing about being a decade or more behind the clinical psychology field is that we can learn from the history and general "truths" about treatments that work (Nathan & Gorman, 2002). The research on psychotherapy in general may provide evidence as to possible reasons why current treatments for domestic violence do not have more potent effects over and above the effects of arrest.

GRASSROOTS MOVEMENT

One major difference in the evolution of psychotherapy and battering interventions is the degree to which politics have influenced their course of development. Politics and IPV have been intertwined historically. Prior to the feminist movement was what we will refer to as the "dark ages," when domestic violence was thought best "left behind drawn curtains" (*State v. Oliver,* 1874, cited in Rosenfeld, 1992, p. 207). In the 1970s, groups of feminist activists worked diligently to create safe havens for women and children in a climate of resistance, indifference, or outright hostility (Curley, 2003). The shelter movement was successful at bringing family violence from the shadows into the public view and protecting victims, at least temporarily. However, they recognized that fundamental societal change would come about not when women would leave abusive relationships but when men would stop hitting women (Curley, 2003).

Thus, shelter workers and feminist advocates were the first to venture into designing interventions with male perpetrators of IPV. Beginning as unstructured consciousness raising and peer self-help groups, they independently grew into more structured formats, infused with feminist beliefs about the role patriarchy plays in violence (Feder & Wilson, 2005).

The most prominent type of clinical intervention with batterers is a feminist psychoeducational approach (Pence & Paymar, 1993). This intervention, originated by the Duluth Domestic Abuse Intervention Project program in Minnesota, is frequently referred to as the Duluth model (see chapter 2 in this volume). According to this model, the primary cause of domestic violence is patriarchal ideology and the implicit or explicit societal sanctioning of men's use of power and control over women. This program is antipsychological (Dutton & Corvo, in press). It eschews diagnoses of the type outlined in the *Diagnostic and Statistical Manual of Mental Disorders* and does not consider the intervention to be therapy. Rather, group facilitators lead consciousness-raising exercises to challenge the man's "right" to control or dominate his partner. Didactic and confrontational approaches are used to attack the man's defenses, excuses, and devaluation of his partner. A fundamental tool of the Duluth model is the "power and control wheel," which illustrates that violence is part of a pattern of behavior, including intimidation, male privilege, isolation, and emotional and economic abuse, rather than isolated incidents of abuse or cyclical explosions of pent-up anger, frustration, or painful feelings (Pence & Paymar, 1993, p. 2). The treatment goals of the Duluth model are to help men refrain from using the behaviors on the power and control wheel that result in authoritarian and destructive relationships and to adopt the behaviors on the "equality wheel," which form the basis for egalitarian relationships (Pence & Paymar, 1993, p. 7).

The feminist approach to batterers' intervention may be more theoretically compatible with a criminal justice perspective than a psychotherapeutic or couples therapy approach (Healey et al., 1998). First, it clearly views domestic violence as criminal behavior, not as the result of a personality disorder or a deficit in couple communication or other relational skills. Second, the goal is accepting responsibility and becoming accountable for one's own violence as opposed to blaming early childhood experiences or some dysfunctional interaction with the victim. Finally, because the cause of battering stems from a societal problem of misogynist and sexist attitudes rather than from individual psychopathology, batterer programs focus on reeducating men rather than providing them with therapy (Austin & Dankwort, 1999). The goal of the feminist approach is to end abusive behavior rather than to heal the batterer (a psychotherapeutic goal) or to improve his relationships (a couples' therapy goal). In addition, it provides a motivational rallying cry for group leaders, inspiring them to see their day-to-day work as having broad societal impact of sociopolitical importance.

WHY DOESN'T THE FEMINIST PSYCHOEDUCATIONAL MODEL WORK BETTER?

Until quite recently, domestic violence researchers appear to have been reluctant to criticize the feminist psychoeducational model; as such, the feminist Duluth-type model remains the unchallenged treatment of choice for most communities. In fact, the states of Iowa, Georgia, and Florida mandate that battering intervention programs adhere to the general tenets of the Duluth model to be state certified (Abel, 2001; Dutton & Corvo, in press; Healey et al., 1998). In a longitudinal study of graduates of the Duluth group program, results showed that completion of the feminist educational intervention had no impact on recidivism after 5 years (Shepard, 1990, cited in Healey et al., 1998). Although psychoeducational interventions integrate well theoretically with criminal justice viewpoints, there are both theoretical and empirically based reasons to question the utility of a purely psychoeducational intervention for domestic violence. Family violence research and intervention has become isolated from general standards of practice in social welfare, criminal justice, public health, psychology, and behavioral intervention, with certifying agencies and advocates mandating training in an ineffective model based on "tautological pseudo-theory" (Dutton & Corvo, in press). "Given our awareness of the limitations of current approaches . . . it is our obligation to apply what we know about the complexity of partner abuse to improve the programs intended to end it" (Stuart, 2005, p. 262).

IS THE DULUTH MODEL SET UP TO FAIL?

Theoretical Reasons for Failure

The underlying theory behind the Duluth model is inherently flawed as a model for effecting behavior change among violent men (Dutton & Corvo, in press; Dutton & Nicholls, 2005). Briefly, the model suggests that all men in our patriarchal society will be violent, yet there is no conclusive research evidence to suggest that males with more sexist attitudes are more likely to be violent (Holtzworth-Munroe, Bates, Smutzler, & Sandin, 1997). Personality factors account for more of the variance in domestic violence than do beliefs about male dominance (Ehrensaft,

Moffitt, & Caspi, 2004; Stuart, 2005). Even if it were true that intimate partner abusers are inherently sexist, impugning the men's characters, either explicitly or implicitly, is probably not the most effective approach for motivating men to participate in treatment. Moreover, predisposing factors, such as deeply entrenched cultural beliefs, are thought to be enduring and not modifiable treatment targets (Stuart, 2005). Further, women's use of violence and violence in homosexual relationships is not adequately addressed. Finally, psychoeducational approaches focus primarily on cognition rather than emotion despite the fact that spousal battery is highly emotionally laden. These group psychoeducational models tend to deal in generalities, not with the idiosyncratic cognitions of the individual (Wessler & Hankin-Wessler, 1989). As such, the psychoeducational model can be criticized for failing to engage and connect with the men on an emotional level. This criticism of leaving emotion out of the therapy can be levied against many other cognitive-behavioral group interventions as well (Babcock & LaTaillade, 2000). Most important, the psychoeducational groups are scripted without considering the unique learning histories of each individual. According to Dutton and Corvo (in press),

> The Duluth model of thoughts and behaviors is simplistic and fails to capture the true complexity of the human intimate relationship. Perhaps this is the central tragedy of the beliefs underlying the Duluth model: that men and women are reduced to socially scripted automatons, without painful personal histories, without current frustrations, and inevitably without meaningful inner lives.

Empirical Reasons for Failure

It is common in the psychotherapy outcome literature to find that different modalities of treatment are equally effective and to conclude that "everybody has won and all must have prizes" (Beutler, 1991, p. 226). This phenomenon of finding comparability in treatment outcomes is referred to as the "dodo bird verdict" (Beutler, 1991; Luborsky et al., 1975). Equivalent effect sizes due to treatment are common results of comparative studies of two active treatments (DeRubeis & Crits-Cristoph, 1998). For example, in the general psychotherapy literature, until the 1990s many researchers concluded that brief psychodynamic approaches were equally effective as compared to cognitive-behavioral therapy for depression and anxiety. Only after a sufficient body of research was consolidated during what Paul (in press) calls the "meta-analytic revolution" did it become evident that cognitive-behavioral therapies outperform psychodynamic and humanistic approaches by approximately two to one (Hunsley & DiGiulio, 2002).

In our meta-analysis of battering outcome studies (Babcock et al., 2004), we could detect no differences between Duluth and cognitive-behavioral therapy group interventions in terms of their effect sizes on impacting violence recidivism. One possible reason is that the domestic violence research field currently lacks a body of research large enough to detect differences between active treatments. This leads to the assumption that over time differential treatment outcomes will emerge, as they did in the general psychotherapy literature. Another possible reason why there appear to be no differences between different types of treatments and why only a small effect due to batterers' interventions overall could be found may be that the differences between two active interventions are more difficult to find than between treatment and no treatment conditions. The entire literature on batterers' intervention is actually pre-dominated by component analysis studies, attempting to measure the additive component of the treatment on top of the legal interventions. That is, even randomized clinical trials employing a no-treatment control group (e.g., Dunford, 2000) are comparing the effects of arrest versus the effects of arrest *plus* a battering intervention program. Since involvement in the legal system is probably beneficial in reducing recidivism (Dutton, 1987), court-ordered treatment programs must reduce abuse recidivism further in order to demonstrate the effectiveness of treatment over and above legal-system interventions (Rosenfeld, 1992). Added to that is the spontaneous violence cessation rate in nonclinical samples of about 35% (O'Leary, Barling, Aria, Rosenbaum, Malone et al., 1989). For batterers' interventions to be proven effective, they must supersede both the spontaneous recovery rate and the effects of legal interventions (i.e., incremental validity).

Activists in the shelter movement and in battering intervention built a crucial platform for bringing public and legal attention to a previously hidden social epidemic. Now the field of IPV is poised to move beyond the highly politicized "prescientific" era and into the "early scientific era" (Paul, in press), spurred on by its own "meta-analytic revolution" (Paul, in press). However, moving beyond politics and fully embracing scientific study in order to create interventions that are based on *evidence* rather than *philosophy* entails a giant step. Over the past century, the field of clinical psychology has experienced its share of political wars between psychologists and psychiatrists and infighting among psychologists of different theoretical camps as it progressed from the dark ages into the scientific era. But perhaps no other field within psychology or criminal justice is more politicized than IPV. The field of battering interventions is "the most politically charged arena I have conducted research in" (Dr. Lynette Feder, personal communication, November 15, 2005). For example, Feder was taken to court in an effort to stop her randomized clinical trial in Broward County, Florida (Feder, 1998; Feder & Forde, 1999). The district attorney charged that such an experiment was both unethical and unnecessary because they "already knew" that their Duluth-based batterer programs worked. The case was dismissed, and Feder proceeded with her federally funded project (Feder, 1998). Such politicized attacks against research studies or researchers are thinly veiled attempts to protect what has become a veritable industry of IPV intervention. Further attempts to thwart progression into the scientific era are to be anticipated.

ON THE ROAD TOWARD THE SCIENTIFIC ERA

Being a decade or more behind most areas of psychotherapy research certainly has its disadvantages. Much of our research energy still is spent describing and operationally defining IPV rather than developing and testing new ways to treat it. Our basic knowledge about violent couples is limited, and our theories are similarly constricted and funding is sparse. More than 40 years ago, Bordin (1966) said, "The present state of our knowledge is such that strong doubts can be expressed about virtually all psychological practices . . . none of them rest upon a firmly verified foundation of knowledge" (p. 199). Similar sentiments can be made of the IPV field today.

One advantage (perhaps the only advantage) of being a decade or more behind is that we can potentially avoid pitfalls along the way if we are cognizant of history. One of the mistakes that happened to the field of psychotherapy research during its early scientific era was "the flight into process" (Zubin, 1964, cited in Paul, in press, p. 124). Rather than examining measurable outcomes assessing change in the targeted, problematic behavior, research attention was instead directed toward naturalistically examining the therapist–client interaction (Paul, in press). However, research on the process of psychotherapy is useless if the therapy does not result in the desired behavior change. In the case if IPV research, our primary goal should be rigorously assessing the measurable outcomes of reducing perpetrators' abuse and increasing victims' safety. Examining the mechanisms of change is a fruitful second step once successful treatments leading to external change have been firmly established.

What We Know About Psychotherapy That Works

One of the most consistent and strongest predictors of therapeutic outcome is the client–therapist alliance (Martin, Garske, & Davis, 2000). The therapeutic alliance, or the bond between therapist and client, has been studied extensively and is highly valued by clinicians from multiple theoretical backgrounds. Clinical psychology research has consistently demonstrated that the strength of the alliance is significantly related to positive outcomes. Conversely, low therapist empathy predicts negative outcomes in diverse therapeutic contexts (Miller, 1985). Many Duluth model group leaders take a confrontational stance, challenging the batterer in order to break through his denial. Anecdotally, we have heard of some group leaders informing the men in the group that they are not their clients. Rather, in their view, the true client is the victim at home. Such statements are barriers to building a strong therapeutic alliance with the men in the group.

Another basic tenet about what leads to effective psychotherapy is that clients' motivation is positively related to outcome. The popularity and success of the stages-of-change model (Prochaska, DiClemente, & Norcross, 1992) has clearly demonstrated that motivation for change can play a crucial role in treatment outcome. First, few intimate partner abusers enter the intervention of their own accord. Most entering battering intervention programs are mandated to do so by the courts or persuaded to do so by their spouse. From the general psychotherapy research literature, we learn that court-mandated psychotherapy (e.g., for substance abuse) is less effective than nonmandated therapy (Finney & Moos, 1998). When individuals feel coerced rather than self-motivated to change, interventions designed to aid them in doing so are not useful.

Like self-help programs, psychoeducational groups work best when participants are highly motivated; some authors suggest that persons who lack motivation to work on their problems be screened out of psychoeducational groups (Sank & Shaffer, 1984; Wessler & Hankin-Wessler, 1989). A well-recognized problem in domestic violence is that most clients are court-ordered or feel coerced into treatment by life circumstances and, therefore, lack motivation for treatment (Daniels & Murphy, 1997). Most clinical research suggests that excessive confrontation is ineffective and that supportive strategies are better able to motivate treatment-resistant clients (Murphy & Baxter, 1997). People rarely listen to alternatives to their own beliefs unless they feel heard and understood (Harway & Evans, 1996). Many batterers react against frequent and intense confrontation with vociferous counterarguments, silence, "phony" agreement, or termination of treatment (Murphy & Baxter, 1997). In addition, teaching batterers to take responsibility for the abuse may have only limited effectiveness on its own because it tends to shame and guilt them and to lead to large dropout rates among already defensive clients (Harway & Evans, 1996).

Most men entering a battering intervention program are not in the "active" stage, ready to change their behavior (Babcock, Canady, Senior, & Eckhardt, 2005; Eckhardt, Babcock, & Homack, 2004; Scott & Wolfe, 2003). Rather, they tend to enter in the "precontemplative" stage, still considering whether their behavior constitutes abuse and, if so, whether it is problematic and worth changing. However, the Duluth model curriculum (Pence & Paymar, 1993) tends to be geared toward action. A confrontational stance of the therapist in these situations has been shown to be counterproductive (Taft, Murphy, King, Musser, & DeDeyn, 2003) and may be expected to have detrimental effects on both the motivation of the client for change and the therapeutic alliance.

A third factor to consider is the general format of domestic violence interventions. The more popular approaches are designed to be psychoeducational as opposed to psychotherapeutic in nature. While psychoeducational interventions have been shown to have positive effects in many situations, such as working with cancer patients (e.g., Edelman, Craig, & Kidman, 2000), psychoeducational approaches have proven to be less effective than cognitive-behavioral interventions in general in treating behavioral or psychological problems (Bechdolf et al., 2004; Neuner, Schauer, Klaschik, Karunakara, & Unni, 2004). For example, of 15 psychosocial interventions for alcohol use disorders, confrontational interventions and educational groups were among the three least effective treatment modalities (Finney & Moos, 1998). Adopting an intervention designed to change belief systems through reeducation rather than therapy designed to change some pathology of the individual has theoretical appeal if one's agenda is to blame violence ultimately on our patriarchal society. However, given our knowledge about the general efficacy of psychoeducation as compared to cognitive-behavioral interventions, it is questionable whether a psychoeducational approach to a serious behavior problem like violence would be most effective. It is possible that the psychoeducational stance toward "re-educating" intimate partner abusers as opposed to "helping and healing" them is not an effective stance in targeting a problem as entrenched and resistant to change as IPV.

A final problem with the format of most batterers' interventions may be that they are conducted in a group rather than a more personal context. Research has demonstrated that psychotherapy delivered in a group format can be efficacious for many internalizing disorders, such as depression and anxiety (Brown & Lewinsohn, 1984; Fuchs & Rehm, 1977); however, in the case of externalizing disorders, group treatments have been shown to be iatrogenic. Possibly the best-known case of this

is with the treatment of conduct disorder in adolescents. When delinquent adolescents were placed in group treatment with similar individuals, deviant behavior was maintained or even increased as a result of the
interactions within the group (e.g., Dishion & Andrews, 1995; Dishion,
McCord, & Poulin, 1999). Within such groups, the individuals with
the most severe behavior problems typically receive the greatest amount
of attention, providing an excellent forum for less severe individuals to
learn new "tricks." It is possible that similar iatrogenic results may be
seen within group interventions for intimate partner abusers as well.
Individuals learn to minimize their own violence in comparison to other
offenders within the group or may learn new ways to control their intimate partners or ways to "beat the system" from other group members.
Individual psychotherapy that incorporates motivational interventions in
the context of a supportive relationship may fare better than current,
more confrontational group psychoeducational programs (Murphy &
Eckhardt, 2005).

WHERE DO WE GO FROM HERE?

It is easy to criticize battering intervention programs and to point out
what they are doing wrong. It is a far more difficult task to set out to
improve them. There are many promising leads as to future directions for
battering interventions. In the next section, we highlight some of these
new directions, including addressing emotions, changing formats, and
tailoring interventions to specific groups.

Some Interventions Do Work

While the effect size due to treatment overall is zero (Feder & Wilson,
2005) to small (Babcock et al., 2004), there are some specific studies
finding large effect sizes. Unfortunately, these studies employed quasi-
experimental designs that potentially inflate the relationship between
treatment and recidivism. Nonetheless, there were two studies that stood
out even among other quasi-experimental studies. First, Morrel, Elliott,
Murphy, and Taft (2003) assigned IPV men to either cognitive-behavioral
or supportive group therapy. Both interventions used motivational interviewing techniques in order to facilitate participant retention (Miller &
Rollnick, 1991). Reminder phone calls and handwritten notes of encouragement both after initial consultation and after missed sessions were
incorporated. Although the two interventions were markedly different,
both produced strong results suggesting that the motivational interviewing
techniques may be important to treatment. The second was a form of rela-

tionship enhancement (Guerney, 1977) modified to teach IPV men how to use interpersonal skills instead of violence. Role play and homework were utilized in this intervention in order to teach emotion-focused approaches that included expressive skills, empathy, communication, and the recognition and regulation of emotion (Waldo, 1988). The large effect size in this study suggests that exploring more emotion-focused approaches may improve the efficacy of the batterers' treatment. Although neither of these two quasi-experimental studies has been replicated, we are cautiously optimistic that adopting a more encouraging, supportive therapeutic stance along with deeper emotion-focused techniques will improve the efficacy of batterers' interventions in the future.

The Role of Emotions in Domestic Violence

Both Duluth-type and cognitive-behavioral interventions may be accused of failing to address adequately the emotional lives of men in their interventions. Two emotions among batterers that often are overlooked in battering interventions are anger and shame. While the evidence is circumstantial, perhaps addressing men's anger and shame—and how they become entwined—will improve the efficacy of battering interventions.

Anger and Anger Management

The role anger plays in IPV is controversial. If anger dysregulation underlies IPV, then anger management might be an effective treatment. While proponents of anger control techniques suggest that there is an important link between anger arousal and IPV that merits clinical attention (Eckhardt, Barbour, & Stuart, 1997; Norlander & Eckhardt, 2005), others criticize this reasoning as circular in that the inability to control anger is employed both as a description of the behavior and as an explanation for it (Feldman & Ridley, 1995; Gelles, 1993). Many jurisdictions have instituted mandates against anger management interventions for IPV. Although targeting anger control only is likely to prove to be too narrow of an approach in effectively intervening with intimate partner abusers, this is not to say that anger should be "off limits" in battering intervention programs.

Although they may not readily endorse being angry on questionnaires, observational research suggests that male intimate partner abusers are more angry than nonviolent men. To date, no research has looked at anger among domestically violent women. IPV men spontaneously articulate more angry statements in response to standardized anger inductions (Costa & Babcock, 2005; Eckhardt, Barbour, & Davison, 1998). They also display more anger during arguments with their partners as compared to nonviolent men. Moreover, these angry displays observed during couples' conflicts are related to the women's reports of their male partners' violence. IPV men may have difficulty recognizing and labeling their anger. Although there is no conclusive evidence that anger causes aggressiveness and violence (Norlander & Eckhardt, 2005), anger management techniques may be useful adjuncts to battering intervention programs and should not be barred from consideration because of knee-jerk responses against anger management treatment.

Shame and Other Primary Emotions

In addition to acknowledging the role that anger plays in IPV, clinicians are beginning to identify and address feelings thought to be a precursor to the expression of anger (Dutton, 1995; Stosny, 1995; Waldo, 1988). For example, Stosny (1995) suggests that anger is a secondary reaction to primary feelings of shame, guilt, and abandonment. Anger has long been thought to be a defensive maneuver to avoid negative self-evaluations (Lewis, 1971), and there is some empirical evidence supporting the notion that anger moderates the relation between anger and abuse (Harper, Cercone, & Arias, 2005). Abusive behavior is understood to be guided by feelings of inadequacy and an inability to sustain attachment. These feelings then lead to emotional dysregulation. IPV men are believed to have difficulty accurately identifying and expressing emotions; therefore, anger ensues because it is the strongest of the emotions. Treatment focuses on men becoming aware of feelings about themselves and using compassion instead of anger when those feelings are experienced (Stosny, 1995). Of course, the group leader must treat the perpetrators with compassion as well to avoid further shaming. Although not yet subjected to the necessary randomized clinical trial, preliminary data are promising, suggesting low dropout rates and decreased physical and psychological abuse (Stosny, 2005).

DIFFERENT FORMATS FOR INTERVENTIONS

A Case for Individual Therapy

Most interventions for domestic violence employ all-male psychoeducational groups focusing on changing attitudes toward women and violence. However, all-male battering intervention groups tend to have at least a 50% dropout rate (O'Leary, Heyman, & Neidig, 1999). They also may elicit negative male bonding (Hart, 1988) that can support the use of violence. For example, one man in Edleson and Tolman's (1992) study went home and told his female partner that "she should stop complaining because the other men in the group beat their wives much worse than he did."

Researchers at the University of Maryland are currently comparing an individualized cognitive-behavioral therapy against the standard group intervention for IPV in a four-year randomized clinical trial (Murphy & Eckhardt, 2005). The individual approach may be especially useful for men classified as being at high risk for reoffending. The treatment manual outlines how to create an atmosphere that encourages men to take responsibility for their abusive behavior, to modify attitudes and emotions that have become extreme, and to instruct men specifically on relationship skills. Results from this study are pending. Although group therapy is cheaper than individual therapy, one-on-one therapy may be more cost effective if it actually works to reduce violence recidivism.

A Case for Couples' Therapy

Most states set standards, guidelines, or mandates that discourage or prohibit the funding of any program that offers couples' or family counseling as a primary mode of intervention (Babcock et al., 2004). There is a strong bias against couples' interventions for domestic violence because it suggests that the woman is somehow, in part, to blame (Schecter, 1987). Another concern is that conjoint treatment may increase the danger of victims of abuse by forcing them to confront their abusers directly (Stith, Rosen, & McCollum, 2003). Alternatively, the victims may be reluctant to speak freely for fear of retaliatory abuse (Stith, McCollum, Rosen, Locke, & Goldberg, 2005).

In cases of characterological violence, pathological features of the abuser are the source of the IPV. A characterologically violent person is likely to be violent in all of his or her intimate relationships. However, in cases of situationally violent couples, the violence may stop when the partners enter new relationships with less volatile partners (Capaldi, Shortt, & Crosby, 2003; Moffitt, Robins, & Caspi, 2001) or when they learn to adopt better communication strategies. Because the violence is tied to poor communication skills, problem-solving techniques, and entrenched patterns of conflict *between two people,* perhaps interventions using a couples' format is warranted (Stith, McCollum, Rosen, & Locke, 2000). In one study, improved communication skills was found to be one of the four variables contributing to change among men who successfully became nonabusive with the help of a battering intervention program (Scott & Wolfe, 2000) for more than 75% of the men. The other three variables were accepting increased responsibility for

their past abusive behavior, development of empathy for their partners' victimization, and reduced dependency on their partners. Moffit
et al. (2001) asserted that abuse is a dyadic process; both partners'
personal characteristics increase abuse risk. Because of this, they concluded, "Policies against treatment of women in abusive couples may
act counter to prevention" (p. 5); they strongly urged prevention programs to involve both sexes.

There is substantial evidence that dysfunctional relationship conflict
plays an important role in situational IPV. For example, in a sample of
11,870 randomly selected military personnel, marital discord was the
most accurate predictor of partner violence (Pan, Neiding, & O'Leary,
1994). For every 20% increase in marital discord, the odds of milder
forms of domestic violence increased by 102% and severe violence by
183%. Violent men offer less social support to their wives as compared
to nonviolent husbands (Holtzworth-Munroe et al., 1997). Instead, they
show more belligerence, contempt, domineering, disgust, anger, and
tension when trying to help solve a problem identified by their wives.
Examining reenactments of couples' arguments, physically aggressive
couples are characterized by reciprocity of hostile affect and by rigid,
highly contingent behavior patterns that were stronger and longer lasting
than those of nonviolent distressed couples (Burman & Margolin, 1993).
Happy couples also tend to reciprocate hostility but are able to exit
these negative interaction cycles quickly (Burman & Margolin, 1993).
Similarly, from observations of couples' arguments in the laboratory, violent couples were found to lack an "exit or withdrawal ritual" from reciprocated or escalating hostility (Cordova, Jacobson, & Gottman, 1993).
Further analyses revealed that violent men reject influence from their
partners, countering even her minor complaints with highly caustic verbal aggression (Coan, Gottman, Babcock, & Jacobson, 1997). Another
hallmark found among violent couples with a violent husband is that
violent *men* make demands, and their *women* withdraw, although the
common pattern found among happy and distressed/nonviolent couples
is the reverse: *Women* make demands, and their *men* withdraw (Babcock,
Waltz, Jacobson, & Gottman, 1993). Research is just beginning to understand the interaction patterns among couples in which the woman is the
primary aggressor (Ridley & Feldman, 2003).

Having conducted observational studies of couples experiencing
IPV, we have come to recognize that violent couples lack some basic
communication skills and that this can become particularly problematic
during conflict when they become angry (Babcock, Green, Webb, &
Yerington, 2005). Clearly, poor communication and problem solving skills are implicated among at least some couples experiencing
IPV. Perhaps ending situational IPV will be facilitated by reducing the

incidence of harmful fights, which is dependent on the cooperation of both partners in breaking the escalating coercive cycle. An intervention designed to reduce marital conflict and improve communication and problem-solving skills may, therefore, be effective in preventing further domestic abuse.

WHO SHOULD BE TARGETED IN INTERVENTIONS FOR DOMESTIC VIOLENCE?

The question remains: For whom would couples' approaches be appropriate? Most researchers and practitioners now agree that there is not just one type of batterer (Gondolf, 1998, Gottman et al., 1995; Hamberger & Hastings, 1986; Hamberger, Lohr, Bonge, & Tolin, 1996; Holtzworth-Munroe & Stuart, 1994; Tweed & Dutton, 1998; Saunders, 1992). Most typologies of domestic violence now recognize that there are at least two types of intimate partner abuse: One that is characterological and one that is situational. The characterological form of domestic violence is characterized as follows:

✓   It tends to be more asymmetrical (there is a clear perpetrator and victim).
✓   It is used in a context of control and domination.
✓   It may be not limited to the family.
✓   The perpetrator tends to minimize the violence and its impact.
✓   The perpetrator may have a diagnosable psychopathology/personality disorder.
✓   The perpetrator tends to have externalized attributions of blame.
✓   There is generally little remorse expressed by the abuser.
✓   The abuser does not think the violence is immoral but rather that it is justified.

The situational form of domestic violence is not just less frequent or severe on a continuum of violence. Recurring, situational IPV is usually sustained by interactive factors, and bilateral violence is its most common form (Dutton & Corvo, in press). It is qualitatively different from the violence committed by characterological batterers (Leone, Johnson, Cohan, & Lloyd, 2004). Previously referred to as "common couples violence" (Johnson & Ferraro, 2000) because of its prevalence, the situational form of couples violence is characterized as follows (for further discussion of typologies of batterers, see chapter 7 in this volume):

✓ It tends to be more reciprocal and symmetrical (there is not a clear perpetrator and victim).
✓ It tends to be limited to the family.
✓ It involves perpetrators who do not minimize the violence and its impact.
✓ It involves perpetrators who have internalized attributions of blame.
✓ It is followed by remorse from both partners.
✓ It does not involve a context of control.

INTERVENTIONS FOR SITUATIONAL VIOLENCE

Most typologies of batterers find that a large proportion (50% in community samples) of men who use violence against their intimate partners do not evidence psychopathology, general violence, irregular patterns of autonomic arousal, or pronounced abandonment fears (Holtzworth-Munroe & Stuart, 1994). These men who batter women have been labeled "family-only batterers" (Holtzworth-Munroe & Stuart, 1994) or even "normal batterers" (Hamberger & Hastings, 1986). The violence perpetrated by these men is less severe and not used in the context of control and domination (Leone et al., 2004); thus, the highly pejorative label "batterer" may not be truly applicable. Breiling (2005) cautions researchers not to blur the distinction between "incidental violence" (situational) and chronic, recidivistic, characterological violence, noting that differential disposition is likely warranted for the two types of offenders.

Unfortunately, the domestic violence field has treated situational and characterological battering as one in the same, assuming that low-level violence will likely escalate into severe domestic abuse (Walker, 1979). However, the two types of violence may be qualitatively different (Johnson & Ferraro, 2000). The violence committed by family-only intimate partner abusers tends to be situational in context. In situational IPV, women are violent at least as often as men, although they usually do less damage (Stith & Straus, 1995; see review by Dutton, 1995). Left without intervention, most of these situationally violent marriages remain stable or deescalate (Feld & Straus, 1989; Jacobson & Gottman, 1998): They do not progress into characterological battery (Dutton & Corvo, in press). Situational violence is likely to be part of a coercive family cycle that contains the characteristics of negative reciprocity, rapid escalation, and lack of withdrawal rituals from the escalating arguments (Jacobson & Gottman, 1998; Patterson, 1976)—habitual patterns of conflict that these couples do not know how to break. Stith et al. (2005) suggested that excluding women from domestic violence interventions is not likely to stop situational violence. While men's treatment groups address men's roles in IPV, they do not address any underlying relationship dynamics that may impact each partner's decision to remain in the relationship despite the violence or that may play a part in maintaining the violence. In fact, research has shown that cessation of partner violence by one partner is highly dependent on whether the other partner also stops hitting (Feld & Straus, 1989; Gelles & Straus, 1988). Estimates are that 21% to 80% of battered women remain with their abusive partner (Ferraro & Johnson, 1983; Snyder & Fruchtman, 1981; Sullivan & Rumptz, 1994). Failing to provide services to both parties in an ongoing relationship may inadvertently disadvantage the female partner who chooses to stay (Ehrensaft et al., 2004). It is for these situationally violent couples for whom couples' interventions may be appropriate.

Stuart (2005) calls for a paradigm shift toward treating both the abusers and partners in couples likely to benefit from some kind of intervention. Hamel (chapter 11 in this volume) would suggest that if the violent partner or partners will not take responsibility for the aggression, conjoint treatment should not be undertaken. We would also specify that conjoint approaches would be appropriate only for couples experiencing situational violence, who want to stay together, and who are not afraid of their partner's abuse. In fact, couples' therapy in these cases is routine. Despite proclamations against couples' therapy in cases of domestic violence, couples' therapists routinely treat violent couples. Approximately 67% of couples seeking outpatient couples' therapy (not for domestic violence) will report some marital violence—if they are asked systematically about the frequency of their use of physically aggressive acts (O'Leary, Vivian, & Malone, 1992). However, many couples' therapists do not assess IPV systematically unless it is a primary presenting problem. Therefore, abusive couples are unwittingly being treated in standard couples' therapy regularly (Heyman & Neidig, 1997). Is this practice harmful? A recent study of integrative behavioral couples' therapy was found to be equally effective at improving relationship satisfaction among couples with low levels of partner violence and did not place them at increased risk (Simpson & Christensen, 2004). Therefore, couples' interventions, even those not specifically targeting domestic violence, may be safe with situationally violent couples and effective at preventing escalation of future violence.

To date, only two studies have investigated couples' therapy designed to treat IPV using some kind of no-treatment comparison group. In his study of Navy personnel, Dunford (2000) found no differences in recidivism rates between men undergoing a men's group, cognitive-behavioral couples' therapy for domestic violence (Geffner & Mantooth, 2000), rigorous monitoring by the commanding officer, and a no-treatment control condition. However, very few couples participated in the conjoint treatment modality (Stith et al., 2003), as wives were not required to attend and few were interested in attending.

Stith, Rosen, McCollum, and Thomsen (2004) compared the effectiveness of their 15-week treatment with couples in a multicouple group format against an individual couples' therapy format using block random assignment. Forty-two couples with mild to moderate violence who chose to stay together were assigned to either individual couple or multicouple format. Nine couples served as a comparison group. At 6-month follow-up, male violence recidivism rates were significantly lower for the multicouple group (25%) than for the comparison group (66%). In contrast, men in the individual couple condition were not significantly less likely to recidivate (43%) than those in the comparison group. Despite a small sample size and nonrandom assignment to the control condition, the results of the study do suggest that a multicouple group format may be efficacious. Compared to couples in the other conditions, among the 16 couples who completed the multicouple treatment, (a) the men had the greatest reduction in negative beliefs about wife beating, (b) men and women had the largest increases in relationship satisfaction, and (c) there was the lowest recurrence of IPV (Stith et al., 2004).

Thus, although adopting a couples' format is not likely to be a panacea, there may be many cases for which intervening with couples makes the most sense. To make couples' therapy more cost effective, a multicouple group format also appears to be promising. Langhinrichsen-Rohling, Turner, and McGowan (chapter 22 in this volume) speculate that couples' therapy may be more potent in reducing child maltreatment than same-sex psychoeducational groups. While no research to date examines the efficacy of couples' approaches when women are the primary aggressor, dyadic interventions may be particularly useful in those cases. Further research is required to ensure that the couples' therapy format is safe and effective for couples experiencing situational violence.

INTERVENTIONS FOR CHARACTEROLOGICAL VIOLENCE

A looming question remains: What is the best intervention for characterological violence? Here we can only speculate. Because the law does not differentiate situational from characterological violence, mandating both types of perpetrators to the same intervention programs, little research addresses differential dispositions for different types of offenders. With typologies (see chapter 7 in this volume) comes the possibility of matching the best treatment to different types of batterers, but as of yet there is limited research to support this notion. Some evidence, however, does tend to bolster the idea that different treatments might be better for different types of men. Eckhardt, Holtzworth-Munroe, Norlander, Sibley, and Cahill (in press) investigated whether readiness to change and batterer subtype would predict completion of a court-mandated batterers' intervention program. While readiness to change was unrelated to treatment disposition, batterer subtype (based on psychopathology) predicted treatment completion and rearrest. Both the borderline/dysphoric and the generally violent/antisocial subtypes of batterers (i.e., the characterological batterers) were more likely to drop out of the program and to be rearrested. Saunders (1996) has also demonstrated the clinical utility of taking personality disorder characteristics into account in predicting treatment outcome. Antisocial batterers showed better outcomes in feminist-cognitive-behavioral group, whereas "dependent" batterers (thought to roughly parallel the borderline/dysphoric type of Holtzworth-Munroe & Stuart, 1994) showed more positive outcomes in a psychodynamic-process group treatment. Gondolf (1998), on the other hand, conducted a factor analysis of scores on the Millon Multiaxial Clinical Inventory (Millon 1994) subscales to generate four types that reflect the prevailing personality types for batterers. He characterized types as: (a) little psychopathology, (b) antisocial/narcissistic, (c) avoidant/dependent, and (d) severe pathology. Results showed no evidence that one "type" of batterer did better in one program approach or another (i.e., didactic vs. process).

Further investigations into the influence of batterer subtypes, batterer characteristics, and treatment effectiveness are warranted. Research funding priorities at the National Institute of Mental Health are geared toward understanding and developing interventions to reduce recidivism among characterologically violent individuals, as they tend to commit the most serious crimes and suffer from identifiable mental disorders (Breiling, 2005). Other researchers are applying interventions developed for borderline personality disorders to cases in IPV (Fruzetti, 2001; Rathus, 2001). Batterers with borderline features, such as abandonment fears and jealousy, may need a dialectal behavioral therapy (Linehan, 1993) component in treatment. Both borderline personality disordered clients and many batterers display difficulty regulating their emotions, especially when confronted with real or imagined rejection or abandonment by an intimate (Dutton & Browning, 1988). Failure to modulate affect in such situations may lead to escalation of the emotion and ultimately to acting on it in an inappropriate way, such as being violent (Waltz, 1999). Therefore, therapeutic approaches that are effective in teaching affect regulation for clients with borderline personality disorder may also be effective with at least some characterologically violent batterers (Waltz, 1999).

Adapting therapeutic techniques for the treatment of personality disorders to fit subtypes of characterologically violent intimate partner abusers may prove efficacious. Unfortunately, to date there are no empirically supported psychotherapeutic interventions for antisocial personality disorder, although there is some agreement that a structured cognitive-behavioral treatment may be the best approach (Crits-Christoph & Barber, 2002; Saunders, 1996). Because psychopharmacological treatments may be effective for patients with histories of impulsivity and aggression (Coccaro & Kavoussi, 1995; Sheard et al., 1976), perhaps medications such as lithium or fluoxetine could prove efficacious in decreasing recidivism among antisocial batterers. In the end, personality disorder features among the more severely violent individuals may not only elucidate effective treatments for the most difficult-to-treat cases of intimate partner abuse but also prove to be informative in the development of new treatments for personality disorders.

TAILORING FOR SPECIFIC CULTURAL GROUPS

Batterer treatment programs, as they are currently being offered, assume that their interventions will be equally effective across all offenders regardless of socioeconomic status and individual or ethnic background (Babcock & LaTaillade, 2000). As such, treatment providers fail to measure or consider environmental conditions that potentially exacerbate couple and family distress, thus rendering treatment potentially inapplicable to "all but the most assimilated people of color" (Cross, Bazron, Dennis, & Isaacs, 1989, p. 23). Few batterer treatment programs make any special effort to accommodate the needs of ethnic minority populations (Williams & Becker, 1994). Treatment recommendations for ethnic minorities include (a) employing staff who are culturally diverse and knowledgeable of and comfortable with differences among and within ethnic groups and cultures, (b) amending current "color-blind" interventions with communities of color to be more appropriate to the concerns and needs of these populations (e.g., including kinship and family networks as part of treatment and incorporating traditional cultural practices that are antithetical to use of violence), and (c) developing community-based approaches to primary prevention (Babcock & LaTaillade, 2000; see also chapter 27 in this volume).

Tailoring battering intervention groups for ethnic minorities may be a promising future direction. However, a recent randomized clinical trial testing one such intervention tailored specifically for African American men found no benefit with a culturally focused intervention (Gondolf, 2005a, 2005b). African American batterers were randomly assigned to either (a) a culturally focused, all–African American group; (b) conventional counseling in an all–African American group; or (c) conventional counseling in mixed racial groups. None of the groups were significantly different from each other in terms of recidivism 12 months posttreatment. There was some indication that conducting treatment as usual with an all–African American group of men fared the worst (Gondolf, 2005b). Despite good intentions, this culturally tailored intervention failed in its primary mission of making the women safer. Men with high racial identification were more likely to complete the program in the culturally focused group compared with the other groups (Gondolf, 2005a). Keeping men in batterers' programs may be an important first step. However, keeping African American men in a treatment program that proves to be no more effective than our relatively ineffective treatments as usual cannot be tallied a success. While this one intervention tailored for African American me failed, the jury is still out as to whether tailoring interventions to specific cultural groups will improve battering intervention programs.

WOMEN ARRESTED FOR DOMESTIC VIOLENCE

We know frustratingly little about male intimate partner abusers and how best to treat them, and we know even less about female perpetrators. Attention to women's roles in IPV, until quite recently, was eschewed. It was seen as victim blaming, diverting funds away from the larger problem of violence against women, antifeminist, and antithetical to the cause of the battered women's shelter movement (Curley, 2003). While the domestic violence field has focused on male-perpetrated violence, several researchers in recent years have found that women also engage in domestic violence and that this violence is usually not in self-defense (Babcock, Miller, & Siard, 2003; Johnson, 1995; Steinmetz, 1978). In the 1970s, Steinmetz (1978) called for public policy to deal with men battered by their wives, but as of yet, no major initiative has been established to help with this often-ignored population.

Fortunately, researchers and clinicians are beginning to examine women's perpetration of IPV so that new treatments can be developed to effectively treat this special population (Hamel, 2005; chapter 11 in this volume). Women arrested for domestic violence have been found to have a high prevalence of abuse experiences (Abel, 2001; Babcock et al., 2003) that may warrant special, clinical attention. Compared to men arrested for domestic violence, female arrestees are less likely to have a history of criminality, drug abuse, and deviant peer affiliations (Henning & Feder, 2004). As is the case with male perpetrators, women arrested for IPV appear to be a heterogeneous lot. Whereas some may be falsely arrested in cases of self-defense, others, by their own admission, report more instrumental reasons for their violent acts (Babcock et al., 2003). If some IPV is of the situational type that emerges in the process of couples' conflict, then examining women's roles in conflict is appropriate. Teaching women how to better communicate and avoid violence would be appropriate in individual or conjoint therapy. Treating all female per-petrators of intimate partner abuse as victims, explaining away their violence as self-defense, is a disservice if our goal is to decrease family violence (Ehrensaft et al., 2004). Further, research suggests that there are women who commit severe violence against nonoffending male partners; this is further found in lesbian relationships (for a review, see Dutton & Nicholls, 2005). Again, as is the case with male perpetrators, programs need to distinguish between situational violence and characterological battering among female perpetrators of IPV.

CONCLUSIONS

We have offered several suggestions for new ways of working with both male and female perpetrators of IPV. While the body of research available to draw from when developing interventions may not be as large as other areas, such as depression or anxiety, clear advances have been made over the past several years in understanding factors related to domestic vio-lence. Appreciating the heterogeneity among perpetrators of IPV in terms of psychopathology, ethnicity, and gender is important. However, we lag behind in developing efficacious interventions for these identified sub-groups. Subtyping perpetrators (see chapter 7 in this volume) will likely only prove clinically useful once we have established functional relation-ships between the subgroups' issues and their abuse. Basic research on emotions and emotional dysregulation as well as couples' communication skills can also inform the development of new battering interventions. Anger and shame may prove to be clinically useful treatment targets for battering interventions. With our improved knowledge of factors influenc-ing domestic violence perpetration and increasing dissatisfaction with the status quo, it appears that we are poised to break from our "prescientific" tendency to cling to theories that clearly do not address our needs and to build on our research base to design new, more effective interventions.

Unfortunately, current research on interventions tells us more about what doesn't work than what are effective ways to stop family violence. Lessons learned from the general psychotherapy literature may help us develop new, effective interventions. Currently, the psychotherapy field is in what Paul (in press) calls the evidence-based practice movement. Although we have a long way to go, the IPV field is moving away from choosing interventions based on ideology toward choosing those based on scientific evidence. As such, the main goal for researchers is to develop new interventions and test them rigorously in randomized clinical trials, discarding those that prove to be ineffective and widely disseminating those that decrease IPV. Dissemination and policy change can be spearheaded by the family violence advocates provided that researchers can inspire the advocates to direct their energy toward promoting evidence-based practices. This task should not be too difficult. At the end of the day, the most inspirational idea is knowing that what we do to stop intimate partner abuse actually *works*.

REFERENCES

Abel, E. M. (2001). Comparing the social service utilization, exposure to violence, and trauma symptomology of domestic violence female "victims" and female "batterers." *Journal of Family Violence, 16*, 401–420.

American Cancer Society. (2004). *Cancer facts and figures 2004*. Retrieved from http://www.cancer.org/downloads/STT/CAFF_finalPWSecured.pdf.

Austin, J. B., & Dankwort, J. (1999). Standards for batterer programs: A review and analysis. *Journal of Interpersonal Violence, 14*, 152–168.

Babcock, J. C., Canady, B., Senior, A. C., & Eckhardt, C. I. (2005). Applying the transtheoretical model to female and male perpetrators of intimate partner violence: Gender differences in stages and processes of change. *Violence and Victims, 20*, 235–251.

Babcock, J. C., Green, C. E., & Robie, C. (2004). Does batterers' treatment work? A meta-analytic review of domestic violence treatment outcome research. *Clinical Psychology Review, 23*, 1023–1053.

Babcock, J. C., Green, C. E., Webb, S. A., & Yerington, T. P. (2005). Psychophysiological profiles of batterers: Autonomic emotional reactivity as it predicts the antisocial spectrum of behavior among intimate partner abusers. *Journal of Abnormal Psychology, 114*, 445–455.

Babcock, J. C., & LaTaillade, J. (2000). Evaluating interventions for men who batter. In J. Vincent & E. Jouriles (Eds.), *Domestic violence: Guidelines for research-informed practice* (pp. 37–77). Philadelphia: Jessica Kingsley Publishers.

Babcock, J. C., Miller, S. A., & Siard, C. (2003). Towards a typology of abusive women: Differences between partner-only and generally violent women in the use of violence. *Psychology of Women Quarterly, 27*, 153–161.

Babcock, J. C., Waltz, J., Jacobson, N. S., & Gottman, J. M. (1993). Power and violence: The relation between communication patterns, power discrepancies, and domestic violence. *Journal of Consulting and Clinical Psychology, 61*, 40–50.

Bechdolf, A., Knost, B., & Kuntermann, C. (2004). A randomized comparison of group cognitive-behavioural therapy and group psychoeducation in patients with schizophrenia. *Acta Psychiatrica Scandinavica, 110*, 21–28.

Beutler, L. E. (1991). Have all won and must all have prizes? Revisiting Luborsky et al.'s verdict. *Journal of Consulting and Clinical Psychology, 59*, 226–232.

Bordin, E. S. (1966). Curiosity, compassions, and doubt: The dilemma of the psychologist. *American Psychologist, 21*, 116–121.

Breiling, J. (2005, November). *Recruiting representative community samples for studies of family violence: Is it possible? Is it worth the effort? Will it be funded?* Panel discussion at the annual meeting of the Association for Behavioral and Cognitive Therapies, Washington, DC.

Brown, R. A. & Lewinsohn, P. M. (1984). A psychoeducational approach to the treatment of depression: Comparison of group, individual, and minimal contact procedures. *Journal of Consulting and Clinical Psychology, 52,* 774–783.

Browne, A. (1993). Violence against women by male partners: Prevalence, outcomes, and policy implications. *American Psychologist, 48,* 1077–1087.

Burman, B., & Margolin, G. (1993). America's angriest home videos: Behavioral contingencies observed in home reenactments of marital conflict. *Journal of Consulting and Clinical Psychology, 61*(1), 28–39.

Capaldi, D. M, Shortt, J. W., & Crosby, L. (2003). Physical and psychological aggression in at-risk young couples: Stability and change in young adulthood. *Merrill-Palmer Quarterly, 49,* 1–27.

Coan, J., Gottman, J. M., Babcock, J., & Jacobson, N. S. (1997). Battering and the male rejection of influence from women. *Aggressive Behavior, 23,* 375–388.

Coccaro, E. F., & Kavoussi, R. J. (1995, May 20–25). *Fluoxetine in aggression in personality disorders.* Presented at the American Psychiatric Association 148th Annual Meeting, Miami, Florida.

Cordova, J. V., Jacobson, N. S., & Gottman, J. M. (1993). Negative reciprocity and communication in couples with a violent husband. *Journal of Abnormal Psychology, 102,* 559–564.

Costa, D. M., & Babcock, J. C. (2005). *Articulations and psychophysiological reactivity of batterers in response to a standardized anger induction.* Manuscript submitted for publication.

Crits-Christoph, P., & Barber, J. P. (2002). Psychological treatments for personality disorders. In P. E. Nathan & J. M. Gorman (Eds.), *A guide to treatments that work* (2nd ed., pp. 611–623). New York: Oxford University Press.

Cross, T., Bazron, B., Dennis, K., & Isaacs, M. (1989). *Towards a culturally competent system of care.* Washington, DC: CASSP Technical Assistance Center.

Curley, C. (2003). *Safe haven shelter for battered women—Acknowledging 25 years.* Retrieved May 10, 2006, from http://www.safehavenshelter.org/about_us/history.html.

Daniels, J. W., & Murphy, C. M. (1997). Stages and processes of change in batterers' treatment. *Cognitive and Behavioral Practice, 4,* 123–145.

Davis, R. C., Taylor, B. G., & Maxwell, C. D. (2001). Does batterer treatment reduce violence? A randomized experiment in Brooklyn. *Justice Quarterly, 18,* 171–201.

DeRubeis, R. J., & Crits-Cristoph, P. (1998). Empirically supported individual and group psychological treatment for adult mental disorders. *Journal of Consulting and Clinical Psychology, 66,* 37–52.

Dishion, T., & Andrews, D. W. (1995). Preventing escalation in problem behaviors with high-risk young adolescents: Immediate and 1-year outcomes. *Journal of Consulting and Clinical Psychology, 63,* 538–548.

Dishion, T., McCord, J., & Poulin, F. (1999). When interventions harm: Peer groups and problem behavior. *American Psychologist, 54,* 755–764.

Dunford, F. W. (2000). The San Diego Navy experiment: An assessment of interventions for men who assault their wives. *Journal of Consulting and Clinical Psychology, 68,* 468–476.

Dutton, D. G. (1987). The criminal justice system response to wife assault. *Law and Human Behavior, 11,* 189–206.

Dutton, D. G. (1995). *The batterer: A psychological profile.* New York: Basic Books.

Dutton, D. G. (1998). *The abusive personality: Violence and control in intimate relationships.* New York: Guilford Press.

Dutton, D. G., & Browning, T. J. (1988). Concern for power, fear of intimacy, and aversive stimuli for wife assault. In G. Hotaling, D. Finkelhor, J. T. Kirkpatrick, & M. A. Straus (Eds.), *Family abuse and its consequences: New directions in research* (pp. 163–175). Newbury Park, CA: Sage.

Dutton, D. G., & Corvo, K. (in press).Transforming a flawed policy: A call to revive psychology and science in domestic violence research and practice. *Aggression and Violent Behavior.*

Dutton, D. G., & Nicholls, T. L. (2005). The gender paradigm in domestic violence research and theory: Part 1—The conflict of theory and data. *Aggression and Violent Behavior, 10*(6), 680–714.

Eckhardt, C. I., Babcock, J. C., & Homack, S. (2004). Partner assaultive men and the stages and process of change. *Journal of Family Violence, 19,* 81–93.

Eckhardt, C. I., Barbour, K. A., & Davison, G. C. (1998). Articulated thoughts of maritally violent and nonviolent men during anger arousal. *Journal of Consulting and Clinical Psychology, 66,* 259–269.

Eckhardt, C. I., Barbour, K. A., & Stuart, G. L. (1997). Anger and hostility in maritally violent men: Conceptual distinctions, measurement issues, and literature review. *Clinical Psychology Review, 17,* 333–358.

Eckhardt, C. I., Holtzworth-Munroe, A., Norlander, B., Sibley, A., & Cahill, M. (in press). Readiness to change: Partner violence subtypes, and treatment outcomes among men in treatment for partner assault. *Violence and Victims.*

Edelman, S., Craig, A., & Kidman, A. D. (2000). Group interventions with cancer patients: Efficacy of psychoeducational versus supportive groups. *Journal of Psychosocial Oncology, 18,* 67–85.

Edleson, J., & Tolman, R. (1992). *Intervention for men who batter: An ecological approach.* Newbury Park, CA: Sage.

Ehrensaft, M. K., Moffitt, T. E., & Caspi, A. (2004). Clinically abusive relationships in an unselected birth cohort: Men's and women's participation and developmental antecedents. *Journal of Abnormal Psychology, 113*(2), 258–270.

Feder, L. (1998). Using random assignment in social science settings. *Professional Ethics Report, 11*(1), 1, 7.

Feder, L. & Dugan, L. (2002). A test of the efficacy of court-mandated counseling for domestic violence offenders: The Broward Experiment. *Justice Quarterly, 19,* 343–375.

Feder, L., & Forde, D. (1999, July). *A test of the efficacy of court-mandated counseling for convicted misdemeanor domestic violence offenders: Results from the Broward Experiment.* Paper presented at the International Family Violence Research Conference, Durham, NH.

Feder, L., & Wilson, D. B. (2005). A meta-analytic review of court-mandated batterer interventions programs: Can courts affect abusers' behavior? *Journal of Experimental Criminology, 1,* 239–262.

Feld, S. L., & Straus, M. A. (1989). Escalation and desistance of wife assault in marriage. *Criminology, 27,* 141–161.

Feldman, C. M., & Ridley, C. A. (1995). The etiology and treatment of domestic violence between adult partners. *Clinical Psychology: Science and Practice, 2,* 317–348.

Ferraro, K., & Johnson, J. (1983). How women experience battering: The process of victimization. *Social Problems, 30,* 325–339.

Finney, J. W., & Moos, R. H. (1998). Psychosocial treatments for alcohol use disorders. In P. E. Nathan & J. M. Gorman (Eds.), *A guide to treatments that work* (pp. 156–166). New York: Oxford University Press.

Ford, D. A., & Regoli, M. J. (1993). The criminal prosecution of wife batterers: Process, problems, and effects. In N. Z. Hilton (Ed.), *Legal responses to wife assault* (pp. 127–164). Newbury Park, CA: Sage.

Fruzetti, A. E. (2001, November). *Dialectical behavior therapy adapted for treatment of partner-violent men.* Panel discussion at the Association for the Advancement of Behavior Therapy Convention, Philadelphia.

Fuchs, C. Z., & Rehm, L. P. (1977). A self-control behavior therapy program for depression. *Journal of Consulting and Clinical Psychology, 45*, 206–215.

Geffner, R., & Mantooth, C. (2000). *Ending spouse/partner abuse: A psychoeducational approach for individuals and couples.* New York: Springer.

Gelles, R. J. (1993). Alcohol and other drugs are associated with violence: They are not its cause. In R. J. Gelles & D. R. Loseke (Eds.), *Current controversies on family violence* (pp. 182–196). Newbury Park, CA: Sage.

Gelles, R. J., & Straus, M. A. (1988). *Intimate violence.* New York: Simon & Schuster.

Gondolf, E. W. (1998, June/July). Do batterer programs work? A 15 month follow-up of a multi-site evaluation. *Domestic Violence Report, 3*, 64–65, 78–79.

Gondolf, E. W. (2005a). Culturally-focused batterer counseling for African-American men. Final report to the National Institute for Justice. Summary retreived from http://www.ojp.usdoj.gov/nij/vawprog/vaw_portfolio.pdf.

Gondolf, E. W. (2005b, July). *Program completion, re-assault, and re-arrest in a clinical trial of culturally-focused batterer counseling.* Panel discussion at the 9th International Family Violence Research Conference, Portsmouth, New Hampshire.

Gottman, J. M, Jacobson, N. S., Rushe, R. H., Shortt, J. W., Babcock, J. C., LaTaillade, J. J., et al. (1995). The relationship between heart rate reactivity, emotionally aggressive behavior, and general violence in batterers. *Journal of Family Psychology, 9*(3), 227–248.

Guerney, B. G. (1997). *Relationship enhancement: Skill training programs for therapy, problem prevention, and enrichment.* San Francisco: Jossey-Bass.

Hamberger, L. K., & Hastings, J. E. (1986). Personality correlates of men who abuse their partners: A cross-validation study. *Journal of Family Violence, 1*, 323–341.

Hamberger, L. K., Lohr, J. M., Bonge, D., & Tolin, D. F. (1996). A large sample empirical typology of male spouse abusers and its relationship to dimensions of abuse. *Violence and Victims, 11*, 277–292.

Hamel, J. (2005). *Gender-inclusive treatment of intimate partner abuse: A comprehensive approach.* New York: Springer.

Harper, F. W. K., Cercone, J. L., & Arias, I. (2005). The role of shame, anger, and affect regulation in men's perpetration of psychological abuse in dating relationships. *Journal of Interpersonal Violence, 20*, 1648–1662.

Hart, B. (1988). *Safety for women: Monitoring batterers' programs.* Harrisburg: Pennsylvania Coalition Against Domestic Violence.

Harway, M., & Evans, K. (1996). Working in groups with men who batter. In M. P. Andronico (Ed.), *Men in groups: Insights, interventions, and psychoeducational work* (pp. 357–375). Washington, DC: American Psychological Association.

Healey, K., Smith, C., & O'Sullivan, C. (1998). *Batterer intervention: Program approaches and criminal justice strategies.* Report to the National Institute of Justice, Washington, DC.

Henning, K., & Feder, L. (2004). A comparison of men and women arrested for domestic violence: Who presents the greater threat? *Journal of Family Violence, 19*, 69–80.

Heyman, R, E., & Neidig, P. H. (1997). Physical aggression couples treatment. In W.K. Halford & H. Markman (Eds.), *Clinical handbook of marriage and couples' interventions* (pp. 589–617). New York: Wiley.

Holtzworth-Munroe, A., Bates, L., Smutzler, N., & Sandin, E. (1997). A brief review of the research on husband violence: Part I: Maritally violent versus nonviolent men. *Aggression and Violent Behavior, 2*, 65–99.

Holtzworth-Munroe, A., & Stuart, G. L. (1994). Typologies of male batterers: Three sub-types and the differences among them. *Psychological Bulletin, 116,* 476–497.

Hunsley, J., & DiGiulio, G. (2002). Dodo bird, phoenix, or urban legend? The question of psychotherapy equivalence. *Scientific Review of Mental Health Practice, 1,* 11–22.

Jacobson, N. S., & Gottman, J. M. (1998). *When men batter women: New insights into ending abusive relationships.* New York: Simon & Schuster.

Johnson, M. P. (1995). Patriarchal terrorism and common couple violence: Two forms of violence against women. *Journal of Marriage and the Family, 57,* 283–294.

Johnson, M. P., & Ferraro, K. (2000). Research on domestic violence in the 1990s: Making distinctions. *Journal of Marriage and the Family, 62,* 948–963.

Kuhn, T. (1962). *The structure of scientific revolutions.* Chicago: University of Chicago Press.

Leone, J. M., Johnson, M. P., Cohan, C. L. & Lloyd, S.E. (2004). Consequences of male partner violence for low-income minority women. *Journal of Marriage and Family, 66,* 472–490.

Lewis, H. B. (1971). *Shame and guilt in neurosis.* New York: International Universities Press.

Linehan, M. M. (1993). *Cognitive behavioral therapy of borderline personality disorder.* New York: Guilford Press.

Lipsey, M. W., & Wilson, D. B. (1993). The efficacy of psychological, educational and behavioral treatment. *American Psychologist, 48,* 1181–1201.

Loesel, F., & Koeferl, P. (1987). Evaluationsforschung zur sozialtherapeutischen Anstalt: Eine meta-analyse. [Evaluation research on the social-therapeutic prison: A meta-analysis.] *Gruppendynamik, 18,* 385–406.

Luborsky, L., Singer, B., & Lubosrksy, L. (1975). Comparative studies of psychotherapies: Is it true that "everyone has won and all must have prizes?" *Archives of General Psychiatry, 32,* 995–1008.

Martin, D. J., Garske, J. P., & Davis, M. K. (2000). Relation of the therapeutic alliance with outcome and other variables: A meta-analytic review. *Journal of Consulting and Clinical Psychology, 68,* 438–450.

Miller, W. R. (1985). Motivation for treatment: A review with special emphasis on alcohol-ism. *Psychological Bulletin, 98,* 84–107.

Miller, W. R., & Rollnick, S. (1991). *Motivational interviewing: Preparing people to change addictive behavior.* New York: Guilford Press.

Millon, T. (1994). *Manual for the MCMI-III* (3rd ed.). Minneapolis, MN: National Computer Systems.

Moffitt, T. E., Robins, R. W., & Caspi, A. (2001). A couples analysis of partner abuse with implications for abuse-prevention policy. *Criminology Public Policy, 1,* 5–36.

Morrel, T. M., Elliott, J. D, Murphy, C. M., & Taft, C. (2003). A comparison of cognitive-behavioral and supportive group therapies for male perpetrators of domestic abuse. *Behavior Therapy, 24,* 77–95.

Murphy, C. M., & Baxter, V. A. (1997). Motivating batterers to change in the treatment context. *Journal of Interpersonal Violence, 12,* 607–619.

Murphy, C. M., & Eckhardt, C. I. (2005). *Treating the abusive partner: An individualized cognitive-behavioral approach.* New York: Guilford Press.

Nathan, P. E., & Gorman, J. M. (2002). *A guide to treatments that work* (2nd ed.) New York: Oxford University Press.

Neuner, F., Schauer, M., Klaschik, C., & Unni, E. T. (2004). A comparison of narrative exposure therapy, supportive counseling, and psychoeducation for treating posttrau-matic stress disorder in an African refugee settlement. *Journal of Consulting and Clinical Psychology, 72,* 579–587.

Norlander, B., & Eckhardt, C. (2005). Anger, hostility, and male perpetrators of intimate partner violence: A meta-analytic review. *Clinical Psychology Review, 25,* 119–152.

O'Leary, K. D., Barling, J., Aria, I., Rosenbaum, A., Malone, J., & Tyree, A. (1989). Prevalence and stability of physical aggression between spouses. A longitudinal analysis. *Journal of Consulting and Clinical Psychology, 57*, 263–268.

O'Leary, K. D., Heyman, R. E., & Neidig, P. H. (1999). Treatment of wife abuse: A comparison of gender-specific and conjoint approaches. *Behavior Therapy, 30*, 475–506.

O'Leary, K. D., Vivian, D., & Malone, J. (1992). Assessment of physical aggression in marriage: The need for a multimodal method. *Behavioral Assessment, 14*, 5–14.

Palmer, S. E., Brown, R. A., & Barrera, M. E. (1992). Group treatment program for abusive husbands: Long-term evaluation. *American Journal of Orthopsychiatry, 62*, 276–283.

Pan, H. S., Neidig, P. H., & O'Leary, K. D. (1994). Predicting mild and severe husband-to-wife physical aggression. *Journal of Consulting and Clinical Psychology, 62*, 975–981.

Patterson, G. R. (1976). *Families, applications of social learning to family life.* Champaign, IL: Research Press.

Paul, G. L. (in press). Psychotherapy outcome can be studied scientifically. In S. O. Lilienfeld & W. O'Donohue (Eds.), *The great ideas of clinical science: The 18 concepts every mental health researcher and practitioner should understand.* New York: Brunner-Routledge.

Pence, E., & Paymar, M. (1993). *Education groups for men who batter: The Duluth model.* New York: Springer.

Prochaska, J. O., DiClemente, C. C., & Norcross, J. C. (1992). In search of how people change: Applications to addictive behaviors. *American Psychologist, 47*, 1102–1114.

Rathus, J. H. (2001, November). *Dialectic behavior therapy adapted for the treatment of partner-violent men.* Panel discussion at the Association for the Advancement of Behavior Therapy, Philadelphia.

Ridley, C. A., & Feldman, C. M. (2003). Female domestic violence toward male partners: Exploring conflict responses and outcomes. *Journal of Family Violence, 18*, 157–170.

Rosenfeld, B. D. (1992). Court-ordered treatment of spouse abuse. *Clinical Psychology Review, 12*, 205–226.

Rosenthal, R. (1995). Writing meta-analytic reviews. *Psychological Bulletin, 118*, 183–192.

Rosnow, R. L., & Rosenthal, R. (1988). Focused tests of significance and effect size estimation in counseling psychology. *Journal of Counseling Psychology, 35*, 203–208.

Sank, L. I., & Shaffer, C. S. (1984). *A therapist's manual for cognitive behavior therapy in groups.* New York: Plenum Press.

Saunders, D. G. (1992). A typology of men who batter women: Three types derived from cluster analysis. *Journal of Orthopsychiatry 62*, 264–275.

Saunders, D. G. (1996). Feminist-cognitive-behavioral and process-psychodynamic treatments for men who batter: Interaction of abuser traits and treatment model. *Violence and Victims, 11*, 393–414.

Schecter, S. (1987). Empowering interventions with battered women. In S. Schecter (Ed.), *Guidelines for mental health professionals* (pp. 9–13). Washington, DC: National Coalition Against Domestic Violence.

Scott, K. L., & Wolfe, D. A. (2000). Change among batterers: Examining men's success stories. *Journal of Interpersonal Violence, 15*(8), 827–842.

Scott, K. L., & Wolfe, D. A. (2003). Readiness to change as a predictor of outcome in batterer treatment. *Journal of Consulting and Clinical Psychology, 71*, 879–889.

Sheard, M. J., Marini, J. L., Birdeges, C. I., & Wagner, E. (1976). The effect of lithium on impulsive aggressive behavior in man. *American Journal of Psychiatry, 133*, 1409–1413.

Shepard, M. (1990). *Predicting batterer recidivism five years after community intervention.* Unpublished report.

Simpson, L. E., & Christensen, A. (2004, November). Low-level violence among distressed couples: What is the impact on treatment outcomes? In L. E. Simpson (Chair), *Comorbidity of domestic violence and couple distress: Development over time and context, the role of psychological abuse, and treatment issues.* Symposium conducted at the Association for the Advancement of Behavior Therapy Convention, New Orleans, LA.

Smith, M. L., Glass, G. V., & Miller, T. (1980). *The benefits of psychotherapy.* Baltimore: Johns Hopkins University Press.

Snyder, D. K., & Fruchtman, L. A. (1981). Differential patterns of wife abuse: A data-based typology. *Journal of Consulting and Clinical Psychology, 49,* 878–885.

Steinmetz, S. K. (1978). The battered husband syndrome, *Victimology, 2,* 499–509.

Stith, S. M., McCollum, E. E., Rosen, K. H., & Locke, L. D. (2000). *Domestic violence focused couples treatment.* Unpublished manual.

Stith, S. M., McCollum, E. E., Rosen, K. H., Locke, L., & Goldberg, P. (2005). Domestic violence focused couples treatment. In J. Lebow (Ed.), *Handbook of clinical family therapy* (pp. 406–430). New York: John Wiley & Sons.

Stith, S. M., Rosen, K. H., & McCollum, E. E. (2003). Effectiveness of couples treatment for spouse abuse. *Journal of Marital and Family Therapy, 29,* 407–426.

Stith, S. M., Rosen, K. H., McCollum, E. E., & Thomsen, C. J. (2004). Treating intimate partner violence within intact couple relationships: Outcomes of multi-couple versus individual couple therapy. Special issue: Implications of Research with Diverse Families. *Journal of Marital and Family Therapy, 30,* 305–318.

Stith, S. M., & Straus, M. A. (1995). Introduction. In S. M. Stith & M. A. Straus (Eds.), *Understanding partner violence: Prevalence, causes, consequences, and solutions* (pp. 1–11). Minneapolis, MN: National Council on Family Relations.

Stosny, S. (1995). *Treating attachment abuse: A compassionate approach.* New York: Springer.

Stosny, S. (2005). Group treatment of intimate partner abusers. In G. L. Greif & P. H. Ephross (Eds.), *Group work with populations at risk* (2nd ed., pp. 226–237). New York: Oxford University Press.

Straus, M. A., & Gelles, R. J. (1990). Societal change and change in family violence from 1975–1985 as revealed by two national surveys. In M. A. Straus & R. J. Gelles (Eds.), *Physical violence in American families* (pp. 113–131). New Brunswick, NJ: Transaction Publishers.

Stuart, R. B. (2005). Treatment for partner abuse: Time for a paradigm shift. *Professional Psychology: Research and Practice, 36,* 254–263.

Sullivan, C. M., & Rumptz, M. H. (1994). Adjustment and needs of African-American women who utilized a domestic violence shelter. *Violence and Victims, 9*(3), 275–286.

Taft, C. T., Murphy, C. M., King, D. W., & DeDeyn, J. M. (2003). Process and treatment adherence factors in group cognitive-behavioral therapy for partner violent men. *Journal of Consulting and Clinical Psychology, 71,* 812–820.

Tweed, R. G., & Dutton, D. G. (1998). A comparison of impulsive and instrumental subgroups of batterers. *Violence and Victims, 13,* 217–230.

U.S. Attorney General. (1994). *Task Force on Family Violence: Final report.* U.S. Department of Justice.

Waldo, M. (1988). Relationship enhancement counseling groups for wife abusers. *Journal of Mental Health Counseling, 10,* 37–45.

Walker, L. E. (1979). *The battered woman.* New York: Harper & Row.

PART II

Assessment and Treatment

CHAPTER 11

Gender-Inclusive Family Interventions in Domestic Violence: An Overview

John Hamel

Current policy toward domestic violence, including criminal justice and mental health responses that favor psychoeducational same-sex group treatment for perpetrators (usually for men) and victim services for victims (almost always women), has proven to be shortsighted and limited in its effectiveness (Babcock, Green, & Robie, 2004; Mills, 2003). In this chapter, a critical review is undertaken of family interventions in domestic violence from the advocacy model to past and recent alternative treatment approaches that take into consideration the systemic, interactive, and complex nature of family violence. Afterward, procedures for assessment and treatment are outlined on the basis of a new, research-based *gender-inclusive* systems model.

THE EVOLUTION OF FAMILY INTERVENTIONS

Ascendancy of the Patriarchal Paradigm

With the advent of the shelter movement in the 1970s, a rapidly growing number of studies on domestic violence began to appear in books and academic journals. Almost immediately, this research fell into one of two distinct schools of thought. The "gender" or "patriarchal" view, based largely on studies of battered women (e.g., Dobash & Dobash, 1979; Martin,

1976; Walker, 1979), equated domestic violence with "wife abuse" and located its etiology in male dominance and patriarchal social structures. In contrast, the work of Straus, Gelles, and Steinmetz (1980) amassed data from large representative sample surveys (e.g., the National Family Violence Surveys [NFVS]), with questions on partner abuse framed within the context of escalated conflict. More important, partner abuse was regarded as only part of the broader problem of family violence in which fathers or mothers might be perpetrators of partner as well as child abuse.

This promising family violence research was soon upstaged by the patriarchal view, which began to shape the core arrest and intervention policies adopted during the past quarter century. Ironically, the NFVS data were widely cited by battered women's advocates who could cite its high prevalence rates for male-perpetrated violence while conveniently ignoring the comparable data on women. The far lesser overall prevalence rates of crime studies, such as the National Crime Victimization Survey, were also ignored, but not so the large gender differences. Thus, proponents of the patriarchal paradigm could pick and choose statistics in such a way that, although misleading, would be sure to advance their cause.

Early Systems Theorists

In the early 1980s, before that paradigm established its stranglehold on research, before its principles became codified into law, and before the psychoeducational same-sex group model became the state-mandated treatment for all domestic violence perpetration, a small number of pioneers published writings espousing a radically different approach based on conflict and general systems theory. The work of Giles-Sims (1983) clearly fell in the gender/patriarchal camp in its exclusive focus on male-perpetrated battering and the assumption that the causes of abuse could be found in male dominance. However, Giles-Sims theorized that such abuse cannot be fully understood according to traditional cause-and-effect explanations; rather, wife battering is a relational and societal problem best explained according to systems principles:

> We know that those people who were abused as children have higher rates of abusing their own children or their spouses than those people who were not abused as children (Straus et al., 1980). A cause-effect interpretation suggests that being abused as a child causes one to abuse one's own child or one's spouse. However, not all people who were abused as children abuse their children or beat their spouses. Some that were not abused as children do abuse their children and/or their spouses. Abuse or nonabuse, therefore, is not completely determined by the earlier behavior. A theoretical gap exists to explain these cases. (pp. 18–19)

This gap may be bridged by conceptualizing relationships as a *system,* one that may be either open or closed, and by considering the role of *feedback,* a general systems theory term referring to the response of one human being to another's behavior. Negative feedback reduces—and positive feedback increases—the probability that a behavior will be repeated. Systems seek homeostatis, or balance, in achieving their goals. In abusive relationships, the goals of the more powerful person tend to prevail, and violence may be used to maintain that homeostasis. Systems are said to be closed when the individuals engage in highly repetitive patterns of interaction, and new behavior tends to be met with negative feedback (e.g., the woman wants to work outside the home, but her husband discourages or physically assaults her). Giles-Sims (1983) elucidates in his six-stage model of wife battering the reasons why abused women stay and the forces preventing them from leaving. If "the system is relatively open to input from the outside social system," he writes, "then the impact of social norms that discourage severe abuse may be felt sooner, and change may occur in that pattern" (p. 11). Crises develop when the victim attempts to leave the system altogether or, during conflict, when one person's response intensifies the other's previous response in positive feedback loops and the conflict escalates to a dangerous new level.

Lane and Russell (1989) proposed a far more radical theoretical model, allowing for the much greater involvement of women in the initiation and maintenance of violence in relationships. They were among the first to suggest that there are different types of abuse, a notion central to the later work of Michael Johnson (Johnson & Leone, 2005), and they explained both within a systemic framework. The fixation on delineating victims and perpetrators, they argued, fails fully to capture the nuances and dynamics of couples in relation to one another. In a *complementary* relationship, the violence is unilateral, and the dynamic is one akin to a predator and its prey; in a *symmetrical* one, both parties are abusive and struggle to control the relationship. Women, in other words, are not always victims.

Fran Deschner (1984) was among the first to incorporate systemic principles into clinical application. In her book *The Hitting Habit* (1984), she outlines a sensible course of treatment consisting of separate same-sex groups for each partner followed by a multicouples group format in which everyone is taught prosocial relationship skills. Other important innovators were Neidig and Friedman, whose book *Spouse Abuse* (1984) remains to this day one of the clearest, most thorough, and most practical manuals on abuse prevention and treatment to be found anywhere. While not dismissing the role of patriarchal factors (or individual psychopathology), the authors emphasized the mutual, escalating nature of violence and the responsibility that *both* partners have for getting it under control:

> The unilateral view of spouse abuse, with its emphasis on societal factors as causing males to be abusive, may reduce the husband and wife's sense of guilt and responsibility while increasing their feelings of helplessness. Additionally, treatment that takes the unilateral view of violence encounters the following problems that can be avoided if the interpersonal perspective is maintained. First, there is the implication that there are fixed "victim" and "perpetrator" roles. Victims may assume that they can legitimately seek retribution or punishment, which can in turn lead to additional violent attempts to settle the score. Second, if the violence sequence is punctuated too narrowly, if either party only views the incident from his own perspective, and if interactional variables are not attended to, the violence may appear as if it erupted spontaneously and is beyond the influence of both parties. This perception is a therapeutic dead end. Third, when positive relationship factors and the contribution of both spouses to the conflict escalation process are ignored, women tend to be viewed as helpless, childlike victims, thus perpetuating conditions that may contribute to additional violence. (pp. 3–4)

Their treatment program eschews simplistic solutions along gender lines, such as the "reeducation" of male perpetrators according to feminist sociopolitical theory (e.g., Pence & Paymar, 1993). Within the format of a 10-week multicouples format, both partners are encouraged to take personal responsibility for the violence, reduce their need to control their partner, and seek and employ broader and healthier support systems. They are also taught a variety of anger management, stress reduction, communication, and conflict resolution skills.

Chloe Madanes (1990) works with the entire family, employing the theoretical principles and interventions of strategic therapy to better understand the contradictory impulses driving family conflict. "How," she asks, citing the connection between violence and love in family relationships, "does a therapist steer people toward love and away from violence when there is so often such a fine line between the two?" (p. 6). The key, she suggests, is in understanding the core motives that drive family members, which she frames as the four dimensions of family interaction. The first involves the struggle over power and the abuse that ensues when an individual attempts to control his or her own life and the lives of others. In the second, an individual's need to be loved may lead, for example, a child to hit his or her sibling as a means to get parental attention. The third dimension involves a parent's wish to love and protect his or her children, which may include spanking the children "for their own good," sometimes leading to escalated stress, conflict, and abuse. The therapist's task is to help family members understand, curb, and redirect these impulses and to encourage their natural tendencies to repent and forgive, the predominant motives in the fourth and final dimension.

Objections to Systems Theories

Battered women's advocates and feminist academics wedded to the patriarchal view of domestic violence were quick to critique systems formulations and the intervention strategies derived from them. Essentially, their objections centered on the issue of *responsibility:* If patriarchal structures cause and perpetuate domestic violence, then men are always responsible for the abuse in any given relationship. We now know that patriarchal structures account for only a partial explanation and that institutionalized power does not necessarily translate to personal power. Perhaps because of collective guilt over the historical maltreatment of women, objections such as the following from Bograd (1984) were readily accepted at the time:

> Systems language can . . . focus attention away from important dimen-
> sions of battering. For example, to state that a woman remains in a
> violent relationship because abusive transactions satisfy needs at the
> systems level neglects that "needs of the system" may be less critical in
> maintaining battering than the husband's control of physical and mate-
> rial resources, which restricts the wife's freedom to leave or to modify
> the relationship. . . . While not dismissing the possibility that battering
> is sometimes mediated by dysfunctional family processes or structures,
> feminists posit that battering is due more to the power inequality that
> is the context of almost all marriages. . . . By neglecting social factors,
> family therapists reduce the causes of wife battering to intrafamilial
> factors. But violence and power are not simply functions of individuals
> and marital systems. Though the individual family may be the stage of
> violence behavior, it may not be its source. (pp. 562–563)

Until relatively recently, when governing bodies for the various mental health disciplines began to mandate domestic violence education program for their members, therapists as a whole were unfamiliar with the dynamics of domestic violence and rarely asked their clients about its occurrence (e.g., Aldorondo & Straus, 1994). But the problem was far more egregious than one of simple ignorance. Hansen and Harway (1995) suggest that therapists are encouraged to focus on pathological factors, which can be diagnosed and therefore billed, as opposed to situational factors or criminal behavior, such as wife beating, which cannot. Furthermore, the theories and clinical methods of most therapists, according to critics, actively supported the maintenance of social and familial structures harmful to women. Hansen (1995) charged that psychodynamic theories, anchored in early childhood mother–child relationships, put the blame on mothers for any subsequent developmental disturbance—and this included the now discredited notion of a "schizophregenetic mother" responsible for causing an essentially hereditary mental illness.

Critics were especially suspicious of family therapy. Minuchin's structural model, they charged, propped up patriarchal structures, and Bowen's goal of differentiation was at its core male oriented:

> Bowen's (1978) theory recognized the ideal individual as detached and objective and the more pathological individual as emotionally reactive to the affect of others. Mothers were consistently identified as having the primary emotional relationships with the child and thus having the primary responsibility for the success of the differentiation process. In addition, the opportunities for separation and identity development outside the primary relationship were clearly greater for male children. Though these opportunities were never specified as "male opportunities," women who sought them were suggested to have other problems, such as role confusion. (Hansen, 1995, pp. 71–72)

In retrospect, one can appreciate how the needs of women may have been minimized in such an environment, given the cultural context of those times (prior to the increasing access by women to meaningful work opportunities and the greater involvement of fathers in parenting) and refinements in the theory and practice of family therapy. But to its critics, conjoint therapy, regardless of how it is conducted, is contraindicated because it gives the impression, by virtue of both parties being in the room together, that both are to blame. Furthermore, the very language of systems parlance—neutral terms such as "feedback loops" and "homeostasis"— seemed cold and amoral and failed to capture the real pain suffered by victims. And because wives tend to be more emotionally forthcoming, the therapeutic focus turns to their issues rather than to those of the battering husband (Bograd, 1984).

The Advocacy Approach to Intervention

As a result of these objections, interest in systemic approaches quickly subsided. Intervention in spouse abuse was limited to shelter-based peer support groups for female victims and the treatment of male batterers in same-sex psychoeducational programs. As the effects of domestic violence on children became more widely known (Wolak & Finkelhor, 1998), the prevailing model expanded to include therapy for the nonoffending parent and her children. One such program (Van Horn, Best, & Lieberman, 1998), centered in a San Francisco hospital, consisted of weekly mother–child sessions for a period of 1 year. Mothers were helped to heal from their abuse as they acquired more appropriate parenting skills and learned to better manage both their children's aggression and their own anger toward them. The recent book by Dalpiaz (2004), herself a battering victim, eloquently explores the dysfunctional aftermath of abuse, including the complex and often contradictory feelings that persist long after the batterer has physically left.

Also deemed acceptable by women's advocates have been supportive/educational children's groups. The program described by Jaffe, Wolfe, and Wilson (1990) taught children between the ages of 8 and 13 about the nature of family violence and how to label and express feelings such as anger, improve their social skills with peers and adults, and how to stay safe in an abusive environment. Similar programs have been developed by Johnston and Roseby (1997) and others, among them Perilla (2000) whose agency worked primarily with Latino families, treating offenders, adult victims, and children in separate but concurrent groups.

Hybrid Approaches

Common to all advocacy approaches has been the segregation of perpetrators and victims and a disdain for systemic theories, with the notable exception of Rivett and Rees's (2004) interesting attempt to explain Duluth-style men's treatment groups as a sort of family system. But while the advocacy approach continued to dominate, a small handful of feminist researchers and clinicians revisited the possibilities of conjoint and family therapy. Eschewing an "either/or" mind-set, a group of family therapists at the Ackerman Institute for the Family founded the Gender and Violence Project and adopted a "both/and" view of violence. Their treatment model for battering included what others have called a *reconstructive approach* (Geffner, Barrett, & Rossman, 1995), in which abuse is explained by individual, or linear, factors as well as family, or circular, factors. Reconstructive therapy encourages, within appropriate safety guidelines, conjoint and family work but is firmly grounded in feminist advocacy ideology with a therapist-advocate rather than neutral observer. Greenspun (2000) summarized the new systems/feminist hybrid as follows:

1. We believe that violence is multiply determined. It is the outgrowth of both male abuse of power over women *and* the result of escalations within the dyad based on relational dynamics. In addition, individual factors, such as internalizations of early relationships, neurobiological predisposition and trauma history,

further contribute to the use of violence and can become points of intervention.

2. We view violence by men against their intimate partners as both an instrumental *and* an expressive act, rather than one or the other. Men wield violence and threats in order to intimidate and control women, but they may also experience the moment of violence as a loss of control.

3. Social control, resocialization to egalitarian viewpoints, and psychological exploration can all serve as useful interventions in order to stop male violence. A comprehensive therapy must be able to utilize all these approaches when necessary in order to address the variety of factors that lead to violence.

4. Couple (conjoint) therapy can be employed as a treatment approach, but *only* when a clear moral framework is utilized that holds the man fully accountable for his use of violence. In this sense, the therapist cannot maintain the usual neutrality most often associated with couples therapy. Understanding the psychological and relational underpinnings should be used to deter the violence, but never to excuse it. *If the man will not take responsibility for his aggression, conjoint treatment should not be undertaken* (p. 158).

Once it was reaffirmed that only the man is responsible for the violence, the Ackerman school was free to expand treatment possibilities, secure in its feminist credentials. Its most notable exponent, Virginia Goldner (1998), emphasized the practical advantages of conjoint therapy as something good for women because it helped reduce violence against them:

Although we always insist on the punctuation that a man's violence is not *caused* by the relationships he forms, it is, nonetheless, woven into the confusing melodrama of the couple's involvement. As a result, the obsessive power of the relationship must be addressed if second-order change around the man's violence is to occur. This cannot be done by seeing each partner separately since it is only by observing the particular, idiosyncratic "pull" of the relationship in *statu nascendi* that its power to possess comes into focus. As systems therapists have often demonstrated, a picture is worth a thousand words, especially since the partners themselves typically cannot see the context that is shaping their behavior.

Such couples bond to one another with a monumental intensity that makes separation both unlikely and very dangerous. Given the level of risk, it is mere common sense to argue that developing a therapeutic alliance with *both* partners is vitally important. . . . It strains common sense to argue that separating them in treatment necessarily promotes safety. After their respective sessions, the two end up at home together anyway, often not any more enlightened about the specifics of their escalation process, and its dangerous moments. (pp. 265–266)

Notwithstanding its narrow focus on male battering, the Ackerman school and its offshoots represented a radical departure from mainstream intervention. By examining childhood abuse, dependency needs, and fear of intimacy, Goldner and her colleagues clearly "raised the bar" for the next generation of domestic violence clinicians, emboldening others to work systemically with violent couples (e.g., Singer, 1997). Successful programs would also be developed employing a multicouple format, but these have generally been limited to providing support and teaching anger management and conflict resolution skills (e.g., Geffner & Mantooth, 2000; O'Leary, Heyman, & Neidig, 1999) rather than exploring underlying issues or providing a corrective emotional experience. That is not to suggest that the latter format is any less effective; act, at Virginia Tech University, Stith, Rosen, and McCollum (2004) reported superior treatment outcomes in terms of lower male offender recidivism for the multi-couples modality compared to standard couples counseling. In fact, both formats are valuable, depending on the needs of the couple.

In New Zealand, Downey (1997) and her staff at the Berry Street MATTERS center have incorporated the core principles of the Ackerman school into their program for teens and their families. Thus, adolescent violence can be explained by socioeconomic factors, drug and alcohol abuse, early parent–child relationships, and the witnessing and experiencing of abuse and neglect—and by patriarchal structures and family dynamics. Spousal abuse by women is not under consideration; any modeling of abuse—and its subsequent intergenerational transfer—can be found exclusively in the father's violence toward the mother. Remarkably, despite its feminist ideological constraints, the MATTERS program broke therapeutic ground in acknowledging the *reciprocal* nature of family violence, a theme that will be picked up in a later section of this chapter. After reflecting on the existing family violence literature, she suggests some far-reaching implications for treatment:

> There are reports that adolescent violence may be retaliation for being struck or that the adolescent's violence may lead the parent to strike back, which cloud the issue of responsibility for the violence. Other authors surmise that the violent behaviour of adolescents could increase stress and conflict in families rather than that the stress and conflict cause the violence. (p. 75)
>
> Adolescents do not fit the typical conception of a perpetrator (who is physically and socially more resourced) and parents do not fit the idea of the physically and socially vulnerable victim. To deal with violence in the therapy room there has to be a complex understanding

of it, such that we can affirm that violence is wrong and assign responsibility to the person who is acting violently, while at the same time
employing our usual skills to assist people to have the relationships
they desire. This is particularly true with adolescents, where we can
see the hurt child so clearly when the adolescent is at the turning point
from victim to perpetrator. There has to be the most comprehensive
theory possible without compromising the moral position that people
must take responsibility for their actions. (p. 77)

Drawn from both the advocacy and reconstructive approaches and
Robert Geffner's work with male offenders and their spouses at the East
Texas Crisis Center in the 1980s (Geffner, Mantooth, Franks, & Rao,
1989), the multisystems perspective proposed a three-stage course of
treatment designed to promote safety while facilitating change (Geffner
et al., 1995): creating a context for change, challenging patterns and
expanding realities, and consolidation. Their list of preconditions, drawn
from multiple clinical research sources, is a well-thought-out and useful
guide for any clinician contemplating family work (Table 11.1).

Research at the Crossroads

Less overtly ideological than the Ackerman model and having broadened
the scope of treatment from the couple to the entire family, the work
of Geffner et al. brought us to the verge of a truly modern, empirically

TABLE 11.1   Preconditions for Conducting Family Therapy

✓ Victim and perpetrator want this type of treatment.

✓ The victim is aware of potential dangers, and has a safety plan.

✓ An adult must accept responsibility in cases of child abuse.

✓ There are no custody issues if the parents are going through a divorce.

✓ Results of a lethality evaluation indicate a low probability of danger.

✓ Perpetrator does not have obsessional thoughts about the victim.

✓ The therapists have been trained in both domestic violence and family
therapy.

✓ None of the clients are abusing drugs or alcohol.

✓ Treatment is mandated in cases of substance abuse.

✓ Neither of the partners exhibits psychotic behavior.

grounded, *gender-inclusive* approach. But this was a decade ago, and since then progress in the development of family therapy for domestic violence has come to a standstill. With the exception of Rybski's (1998) structured group program for adolescents and their parents (based on the work of Neidig and Friedman [1984]), Caffaro and Conn-Caffaro's (1998) volume on sibling abuse, the narrative therapy approach for couples developed by Ziegler and Hiller (2002), this author's *Gender-Inclusive Treatment of Intimate Partner Abuse* (Hamel, 2005), and Potter-Efron's outstanding *Handbook of Anger Management* (2005), one is pressed to find anywhere in the family violence literature treatment approaches that are both systemic *and* take seriously violence perpetrated by women. Today, there seems to be implicit agreement among researchers and clinicians that it is permissible to explore options of couples and family intervention and even acknowledge that women can be physically abusive as *long as it is understood that men are always the dominant aggressors and that the safety of women is always the primary consideration.*

These assumptions exist frankly because of the considerable influence by battered women's advocates on public policy, which has created a climate of fear within the research community to remain "politically correct," but they have also been buttressed by the work of Michael Johnson (Johnson & Leone, 2005). It was Johnson who formulated the now popular distinction between *intimate terrorism,* a pattern of severe physical abuse combined with highly controlling behavior presumed to be male perpetrated, and *common couple violence,* involving less serious abuse arising from escalated mutual conflict, perpetrated equally by men and women. Although his studies are deeply flawed and based on selected samples and although recent research with more representative community samples has found comparable numbers of "intimate terrorists" between the genders (Graham-Kevan & Archer, 2005; see also chapter 7 in this volume), Johnson's typology has emerged as the only widely acceptable alternative to the patriarchal paradigm (e.g., Greene & Bogo, 2002; Philpot, Brooks, Lusterman, & Nutt, 1997).

THE GENDER-INCLUSIVE APPROACH

The accumulated body of data from family violence research conducted over the past three decades, including batterer treatment outcome studies, the literature on prevalence and context in intimate partner abuse and its effects on children, as well as research on child abuse and neglect, is summarized in Table 11.2. For overviews, the reader is referred to Dutton and Nicholls (2005), the treatment manual by Hamel (2005), this book's introduction, as well as chapters 2, 3, 8, and 10 in this

TABLE 11.2   Gender-Inclusive Research Findings

✓ Both men and women can be victims and/or perpetrators.

✓ Victim/perpetrator distinctions are overstated, and much partner violence is mutual. Even when the violence is unilateral, overall *abuse* is often bilateral.

✓ Both genders are physically and emotionally impacted by abuse. Women suffer the greater share of physical injuries and express overall higher levels of fear.

✓ Men engage in higher levels of sexual coercion and can more readily intimidate physically, but women and men overall engage in comparable levels of controlling and abusive behaviors.

✓ The causes of partner abuse are varied but similar across gender, and patriarchal explanations are insufficient.

✓ Men and women have similar motives in perpetrating violence. "Gendered" violence may be male or female perpetrated.

✓ There is no automatic power imbalance favoring the man that would preclude couples or family counseling; the dominant aggressor may be male or female.

✓ Regardless of perpetrator gender, child witnesses to partner abuse are adversely affected and are at risk for experiencing and perpetrating partner abuse as adults.

✓ There is a high correlation between perpetration of partner abuse and child abuse for both men and women.

✓ Family violence is a complex phenomenon, mediated by stress, with reciprocal interactions between the individual members.

✓ The victim of one person's abuse maybe a perpetrator toward another in the same family, and victims who leave may become perpetrators in subsequent relationships.

volume. The systemic, gender-inclusive approach to domestic violence is based on this research. It is empirically rather than ideologically driven, drawing heavily on previous models, but represents a significant departure in other respects.

Family Violence Assessments: Who Comes In?

There are numerous reasons why partner and child abuse are underdetected (Aldorondo & Straus, 1994). Client-based reasons include the belief that violence is excusable, the desire to make a good impression, fear of further victimization, and dependency needs. Among the therapist-based reasons are using inappropriate terminology (e.g., using vague terms such as "battering" rather than asking specific questions about discrete acts of violence) and failure to ask or even see both partners. When therapists do ask about violence, it is usually about violence directed against the mother or the children; adult male victims are an afterthought at best. Seeing multiple family members increases the odds that abuse by *either* parent or other family members will be discovered. Children, particularly teens, are less concerned about making a good impression and may be more honest. An operating principle is *for the clinician to interview as many family members—and in whatever combination—that will yield the maximum information about the family system without compromising anyone's safety or unnecessarily alienating key family members.*

Who is seen during the assessment process depends on a number of factors: (a) the nature of the presenting problem, (b) legal constraints, and (c) client resistance. The clinician must ascertain who *should* be seen and who *can* be seen. Unless the clinician is working specifically with a violent population (e.g., he or she is a batterer intervention provider), the presenting problem may not be partner or child abuse. Adults seek help for depression but are not immediately forthcoming about their victimization at the hands of their partner, which may have caused the depression. Parents who bring their son in for hitting his younger brother may have previously been abusive to the children or each other. The adolescent girl brought in for drug use and curfew violations may be trying to escape a dysfunctional family system, in which emotional and physical abuse is perpetrated and reciprocated among all the family members.

The clinician must therefore be on the lookout for any signs of abuse. Among the risk factors for intimate partner abuse are high conflict and relationship dissatisfaction; whether one partner is afraid of the other; aggressive personality or evidence of certain psychopathology, such as bipolar disorder, attention-deficit/hyperactivity disorder, and personality disorder, particularly the "cluster B" group in the *Diagnostic and Statistical Manual of Mental Disorders* (4th ed.); violence in family of origin or violence in previous adult relationships; low socioeconomic status; any alcohol or drug abuse; and corporal punishment. Risk factors for child abuse are similar (Merrill, Crouch, Thomsen, & Guimond, 2004), and checklists are available (Milner and Chilamkurti, 1991.) Whenever, in fact, evidence is found for *any* type of abuse, the clinician should investigate the possibility that other types of abuse also exist. A more thorough discussion of risk factors, including how to conduct a lethality assessment, can be found in chapter 12 in this volume.

When clients are court-referred after a conviction for spousal abuse, there may be legal prohibitions against seeing perpetrator and victim together in the same session. The clinician may attempt to see the victim separately, if he or she is willing to oblige, or conduct an interview on the telephone. Collateral sources may be helpful. These would include contact with other mental health professionals previously or currently involved with the client and/or victim and a review of documents from agency sources such as probation or Child Protective Services. In cases involving voluntary clients, the clinician may have legal access to key family members who are nonetheless resistant to treatment. Strategies for engaging clients in treatment and building a therapeutic alliance can be found in Hamel (2005). One option is to conduct interviews separately with whomever is willing to participate and to collect the information piecemeal. This author has had success in securing the participation of key but resistant family members by soliciting their "expertise" as crucial to the success of therapy.

Exploring the Family System

During the assessment process, the clinician will need to explore the important areas of family functioning that can directly or indirectly lead to conflict, abuse, and violence. They are the following:

1. Each Individual's Ability to Cope with Anger, Stress, and Conflict
   Who has poor impulse control and tends to react to the slightest provocation by yelling, throwing things, or worse? In periods of high stress, are there certain family members around whom everyone must "walk on eggshells" lest they suddenly act out? Is there one "primary aggressor" whose internally driven aggressive impulses generate the bulk of family conflict and dysfunction?

2. Family Beliefs About Anger and Violence
   Is corporal punishment the preferred means of discipline? Are outbursts of verbal or physical abuse overtly disapproved but tacitly allowed when someone has been "pushed over the limit"? Are certain transgressions, such as flirting, "fair game" for violence? Is violence by the father minimized because of society's glorification of male violence, or is the mother's violence ignored because it is less physically damaging?

3. Family Structure (see also chapter 23 in this volume)

   Differentiation and Organization—Are each family member's roles clearly defined and appropriate for their abilities and developmental level? In unhealthy families, roles are unfulfilled (e.g., the mother who neglects her children because of chronic substance abuse) and definitions blurred or reversed (e.g., the child who takes care of a battered mother or the chronically unemployed father who likes to "hang out" with his son to play video games).

Boundaries and Hierarchies—Emerging research (see chapter 8 in this volume) finds associations between family conflict and boundary problems. The clinician needs to ask, Is there a clear boundary between the parental system and the child subsystem so that parental authority is maintained yet permeable enough to allow for necessary information and communication from the children? Is there overinvolvement (enmeshment) or underinvolvement (disengagement) between individuals in the two subsystems? Is there an inappropriate alliance between a parent and child, causing the triangulation of another? In healthy families, the parental subsystem is not only separate from but also above the child subsystem in the vertical hierarchical organization of its members.

Accessibility to Outside Influence—Are the boundaries with the outside world also appropriately permeable, allowing for the privacy and integrity of the family while allowing input necessary for growth and change? Or does a family code of secrecy prevent victims from accessing help against abuse?

Adaptability—How capable is the family system of adapting to stress and changes in circumstances? Can it maintain an optimum equilibrium of functioning, allowing for stability but flexible enough to grow and to increase its available set of responses?

4. Relationship Dynamics (see also chapters 6 and 9 in this volume)

   These include attachment styles (secure, anxious, avoidant, and disorganized), communication and emotion expression, and how conflicts are handled. Is a particular relationship characterized by a control–compliance or control–control dynamic? When one person attacks, does the other counterattack, defend, or else withdraw altogether? To what extent does fear of abuse (physical or emotional) shape any individual's behavior?

5. The Function of Each Person's Behavior in the Family Context

   What are the likely repercussions within the family system for a given behavior? Consciously or unconsciously, human beings tend to do things for which there is some "payoff." An adolescent, for instance, may become violent toward his or her parents as a way to prevent them from divorcing. A victim may consciously initiate a fight in order to "get it over with" before an important event (e.g., Christmas).

A number of questionnaires are available to the clinician conducting an assessment. To secure information about intimate partner abuse, recommended instruments are the Conflict Tactics Scales (CTS; verbal and physical abuse prevalence rates), CTS-2 (verbal, physical, sexual, and psychological abuse and extent of injury), the Controlling and Abusive Tactics Questionnaire (CAT; abuse and control), and the Anger Styles Questionnaire developed by Potter-Efron (2005). The standard instrument for measuring child abuse is the CTS-PC. A complete, step-by-step family violence assessment protocol can be found in Hamel (2005), including questions to ask children and reproductions of the previously mentioned instruments (or information on how to order them). Children and adolescents may be quite forthcoming about their parent's violence but not their own. At the MATTERS Program in New Zealand (Sheehan, 1997), the staff employ several sets of questions to obtain information while engaging the cooperation of adolescent perpetrator clients. A partial list, some of them applicable when working with other types of family violence, can be found in Table 11.3.

Primary Aggressor Assessment, Responsibility, and Empowerment

In justifying a couples approach to domestic violence, Goldner (1998) cited the "obsessive power of the relationship" and the "confusing melodrama of the couple's involvement" (p. 265) but also made it clear that a man's violence is not *caused* by his relationship problems. In the gender-inclusive perspective, violence by the man *or* the woman—or by any of the children—may in fact be at least partially caused by stress and relationship issues, and physical aggression may be a response to verbal or emotional abuse or to controlling behavior. However, it is equally true that violence is itself a cause of stress and relationship problems—in the same manner that personal problems (e.g., anxiety, depression, and unsatisfactory peer relations) may lead to excessive drinking, and excessive drinking in turn brings it own share of dysfunction (e.g., more depression or job problems). In any case, stress cannot be cited as an excuse for engaging in violent behavior (Stith & Rosen, 1990).

One must attend to both the abuse and the factors that contribute to and that are caused by the abuse. However, it is important to point out that although family abuse is often reciprocal and mutual and systemic factors serve to perpetuate abusive systems, violence is also caused and maintained by factors inherent in the *individual,* among them distorted

TABLE 11.3   Engagement and the Joining Process

A. Questions that help lessen a child's anxiety about entering treatment:

"Do you feel like you're in the hot seat?"

"What do you think your parents want to say to me?"

"Do you think I'll hear your side of the story, or only your parents' side?"

B. Questions that elicit a child's "honorable self," capable of empathy:

"What was it like when you hit your mum? How did you feel afterward?"

"When you're feeling angry, do you ever notice any other feelings there as well?"

"How would you know if anyone in the family was feeling scared of you?"

C. Questions that help bring forth the child's "agentive self," capable of taking action to end the violence:

"At what point did you choose to hit your dad? Looking back, could you have chosen to act differently?

"Can you think of a time when you wanted to hit your mum but chose not to?

"What did you do instead? Was it a better idea or not?"

D. Questions that elicit the parents' and siblings' experiences of living with a violent child:

"What was it like for you when your daughter was being violent?"
"What will it do to your relationship if nothing changes?"

"Does your sister's violence stop you from being her friend?"

E. Questions that encourage change by helping family members notice improvement:

"Who will notice first if Jason is making an effort to control his violence?"

"Do you think your mum and dad see you differently when you are controlling your anger?"

"Now that Kylie is making an effort, are other people in the family acting differently too?"

Source: Sheehan (1997, pp. 85–86).

and antisocial attitudes, a need to dominate, and poor impulse control (Dutton, 1998). Perpetration of abuse should thus be considered a separate problem (Geller, 1998). In deciding who should be treated specifically for the abuse (e.g., through referral to an anger management or batterer program), one may begin with the work of Appel and Holden (1998), who propose five possible models of co-occurring spousal and child abuse. Their scheme, with some modification to bring it line with gender-inclusive research, is as follows:

✓ *Single Perpetrator*—One parent abuses the other parent and the children.
✓ *Sequential Perpetrator*—One parent abuses the other parent, who in turn abuses the children.
✓ *Dual Perpetrator*—One parent abuses the other parent, and both parents abuse the children.
✓ *Marital Violence*—The parents mutually abuse one another and the children.
✓ *Family Dysfunction*—Both parents abuse one another and the children, and the children abuse one or both of the parents and/ or each other.

Although the last model is the most inclusive, it is often one of the other models that best explains the abuse in a particular family. To account for all possible combinations of family violence, this scheme may be expanded to include, for example, child abuse without partner abuse and partner abuse without child abuse as well as child-perpetrated violence when there is no child abuse. Appel and Holden (1998) also point out that families are fluid, not static, entities and may pass through several models.

In identifying the pathways for abuse, one important consideration is determining the *primary aggressor.* This is not always the biggest person or the one who yells the loudest. The primary aggressor is *the one who tends to initiate the abuse and whose behavior has the greatest impact on the family system.* As the family dysfunction model suggests, this could certainly be a child, but a child would rarely be considered the *dominant aggressor,* a legal term referring to who has the greater power and is the greater threat in an intimate partner relationship. Dad may be the primary (and dominant) aggressor if, for instance, he initiates the verbal and physical aggression toward his partner, controls the household money, and has an authoritarian parenting style. Mom may retaliate at times by hitting back or may yell at the children, and she may in fact require some help with her own issues and be a key to the family's overall treatment success, but unless dad's anger and violence is specifically addressed as a separate problem, the outcome is likely to be poor. In another family, if dad has thrown things but this was in response to a constant barrage of verbal and emotional abuse from a partner who insists on making all the family decisions, then mom would be regarded as the primary and dominant aggressor. Of course, there are times when neither party can be considered dominant because both engage in various types of abusive and controlling behaviors (e.g., dad slams doors, has grabbed mom by the arm, controls the finances, and uses the "silent treatment," and mom initiates the verbal abuse, constantly checks on his whereabouts, and has allied herself with the children).

Research indicates that distinctions between "perpetrator" and "victim" are grossly overemphasized. In the gender-inclusive perspective, everyone is responsible for their behavior. Some individuals obviously need to be protected and given appropriate resources. Individuals who stay out of fear or because of pressing financial reasons may need special assistance in leaving their relationship (e.g., with restraining orders or refuge in a shelter). But they are nonetheless responsible for their own well-being, and to the extent that a victim remains in a relationship for personal and less pressing reasons, it would seem prudent—indeed, required—to help them evaluate their choices (Mills, 2003; Peled, Eisikovits, Enosh, & Winstok, 2000). We ought to be careful not to pathologize victims (Hansen, 1995), but asking a client to address the personality characteristics that make them prone to finding abusive partners is to empower them, not blame them. Do we ignore a victim's dependency issues because it is not "politically correct"? We cannot discount the strong likelihood that an untreated victim will at some point retaliate the abuse against either their partner or the children or leave the abuser only to later involve themselves in another abusive relationship, subjecting the children to further dysfunction. Children don't care "who started it" or how long the parent has been a victim.

We need to distinguish between true victims who unnecessarily blame themselves out of fear of the abuser, dependency needs, or denial of the abuse from situations in which a "victim" feels appropriately guilty for engaging in abuse of his or her own. Taking responsibility means accepting the consequences of one's actions regardless of victim or perpetrator status: A person whose nagging results in being physically assaulted has contributed to the cycle of violence, but this should imply neither that he or she is responsible for their partner's behavior nor that the partner's behavior should be minimized. Clearly, that victim can claim the "moral high ground." But the task of a clinician is to facilitate change, not make moral judgments. By failing to understand that systems theory is first and foremost *a means of understanding* and not a specific set of treatment recommendations and by confusing "cause" and "blame" (Felson, 2002), victim advocates have severely restricted our common efforts to combat family violence.

Treatment Options

Once the clinician has a working understanding of the family's abuse dynamics, he or she can proceed to formulate a treatment plan. Treatment may be carried out in any number of modalities, sequentially or concurrently, in whatever combinations are most promising for success. On a spectrum from most inclusive to least, those modalities are the following:

- ✓ Therapy with the entire family
- ✓ Therapy with several family members (e.g., parents and one child or one parent and the children)
- ✓ Couples counseling (includes the dyad by itself or part of a multicouples group or anger management parenting group)
- ✓ Other dyads (e.g., parent and child or two siblings)
- ✓ Counseling with several family members but individually
- ✓ Separate anger management/batterer group participation for the primary aggressor(s)
- ✓ Therapy group for the child

Safety and the Course of Treatment

It should be emphasized that "most inclusive" is not always what is best. Seeing the entire family is usually a good idea, for example, when there is a high degree of reciprocal abuse or when the clinician needs the assistance of additional family members to confront resistance and denial. In other cases, the dysfunction is more or less contained among a segment of the family (e.g., two siblings, the parents, or one parent and a child), and it would be more expeditious to narrow the treatment focus, at least initially. Of course, family therapy may be contraindicated when one or more of the preconditions outlined in Table 11.1 have not been met. One of the most important concerns is safety. Participants cannot be expected to engage honestly in the process when they feel threatened by an untreated parent (or child or sibling). Battered women have often reported violence directed against them following a family session (Adams, 1988; Pagelow, 1981), but this is not a gender-specific phenomenon, and it matters little if that threat is physical (dad has choked mom, requiring her hospitalization, or mom has punched her daughter in the face) or emotional (mom calls her son a "little shit" or dad routinely threatens to abandon the family).

Vetere and Cooper (2001) caution clinicians to be aware of nonverbal signs of intimidation: "If the perpetrator stops physically violent behaviour but continues to intimidate—through attitude, facial expression, physical posture and use of language—then only partial change has been achieved" (p. 391). In such cases, the clinician has the choice of separating the couple or, if appropriate, confronting the behavior directly, thus allowing for the

possibility of insight and the corrective emotional experience for both partners that might alter a long-standing relationship dynamic.

As Goldner (1998) has articulated, safety is hardly promoted when
the clinician refuses conjoint counseling against the victim's wishes, considering that the couple will simply continue the violence outside the
office, where it cannot easily be monitored. And Potter-Efron (2005) suggests that conjoint therapy may be required for even the most violent
couples as a "last resort" when everything else has been tried (e.g., several rounds of batterer group or separate victim services). The clinician
can foster a feeling of safety in victimized family members by clearly
articulating his or her position that violence is unacceptable, by offering
a safety plan, and by encouraging them to call the police should they be
reassaulted. Safety will also be promoted if the course of treatment follows the author's three-phase approach (Table 11.4), which emphasizes
skill building and the reestablishment of trust and confidence among the
family members in the first phase and greater exploration of underlying
issues and dynamics in the following phases.

CASE EXAMPLES

CASE 1: DUAL PERPETRATOR MODEL

Joe and Evelyn Mitchell brought their 12-year-old son, Drake, to a private practice marriage and family therapist, seeking help for his school
problems. A middle-aged insurance salesman, Joe tried to project an outward demeanor of strength and confidence but was overshadowed by
his extremely high-strung, domineering wife, a real estate broker who
did most of the talking during the first session. It was also apparent that
Joe had been suffering from depression. While answering the therapist's
questions about his poor school attendance and failing grades, Drake
revealed that he sometimes "lost it" with friends whom he perceived as
disloyal. The therapist asked Drake if there was anyone else in his life who
sometimes "lost it," and he disclosed, hesitantly, that mother "screams
at dad and sometimes hits him with things." It was revealed that Evelyn
also yelled at Drake and had in fact physically abused him for years with
hairbrushes and other household objects. The week before, when he lied
to her about his school attendance, she had slapped him hard enough
to cause a bloody nose. And Joe had on occasion pushed and grabbed
Drake, typically when under pressure from mom, once bruising his arm
when he refused to clean up his room.

After the first session, the therapist asked to meet with the couple
without their son. Results of the CTS and CAT confirmed that Evelyn

TABLE 11.4   Phases of Treatment

I	II	III
Overall approach:	Overall approach:	Overall approach:
Psychoeducational	Psychoeducational/ cognitive	Cognitive/ insight oriented
Goals:	Goals:	Goals:
Eliminate physical aggression	Begin to reduce verbal/ psychological aggression	Eliminate verbal/ psychological aggression
Avoid secondary problems Minimum ventilation of affect	Continue avoiding secondary problems but begin addressing lesser primary problems	Begin addressing core issues
Build confidence and trust	More ventilation of affect	Full expression of affect encouraged
Focus on content	Continue trust and confidence building	Greater attention to process
Learn how anger works, conflict escalation dynamics, role of stress, impact of control and "dirty fighting" tactics, and equalitarian decision making	Continued focus on content; limited discussion of process Identify and challenge "self-talk"	Identify belief systems underlying distorted self-talk
Acquire basic anger manage-ment, communication and conflict containment skills	Expand communication skills and learn conflict resolution and problem solving techniques Assertiveness training	Begin addressing and working through childhood-of-origin issues
Type of change sought:	Type of change sought:	Type of change sought:
First order, behavioral, immediate	First order, behavioral, some internal	Second order, systems level, internal

was the dominant aggressor in the family, scoring high on the CAT dimensions of diminishment of self-esteem (berating Joe for not bringing in enough income and ridiculing his sexual performance) as well as isolation and jealousy (she constantly questioned his whereabouts and accused him of having affairs). Although severely abused (on one occasion he incurred a deep gash in his head from a fireplace poker), Joe refrained from hitting back, too scared that if he were to do so she would leave him. Raised to not "air your dirty laundry," he never thought of calling the police or sought any type of assistance from extended family or from professionals, bearing the twin burdens of family violence and his own depression in secret. His role, he told the therapist, was to be "the strong one." Meanwhile, because of the long-standing alliance between father and son, Evelyn felt painfully alienated, and when they would dismiss her as "crazy" and threatened to move out together, the old shame and hurt of having lived with an abusive schizophrenic mother and having been abandoned at age seven by her father resurfaced again. This rejection made her more angry and justified her criticisms of Joe, causing him to withdraw, which in turn led Evelyn to lash out in desperate bids for attention.

Because of the seriousness of Evelyn's violence and poor impulse control, the therapist referred her to a one-year domestic violence/anger management group. The local battered woman's shelter did not offer support groups for men, but a concerned worker offered to see Joe on an individual basis, providing him support and helping him understand the issue around his victimization. Claiming that the counseling was "repetitive," he terminated after six weeks. (Later, he admitted to having felt uncomfortable in the role of "victim.") But the family came in together for another three months, during which time Evelyn ceased her physical assaults and most of her verbal abuse, and the parents were able to work on a parenting plan to deal with Drake's school problems. In doing so, the family hierarchy was restructured to bolster the parental subsystem. Evelyn was asked to come in for a few sessions separately with Drake, and over time (but not without some setbacks) the mother was able to build a loving and healthy relationship with her son.

Encouraged with this success, the couple agreed to come in for conjoint sessions and work on their own relationship. Over the next 14 months, the focus was first on Evelyn and on consolidating the progress she made on managing her anger; then it shifted to Joe, who found the reconciliation between mother and son somewhat threatening. Joe's own dependency needs emerged, as did his fears of intimacy. By helping Joe learn to better assert himself and set limits on his wife's aggression while encouraging him to accept appropriate bids for love and attention, he gradually overcame his depression and became the genuinely strong and compassionate man he had always wanted to be.

CASE 2: FAMILY DYSFUNCTION

Matt, a 29-year-old construction worker, was referred to a batterer intervention program (BIP) at the insistence of his wife, Jackie, a stay-at-home-mom, for having shoved her. During the intake process, Matt complained to the BIP counselor that he had already done a batterer program and that for the past two years it had been his wife who "caused all the problems." It began, he said, with sabotaging behaviors (e.g., standing in front of the door when he attempted to take a time-out) and later turned into verbal put-downs, throwing things, and finally hitting. The BIP counselor at first assumed that Matt was in denial (like a lot of the men he worked with) until a phone consultation with Jackie revealed a more complex picture.

Meanwhile, Jackie had expressed dissatisfaction with her shelter support group, where her own problems with anger, against Matt as well as the children, seemed to be minimized. On the CTS and CTS-PC, it was revealed that Matt had punched Jackie 5 years before, an incident for which he was arrested, and had frequently used a belt to discipline their 13-year-old son, Andy. In the past, both parents had frequently yelled, and sometimes Jackie initiated. But the CAT also indicated that Matt often used nonverbal intimidation around Jackie (e.g., cornering her in the kitchen and literally getting into her face) and that he controlled the family finances, withholding his wife's "allowance" when she gave him "a hard time." As a result of his involvement with the batterer group, Matt eventually let go of his need for control and never hit Jackie again. Wanting more information, the therapist invited the entire family to come to the next session, and the full picture of the family's violence and dysfunction began to emerge, one that over the years had clearly shifted from a single perpetrator to a family dysfunction model.

The pushing incident, it turned out, occurred when Matt restrained Jackie from hitting their 11-year-old daughter, Viola, after Viola had slapped her mother and called her a "bitch." While attempting to separate wife and daughter, Matt blamed Jackie for letting the conflict escalate, and that's when Jackie began to slap and kick her husband. When Matt pushed her away, she fell against a bookcase. Probing for antecedents, the therapist learned that earlier that day Viola had been yelling at Andy for using her Walkman without permission. Because of his age, it was Andy whom the parents typically punished whenever the siblings didn't get along, but on this occasion the parents had decided to side with Andy after finding out that Viola had retaliated by ripping up one of his crucial homework assignments. Viola indeed had been the favored child, and for years Andy had deeply resented her. Fearing his father's wrath, he would rarely confront her directly. Instead, he would engage in passive-aggressive behavior, such as burying her dolls in the backyard. But now, having just experienced a sudden growth spurt, emboldened by his father's nonviolence, and having internalized dad's previously abusive coping style, Andy began to strike out physically against his sister and his mother.

Viola had previously acted as the family peacemaker when dad had been violent. She had joined mom in some counseling sessions at the shelter and had even become a confidante. But when mom restricted her involvement with a new, more delinquent peer group in middle school, Viola turned on her. Recognizing the dangerous, escalating nature of these shifting dynamics, the therapist requested that everyone come in together for therapy. Partly during these sessions and in the course of a separate 26-week family violence parent program for Matt and Jackie, the therapist educated them about family abuse dynamics, the intergenerational cycle of violence, and prosocial ways with which to handle conflict. Adjunct sessions with Andy and Viola were helpful in shoring up the sibling subsystem and to reduce the enmeshment between mother and daughter. Later, conjoint sessions with the parents addressed some of the issues in their relationship, including Jackie's lingering difficulties in trusting Matt not to be violent as well as Matt's plummeting self-esteem following an extended layoff from his job. The therapist helped the couple adjust to the stress of changing gender roles when Jackie found work as a legal secretary (something that Matt initially protested). Within six months, Matt had found another job and in the meantime had spent valuable and needed time mending his relationships with his children.

REFERENCES

Adams, D. (1988). Treatment of men who batter: A profeminist analysis. In K. Yllo & M. Bograd (Eds.), *Feminist perspectives on wife abuse* (pp. 176–199). Newbury Park, CA: Sage.

Aldorondo, E., & Straus, M. (1994). Screening for physical violence in marital therapy. *Family Process, 33,* 425–439.

Appel, A., & Holden, G. (1998). The co-occurrence of spouse and physical child abuse: A review and appraisal. *Journal of Family Psychology, 12*(4), 578–599.

Babcock, J., Green, C., & Robie, C. (2004). Does batterer's treatment work? A meta-analytic review of domestic violence treatment. *Clinical Psychology Review, 23,* 1023–1053.

Bograd, M. (1984). Family systems approaches to wife battering: A feminist critique. *American Journal of Orthopsychiatry, 54,* 558–568.

Caffaro, J., & Conn-Caffaro, A. (1998). *Sibling abuse trauma: Assessment and intervention strategies for children, families and adults.* Binghamton, NY: Haworth Maltreatment & Trauma Press.

Dalpiaz, C. (2004). *Breaking free, starting over: Parenting in the aftermath of family violence.* Westport, CT: Praeger.

Deschner, F. (1984). *The hitting habit: Anger control for battering couples.* New York: Simon & Schuster.

Dobash, R. E., & Dobash, R. P. (1979). *Violence against wives: A case against the patriarchy.* New York: Free Press.

Downey, L. (1997). Adolescent violence: A systemic and feminist perspective. *Australian and New Zealand Journal of Family Therapy, 18*(2), 70–79.

Dutton, D. (1998). *The abusive personality.* New York: Guilford Press.

Dutton, D., & Nicholls, T. (2005). A critical review of the gender paradigm in domestic violence research and theory: Part I—Theory and data. *Aggression and Violent Behavior, 10,* 680–714.

Felson, R. (2002). *Violence and gender reexamined.* Washington, DC: American Psychological Association.

Geffner, R., Barrett, M., & Rossman, R. (1995). Domestic violence and sexual abuse: Multiple systems perspectives. In R. Mikesell, S. McDaniels, & D. Lusterman (Eds.), *Integrating family therapy: Handbook of psychology and systems theory* (pp. 501–517). Washington, DC: American Psychological Association.

Geffner, R., & Mantooth, C. (2000). *Ending spouse/partner abuse: A psychoeducational approach for individuals and couples.* New York: Springer.

Geffner, R., Mantooth, C., Franks, D., & Rao, L. (1989). A psychoeducational, conjoint therapy approach to reducing family violence. In P. Caesar & L. Hamberger (Eds.), *Treating men who batter: Theory, practice and programs* (pp. 196–235). New York: Springer.

Geller, J. (1998). Conjoint therapy for the treatment of partner abuse: Indications and contraindications. In A. Roberts (Ed.), *Battered women and their families* (2nd ed., pp. 76–96). New York: Springer.

Giles-Sims, J. (1983). *Wife battering: A systems theory approach.* New York: Guilford Press.

Goldner, V. (1998). The treatment of violence and victimization in intimate relationships. *Family Process, 37*(3), 263–286.

Graham-Kevan, N., & Archer, J. (2005, July 10–13). *Using Johnson's domestic violence typology to classify men and women in a non-selected sample.* 9th International Family Violence Research Conference, Portsmouth, New Hampshire.

Greene, K., & Bogo, M. (2002). The different faces of intimate violence: Implications for assessment and treatment. *Journal of Marital and Family Therapy, 28*(4), 455–466.

Greenspun, W. (2000). Embracing the controversy: A metasystemic approach to the treatment of domestic violence. In P. Papp (Ed.), *Couples on the fault line: New directions for therapists* (pp. 154–179). New York: Guilford Press.

Hamel, J. (2005). *Gender-inclusive treatment of intimate partner abuse: A comprehensive approach.* New York: Springer.

Hansen, M. (1995). Feminism and family therapy: A review of feminist critiques of approaches to family violence. In M. Hansen & M. Harway (Eds.), *Battering and family therapy* (pp. 69–81). Newbury Park, CA: Sage.

Hansen, M., & Harway, M. (1995). Intervening with violent families: Directions for future generations of therapists. In M. Hansen & M. Harway (Eds.), *Battering and family therapy* (pp. 227–251). Newbury Park, CA: Sage.

Jaffe, P., Wolfe, D., & Wilson, S. (1990). *Children of battered women.* Newbury Park, CA: Sage.

Johnson, M., & Leone, J. (2005). The differential effects of patriarchal terrorism and common couple violence. *Journal of Family Issues, 26*(3), 322–349.

Johnston, J., & Roseby, V. (1997). *In the name of the child.* New York: Free Press.

Lane, G., & Russell, T. (1989). Second-order systemic work with violent couples. In P. Caesar & K. Hamberger (Eds.), *Treating men who batter* (pp. 134–162). New York: Springer.

Madanes, C. (1990). *Sex, love and violence: Strategies for transformation.* New York: Norton.

Martin, D. (1976). *Battered wives.* San Francisco: Volcano Press.

Merrill, L., Crouch, J., Thomsen, G., & Guimond, J. (2004). Risk for intimate partner violence and child physical abuse: Psychosocial characteristics of multirisk male and female navy recruits. *Child Maltreatment, 9*(1), 18–29.

Mills, L. (2003). *Insult to injury: Rethinking our responses to intimate abuse.* Princeton, NJ: Princeton University Press.

Milner, J., & Chilamkurti, C. (1991). Physical child abuse perpetrator characteristics: A review of the literature. *Journal of Interpersonal Violence, 6,* 345–366.

Neidig, P., & Friedman, D. (1984). *Spouse abuse: A treatment program for couples.* Champaign, IL: Research Press.

O'Leary, K., Heyman, R., & Neidig, P. (1999). Treatment of wife abuse: A comparison of gender-specific and conjoint approaches. *Behavior Therapy, 30,* 475–505.

Pagelow, M. (1981). *Woman-battering: Victims and their experiences.* Beverly Hills, CA: Sage.

Peled, E., Eisikovits, Z., Enosh, G., & Winstok, Z. (2000). Choice and empowerment for battered women who stay. *Social Work, 45*(1), 9–25.

Pence, E., & Paymar, M. (1993). *Education groups for men who batter: The Duluth model.* New York: Springer.

Perilla, J. (2000). Cultural specificity in domestic violence interventions: A Latino model. *The Family Psychologist, 16,* 6–7.

Philpot, C., Brooks, G., Lusterman, D., & Nutt, R. (1997). *Bridging separate gender worlds: Why men and women clash and how therapists can bring them together.* Washington, DC: American Psychological Association.

Potter-Efron, R. (2005). *Handbook of anger management: Individual, couple, family and group approaches.* New York: Haworth Press.

Rivett, M., & Rees, A. (2004). Dancing on a razor's edge: Systemic group work with batterers. *Journal of Family Therapy, 26,* 142–162.

Rybski, N. (1998). *An evaluation of a family group therapy program for domestically violent adolescents.* Unpublished doctoral dissertation, University of Arizona, Tucson.

Sheehan, M. (1997). Adolescent violence—Strategies, outcomes and dilemmas in working with young people and their families. *Australian and New Zealand Journal of Family Therapy, 18*(2), 80–91.

Singer, M. (1997). Saving face: Applying a systemic approach to domestic violence. *Journal of Systemic Therapies, 16*(3), 229–245.

Stith, S., & Rosen, K. (1990). Family therapy for spouse abuse. In S. Stith, M. Williams, & K. Rosen (Eds.), *Violence hits home: Comprehensive treatment approaches to domestic violence* (pp. 83–99). New York: Springer.

Stith, S., Rosen, K., & McCollum, E. (2004). Treating intimate partner violence within intact couples relationships: Outcomes of multi-couple versus individual couple therapy. *Journal of Marital and Family Therapy, 30*(6), 305–315.

Straus, M., Gelles, R., & Steinmetz, S. (1980). *Behind closed doors: Violence in the American family.* Newbury Park, CA: Sage.

Van Horn, P., Best, S., & Lieberman, A. (1998, November). *Breaking the chain: Preventing the transmission of trauma in children of battered women through parent-child psychotherapy.* Paper presented at the 14th annual meeting of the International Society for Traumatic Stress Studies, Washington, DC.

Vetere, A., & Cooper, J. (2001). Working systemically with family violence: Risk, responsibility and collaboration. *Journal of Family Therapy, 23,* 378–396.

Walker, L. (1979). *The battered woman.* New York: Harper & Row.

Wolak, J., & Finkelhor, D. (1998). Children exposed to partner violence. In J. Jasinski & L. Williams (Eds.), *Partner violence: A comprehensive review of 20 years of research* (pp. 184–209). Thousand Oaks, CA: Sage.

Ziegler, P., & Hiller, T. (2002, March/April). Good story/bad story: Collaborating with violent couples. *Psychotherapy Networker,* pp. 63–68.

CHAPTER 12

Violence Risk Assessments With Perpetrators of Intimate Partner Abuse

Tonia L. Nicholls, Sarah L. Desmarais, Kevin S. Douglas,
and P. Randall Kropp

Readers likely will be familiar with the idea that many police officers consider domestic violence calls to be among the most difficult and dangerous situations to which they must respond. Officers attending domestic disputes often are confronted with tales of "he said, she said" and the burden of disentangling the truth from blame, denial, and minimization. The challenges inherent in assessing the ongoing risk presented by an individual with a history of offending against his or her partner is no less challenging farther along in the system when victim safety workers, psychologists, psychiatrists, judges, and probation officers have the responsibility of determining the risk the perpetrator presents for the victim; this is even more complicated, perhaps, in cases characterized by mutual abuse.

Accurate risk assessments with perpetrators of intimate partner abuse are important for a variety of diverse reasons. A proper assessment should lead to informed safety planning for the victim and case management for the perpetrator. Good risk evaluations can help ensure the appropriate division and provision of scarce resources to those individuals and families in greatest need. The information gleaned from a violence risk evaluation can be essential for assisting victims

The authors are grateful to the Michael Smith Foundation for Health Research, the Social Sciences and Humanities Research of Council of Canada, and the British Columbia Mental Health and Addictions Services for their support.

and their advocates in relevant civil (e.g., divorce or custody disputes) and criminal proceedings. It can also be essential in protecting professionals at risk of liability (e.g., duty to warn and protect). In sum, it is essential for professionals working with perpetrators and victims to have a valid and reliable means of determining the potential for serious harm in cases of intimate partner abuse both to prevent tragedies and to maintain the community's trust in the mental health and criminal justice systems.

In this chapter, we remind the reader that violence risk evaluation is a complex process, and we provide a review of judgment errors, common in human decision making, that can limit professionals' abilities to make accurate assessments of risk. We demonstrate how (unconscious) cognitive simplification strategies can backfire to increase the likelihood of errors and, conversely, how applying principles from theory and research to risk judgments can improve decision-making accuracy. This sets the stage for a brief review of the necessity for applying structured professional judgment and evidence-based practice in the assessment and management of intimate partner violence. This is based on the foundation of research that grew out of the formal risk assessment for general criminal violence literature and the more recent empirical examination of predictors of intimate partner abuse perpetration. A review of select instruments intended to inform partner assault risk assessments provide the reader with an introduction to the available tools and their empirical efficacy. We assert that mental health professionals, police officers, and other advocates are most likely to be successful in preventing harm if they make use of such evidence-based, formalized risk instruments.

PITFALLS TO AVOID IN CONDUCTING RISK ASSESSMENTS: JUDGMENT ERRORS IN HUMAN DECISION MAKING AND COGNITIVE SIMPLIFICATION STRATEGIES THAT CAN BACKFIRE

Risk assessment is a decision-making process through which we determine the "best" course of action by estimating, identifying, qualifying, or quantifying risk. When confronted with making any decision, we naturally (and appropriately) look for ways to decrease the amount of cognitive or mental effort needed. To do so, we use *heuristics,* which are guidelines or "rules of thumb" based on personal knowledge and experience that allow us to make "educated guesses" (Kahneman & Tversky, 1973). For the most part, these heuristics lead to efficient decision making but may contribute to judgment errors.

The *availability heuristic* (Tversky & Kahneman, 1973) describes how we make judgments about frequency and probability: We estimate the probability of a particular outcome on the basis of how easily we can imagine that outcome occurring. For example, all diagnostic categorizations in psychology and medicine are influenced by the options that readily come to mind. In risk assessment, we are charged with imagining *plausible* scenarios within which: (a) the perpetrator reoffends and/or (b) the victim is revictimized. It is on the basis of those scenarios that decisions are made with respect to sentencing, treatment, and release, for example. The implications of the availability heuristic are such that emotionally charged possibilities will be perceived as more likely because of their saliency. In addition, the outcomes that are most likely to come to mind will be those that fit within our framework or stereotypes of intimate partner abuse. Situations in which a female victim is abused by her male partner, for instance, are likely easier for most people to imagine than a scenario in which a male victim is abused by his female partner, unless it is in self-defense. Hence, the potential for a biased assessment reflecting errors arising from the availability heuristic becomes clear.

Similarly, the *representativeness heuristic* describes how we make decisions or categorical judgments on the basis of the extent to which something is perceived as being representative of or similar to a particular category. These judgments often are made on superficial qualities, and this contributes not only to stereotyping but also to our tendency to presume categories or groups to be like individual members. Literature to date has tended to promote stereotypical thinking about victims and perpetrators (e.g., males are presumed to be the aggressors, females the victims; for reviews, see Dutton & Nicholls, 2005, and the other chapters in this volume). Finally, *adjustment and anchoring* describes our tendency to start with an implicitly suggested reference point (the anchor) and make adjustments to it to reach decisions or judgments. For example, information acquired early in the process of an assessment can disproportionately influence how we interpret and weigh subsequent information (e.g., Friedlander & Stockman, 1983). Labels and stereotypes (e.g., men are aggressive and women are nurturing), for example, can act as psychological anchors.

Decisions can be further influenced by cognitive biases. For example, *confirmatory or confirmation bias* (Wason, 1960) is the process through which we tend to seek information that confirms our expectations and ignore information that is relevant but disconfirming. In risk assessments, this bias may direct our attention, resulting in the selective focus on evidence and information that confirms our initial judgment. We run the risk of perceptually distorting irrelevant, neutral, or disconfirming information in such a way that we see it as irrelevant or even as confirmation of the preexisting hypothesis. The very fact that we are conducting a risk assessment suggests a history of abusive behavior or a belief that this individual could recidivate. In such a case, the assessor may overestimate the likelihood that the target will behave in ways that confirm the initial hypothesis (i.e., that the perpetrator will necessarily abuse his or her partner again).

Response bias is a tendency to answer questions in a socially desirable or self-promoting manner. Response bias can affect risk assessments if respondents (e.g., victims, perpetrators, or children) answer questions in a way that they think the assessor wants them to answer or in a way that they think will produce a more desirable decision, whether or not they are deliberately trying to mislead the interviewer. *Diagnostic overshadowing,* on the other hand, is a bias on the assessor's part that negatively affects judgment accuracy about concomitant mental illness (e.g., Walker & Spengler, 1995). Overshadowing occurs when a client's problematic behaviors are attributed to some presumed explanation, with no attempt made to search for alternative explanations and/or the etiology of the problem.

Finally, *hindsight bias* (or the "knew-it-all-along" effect) occurs when we perceive events that have already happened as being relatively inevitable and predictable. In risk assessment, we tend to falsely believe that we would have predicted the outcome of an event, potentially overestimating the accuracy of assessments. Moreover, stereotypes associated with personal characteristics, such age, gender, and culture, also may bias clinical decision making. For example, the traditional view of domestic violence is that of a man aggressing against a female partner. Instances of female aggression against a male partner are usually attributed to self-defense, ignoring the potential risk posed by the female partner (for a review of the gender paradigm, see Dutton & Nicholls, 2005).

METHODS FOR REDUCING RELIANCE ON HEURISTICS AND BIASES TO IMPROVING DECISION-MAKING ACCURACY

Principles drawn from decision theory suggest methods to reduce reliance on heuristics and other biases known to negatively impact on the validity and reliability of risk assessments. The first principle calls for continued education and training. High levels of *domain-specific knowledge of decision-makers* (or expertise) can potentially increase decisional quality (e.g., continuing education credits, attending professional conferences, or reading the literature). Under a *production systems framework,* domain-specific knowledge facilitates recognition of common informational patterns and search strategies (Devine & Kozlowski, 1995). Knowledge may increase the ability to locate decision-relevant information (Barrick & Spilker, 2003). In some contexts, however, experts do not perform as well as amateurs, leading to a *process-performance paradox* (Onkal, Yates, Simga-Mugan, & Oztin, 2003). This can occur in low structure conditions when making ambiguous judgments, especially about low baserate behavior (Devine & Kozlowski, 1995; e.g., homicide by intimate partners) or if search strategies are suboptimal (i.e., are not guided or directed), such as in the absence of risk assessment guidelines.

This leads to the second informative principle from decision theory—the *structure of the decision-making task*. Structure as a task domain consistently has been shown to increase consistency of judgments (Payne, Bettman, & Luce, 1998). Structure can vary from ill to well defined as a function of the number of "constraints" left unspecified in a decision task. "Constraints" may come in the form of guidelines detailing risk variables that have been empirically shown to have a strong association with intimate partner abuse perpetration and recidivism (reviewed in the following sections of this chapter). Imposing such constraints should reduce the possible number of alternative judgments and reliance on heuristics and, ultimately, increase judgment quality and consistency (Barrick & Spilker, 2003; Devine & Kozlowski, 1995). Structure reduces cognitive burden and can increase access to "low availability" information by increasing *information search scope*, hence reducing availability bias (Benbasat & Lim, 2000). Finally, theory and research suggests that *consideration of alternatives* to one's initial decision can reduce reliance on heuristics and increase judgment quality and accuracy by precluding the premature settling on a decision (Hirt, Kardes, & Markman, 2004; Payne et al., 1998; Yaniv, 2004). Most of the remainder of this chapter is devoted to explicating how structure can be used in domestic violence risk assessments to increase decisional quality.

GENERAL APPROACHES TO VIOLENCE RISK ASSESSMENT: AN OVERVIEW OF LEADING METHODS

Approaches to violence risk assessment can be divided into two primary categories: actuarial and clinical. The essence of what distinguishes these two approaches is that the actuarial approach combines risk factors through the use of explicit combinatory rules (i.e., algorithm or equation) (Grove & Meehl, 1996; Meehl, 1954), whereas the clinical approach has been described as an "informal, in the head, impressionistic, subjective conclusion, reached (somehow) by a human clinical judge" (Grove & Meehl, 1996, p. 294). By contrast, the traditional actuarial approach is "a formal method, [that] uses an equation, a formula . . . to arrive at a probability or expected value, of some outcome" (Grove & Meehl, 1996, p. 294). Despite this alluring characteristic, the actuarial approach has its own unique problems, as described here.

Unaided clinical judgment is particularly susceptible to the judgmental biases and heuristics discussed previously. Lacking structure, it has been shown on numerous occasions to be less reliable and valid than more structured (typically actuarial) approaches (Grove, Zald, Lebow, Snitz, & Nelson, 2000). Because there are no clear rules for combining information, it also suffers from lack of transparency, no mechanism by which established risk factors are considered, and no guarantee that treatment-relevant risk factors form part of the risk assessment.

In response to the problems identified with clinical judgment, alongside condemning statements that only one in three predictions were accurate (Monahan, 1981) and that making clinical predictions of violence was akin to "flipping coins in the courtroom" (Ennis & Litwack, 1974), structure in risk assessment emerged in the 1990s. Actuarial prediction instruments were developed with the promise of offering more reliable and valid predictions. In the general interpersonal aggression literature, such instruments were typified by the *Violence Risk Appraisal Guide* (VRAG; Harris, Rice, & Quinsey, 1993; Quinsey, Harris, Rice, & Cormier, 1998, 2006). This instrument, containing 12 weighted variables calibrated on a sample of 618 forensic patients and criminal offenders receiving treatment or assessment, attained quite high prediction levels in development samples and could be scored reliably.

While the actuarial approach appeared to address the main problems of unaided clinical prediction (i.e., low reliability and validity), it suffers from other problems. For instance, algorithms optimized in any given research sample are destined—almost axiomatically—to degrade in accuracy on cross validation. A recent example from the violence risk assessment literature makes the point. In one set of samples, the MacArthur study of mental disorder and violence derived a prediction instrument and method that achieved high accuracy in classifying who would be violent after release from a psychiatric hospital—1% in the "low risk" group and 76% in the "high risk" group (Monahan et al., 2001). On cross validation in a new sample, there was an observed rate of violence of 9% and 35% to 49% (depending on variations in method) in these two groups (Monahan et al., 2005), showing substantial "validity shrinkage." This shrinkage stems from the inherent capitalization on chance in many actuarial procedures as well as the inherent instability of many statistical weighting procedures (i.e., beta weights from regression models).

Second, actuarial predictive models have been criticized for tending to downplay risk factors that are relevant to violence reduction or risk management (Douglas & Kropp, 2002; Douglas, Webster, Hart, Eaves, & Ogloff, 2001; Dvoskin & Heilbrun, 2001; Hart, 1998). As such, they often consist largely of static, unchangeable risk factors (i.e., a history of violence) at the expense of risk factors that directly relate to risk reduction opportunities (e.g., anger). In other words, they focus on *risk status* rather than *risk state* (Douglas & Skeem, 2005; Skeem & Mulvey, 2002)—emphasizing unchanging, *inter*individual differences in risk level rather than dynamic (changeable through intervention) *intra*individual differences in risk as well. It is also noteworthy that most violence risk assessment and management strategies fail to consider protective factors or strengths that clients have available to them that might serve to buffer risk (Nicholls, Brink, Desmarais, Webster, & Martin, in press; Webster, Martin, Brink, Nicholls, & Middleton, 2004).

In a related sense, a third problem with actuarial models is that they often fail to include low base rate but potentially vital case-related information. Homicidal ideation or intent is not included on *any* actuarial instrument the authors are aware of—most likely because it is relatively rare and hence unlikely to make it into a regression equation (or other purely empirical item selection method—the method typically used to construct actuarial instruments). If an item is not represented on an actuarial instrument, some commentators would argue that it simply is not relevant (Quinsey et al., 1998). Yet, as others have asked (Hart, 1998), if a person makes a genuine threat to kill another person, does it matter what score he or she has on *any* risk assessment instrument? Prudent and ethical decision making would require a decision of high risk in such circumstances, a practice eschewed by a strict actuarial approach. Meehl (1954) and others (Quinsey et al., 1998) would likely argue that such cases might represent so-called broken-leg examples (i.e., the rare exception that will obviate the need for an actuarial prediction). Yet clinicians are duty bound (ethically, morally, and legally) to make *case-specific* decisions and not simply to follow test information. In any area of psychological or psychiatric decision making, clinicians rather than tests *must* make the final decision, and this includes deciding when test results are not applicable or informative.

The problems associated with both unaided clinical judgment and pure actuarial approaches spurred the development of a model that attempts to reflect the strengths of both approaches (discretion and relevance to treatment, on the clinical side, and satisfactory reliability and predictive validity on the actuarial side) while at the same time minimizing the weaknesses of each approach. This model is called structured professional judgment, or SPJ (Borum, 1996; Douglas & Kropp, 2002; Hart, 1998).

SPJ instruments might best be considered professional guidelines or "aides-mémoire" rather than formalized tests, although their evaluation requires formal analysis of reliability and predictive validity. Instruments developed under the SPJ approach attempt to minimize problems in generalizability associated with actuarial models by using rational item selection, a procedure that involves selecting items with broad empirical support in the empirical and professional literatures. They also use unit weighting to avoid incorporating the instability associated with many optimized weighting procedures, hence drawing on what Dawes (1979) called the "robust beauty of improper [i.e., nonweighted] linear models" (p. 579). Grann and Långström (in press) showed that the unit weighting associated with one SPJ instrument outperformed four different sets of cross-validated weights derived from various weighting procedures (i.e., logistic regression and neural network analyses). In fact, the more complex the weighting, the poorer the performance of the instrument.

The SPJ model incorporates a good deal of structure to reflect the behavior decision literature as well as the prediction literature, suggesting that unaided or unstructured decisions lack acceptable reliability and validity. Structure is provided in terms of (a) specifying, *at a minimum*, which risk factors should be considered in every risk assessment; (b) providing explicit operational definitions and coding procedures for each item; (c) providing guidance for how to arrive at a final decision; and (d) providing professional manuals that specify user qualifications, assessment methods, and general information about risk assessment for the type of violence under consideration.

In terms of using SPJ instruments, evaluators indicate which risk factors are present for an individual, delineate how each risk factor is relevant for the individual (narratively), and specify concomitant risk management strategies. Emphasis is placed on linking risk management strategies with dynamic risk factors. Appropriate professional discretion is embodied in the SPJ model in its final decision scheme: Based generally on the number of risk factors present, their relevance and salience for the individual under consideration, and the anticipated intensity and type of intervention and management required to maintain risk at an acceptable level, evaluators make decisions of low, moderate, or high risk. There are no "bright-line" numeric cutoffs since, in principle, a single risk factor could place a person at high risk (i.e., genuine homicidal intent). Generally, however, the more risk factors present, the greater the risk. Evaluators also are encouraged to incorporate "other considerations" into their decisions (i.e., risk factors present in the case that are not included items on the instrument, or case-specific risk variables).

A number of risk assessment guides have been developed under the SPJ approach: *Early Assessment Risk List for Boys, Version 2* (EARL-20B; Augimeri, Koegl, Webster, & Levine, 2001); *HCR-20* (Webster, Douglas, Eaves, & Hart, 1997); *Structured Assessment of Violence*

Risk in Youth (SAVRY; Borum, Bartel, & Forth, 2002); *Sexual Violence Risk—20* (SVR-20; Boer, Hart, Kropp, & Webster, 1997); *Risk for Sexual Violence Protocol* (Hart et al., 2003); *Spousal Assault Risk Assessment Guide* (SARA; Kropp, Hart, Webster, & Eaves, 1999); and the *Short-Term Assessment of Risk and Treatability* (START; Webster et al., 2004). The SARA and other domestic violence instruments are described in detail later in this chapter.

A good deal of research has accrued on instruments developed under this model, suggesting that, generally, the sum of risk factors on the instruments predict violence with moderate to strong effect sizes and hence constitute a reasonable platform upon which to base decisions (for independent reviews, see Arbisi, 2003; Buchanan, 2001; Cooper, 2003; Mossman, 2000; Witt, 2000; for a summary of research on the HCR-20, see Douglas, Guy, & Weir, 2005). Several studies also indicate that the structured decisions of low, moderate, and high risk generated under this model are significantly predictive of violence and add incrementally to the numeric (i.e., actuarial) use of the instruments (de Vogel, de Ruiter, Hildebrand, Bos, & van de Ven, 2004; Douglas, Ogloff, & Hart, 2003; Douglas, Yeomans, & Boer, 2005; Fujii, Lichton, & Tokioka, 2004; Kropp & Hart, 2000). Finally, preliminary research suggests that this model can inform the appropriate amount and type of intervention and thereby actually decrease recidivism in cases of partner abuse (Kropp & Belfrage, 2004).

Despite this body of research and attempts made to minimize weaknesses associated with other approaches, the SPJ model contends with some of its own challenges. These include a lower-than-preferable interrater reliability in some studies of the final structured decisions of low, moderate, and high risk (.41 in Douglas et al., 2005; .63 in Douglas et al., 2003). These decisions most appropriately should be considered "single items" in that reliability estimates are not derived from summing other individual items. As such, they can be considered fair to good (Cicchetti & Sparrow, 1981; Landis & Koch, 1977). Other reliability estimates of the SPJ decisions are higher (de Vogel et al., 2004; Fujii et al., 2004). Further, interrater reliability of SPJ measures' scales tends to be higher—in the .80s typically (Douglas, 2002). Despite this, the SPJ approach perhaps could benefit from increasing the structure somewhat on its final decisions while still striving to permit appropriate professional discretion.

ASSESSING MEN AND WOMEN FOR RISK OF PERPETRATING ABUSE IN INTIMATE RELATIONSHIPS

Although formalized risk assessment approaches have informed general criminal violence risk evaluations for several decades (e.g., Monahan,

1981), the application of similar approaches to the domestic violence field is relatively recent (Campbell, 2004; Kropp, 2004). Clearly, the youth of the field is a disadvantage in many respects (e.g., there is insufficient research to indicate a "gold standard" assessment tool), but the domestic violence field has the advantage of being able to learn from related fields (e.g., general violence risk assessment with psychiatric patients, e.g., Monahan et al., 2001; sex offenders, e.g., Quinsey et al., 1998, 2006), and much is known about individual risk factors associated with intimate partner abuse (Dutton & Kropp, 2000; Hilton et al., 2004; Kropp, 2004; Riggs, Caulfield, & Street, 2000; Schumacher, Feldbau-Kohn, Slep, & Heyman, 2001).

The Accuracy of Victims' Perceptions of Their Abusers' Risk

An interesting finding from both general risk assessment work (e.g., Skeem, 2005) and the domestic violence field is the contribution that perpetrators and victims of violence can make to the accuracy of violence risk judgments. A small number of well-designed studies have examined the predictive accuracy and incremental validity achieved by considering the risk assessment of domestic violence victims. In general, women have been found to be good at recognizing their male partners' risk of reassault (Goodman, Dutton, & Bennett, 2000; Heckert & Gondolf, 2004; Weisz, Tolman, & Saunders, 2000). Notably, however, there may be a difference in victims' capacities to identify men at risk of reassault versus men capable of killing them. In a study of intimate partner homicide, Campbell et al. (2003) reported that only about half of the women who were murdered or almost killed as a result of injuries sustained at the hand of their abuser acknowledged that their partner was capable of killing them. Specifically, 47% of the femicide victims (according to proxy informants) and 53% of attempted femicide victims accurately predicted their risk before the lethal or near lethal event.

Relevant literature suggests that while a consideration of victims' perceptions is clearly desirable from the perspective of increasing violence risk assessment accuracy and for improving the therapeutic/professional alliance with the victim, an examination of the victim's assessment of their abuser's violence risk potential is *necessary but certainly not sufficient*. Theoretical, empirical, and qualitative evidence suggests that victims of intimate abuse often underestimate their abuser's risk potential. We agree with Campbell (2004), who cautioned that mental health professionals are most likely on safest ground when they combine an empirically validated measure intended to assess domestic violence (e.g., the SARA and the Danger Assessment, discussed later in this chapter) in addition to considering the opinion of the victim. It is also important to remember, however, that victims often are unable or unwilling to provide information because of concerns about confidentiality and safety or because of a general reluctance to participate in the criminal justice system (Kropp, 2004). In such cases, risk assessments might be compromised by a lack of reliable information.

Instruments for Assessing Risk of Partner Abuse

Evidence of the recent explosion of development and research in the area of risk assessments for domestic violence can be found in the publication of several comprehensive reviews of the literature (e.g., Kropp, 2004). Dutton and Kropp (2000) reported that there has been a proliferation of domestic violence risk, lethality, and prediction scales. More recently, Hilton et al. (2004) examined many of the same instruments. The scales reviewed here provide information on some popularly used as well as new risk measures that have been developed in response to changing needs. We also highlight some key issues in the use of risk assessment and risk prediction measures. We caution readers that most of these instruments are fairly new and that further validation efforts are needed. Assessors should also be mindful that different instruments are intended for unique purposes, including assessing risk of future partner abuse versus femicide, and that little if any empirical evidence exists to support the use of these instruments with female perpetrators.

The Spousal Assault Risk Assessment Guide (SARA; Kropp et al., 1999)

The SARA is a 20-item SPJ instrument designed to assess adult males for risk of abuse against female intimate partners. Items on the SARA were identified primarily from the scientific and professional literatures on characteristics of assaultive men and the predictors of violent crime. Part 1 consists of 10 general violence risk factors: past assault of family members, past assault of strangers or acquaintances, past violation of conditional release, recent relationship problems, recent employment problems, victim of or witness to family violence as a child or adolescent, recent substance abuse, recent suicidal or homicidal ideation/intent, recent psychotic and/or manic symptoms, and personality disorder. Part 2 lists 10 partner violence risk factors, including past physical assault, past sexual assault, past use of weapons and/or credible threats of death, recent escalation in frequency or severity of assault, past violation of "no contact" orders, extreme minimization/denial, and attitudes that support or condone spousal assault. Assessors are instructed to use the item descriptions to form a clinical judgment of low, moderate, or high risk of future spouse abuse. The assessment should reflect multiple sources of information (e.g., victim and offender interviews, a review of criminal records, and other psychological assessments where available). The SARA is available from the British Columbia Institute against Family Violence (http://www.bcifv.org) or Multi Health Systems (http://www.mhs.com).

The SARA has been evaluated in three North American (Hilton, Harris, Rice, Lang, Cormier, et al., 2004; Kropp & Hart, 2000; Williams & Houghton, 2004) and two Swedish (Grann & Wedin, 2002; Kropp & Belfrage, 2004) validation studies. Kropp and Hart (2000) analyzed SARA scores in six samples of adult male offenders (total $N = 2,681$). The distribution of ratings indicated that offenders were quite heterogeneous with respect to the presence of individual risk factors and to overall perceived risk. Structural analyses of the risk factors indicated moderate levels of internal consistency and item homogeneity. Interrater reliability was high for judgments concerning the presence of individual risk factors and for overall perceived risk. SARA ratings significantly discriminated between offenders with and without a history of spousal violence in one sample and between recidivistic and nonrecidivistic spousal assaulters in another. Finally, SARA ratings showed good convergent and discriminant validity with respect to other measures related to risk for general and violent criminality. An unadjusted total of the scores on the 20 items exhibited better interrater reliability (.84) but was unrelated to wife assault recidivism (Kropp & Hart, 2000).

Williams and Houghton (2004), in their evaluation of the *Domestic Violence Screening Inventory* (DVSI), included the SARA in some of the analyses. The results supported the concurrent validity of the SARA, and the area under the curve (AUC) for the SARA in the 18-month follow-up exceeded that of the DVSI (.65 vs. .60, although the difference was not statistically significant). Similarly, Hilton et al. (2004) reported an AUC for the SARA of .64 in a 5-year follow-back study. However, the accuracy of the result was limited by the fact the authors could not guarantee the "integrity" (p. 271) of the SARA scores because they were coded from archival data only. Grann and Wedin (2002) examined the concurrent validity of the SARA in a sample of adult male offenders in Sweden ($N = 88$). Results demonstrated that although the performance of individual items, which were approximated from archival sources, was somewhat poor (e.g., one item was negatively associated with recidivism, and only three items were statistically significant predictors of recidivism), the predictive validity of the total SARA scores was promising, as offenders scoring above the median were 2.5 times more likely to recidivate than those scoring below the median.

Finally, because of calls from the field, particularly from law enforcement agencies, to have briefer risk assessment tools to conduct time-limited assessments, the authors of the SARA have developed the *Brief Spousal*

Assault Form for the Evaluation of Risk (B-SAFER; Kropp, Hart, & Belfrage, 2005). It consists of 10 risk factors that were derived in part from the 20 SARA risk factors using factor analysis. The B-SAFER has been piloted in Canada and Sweden, but no data have yet been published (Kropp, 2004).

The Ontario Domestic Assault Risk Assessment (ODARA; Hilton et al., 2004)[1]

The ODARA is a brief actuarial assessment developed to predict the risk that a man who has assaulted his female partner will do so again. It assesses (a) how likely it is that a man will reassault his partner, (b) how the client's risk level compares with that of other intimate abusers (rank-order statistic), and (c) the anticipated time to reoffense, the number of recidivistic offenses, and the severity of injuries caused. The ODARA is available for use by police, victim services, health care, and correctional services. This measure consists of 13 dichotomous (yes/no) questions identified using multiple regression techniques as most highly predictive of future domestic violence. The questions include an assessment of the accused's history of violence and antisocial behavior (police record for domestic assault, police record for nondomestic assault, prior correctional sentence, prior failure on conditional release, violence outside the home, domestic assault during pregnancy, and substance abuse), details of the most recent assault (physical confinement, threats of harm, and victim reported fearing future assaults at time of the assault), and the victim's personal circumstances (number of children, children from a prior relationship, and barriers to support).

The ODARA is a relatively new instrument; thus, it has not been the focus of much research, so we know relatively little about its psychometric properties. Preliminary validation research using a follow-back design indicates good correspondence between ODARA scores and reoffense rates. Because the ODARA is an actuarial risk assessment tool, it is possible to rank a client's level of risk for repeated domestic violence into one of seven categories of risk. A score of 0 places a man in the lowest-risk category. In the construction sample, "11% of men fell into this category and 5% of these men met the criteria for domestic recidivism within a follow up of about 5 years. A score of 7 or more places a man in the highest risk category; 7% of men fell into this category, and 70% of these men met the criteria for domestic recidivism" (see the ODARA Web site at http://www.mhcp-research.com/odarasum.htm; Hilton et al., 2004).

The Danger Assessment (DA; Campbell, 1986)[2]

The DA is unique from the other instruments we present here because it was specifically developed to evaluate the risk of *femicide* in cases of male-perpetrated abuse in intimate heterosexual relationships. The DA is completed using victim interview or self-report. Its 15 items pertain to a perpetrator's history of relationship and other violence, availability of weapons, substance abuse, suicidality, and jealousy. The relevance of the instrument to other dyads (e.g., gay, lesbian and mutually abusive or female perpetrators/male victims) is unknown. The DA consists of 15 items coded with yes/no responses and is completed in two sections. First, the measure evaluates the severity and frequency of abuse by prompting the woman to indicate on a calendar the approximate days when physically abusive incidents occurred and to rank the severity of the incident on a 1 to 5 scale (1 = slap, pushing, no injuries and/or lasting pain; 5 = use of weapon, wounds from a weapon). The completion of the calendar is intended to "raise the consciousness of the woman and reduce the denial and minimization of the abuse, especially since using a calendar increases accurate recall in other situations" (Campbell, 2004). In the original sample, 38% of women who initially reported there had been no increase in the severity and frequency of abuse changed their response to "yes" after completing the calendar (Campbell, 1986).

The utility of the DA has been examined in several validation studies. Test–retest reliability has ranged from 0.83 to 0.94 (1995; Stuart & Campbell, 1989), and internal consistency ranges from 0.60 to 0.86. (Campbell, 1986, 1995; McFarlane et al., 1996, 1998). Evidence of convergent construct validity has been found in several studies demonstrating that the DA has moderate to strong correlations with instruments measuring severity and frequency of domestic violence (e.g., *Index of Spouse Abuse*, *Conflict Tactics Scales*, and abuse-related injury) (Campbell, 1995).

A large prospective study of reassault also provided independent support for the predictive validity of the DA (Heckert & Gondolf, 2004). Weisz, Tolman, and Saunders (2000) reported a small positive relationship between DA scores and subsequent nonlethal violence or serious threats of violence several months after court disposition. Another study found associations between several DA items and nonlethal assault or threats three months after the arrest of a perpetrator (Goodman, Dutton, & Bennett, 2000). Hilton et al. (2004) asserted that the predictive value of the DA might be limited by items that are actually inversely associated with recidivism (e.g., suicidality), although there is considerable theoretical and empirical evidence of the intermingling of violence to others and suicide (specifically homicide, Hillbrand, 2001; Nicholls, Douglas, Desmarais, Kropp, & Koch, 2006; Webster et al., 2004).

Domestic Violence Screening Inventory (DVSI; Williams & Houghton, 2004)[3]

The DVSI was developed by the Colorado Department of Probation Services. It was designed to be a brief risk assessment instrument that can be completed with a quick criminal history review. It contains 12 social and behavioral factors found to be statistically related to recidivism by domestic violence perpetrators on probation (Williams & Houghton, 2004). The authors also justified including the risk factors on the basis of a thorough review of the literature and in consultation with judges, law enforcement personnel, lawyers, and victim advocates. The social factors include current employment and relationship status. The behavioral items essentially summarize the offender's history of domestic violence/non-domestic violent criminal history. A copy of the DVSI coding sheet is included in an appendix of the Williams and Houghton (2004) validation paper.

The DVSI was validated on a sample of 1,465 male domestic violence offenders on probation, selected consecutively over a 9-month period. Data on reoffending were collected in a 6-month follow-up period from a subsample of the victims ($N = 125$) of these perpetrators and from official records for all perpetrators during an 18-month follow-up period. The results suggest that the DVSI was administered reliably. The DVSI also appears to have adequate concurrent validity, correlating strongly with ratings of risk to spouses on the SARA. Finally, Williams and Houghton (2004) reported statistically significant predictive validity for the DVSI using a prospective design. They reported an AUC of .60 using DVSI scores to predict recidivism. There have been no independent validation studies of the DVSI to date.

THE VALUE OF VIOLENCE RISK ASSESSMENT INSTRUMENTS DEVELOPED TO ASSESS GENERAL OFFENDING

It is clear that when intimate partner violence is a risk, a special-purpose risk assessment instrument such as those reviewed here should be considered. However, as risk of harming intimate partners and risk of harming others often are associated with one another, there is some value in considering general risk assessment instruments as well. That is, being at risk for general offending and violence places one at risk for harming intimate partners as well because a number of risk factors for general interpersonal violence (e.g., personality disorder and anger) are also risk factors for violence against intimate partners. Evaluators might consider actuarial instruments such as those mentioned earlier (Monahan et al., 2005; Quinsey et al., 1998) after thoughtful consideration of whether they apply in the extant case, given the problems noted previously with generalizability and validity shrinkage. Several other instruments (reviewed in the following sections) have been researched considerably in terms of their relationship to violence and other crime. This is likely particularly pertinent if the client has a history of previous violence outside a romantic relationship or general criminal offending (Stalans, Yarnold, Seng, Olson, & Repp, 2004).[4] A couple of limitations should be noted: (a) these instruments typically require that the assessor is a licensed mental health professional; (b) they require purchase of the manual and, in some cases, the forms to complete the assessment; (c) they are also typically more resource intensive than the measures we described previously; and (d) these schemes were not developed specifically to evaluate risk for partner abuse. That being said, there is good reason for those requirements (e.g., sufficient professional training and expertise is required to code many of the items), and there is considerably more research to provide evidence of the clinical utility of these instruments.

The Level of Service Inventory—Revised (LSI-R; Andrews & Bonta, 1995)

The LSI-R is a 54-item instrument intended to be used with criminal offenders. The LSI-R was developed with reliance on a social learning perspective of criminal behavior, along with rational item selection. Hence, despite using numeric cutoffs for classifying people as low, moderate, or high risk, its development procedure likely contributes to its generalizability. Further, a number of the LSI-R's 10 scales tap ostensibly dynamic risk factors (e.g., Attitudes/Orientation, Companions, and Alcohol/Drug Problems), making it relevant to intervention. Most evaluative research has focused on its relationship to general offending (Andrews & Bonta, 1995; Bonta, 1996), although a meta-analytic study reported a mean correlation between the LSI-R and violent recidivism of .29 across nine effect sizes (Gendreau, Goggin, & Smith, 2002). More recent research by Girard and Wormith (2004) also found that the instrument's General Risk/Need score was highly associated with general recidivism and, to a lesser degree, with violent recidivism in both a general offender population and offender subgroups, including domestic violence offenders.

HCR-20: Assessing Risk for Violence (Version 2; Webster et al., 1997)

The HCR-20 violence risk assessment scheme was referred to previously in the discussion of the SPJ model of risk assessment, to which it belongs. It contains 10 historical, largely static risk factors, such as history of violence, and 10 potentially dynamic risk factors, including five that reflect current mental and clinical status (the Clinical scale) and five that reflect future situational risk factors (the Risk Management scale).

Most research on the HCR-20 focuses on mentally disordered offenders, general offenders, forensic psychiatric patients, and civil psychiatric patients (for reviews, see Arbisi, 2003; Buchanan, 2001; Cooper, 2003; Mossman, 2000; Witt, 2000). As described previously, there has been a fair amount of research in support of its relationship to violence in terms of both the risk factors it contains and the structured decisions of low, moderate, or high risk that it facilitates. To date, the utility of the HCR-20 for informing violence risk evaluations with perpetrators of intimate partner abuse has not been tested.

Hare Psychopathy Checklist—Revised (PCL-R; Hare, 1991, 2003) and
   Psychopathy Checklist: Screening Version (PCL:SV; Hart, Cox, &
   Hare, 1995)

Finally, we mention the PCL-R and its shorter counterpart, the PCL:SV. These are not risk assessment instruments but rather measures of the construct of psychopathy, which has been demonstrated through in an impressive body of research to be robustly related to violence and criminal behavior; most studies on the topic use the PCL-R or PCL:SV. As such, psychopathy can be considered just one pathway to violence, including intimate partner violence, but it is an important one. There is fairly consistent evidence that psychopathy is at least moderately strongly related to criminal and violent behavior among offenders, insanity acquittees, civil psychiatric patients, and sexual offenders (for reviews and meta-analyses of the PCL-R and PCL:SV see Douglas, Vincent, & Edens, 2006; Gendreau et al., 2002 [and Hemphill & Hare, 2004, in rebuttal]; Guy, Edens, Anthony, & Douglas, 2005; Hare, 2003; Hemphill, Hare, & Wong, 1998; Salekin, Rogers & Sewell, 1996; Walters, 2003a, 2003b), although some meta-analyses have reported small effect sizes (.16–.21) for violence (Gendreau et al., 2002; Guy et al., 2005). Hilton et al. (2004) have recommended conducting psychopathy assessments in domestic violence cases whenever feasible.

Hilton et al. (2004; see also Harris & Hilton, 2001) make the point that the characteristics of male abusers might not be useful for informing domestic violence risk assessments if they do little to distinguish between men in that population. To clarify, if most abusive men are jealous, using jealousy as a predictor variable will have limited utility as a predictor variable. In contrast, these authors go on to assert that while psychopathy is relatively uncommon in domestically violent men, it could be a powerful predictor of partner violence and femicide because psychopathic batterers could present the greatest violence risk.

The extent to which these instruments can be applied to women is still being explored, and, in many cases, the literature is perhaps best considered to be in its infancy (e.g., we are aware of just one study evaluating the utility of the VRAG with women). For instance, Dutton and Kropp (2000) asserted that because it was designed to predict general violence and criminal recidivism and not partner abuse specifically, the PCL instruments do little to prompt evaluators to collect and consider information pertinent to partner abuse. As with the general violence risk assessment literature progressing at a faster pace than the domestic violence risk assessment literature, we know precious little about the utility of applying current domestic violence assessment instruments to assess future partner abuse risk and lethal violence potential in female perpetrators.

CONCLUSIONS AND IMPLICATIONS

Clinical Implications

There have been several good discussions of the general process of domestic violence risk assessment in the literature (Campbell, 1995, 2004; Dutton & Kropp, 2000; Goldsmith, 1990; Hilton et al., 2004; Kropp, 2004; Saunders, 1992; Sonkin, 1987; Whittemore & Kropp, 2002). Several important themes have emerged. First, it is clear that domestic violence risk assessments must be *comprehensive* and incorporate information from a variety of sources, including perpetrators, partners, collateral informants, and existing records. This is mostly a matter of common sense, and it is consistent with professional ethical principles that discourage assessments that rely on limited information (e.g., American Psychological Association, 2002). Second, most agree that risk assessments should attempt to consider the context of future violence and, whenever possible, offer forecasts of the nature (e.g., assault vs. homicide), frequency, severity, and imminence of future violence (Hart, 1998). Such assessments provide more nuanced and practical information to judges, parole boards, and potential victims than do deterministic "predictions" of the likelihood of violence.

Third, there is considerable consensus that risk assessment approaches must be rooted in the literature. Much is now known about the putative risk factors associated with domestic violence. A good risk assessment should, therefore, consider risk factors that are supported by the empirical or clinical/professional literatures. Fourth, as we have emphasized in this chapter, most of the potential pitfalls of risk assessment can be avoided by imposing some structure on the task. The SPJ approach has been recommended by many (Campbell, 2004; Kropp, 2004) because it allows structure without eliminating flexibility and discretion. Fifth, the ultimate goal of risk assessment is to *prevent* violence. Indeed, this is the goal of all practitioners working with perpetrators and victims. Thus, risk assessments should logically link to specific risk management strategies, such as treatment, supervision, monitoring, and safety planning (Kropp et al., 2005).

As we have discussed, an assessment of partner abuse risk is likely to have increased validity if assessors consider the perspective of both partners. Much partner abuse is reciprocal aggression, and, as such, assessors should always consider the base rates of abuse and violence by men and women. With this in mind, an assessment should involve evaluating both partners for perpetration and victimization, recognizing that one does not rule out the other. The focus should be on ensuring the physical, emotional, and psychological well-being of *all* family members.

An assessment that considers dynamic variables (i.e., changeable and amenable to intervention) will be particularly useful for safety planning, but any violence risk assessment should have a strong foundation in historical predictors (e.g., prior nonfamilial violence) (Webster, Nicholls, Martin, Desmarais, & Brink, in press). We recommend a psychopathy assessment be considered in cases of severe prior violence and/or when a structured instrument indicates the abuser is high risk or there is evidence of severe personality disorder (Hart, 1998), but we recognize that in most cases this will be impractical given limited resources and time. Given some evidence suggesting that lethal violence has unique predictor variables, professionals might also want to consider an assessment of general domestic violence in combination with a review of lethal violence risk. We also caution that some research suggests that combining multiple instruments to inform a single risk assessment can backfire, actually resulting in reduced accuracy (Seto, 2005). It is not yet clear, however, if that is unique to using type-specific assessment instruments (e.g., multiple measures for assessing risk of future partner abuse) as opposed to combining instruments with unique purposes (e.g., a measure of psychopathy and a measure of domestic violence risk).

Future Research

Despite advances in the assessment and management of intimate partner violence, there are several unresolved issues requiring further empirical examination. For instance, there is insufficient evidence (e.g., from cross-validation and prospective studies with large samples) to suggest an instrument that might be considered the gold standard in clinical practice. Relative to the literature examining risk factors for male-perpetrated abuse, there is limited research examining which variables are most predictive of women's risk to reassault or kill their intimate partners (but see chapter 3 in this volume). However, to our knowledge, studies of the predictive validity of spouse abuse instruments (e.g., the SARA or DA) with female offenders have yet to be conducted. "Fortunately, the predictors of violent crime appear to be extremely general" (Hilton et al., 2004, p. 273; see Bonta, Law, & Hanson, 1998; Quinsey et al., 1998), and while it is unclear to what extent existing violence risk assessment instruments can be applied "as is" to provide accurate risk assessments with general female offenders (e.g., Nicholls, Ogloff, Brink, & Spidel, 2005) and women who abuse their intimate partners, it is unlikely that variables known to have utility with male perpetrators would have no relevance to female perpetrators (also see Webster, 1999). That being said, there is considerable debate in the literature about the need for gendered versus nongendered risk assessment instruments that can truly be answered only with well-designed research and meta-analyses. Conversely, we also know considerably less about male victims than we do about female victims.

Policy Implications

Many jurisdictions in North America have implemented mandatory arrest policies, probation, and treatment programs for perpetrators of intimate partner abuse. Babcock and Steiner (1999) estimated that more than 84% of large U.S. municipalities have adopted mandatory arrest policies. In Canada, Kropp and Hart (2000) reported that implementation of criminal justice sanctions and treatment has resulted in assaults by intimate partners constituting more than 80% of all violent crimes reported to the police. Unfortunately, empirical evidence demonstrating the efficacy of interventions with perpetrators is lacking (see chapter 10 in this volume). Temporary civil protection orders have been associated with an *increase* in psychological abuse. Arrest has been found to be a deterrent among men who have an investment in social conformity (e.g., employed batterers) but has also been found to *increase* risk among unemployed perpetrators (Babcock & Steiner, 1999). Babcock and Steiner (1999) reported that incarceration in lieu of treatment was related to an *increase* in recidivism.

Research suggests that treatment programs for abusive males in the health sector have had minimal effects on recidivism. The first formal meta-analysis of treatment outcome studies demonstrated very small effect sizes for interventions with male batterers (Babcock, Green, & Robie, 2004). Kropp and Hart (2000) concluded that perpetrators, even those who have participated in treatment, have the highest rate of recidivism of all violent offenders. In fact, some studies suggest that treatment programs for abusers may increase the victim's risk, given that a perpetrator's participation in treatment often is stated as a reason for returning to the abuser or for offering a false sense of security (Babcock & Steiner, 1999). As such, accurate violence risk assessment methods are essential.

Although beyond the scope of this chapter, we must also look for ways to intervene with victims in order to reduce the risk of recidivistic abuse by identifying victims who are at high risk for future victimization and, more specifically, by identifying their needs. A search for effective strategies for supporting victims is essential. We have begun this process by developing an assessment instrument intended to inform risk assessments with victims of intimate partner abuse (Decision-making in Abusive Relationships Interview [DIARI]; Nicholls et al., 2006). The DIARI is an SPJ instrument intended to evaluate victims of partner abuse and is intended to complement a violence risk assessment with the perpetrator of partner abuse.

As we mentioned in the introduction of this chapter, good risk evaluations can help ensure the appropriate division and provision of scarce resources to those individuals in greatest need and at highest risk. However, with gender-*exclusive* policies the norm, we are disregarding the potential detrimental effects of female perpetration and male victimization and essentially preventing the delivery of effective treatment intervention to high-risk groups (for a review, see Dutton & Nicholls, 2005; Hamel, 2005; chapter 2 in this volume). Policies should make provisions for the assessment and treatment of all family members.

NOTES

1. See http://www.mhcp-research.com/odarapage.htm.
2. The DA is available for free at http://www.dangerassessment.com/WebApplication1/ pages/product.aspx.
3. See http://www.bdsltd.com/bds_dvi.htm.
4. Readers will likely want to consider chapter 7 in this volume on typologies of intimate abusers and chapter 10 in this volume, both of which discuss family-only abusers and generally violent abusers.

REFERENCES

American Psychological Association. (2002). *Ethical principles of psychologists and code of conduct.* Washington, DC: Author.

Andrews, D. A., & Bonta, J. (1995). *The Level of Service Inventory—Revised.* (LSI-R). Toronto, Ontario, Canada: Multi-Health Systems.

Arbisi, P. A. (2003). Review of the HCR-20: Assessing Risk for Violence. In B. S. Plake, J. C. Impara, & R. A. Spies (Eds.), *The fifteenth mental measurements yearbook.* Retrieved May 7, 2003, from http://www.unl.edu/buros.

Augimeri, L. K., Koegl, C. J., Webster, C. D., & Levine, K. S. (2001). *Early Assessment Risk List for Boys (EARL-20B): Version 2.* Toronto, Ontario, Canada: Earlscourt Child and Family Centre.

Babcock, J., & Steiner, R. (1999). The relationship between treatment, incarceration and recidivism on battering: A program evaluation of Seattle's Coordinated Community Response to domestic violence. *Journal of Family Psychology, 13,* 46–59.

Babcock, J. C., Green, C. E., & Robie, C. (2004). Does batterers' treatment work? A meta-analytic review of domestic violence treatment. *Clinical Psychology Review, 23,* 1023–1053.

Barrick, J. A., & Spilker, B. C. (2003). The relations between knowledge, search strategy, and performance in unaided and aided information search. *Organizational Behavior and Human Decision Processes, 90,* 1–18.

Benbasat, I., & Lim, J. (2000). Information technology support for debiasing group judgments: An empirical evaluation. *Organizational Behavior and Human Decision Processes, 83,* 167–183.

Boer, D. P., Hart, S. D., Kropp, P. R., & Webster, C. D. (1997). *Manual for the Sexual Violence Risk—20: Professional guidelines for assessing risk of sexual violence.* Vancouver, British Columbia, Canada: British Columbia Institute Against Family Violence.

Bonta, J. (1996). Risk-needs assessment and treatment. In A. T. Harland (Ed.), *Choosing correctional options that work: Defining the demand and evaluating the supply* (pp. 18–32). Thousand Oaks, CA: Sage.

Bonta, J., Law, M., & Hanson, K. (1998). The prediction of criminal and violent recidivism among mentally disordered offenders: A meta-analysis. *Psychological Bulletin, 123,* 123–142.

Borum, R. (1996). Improving the clinical practice of violence risk assessment: Technology, guidelines, and training. *American Psychologist, 51,* 945–956.

Borum, R., Bartel, P., & Forth, A. (2002). *SAVRY: Manual for the structured assessment of violence risk in youth (Version 1.1).* Tampa: Florida Mental Health Institute, University of South Florida.

Buchanan, A. (2001). Review of the book, *HCR-20: Assessing risk for violence, Version 2. Criminal Behaviour and Mental Health, 11,* S77–S89.

Campbell, J. C. (1986). Nursing assessment of risk of homicide for battered women. *Advances in Nursing Science, 3,* 67–85.

Campbell, J. C. (1995). Prediction of homicide of and by battered women. In J. C. Campbell (Ed.), *Assessing dangerousness: Violence by sexual offenders, batterers, and child abusers* (pp. 96–113). Thousand Oaks, CA: Sage.

Campbell, J. C. (2004). *The danger assessment.* Retrieved January 4, 2006, from http://www.dangerassessment.com/WebApplication1/pages/product.aspx

Campbell, J. C., Webster, D., Koziol-McLain, J., Block, C., Campbell, D., Curry, M. A., et al. (2003). Risk factors for femicide in abusive relationships: Results from a multisite case control study. *American Journal of Public Health, 93,* 1089–1097.

Cicchetti, D. V., & Sparrow, S. A. (1981). Developing criteria for establishing interrater reliability of specific items: Applications to assessment of adaptive behavior. *American Journal of Mental Deficiency, 86,* 127–137.

Cooper, C. (2003). Review of the HCR-20: Assessing Risk for Violence. In B. S. Plake, J. C. Impara, & R. A. Spies (Eds.), *The fifteenth mental measurements yearbook.* Retrieved May 7, 2003, from http://www.unl.edu/buros.

Dawes, R. M. (1979). The robust beauty of improper linear models in decision making. *American Psychologist, 34,* 571–582.

Devine, D. J., & Kozlowski, S. W. J. (1995). Domain-specific knowledge and task characteristic in decision making. *Organizational Behavior and Human Decision Processes, 64,* 294–306.

de Vogel, V., de Ruiter, C., Hildebrand, M., Bos, B., & van de Ven, P. (2004). Type of discharge and risk of recidivism measured by the HCR-20: A retrospective study in a Dutch sample of treated forensic psychiatric patients. *International Journal of Forensic Mental Health, 3,* 149–165.

Douglas, K. S. (2002, March). *The HCR-20 violence risk assessment scheme: A synthesized, quantitative review of research and recommendations for future research directions.* Paper presented at the Second Annual International Conference of the International Association of Forensic Mental Health Services, Munich, Germany.

Douglas, K. S., Guy, L. S., & Weir, J. (2005). *HCR-20 violence risk assessment scheme: Overview and annotated bibliography.* Retrieved from http://kdouglas.wordpress.com/hcr-20/.

Douglas, K. S., & Kropp, P. R. (2002) A prevention-based paradigm for violence risk assessment: Clinical and research applications. *Criminal Justice and Behavior, 29,* 617–658.

Douglas, K. S., Ogloff, J. R. P., & Hart, S. D. (2003). Evaluation of a model of violence risk assessment among forensic psychiatric patients. *Psychiatric Services, 54,* 1372–1379.

Douglas, K. S., & Skeem, J. L. (2005). Violence risk assessment: Getting specific about being dynamic. *Psychology, Public Policy, and Law, 11,* 347–383.

Douglas, K. S., Vincent, G. M., & Edens, J. F. (2006). Risk for criminal recidivism: The role of psychopathy. In C. Patrick (Ed.), *Handbook of psychopathy* (pp. 533–554). New York: Guilford Press.

Douglas, K. S., Webster, C. D., Hart, S. D., Eaves, D., & Ogloff, J. R. P. (Eds.). (2001). *HCR-20: Violence risk management companion guide.* Burnaby, British Columbia, Canada: Mental Health, Law, and Policy Institute, Simon Fraser University; Tampa: Department of Mental Health Law and Policy, University of South Florida.

Douglas, K. S., Yeomans, M., & Boer, D. P. (2005). Comparative validity analysis of multiple measures of violence risk in a general population sample of criminal offenders. *Criminal Justice and Behavior, 32,* 479–510.

Dutton, D. G., & Kropp, P. R. (2000). A review of domestic violence risk instruments. *Trauma, Violence and Abuse, 1,* 171–182.

Dutton, D. G., & Nicholls, T. L. (2005). The gender paradigm in domestic violence research and theory: Part 1—The conflict of theory and data. *Aggression and Violent Behavior, 10,* 680–714.

Dvoskin, J. A., & Heilbrun, K. (2001). Risk assessment and release decision-making: Toward resolving the great debate. *Journal of the American Academy of Psychiatry and the Law, 29,* 6–10.

Ennis, B. J., & Litwack, T. R. (1974). Psychiatry and the presumption of expertise: Flipping coins in the courtroom. *California Law Review, 62,* 693–752.

Friedlander, M. L., & Stockman, S. J. (1983). Anchoring and publicity effects in clinical judgment. *Journal of Clinical Psychology, 39,* 637–643.

Fujii, D., Lichton, A., & Tokioka, A. (2004, July). *Structured professional judgment versus actuarial data in violence risk prediction using the Historical Clinical Risk Management—20*. Paper presented at the annual meeting of the American Psychological Association, Honolulu, HI.

Gendreau, P., Goggin, C., & Smith, P. (2002). Is the PCL-R really the "unparalleled" measure of offender risk? A lesson in knowledge cumulation. *Criminal Justice and Behavior, 29,* 397–426.

Girard, L., & Wormith, J. S. (2004). The predictive validity of the Level of Service Inventory—Ontario Revision on general and violent recidivism among various offender groups. *Criminal Justice and Behavior,, 31,* 150–181.

Goldsmith, H. R. (1990). Men who abuse their spouses: An approach to assessing future risk. *Journal of Offender Counseling, Services and Rehabilitation, 15,* 45–56.

Goodman, L. A., Dutton, M. A., & Bennett, L. (2000). Predicting repeat abuse among arrested batterers: Use of the Danger Assessment Scale in the criminal justice system. *Journal of Interpersonal Violence, 15,* 63–74.

Grann, M., & Långström, N. (in press). Actuarial assessment of risk for violence: To weigh or not to weigh? *Criminal Justice and Behavior.*

Grann, M., & Wedin, I. (2002). Risk factors for recidivism among spousal assault and spousal homicide offenders. *Psychology, Crime, and Law, 8,* 5–23.

Grove, W. M., & Meehl, P. E. (1996). Comparative efficiency of informal (subjective, impressionistic) and formal (mechanical, algorithmic) prediction procedures: The clinical-statistical controversy. *Psychology, Public Policy, and Law, 2,* 293–323.

Grove, W. M., Zald, D. H., Lebow, B. S., Snitz, B. E., & Nelson, C. (2000). Clinical versus mechanical prediction: A meta-analysis. *Psychological Assessment, 12,* 19–30.

Guy, L. S., Edens, J. F., Anthony, C., & Douglas, K. S. (2005). Does psychopathy predict institutional misconduct among adults? A meta-analytic investigation. *Journal of Consulting and Clinical Psychology, 73,* 1056–1064.

Hamel, J. (2005). Fixing only part of the problem: Public policy and batterer intervention. *Family Violence and Sexual Assault Bulletin, 21,* 18–31.

Hare, R. D. (1991). *The Hare Psychopathy Checklist—Revised.* Toronto, Ontario, Canada: Multi-Health Systems.

Hare, R. D. (2003). *The Hare PCL-R* (2nd ed.). Toronto, Ontario, Canada: Multi-Health Systems.

Harris, G. T., & Hilton, N. Z. (2001). Theoretical note: Interpreting moderate effects in interpersonal violence. *Journal of Interpersonal Violence, 16,* 1094–1098.

Harris, G. T., Rice, M. E., & Quinsey, V. L. (1993). Violent recidivism of mentally disordered offenders: The development of a statistical prediction instrument. *Criminal Justice and Behavior, 20,* 315–335.

Hart, S. D. (1998). The role of psychopathy in assessing risk for violence: Conceptual and methodological issues. *Legal and Criminological Psychology, 3,* 121–137.

Hart, S. D., Cox, D. N., & Hare, R. D. (1995). *Manual for the Psychopathy Checklist: Screening Version (PCL:SV).* Toronto, Ontario, Canada: Multi-Health Systems.

Hart, S. D., Kropp, P. R., Laws, D. R., Klaver, J., Logan, C., & Watt, K. A. (2003). *The risk for sexual violence protocol.* Burnaby, British Columbia, Canada: Simon Fraser University.

Heckert, D. A., & Gondolf, E. W. (2004). Battered women's perceptions of risk versus risk factors and instruments in predicting repeat reassault. *Journal of Interpersonal Violence, 19,* 778–800.

Hemphill, J. F., & Hare, R. D. (2004). Some misconceptions about the Hare PCL-R and risk assessment: A reply to Gendreau, Goggin, and Smith. *Criminal Justice and Behavior, 31,* 203–243.

Hemphill, J. F., Hare, R. D., & Wong, S. (1998). Psychopathy and recidivism: A review. *Legal and Criminological Psychology, 3,* 141–172.

Hillbrand, M. (2001). Homicide-suicide and other forms of co-occurring aggression against self and against others. *Professional Psychology: Research and Practice, 32,* 626–635.

Hilton, N. Z., Harris, G. T., Rice, M. E., Lang, C., Cormier, C. A., & Lines, K. J. (2004). A brief actuarial assessment for the prediction of wife assault recidivism: The Ontario Domestic Assault Risk Assessment. *Psychological Assessment, 16,* 267–275.

Hirt, E. R., Kardes, F. R., & Markman, K. D. (2004). Activating a mental simulation mindset through generation of alternatives: Implications for debiasing in related and unrelated domains. *Journal of Experimental Social Psychology, 40,* 374–383.

Kahneman, D., & Tversky, A. (1973). On the psychology of prediction. *Psychological Review, 80,* 237–251.

Kropp, P. R. (2004). Some questions about spousal violence risk assessment. *Violence Against Women, 10*(6), 676–697.

Kropp, P. R., & Belfrage, H. (2004, September). *The Brief Spousal Assault Form for the Evaluation of Risk: B-SAFER.* Paper presented at the 2nd International Conference—Toward a Safer Society, Edinburgh, Scotland.

Kropp, P. R., & Hart, S. D. (2000). The Spousal Assault Risk Assessment (SARA) Guide: Reliability and validity in adult male offenders. *Law and Human Behavior, 24,* 101–118.

Kropp, P. R., Hart, S. D., & Belfrage, H. (2005). *The Brief Spousal Assault Form for the Evaluation of Risk (B-SAFER).* Vancouver, British Columbia, Canada: Proactive Resolutions.

Kropp, P. R., Hart, S. D., Webster, C. D., & Eaves, D. (1999). *Manual for the spousal assault risk assessment guide* (3rd ed.). Toronto, Ontario, Canada: Multi-Health Systems.

Landis, J., & Koch, G. G. (1977). The measurement of observer agreement for categorical data. *Biometrics, 33,* 159–174.

McFarlane, J., Parker, B., & Soeken, K. (1996). Abuse during pregnancy: Associations with maternal health and infant birth weight. *Nursing Research, 45,* 37–42.

McFarlane, J., Parker, B., Soeken, K., & Bullock, L. (1992). Assessing for abuse during pregnancy: Severity and frequency of injuries and associated entry into prenatal care. *Journal of the American Medical Association, 267,* 3176–3178.

McFarlane, J., Soeken, K., Campbell, J. C., Parker, B., Reel, S., & Silva, C. (1998). Severity of abuse to pregnant women and associated gun access of the perpetrator. *Public Health Nursing, 15*(3), 201–206.

Meehl, P. E. (1954). *Clinical versus statistical prediction.* Minneapolis: University of Minnesota Press.

Monahan, J. (1981). *Predicting violent behavior: An assessment of clinical techniques.* Beverly Hills, CA: Sage.

Monahan, J., Steadman, H. J., Robbins, P. C., Appelbaum, P. S., Banks, S., Grisso, T., et al. (2005). An actuarial model of violence risk assessment for persons with mental disorders. *Psychiatric Services, 56,* 810–815.

Monahan, J., Steadman, H. J., Silver, E., Appelbaum, P. S., Robbins, P. C., Mulvey, E. P., et al. (2001). *Rethinking risk assessment: The MacArthur study of mental disorder and violence.* New York: Oxford University Press.

Mossman, D. (2000). Commentary: Assessing the risk of violence—Are "accurate" predictions useful? *Journal of the American Academy of Psychiatry and the Law, 28,* 272–281.

Nicholls, T. L., Brink, J., Desmarais, S. L., Webster, C. D., & Martin, M.-L. (in press). The Short-Term Assessment of Risk and Treatability (START): A prospective validation study in a forensic psychiatric sample. *Psychological Assessment.*

Nicholls, T. L., Douglas, K. S., Desmarais, S. L., Kropp, P. R., & Koch, W. J. (2006). *Decision-making in Abusive Relationships Interview (DIARI): Professional guidelines for risk/needs assessments with victims.* Unpublished manuscript.

Nicholls, T. L., Ogloff, J. R. P., Brink, J., & Spidel, A. (2005). Psychopathy in women: A review of its clinical usefulness for assessing risk for aggression and criminality. *Behavioral Sciences and the Law, 23,* 779–802.

Onkal, D., Yates, J. F., Simga-Mugan, C., & Oztin, S. (2003). Professional vs. amateur judgment accuracy: The case of foreign exchange rates. *Organizational Behavior and Human Decision Processes, 91,* 169–185.

Payne, J. W., Bettman, J. R., & Luce, M. F. (1998). Behavioral decision research: An overview. In M. Birnbaum (Ed.), *Measurement, judgment, and decision making: Handbook of perception and cognition* (2nd. ed., pp. 303–359). San Diego, CA: Academic Press.

Quinsey, V. L., Harris, G. T., Rice, G. T., & Cormier, C. A. (1998). *Violent offenders: Appraising and managing risk.* Washington, DC: American Psychological Association.

Quinsey, V. L., Harris, G. T., Rice, M. E., & Cormier, C. A. (2006). *Violent offenders: Appraising and managing risk* (2nd ed.). Washington, DC: American Psychological Association.

Riggs, D. S., Caulfield, M. B., & Street, A. E. (2000). Risk for domestic violence: Factors associated with perpetration and victimization. *Journal of Clinical Psychology, 56,* 1289–1316.

Salekin, R. T., Rogers, R., & Sewell, K. W. (1996). A review and meta-analysis of the Psychopathy Checklist and Psychopathy Checklist—Revised: Predictive validity of dangerousness. *Clinical Psychology: Science and Practice, 3,* 203–215.

Saunders, D. G. (1992). Woman battering. In R. T. Ammerman & M. Hersen (Eds.), *Assessment of family violence: A clinical and legal sourcebook* (pp. 208–235). New York: John Wiley & Sons.

Schumacher, J. A., Feldbau-Kohn, S., Slep, A. M. S., & Heyman, R. E. (2001). Risk factors for male-to-female partner physical abuse. *Aggression and Violent Behavior, 6,* 281–352.

Seto, M. C. (2005). Is more better? Combining actuarial risk scales to predict recidivism among adult sex offenders. *Psychological Assessment, 17,* 156–167.

Skeem, J. (2005, March). *Identifying patients at risk for repeated involvement in violence: Self-perceptions perform better than systematic scales.* Paper presented at the American Psychology-Law Society annual conference, La Jolla, CA.

Skeem, J., & Mulvey, E. (2002). Monitoring the violence potential of mentally disordered offenders being treated in the community. In A. Buchanan (Ed.), *Care of the mentally disordered offender in the community* (pp. 111–142). New York: Oxford University Press.

Sonkin, D. J. (1987). The assessment of court-mandated male batterers. In D. J. Sonkin (Ed.), *Domestic violence on trial: Psychological and legal dimensions of family violence* (pp. 174–196). New York: Springer.

Stalans, L. J., Yarnold, P. R., Seng, M., Olson, D. E., & Repp, M. (2004). Identifying three types of violent offenders and predicting violent recidivism while on probation: A classification tree analysis. *Law and Human Behavior, 28,* 253–271.

Stuart, E. P., & Campbell, J. C. (1989). Assessment of patterns of dangerousness with battered women. *Issues Mental Health Nursing, 10,* 245–260.

Tversky, A., & Kahneman, D. (1973). Availability: A heuristic for judging frequency and probability. *Cognitive Psychology, 5,* 207–232.

Walker, B. S., & Spengler, P. M. (1995). Clinical judgment of major depression in AIDS patients: The effects of clinician complexity and stereotyping. *Professional Psychology: Research and Practice, 26,* 269–273.

Walters, G. D. (2003a). Predicting criminal justice outcomes with the Psychopathy Checklist and Lifestyle Criminality Screening Form: A meta-analytic comparison. *Behavioral Sciences and the Law, 21,* 89–102.

Walters, G. D. (2003b). Predicting institutional adjustment and recidivism with the Psychopathy Checklist factor scores: A meta-analysis. *Law and Human Behavior, 27,* 541–558.

Wason, P. C. (1960). On a failure to eliminate hypotheses in a conceptual task. *Quarterly Journal of Experimental Psychology, 12,* 129–140.

Webster, C. D. (1999, December). *Risk assessment and risk management with women offenders.* Report to the National Parole Board. Correctional Service of Canada.

Webster, C. D., Douglas, K. S., Eaves, D., & Hart, S. D. (1997). *HCR-20: Assessing risk for violence.* Version 2. Burnaby, British Columbia, Canada: Mental Health, Law, and Policy Institute, Simon Fraser University.

Webster, C. D., Martin, M. L., Brink, J., Nicholls, T. L., & Middleton, C. (2004). *Manual for the Short-Term Assessment of Risk and Treatability (START).* Version 1.0. Consultation Edition. Hamilton, Ontario, Canada: St. Joseph's Healthcare; Port Coquitlam, British Columbia, Canada: Forensic Psychiatric Services Commission.

Webster, C. D., Nicholls, T. L., Martin, M. L., Desmarais, S. L., & Brink, J. (in press). Short-Term Assessment of Risk and Treatability (START): The case for a new violence risk structured professional judgment scheme. *Behavioral Sciences and the Law.*

Weisz, A. N., Tolman, R. M., & Saunders, D. G. (2000). Assessing the risk of severe domestic violence: The importance of survivors' predictions. *Journal of Interpersonal Violence, 15,* 75–90.

Whittemore, K. E., & Kropp, P. R. (2002). Spousal assault risk assessment: A guide for clinicians. *Journal of Forensic Psychology Practice, 2*(2), 53–64.

Williams, K. R., & Houghton, A. B. (2004). Assessing the risk of domestic violence reoffending: A validation study. *Law and Human Behavior, 28,* 437–455.

Witt, P. H. (2000). A practitioner's view of risk assessment: The HCR-20 and SVR-20. *Behavioral Sciences and the Law, 18,* 791–798.

Yaniv, I. (2004). The benefit of additional opinions. *Current Directions in Psychological Science, 13,* 75–78.

CHAPTER 13

Male Victims of Domestic Violence

David L. Fontes

People sometimes ask me how I became interested in the topic of male victims of domestic violence. The answer is simple: It was completely by accident. For a number of years, I have worked as the internal Employee Assistance Program (EAP) manager for a state agency in California. The purpose of the EAP office is to help employees who are going through personal or work-related problems in an effort to assist them in resolving their issues so that their job performance will not suffer and management will not have to take formal corrective action against the employees. One day in 1995, I received a call from a manager who was referring one of his employees to my office who had missed several days at work. It was becoming a job performance issue, and the manager was concerned. The manager shared that when he asked his employee why he had missed so many days at work, the employee replied by saying it was due to "family problems." Several days later, I heard a knock on my office door. When I opened it, I was greeted by a 6-foot-tall young Hispanic man. It was the same employee the manager had referred to me a few days earlier. After he took a seat in my office, I invited him to tell me what was going on in his life that had made him miss so many days of work. Hanging his head down a bit and in a soft-spoken voice, he began to share his concern about how his wife was physically disciplining their two young children. He said she would spank them very hard in anger. A few days later, he brought his two children into my office. The children showed me bruises on their backs and told me that their mother

303

had done this to them. After they left my office, I contacted Child Protective Services, the agency that investigates suspected child abuse.

I continued to see the young man, and during the course of one of our meetings I asked him a question I do not believe I had ever asked a man before. I asked him whether his wife ever hit *him* as well as his children. He slowly began to share how his wife had physically assaulted him multiple times over the past seven years and that he never physically assaulted her back. He said he was raised to believe that a man should never hit a woman. He also shared that the police had come to their home three times, but to his frustration, they never arrested his wife. He began to feel that law enforcement either did not care or that they did not really believe he was a victim. In response to his disclosure of being assaulted by his wife, I referred him to our local domestic violence center. Working with this young man had a profound effect on me. I came face-to-face with my own bias with regard to domestic violence. I realized that I did not ask men the same questions I asked women when they told me that they were having marital conflict.

Why did I have this bias? It is probably because I had been taught for years in domestic violence training workshops or presentations that the vast majority of domestic violence victims were women, not men. When the topic of male victims did come up in these workshops, which almost exclusively focused on the female victim, the response was almost always something like this: "Yes, we know that there are male victims of domestic violence, but the percentage is very small, only about 5%, and women who assault their male partners usually do so in self-defense." After doing a few years of research on this topic for my doctoral dissertation, I found that, depending on the data source, both of these statements were just wrong or at least very misleading.

What I have learned in the years that followed my encounter with the young Hispanic man was that a number of shelters have worked with male victims, but it has been by "accident," not by "focus." In other words, if a male victim happens to show up at a domestic violence center, they might try to help him, but are unlikely to have an active outreach program or services specifically set up with his needs in mind. They may have special programs for Hispanic females or African American females but none for male victims. You do not see any posters of men with a bruised face or lacerations, nor do you find such pictures in their brochures. Some men feel they were treated at these shelters and centers more with suspect than with respect.

ADDRESSING THE PROBLEM OF MALE VICTIMS OF DOMESTIC VIOLENCE

If you are going to work with male victims of domestic violence, it is important that you have a good understanding of what randomized survey research tells us about the number of male victims in the general population and what the obstacles are that these men are likely to face in getting the help they need, which may include your own bias on the topic. I am not going to go over the statistics at length in this chapter. If you wish to learn more about the research on male victims and useful arguments that can be given to their detractors and minimizers, I would suggest you read my paper "Violent Touch: Breaking Through the Stereotype," which can be found at http://www.safe4all.org.

In short, what you need to know about the statistics is that there is a difference between archival research, which comes from *reported* cases of domestic violence, and randomized survey research, which captures both reported cases and, more important, those that have not been reported to law enforcement, domestic violence centers, hospital emergency rooms, and the like. What I found is that when you look at archival research, those cases of domestic violence that have been *reported,* males make up between 5% and 15% of the victims of domestic assault (Bennett, 1997; Brown, 1997; California Department of Justice, 1997; McLeod, 1984). But when you look at the vast majority of the randomized survey research, except for the National Crime Victimization Survey (NCVS), you find that men and women are assaulting each other at nearly the same rate, with men the victims in between 35% and 50% of domestic assault (Commonwealth Fund, 1994; Flynn, 1990; Plichta, 1996; Steinmetz, 1978; Stets & Straus, 1990; Straus, 1977; Straus, Kaufman-Kantor, & Moore, 1997; Straus & Gelles, 1986; Tjaden & Thoennes, 1998). I also found from the few studies conducted on why partners assault that only 10% to 20% of women hit their male partners for reasons of self-defense (Carrado, George, Loxam, Jones, & Templar, 1996; Sommer, Barnes, & Murray, 1992). On the other hand, I learned that women are at least twice as likely as men to report being physically injured; 41% of women reported sustaining an injury compared to 19% of men (Tjaden & Thoennes, 1998). This, of course, does not mean that men are not seriously injured by their female partners. They are, and I have interviewed a number of them.

The challenge that faces us now is how to get men to break the silence of their victimization by their female partners. We have spent a lot of time helping women break their silence; it is time we do the same for men. As mentioned earlier, some domestic violence centers will work with a male victim if he happens to show up at their location, but they have no active outreach programs set up with the male victim in mind. This is because they still frame the issue of domestic violence primarily as a gender-specific problem, namely, a woman's issue. As a result, men face a number of obstacles when it comes to getting help or feeling comfortable enough to report their victimization to clinicians, social workers, domestic violence workers, law enforcement officers, district attorneys, and hospital employee (Hines, Brown, & Dunning, in press; Migliaccio, 2002). If you are going to work with male victims, you need to know what these obstacles are. I now review three major obstacles male victims face.

OBSTACLE 1: MEN AND PATRIARCHY

When most partner violence survey data—those who say they have been victims of domestic violence—is compared with archival data—those who say they subsequently *reported* their victimization—it appears that only about 8% to 14% of women who were assaulted actually report their abuse. But the same data comparison also suggests that only about 1% to 3% of men who were assaulted report their abuse. In other words, although only a small percentage of both women and men report being abused by their intimate partner, women do so about five to eight times more often than men (Fontes, 1998). This is also supported by the 1985 National Family Violence Survey, which found that women were nine times more likely than men to report their assaults to the police and five times more likely to discuss the abuse with a friend or relative. (Stets & Straus, 1990). A 1994 CBS movie about a male victim of domestic violence by his wife was appropriately titled *Men Don't Tell.*

Sadly today, society still regards men who report their victimization as *wimps* for letting their wives beat them or for complaining about it. For many men, the saying "Take it like a man" means that one does not complain and does not show vulnerability or any kind of emotional or physical pain, especially if the perpetrator is female. With the prospect of being viewed as a wimp and/or having the assaults by their wives unbelieved or minimized by the general public, by domestic violence workers or feminist advocates, or by law enforcement, it's not surprising that few men report their abuse or discuss it openly. Men have a dilemma because patriarchy socializes them to be *self-sufficient*. This means they should not require help from others—that is, if they are real men. Men are also socialized to be *strong,* physically and emotionally. This means they should not express physical and emotional pain, sadness, or fear—that is, if they are real men. Men are also socialized to be the *protectors* in society, especially of women and children. This means they should not need to be protected, especially from abusive women—that is, if they are real men. Yet to acknowledge being a male victim of domestic violence implies having a need to be helped by others. The victim may see this as not being self-sufficient and therefore not a real man. He has a need to express his physical and emotional pain, sadness, and fear to others, but may see this as evidence that he is not strong and therefore not a real man. He has a need to be protected by society from an abusive and assaultive woman, but may see this as meaning he cannot protect himself or his children and therefore see himself as a wimp and not a real man.

One of the emotions males are trained from a very early age to ignore or at least suppress is fear. While females are generally given permission to feel this emotion, boys and especially men are not. Fear is a perception that one is in some kind of danger or potential danger. However, not all perceptions are accurate. Someone can feel afraid but may not be in any real danger; another can be in real danger but not feel afraid when they should. I have heard some women's advocates say that because a woman has a greater fear of being assaulted or injured by her male partner, she ought to be regarded as more of a victim. Yet there are men who, because of their acculturation in a patriarchal system, do not *feel* afraid of their female partners when in fact they may be in real danger of physical harm. The point is that our concern for male victims of domestic violence should be based not on whether the man is *feeling* afraid of his female partner but rather on whether the abusive behavior warrants our helping him avoid further victimization. A man may be especially reluctant to acknowledge fear before a judge, a jury, peers, or others because he does not want to be seen as a wimp. Fear may be identified as an emotion of vulnerability, and these male victims may not want to appear vulnerable to others.

Males are trained to suppress their pain. An example of this might be when a young boy is hit on the playground by another boy his age. The victim of the blow can do three things. He can strike back and be seen as aggressive; he can proclaim, "That didn't hurt," and be seen as strong; or he can cry and run away and be seen as a wimp. Young boys who do not want to be viewed as either aggressive or wimpy will then choose the second action and proclaim, "That didn't hurt," and be seen as strong in the eyes of peers. What they are in fact doing is denying their pain and choosing not to complain to others about it. So what will this boy do when a *girl* hits him on the playground? What if he grows up and marries an abusive woman? This is the hidden side of domestic violence.

Males are often encouraged to show others how much pain they can endure. Television programs feature young men who allow others to assault their testicles (their reproductive system) to demonstrate that they can withstand such an attack. Similar scenes, also shown in movies and other media, are presented in a humorous way. But there is nothing funny about sexual assault, be it is against a woman or a man. Assaulting a male's reproductive system for reasons *other* than physical self-defense is a form of sexual assault and should be identified as such and not laughed about. I remember overhearing a young woman threatening to hit her boyfriend where "it really hurts" because he said something that *offended* her. In effect, she was threatening a form of sexual assault for what he *said*, not for reasons of defending herself against a physical assault.

In short, patriarchy and men in general do not want society to view males as victims because to be a victim is to be vulnerable, to be vulnerable is to be weak, and to be weak is to be unmanly or, worse, a wimp. One domestic violence counselor said to me, "When men are victims of domestic violence, they are the hidden victims of domestic violence." How true this statement is.

OBSTACLE 2: FEMINISM

While men minimize the effects of being assaulted by females and are unlikely to identify themselves as victims of domestic violence in a patriarchal society, feminists see patriarchy as the root of all evil in the lives of women. For them, domestic violence comes from living in a society that oppresses women in general. They believe that men want power and control over women and explain domestic violence as the result of this desire. One female director of a domestic violence center near Sacramento, California, runs a large court-ordered anger management program that offers group sessions for both male and female offenders every week. She shared with me that in her experience, about 15% of the men abused their female partners because they felt they had the *male privilege* to do so. This fits well into the feminist model. Yet if her analysis is accurate and about 15% of men she works with assault their female partners for reason of male privilege, that would suggest that the other 85% abuse their female partners for reasons that do not fit the feminist model. Unfortunately, most batterer intervention and anger management programs for men have been designed on the basis of the feminist model and not on other alternatives, such as the family system model, the learning theory model, the socioeconomic model, the organic brain model, and the psychological model, which includes research into personality disorders. This director also told me that a large number of the female perpetrators she works with slap their male partners when they behave badly, and said these women dismiss such assaults by calling them "soap opera" slaps. This is an example of what may be called *female privilege*, and it is becoming a disturbing trend in our society today.

John Hamel (2005) has determined that the tactics in the classic "power and control wheel," typically applied to male perpetrators, can be used with female perpetrators as well. He explains how a woman can physically intimidate her male partner by smashing things and threatening to injure him while he is asleep. She can emotionally abuse him by putting him down, by saying he is not being a good provider, by saying that he is not a good sex partner, by insisting on talking to him at 2:00 a.m. when he needs to get up at 5:00 A.M. for work, by being jealous of him with other people, or by threatening to get primary physical custody of the children in family court. This last threat gives women a lot of power and control. The perception is that, unless the woman is drug involved or has a psychiatric disability, family courts will give her primary physical custody of their children. One man I have worked with shared how the very week his wife was *convicted* of domestic violence against him by a criminal court, the family court gave her 85% physical custody of his children. Fathers are torn between leaving their violent wives or losing primary physical custody of their children. I know of a number of fathers who chose to stay with their assaultive wives in silence in order to be with their children. In a number of cases, they stay to also protect their children from the abuse their mothers perpetrate upon them. This can also be said for women who stay in abusive environments with their male partners, but that is the point: This situation exists for both genders, not just women.

Society has a greater tolerance for female violence than male violence, probably because of the assumption that men suffer less physical injuries and that men can "take it better" or more easily defend themselves. But what I have found is that if a man does physically defend himself by grabbing the woman's forearms to stop her blows and she develops bruises on her arms, or if he tries to push her away from the door so he can escape because she is blocking the doorway while hitting him, he is the one, not she, who is likely to be arrested and go to jail if the police are called. It becomes a no-win situation. The truth is that a number of men are afraid to call the police because of the biased feminist training they believe law enforcement officers have received. They worry that they will be the ones the officer arrests and not the woman whom they initially reported.

In the early 1970s, I remember some feminists saying that women will never be free until men are liberated from patriarchy. They said this because they saw that some aspects of patriarchy also caused men to suffer. We need to understand that a part of the patriarchal system has to do with the protection of women and children and providing for their welfare. Today's feminist groups actually appeal to this part of patriarchy in male legislators to get the sympathy, funding, and laws they want for the protection of women. Although their arguments, ironically, feed into the very patriarchal attitudes that they want to dismantle, they work in their favor when it comes to getting help from male lawmakers. I am very pleased that women are getting the funding to help them escape domestic violence, but should not the funding be used to help both male and female victims with the same level of focus and outreach?

The women's movement envisioned a world where women are treated with equal respect and where their voices have equal value. It is absolutely true that, not long ago, women could not own property, could not vote for public officials, and were treated like second-class citizens. Through the efforts of many women *and* men of goodwill who spoke up against this unfairness, much has changed in a relatively short period of time. Recently, however, a troubling trend has developed. Today I believe a growing number of feminists have devalued the voices of men, and the only voices they will listen to are from those who agree with their worldview. Giving equal value to the voice of women is one thing; making their voices more valuable than the voices of men is quite another.

A number of women, among them Christina Hoff-Sommers (1994) and Cathy Young (1999), have challenged this recent devaluation of men in our society and have criticized some of the feminist activists. Hoff-Sommers, who devotes an entire chapter in her book *Who Stole Feminism?* (1994) to the topic of male victims of domestic violence, addresses the feminist spin and the misleading information given in women's studies courses at our colleges today. Identifying as an "equity" feminist as opposed to what she calls a "gender" feminist, she makes the point that if feminists do not start presenting all the gender research data and historical events accurately and honestly the feminist movement as a whole will lose credibility. Some would argue that it already has. Women like Hoff-Sommers and men like Warren Farrell (1988) (who at one time was a board member of the National Organization for Women) have addressed the devaluation of males in our society and provided a counterbalance to the *gender*-feminist worldview. It might be said that while patriarchy does not want society to view men as victims, gender feminism does not want society to view women as perpetrators, especially of domestic violence. Where attention goes, funding flows, and where funding flows, programs grow. As a result, almost all—if not all in some quarters—of the attention regarding the topic of domestic violence has been focused on the female victim and the male perpetrator but not the other way around.

I am pleased that so many female victims, some of whom I have helped myself, have found the resources they need, but we should be concerned about all victims of domestic violence, including males. Unfortunately, when one hears the neutral term *"victim" of domestic violence,* the mental picture that comes to mind is anything but neutral, but rather that of an injured woman and not of an injured man. Gender feminists view any discussion of male victims as a threat to their paradigm and movement. An example is the well-known organization

Family Violence Prevention Fund (1997), which produced a booklet titled *The Backlash Book: A Media and Political Guide for Battered Women's Advocates*. In this booklet, the authors interpret the simple assertion that "women are as likely to commit violence in relationship as men" (p. 7) as a threat to the feminist movement and as coming from the political "far right." It is common practice to minimize and devalue those who seriously discuss the need to help male victims by placing them in a category that many in society are likely to object to, such as Christian conservatives or right-wing fanatics. This is exactly what the writers of the *Backlash* booklet do. They want people to believe that any discussion about the seriousness of male victimization comes from conservative Christians or the far right. They write, "Today, the backbone of the far right movement is an uncommon marriage between conservative Christian Churches and a range of Theo-Political Organization" (p. 2). They include as part of this right-wing movement women such as Christina Hoff-Sommers and Cathy Young, both of whom I have spoken with and respect for having the courage and integrity to tell the whole truth about domestic violence. I do not know whether these women are conservative Christians or part of the so-called far right. In any case, what does that have to do with helping male victims? If most of the domestic violence shelters and centers are run by advocates such as those who wrote *Backlash*, it will be difficult to get some positive movement toward helping male victims of domestic violence in our communities.

Gender feminists have become a formidable obstacle in addressing the needs of male victims. Several years ago, there was a display board discussing the plight of male victims at a California statewide sponsored conference on domestic violence. The person who was overseeing the display walked away for just a moment; when he returned, the display had been defaced with a large number of feminist stickers. When one of the conference leaders was informed of the defacing, she was understandably upset about the behavior of these immature feminists.

OBSTACLE 3: GENDER POLITICS

Politics can be difficult, but gender politics can be brutal. I remember a domestic violence worker telling me that the money they raised was for female victims, and if male victims want help then they need to raise their *own* money. This was a pretty cold statement but perhaps the attitude of many other domestic violence workers. When it comes to domestic violence, gender politics goes something like this: "For every dollar we spend on helping a male victim of domestic violence in our center, it would mean one less dollar we can spend on helping a female victim of domestic violence, and that is just unacceptable!"

The feminist movement has become so enmeshed in the domestic violence movement that they have become one and the same. This is because feminists have defined domestic violence as being an issue of male oppression of women, which leads to violence against women. Thankfully, not everyone in a particular domestic violence shelter shares the limited gender-feminist view. A number of domestic violence workers have confided in me that they were afraid to challenge the feminist model or to rock the boat by disagreeing with their coworkers or the leaders in the shelter movement. One domestic violence worker told me that she agrees with my message and data but that she would be ostracized by her colleagues if she spoke up against their bias. I have known shelter workers who quit their jobs because they were tired of the gender politics. I am a friend of a female victim of domestic violence who founded a large and well-known domestic violence center and shelter in California in the mid-1970s. She told me that about two years after she started the shelter, she had to leave this place that she herself founded because radical feminists got on their board of directors and replaced her family system approach of treatment with a gender-feminist model.

Even if this year's research shows the number of female victims increasing relative to males, why should that matter when it comes to the general funding of services for all domestic violence victims? I am convinced that most women's advocates want funding primarily—if not exclusively—for those whom they deem to be the *real* victims of domestic violence, namely, women. Even if they truly believe the archival data and the NCVS statistics that only 5% to 15% of the victims of domestic violence are male, should they not try to reach out to these men anyway? Let us compare this 5% to 15% male victims to the number of female AIDS patients in California, which by 1996 had risen to 10.6%. (California Department of Health Services, 1997). There has been considerably more literature for women with AIDS, and more reports about their plight, than for male victims of domestic violence. Would it not be wrong to say, "We cannot have an outreach program for female AIDS patients because it would reduce the funding for the *real* victims of AIDS, namely, gay men." Yet this argument is used to minimize their focus of male domestic violence victims. I am pleased that women in abusive relationships have, in the past 30 years, finally been getting the assistance they need. It is not the intent of this chapter to minimize the struggles that many women suffer every day living with violent partners. However, until we regard domestic violence as a relationship-system collapse and not as a gender-specific issue, few changes will occur in the political or social discourse, and we will not significantly reduce violence in couples and families.

These three major obstacles—men and patriarchy, feminism, and gender politics—all work against male victims getting the kind of assistance, and outreach programs they need in our communities. There are men who in a patriarchal culture do not want society to view them as victims of domestic violence. There are women in the gender-feminist culture who do not want society to view women as perpetrators of domestic violence. Finally, gender politics seeks to ensure that all funding is directed toward the *real* victims of domestic violence, namely, women.

TREATING THE MALE VICTIM OF DOMESTIC VIOLENCE

The first thing I would suggest doing when working with a man you suspect is a victim of domestic violence or who claims to be a victim is to ask him the same questions you would typically ask women regarding their victimization. You may want to use something like the Conflict Tactics Scales (CTS), or the CTS-2, developed by Murray Straus at the Family Research Laboratory at the University of New Hampshire (Straus & Douglas, 2004). When using these instruments, you will be asking about specific aggressive actions, such as whether the man has ever been pushed, hit, or slapped; had a hard object thrown at him; been hit with a hard object; or been threatened with physical assault by a female intimate partner. If you have been struggling with or outright rejecting the notion that there are nearly as many male victims of domestic assault as women, you may begin to hear a side of domestic violence that you have not heard before. You will also notice how a number of men, after admitting to having been assaulted, will try to minimize the impact on their lives and make sure you do not consider them victims. The point is that you need to ask *specific questions*; do not simply ask, "Are you a victim of domestic violence?" Men are not socialized to see themselves as victims: "That's what happens to women, not men." If you ask a man if he has been a victim of domestic violence, he will probably say no, unless she used a knife or gun on him. I heard a man at a domestic violence steering committee meeting say that his female partner had pointed a gun at him but that he did not think of himself as a victim of domestic violence at the time of the incident.

Second, share with him that he is not alone. Part of helping men is *educating* them about what domestic violence is, just as we do with women who seek our help. This is why those who work with male victims need to have an accurate statistical understanding that is free of gender spin or bias. You can inform the man that survey research suggests that between "36% and 50% of victims of domestic violence are males, and some studies show even higher rates." This helps him to feel like he is not such an oddity. Third, tackle the "wimp factor." As hard as it is for a woman to acknowledge that she is a victim of domestic violence and to decide finally to get help, I believe it is even harder for the man because of his gender socialization. Empathize with the shame and embarrassment he feels when talking about the physical abuse he has received from the very woman who society tells him to protect. It is hard enough to act strong and to suppress your emotional pain when another male assaults you, but to have a woman assault you is even harder to acknowledge, and so is the pain that comes with it. Clearly state to the man that no woman has a right to slap or assault him and that this is what we call domestic violence, regardless of the level of physical injury to him. Also impress upon him that whether it is a man assaulting a woman or the other way around, children who witness domestic violence are given the wrong message, that conflict between intimate partners can be resolved with physical abuse.

Next, share with him stories of other men who have been abused by their partners, including some of those with whom you have worked—of course, without giving identifiable information about the men for reasons of confidentiality. "Taking it like a man" should not mean denying their victimization or the emotional and physical pain they carry deep inside themselves and often in silence. Have them read articles about male victims or the book *Abused Men* (Cook, 1997). They can also be encouraged to visit Web sites sympathetic to male victims of domestic violence, such as http://www.safe4all.org, http://www.favtea.com, or http://www.menshealthnetwork.org, or they can contact the Domestic Abuse Helpline for Men and Women at 1-888-743-5754. Then let the man express his anger over the double standard of justice he may have experienced by law enforcement or by the court system. I do not believe that law enforcement officers are getting the training they need to properly deal with abused men or even to recognize them as possible victims and women as a possible perpetrators. Most of the training law enforcement officers receive focuses on the female victim. Presenters want them to share their belief that men make up only a *small* percentage of victims of domestic assault, as low as 5%. Although this statistic is not supported by most scientific survey research, law enforcement officers may be disinclined to question it. After all, men are nine times less likely than women to contact the police when they are victimized by their partner, so it stands to reason that most of the cases these officers find themselves involved with are of female victims. It would be nice to see local media outlets and law enforcement join together and add to their community outreach efforts discussions about the needs of male victims, breaking through the stereotype and giving the topic equal attention. I believe it would generate calls from male victims seeking help and wanting to tell others about their stories.

Some women manipulate the law enforcement system in order to get the man into trouble. In 1998, the *Sally Jessie Raphael* television show featured a woman who admitted on national television that she had lied about being abused by her male partner when in fact *she* was the perpetrator. Tragically, her male partner was willing to go to jail because he "loved" her and did not want to confront her with the truth of the abuse. Women like this may count on the police to identify their partners as the abusers and they themselves as the victims even when they are the perpetrators. These women may also fail to take responsibility when the abuse is mutual. One clinical director of a large domestic violence shelter in California told me that most of the women they work with at their center are also perpetrators, but they have to list them as victims. In light of research suggesting that 36% to 50% of victims of domestic assault are men, but that only a small percentage of these men call the police compared to women, law enforcement needs to examine why this is the case and find ways to reach those male victims who are currently afraid to call for help.

Men are more likely to express anger than other emotions. When working with the male victim, encourage him to go behind the anger to the fear and sadness of being a victim of domestic violence in a society that may be biased against him. Talk about his fear of not being believed when he shares his victimization before a judge and jury, a fear that people will see him as a wimp and not as a real man, and that even if his female partner does get arrested and the criminal court convicts her of domestic violence, family court may still give her primary physical custody of his children. These men have a lot of fears, some expressed and some hidden, many of them valid. District attorneys do not like law enforcement officers to arrest both the man and the woman when there is mutual abuse, which, according to the research, is at least 50% of the time (Straus, 1992), because it complicates the case. They may prefer having just one victim and one perpetrator when they go before the judge. And if they do convict both the male and the female of domestic violence and both are required to go to jail, who will take care of their children? I wonder how many men are willing to take the "fall" in a mutual abuse case or even when they are not the perpetrator just so their children do not have to see their mother go to jail. So encourage the male victim to share his anger, fear, and grief over the abuse he has sustained and perhaps the abuse he may have received from a biased legal system.

Treat these men with respect and not suspicim. I try to trust people until there is evidence to the contrary. There may be men who lie or only partially tell the truth, but this is no different than the women who choose to lie or who tell only part of the truth. When a male victim senses that you believe his story, he is more likely to open up to you and feel that he is finally being taken seriously. There was a time when we did not believe women who sought assistance or we minimized their pain. That attitude has been changing for the better. Male perpetrators are getting help in batterer intervention and anger management programs in learning new skills to handle their aggressive impulses and deal with partner conflict, and more female victims feel safe enough to come forward for help. It is now time to help the male victim feel equally safe to come forward. This will, it is hoped, also create more interest in developing services for the female perpetrator. One woman called me and said she was a perpetrator of domestic violence and was trying to find someplace that provides counseling to women with anger management problems. She said that if she did not get help, things would get worse between her and her male partner. She went to the local domestic violence center, but they tried to convince her that she was a victim and not a perpetrator. She finally did find a place that works with women perpetrators, but only after a great deal of effort. Raising the awareness of male victims not only will help men but also will automatically raise awareness about female perpetrators, who have their own needs.

Finally, network with others who work with male victims of domestic violence. Join organizations and groups that are completely gender *inclusive* in their beliefs and efforts and do not treat domestic violence as a gender-specific phenomenon. At times, you may feel alone in fighting the system and the stereotypes. Try to locate supportive resources for the male victim, including qualified attorneys who are willing to help him get restraining orders against his abusive female partner or to secure primary physical custody of his children. As domestic violence workers know, developing support groups for female victims helps them to realize that they are not alone in their struggle. This is just as true for male victims. Being able to talk about their abuse in front of other men may initially be difficult, but over time it will help them better take care of themselves and their children. This area of working with male victims of domestic violence is an opportunity for interested people to get involved, and to create a specialized niche for themselves in the community.

Goodwill Toward Men is the title of a book by Jack Kammer. Men are people too. They are your fathers, your brothers, your sons, and your grandsons. When men inform you that they are having "marital problems," ask them whether the conflict also included physical abuse of any kind and in either direction. The next time you hear domestic violence workers say that they work with male victims of domestic violence, ask them about their active outreach program for male victims and how their literature and posters encourage this population to seek help. Ask them how many male victims have participated in their special television programs or public awareness presentations on the topic of domestic violence. Do not accept the answer that they do not know of such victims.

Tell them that if they can create an active outreach program designed with the male victim in mind, men will start to come forward, and as they work with them over time, some will be willing to discuss their stories publicly at workshops, presentations, and media events.

Until there are active and public outreach programs and services for male victims in the community, it is doubtful that males will come forward. Women did not come forward for help in the numbers we see today until we implemented active outreach programs and services for them. The domestic violence movement must be fully inclusive of all victims and perpetrators of violence and abuse. As stated earlier, whether it is dad or mom who assaults the other, the child who witnesses the abuse learns that violence is an acceptable way to resolve conflict between people. This is not the lesson we want children to learn. In the 1970s, many in the women's movement invited men to be more open in sharing their emotions and feelings. Now that men are starting to share their feelings and may even share the abuse they have received from their female partners, is anyone really listening, and do they have the will to help them—not by accident but by focus?

REFERENCES

Bennett, R. (1997, January). A new side to domestic violence. *The Family Bulletin,* 4–5.

Brown, M. (1997, December 7). Arrests of women soar in domestic abuse cases. *Sacramento Bee,* pp. A1, A14.

California Department of Justice, Criminal Justice Statistics Center. (1997, April 21). Special run.

Carrado, M., George, M. J., Loxam, E., Jones, L., & Templar, D., (1996). Aggression in British heterosexual relationships: A descriptive analysis. *Aggressive Behavior, 22,* 401–415.

Commonwealth Fund. (1994). *Violence against women in the United States: A comprehensive background paper.* New York: Columbia University: Commission on Women's Health.

Cook, P. (1997). *Abused men: The hidden side of domestic violence.* Westport, CT: Praeger.

Family Violence Prevention Fund. (1997). *The health care response to domestic violence: Fact sheet.* San Francisco: Author.

Farrell, W. (1988). *Why men are the way they are.* New York: Berkeley Publishing Group.

Flynn, C. P. (1990). Relationship violence by women: Issues and implications. *Family Relations, 39*(2), 194–198.

Fontes, D. L. (1998). *Domestic violence against men: Development of a comprehensive partner conflict survey.* ProQuest, LDO3897.

Hamel, J. (2005). *Gender inclusive treatment of intimate partner abuse: A comprehensive approach.* New York: Springer.

Hines, D., Brown, J., & Dunning, E. (in press). Characteristics of callers to the domestic abuse helpline for men. *Journal of Family Violence.*

Hoff-Sommers, C. (1994). *Who stole feminism? How women have betrayed women.* New York: Simon & Schuster.

McLeod, M. (1984). Women against men: An examination of domestic violence based on an analysis of official data and national victimization data. *Justice Quarterly, 1,* 171–193.

Migliaccio, T. (2002). Abused husbands: A narrative analysis. *Journal of Family Issues, 23,* 26–52.

Plichta, S. B. (1996). Violence and abuse: Implications for women's health. In M. Falik & K. S. Collins (Eds.), *Women's health: The commonwealth fund survey* (pp. 237–270). Baltimore, MD: John Hopkins University Press.

Sommer, R., Barnes, G., E., & Murray, R. P. (1992). Alcohol consumption, alcohol abuse, personality and female perpetrated spouse abuse. *Personality and Individual Difference, 13*(12), 1315–1323.

Steinmetz, S. K. (1978). The battered husband syndrome. *Victimology, 2,* 499–509.

Stets, J., & Straus, M. A. (1990). Gender differences in reporting marital violence and its medical and psychological consequences. In M. Straus & R. Gelles (Eds.), *Physical violence in American families: Risk factors and adaptations to violence in 8,145 families* (pp. 151–166). New Brunswick, NJ: Transaction Publishers.

Straus, M. A. (1977). Wife beating: How common and why? *Victimology, 2,* 443–458.

Straus, M. A. (1992). Yes, physical assaults by women partners: A major social problem. In M. Walsh (Ed.), *Women, men, and gender: Ongoing debates* (pp. 210–221). New Haven, CT: Yale University Press.

Straus, M., & Douglas, E. (2004). A short form of the revised conflict tactics scales, and typologies for severity and mutuality. *Violence and Victims, 19*(5), 507–520.

Straus, M. A., & Gelles, R. (1986). Societal changes and change in family violence from 1975 to 1985 as revealed by two national surveys. *Journal of Marriage and the Family, 48,* 465–479.

Straus, M., Kaufman-Kantor, G., & Moore, D. (1997). Change in cultural norms approving marital violence from 1968 to 1994. In G. Kaufman Kantor & J. Jasinski (Eds.), *Out of the darkness: Contemporary perspectives on family violence* (pp. 3–16). Thousand Oaks, CA: Sage.

Tjaden, P., & Thoennes, N. (1998, November). *Prevalence, incidence, and consequences of violence against women: Findings from the National Violence Against Women Survey* (NCJ 172837). Washington, DC: National Institute of Justice.

Young, C. (1999). *Ceasefire! Why women and men must join forces to achieve true equality.* New York: Free Press.

CHAPTER 14

Domestic Violence in Ethnocultural Minority Groups

Kathleen Malley-Morrison, Denise A. Hines, Doe West,
Jesse J. Tauriac, and Mizuho Arai

The United States has among the highest rates of violence, including domestic violence, in the industrialized world. Intimate partner homicide is the seventh leading cause of premature death for women in the United States (Greenfeld et al., 1998), with approximately 4,000 women murdered every year. This rate is five times that of all the other high-income countries combined (Hemenway, Shinoda-Tagawa, & Miller, 2002). Although perpetrators of male homicide, which is five times the rate of female homicide, are typically other males, American men may be at greater risk of violence from their wives than men in other countries (Kumagai & Straus, 1983).

To what extent is the pattern of high levels of domestic violence in the United States consistent across ethnic groups? The answer to this question varies, depending on the methods used to collect the data and from whom the data are collected—for example, whether the sample is nationally representative or a small convenience sample. A recent report from the U.S. Department of Justice indicates that among family violence cases reported nationally, non-Hispanic Whites, Blacks, Native American Indians, and Alaskan Natives tended to be overrepresented in relation to their numbers within the population, whereas Hispanic Whites and Asians and Pacific Islanders were underrepresented (Durose et al., 2005). However, the cases reported to the criminal justice system are likely to be gross underestimates of actual levels of domestic violence because most cases are never reported to the police. Self-report surveys, such as the National Violence Against Women (NVAW) survey and the National Family Violence Surveys, yield considerably higher estimates of domestic violence in both minority and majority communities. The NVAW survey indicated that Asian American women, like Asian American men, perpetrated relatively low rates of intimate violence in comparison to their proportion in the population and to other ethnic groups (Tjaden & Thoennes, 2000). Specifically the lifetime rate of intimate victimization of Asian Pacific Islander women was 15.0% compared with rates of 24.8% for White women, 29.1% for African American women, and 37.5% for American Indians and Alaskan Natives. Similarly, the lifetime rates for total intimate victimization was 3.0% for Asian Pacific Islander men compared to 7.5% for White men, 12.0% for African American men, and 12.4% for American Indian and Alaskan Native men.

In this chapter, we focus on the predictors and correlates of domestic violence in these four major ethnic minority groups within the United States—Native American Indians, African Americans, Hispanics/Latinos, and Asian Americans/Pacific Islanders. Although all these groups are themselves extremely diverse in regard to ethnicity, SES, and experiences with the European American majority community, they share a history of oppression, discrimination, and systemic (government-sponsored or condoned) violence—all of which have had an impact on their lives and intimate relationships. We also briefly address issues in the prevention and treatment of domestic violence in these communities and include any available information on intimate abuse of men.

NORTH AMERICAN NATIVE AMERICAN COMMUNITIES

Historically, Native American Indian communities had rich and vibrant cultures emphasizing cooperation, noncompetition, sharing, humility, spirituality, living in harmony with all of creation, maintaining optimism and contentment with life, strict religious practices and rituals, and not hurting others—values that helped them endure European invasion and domination (Bigfoot, 2000; Carson, 1995; Malley-Morrison & Hines, 2004). In general, before European contact, Native American Indians had a tradition of relative equality and complementarity between the sexes. Some Indian nations were governed by women; in others, women held positions as healers and spiritual leaders or at least had a say in tribal decision making. Although abuse of women probably occurred in some communities, wife batterers were considered irrational, and their wives could exile them from the family (Sacred Shawl Women's Society, 2002).

Many of these traditional community and family values and practices were severely disrupted by the arrival of European settlers, who forced the Native people off their ancestral lands, imposed foreign and oppressive governmental laws and regulations, mandated the education of Native American Indian children in White schools, refused to include the women in decision-making conferences, and to a considerable extent destroyed the Native American Indian language and religion (Norton & Manson, 1995). The repercussions of these practices continue today and are reflected in substandard housing, poverty, unemployment, substance abuse, malnutrition, inadequate health care, and shortened life expectancy.

Domestic Violence in Native American Life Today

Native American Indians experience a per capita rate of violence more than twice that of other U.S. resident populations (120:1,000 for those aged 12 and over, which is two and a half times the rate for others) (Bureau of Justice Statistics, 1999). In a recent Department of Justice report, the intimate victimization rate of 23 victims per 1,000 Native females was more than twice that of Black women, the next highest group (Rennison, 2001). According to the NVAW survey, more than 30% of Native American Indian women reported physical assaults from their husbands at some point in their lifetimes compared to 22.1% of women overall. Native American Indian women are also sexually victimized by an intimate partner at a significantly higher rate than women of other races (Tjaden & Thoennes, 2000). However, there is also evidence that rates of wife abuse may vary significantly across tribes. For example, at least as recently as the 1980s, the Iroquois, Fox, and Papago had no or minimal levels of wife abuse (Levinson, 1989).

The 1985 National Family Violence Resurvey revealed that for Native American Indians, 15.5% of couples (or 37,000 overall) compared to 14.8% of White couples experienced violence in the previous year, and 7.2% of Native couples (18,000) compared to 5.3% of White couples experienced severe violence (Bachman, 1992). The NVAW survey showed that 11.4% of Native American Indian husbands were the victims of husband abuse at some point in their lifetimes, a rate not significantly different from that in other ethnic groups (Tjaden & Thoennes, 2000). Again, there is evidence of differences in the rates of husband abuse across tribes: Among Apaches, 50% of men reported a physical assault from their wives in the previous year, and 57.5% reported a physical assault at some point in their current relationships (Hamby & Skupien, 1998). Among southwestern Native American Indians, approximately 91% of men reported being the victims of intimate violence over the course of their lifetimes. Overall, the majority of the reported perpetrators of abuse against Native American Indian husbands are from other ethnic groups (Greenfeld & Smith, 1999).

The most commonly identified correlate of domestic violence in Native American Indian communities is alcohol abuse. Overall, Department of Justice reports reveal that about half the victims of intimate violence reported a drinking offender; however, approximately 75% of Native American Indian victims indicated that the offender was drinking at the time of the offense (Greenfeld & Smith, 1999). Moreover, alcohol consumption may also be a *consequence* of wife abuse. In one study, Native women who reported a history of domestic violence also reported more problems with alcohol than women without this history (Norton & Manson, 1995). Other consequences of wife abuse include physical injuries, depression, stress, symptomatology for posttraumatic stress disorder (PTSD), and suicidality (Hamby & Skupien, 1998).

Interventions and Treatments

Since 1995, the U.S. Department of Justice has funded dozens of STOP Violence Against Women grants in Native American Indian communities— including 98 programs in 1998 alone (Centers for Disease Control, 2001). It has also provided support for (a) the development of a Tribal Court Bench Book (Northwest Tribal Court Judges Association, 1999), (b) recommendations to tribal courts for dealing with domestic violence cases (Tribal Court Clearinghouse, 2001), and (c) the development of the Violence Against Indian Women sample tribal code. A recent evaluation of tribal codes revealed that none fully complied with all model code standards, but five (Jicarilla Apache, White Mountain Apache, Northern Cheyenne, Confederated Tribes of Siletz Indians, and Cangleska) met many of the criteria (National American Indian Court Judges Association, 2001).

Among Native Americans, especially male victims, reporting domestic violence to a system outside the tribal structure holds special concerns. "Indian nation citizens often refuse to report due to fear that their needs cannot or will not be met by service providers having access to Indian country. Certain law enforcement professionals, for example, may feel that Indian people are naturally violent or that 'Indian men always beat their wives/children/relatives'" (Native American Circle, 2001, sec. 1, p. 8). Moreover, indigenous peoples have many reasons to be fearful of governmental institutions in the United States. "One of the crucial things many professionals do not understand is that Native Americans have a legitimate reason to distrust 'the system.' After all, memories—both per-sonal and cultural—of forced sterilization and other violent 'treatment' procedures are not so far in the distant past for many Native Americans" (The Circle On-Line, July 1999, p. 8, cited in Bhungalia, 2001).

Most of the treatment programs available to Native American Indians tend to be gender based in their language and outreach, further isolating males who may be living as the victims of violence among inti-mates who feel that maintaining the family and eliminating all violence is of primary concern. One well-noted and respected intervention program, "Mending the Sacred Hoop," seeks to change the systemic response to domestic violence and help members of the Native American community restore some of their original teachings, beliefs, and cultural and moral values. On their Web site (http://www.msh-ta.org), they state, "We work to improve the safety of Native women who experience battering, sexual assault, and stalking by assisting tribes with training, technical assistance and resource materials that specifically address violence against American Indian/Alaskan Native women. . . . The challenge for our Nations is to reclaim traditional views of women, developing a Native justice response that is an effective means of accountability and ending violence against Native women." The very language in this outreach effort is so gender specific that males needing support or information may avoid seeking it there.

AFRICAN AMERICAN COMMUNITIES

Although many of the African Americans today have ancestors who were brought to this country as slaves, many others are immigrants who came to the United States voluntarily either before or after the civil rights movement. Regardless of the circumstances bringing people of color to the United States, discriminatory practices and prejudice continue to take a toll on their lives. Prevalence studies reveal rates of aggression against Black wives ranging from around 7% for severe physical aggres-sion (Hampton & Gelles, 1994) to more than 70% for verbal/symbolic aggression (Straus & Sweet, 1992). Rates of violence of Black wives against Black husbands are also relatively high, with violence rates of 30% for female-to-male partner violence (Caetano, Cunradi, Schafer, & Clark, 2000) and severe assault rates of 7.6% by Black wives against their husbands (Straus, Gelles, & Steinmetz, 1980). In 1996, women's rates of nonlethal intimate violence were highest among the following groups: Black women, women aged 16 to 24, women in the lowest income cat-egories, and women residing in cities (Chaiken, 1998). An analysis of verbal/symbolic aggression indicated that neither race nor socioeconomic class was significantly related to nonphysical forms of aggression (Straus & Sweet, 1992).

Nationally representative surveys of community samples have generally shown that rates of spousal violence are significantly higher in African American than in European American communities—rates that ignore the confounding roles of socioeconomic status (SES) and community context with race and ethnicity (Malley-Morrison & Hines, 2004). In 2003, Black households reported the lowest median income ($29,688) of any racial group—an income that was only 62% of the median for non-Hispanic White households ($47,876). The poverty rate for Blacks in 2003 (24.4%) was three times the rate for non-Hispanic Whites (8.2%) (U.S. Census Bureau, 2004). In most cases, ethnic differences in domestic violence rates diminish or disappear when statistical models control for sociodemographic variables (e.g., Coker, Smith, McKeown, & King, 2000). Using data from the National Survey of Families and Households and the 1990 U.S. Census to examine the role of ecological context in levels of domestic violence, Benson, Wooldredge, Thistlewaite, and Fox (2004) found that for both African Americans and European Americans, rates of domestic violence are similarly influenced by individual-level risk factors (e.g., age, subjective financial strain, male job instability, male education, and male drinking problems). When European Americans were compared to African Americans in similar ecological contexts, the correlation between race and domestic violence either was substantially reduced or disappeared altogether.

Community studies of convenience samples have produced conflicting findings. Some investigators (e.g., Bauer, Rodriguez, & Perez-Stable, 2000) found no differences between European American and African American women in prevalence of abuse. Lockhart (1985) found significant race differences only within the middle class, where the Black women reported more husband-to-wife violence than the White women. Other researchers (e.g., Weinbaum, Stratton, Chavez, Motylewski-Link, Barrera, et al., 2001) have also reported that African American women experienced significantly higher rates of intimate partner violence than non-Hispanic White women. On the other hand, some investigators (e.g., O'Campo et al., 1995) found that following controls for neighborhood variables, the risk of partner-perpetrated physical violence was significantly higher in White than in Black women.

In addition to SES and contextual variables, forms of racial oppression place African Americans at higher risk for domestic violence. Zamel and Stevenson (2005) found that, among African American adolescent males, hypermasculine expressions (including aggressiveness, fearlessness, and self-reliance) were often preceded by feelings of shame due to covert or overt discrimination, which threatened their self-worth, feelings of power, or sense of agency. These hypermasculine attitudes and beliefs are positively correlated with physical and sexual aggression and alcoholism (Zamel & Stevenson, 2005). Moreover, because of structural forces and "last hired, first fired" policies, many African American males face chronic unemployment or underemployment—stressors that are significantly associated with domestic violence (Boyd-Franklin, 2003a; Malley-Morrison & Hines, 2004) and contribute to the shortage of eligible Black men within African American communities (Boyd-Franklin, 2003a). This shortage pressures many African American women to remain in violent relationships and to attribute violence from their intimates to centuries of racial oppression of the Black community (Daly, Jennings, Beckett, & Leashore, 1995).

The research provides no support for a conclusion that African Americans have an inherent biological or cultural propensity for violence; rather, the stressors and oppressive systemic forces that disproportionately affect African Americans place them at greater risk for domestic violence (Malley-Morrison & Hines, 2004; West, 2004). Nevertheless, it is crucial that domestic violence within African American communities be addressed, as the outcomes are devastating. Murder by intimate partners is the leading cause of death among African American females between 15 and 45 years of age (West, 2004). In 1996, per capita rates of intimate murder were eight times higher in African American than European American males and three times higher in African American than European American females (Chaiken, 1998). Abused Black women appear to be at heightened risk for PTSD (e.g., Dutton, Goodman, & Bennett, 2001), depression (Dutton et al., 2001), serious injuries, substance abuse, HIV (Cohen et al., 2000), and suicide attempts (Kaslow, 2002). Moreover, despite the overrepresentation of African American male victims of domestic violence and female-perpetrated homicides, there is a dearth of literature on Black male victims (Light-Allende, 2004). This omission seems to reflect an assumption that males alone are responsible for intimate violence and are not themselves harmed by abuse. On the contrary, data show that for African American males as well as females, "involvement in abusive relationships is likely to result in depression, stress, and alcohol abuse" (Huang & Gunn, 2001, p. 809)—outcomes placing the entire family system at risk.

Selected Prevention and Intervention Programs

African American communities have developed natural networks and numerous coping strategies to survive centuries of slavery and racist oppression (Stewart, 2004). Community members often share resources and make extensive efforts to support one another. To help African Americans deal with family violence, mental health workers should (a) focus on and help mobilize their inherent strengths and survival skills and (b) enlist assistance from family members, local religious leaders, and trusted community elders and advocates (Boyd-Franklin, 2003b). Moreover, it is important to target media outlets and partner with prominent African American community organizations (e.g., churches, public agencies, barbershops, salons, community centers, and social groups) to educate the public about violence (Bent-Goodley, 2004; Stewart, 2004).

Training practitioners, social workers, and shelter staff to be culturally sensitive is crucial in order to counsel Black victims of intimate partner abuse effectively. Many poor African Americans have been pathologized and labeled as "deviant," "lazy," or "disorganized" by mental health workers, leading to strong feelings of distrust and suspicion toward these professionals. Although some practitioners have described these fears as "paranoia" or "antipsychiatry" (Baker & Bell, 1999, p. 365), this distrust is often a "healthy cultural paranoia" in reaction to oppressive policies that have targeted peoples of African descent for generations (Boyd-Franklin, 2003b). Many events endure in the collective memory of African Americans, including slavery, segregation, and unethical medical studies, such as the 40-year government-supported Tuskegee experiment that misled and withheld treatment from African Americans diagnosed with syphilis (West, 2004).

Tricia Bent-Goodley (2004) described the not-too-uncommon experience of African American women being denied housing at shelters because of workers' stereotypical assumptions about Black women's ability to be strong and endure hardship. Support for male victims is even less available. Moreover, African American males are often socialized to control hurt and pain and not to acknowledge "weakness" (Boyd-Franklin, 2003a). As a result, Black males may be less likely to disclose or seek out assistance when victimized.

Many within the African American community are leery of social service agencies because of differential treatment by the child welfare system, disproportionately higher out-of-home placement of African American children, and arrest rates of African American males for domestic violence (e.g., Bent-Goodley, 2004). Therapists must work hard to establish rapport with African American clients and to create a comfortable atmosphere that engenders communication and trust (Baker & Bell, 1999). The use of clear language when communicating about domestic violence is also essential. Three domestic violence focus groups with African American women identified the need to clarify terminology and avoid assumptions that domestic violence terminology means the same thing to all people (Bent-Goodley, 2004). In fact, among participants in the focus groups, there was a belief that being pushed, slapped, or shoved by an intimate did not constitute domestic violence.

Therapists should not ignore or underestimate the connection between frustration and rage due to discrimination and oppression and male or female battering behavior (Stewart, 2004). Even many educationally and financially successful middle- and upper-class African Americans continue to encounter and feel enraged about overt and covert racial assaults, tokenism, and glass ceilings encountered at the workplace (Cose, 1993). These pressures mount and sometimes result in African American women and men experiencing "a sense of powerlessness in their interactions with the world that they angrily act out in their intimate relationships" (Boyd-Franklin, 2003a, p. 93). Hardy and Laszloffy (1995) described four steps in a sociocultural approach to working with African American families who are experiencing misdirected rage: (a) identifying rage and its connection to presenting problems, (b) validating rage as a natural and rational response to the painful degradation of racial oppression, (c) identifying other related emotions, and (d) developing constructive ways of channeling rage.

HISPANIC/LATINO COMMUNITIES

The Hispanic/Latino population in the United States is mostly young, part of a large household, urbanized, and poor—factors of great relevance to domestic violence; however, these characteristics vary considerably across Hispanic/Latino communities. In general, Cubans and Central/South Americans mirror the U.S. population in age, income, education, and employment, whereas Mexicans and Puerto Ricans typically fall below the U.S. population average.

Cultural Values

Although Hispanics/Latinos in the United States are heterogeneous, they tend to share several cultural values with important implications for domestic violence: familism (reliance on the family as their source of emotional, structural, and material support), machismo, marianismo, and fatalism. For example, familism can play a role in a wife's unwillingness to leave an abusive situation; conflicts are supposed to be handled within the family without external help (Campbell, Masaki, & Torres, 1997). On the other hand, familism can provide a buffer to external stressors (e.g., poverty, joblessness, and isolation) contributing to family violence (Vasquez, 1998). In its positive sense, machismo includes notions of honor, pride, responsibility, and obligation to the family (Perilla, 1999). However, its negative side involves expectations that the macho Latino will be violent and domineering, a sexually hot-blooded womanizer, drunken, and harsh with children (Vasquez, 1998). Men who internalize this stereotype may sexually maltreat their wives because they are "supposed to" (Perilla, 1999), and many Latinas may excuse such violence because they see it as culturally prescribed (Campbell et al., 1997). Marianismo, the female counterpart of machismo, is the cultural prescription that Latinas emulate the Virgin Mary's moral integrity and spiritual strength through self-sacrifice for their families (Comas-Diaz, 1995). It encompasses a willingness to tolerate a husband's bad habits, comply with his decisions, and support him unwaveringly (Campbell et al., 1997). Finally, many Latino Catholics believe that even negative events are God's will and that suffering is part of one's destiny. This *cultural fatalism* may have grown out of a history of domination and political control of Hispanic people—it was their way of adapting to situations they could not control (Campbell et al., 1997). Unfortunately, fatalism also has negative implications for individuals in violent families— they may not seek help because they believe it is God's will that they endure suffering now to gain spiritual rewards later.

Domestic Violence Rates

Domestic violence rates in Hispanic/Latino communities vary considerably, depending on such factors as immigration and SES. For example, Mexican and Puerto Rican men are significantly more likely to assault their wives if they were born in the United States (Kaufman Kantor, Jasinski, & Aldarondo, 1994). Latinos living in the United States who are highly acculturated or not acculturated at all have lower rates of both husband and wife abuse than do medium-acculturated Latinos (Caetano, Schafer, Clark, Cunradi, & Raspberry, 2000).

    According to a recent NVAW survey, lifetime rates of physical assault by husbands were around 21% and not significantly different for Hispanic and non-Hispanic female victims (Tjaden & Thoennes, 2000). However, the non-Hispanic group included Whites, Blacks, Asians, and Native Americans if they did not report coming from a Spanish-speaking country. This type of "ethnic lumping" does not allow for meaningful comparisons across major ethnic groups. In a representative sample of Whites and Hispanics who completed the Conflict Tactics Scales (a self-report measure of use of aggressive behaviors in family relationships) in either English or Spanish, Hispanics did not differ from Whites in rates of wife abuse when the following factors were held constant: norms regarding violence, age, and economic stressors. Yet within the Hispanic communities, several meaningful differences emerged: 20.4% of Puerto Ricans, 10.5% of Mexican Americans, and 2.5% of Cubans reported abusive tactics with wives (as compared to 9.9% of Whites) (Kaufman Kantor et al., 1994). Among undocumented and recently documented Latinas, 60% experienced dominance and isolation from their spouses, and 40.7% experienced other types of emotional and verbal abuse (Hass, Dutton, & Orloff, 2000). Still higher rates of emotional abuse were observed among battered women: 94.2% experienced verbal/emotional abuse, and there were no ethnic differences in this rate (Krishnan, Hilbert, & Van Leeuwen, 2001).

Husband Abuse

The limited research on husband abuse suggests that it is a problem. The Department of Justice reported that between 1993 and 1998, there were approximately 1.5/1,000 male Hispanic victims of intimate violence, which is comparable to the rate of non-Hispanics (Rennison & Welchans, 2000). The NFVS showed that Hispanic women were significantly more likely than White women to abuse their husbands physically (16.8% vs. 11.5%, respectively) and to inflict severe physical abuse (7.8% vs. 4%, respectively). Nationwide, these numbers project to 504,000 physically abused and 234,000 severely physically abused Hispanic husbands (Straus & Smith, 1990). The 1995 National Study of Couples also reported a rate of husband abuse among Hispanic men (21%) that was higher than that of White men (15%) (Caetano, Schafer, et al., 2000). Again, rates tend to vary across groups. In a survey of Los Angeles residents, Mexican-born Mexican Americans had the lowest rate of husband abuse, whereas U.S.-born Mexican Americans had the highest. Whites fell somewhere in between those two groups (Sorenson & Telles, 1991).

Predictors of Spousal Abuse

The most consistent predictors of both husband and wife abuse in Latino/Hispanic communities are low income (Cunradi, Caetano, Clark, & Schafer, 2000), high financial strain (Neff, Holamon, & Schluter, 1995), and impoverishment (West, Kaufman Kantor, & Jansinski, 1998). At the same time, perhaps because of the threat to husbands' machismo, one study showed that the greater the contribution of Latina wives to family income, the more physical abuse they experienced from their husbands (Perilla, Bakeman, & Norris, 1994). Unemployed Latino husbands commit more wife abuse than employed husbands (Cunradi et al., 2000), and wives abuse employed husbands more than unemployed ones (Straus & Smith, 1990). Furthermore, employed Latinas were more likely to abuse their husbands than retired wives, and the more educated the Latina, the more abusive she was toward her husband (Cunradi et al., 2000).

In comparison to White battered women, Latina battered women are significantly more likely to come from male-dominated marriages

(West et al., 1998). A strong predictor of wife or husband abuse in the population at large that is also found among Latinos is abuse by the other partner (Neff et al., 1995). Alcohol use and abuse predicts both wife and husband abuse (Caetano, Cunradi, et al., 2000). Among nationally representative samples of Hispanics, the experience of violence in the family of origin is associated with the perpetration of both husband and wife abuse (Caetano, Schafer, et al., 2000; Straus & Smith, 1990). In one study, 92% of Latino male batterers had witnessed their fathers beating their mothers (Perilla, 1999).

Interventions

Hispanics may be the least likely of the major ethnic groups in this country to utilize the services offered to them (Ginorio, Gutierrez, & Acosta, 1995). Because Hispanic men have the reputation in the majority culture of being hypermasculine (violent, sexual, and drunken), wives fear that by reporting their husbands to the police, they will be reinforcing these perceptions and betraying their ethnic group (Kanuha, 1994). Among more recent Latina immigrants, language barriers, lack of transportation, and lack of knowledge of existing support and legal services may impede battered women from seeking the help they need. Moreover, failure to utilize resources, particularly for recent immigrants, may be related to experiences in their countries of origin, where the government and police were oppressive and inspired a fear of authorities (Gonzalez, 2002). A second reason may be fear of deportation. Batterers may threaten to contact the Immigration and Naturalization Service if the wives try to report or leave them (Gonzalez, 2002). Cultural barriers to help seeking include the cultural value of an intact family (familism); because it is traditionally the woman's responsibility to keep the family together (marianismo), many Latinas feel that they cannot break up the family by leaving their batterers (Torres, 1987). Furthermore, Latinas often drop out of treatment because the majority culture tends to offer mental health treatments on the basis of a medical model perceived as too impersonal. Latinas may prefer folk remedies that are rarely available in Western psychology (Kanuha, 1994; Vasquez, 1998). Moreover, Latinos generally believe that wife abuse affects not only the victimized woman but also the whole family. The North American method of dealing with wife assault, which often involves putting the husband in jail and/or putting the wife in a shelter and removing the children from the home, clashes with Latino cultural values. Latinos perceive this approach as an "anti-male" means of breaking up the family, the most vital social structure in their communities, and would rather find methods designed to heal the batterer and the family (Malley-Morrison & Hines, 2004).

The most common response to the push for culturally sensitive services has been to offer bilingual services. When non-English-speaking Latinos are offered a bilingual therapist, their dropout rates are lower, they stay in treatment longer, and they improve psychosocially. In response to the incongruency between the majority culture's feminist approach to wife abuse and the Hispanics' cultural emphasis on maintaining the family, many leading members of the Latino community have initiated domestic violence programs that encompass the entire family. Julia Perilla (2000) designed a domestic violence program that includes two women's groups, two men's groups, and four children's groups that meet concurrently at a local Latino Catholic mission and incorporates the religious beliefs of many Latinos. These groups focus on many social forces, such as power imbalances in relationships and patriarchal cultural traditions, which can perpetuate domestic violence through the generations. Furthermore, the men's group has a substance abuse component that addresses the high correlation between substance abuse and wife abuse. Preliminary evidence shows great success: The men stop using violence within one or two weeks and are still violence free six months after completing the program. The wife abuse recidivism rate is less than 2%, and many of the men stop or considerably reduce their use of alcohol and other drugs.

A culturally specific treatment program for Latino men who batter, developed by Carillo and Goubaud-Reyna (1998), incorporates many traditional Latino beliefs, including the real definition of machismo, through the use of stories from ancient times, prayer, and healing circles. These methods give batterers a clearer perspective on the causes of their violence, its relation to their history, and its consequences so that they can change their behavior and provide a better example for future generations. Programs for Latina batterers are likely to be slower to develop than programs for other female batterers, in part because the culture is even more patriarchal in structure than in the White, Black, or Native American cultures and has a more macho patriarchy than in Asian cultures. In addition, the emphasis on both machismo and marianismo is likely to lead to great reluctance to acknowledge and treat female abusers among Latinos.

ASIAN AMERICAN COMMUNITIES

Although it is widely assumed that Asian Americans share similar cultural values and experiences, there are ethnic differences among subgroups. For example, Confucianism appears to have had a stronger influence on the traditional family system in Korea than in Vietnam. After marrying, Vietnamese women can retain stronger kinship ties to their family of origin than Korean women, who are expected to live with their in-laws if they marry an elder son (Hurh, 1998). Immigrant Asian groups (such as Koreans, Chinese, and Indians) differ significantly from refugee Asian groups (such as Vietnamese and Cambodian) in relation to education and economic achievement. For example, a higher proportion of Asian Indians, Chinese, and Japanese, as compared to the overall American population, graduate from college and receive postgraduate education or training. However, in Massachusetts, 85.7% of Cambodian females and 71% of Vietnamese females have *less than a high school* education. Data also suggest that Asian Americans as a group have the highest average family income in the United States, but Southeast Asians are among the poorest Americans. Because of racial discrimination and lack of proficiency in the English language, many Asian immigrants experience unemployment or underemployment (Arai, 2005). Often, unskilled jobs are more accessible to immigrant women than to men. As a result, gender role reversals and an improved social status for immigrant women may occur; for some families, these drastic changes produce family conflict and contribute to domestic violence (Yick, Shibusawa, & Agbayani-Siewert, 2003).

Domestic Violence Rates

Estimates of the prevalence of spousal abuse in Asian Americans vary considerably, depending on the source. For example, data from the NVAW survey (Tjaden & Thoennes, 2000) indicate that Asian American/Pacific Islander women have significantly lower lifetime victimization rates and fewer physical assaults than women from other ethnic groups. By contrast, studies with state and local community and refugee samples suggest that the rates are considerably higher. Rates of partner abuse from self-report studies range from 20% to 80% of Asian American women, depending on country of origin, for example, 80% in a sample of Japanese American women (Yoshihama & Horrocks, 2002), 60% in a sample of Korean American women (Song, 1996), 40% of a South Asian American sample (Raj & Silverman, 2002), and 50% of a sample of Vietnamese women (Bui & Morash, 1999). In samples of Vietnamese women recruited from a domestic violence center and a civic organization, nearly all the women in both samples had experienced physical and/or verbal abuse (Tran & Des Jardins, 2000). Thus, the actual magnitude of physical violence against Asian American women is probably much higher than the reported cases indicate (e.g., Yoshihama, 2000).

Although there is much less evidence concerning husband abuse than wife abuse in Asian American communities, the rates appear to be rather low. In one study with a nonrepresentative sample of Korean Americans, some aggression against husbands was found in 8% of the wives (Kim & Sung, 2000), but fewer than 1% of the sample reported severe physical aggression of husbands. In a community sample of Vietnamese American couples, physical aggression against partners was reported relatively infrequently but somewhat more often by women than by men (Segal, 2000). Additionally, overall reported rates of psychological maltreatment were very similar across gender, although wives tended to shout and husbands to swear.

There are several reasons why intimate violence, particularly violence against wives, occurs in Asian American communities (Asian Task Force Against Domestic Violence, 2000). Vietnamese respondents tend to believe that men have the right to discipline their wives, can expect sex whenever they want, and are the ruler of the house and that wives deserve beatings. Among Korean respondents, males are more likely than females to hold supportive attitudes toward domestic violence. It appears that male Korean immigrants feel powerless because of their immigrant status and displace their frustration and anger onto wives. South Asian respondents reported that women become property of their husbands after marriage and cannot turn to their families for help.

Many Asian immigrants are reluctant to seek assistance from social service agencies because of language and cultural barriers (Baba & Murray, 2003). In addition, traditional Asian values emphasizing close family ties, harmony, and saving face may discourage Asian women from disclosing physical and emotional abuse by intimates (Office of Minority Health, 2004). Moreover, according to Confucian principles, marital relationships are regarded as secondary to parent–child relationships. Asian American wives who are abused may feel they have no right to report the abuse, and Asian American men may not view partner or marital violence as a violation of women's rights (Yick et al., 2003).

Selected Intervention and Prevention Programs

As with the other ethnic groups, efforts to help Asian American victims of family violence should be culturally sensitive. Seeking outside assistance is new and risky for them because it is seen as bringing shame to their families. Practitioners should help victims develop trust by acknowledging the victims' feelings of shame and loss of face about seeking help (Yick et al., 2003). It is also important that intervention and prevention programs provide services such as bilingual assistance; financial, medical, and social services; child care; and shelters that have experience in working with Asian women. Yick et al. (2003) suggested that the words "abuse" and "battering" are socially and culturally constructed terms rather than terms Asian Americans use in daily conversations. Therefore, practitioners from intervention programs should ask specific behaviorally oriented questions using phrases, such as "Has your husband caused some type of injury to you?" rather than "Has your husband ever abused you?" (Yick et al., 2003). Similarly, health care practitioners might ask Asian American men if a wife or girlfriend is hitting them or anyone they know. Because of patriarchal assumptions, maltreated men are unlikely to disclose their victimization but may be somewhat more likely to do it indirectly ("I know a man who . . . ") than directly. In addition, for many Asian Americans, somatic complaints and symptoms are indicators of anxiety and depression that may be caused by family violence; consequently, attention should be paid to somatic symptoms.

Asian Americans tend to underutilize therapeutic services, and several barriers to providing psychological therapy to Asian Americans have been identified (Mays & Albee, 1992). Asian Americans prefer to rely on informal assistance from family members and respected elders who share their cultural values. Many Asian Americans who have had frustrating interactions with Americans are distrustful of institutions such as hospitals and community mental health centers that they find intimidating and foreign. Moreover, if they suffer from unemployment and underemployment, they generally do not have health insurance.

Sue et al. (2005) suggested that many mental health professionals have biased assumptions about various ethnic minorities. For example, a mental health professional who does not understand that Asian Americans value collectivistic identity might see them as "overly dependent, immature, and unable to make decisions on their own. Likewise, such a person might perceive restraints of strong feelings—a valued characteristic among some Asian groups—as evidence of being inhibited, unable to express emotions or repressed" (p. 58).

For Asian Americans, with their strong emphasis on the value of the family, a family system approach can be used as a form of group-oriented strategy to prevent or respond to family violence. Opportunities for Asian Americans to network with other Asian Americans to build a multicultural supportive community would also be helpful, as would efforts by practitioners to provide empowering services such as knowledge or information about where and how to obtain resources such as jobs, health care, and education (Arai, 2005). Intervention techniques such as family structural therapy, group therapy, and psychoeducational workshops may prove useful to domestic violence situations in Asian American families through restoring orderly hierarchical family relationships, teaching new roles, modifying family functions, changing the family's perception of itself from incomplete extended family unit into an altered but functional family system, and building a new sense of belonging in the community, which may prevent family violence.

CONCLUSIONS

In this chapter, we have placed considerable emphasis on the historical, political, and socioeconomic forces associated with domestic violence in the major ethnic communities within the United States. One of the limitations of the traditional feminist view of domestic violence is that it overlooks the extent to which throughout history men have been victims of violence across the globe. We should not blame all men for violence; the problem is not so much patriarchy as oligarchy—the control of the many by the few and the propensity of the power elites to use and justify the use of violence to achieve their goals of power and control. Violence does breed violence, and violence at any level of society (ranging from the individual to the nation) can engender violence at other levels through the frustration, anger, and despair it generates as well as through the models and rationales for violence it produces. The causal role that societal violence and systemic injustice may play in domestic violence never excuses that violence, a position that has been well articulated within African American communities. However, a recognition that the causes of domestic violence are multiple and complex and occur at every level of the ecological framework (macrosystem, exosystem, microsystem, and individual/developmental) is as important to its eradication as the development of domestic violence laws and training programs (for an extensive discussion of intervention and prevention programs aimed at all ecological levels for ethnic minority victims of domestic violence, see Malley-Morrison & Hines, 2004).

Moreover, within an ecological system that has many supports for violence, it is essential to address issues related to violence by women. Since the advent of mandatory arrest policies for domestic violence, increasing numbers of women have been prosecuted for spousal abuse offenses (Hamberger & Arnold, 1990). Services to help assaultive women resolve domestic encounters nonviolently (e.g., a 36-week-long intervention in Denver that is a modified version of a male batterers' program and a 20-week-long anger management program at the University of Massachusetts Medical Center with a strong cognitive-behavioral emphasis) are rare indeed, and there appear to be no outcome studies published on the effectiveness of female batterers' programs (Dowd, 2001). Even women who want treatment for anger management have trouble accessing it and probably have to get it through private counselors, not the services that are usually available to male batterers. It is ironic that a system set up by feminists discriminates against women because instead of making the services that are available to male batterers also available to women who want/need them, they make these women utilize expensive private counselors to deal with their anger management and abusive behavior problems.

REFERENCES

Arai, M. (2005). The impact of culture on women's meanings and experiences of work: Asian American and Asian immigrant women. In M. P. Mirkin, K. L. Suyemoto, & B. F. Okun (Eds.), *Psychotherapy with women: Exploring diverse contexts and identities* (pp. 185–197). New York: Guilford Press.

Asian Task Force Against Domestic Violence. (2000). *Family violence report*. Retrieved August 28, 2005, from http://www.atask.org/Resources.htm.

Baba, Y., & Murray, S. B. (2003). Spousal abuse: Vietnamese children's reports of parental violence. *Journal of Sociology and Social Welfare, 30*(3), 97–122.

Bachman, R. (1992). *Death and violence on the reservation.* New York: Auburn House.

Baker, F. M., & Bell, C. C. (1999). Issues in the psychiatric treatment of African Americans. *Psychiatric Services, 50*(3), 362–368.

Bauer, H. M., Rodriguez, M. A., & Perez-Stable, E. J. (2000) Prevalence and determinants of intimate partner abuse among public hospital primary care patients. *Journal of General Internal Medicine, 15*, 811–817.

Benson, M. L., Wooldredge, J., Thistelwaite, A. B., & Fox, G. L. (2004). The correlation between race and domestic violence is confounded with community context. *Social Problems, 51*(3), 326–342.

Bent-Goodley, T. B. (2004). Perceptions of domestic violence: A dialogue with African American women. *Health and Social Work, 29*(4), 307–316.

Bhungalia, L. (2001). Native American women and violence. *National Now Times.* Retrieved May 20, 2006, from http://www.now.org/nnt/spring-2001/nativeamerican.html.

Bigfoot, D. S. (2000). *History of victimization in Native communities.* Native American Topic-Specific Monograph Series. Norman: University of Oklahoma Health Sciences Center.

Boyd-Franklin, N. (2003a). *Black families in therapy* (2nd ed.). New York: Guilford Press.

Boyd-Franklin, N. (2003b). Race, class, and poverty. In F. Walsh (Ed.), *Normal family processes* (3rd ed., pp. 260–279). New York: Guilford Press.

Bui, H. N., & Morash, M. (1999). Domestic violence in the Vietnamese immigrant community. *Violence Against Women, 5*(7), 769–795.

Bureau of Justice Statistics. (1999). *American Indians and crime.* Retrieved May 20, 2006, from http://www.ojp.usdoj.gov/bjs/abstract/aic.htm.

Caetano, R., Cunradi, C. B., Schafer, J., & Clark, C. L. (2000). Intimate partner violence and drinking patterns among white, black, and Hispanic couples in the U.S. *Journal of Substance Abuse, 11*, 123–138.

Caetano, R., Schafer, J., Clark, C. L., Cunradi, C. B., & Raspberry, K. (2000). Intimate partner violence, acculturation, and alcohol consumption among Hispanic couples in the United States. *Journal of Interpersonal Violence, 15*, 30–45.

Campbell, D. W., Masaki, B., & Torres, S. (1997). Changing domestic violence perceptions in the African American, Asian American, and Latino communities. In E. Klein, J. Campbell, E. Soler, & M. Ghez (Eds.), *Ending domestic violence: Changing public perceptions/halting the epidemic* (pp. 64–87). Thousand Oaks, CA: Sage.

Carillo, R., & Goubaud-Reyna, R. (1998). Clinical treatment of Latino domestic violence offenders. In R. Carrillo & J. Tello (Eds.), *Family violence and men of color* (pp. 53–73). New York: Springer.

Carson, D. K. (1995). American Indian elder abuse: Risk and protective factors among the oldest Americans. *Journal of Elder Abuse and Neglect, 7*, 17–39.

Centers for Disease Control. (2001). *American Indian/Alaska Natives and intimate partner violence.* Retrieved September 1, 2001, from http://www.cdc.gov/ncipc/factsheets/natamer.htm.

Chaiken, J. M. (1998). *Violence by inmates: Analysis of data on crimes by current or former spouses, boyfriends, and girlfriends.* Washington, DC: U.S. Department of Justice, Bureau of Justice Statistics. (NCJ No.167237).

Cohen, M., Deamant, C., Barkan, S., Richardson, J., Young, M., Holman, S., et. al. (2000). The domestic violence and childhood sexual abuse in HIV-infected women and women at risk for HIV. *American Journal of Public Health, 90, 560–565.*

Coker, A. L., Smith, A. L., McKeown, R. E., & King, M. J. (2000). Frequency and correlates of intimate partner violence by type: Physical, sexual, and psychological battering. *American Journal of Public Health, 90, 553–559.*

Comas-Diaz, L. (1995). Puerto Ricans and sexual child abuse. In L.A. Fontes (Ed.), *Sexual abuse in nine North American cultures: Treatment and prevention* (pp. 31–66). Thousand Oaks, CA: Sage.

Cose, E. (1993). *The rage of a privileged class.* New York: HarperCollins.

Cunradi, C. B., Caetano, R., Clark, C., & Schafer, J. (2000). Neighborhood poverty as a predictor of intimate partner violence among White, Black, and Hispanic couples in the United States: A multilevel analysis. *Annals of Epidemiology, 10,* 297–308.

Daly, A., Jennings, J., Beckett, J. O., & Leashore, B. R. (1995). Effective coping strategies of African Americans. *Social Work, 40*(2), 240–248.

Dowd, L. (2001). Female perpetrators of partner aggression: Relevant issues and treatment. *Journal of Aggression, Maltreatment, and Trauma, 5,* 73–104.

Durose, M. R., Harlow, C. W., Langan, P. A., Motivans, M., Rantala, R. R., & Schmitt, E. L. (2005). *Family violence statistics: Including statistics on strangers and acquaintances.* Washington, DC: U.S. Department of Justice, Office of Justice Statistics.

Dutton, M. A., Goodman, L. A., & Bennett, L. (2001). Court-involved battered women's responses to violence: The role of psychological, physical, and sexual abuse. In K. D. O'Leary & R. D. Maiuro (Eds.), *Psychological abuse in violent domestic relationships* (pp. 177–195). New York: Springer.

Ginorio, A. B., Gutierrez, A. M., & Acosta, M. (1995). Psychological issues for Latinas. In H. Landrine (Ed.), *Bringing cultural diversity to feminist psychology: Theory, research, and practice* (pp. 241–263). Washington, DC: American Psychological Association.

Gonzalez, G. (2002). *Barriers and consequences for battered immigrant Latinas.* Retrieved February 24, 2002, from http://www.aad.berkeley.edu/96journal/gloriagonzalez. html.

Greenfeld, L. A., Rand, M. R., Craven, D., Klaus, P. A., Perkins, C. A., Ringel, C., et al. (1998). *Violence by intimates.* Washington, DC: U.S. Department of Justice, Office of Justice Programs, Bureau of Justice Statistics.

Greenfeld, L. A., & Smith, S. K. (1999, February). *American Indians and crime* (NCJ 173386). Washington, DC: U.S. Department of Justice, Office of Justice Programs, Bureau of Justice Statistics.

Hamberger, L. K., & Arnold, J. E. (1990). The impact of mandatory arrest on intimate partner violence perpetrator counseling services. *Family Violence Bulletin, 6,* 10–12.

Hamby, S. L., & Skupien, M. B. (1998). Domestic violence on the San Carlos Apache reservation: Rates, associated psychological symptoms, and current beliefs. *The IHS Provider, 23,* 103–106.

Hampton, R. L. & Gelles, R. J. (1994). Violence toward Black women in a nationally representative sample of Black families. *Journal of Comparative Family Studies, 25,* 105–119.

Hardy, K. V., & Laszloffy, T. A. (1995). Therapy with African Americans and the phenomenon of rage. *In Session: Psychotherapy in Practice, 4*(1), 57–70.

Hass, G. A., Dutton, M. A., & Orloff, L. E. (2000). Lifetime prevalence of violence against Latina immigrants: Legal and policy implications. *Domestic Violence: Global Responses, 7,* 93–113.

Hemenway, D., Shinoda-Tagawa, T., & Miller, M. (2002). Firearm availability and female homicide victimization rates among 25 populous high-income countries. *Journal of the American Medical Women's Association, 57,* 100–104.

Huang, C. J., & Gunn, T. (2001). An examination of domestic violence in an African American community in North Carolina: Causes and consequences. *Journal of Black Studies, 31*(6), 790–811.

Hurh, W. M. (1998). *The Korean Americans.* Westport, CT: Greenwood Press.

Kanuha, V. (1994). Women of color in battering relationships. In L. Comas-Diaz & B. Greene (Eds.), *Women of color: Integrating ethnic and gender identities in psychotherapy* (pp. 428–454). New York: Guilford Press.

Kaslow, N. J. (2002). Risk and protective factors for suicidal behavior in abused African American women. *Journal of Consulting and Clinical Psychology, 70,* 311–319.

Kaufman Kantor, G., Jasinski, J. L., & Aldarondo, E. (1994). Sociocultural status and incidence of marital violence in Hispanic families. *Violence and Victims, 9,* 207–222.

Kim, J. Y., & Sung, K. (2000). Conjugal violence in Korean American families: A residue of cultural transition. *Journal of Family Violence, 15*(4), 331–345.

Krishnan, S. P., Hilbert, J. C., & VanLeeuwen, D. (2001). Domestic violence and help-seeking behaviors among rural women: Results from a shelter-based study. *Family and Community Health, 24,* 28–38.

Kumagai, F., & Straus, M. A. (1983). Conflict resolution tactics in Japan, India, and the USA. *Journal of Comparative Family Studies, 14*(3), 377–387.

Levinson, D. (1989). *Family violence in a cross-cultural perspective.* Newbury Park, CA: Sage.

Light-Allende, K. (2004). Relationship violence: Women perpetrators. *Dissertation Abstracts International: Section B: The Sciences and Engineering, 65*(4-B).

Lockhart, L. L. (1985). Methodological issues in comparative racial analyses: The case of wife abuse. *Social Work Research and Abstracts, 21*(2), 35–41.

Malley-Morrison, K., & Hines, D. A. (2004). *Family violence in a cultural perspective.* Thousand Oaks, CA: Sage.

Mays, V. M., & Albee, G. W. (1992). Psychotherapy and ethnic minorities. In D. K. Freedhelm (Ed.), *History of psychotherapy: A century of change* (pp. 552–570). Washington DC: American Psychological Association.

National American Indian Court Judges Association. (2001). *Violence against Indian women tribal code project.* Retrieved September 16, 2001, from http://www.naicja.org/vawa/htm.

Native American Circle. (2001), *Domestic violence: Prevention and intervention programs in Native American communities.* Retrieved August 1, 2005, from http://www.nativeamericancircle.org/pdf/1DomesticViolence.pdf.

Neff, A. J., Holamon, B., & Schluter, T. D. (1995). Spousal violence among Anglos, Blacks, and Mexican Americans: The role of demographic variables, psychosocial predictors, and alcohol consumption. *Journal of Family Violence, 10,* 1–21.

Northwest Tribal Court Judges Association. (1999). *Tribal court bench book for domestic violence cases.* Washington, DC: Violence Against Women Grants Office.

Norton, I. M., & Manson, S. M. (1995). A silent minority: Battered American Indian women. *Journal of Family Violence, 10,* 307–318.

O'Campo, P., Gielen, A. C., Faden, R. R., Xue, X., Kass, N., & Wang, M. C. (1995). Violence by male partners against women during the childbearing years: A contextual analysis. *American Journal of Public Health, 85,* 1092–1097.

Office of Minority Health. (2004). Highlights in minority health. Retrieved August 28, 2005, from http://www.cdc.gov/omh/Highlights/2004/HOct04.htm.

Perilla, J. L. (1999). Domestic violence as a human rights issue: The case of immigrant Latinos. *Hispanic Journal of Behavioral Sciences, 21,* 107–133.

Perilla, J. L. (2000). Cultural specificity in domestic violence interventions: A Latino model. *The Family Psychologist, 16,* 6–7.

Perilla, J. L., Bakeman, R., & Norris, F. H. (1994). Culture and domestic violence: The ecology of abused Latinas. *Violence and Victims, 9,* 325–339.

Raj, A., & Silverman, J. G. (2002). Violence against immigrant women: The roles of culture, context, and legal immigrant status on intimate partner violence. *Violence Against Women, 8,* 367–398.

Rennison, C. M. (2001). *Intimate partner violence and age of victim, 1993–99.* U.S. Department of Justice, Office of Justice Programs, Bureau of Justice Statistics, Special Report, NCJ 187635.

Rennison, C. M., & Welchans, S. (2000). *Intimate partner violence.* Retrieved February 12, 2003, from http://www.ojp.usdoj.gov/bjs/abstract/ipv.htm.

Sacred Shawl Women's Society. (2002). *A sharing: Traditional Lakota thought and philosophy regarding domestic violence.* Pine Ridge, SD: Author.

Segal, U. A. (2000). A pilot exploration of family violence among non-clinical Vietnamese. *Journal of Interpersonal Violence, 15*(5), 523–533.

Song, Y. I. (1996). *Battered women in Korean immigrant families: The silent scream.* New York: Garland.

Sorenson, S. B., & Telles, C. A. (1991). Self-reports of spousal violence in a Mexican-American and Non-Hispanic White population. *Violence and Victims, 6,* 3–15.

Stewart, P. E. (2004). Afrocentric approaches to working with African American families. *Journal of Contemporary Social Services, 85*(2), 221–228.

Straus, M., Gelles, R., & Steinmetz, S. (1980). *Behind closed doors: Violence in the American family.* Newbury Park, CA: Sage.

Straus, M. A., & Smith, C. (1990). Violence in Hispanic families in the United States: Incidence rates and structural interpretations. In M. A. Straus & R. J. Gelles (Eds.), *Physical violence in American families: Risk factors and adaptations to violence in 8,145 families* (pp. 305–313). New Brunswick, NJ: Transaction Publishers.

Straus, M. A., & Sweet, S. (1992). Verbal symbolic aggression in couples: Incidence rates and relationships to personal characteristics. *Journal of Marriage and the Family, 54,* 346–367.

Sue et al. (2005)

Tjaden P., & Thoennes, N. (2000). *Extent, nature, and consequences of intimate partner violence: Findings from the National Violence Against Women Survey.* Retrieved January 10, 2003, from http://www.ojp.usdoj.gov/nij/victdoc.htm#2000.

Torres, S. (1987). Hispanic-American battered women: Why consider cultural differences? *Response to the Victimization of Women and Children, 10,* 20–21.

Tran, C. G., & Des Jardins, K. (2000). Domestic violence in Vietnamese refugee and Korean immigrant communities. In J. L. Chin (Ed.), *Relationships among Asian American women* (pp. 71–96). Washington, DC: American Psychological Association.

Tribal Court Clearinghouse. (2001). *Domestic violence.* Retrieved September 16, 2001, from http://www.tribal-institute.org/lists/domestic.htm.

U.S. Census Bureau. (2004). *Income, poverty, and health insurance coverage in the United States: 2003.* Retrieved August 5, 2004, from http://www.census.gov/prod/2004pubs/p60–226.pdf.

Vasquez, M. J. (1998). Latinos and violence: Mental health implications and strategies for clinicians. *Cultural Diversity and Mental Health, 4,* 319–334.

Weinbaum, Z., Stratton, T.L., Chavez, G., Motylewski-Link, C., Barrera, N., & Courtney, J. G. (2001). Female victims of intimate partner physical domestic violence (IPP-DV), California 1998. *American Journal of Preventive Medicine, 21,* 313–319.

West, C. M. (2004). Black women and intimate partner violence: New directions for research. *Journal of Interpersonal Violence, 19,* 1487–1493.

West, C. M., Kaufman Kantor, G., & Jansinski, J. L. (1998). Sociodemographic predictors and cultural barriers to help-seeking behavior by Latina and Anglo American battered women. *Violence and Victims, 13,* 361–375.

Yick, A. G., Shibusawa, T., & Agbayani-Siewert, P. (2003). Partner violence, depression, and practice implications with families of Chinese descent. *Journal of Cultural Diversity, 10*(3), 96–104.

Yoshihama, M. (2000). Reinterpreting strength and safety in socio-cultural context: Dynamics of domestic violence and experiences of women of Japanese descent. *Children and Youth Services Review, 22*(3), 205–227.

Yoshihama, M., & Horrocks, J. (2002). Post-traumatic stress symptoms and victimization among Japanese American women. *Journal of Consulting and Clinical Psychology, 70*(2), 205–215.

Zamel, P. C., & Stevenson, H. C. (2005, August). Hypervulnerable youth in a hypermasculine world: Effects of invulnerability training, racism and violence on African American adolescent males. In H. C. Stevenson (Chair), *Adolescents making meaning—Issues of race, gender, and identity.* Symposium conducted at the annual convention of the American Psychological Association, Washington, DC.

CHAPTER 15

Systems Considerations in Working With Court-Ordered Domestic Violence Offenders

Lonnie Hazlewood

A DEVELOPING CLINICAL PERSPECTIVE

As we suggested in *The Violent Couple* (Stacey, Hazlewood, & Shupe, 1994), the family violence field at that time was evolving through three stages: the female victim-oriented stage, the male-perpetrator-oriented stage, and the systems stage. The systems stage is well started and now gathering momentum with many practitioners who understand the need for flexibility in therapeutic approaches to family violence and for models that go beyond the victim–perpetrator conception.

My clinical perspectives have been informed by Thomas S. Kuhn's influential book *The Structure of Scientific Revolutions,* which urges the reader to consider that every current state of knowledge is relative and incomplete based on a model or paradigm of how things work. The current paradigm helps organize knowledge and influences how subsequent questions are asked. The current paradigm also discourages other questions and inquiries about the issue. This leads to gaps in research that cannot be explained by the dominant model and that accumulate and lead to the emergence of another paradigm that more fully explains the phenomenon being studied. In this way, scientific knowledge continues to evolve and regenerates. This understanding has helped me resist ideological and philosophical ways of understanding domestic violence and to accept empirical and experiential information and new ways of understanding domestic violence as they emerge.

In 1980, when I began work in the family violence field, the victim stage was dominant with a single causative etiology of patriarchal culture and the associated concept of male privilege. Having come to the field with a somewhat traditional education in social psychology and training in the major psychodynamic theories of the 1970s, gender socialization by a patriarchal culture was for me an intriguing and compelling explanation for family violence. My mentors in this education, Debbie Tucker, Barbara Hart, and Judy Reeves, opened my eyes to a revealing look at men and masculinity and the gender role socialization of men that emphasized male domination and control of women. However, within a short period of time working directly with men accused and convicted of domestic assault and their intimate partners and other family members, it was apparent that this paradigm did not completely account for the complex interactions of the relationships and families involved.

I took what I thought was a logical and simple strategy and began to interview intimate partners and other family members of offenders court-mandated to treatment in our Family Violence Diversion Network about what went on during abusive and violent episodes. I began to quantify these responses using a scale that I developed based on the Center for Social Research's Abuse Index (Shupe, Stacey, & Hazlewood, 1987). This abuse index, which had been developed to quantify men's controlling and abusive behaviors toward women who had sought refuge in shelters, was changed to ask both partners how often they engaged in each behavior of abuse, control, and violence and how often their partner engaged in each item. This allowed a direct comparison of couples' responses. This approach was questioned and criticized by members of the shelter movement and was regarded as antifeminist. The message seemed to be that if women were asked about their abuse or violence, they might think they were responsible for their partner's abuse and violence against them. However, this simple but controversial step yielded important data that I later learned were consistent with data from the National Family Violence Survey (Straus, Gelles, & Steinmetz, 1980) and other studies (Breen, 1985; chapters 1, 2, 3, and 4 in this volume). Women admitted engaging in verbal abuse, controlling behaviors, and physically violent assaults on their male partners. They also admitted to often having initiated these behaviors. See Table 15.1 for results of a group analysis of this data. The men's responses, indicating even higher levels of verbal and physical abuse and controlling behaviors by the wives/girlfriends, can be found in Stacey et al. (1994).

These were startling findings and unanticipated in a population of men who had been identified by the criminal justice system as violent and

TABLE 15.1   Family Violence Diversion Network Abuse Reports

Items Measuring Physical Violence by the Wife/Girlfriend and by Husband/ Boyfriend as Reported by the Wife/Girlfriend

Item	Female (%)	Male (%)
Hitting or destroying household things	44	83
Physically holding or restraining	28	87
Pushing or shoving	53	92
Throwing household things	49	73
Destroying personal belongings	35	66
Slapping	47	74
Kicking	39	66
Punching with fist to body	32	66
Punching with fist to head	21	67
Burning	7	29
Forced sex	8	51
Choking	13	61
Biting	23	37
Using a weapon	12	40

Items Measuring Psychological Abuse by the Wife/Girlfriend and by Husband/ Boyfriend as Reported by the Wife/Girlfriend

Item	Female (%)	Male (%)
Deny rights to privacy by going through pockets, billfolds, etc.	66	73
Deny freedom of activities (Can you go where you want to go?)	37	72
Deny access to family members	20	47
Deny access to friends	31	63
Deny access to jointly held money	17	57
Deny input on financial decisions	20	63
Censor phone calls or communication with family and/ or friends	24	60
Withdraw emotionally as punishment or disapproval	72	84
Withhold sex as punishment/disapproval	48	44
Verbal abuse (name-calling, belittling, insulting)	92	98
Make verbal threats to use physical violence	46	77
Make verbal threats to use a weapon	30	59
Make verbal threats to kill	22	62

by victim advocates as woman batterers. It was expected that this population would evidence relatively unilateral abuse—that is, male-toward-female abuse. It was recognized that men's physical violence outpaced that of their intimate partners, and our measures showed that men caused more serious injuries. However, men reported significant levels of isolating and controlling behaviors by their intimate partner as well physical violence.

As a result of this new information, a new therapeutic view began to develop—a multicausative, family systems one in which there may be many causative factors in any one domestic violence event, including but not limited to patriarchal learning of both men and women, social learning and modeling of violence responses in the family of origin, conflict escalation, alcohol and other substances of abuse, and stress that interacts with relational and family dynamics to produce abuse and violence. Accordingly, my domestic violence treatment model was extended to interview whenever possible intimate partners of the men in treatment and to provide individual, couples, and family counseling when the safety of the most vulnerable family members could be ensured. The women interviewed were given assurances that the information they provided would not be given to their male partner or the criminal justice system and would be used only if they gave consent to release the information for a specific use. Intimate partner contact monitoring was instituted on a regular basis throughout the time their male partners were in the program, usually by telephone interviews, to determine if abuse and/or violence were continuing. This allowed the development of safety plans when this was necessary to prevent further violence and to make referrals for safe shelter or other social agencies. When given a release to do so, we could also plan an intervention strategy to deal with the abuse, violence, or other issues found during monitoring. For the most part, women who were contacted welcomed the chance to talk about what was happening at home, and despite our best efforts to limit these monitoring contacts to violence and abuse in the home, our counselors found themselves involved in a myriad of couples' conflicts and family problems.

THE CRIMINAL JUSTICE RESPONSE

The criminal justice response to domestic violence has evolved over the past 20 years and led directly to the male-perpetrator-oriented phase and the development of batterer intervention programs. The criminal justice response to domestic violence has been characterized by three broad stages: nonintervention, mediation and proarrest (Erez, 2002).

After the legal right of a husband physically to chastise his wife was taken away at the beginning of the 19th century, the justice response was one of nonintervention. The courts appeared to recognize a husband's right to force his wife to "behave" and "know her place" (*Joyner v. Joyner*) and would not intervene in family conflicts unless some serious injury or excessive violence was used (*State v. Oliver,* 1979).

The second stage, mediation response to domestic violence, began in the 1960s as professionals in the social sciences and psychology fields began to suggest that police use crisis intervention and mediation in responding to "family disturbances" (Bard, 1970). This approach used the police to separate the conflicting family members, mediation between the parties, and referral to social service agencies (Erez & Belknap, 1995) to continue appropriate interventions. The use of mediation and crisis intervention was successful in the sense that it reduced arrest rates for domestic assault and kept these cases out of criminal courts.

The third and current response to domestic violence by the criminal justice system is aggressive arrest policies, mandatory prosecution, and counseling of offenders. This response dovetails nicely with the patriarchal interpretation of domestic violence and a perpetrator–victim scenario that is at the core of our criminal justice system. State legislatures have changed assault laws or created new ones specific to domestic violence to support these polices. Correspondingly, the arrest rate in domestic violence misdemeanor assaults soared by 70% between 1985 and 1989 (Sherman, 1992). A number of other corollary interventions, both legal and psychosocial, have also accompanied the arrest strategy to domestic violence, including but not limited to the following:

1. Encouraging the filing of protective orders by the presumed victim and emergency protective orders filed directly by the court as well as no-contact conditions of adjudication that create a legal barrier between intimate partners, husbands and wives, and victims and offenders
2. Automatic domestic assault filing by the police regardless of the wishes of the alleged victim and no-drop policies by the jurisdiction's prosecutors, again taking the alleged victim out of the criminal process
3. Changes in spousal testimony laws that allow a spouse to testify before the court against the other spouse in domestic violence cases
4. Legislation that allows prosecutors to enhance a subsequent misdemeanor domestic assault to a felony
5. Diversion or mandatory assignment of male abusers to what became known as batterer intervention programs for counseling
6. A "fast track" adjudication of domestic assaults after arrest of domestic violence perpetrators, which did not prove to be as

effective as originally thought (Binder & Meeker, 1992) in deter-
ring future assaults
7.   The implementation in about a dozen states of domestic violence
     guidelines that restrict the use of nonfeminist models of batterer
     treatment
8.   Restrictions on those accused of domestic violence in parental
     visitation of children

Little attention socially or in the research has been given to the cost
of these new strategies on men, families, and children. Not only is there
considerable financial cost to obtain legal defense for oneself (if one has
the means to do so), but there are many other costs, financially, socially,
and psychologically. Since about 94% (Boland, Brady, Tyson, & Bassler,
1982) of criminal convictions are obtained by plea bargain even when a
defense attorney is retained, there is no hearing of the facts of these cases
in an open forum. There is great pressure to adjudicate these cases without trial because setting even a small percentage of these cases for a trial
by jury or judge would create a logjam of cases, taking years to process in
most jurisdictions. Financial and other resources and incentives are often
not available to a victim who chooses to remain with a partner accused
or convicted of a domestic assault. There is a long-term financial burden
on the family in court costs, probation fees, counseling requirements, and
loss of or inability to find a job with a criminal record and the hours that
must often be spent doing community service. What long-term effects
does this have on a family's ability to provide a quality life for themselves
and their children? Does it increase the probability of children living in
poverty? In addition, many families find it difficult to find housing when
a member has been convicted of a domestic violence offense, especially if
that offense is a felony or enhanced felony, because many landlords are
now conducting criminal background checks and are denying housing to
certain criminal classifications, including assault.

TREATMENT APPROACHES TO DOMESTIC VIOLENCE

Batterer intervention programs and other therapeutic responses ought to
provide salient and effective approaches to eliminating and ameliorating
abuse and violence in intimate and family relationships and the devastating effects such violence has on the individuals, children, and families
involved. Even though there may be conflicts and controversy between
various stakeholders over the specifics of how to do this, there is general
agreement in this overall goal. There is less agreement between shelter
staff and batterer treatment programs and other competing professional

and community interests regarding other goals, such as couple and family reconciliation.

Regardless of the clinical setting in which one approaches domestic violence or the theoretical and psychotherapeutic basis of intervention, there are essential features of the intervention that must be considered. These consist of risk/danger/lethality assessment and treatment methods, including group, individual and couple/family strategies.

Since a core value of domestic violence intervention is protection of the victim, some form of risk assessment is a necessary starting point for treatment. These assessments are also undertaken to assign the treatment candidate the appropriate type and duration of treatment; to help the police, courts, and probation officers identify those offenders who need closer supervision; and to help specify which victims need to develop immediate safety plans (Weisz, Tolman, & Saunders, 2000).

Risk assessment in domestic violence can be defined as "the formal application of instruments to assess the likelihood that intimate partner violence will be repeated or escalated. This term is synonymous with dangerousness assessment and encompasses lethality assessment, the use of instruments specially developed to identify the potentially for a lethal situations" (Roehl & Guertin, 2002, p. 171). This process compares the accused or convicted domestic violence treatment candidate against known characteristics or risk markers of those who have assaulted or murdered their intimate partner. A number of these instruments have been developed in recent years, including the Domestic Violence Screening Instrument, the Spousal Assault Risk Assessment, the Danger Assessment Scale (Campbell, 1986; Campbell, Webster, Koziol-Mclain, Block, Campbell, et al., 2003), and the checklist of risk factors developed by the Pennsylvania Coalition Against Domestic Violence (Hart, 1990). Further discussion of assessment procedures can be found in chapters 11 and 12 in this volume.

In addition to this type of risk assessment, one also needs to consider personality characteristics and types that have been linked to domestic violence (Dutton, 1998) and the potential for future violence (Meloy, 1992). Primary considerations have to do with the diagnosis of borderline personality and attachment issues. A very good treatment of these factors can be found in Dutton's book *The Abusive Personality* (1998).

It is also very important to add the identified victim's prediction of risk and danger to these assessments since some studies have found that predicting severe violence is improved by combining risk marker identification with a victim's general rating of danger (Weisz et al., 2000). Gondolf, in his 2002 multisite, four-year follow-up study of batterer intervention programs, found that women's perception of safety and the probability of reassault was the most consistent and strongest risk marker (Gondolf, 2002). When victims cannot be interviewed, other family members of the treatment candidate can be a good check on the veracity of the responses given to risk assessment questions by the candidate. Whenever possible, police reports of intimate partner violence, victim statements, and criminal history searches are also important adjuncts to these instruments.

Finally, risk assessment must be an ongoing process that continues during the course of treatment. This can be most reliably accomplished by regular intimate partner monitoring. Situational contexts often change related to weapons access, attachment losses, escalation of violence, and exposure of the victim to perpetrator secrets (affairs, criminal activity or incest). Among the most important changes that may increase risk are victim's suicide attempts and substance abuse. Risk of reassault or homicide is not a static process but a dynamic one that can change rapidly, depending on situational circumstances of the couple and/or family.

Although the risk assessment approach is an improvement on past attempts to predict future violent behavior and is an important step in the treatment of domestic violence perpetrators, there are obvious weaknesses to this approach. Current risk assessment instruments are based primarily on male risk factors for future violence, and not much has been done to determine if these same risk factors hold true for female-perpetrated violence. Although risk assessment instruments are superior to clinical judgment, these instruments make significant levels of misclassifications (Gondolf, 2002) for both false positives and false negatives. Risk assessment is in its early stages of development (Weisz et al., 2000), and there is little research on the validity, reliability, and predictive accuracy of this process (Roehl & Guertin, 2002).

As Dutton and Kroop (2000) have observed,

> Properly applied, the practice of risk assessment can serve as a paradigm for effective case management of spousal assaulters. It can serve as the basis for release planning, treatment placement, and safety planning for the victim. Improperly applied, it can mislead the courts, victims and offenders into falsely believing in an infallible science that does not yet exist. (p. 180)

Even when risk assessment is not used to determine a treatment path, it is important that domestic violence service providers know who among those being treated represent the most serious threat of serious injury or lethality. All providers, including those providing "one size fits all" same-sex group treatment of offenders populations have a professional duty to determine to the best of their ability who is most dangerous in order to provide partner and family safety planning.

GROUP TREATMENT

The patriarchal causative model proposed by feminists, stated briefly, is that men go through a gender role socialization process that teaches them to believe in their right as males to exercise power and control over women. There is a related complex of beliefs that is not only present in men but also expressed by the institutions of society and culture. The Duluth model (Pence & Paymar, 1993) is the most widespread same-sex group treatment approach based on this analysis of domestic violence. Activists in the battered women's movement and battered women in Duluth, Minnesota, relying heavily on the work on Dobash and Dobash (1979), developed this model. It rejects treatment based on insight models, family systems theory, or cognitive-behavioral models in favor of a sociopolitical model with the so-called power and control wheel, describing male-perpetrated abuse and control behaviors, as a central feature. Its goal is to challenge and change traditional patriarchal beliefs held by men and the behaviors associated with power and control of women. It denies or rejects violence committed by women and therefore is inappropriate in the treatment of heterosexual female, lesbian and gay offenders.

A second causative model used in same-sex group treatment programs is the social learning theory and generational transfer model. Work by Leonard Berkowitz, Albert Bandura, Richard Walters, Robert Baron, and many others during the 1960s and 1970s contended that violent behavior is learned, similar to other complex human behavior. Consequently, any behavior can be changed (Rotter, 1982) and new behaviors acquired. This theory led to a group of therapeutic strategies known as cognitive-behavioral therapies (Bush, 2003) and was used in same-sex group treatment of male offenders, sometimes referred to as psychoeducational groups, to teach anger management skills and encourage new communication, assertiveness, conflict resolution behaviors, and other positive relationship behaviors.

Although there is a scattering of other approaches to domestic violence same-sex group treatment (e.g., modified Duluth model, art therapy, psychodrama, psychodynamic process group, mixed-gender group, or some combination of approaches), these programs have gained little attention from researchers. In the past few years, there has been an increase in the number of same-sex group treatment for female offenders. So far, however, research is lacking in the effectiveness of these groups. Preliminary research suggests that women arrested for partner abuse evidence high levels of psychopathology (Simmons, Lehmann, & Cobb,

2004) but, like male offenders, are a heterogeneous population, ranging from "family only" types with less severe abuse histories to much more violent women with a history of arrests for criminal activity (Babcock, Miller, & Siard, 2003).

Same sex group treatment of men has demonstrated moderate effectiveness in diminishing and eliminating future abuse and violence. My own work with Stacey and Shupe (Shupe et al, 1987; Stacey et al, 1994) on outcomes of a specific psychoeducational model program in Austin, Texas, showed that about 70% (partner's report) versus 82% (men's report) of program completers had not used physical violence on follow-up. Of those who did commit physical violence after program completion, their assaults were either less severe (70%) or about the same (30%) according to partner reports, and 78.5% and 21.5%, respectively, according to men's reports. We also found significant positive differences between program completers and those not completing treatment. Of the follow-up sample of noncompleters, almost 67% of female partners and nearly 45% of men reported continuing physical violence.

Gondolf (2002) found slightly higher rates of reassault of 39% in his multisite study that also used male abuser and female partner reports as well as police arrest records. He concluded that these "well established" programs contributed to short-term cessation of violence and also found that dropouts from these programs, as well as "voluntary" participants, had higher rates of reassault. Even though there were considerably higher rates for verbal abuse and threats, 70% of women on follow-up reported feeling safe with their partner.

A study funded by the National Institute of Justice (Jackson et al., 2003) on two batterer intervention programs, one in Brooklyn, New York, the other in Broward County, Florida, reported similarly low levels of reassault after assignment to one of the two programs but little difference at 6- and 12-month follow-ups when compared to a control group of domestic violence offenders assigned to community service instead of treatment. In studying four experiments using control groups, Bennet and Williams (2001) found that batterer intervention programs have a modest but positive effect on stopping future violence. (Interested readers may want to read chapter 10 in this volume for a review of batterer intervention program outcome studies.) We therefore ought not abandon the batterer intervention model, but, for it to be more effective, it will need significant restructuring and rethinking along the lines of gender-inclusive treatment.

The recognition of the contribution of alcohol and substance abuse and dependency was slow to emerge in same-sex group treatment of domestic violence offenders because of the dominance of the patriarchal model that rejected other possible influences or causal explanations for male violence.

However, there is a large body of evidence showing a robust relationship (if not causation) between these co-occurring conditions. Alcohol, as the most available and socially sanctioned substance, is a factor in at least 50% of violent behaviors (Roy, 1992), and 40% of batterers are classified as heavy or binge drinkers (Kantor & Straus, 1989). A study for the Institute for Teaching and Research on Women (1993) of 232 domestic violence offenders found that 54% used one or more substances, with alcohol being the largest percentage, and 38% reported drinking at the time of the domestic assault. Thirty-nine percent of incarcerated batterers were found to be alcoholic, and all but one of the subjects reported being drunk at the time of the serious assault. More than half the defendants accused of murdering their spouses were drinking, as were almost half the victims (Bureau of Justice Statistics, 1994). Gondolf (2002) found that drunkenness was the most important predictor of reassault for domestic violent offenders in treatment. About 25% of men and women reported alcohol as a factor in creating violent interactions after treatment (Shupe et al., 1987). As Labell (1979) noted,

> Probably the largest contributing factor to domestic violence is alcohol. All major theorists point to the excessive use of alcohol as a key element in the dynamics of wife beating. However, it is not clear whether a man is violent because he is drunk or whether he drinks to reduce his inhibitions against his violent behavior. (p. 264)

A more extensive discussion of this topic can be found in chapter 20 of this volume.

Where legally permissible, significant programmatic changes need to be considered either at the community level, in centralized assessment and referral systems, or at the program level to include gender-inclusive principles. First, assessment should include an interview not only with the identified victim but also, when possible, with the children or other witnesses to the abusive event. This is a process that should be done through police investigation, but too often police educated in the patriarchal view of domestic violence are trained to look for evidence of male wrongdoing rather than ascertain who is the most likely person to have committed the assault, and are too busy or lack the motivation to pursue a more thorough investigation of the facts. This process needs to include a risk assessment that leads to a referral for treatment involving differing approaches and durations.

Also important are attempts to understand couples and family abuse dynamics within a gender-inclusive perspective. I have devised a conflict tactics type of survey in my Domestic Violence Threat Containment Intensive Treatment Program in Austin, Texas, that is based on the Center

TABLE 15.2   Abuse Index Questionnaire, Revised (AI-2)

AI-2

Name: _____   Date: _____

    The following questions are concerned with certain behaviors that you and your partner may engage in. Please respond to the following items by placing the number that best describes how often you do that behavior with your partner in column A. In column B put the number that best describes how often you do the behavior *first* during an interaction with your partner. In column C put the number that best describes how often you think your partner engages in that behavior and in column D place the number that best describes how often your partner does the behavior *first* during an interaction.

Key for columns A and C:

Never	Once	Once a month	2–3 times monthly	Weekly	2–3 times Weekly	Daily
0	1	2	3	4	5	6

Key for columns B and D:

Never	Once	1 in 4 times	Half the time	About 3 in 4 times	Most of the time	All the time
0	1	2	3	4	5	6

What you do: What your partner does to you:

A	B		C	D
___	___	Deny rights to privacy by going through pockets, billfold, purse, mail, etc.	___	___
___	___	Checking up or monitoring social contacts and whereabouts	___	___
___	___	Deny freedom of activities (can you go where you want to?)	___	___
___	___	Deny access to family members	___	___
___	___	Deny access to friends	___	___
___	___	Deny access to jointly held money	___	___
___	___	Deny input on financial decisions	___	___
___	___	Censor phone calls or communications with family and friends	___	___
___	___	Withdraw emotionally as punishment of disapproval	___	___
___	___	Withhold sex as punishment or disapproval	___	___
___	___	Use verbal abuse such as name calling, belittling, insulting, unjust criticism	___	___
___	___	Make verbal threats to use physical violence	___	___
___	___	Hit or destroy household things	___	___
___	___	Damage or destroy personal belongings	___	___
___	___	Physically holding or restraining	___	___
___	___	Pushing or shoving	___	___

(Continued)

TABLE 15.2   (Continued)

___ ___	Throwing household things
___ ___	Throwing household things at someone
___ ___	Slapping
___ ___	Kicking to legs, arms, or body
___ ___	Kicking to head
___ ___	Punching with fist to body
___ ___	Punching with fist to head
___ ___	Burning
___ ___	Forcing sexual activity
___ ___	Choking
___ ___	Biting
___ ___	Making a verbal threat to kill
___ ___	Making a verbal threat to use a weapon
___ ___	Making a verbal threat to use a gun or knife
___ ___	Making a physical threat to use a weapon (object is in hand or close by)
___ ___	Making a physical threat to use a gun or knife (pointed gun or held knife)
___ ___	Used a weapon

Please give specifics (what weapon and how used):_____

Please check each kind of injury you and your partner have had related to physical violence between you.

You have had		Partner has had
___ None		___ None
___ Bruises		___ Bruises
___ Multiple bruises		___ Multiple Bruises
___ Scratches		___ Scratches
___ Cuts		___ Cuts
___ Cuts with Stitches		___ Cuts with stitches
___ Burns		___ Burns
___ Black eye(s)		___ Black eye(s)
___ Bloody nose		___ Bloody nose
___ Split lip		___ Split lip
___ Broken bone(s)	-Please specify-	___ Broken bone(s)
___ Other injuries	-Please specify-	___ Other injuries

Did you have medical treatment for any of these injuries? Please specify below.

Treatment by a physician:
Treatment at the emergency room:
Treatment by EMS at the scene:

Did your partner have medical treatment for any of these injuries? Please specify below.

Treatment by a physician:
Treatment at the emergency room:
Treatment by EMS at the scene:

for Social Research abuse scale (Shupe & Stacey, 1984). It attempts to capture the types of abuse and violence between intimates, who and how often each initiated physical violence, and the types of injuries sustained. It is reproduced in Table 15.2. Each member of the couple completes this scale. This provides important information about couples abuse and differentiates the various types of domestic violence: single unidirectional abuse and violence, escalation of violence from verbal and psychoemotional abuse, and mutual abuse and violence. This type of information is also important in determining a treatment approach.

Treatment should be tailored to client needs, including variation in the duration of same-sex group treatment, depending on the individual's assessment. Those men who commit single acts or mild levels of violence (e.g., restraining, pushing, shoving, or slapping with no history of injury or those using size and strength against their partner when no physical contact is made, as in interfering with a 911 call) are appropriate for short-term approaches, whereas those men who cause higher levels of injury and represent a greater threat need to undergo intermediate or long-term programs. In either case, those leading or supervising batterer intervention program groups who want to apply gender-inclusive and systemic principles must be prepared to listen to men's experiences without defensiveness or ideological positions to protect. Men usually arrive to these groups with resentments, emotional wounds, significant untreated individual/couple/family dysfunction, and alcohol and substance abuse problems.

There is a difference between responsibility and blame. If your demeanor and presentation project blame and fault, you will find it difficult to form any kind of therapeutic alliance with the group members. Taking responsibility for one's thoughts, feelings, and actions is an empowering process that leads to an assumption that one can control oneself, whereas blame and fault produce shame, which can lead to anger and rage. This does not mean that someone who has committed abuse or violence should be protected from the natural emotional consequence of guilt and remorse. It means interacting with men in ways that show that you as the group leader know they are responsible for choosing how they respond to their intimate partner and other family members while validating their own experiences of abuse and injustice.

One method for promoting responsibility taking by group members is to correct language usage from an external agent of control to an internal one. Often a group member will describe his abuse or violence as caused by his intimate partner, as in "She pushed my button," "She put me in jail," or "She made me angry." This can be reframed by asking the person to rephrase their statement using *I,* as in "I reacted when she said or did something" and "I got angry." There are opportunities in many other situations to make linguistic redefinitions of causation. One must continually stress the individual's primary ownership of his behavior without invalidating the reality of the external circumstance or the group member's reaction to it.

Misidentifying the causation of one's responses to external stimuli in interpersonal interactions leads to feelings of powerlessness, produces faulty coping responses, and ends in externalizing blame and attempts to control. If I am made to be angry, I have no control over my response and have to change or control the external cause not to be angry. Most people can easily understand the self-defeating nature of this strategy since control of another person is an impossible task that leads to further frustration and anger. An accurate identification of causation for behavior (i.e., this response was learned in the past) leads to more adaptive responses centered within the individual. Perception, beliefs, cognitions, and behavior can be changed in ways that lead to successful coping with situations the individual experiences as provocative.

Clients court-mandated to a domestic violence program are often resentful. An immediate source of resentment has to do with the criminal justice system, which has precipitated their referral for treatment. It is unadvisable to align oneself with this system since most program participants already see the program and group leader as part of it. One can empathize with a client's resentments toward the criminal justice system while continuing to hold that individual responsible for his or her choices. Assumptions of legal guilt are counterproductive and can lead to power struggles between the client/group and the leader. The high rate of plea bargaining can certainly produce a significant number of false positives for domestic violence, and those referred to treatment from pretrial diversion processes and conditions of bond have not been adjudicated. A group leader can acknowledge these truths without colluding and still hold a participant responsible for the choice of being in the program. After all, one has a choice in our justice system to accept an offer to plead guilty or no contest to a criminal charge for a known outcome or to plead not guilty and risk the consequences, and this can be stressed with those who voice resentment.

Also brought up as a source of resentment is the cost of treatment and the profit motive of the provider. As one man recently stated in group, "I told the judge that the whole thing was just about money and putting asses in classes." These inquiries need to be met honestly and nondefensively even when it is stated in an insulting way. The group leader can respond straightforwardly to these statements —"You're right. I would not be here if I were not being paid"—and for private program providers there is indeed a profit motive like any other business. One does not need to be ashamed of this truth in a capitalistic society.

Another common refrain from men in same-sex groups is, "Why doesn't she have to attend counseling? she's part of the problem too." The group leader can reply that victims of other crimes such as robbery are not required to attend counseling. It can also be pointed out that individual counseling for his intimate partner is available and that couples counseling can be pursued outside the program. A list of referrals is helpful, especially those that include low-fee or sliding scale–fee options. The group leader also needs to redirect this inquiry and reiterate that the group program has the specific goal of eliminating abuse and violence and is not intended as a cure for all problems in a couple or family (Hamel, 2005).

A corollary complex of complaints about intimate partners of men in group who are in intact relationships includes: "I'm changing but she isn't," "She won't let me leave when I get too angry," "She threatens to call the police if I don't do what she wants," and "I'm afraid she might make a false accusation." In my clinical experience, these complaints are reasonable and often true. A response from the group leader that says verbally or nonverbally that "I don't believe you" or "I'm not interested" is counterproductive to positive change. If a program is having contact with the partner at intake, program strategies can include dispensing advice such as, "When he gets too angry and may become abusive or violent, he is instructed to leave the scene, and we really need your help in allowing him to leave. This is for your safety." The group leader can encourage a man to continue his efforts by pointing out that he is part of a system and that a change initiated in any part of the system leads to adaptation and change by other components of the system and that it may take time before he sees success from his efforts. Typically, there are small, unnoticeable incremental changes that are taking place but are unnoticed until the change accumulates to a level that is recognizable. Another group strategy is to point out the man's choice of leaving the relationship if he is fearful of his partner making false accusations against him or threatening to call the police for nonviolent acts of which she disapproves. Not only does this intervention provide a viable option on which he may take action, but it also serves to uncover important issues of dependency.

Recent interactions in one of my men's groups provide a good example of this process.

CASE EXAMPLE 1

Carlos had complained for several group sessions about the verbally abusive, threatening, controlling, and physically aggressive behaviors of his intimate partner, Yolanda. His complaints were serious, and he was obviously upset over her yelling, insults, regular accusations of sexual infidelity, taking his cellular phone and going through the telephone numbers on calls he made and received, and threatening to call the police and have him arrested. He denied any physical violence in his response, but he admitted at times he yelled back and called Yolanda names. Each time Carlos brought these complaints to group, an intervention was attempted to help him focus on himself and how he responded to these incidents of abuse. He was required to own his response by using "I statements"; his stop signs were readjusted to be aware of his anger before he yelled or used verbal abuse, and he was helped to identify the vulnerable feeling(s) under his anger and asked to communicate these feelings to Yolanda. The last intervention completely failed, considering that she was not understanding of his feelings or remorseful for the impact her behavior had on him. Carlos reported that she responded in no uncertain terms that he was weak for expressing these feelings and made fun of him for not acting like a man and just taking it. His report of her reaction was difficult to believe, and a partner contact monitoring was initiated to get her side of this interaction.

When contacted, Yolanda was furious that she was asked about this and screamed a few expletives and hung up. In subsequent group sessions, Carlos was asked why he stayed in this relationship, in which there was regular verbal and emotional abuse and threats to send him to jail by a false allegation of violence. His peers in group also questioned his reasons for staying and urged him to leave. This prompted an insightful discussion of his dependencies on Yolanda, his fears of being alone, the unusual dynamics of their relationship, and his beliefs about himself and love. Although Carlos separated from Yolanda after a particularly bad period in which he stated he could no longer take the ongoing yelling and insults between them, he returned two weeks later when she called him many times a day telling him to do so. She also came to his job site. I had urged him to at least get a commitment from Yolanda to attend relationship counseling before he agreed to return, but she refused. However, this intervention had some positive outcomes. For example, he now chooses to stay in this relationship and no longer feels stuck without a choice, and he also admits there are dysfunctional dynamics at work both within himself and in their relationship that he hopes to change over time. In short, Carlos is beginning to take responsibility for his life.

The use of intimate partner contact monitoring should be an indispensable part of any program that seeks to use gender-inclusive principles in men's group treatment. However, contact with the identified victim may be difficult in domestic violence treatment communities that support separation strategies or in jurisdictions where there are legal prohibitions against this procedure. Partner contact monitoring provides a means to check out the veracity of men's statements in group, yielding valuable information about the current level of abuse, and is indispensable in safety planning and the implementation of other interventions for the partner. It helps the provider to learn about important couples dynamics and to make referrals for alcohol and substance abuse problems and for individual and couples counseling, and it provides information for partners about the treatment program.

CASE EXAMPLE 2

As a result of his third domestic assault, which had been enhanced to a felony, the court referred Dale to the Domestic Violence Threat Containment Intensive Treatment Program. During the intake and screening process, he denied responsibility for the current domestic assault but admitted being abusive and violent in other incidents. He also reported that his wife, Debbie, often initiated physical violence by throwing things at him or hitting him. He described the most common process of violence and abuse as almost always occurring when he and Debbie drank. He stated that sometimes when they became intoxicated, Debbie would accuse him of having affairs or interest in other women. She sometimes would threaten to call the police and report an assault to punish him. He would deny these accusations or refuse to talk with her about them, fearful that this would lead to an escalation and end in violence or being arrested. He reported that when he tried to leave the scene, as a previous domestic violence prevention program had instructed him, Debbie would block the doorway, cling to him, hide the car keys, and increase her threats to call the police. There had been at least 10 calls to the police, and he had been arrested four times. Dale felt trapped in his marriage of 12 years. He loved his wife and wanted to be a full-time father to his children.

When Debbie was contacted as part of the intake and screening process to get her description of events at home, she readily admitted that when she drank too much, she sometimes accused Dale of messing around on her. She stated that Dale had an affair before they got married and that she had not been able to get over it completely and trust him again. As far as she knew, he had not had another affair, although she thought about it a lot. She also admitted that she often started the fights by throwing things and trying to slap his face. Sometimes, he would get angry with her and retaliate by pushing her away from him and had on some occasions hit her back. When asked about what role their drinking played in their conflicts, she denied having a drinking problem but stated that she did experience more intense fear of Dale having an affair when drinking. She felt guilty about getting Dale in trouble and complained that prosecutors would not drop the case as she requested.

Debbie was asked to let Dale leave the scene if he got too angry or upset, knowing that he would return when he had calmed down. She was also told that this was a temporary strategy and that the program hoped to give Dale better ways to communicate and resolve the problems in their marriage. She agreed to allow this "time-out" to keep disagreements from escalating to abuse or violence. Subsequent to partner monitoring, Debbie was given referrals for AA women's groups and encouraged to understand why she was fearful and angry with Dale for his past affair. During one monitoring, she talked about her parents' split and her father's alcoholism. It was suggested that there might be a connection between that family-of-origin experience and her current fears of abandonment. She accepted a referral to her employee assistance program (EAP) to help her understand this possible connection with her current marital problems.

Dale had to be challenged and confronted in group several times for viewing Debbie and her jealousy and drinking as the cause of his problems with past violence and abuse. He was asked to make "I statements" when describing his relationship, and as he continued the group program, he was able to examine his angry response to his wife's accusations and threats. He came to realize that he felt hurt by Debbie's accusations of infidelity and helpless at his inability to earn her trust. He was given a homework assignment to talk with Debbie (when she was not drinking) about his feelings and to listen to her response without interruption.

On the next monitoring call, Debbie reported improvement in her marriage. She gave credit to Dale for expressing his feelings and stopping drinking. She also stated that she had followed through with EAP counseling and now realized the role she and her own drinking had played in past escalations of conflict. She had begun to attend a women's AA group at the added urging of her EAP counselor and was confronting her drinking problem.

At the last monitoring, Debbie reported no violence and little verbal abuse in their marriage. She stated that Dale usually did not have to leave the scene and that they were talking over issues that had been overshadowed by their drinking and fighting in the past. She expressed little fear of Dale or of future violence.

About a year later, Dale and Debbie sent a card thanking the program for the help they had received. They were alcohol abstinent and reported no significant escalation of arguments. Trust had returned to their marriage.

REFERENCES

Babcock, J., Miller, S., & Siard, C. (2003). Toward a typology of abusive women: Differences between partner-only and generally violent women in the use of violence. *Psychology of Women Quarterly, 13*, 46–59.

Bard, M. (1970). *Training police as specialists in family crisis intervention* (NCJ 50). Washington, DC: U.S. Department of Justice, Law Enforcement Assistance Administration.

Bennet, L., & Williams, O. (2001). Intervention programs for men who batter. In C. M. Renzetti & E. L. Edleson (Eds.), *Sourcebook on violence against women* (pp. 261–267). Newbury Park, CA: Sage.

Binder, A., & Meeker, J. S. (1992). On the implications of the domestic violence experiment replications: Comment. *American Sociological Review, 58*(6), 886–888.

Boland, B., Brady, E., Tyson, H., & Bassler, J. (1982). *The prosecution of felony arrests.* Washington, DC: Institute for Law and Research.

Breen, R. N. (1985). Premarital abuse: A study of abuse within dating relationships of college students. Unpublished manuscript, University of Texas at Arlington, Arlington, Texas.

Bureau of Justice Statistics. (1994). *Violence against women* (NCJ NCJ-149259). Washington, DC: Author.

Bush, J. W. (2003). *Learning theory: A fuller explanation of cognitive behavioral therapy.* New York: Institute of Cognitive Behavioral Therapy.

Campbell, J. (1986). Nursing assessment for risk of homicide with battered women. *Advances in Nursing Science, 8*(4), 36–51.

Campbell, J., Webster, D., Koziol-Mclain, J., Block, C., Campbell, D., Curry, M., et al. (2003). Risk factors for femicide in abusive relationships: Results from a multisite case control study. *American Journal of Public Health, 93*(7), 1089–1097.

Dobash, R. E., & Dobash, R. P. (1979). *Violence against wives: A case against the patriarchy.* New York: Free Press.

Dutton, D. (1998). *The abusive personality: Violence and control in intimate relationships.* New York: Guilford Press.

Dutton, D., & Kroop, R. (2000). A review of domestic violence risk instruments. *Trauma, Violence and Abuse, 1*(2), 171–181.

Erez, E. (2002). Domestic violence and the criminal justice system: An overview. *Online Journal of Issues in Nursing, 7*(1), manuscript 3. Retrieved June 17, 2005, from http://www.nursingworld.org/ojin/topic17/tpc17_3.htm.

Erez, E., & Belknap, J. (1995). Policing domestic violence. In W. Bailey (Ed.), *Encyclopedia of police science* (2nd ed., pp. 223–231). New York: Garland.

Gondolf, E. (2002). *Batterer intervention systems: Issues, outcomes and recommendations.* Thousand Oaks, CA: Sage.

Hamel, J. (2005). *Gender-inclusive treatment of intimate partner abuse: A comprehensive approach.* New York: Springer.

Hart, B. (1990). Assessing whether batterers will kill. *Pennsylvania Coalition Against Domestic Violence.* Retrieved September 4, 2005, from www.mincava.umn.edu/documents/hart/hart.html.

Institute for Teaching and Research on Women. (1993, Spring). Domestic violence and substance abuse. *ITROW News, 3*(1), 7.

Jackson, S., Feder, L., Forde, D., Davis, R., Maxwell, C., & Taylor, B. (2003). *Batterer intervention programs: Where do we go from here?* National Institute of Justice, NIJ 195079.

Kantor, G., & Straus, M. A. (1989). Substance abuse as a precipitant of wife abuse victimizations. *American Journal of Drug and Alcohol Abuse 15*, 173–189.

Labell, L. S. (1979). Wife abuse: A sociological study of battered women and their mates. *Victimology, 4*(2), 258–267.

Meloy, R. (1992). *Violent attachments.* Northvale, NJ: Jason Aronson.

Pence, E., & Paymar, M. (1986). *Power and control: Tactics of men who batter.* Duluth, MN: Program Development, Inc.

Roehl, J., & Guertin, K. (2002). Intimate partner violence: The current use of risk assessments in sentencing offenders. *Justice System Journal, 21*(2), 171–198.

Rotter, J. B. (1982). *The development and application of social learning theory.* New York: Praeger.

Roy, M. (1992). *Children in the crossfire: Violence in the home: How does it affect our children?* Deerfield Beach, FL: Health Communications, Inc.

Sherman, L. (1992). *Policing domestic violence.* New York: Free Press.

Shupe, A., & Stacey, W. (1984). *The family secret: Domestic violence in America.* New York: Farrar, Straus and Giroux.

Shupe, A., Stacey, W., & Hazlewood, L. (1987). *Violent men, violent couples: The dynamics of domestic violence.* Lexington, MA: D.C. Heath.

Simmons, C., Lehmann, P., & Cobb, N. (2004, September 18). *Personality profiles and attitudes toward violence of women arrested for domestic violence: How they differ from and are similar to men arrested for domestic violence.* Paper presented at the FVSAI 9th International Conference on Family Violence, San Diego, California.

Stacey, W., Hazlewood, L., & Shupe, A. (1994). *The violent couple.* Westport, CT: Praeger.

Straus, M. A., Gelles, R. J., & Steinmetz, S. (1980). *Behind closed doors: Violence in the American family.* Garden City, NY: Anchor.

Weisz, A. N., Tolman, R. M., & Saunders, D. G. (2000). Assessing the risk of severe domestic violence: The importance of survivors' predictions. *Journal of Interpersonal Violence, 15*(1), 75–90.

CHAPTER 16

Treatment of Psychological and Physical Aggression in a Couple Context

K. Daniel O'Leary and Shiri Cohen

WHO ARE APPROPRIATE CANDIDATES FOR TREATING AGGRESSION CONJOINTLY?

Men and women who are in relationships characterized by psychological aggression and infrequent, mild levels of physical aggression are good candidates for conjoint treatment in a dyadic context. These individuals are often physically aggressive only against their partners, and they are often those who seek therapy for marital problems. Further, they would not voluntarily seek out help in batterers programs, and they would often drop out of such programs if mandated to them. In relationships characterized by infrequent and mild levels of physical aggression, the psychological and physical aggression is typically engaged in by both partners (O'Leary, Vivian, & Malone, 1992). While outcome studies have not yet evaluated services for only mild and infrequent physical aggression, these individuals appear to be the very ones for whom interventions could prevent escalation to more serious and frequent aggression (O'Leary & Vega, 2005). And controlled outcome research with no treatment or delayed treatment control groups would be more feasible with such populations.

In a related fashion, Hamel (2005) describes treatment options as indicated according to the type of violence, and he argues that couples interventions by clinicians who are experienced in partner violence dynamics are appropriate for couples in which there is mutual aggression by both partners and high-conflict violence (defined as verbal and symbolic aggression, or aggression leading to negligible or no injury). Furthermore, conjoint or dyadic treatment is contraindicated in cases of unilateral or mutual severe battering (Hamel, 2005).

We do not believe that men or women who cause significant injury and engender fear in their partners are appropriate candidates for therapy in a conjoint context. There are no empirical outcome data regarding fear and injury predicting outcome of couples therapy, but our clinical experience and data to be described here lead us to believe that such individuals are not appropriate candidates for treatment in a couple context. Men who engage in such behaviors are described as batterers (Jacobson & Gottman, 1998), and, in our opinion, they need individual help and/or need to be the subject of legal actions. While less frequently an issue, a similar standard should apply to women; namely, if she has injured her partner in a serious way or caused fear in the partner, she is not an appropriate candidate for therapy in a couple context. Fear of the partner should be assessed individually, especially the female in heterosexual relationships and the one who seems less powerful in homosexual relationships. We also recommend that information on fear of the partner be obtained both in an interview and in a self-report format, and we have a self-report assessment designed for this purpose (Cohen & O'Leary, 2005).

As we have reviewed elsewhere, pretreatment symptomatology has been shown to predict reduced responsiveness, higher dropout rates, and greater relapse for many psychosocial and psychopharmacological interventions, such as those for social phobia, depression, panic disorder, obsessive-compulsive disorder, eating disorders, and cocaine addiction (Woodin & O'Leary, 2006). Given the generality of this finding, it should not be surprising that pretreatment levels of physical aggression would also predict posttreatment and follow-up levels of physical aggression against a partner. In the context of an evaluation of treatment for partner aggression, we found that elevated aggression levels in the year and weeks before treatment were associated with a range of aggression indices at posttreatment and one-year follow-up. At pretreatment, higher levels of mild and severe physical aggression placed both husbands and wives at greater risk for continued elevated mild and severe aggression during treatment and in the following year. In addition, psychological aggression by the wife at pretreatment was associated with elevated levels of husband and wife psychological and physical aggression at the posttreatment time points, even when controlling for levels of husband aggression at pretreatment (Woodin & O'Leary, 2006). Therefore, we believe that treatment in a couple context should take place when the physical aggression has not been very frequent.

In addition, men and women who have very little control of their anger outbursts at home or in a therapy session are not good candidates for treatment in a couple context since psychological aggression perpetrated by women was a predictor of their own physical aggression both cross sectionally and longitudinally (Woodin & O'Leary, 2006). As reflected in a large meta-analysis of all published studies in which men's and women's behavior was coded in a conjoint problem-solving task, women showed more displays of negative affect (e.g., critical comments and demandingness) (Woodin, 2006). Thus, a clinician should be especially attuned to the ways in which the female may not be able to control her own anger since anger outburst by either party can lead to deleterious escalation of verbal aggression, and anger outbursts have negative impacts on both marital satisfaction and partner aggression.

WHAT EVIDENCE SUPPORTS A COUPLE-BASED APPROACH?

There is a body of literature that strongly suggests that treatment of men and/or women who are physically aggressive in a couple context is useful. Two studies have compared gender-specific treatments with treatments in a couple context when both interventions were delivered in a multicouple group format (Brannen & Rubin, 1996; O'Leary, Heyman, & Neidig, 1999). Both studies showed significant reductions in physical aggression following both treatment formats, and in the latter study there was evidence that men took more responsibility for their aggressive behavior. Further, the O'Leary et al. study showed that women's aggression was reduced as well as men's aggression, and they were not different from one another at pre- or posttreatment.

There are no controlled outcome studies with random assignment to waiting list control groups or no-treatment groups for physically aggressive behavior, but Stith and her colleagues (Stith, Rosen, McCollum, & Thomsen, 2004) compared treatment in a couple context with a nonrandomly assigned control group of nine couples who were eligible for treatment but did not attend the treatment. Couples treatment took place in a multicouple group therapy and in an individual couple format. At six months follow-up, recidivism of the multicouple treatment ($n = 16$) fared better (25%) than the comparison group ($n = 9$), who had a recidivism rate of 66%. However, the recidivism (43%) of individual couple treatment ($n = 14$) was not different from the comparison ($n = 9$) group (66%). And the individual and multicouple group did not differ from one another at six months follow-up. In the two-year follow-up, the recidivism was as follows: multicouple (13%; $n = 8$), individual couple (0%; $n = 11$), and comparison group (50%; n = 4). While the n's in the different groups are small and one can reach only tentative conclusions based on the research, the data suggest that the couples therapy in either format has positive effects on reducing men's aggression against partners.

In addition, Christensen and his colleagues (Doss, Thum, Sevier, Atkins, & Christensen, 2005) have compared marital therapy of an acceptance variety (called integrative behavior couples therapy) and a standard cognitive-behavioral marital therapy. Couples were accepted into treatment if they were martially discordant, and couples were screened out if they had moderate to severe violence as reported by the wife (more than six episodes of mild levels of physical aggression in the past year [pushing, shoving, grabbing]; more than two episodes of moderate physical aggression in the past year [slapping] or any episode of severe physical aggression (beating, use of knife or gun) ever in the relationship. The study was a large outcome intervention, and in subsidiary analyses presented at a conference (Simpson & Christensen, 2004), physical aggression was used as a predictor of treatment outcome. Both the acceptance therapy and the standard behavior marital therapy led to significant improvements in marital satisfaction. A dichotomous measure of physical aggression did not predict outcome when outcome was measured as marital satisfaction or divorce. Psychological aggression decreased in the intervention, although physical aggression did not (probably because it was at such a low level initially). Thus, therapy can take place in a couple context where some levels of physical aggression exist without its having adverse consequences and in fact having positive outcomes.

The intervention that is couple based can take place with one therapist and a couple or with a therapist(s) and a group of couples. While our own outcome research has been on couples in groups, treatment in our clinic is for individual couples. Murphy and Eckhardt (2005) have presented arguments regarding why treatment in a group format may be less effective than providing such treatments in a nongroup format. Basically, the group format is not flexible regarding topics covered, and the formation of groups per se often presents major problems for serving clients. Further, an individual intake approach that used a motivational interview format fared better in stimulating client involvement in treatment than an intake approach relying on a group format. However, at this point there is almost no research addressing this treatment comparison.

ARGUMENTS FOR TREATING PSYCHOLOGICAL AND PHYSICAL AGGRESSION IN A COUPLE CONTEXT

A main argument for using a treatment in a couple context is that marital problems are one of the biggest risk factors for partner aggression.

For example, Pan, Neidig, and O'Leary (1994) found that marital problems dramatically raised the risk for men's physical aggression against a partner. In a sample of 11,000 military men, for every 20% increase in marital discord, the odds of being mildly physically aggressive increased by 102%, and the odds of being severely aggressive increased by 183%. In numerous studies, marital problems have correlated highly with partner aggression. Further, arguments between partners are the single most important precipitating event preceding physical aggression against a partner. And, if one could reduce arguments in a relationship, it makes logical sense that physical aggression could thereby be reduced.

A second argument for conjoint treatment is that many studies with community samples have shown that physical aggression is as commonly engaged in by women as by men, suggesting the possibility that, in many couples, the aggression is not a one-sided problem but one of a dyadic nature occurring as a result of dynamics within the couple. The conclusion that women engage in physical aggression as much as men in intimate relationships was reached more than two decades ago by Straus, Gelles, and Steinmetz (1980) in the first large representative community sample study of approximately 2,000 individuals. This result was replicated in a follow-up to that study a decade later (Straus & Gelles, 1990). Further, a meta-analysis largely of community and nonclinical samples (i.e., not of battered women) shows that this conclusion has held up across a wide range of studies (Archer, 2000). In a sample of engaged partners from the community, we found that women were at least as likely as men to engage in physical aggression through the first 30 months of marriage (O'Leary et al., 1989). Further, research by others found similar results with newlyweds in the United States (Lawrence & Bradbury, 2001; O'Leary, Barling, Arias, Rosenbaum & Tyree, 1989; Straus, 1993) and New Zealand (Moffitt, Robins, & Caspi, 2001). The findings that women engage in aggression equally as much as men suggests that treating this problem with gender-specific approaches for both partners may not address the dynamics within the relationship that contribute to their aggressive behavior.

Some qualifications about this conclusion are in order, and they have been noted in an earlier discussion on the prevalence of aggression issue (Archer, 2000). The conclusion that women are as likely to physically aggress as men does not generalize to sexual aggression in community samples (O'Leary, 2000). Although based on limited data, males report engaging in sexual aggression more frequently than females (White & Kowalski, 1994). A second qualification regarding the relatively high percentage of women who engage in physical aggression against their partners is that various studies with community samples have shown that men are more likely to inflict injury than women. This has been found with dating (Foshee, 1996), community (Stets & Straus, 1990), marital therapy (Cascardi, Langhinrichsen, & Vivian, 1992), and mandated treatment samples (Cantos, Neidig, & O'Leary, 1994). In one study of young couples from a representative sample in which there was no overall difference in percentages of men and women who engaged in physical aggression (Ehrensaft, Moffitt, & Caspi, 2004), women who reported being in a physically abusive relationship were significantly more likely than men to have needed medical care (24% of women vs. 3% of men, $p < .05$). However, it is also important to emphasize that the vast majority of women in community samples who report that their partners engaged in physical aggression against them do not report injuries (Stets & Straus, 1990).

A third argument for conjoint treatment is that the strongest predictor of physical aggression by men is physical and/or psychological aggression by women and vice versa. A number of investigators have found that if physical aggression occurs within a dyad, it tends to be engaged in by both partners in the dyad. Most measures of physical aggression against the partner, such as the Conflict Tactics Scales (Straus, Hamby, Boney-McCoy, & Sugarman, 1996), assess whether acts of physical aggression have occurred within the past year. Finer-grained measurement of dyads is needed to determine how many incidents of mutual physical aggression occur. However, one way to obtain an overall idea of the mutuality of aggression is to examine the extent to which physical aggression is engaged in over a year by men only, women only, or both (Straus, 1993). Using the self-reports of women in the National Family Violence Survey who reported the presence of any physical aggression in the dyad, the husband alone was physically aggressive in 26% of the cases, the wife alone was physically aggressive in 26% of the cases, and both partners were physically aggressive in approximately 48% of the cases. Even when Straus examined reports by wives who indicated that severe physical aggression occurred, the percentages of severe physical aggression by males only was 35%, by females 29%, and by both 35%.

Several additional arguments for conjoint treatment have been proffered by Stith, Rosen, and McCollum (2003). First, typological classifications of batterers suggest that family-only batterers with little psychopathology or violence outside the home may be amenable to conjoint treatment approaches (Holtzworth-Munroe & Stuart, 1994). Second, men-only treatment groups may inadvertently lead some men to support one another's negative attitudes and aggressive behaviors toward women, resulting in an iatrogenic effect and potentially placing some women at greater risk of harm (e.g., Edleson & Tolman, 1992).

SCREENING APPROPRIATE CLIENTS FOR COUPLE TREATMENT

In selecting clients for couple treatment designed to reduce psychological and physical aggression, we suggest that all individuals have interviews and that they complete standardized self-report assessments. Our interviews follow a format in which individuals are asked about the following:

Precipitants of coming for treatment now
Major problems in the marriage
Major psychological problems of each partner (e.g., depression, mania, anger outbursts)
Presence or absence of drug use, alcohol abuse, and affairs
Extent of psychological and physical aggression

Standardized assessments would include the Conflict Tactics Scales 2 (CTS2) to assess psychological and physical aggression as well as injury (Straus et al., 1996). The CTS2 assesses sexual aggression, but it had very low internal consistency in a large community sample, whereas the psychological and physical aggression scales had strong internal consistencies (O'Leary & Williams, in press). Further, we have found that the test–retest reports of psychological and physical aggression were over .70 (Vega & O'Leary, in press). The CTS2 had higher internal consistencies in a dating sample on the sexual aggression scale than found in a community sample, but the community sample is much more similar to a sample of married individuals who would be seeking treatment. If the clinician is concerned about the presence of significant sexual aggression, it would be useful to consider scales such as that of Koss and Gidycz (1985) and a variation of the Koss scale used by Meyer, Vivian, and O'Leary (1998).

In addition, we suggest that both partners complete a self-report assessment of fear of the partner's physical and emotional abuse. We also believe that it is important to assess whether a partner fears expressing his or her opinion in a therapy session and specifically of how the information expressed might be used against him or her later. We recommend that a clinician screen out couples in which one partner is fearful of the other in any one or more of these realms (physical aggression, emotional abuse, and expression of opinions in therapy and consequences thereof) since treatment in a dyadic context relies on the ability of partners to be able to communicate with one another. Our assessment is a 25-item self-report scale that has high internal consistency (total scale: $\alpha = 0.90$; subscales: $\alpha = 0.72$ physical/sexual abuse; $\alpha = 0.90$ emotional abuse; $\alpha = 0.92$ expression) and good construct validity (Cohen & O'Leary, 2005).

We also routinely have both partners complete some standardized assessment of overall relationship satisfaction. A measure that has become a standard in the field is the Dyadic Adjustment Scale (DAS; Spanier, 1976), a 32-item measure of overall satisfaction. For clinical purposes, one can simply use the single one-item, global assessment of relationship quality of the DAS. Other measures include the Quality of Marriage Index, which is a six-item assessment (Norton, 1983) that will provide one with an overall assessment of marital quality.

A DYADIC TREATMENT MODEL

The focus of our treatment is to help spouses reduce and/or eliminate psychological and physical aggression in the home (O'Leary et al., 1999). Other purposes include having each partner accept responsibility for his or her own psychologically and physically aggressive behavior. Alternatively stated, our goal is to have each individual accept responsibility for escalation of angry interchanges and resulting physical aggression. In addition, the therapist strives to have the men and women recognize and control self-angering thoughts, to communicate more effectively, and to increase caring and mutually pleasurable activities. Finally, the therapists work with clients to help them treat their partners with respect. In contrast to gender-specific treatments for reducing physical aggression against a partner, in the dyadic treatment model each partner is held responsible for his or her own contribution to the process of conflict escalation. And, importantly, each partner is held responsible for his or her physical aggression. While the greater impact of physical aggression of men against women is emphasized, the negative consequences of physical aggression by either partner are also stressed.

OVERVIEW OF TREATMENT PROGRAM

While our treatment program is not a family treatment per se in that it does not directly treat the children of aggressive partners, we routinely emphasize the children as a critical motivational factor for parents to cease their aggressive behavior. More specifically, we stress to both parents the potential and likely danger of their children modeling their aggressive behavior in the future and thereby continuing the cycle of violence. We believe that this allows the couple to see the truly toxic nature of their own behavior, and the emphasis of the adverse effects of modeling aggressive behavior often provides a powerful source of motivation for change.

As will be discussed in greater depth in the description of the intervention process itself, it is important to address specific problems that are important to each specific couple. However, it is important to note that there are several overarching goals that are important in therapy for couples. While specific issues may vary, most will typically fit into one of the broader goals of the program:

1. Decreasing psychological aggression
2. Decreasing/eliminating physical aggression
3. Increasing hope for and commitment to the relationship
4. Increasing overall satisfaction with the relationship
5. Increasing positive/loving feelings

The treatment program described herein is based on 15 to 20 one-hour conjoint sessions, although the course of therapy may vary, depending on the needs of the individual couple, and the length of the sessions may vary, depending on the couple. In the next several sections, we describe the various stages of our treatment program, with an emphasis on the initial and middle stages of treatment. The latter stages are only briefly summarized.

INITIAL STAGES OF TREATMENT

Establishing a Therapeutic Bond

Across various types of therapy, the therapeutic bond has been shown to be a significant factor in the success or failure of treatment. In the marital therapy arena, Johnson and Talitman (1997) found that the strength of the therapeutic alliance was a positive predictor of posttreatment marital satisfaction, accounting for 22% of the variance. In couples therapy, it has been argued that treatment works optimally when there is a positive alliance between each spouse and the therapist (Pinsof & Catherall, 1986). And the formation of a positive alliance has proven of value in predicting decreases in husband-to-wife psychological aggression as well as mild and severe physical aggression (Brown & O'Leary, 2000).

It is particularly important for the therapist to generate a sense that the clients are liked and their opinions valued. In response to dealing with issues of anger and aggression in relationships, the therapist will necessarily impose some value judgments on the relationship (e.g., aggression is clearly inappropriate and unacceptable; each partner should take responsibility for maladaptive elements of his or her own behavior rather than blaming and attempting to change his or her partner). However, as a therapist, it is important to be able to express caring and concern without being overly judgmental (i.e., imposing value judgments in areas that clearly do not affect the health, safety, and well-being of the clients). The dropout rate in some treatment programs for batterers is 50% or higher, and some research indicates that part of the reason for dropouts is a sense that the therapist is judging the client as wholly culpable for all the arguments and all the aggression in the relationship (Murphy & Baxter, 1997).

In addition, in many cases only one partner is highly motivated to seek therapy, while the other partner attends largely because of pressure from his or her partner. In such cases, it is necessary to establish an alliance with the partner who appears less committed to therapy while being careful not to alienate the other partner. Many marital therapists have addressed this issue (e.g., Rathus & Sanderson, 1999). Similarly, it is not uncommon for one member of the dyad to attempt to engage the therapist in a manner that elicits his or her approval as if to gain an ally against the other partner, a process often called "triangulation." Insofar as possible, the therapist should try to develop equal levels of rapport with each partner, provide relatively equal time for each partner to speak, and steer couples away from a blaming attitude toward a focus on making personal changes to improve the relationship.

Examining the Origins of Each Partner's Interacting Styles

Many of the interaction patterns between partners may be rooted in each partner's earlier relationships, as these early and sometimes formative relationships often serve to provide a template for later interaction styles with romantic partners. It seems to us that in order to help partners reduce negative interaction patterns, it is helpful for them to have an understanding of the ways in which they interact and to understand the origin of their interaction patterns. Toward this goal, questions like the following become relevant:

How did your mother and father interact?
What was your style of interacting with your partner when you first met him or her, and how did that change across time?
Do you have a style that you believe is domineering and/or critical? (What parts of your interpersonal style might be seen as domineering and/or critical?)

There can be great utility in assisting clients to understand their own personality and interaction style, how they developed that particular style, how they may be predisposed to interpret input from others, and how they may tend to be perceived by others. Often people have a very poor understanding of how others perceive them. Thus, if a person can be helped to see that others experience them as "dominant yet affectionate" or as "dominant and aloof," they may begin to reevaluate desirable areas of personal change. In addition, the emphasis on each person as an individual is a way to minimize the tendency of many clients to blame their partner for their marital problems.

It is often the case that recognizing and labeling personal characteristics (e.g., recognizing oneself as "critical and having a bad temper") can help provide lasting effects, even after one leaves therapy. Often, the therapeutic process falls into the trap of simply solving the "problem of the day," while long-term themes are lost or the need for long-term change is ignored. As such, it may be important for the client to have a mental self-image or self-labels that are accurate. With the aid of self-labels based on realistic feedback, the client may be able to self-correct his or her behavior more readily than if he or she did not have such labels.

Developing a Mutually Agreed-On Treatment Plan: Goals and Methods of Treatment

At the beginning of treatment, the therapist should explain the rationale for treating aggression in a couples context, including an explanation of the dyadic nature of aggression between partners. It is likely that, in any relationship, each partner will sometimes act, whether intentionally or inadvertently, in a manner that is hurtful to the other partner. This program is designed to identify and reduce these behaviors, which we feel are at least partly rooted and maintained in a dyadic context.

The overarching method of helping the clients reach their goals is dyadic; that is, this therapeutic model utilizes both partners. It does not attempt to achieve relationship goals through individual therapy, though in some cases adjunctive individual therapy may be useful or necessary. Clients often enter marital therapy with the goal of prompting the therapist to identify the partner as the one in need of help. While partner blaming must be avoided so as to help each partner take responsibility for his or her own behavior, there are, in fact, occasions in which one partner may need individual therapy as a precursor or as a continuing adjunct to relationship therapy. For example, individuals with bipolar disorders, severe depression, obsessive-compulsive behaviors, or other psychiatric and/or personality disorders will need treatment outside the context of relationship therapy. However, in many cases, dyadic therapy can proceed even when individual problems have an impact on the relationship. Halford (2001) has written cogently about the ways in which marital clients can learn to help themselves. Such an emphasis in therapy can help change the focus from partner blaming to focus on oneself. Since partner blaming has been shown to be etiologically related to the development of marital discord (Bradbury & Fincham, 1990), it is important to reduce partner blame whenever possible. In order to place emphasis on the individuals rather than on the partner, the therapist must take a very active role in pursuing with each partner the question, "What are you willing to change to improve yourself and the relationship?"

Finally, agreement on the methods of achieving the therapeutic goals is important so that the clients know what will be expected of them. They also need to know that we place emphasis on individual contributions to solving relationship problems. They should know that repeated blaming of the other partner for all the relationship problems will interfere with therapeutic progress. Finally, the therapist and clients must agree on ground rules for therapy, including a focus on personal responsibility for one's own behavior, examination of the impact that one's behavior has on the partner, and the importance of communicating in an open, honest, and respectful way.

Establishing Hope

To inspire confidence in them and in the treatment program, therapists should discuss the extent to which they know that the kinds of problems presented by the client can be changed. A therapist should be able to address the issue of establishing hope for an individual or a couple after having done the following:

1. Discovered how much caring/love still exists
2. Discovered how much marital discord exists
3. Discovered how committed the individuals are to the relationship

Knowing how the two partners feel about these matters, the therapist should provide the clients with as much *realistic* hope as possible. Since hope appears to be central to success in many kinds of therapy, the therapist should provide specific information to the clients about the reasons that he or she believes that there is hope in the relationship. Experienced therapists can often rely on past cases and positive changes that they have seen. Less experienced therapists can express knowledge of the current literature on relationship therapy and describe the kinds of change that are typically found with such therapy. For example, reducing psychological aggression has been documented to increase marital satisfaction (O'Leary et al., 1999), and there is a large body of literature showing that couples therapy can increase relationship satisfaction (Jacobson & Addis, 1993; Shadish, Ragsdale, Glaser, & Montgomery, 1995).

MIDSTAGES OF TREATMENT

Teaching Time-Outs in Session

Given that couples in need of this treatment program are likely to have basic communication difficulties, compounded by problems with self-control of impulses and/or anger escalation, it is vital to prevent session dialogues from becoming damaging in any way. Accordingly, each partner should begin to accept responsibility for removing him or herself from situations prior to becoming psychologically or physically aggressive. Although it is obviously more ideal for the partners to be able to continue discussing an issue until a resolution is reached, this will not always be possible, especially in the earlier stages of therapy. As such, couples may implement a policy of taking time-outs if either partner feels that they may soon become aggressive or if either partner becomes uncomfortable with the interaction at hand.

Initially, the therapist should be responsible for imposing time-outs when he or she observes that the couple is beginning to escalate. When a time-out is imposed in session, the therapist should make clear why a time-out is necessary, which partner should leave the room and for how long (i.e., either a specified amount of time or until the partner feels fully calmed down), and what each partner can be thinking about in terms of their contribution to the escalation. This serves as a model for how the partners can begin to use time-outs on their own outside of session. When conducted outside of session, it is important for partners to agree with each other on how and when time-outs will be taken. For example, in initiating a time-out period, the initiating partner should state that he or she needs a time-out and should articulate for how long he or she will be away (typically no more than 2 hours), where he or she will be, when he or she will return. It is also important that both parties agree to readdress the issue within 24 hours after the time-out.

Increasing Discussions of Positive Attributes of Partners

Clients typically want to tell therapists what bothers them most but often have difficulty remembering or acknowledging the positive elements of their relationship. However, asking about positive elements of the relationship or positive characteristics of the partner is important in getting a more complete and accurate picture of the relationship, particularly in terms of helping them to remember what initially brought them together. More important, remembering positive aspects of the relationship can remind the clients of how positive their relationship has been and perhaps can be again in the future.

Increasing Daily Positive Interchanges

In a manner similar to the concept of "caring days" described by Beach, Sandeen, and O'Leary (1990), couples should be encouraged to make a conscious effort to increase the number of prosocial behaviors done for one's partner. For example, each partner can be asked to do, every day, at least three things that he or she knows is pleasing to one's partner. Of course, a prelude to this exercise can include having each partner disclose, in a self-focused and noncritical manner, things that he or she enjoys. This overt disclosure can avoid problematic situations in which partners mistakenly believe that a particular behavior is pleasing to their partner. Especially when this technique is first implemented, a focus should be kept on keeping the prosocial behaviors simple.

In addition to doing things *for* each other, couples can be encouraged to find more mutually enjoyable activities to do *with* each other. This too can have a powerful effect in beginning to turn negative exchanges into more positive ones and increase positive feelings of each person toward his or her partner. It is worth noting that in the use of caring days, sexual contact should not be bargained for and should be approached carefully. It is frequently the case among couples who are experiencing a reduction in sexual activity as a result of discord that when the discord is alleviated, sexual activity resumes.

Helping Partners Listen and Understand One Another

There is significant research indicating that children and adults who are able to empathize with another person's feelings and point of view are less likely to be hurtful to others (Kendall & Panichelli-Mindel, 1995; Spivack & Shure, 1982). In addition, viewing a partner's intentions as malevolent will predictably result in increased negative emotion regardless of the partner's actual motives. Marital therapists have long used communication exercises, and there are numerous exercises available to therapists. In our opinion, it seems best to provide feedback about interaction and communication style as the therapy process unfolds rather than have couples engage in a series of communication exercises. Further, very often partners know what the other would like them to do. They simply do not want to act in a manner that fulfills those desires. Thus, a major challenge for therapists is to discover ways to motivate clients to want to change.

Highlighting Treatment Gains and Skills Learned

As treatment ends, it is important for the therapist to instill a sense of confidence in the couple's ability to maintain change. In part, this can be done by highlighting the positive changes made by each partner during the course of treatment as well as the skills they have acquired that will enable them to be more prepared for future relationship difficulties.

FOLLOW-UP

Given the difficult and perhaps resistant nature of treating partner aggression, it can be valuable to follow up with couples in our treatment program after terminating treatment. Follow-up generally involves scheduling periodic "checkup" sessions with the couple (preferably in person, but this can also be done by phone) to monitor maintenance of change. If the therapist determines that one or both partners are regressing into increasingly aggressive behavior, it may be therapeutically indicated to reintroduce regular appointments for further work until the couple is able to demonstrate that they have mastered the necessary skills to desist their aggressive behavior. At that time, the couple can be phased out of treatment.

REFERENCES

Archer, J. (2000). Sex differences in aggression between heterosexual partners: A meta-analytic review. *Psychological Bulletin, 126*, 651–680.

Beach, S. R. H., Sandeen, E., & O'Leary, K. D. (1990). *Depression in marriage.* New York: Guilford Press.

Bradbury, T. N., & Fincham, F. F. (1990). Attributions in marriage: Review and critique, *Psychological Bulletin, 107*, 3–33.

Brannen, S. J., & Rubin, A. (1996). Comparing the effectiveness of gender-specific and couples groups in a court-mandated-spouse-abuse treatment program. *Research on Social Work Practice, 6*, 405–424.

Brown, P. D., & O'Leary, K. D. (2000). Therapeutic alliance: Predicting continuance and success in group treatment for spouse abuse. *Journal of Consulting and Clinical Psychology, 68*, 340–345.

Cantos, A. L., Neidig, P. H., & O'Leary, K. D. (1994). Injuries of women and men in a treatment program for domestic violence. *Journal of Family Violence, 9*, 113–124.

Cascardi, M., Langhinrichsen, J., & Vivian, D. (1992). Marital aggression: Impact, injury, and health correlates for husbands and wives. *Archives of Internal Medicine, 152,* 1178–1184.

Cohen, S., & O'Leary, K. D. (2005). *Development and validation of the Fear of Partner Scale.* Unpublished manuscript, Stony Brook University, Stony Brook, New York.

Doss, B. D., Thum, W. M., Sevier, M., Atkins, D., & Christensen, A. (2005). Improving relationships: Mechanisms of change in couple therapy. *Journal of Consulting and Clinical Psychology, 73,* 624–633.

Edleson, J. L., & Tolman, R. M. (1992). *Intervention for men who batter: An ecological approach.* Newbury Park, CA: Sage.

Ehrensaft, M., Moffitt, T., & Caspi, A. (2004). Clinically abusive relationships in an unselected birth cohort: Men's and women's participation and developmental antecedents. *Journal of Abnormal Psychology, 113,* 258–271.

Foshee, V. (1996). Gender differences in adolescent dating abuse prevalence, types, and injuries. *Health Education Research, 11*(3), 275–286.

Halford, K. (2001) *Brief therapy for couples.* New York: Guilford Press.

Hamel, J. (2005). *Gender inclusive treatment of intimate partner abuse: A comprehensive approach.* New York: Springer.

Holtzworth-Munroe, A., & Stuart, G. L. (1994). Typologies of male batterers: Three subtypes and the differences among them. *Psychological Bulletin, 116,* 476–497.

Jacobson, N. S., & Addis, M. E. (1993). Research on couple therapy: What do we know? Where are we going? *Journal of Consulting and Clinical Psychology, 61,* 85–93.

Jacobson, N. S., & Gottman, J. (1998). *When men batter women: New insights into ending abusive relationships.* New York: Simon & Schuster.

Johnson, S. M., & Talitman, E. (1997). Predictors of success in emotionally focused marital therapy. *Journal of Marital and Family Therapy, 23,* 135–152.

Kendall, P. C., & Panichelli-Mindel, S. M. (1995). Cognitive-behavioral therapies with children and adolescents: An integrative overview. In H. P. van Bilsen, P. C. Kendall, & J. H. Slavenburg (Eds.), *Behavioral approaches for children and adolescents: Challenges for the next century* (pp. 1–18). New York: Plenum Press.

Koss, M. P., & Gidycz, C. A. (1985). Sexual experiences survey: Reliability and validity. *Journal of Consulting and Clinical Psychology, 53,* 422–423.

Lawrence, E., & Bradbury, T. N. (2001). Physical aggression and marital dysfunction: A longitudinal analysis. *Journal of Family Psychology, 15,* 135–154.

Meyer, S. L., Vivian, D., & O'Leary, K. D. (1998). Men's sexual aggression in marriage: Couples' report. *Violence Against Women, 4,* 415–435.

Moffitt, T. E., Robins, R. W., & Caspi, A. (2001). A couples analysis of partner abuse with implications for abuse prevention. *Criminology and Public Policy, 1,* 5–36.

Murphy, C. M., & Baxter, V. A. (1997). Motivating batterers to change in the treatment context. *Journal of Interpersonal Violence, 12,* 607–619.

Murphy, C. M., & Eckhardt, C. I. (2005). *Treating the abusive partner: An individualized cognitive-behavioral approach.* New York: Guilford Press.

Norton, R. (1983). Measuring marital quality: A critical look at the dependent variable. *Journal of Marriage and the Family, 45,* 141–151.

O'Leary, K. D. (2000). Are women really more aggressive than men in intimate relationships? Comment on Archer (2000). *Psychological Bulletin, 126,* 685–689.

O'Leary, K. D., Barling, J., Arias, I., Rosenbaum, A., Malone, J., & Tyree, A. (1989). Prevalence and stability of physical aggression between spouses: A longitudinal analysis. *Journal of Consulting and Clinical Psychology, 57,* 263–268.

O'Leary, K. D., Heyman, R. E., & Neidig, P. H. (1999). Treatment of wife abuse: A comparison of gender-specific and conjoint approaches. *Behavior Therapy, 30,* 475–505.

O'Leary, K. D., & Vega, E. M. (2005). Can partner aggression be stopped with psychosocial interventions? In W. Pinsof & J. Lebow (Eds.), *Family psychology: The art of the science* (pp. 243–263). New York: Oxford University Press.

O'Leary, K. D., Vivian, D., & Malone, J. (1992). Assessment of physical aggression in marriage: The need for a multimodal method. *Behavioral Assessment, 14,* 5–14.

O'Leary, K. D. & Williams, M. C. (in press). Agreement about acts of aggression in marriage. *Family Psychology.*

O'Leary, K. D., & Woodin, E. M. (in press). Partner aggression severity as a risk-marker for male and female violence recidivism. *Journal of Marital and Family Therapy.*

Pan, H., Neidig, P. H., & O'Leary, K. D. (1994). Predicting mild and severe husband to wife physical aggression. *Journal of Consulting and Clinical Psychology, 62,* 975–981.

Pinsof, W. M., & Catherall, D. R. (1986). The integrative psychotherapy alliance: Family, couples, and individual therapy scales. *Journal of Marital and Family Therapy, 12,* 137–151.

Rathus, J. H., & Sanderson, W. C. (1999). *Marital distress: Cognitive behavioral interventions for dysfunctional couples.* Northvale, NJ: Jason Aronson.

Shadish, W. R., Ragsdale, K., Glaser, R. R., & Montgomery, L. M. (1995). The efficacy and effectiveness of marital and family therapy: A perspective from meta-analysis. *Journal of Marital and Family Therapy, 21,* 345–360.

Simpson, L. E., & Christensen, A. (2004, November). *Low-level violence among distressed couples: What is the impact on treatment outcomes?* Symposium presented at the 38th annual meeting of the Association for the Advancement of Cognitive and Behavior Therapy, New Orleans, LA.

Spanier, G. B. (1976). Measuring dyadic adjustment: New scales for assessing the quality of marriage and similar dyads. *Journal of Marriage and the Family, 38,* 15–28.

Spivack, G., & Shure, M. B. (1982). The cognition of social adjustment: Interpersonal cognitive problem-solving thinking. In B. B. Lahey & A. E. Kazdin (Eds.), *Advances in clinical psychology* (Vol. 5, pp. 323–369). New York: Plenum Press.

Stets, J. E., & Straus, M. A. (1990). Gender differences in reporting marital violence and its medical and psychological consequences. In M. A. Straus & R. J. Gelles (Eds.), *Physical violence in American families: Risk factors and adaptations to violence in 8,145 families* (pp.151–165). New Brunswick, NJ: Transaction Publishers.

Stith, S. M., Rosen, K. H., & McCollum, E. E. (2003). Effectiveness of couples treatment for spouse abuse. *Journal of Marital and Family Therapy, 29,* 407–426.

Stith, S., Rosen, K., McCollum, E., & Thomsen, C. (2004). Treating intimate partner violence within intact couple relationships: Outcomes of multi-couple versus individual couple therapy. *Journal of Marital and Family Therapy, 30*(3), 305–318.

Straus, M. A. (1993). Physical assault by wives: A major social problem. In R. J. Gelles & D. R. Loseke (Eds.), *Current controversies on family violence* (pp. 67–87). Newbury Park, CA: Sage.

Straus, M. A., & Gelles, R. J. (Eds.). (1990). *Physical violence in American families: Risk factors and adaptation to violence in 8,145 families.* New Brunswick, NJ: Transaction Publishers.

Straus, M. A., Gelles, R. J., & Steinmetz, S. K. (1980). *Behind closed doors: Violence in the American family.* Garden City, NY: Anchor Books/Doubleday.

Straus, M. A., Hamby, S. L., Boney-McCoy, S., & Sugarman, D. B. (1996). The revised Conflict Tactics Scale (CTS2): Development and preliminary psychometric data. *Journal of Family Issues, 17,* 283–316.

Vega, E. M., & O'Leary, K. D. (in press). Test-retest reliability of the revised Conflict Tactics Scales. *Journal of Family Violence.*

White, J. W., & Kowalski, R. M. (1994). Deconstructing the myth of the non-aggressive woman. *Psychology of Women Quarterly, 18,* 487–508.

Woodin, E. M. (2006). *Observed marital conflict: A meta-analysis of gender differences and links with relationship satisfaction.* Unpublished manuscript, Stony Brook University, Stony Brook, NY.

Woodin, E. M., & O'Leary, K. D. (2006). Partner aggression severity as a risk-marker for male and female violence recidivism. *Journal of Marital and Family Therapy, 32,* 283–296.

CHAPTER 17

Couple Violence and Couple Safety: A Systemic and Attachment-Oriented Approach to Working With Complexity and Uncertainty

Arlene Vetere and Jan Cooper

The Reading Safer Families project was established more than nine years ago. We provide an independent, community-based therapeutic service to men, women, and children in families where violence is of concern. We work with both victims and perpetrators, of all ages and both genders. Much of our risk assessment work has been conducted within the U.K. family court system. We are both systemic family therapists; Arlene is also a clinical psychologist, and Jan also is a social worker.

Much of our work with couples in the Reading Safer Families project has been with White, European, opposite-sex couples. In all our work with couples, including minority group couples and same-sex couples, we put safety first. Whatever the cultural and subcultural differences in expectations and patterns of relating within and between couples and their extended families, our U.K. legal framework is our highest context marker. Domestic violence is a crime. Our moral belief is that no one should live in fear of the person or the people he or she loves. Our responsibility as therapists is to create a context for safe practice and to help the perpetrator stop the violence and abuse. The couple's responsibility is to put safety first and for the perpetrator to take full responsibility for his or her violent actions and to hold oneself accountable. We make these positions clear at the start of our work to our clients and within the professional network. If safety can be achieved, we may consider the possibility of further therapeutic work with the couple that helps them address and deal with the multiple legacies of past violence and abuse. At all times, we keep the safety of the children in mind: the children of the couple and the couple as children once themselves.

As we are writing this chapter from the U.K./European perspective of law, politics, and practice, we thought it was important to underline how the zero-tolerance campaign in the United Kingdom has been crucial for our context as well. This campaign provided the necessary platform on which to raise public awareness and to recruit and encourage the political will to outlaw physical and sexual assault by men to their women partners. This platform made safety the highest priority and has been extended now to include other forms of psychological abuse, to be gender inclusive (i.e., to consider abuse by women toward their men partners), and to take seriously the intergenerational impacts for children as witnesses to domestic violence, whoever the perpetrators.

In our professional lives, we have been indebted to and influenced by the rigor of feminist thinking in many disciplines. Historically in the United Kingdom, as in many other countries, the responses to domestic violence have overwhelmingly been made toward women whose male partners have been violent to them. Few service protocols have been established for working with men in this context. Interventions for men continue to be largely through the criminal justice system, such as men's groups in association with the Probation Service or Forensic Service. On the one hand, services for men are seen as an essential part of a community response, but, on the other, the rationale offered for working with men is that the work is essential to help protect women and children. We would extend the moral argument, however, and assert that men are entitled to therapeutic services in their own right. Not to do so and to tell men that we provide a service to them only to keep women and children safe potentially compromises the development of trust within any intervention or service offered. Therapeutically, this would seem to us to inhibit understanding, compassion, and human engagement, as trust is needed to help the men develop a sense of confidence and self-respect, the lack of which often underlies abusive behavior, alongside any felt entitlement to abuse those whom they love (Vetere & Cooper, 2004).

In this chapter, we focus on our work with couples where one or both partners has behaved in physically and emotionally abusive ways. Our definition of violence encompasses physical harm and threats of harm, coercion, humiliation, and other forms of emotional and economic abuse. We use an extended example to show how we weave theory and practice in the context of ongoing risk assessment and risk management. Although much of our work is with men as partners and fathers, we do also work with women who are violent. We have chosen our example to illustrate the complexity around working with a couple where both the man and the woman have behaved violently.

We have written extensively elsewhere on how we create safety for therapeutic work through an interlocking methodology of risk assessment and risk management, responsibility for behavior, and collaborative practice (Cooper & Vetere, 2005; Vetere & Cooper, 2001, 2003). We outline briefly the key features of our approach to safe practice. We do not undertake couples therapy unless and until we can establish safety, help stop the violence, and be as sure as possible that the adults and children are safe. Although we will never know the full extent of the violence, we do know that violence has occurred. This gives us an advantage. It means that we can openly and carefully speak about safety, responsibility, and accountability in our first meeting with a couple (Jory & Anderson, 1999).

BUILDING A SAFE CONTEXT FOR PRACTICE

Risk Management and Risk Assessment

As independent practitioners, we do not work with couples on our own, isolated from the professional network and the community of concern. We use the psychodynamic concept of the stable third to help us understand and manage anxiety and risk in the professional network, for the couple and their children, for ourselves, and for their wider families. The stable third is someone known to the couple and trusted by them and the professional network. This could be a person or a team, but it is someone who knows the family, can visit the family home and see the children (if there are any), can provide a third point of view about what is happening, and, if necessary, can help corroborate whether violence has ceased. It is not enough that the couple tell us that the violence has stopped. The person who is the stable third is often a health visitor, a social worker, an elder in the faith community, a trusted grandparent, and sometimes a family doctor—very often it is the referrer. We hold regular reviews with the couple and the referrer/stable third to assess how the work is progressing, to examine the risks for all participants of a recurrence of violence, and to plan the next stage of the work. We establish a no-violence contract in the first meeting and work to help the couple put safety first (for a full description, see Cooper & Vetere, 2005). If the no-violence contract is broken, we call an immediate review with the couple and the referrer/stable third to decide whether we continue with the assessment process. We do not abandon people, but we may offer short-term individual work or refer for group work instead.

We always carry out assessments for the possibility of therapeutic work with the couple first, even if another agency has done a risk assessment of further violence. We meet the couple separately and together. We take at least six sessions for assessments. This gives all of us time to get to know each other and to assess their intentions and commitment to safety, the perpetrator's ability to take responsibility for his or her actions, and his or her capacity to learn and change. We do not undertake therapeutic couples work until we have established the no-violence contract and can see it hold alongside their commitment to want to work with us. We use the last or the worst episode of violence to help us understand the distal and proximal triggers for violent behavior, to hold people responsible for their behavior, and to develop a safety plan to help the couple deescalate negative patterns of interaction and to learn to prevent them. We rehearse the safety plan and anticipate difficulties with implementing it. We do this whether the couple continue to live together or are in the process of separation. We develop no-violence contracts for all contexts in which couples may meet, such as in the street or at contact handover. At all times, we are clear about our shared moral and legal responsibilities for safety and for holding perpetrators of violent behavior accountable for their actions regardless of how we understand such behaviors to develop.

When conducting assessments around the risk of further violence, we take account of repeated violence and the contexts in which violent behavior is perpetrated. We observe people's ability to manage their anger and arousal in their meetings with us and their emotional capacity to empathize with their victim's experience. We are careful to explore their ability to reflect on past experience and show evidence of learning, and we seek some indication of internal motivation for change. Many of the couples we work with are externally motivated insofar as someone else is insisting the perpetrator change his or her behavior—we look for the capacity for reflective self-function (Fonagy & Target, 1997) and evidence that violence comes out of a "hot place" of emotional arousal rather than being used instrumentally in calculated attempts to control others.

Responsibility

When assessing for responsibility, we want some acknowledgment that there is a problem! If the perpetrator persists in blaming others for his or her violence, we would see this as a contraindication for safe practice. Along with this acknowledgment, we also seek the perpetrator's ownership of his or her relational contribution to the problem—his or her violent behavior has both direct and indirect effects on people and the felt quality of relationships. We need to see that the perpetrator can take responsibility for safety and that victims can take their entitlement to safety seriously. We do not meet children with parents until we are sure that the adults can keep them safe. We explore how the couple as parents take personal and coparental responsibility for the safety and well-being of their children. We want to know what people have tried, and we work hard to give them credit for their attempts at problem solving around their children. We speak with parents about the effects of domestic violence on their children as they grow up and reflect with the parents on the intergenerational impact of their own childhood experiences of witnessing domestic violence. We engage parents around the hoped-for futures of their children and what they hope their children will learn from them. We underpin our attempts to promote responsibility by paying attention to how people talk about their actions. We notice attempts to deny or minimize actions, to evade responsibility by using explanation as an excuse, and to blame others. We pause and deconstruct the use of language in these moments and invite the couple, as appropriate, to develop their curiosity in how language both constructs and reflects social experience. Thus, we can see how extended assessments carry enormous therapeutic potential.

Collaboration

We try to promote transparent and collaborative practice in a number of ways. We are clear about our moral position on the use of violence in the family and the community and why we do this work. We are prepared to debate the moral dilemmas around the use of violence in the multicontextual society in which we live and how we act as agents of social control. We explain why we do not give confidentiality in our work when safety is the issue and how we can negotiate what can be held confidential in the work as we progress. We encourage our clients to ask us questions about why we practice as we do. We help them develop their capacity to see professional workers as potentially helpful, particularly for those couples whose children are subject to social services care proceedings, and to develop their ability to cooperate with professional workers. We often find ourselves using our systemic thinking to help couples and parents understand and navigate successfully the workings of the professional system. Exposure to professional scrutiny can evoke feelings of shame, and most couples find themselves under duress during this process. In our work, we pay attention to this process.

We always work in the room together as lead therapist and in-room consultant. We have developed and elaborated a systemic reflecting process that extends to our written work and court reports. When working therapeutically, one of us takes the role of lead therapist and the other the role of in-room consultant for every couple and family we see. This practice allows us to harness the multiple points of view available within the room by offering opportunities for everyone to speak and to listen. When we invite the couple to listen to us reflect on the conversation so far, they hear us develop our ideas in front of them. This could be an unusual experience for them. When they offer feedback on our reflections, they are promoting their capacity for reflection, and a shared process of interleaving ideas evolves as we continue to meet together. The emotional experiences contained within the different roles and perspectives are different, and developing this understanding among all of us offers both containment and a context for therapeutic growth. In our supervision, we notice and expand on differences of perception, understanding, and experience between us in an attempt to prevent a too comfortable and cozy relationship in our work that could lead us to be less watchful and careful around safety issues.

Intimacy and Fear

As feminist practitioners ourselves, we appreciate the work of feminist writers in the social sciences who have deconstructed the contexts of patriarchy that contribute to the socialization of boys and girls and women and men (Goldner, Penn, Sheinberg, & Walker, 1990). In particular, the construct of entitlement, held by some men, has been helpful in understanding how some people come to believe they can use physical violence to control others in the family. Such entitlement can be seen to be embedded within our social and political contexts and embodied in how we treat others. However, if such patriarchal discourses are prevalent, all of us are to some extent subject to their influence. Thus, we agree with Don Dutton (2003) when he says that we need to go beyond the deconstruction of power and control in societal and family relationships to explain why some men and some women behave abusively in the context of intimate relating and others do not. He has suggested that there is something about the experience of relationship intimacy that needs to be understood. This points us to attachment theory as a theory of adult love (Bowlby, 1988; Crittenden, 1997; Johnson, 2002).

In this section, we want to examine intimate relating using ideas from attachment theory in the context of a systemic approach to therapeutic work with couples. Attachment theory helps us theorize emotion and emotional responsiveness. It is a theory of the social regulation of emotion across the life span. Since many of the couples we meet are traumatized as part of exposure to continuous trauma, past trauma, and intergenerational trauma, we look to trauma theory to help us understand and unravel intergenerational legacies (Herman, 1992; Horowitz, 1986). In doing this work, we too are indirectly exposed to trauma and are at risk of secondary traumatization (Figley, 1995).

Attachment theory proposes that adults give and receive love, comfort, support, and protection in their intimate relationships (Hazan & Shaver, 1987; Johnson, 2002). Just as attachment is theorized to be crucial to the survival of the infant and to the psychological adjustment of the developing child, so it is theorized that adult attachment processes are representational and about caregiving, sex, and affection across the life span. Emotional security and the expectation of partner accessibility and responsiveness are seen to underpin confidence and trust in intimate relating and reinforce our sense of ourselves as lovable people. In an emotionally secure relationship, we can deal with occasional emotional upsets when we feel well regarded by our partner. Without such emotional security, when partners are increasingly unresponsive, we can feel afraid and respond in anxious and fearful ways or with emotional numbness and distancing. Gottman (1999) suggested that emotional distance per se contributes more to relationship deterioration than conflictual relating. What seems to matter is whether couples can repair the rift following conflict.

Helping couples develop a sense of emotional connection is contraindicated *initially* when abuse is known to have occurred, in case emotional vulnerability is used to further attack a partner. In our experience of working with couples, they do not enjoy secure attachment relationships and desperately seek comfort and reassurance in ways often masked, disguised, and misunderstood. Attachment insecurity is thought to be a key factor in maintaining couple distress. In our work, we observe systemic patterns of insecure relating characterized by emotional pursuit and emotional withdrawal and by mutual withdrawal, often accompanied by blame, counterblame, and hidden shame. Continuous fear of loss and abandonment can give rise to anger. We see anger and frustration expressed as hope in the angry pursuit of a partner: "What do I have to do to get you to pay attention to me!" We see the anger of despair in the contemptuous dismissal of a partner's overture: "I don't need you!" Attachment theory suggests that at the heart of such misery is the wish to have a connection with the partner. Systemic thinking points up the perceptual bias under conditions of emotional arousal to pay attention to the nonverbal communication in a message—so we notice the contempt in the voice rather than see the wish for connection. Trauma theory suggests that fear constrains and slows information processing. When we are afraid, for whatever reason, we are preoccupied with regulating our fear and protecting ourselves from threat. We are literally unable to see and respond to relationship attachment cues. Couples therapists are process consultants who work within and between, moving from the representational to the interpersonal. In the safety of the therapeutic alliance, we slow these processes and patterns and help couples develop shared understandings that help regulate and integrate emotional responses. Learning to comfort each other and to self-soothe is based in part on the ability to stand in the emotional shoes of the other. This goes beyond empathy as partners learn to bear and tolerate each other's negative emotional states. It is our task as therapists to reach underneath distressed patterns of communication to search out the longings and needs for comfort and soothing.

However, as therapists, we can work in this way only if safety can be achieved, and, even then, the legacy of shame and humiliation might be too much to overcome. For example, following the cessation of physical violence from the man, we may find that the woman will not give up practices of humiliation. The wish to pay back past hurts is strong. We find that couples will go to the edge of separation when they contemplate whether they have a shared future together and doubt whether they can overcome the fear of further assault to create mutual trust. It may be that the best outcome is found in helping the couple separate safely. In the following example, we show how we used attachment thinking to help us understand the complex patterns of relating that we observed in a couple where both partners had struggled with problems of violence.

COMPLEXITY AND UNCERTAINTY: WORKING WITH JANE AND JOHN

The Referral

Jane and John were referred to us by John's general practitioner (GP). They are a White couple, born in the United Kingdom, and both in their mid-30s. Jane had visited her GP in the past with bruising but had always minimized the events. In this incident, John had physically attacked Jane when she roused him from a drunken sleep. The attack was so severe that she needed to be hospitalized overnight. Jane went to live with her close woman friend for a few weeks. John was upset, full of apologies, and desperate for them both to be reunited. He felt a deep sense of shame for what he had done and was shamed within his community. Their mutual friends made it clear to him that his behavior was totally unacceptable. With the support of his sister, John went to his GP seeking help so that he would never do this again. The GP contacted us with a view to working therapeutically with John and, possibly at some point, with Jane. When we work with men around issues of safety and they have a partner, we like to get a clear commitment to safety from both of them—in this case for him to take responsibility for his safety around others and for her not to take risks with her own safety. We agreed to meet with John but made it clear that we do not do long-term psychotherapeutic work with men on their own. After five meetings with us, John asked if Jane could come to the sessions so that we could work with them as a couple. We agreed, and John's family GP agreed to be our stable third.

Comment

At this very early stage, we were struck by the tangible sense of shame John felt and how he had been shamed and shunned by others. We wondered about an intergenerational legacy of shame and shaming in his family of origin and how his relationship with his mother and father may have impacted on his current sense of vulnerability. John's sister was extremely supportive of him, and his GP was a woman, as are we both women! So we had an idea that he could risk trusting women. John took the initiative in seeking help from his GP so that he could put a stop to such behavior. He had taken early steps toward responsibility. In our first meetings, he made no attempt to minimize the force and effects of his attack on Jane.

Background

Both John and Jane maintained their own homes in their community, although both lived in John's house. Jane had moved into John's house without discussion or planning—she told us that she arrived one day on his doorstep with a suitcase and that he had agreed. Jane shared her own house with a close woman friend who paid rent to Jane. Both women had moved to this community from another region of the United Kingdom.

John had a young daughter by a previous relationship. He had established a regular pattern of contact for one weekend every month and seemed to work in cooperation with his former wife around his daughter's needs. He maintained this pattern of contact during our therapeutic work with him. We had no reason to believe that John's relationship with his daughter was unsafe in any way, and with permission we checked this out with a number of informants. Jane struggled with her relationship with his daughter, seeing it as a duty if she wanted to live with John rather than as a pleasure or a relationship she could develop. However, she did not try to prevent the contact. Sometimes she would go to stay with friends when his daughter was staying home, and sometimes she would go back to live in her own house in the company of her woman friend.

Comment

It is probably fair to say that Jane did not like her own company. We wondered about her past experiences of being parented, for she seemed so unable to bear John's caring (both physically and emotionally) for his daughter. We wondered if watching John look after his little girl evoked feelings of grief (and anger?) for her lack of comfort and security as a child. We wondered if she resented John's daughter, and, if so, how that impacted on her felt sense of intimacy with John. Did she need him to give her all his emotional attention? We wanted to know more about her past experiences of adult love and of being looked after as a child. In sum, we wondered if she felt she was unlovable and could not rely on others to be responsive.

The Crisis

The crisis was triggered by two factors. One was their pattern of heavy social drinking on the weekends, and the other was the tension in their relationship around their inability to make a commitment to each other. Both were in full-time paid employment, but John saw Jane as being the more successful of the two, as her income was higher. They worked hard and played hard. They met at the pub for drinking sessions with their friends on the weekends. Their apparent indecision about their relationship seemed hard to understand, as they were clearly passionate about each other and talked and acted as if they wanted to be together. We noted early on in our couples meetings how Jane described her retreat to her own home when she and John had an argument.

The incident that led to the attack on Jane, her hospitalization, and her decision to move back with her woman friend, albeit temporarily, occurred on a weekend. Both had gone out drinking, this time with separate groups of friends, and had agreed to meet later in the evening at a prearranged venue. Jane had gone to meet John as agreed, but he did not show up. She had been drinking. It transpired that he had drunk too much earlier in the evening, and his friends had taken him home to "sleep it off." She went back to his house, found him asleep in bed, and yanked the pillow out from under his head to wake him. He awoke and assaulted her. She ran to the neighbor's house for help. Subsequently, John maintained that Jane had thrown her stiletto-heeled shoe at him, and Jane always denied this, although she agreed with the description of "yanking the pillow." This difference in their accounts continued to rankle between them.

Comment

Jane seemed to be angry and disappointed when John did not arrive for their meeting. It was as if she felt let down and abandoned by him. When she rushed home to find him and confront him, she did so both in extreme anger and in anxiety to check that he was alright. She found him asleep, almost as if he was unconcerned about her and for her. It would seem that her anger and disappointment overrode her concern for him in that moment. Both were disinhibited with the effects of alcohol consumption.

As systemic therapists, we noted the continuing impact of this disagreement about what *actually* happened between them as they told it. It was as if John needed Jane to acknowledge she had hurt him too. He held his responsibility for assaulting and hurting her uppermost and did not flinch from his commitment to be accountable to her and to others. But he seemed to need her to acknowledge that her actions had wounded him. She could not acknowledge that for fear it would diminish his responsibility toward her. Thus, we see how ideas of responsibility and entitlement can be powerfully emotionally laden with meanings that pre-date their relationship and that are reworked in their current relationship.

We wanted to talk with them about safety. How can we keep safety in mind in these moments of anger and despair? How can we prevent the escalation of conflict and misunderstanding or, if not prevent it, reduce the negative intensity and impact? Our view is that both Jane and John are entitled to be safe in their intimate relationships, but we thought that neither of them held a sense of entitlement to be safe, to be kept safe, and to feel they could seek safety and comfort in intimacy.

We would seek to work toward this as long as we could help them prioritize safety. We had noted a pattern of mutual withdrawal during conflict and times of hurt, with Jane retreating to her own home and seeking solace with her woman friend. As a couple, they struggled to find ways to comfort each other when they were upset and hurt with each other. Both seemed to lean toward a dismissing and avoidant style of emotional relating when threatened with feelings of abandonment and rejection during conflict, but Jane would pursue him with energy and anger at first, perhaps showing her preoccupation and anxiety around feelings of loss. Her critical pursuit of him, as he saw it, appeared to reinforce his view that the safest thing he could do in those moments was to emotionally withdraw to protect both himself and her. His withdrawal was then felt by her as acute rejection, and she would then retreat to seek comfort from her friend. We needed to know more about the developmental origins of these patterns of relating.

Childhood Experiences

In their childhoods, both Jane and John been victims and witnesses of different forms of domestic violence. John was the younger of four brothers and had a twin sister. His father had been violent to all his sons and to his wife but not his daughter. John told us how his father had always told him to protect his sister and keep her safe. We discovered that John had not been able to reflect consciously on this paradox for what it meant for either him or other family members. John's mother had been intimidated by his father and had been an unspeaking witness to his violence to their sons. In trying to understand both his father's and his mother's silence, John said that he understood his mother's silence to be fear, but he also knew that she was distressed and moved for her sons while passive with fear and apprehension for herself. He thought that she had believed his father was entitled to treat their sons that way, as boys needed a firm hand from their father. John told us the violence toward all of them stopped when his older brother reached manhood and stood up to his father by beating him up in return. John told us that his father was "as good as gold" after that. So we see how greater strength and violence is used in families to stop the violence. John said there was no discussion within the family of his father's violence at that time or at any time since. Talking with us appeared to be the first time he had been able to create the mental space to reflect on the meaning of these events. John's parents had died a few years ago. He had good relationships with his brothers and sister, who lived nearby.

Jane was an only child. Her parents had separated when she was seven and spent years going through a long and acrimonious divorce process. Her parents had competed with each other for her attention and love, her father by showering her with presents and toys and her mother by making her a confidante and telling her how awful her father had been as a husband. Jane described her father as a man of unpredictable tempers and rages and her mother as a woman who sought comfort in alcohol and who abused alcohol for most of her childhood years. Her mother was therefore also unpredictable and unreliable in her care of Jane but also very needy of her daughter's love and support. Jane's father remarried, and Jane remembers never having time with her father on her own, as his new wife was always present. Jane said she resented this.

Comment

Attachment theory suggests that attachment behavior is a lifelong developmental process of the social regulation of emotion and behavior embedded in family life. Intense and/or unbearable anxiety can be experienced by the child when parents are distressed and harmed. For both John and Jane, they lived with parents who were not able to create an emotionally predictable pattern of caring for them throughout their childhoods. We might speculate that their signals of distress as children were not so easily noticed and contained and soothed. When reassuring communication was offered to them, they had a dilemma about whether they could trust it, particularly as their parents were not safe. We suggest that we see an adult version of this pattern in their relationship with each other and, in their different ways, in their growing relationship with us. Our task as therapists was to help them find ways to think about thinking—to seek to understand the representational nature of mental states both of each other and of important family members in the past. This capacity is protective and helps further develop a sense of resilience. We saw both John and Jane as resilient and hopeful about each other and their respective futures. Systemically speaking, both wished to draw forth positive ghosts from their pasts, looking for kindness, comfort, and support for their troubles in the present.

The Process of Therapy

We began with an assessment for the safety of couples work. In the process of therapy, we attempted to understand the crisis and the effect it was having on their lives both separately and in their relationship. We understood that they had not made an explicit decision to live together but that Jane had gradually moved more and more of her possessions to John's house, without his commenting, complaining, or approving, nor did she seek any conversation about her actions. Jane was very feisty and spoke with authority for herself. She held John responsible for his violent actions without diminishing what he had done. However, when we worked in the area of mutual decision making and responsibilities, it was harder for her.

John told us some way into the therapy that Jane was often violent to him. He said that she often hit him but that he was not so concerned about that because it did not hurt him. We often hear this point of view expressed by men. What concerned him more was when Jane threw things, deliberately broke his possessions, and refused to speak to him. He worried about their safety when she would deliberately brake the car, when driving fast, without any warning.

We asked ourselves, Why had we not asked more about the possibility that Jane may be violent toward John? Her violence was an invisible piece in the interlocking pieces of their relationship. We had to admit that we had not focused on Jane as a potentially violent person to John. When we explored this further with her, we learned that she had been referred for anger management at her place of work by her employers. We wondered if the original attack on Jane by John was so severe that we stopped thinking about Jane. Or was it that we worked with John first and that as he took complete responsibility and was so contrite, we were lulled into complacency by his responses? Or was it that we were being blind to women's violence? However, when we took her responsibility for her violence as seriously as his, she felt betrayed by us and attacked our ideas and our stance. When we asked John why he had not told us, he said that his original abuse of Jane was so bad that nothing that Jane did to him could be as bad. He wanted to protect himself from being seen as a man who was abused by his woman, and he wanted to protect her because he thought that the revelation would make their relationship vulnerable and that they would have no future together.

Comment

We considered their capacity for empathic reflection. Did they struggle to imagine what others might feel like when they are frightened? As partners, could they go beyond standing in each other's emotional shoes, so to speak, and actually tolerate and bear each other's powerful negative emotional states? Their capacity to comfort and soothe each other was not developed between them. Attachment thinking suggests we are impelled to seek comfort, security, and safety across the life span, yet in their case they could not trust it. The emotional contract on which they based their life together was implicit rather than explicit, with powerful unspoken feelings underlying and coursing through their actions. If psychotherapy, broadly speaking, is to put thinking into the emotional flow in a couple's relationship—to imagine and to hold alternative hypotheses about each other—our attempts to help them connect their feelings, thoughts, and actions foundered on Jane's sense of betrayal by us. In many ways, Jane's behavior reminded us of Pat Crittenden's (1997) description of endangered children whereby the child learns feisty, controlling, and aggressive ways of relating in order to secure some attention and comfort in the face of emotional inconsistency from caregivers. As an adult, her choice of John as a partner, with his tendency toward a dismissing emotional style of intimate relating, served to reinforce her fears about the emotional unavailability of others and her own unlovability.

Therapists' Dilemmas

As therapists, we strongly questioned ourselves for not having asked obvious questions. We searched for reasons why. We also found ourselves in the firing line from Jane and needing to stoutly defend ourselves and our beliefs about the seriousness of women's violence and the need for women to be accountable in their own right. She asked us how we could do this to her, as two women ourselves. Jane thought we were diminishing John's responsibility by our stance, and we were saddened at not being able to find a way of talking these moral dilemmas through with her. It seemed as if she could not trust us either. She did, however, agree to our referring her to an adult psychotherapist so that she could reflect on her own emotional experiences both now and in the context of her past family life. We hoped she could construct this as an act of caring and comfort enabling on our part. John, for his part, decided their relationship was unsafe, and he took steps to end their relationship. We continued to work with him on maintaining the no-violence contract and to uphold his wish to end violence for any future intimate partnerships.

On reflection, we learned so much from Jane and John about anger and violence within a relationship and about risk, responsibility, and collaboration on the part of clients as well on the part of us as therapists. As a result of our experiences, we are more inclined to assess earlier for the possibility of a woman's violence to her man partner and to try to promote discussion about the different ways in which we respond to conflict and initiate conflict within our framework of safety.

REFERENCES

Bowlby, J. (1988). *A secure base.* New York: Basic Books.

Cooper, J., & Vetere, A. (2005). *Domestic violence and family safety: A systemic approach to working with violence in families.* London: Whurr/Wiley.

Crittenden, P. (1997). Truth, error, omission, distortion, and deception: The application of attachment theory to the assessment and treatment of psychological disorder. In S. Dollinger & L. DiLalla (Eds.), *Assessment and intervention issues across the lifespan* (pp. 35–75). Hillsdale, NJ: Lawrence Erlbaum Associates.

Dutton, D. (2003). *The abusive personality.* New York: Guilford Press.

Figley, C. R. (Ed.). (1995). *Compassion fatigue: Coping with secondary traumatic stress disorder in those who treat the traumatised.* New York: Brunner-Mazel.

Fonagy, P., & Target, M. (1997). Attachment and reflective function: Their role in self organisation. *Development and Psychopathology, 9,* 679–700.

Goldner, V., Penn, P., Sheinberg, M., & Walker, G. (1990). Love and violence: Gender paradoxes in volatile attachments. *Family Process, 29,* 343–364.

Gottman, J. (1999). *The marriage clinic: A scientifically based marital therapy.* New York: Norton.

Hazan, C., & Shaver, P. (1987). Conceptualising romantic love as an attachment process. *Journal of Personality and Social Psychology, 52,* 511–524.

Herman, J. L. (1992). *Trauma and recovery.* New York: Basic Books.

Horowitz, M. J. (1986). Stress response syndromes: A review of posttraumatic and adjustment disorders. *Hospital and Community Psychiatry, 37,* 241–249.

Johnson, S. (2002). *Emotionally focused couple therapy with trauma survivors: Strengthening attachment bonds.* New York: Guilford Press.

Jory, B., & Anderson, D. (1999). Intimate justice II: Fostering mutuality, reciprocity, and accommodation in therapy for psychological abuse. *Journal of Marital and Family Therapy, 25,* 349–364.

Vetere, A., & Cooper, J. (2001). Working systemically with family violence: Risk, responsibility and collaboration. *Journal of Family Therapy, 23,* 378–396.

Vetere, A., & Cooper, J. (2003). Setting up a domestic violence service: Some thoughts and considerations. *Child and Adolescent Mental Health, 8,* 61–67.

Vetere, A., & Cooper, J. (2004). Wishful thinking or Occam's razor? A response to "Dancing on a razor's edge: Systemic group work with batterers." *Journal of Family Therapy, 26,* 163–166.

CHAPTER 18

Dangerous Dances: Treatment of Domestic Violence in Same-Sex Couples

Vallerie E. Coleman

OVERVIEW OF VIOLENCE IN LESBIAN AND GAY COUPLES

The existence of same-sex domestic violence challenges the traditional assumption that domestic violence is rooted primarily in men's patriarchal privilege. While the role of patriarchy in perpetuating and maintaining domestic violence cannot be underestimated, battering in lesbian and gay relationships brings to light the need for a multidimensional understanding of domestic violence. In order to address the complex individual, relational, and societal variables that underlie the perpetration of battering, we must creatively broaden both our theoretical understanding of domestic violence and our treatment modalities. Although domestic violence also occurs in bisexual and transgender relationships, this chapter focuses specifically on how, under certain circumstances, couple therapy can be a safe and effective treatment modality for lesbians and gay men.

Studies examining same-sex domestic violence have found that the frequency and severity of violence in gay and lesbian relationships is comparable to those of heterosexual relationships (Coleman, 1991; Gardner, 1989; Lie, Schilit, Bush, Montagne, & Reyes, 1991; Waldner-Haugrud, Gratch, & Magruder, 1997), with rates of emotional abuse generally exceeding those of physical and sexual abuse (Burke & Follingstad, 1999;

Coleman, 1991; Merrill & Wolfe, 2000; Renzetti, 1988). Similarly, milder forms of violence (pushing, slapping, hitting, restraining) typically exceed rates of severe violence (use of a weapon, hitting with an object) (Burke & Follingstad, 1999; Coleman, 1991; Merrill & Wolfe, 2000; Renzetti, 1988; Waldner-Haugrud et. al., 1997).

Research has demonstrated that the factors that determine relationship quality are similar across couple types, and, analogous to heterosexual relationships, gay men and lesbians tend to have satisfying, long-term relationships (Gottman, 2004; Kurdek, 1994). Despite the numerous similarities between opposite-sex and same-sex relationships, there are a number of significant differences that must be taken into consideration. First and foremost, throughout their lives, gay men and lesbians must battle both external and internalized heterosexism and homophobia.[1] As I have stated elsewhere (Coleman, 2003), "Core experiences of sexual orientation/identity that are not mirrored and accepted (either consciously or unconsciously) by one's primary caretakers result in significant experiences of mis-attunement which must be split-off and sequestered in one's internal world" (p. 172). This lack of mirroring and attunement has profound implications for one's style of attachment and capacity for affect regulation. An insecure attachment style, which is further exacerbated by societal and cultural devaluation, can create significant relational challenges for lesbian and gay couples. For instance, as stated by Alonzo (2005), "the very real threat of anti-gay violence, the omnipresent possibility of disapproving attitudes from others, and the fear of discovery in a potentially hostile environment lead gay and lesbian couples to disguise, minimize, or deny their relationships" (p. 372).[2]

The paucity of domestic violence resources for lesbians and gay men is also a significant difference. Compared to the resources available for heterosexual battered women, there are very few service providers for lesbians and gay men. While lesbians may be able to obtain services through a battered women's shelter, they may have to "come out" and face further oppression. Additionally, special steps must be taken by battered women's shelters to ensure that a lesbian woman's batterer does not gain access to the shelter. Services for gay men are even more marginalized, as throughout the United States there are less than a handful of safe homes for battered gay men. Moreover, many gays and lesbians do not have the support of their families of origin and risk losing other support networks if they disclose that there is violence in their relationship. For lesbians and gay men of color, this is often amplified by experiences of racism within the gay community and society at large. In addition, many communities of color are rife with "negative and hostile attitudes toward homosexuality," further exacerbating levels of isolation and reinforcing dependence on the batterer (Waldron, 1996). Same-sex-specific tactics are often used by batterers to control and disempower their partner, for example, threatening to "out" one's partner at work; telling them that no one will believe them because they are just a "fag," "dyke," and so on; or threatening that their children will be taken away because of their sexual orientation. Such threats can be exponentially terrifying for those men and women in rural and small-town settings where high levels of homophobia exist and there are few or no gay/lesbian communities.

Minimization and denial are common defense mechanisms in any domestic violence situation; however, for gay men and lesbians, gender-based myths increase the denial of same-sex battering. In combination with societal myths that minimize same-sex domestic violence (boys will be boys; girls can't/don't really hurt each other), heterosexist portrayals of battering and the paucity of same-sex domestic violence services result in a general lack of awareness regarding gay and lesbian domestic violence (McLaughlin & Rozee, 1996). Furthermore, butch/femme stereotypes perpetuate the belief that the batterer in a same-sex relationship must be the larger, more stereotypically masculine partner. One must be mindful not to minimize the psychological terror and physical damage that a batterer can do to her or his partner regardless of their size or appearance.

An in-depth discussion of differences between lesbian and gay male relationships is beyond the scope of this chapter; however, I briefly highlight some issues for consideration. It is recommended that readers further familiarize themselves with the available gay-affirmative literature on homosexuality and same-sex couples.

Issues Specific to Gay Male Couples

Areas that become problematic for gay men are managing the impact of male socialization and internalized homophobia, navigating levels of monogamy or nonmonogamy in their relationships, and dealing with the impact of HIV and AIDS (Alonzo, 2005; Meyer & Dean, 1998). Alonzo (2005) has coined the term "masculine imperative" to describe the "pressure within larger gay male communities for men to adhere to a rigid attitudinal and physical presentation to the world" that idealizes "hypermasculine" physical qualities (p. 376). Such stereotypical models of masculinity can make intimacy and emotional expression difficult in the context of a relationship. Moreover, such male socialization can lead men to deny their vulnerability. As noted by Letellier (1994), men are frequently unable to see themselves as victims because to do so is equated with weakness and femininity. Similarly, they are apt to experience such sex role stereotyping from law enforcement and others. Merrill and Wolfe (2000) give the example of a man with a bleeding bite wound from his partner who was told by the responding officer that he would "need to learn to defend himself better" (p. 7).

In general, gay male relationships do not follow the same ideal of monogamy that is normative for heterosexual relationships. There is a great deal of variation in the ways that gay men define their relational boundaries. Some maintain monogamous relationships, while others agree to keep their emotional relationship primary but agree on guidelines for extradyadic sexual encounters (e.g., only as a threesome, only on business trips, only one night stands, and so on) (Alonzo, 2005). As noted by Alonzo (2005), research demonstrates that, in general, "nonmonogamous couples do not experience less satisfaction than their monogamous counterparts" (p. 377).

HIV and AIDS have affected virtually every gay man in one way or another and can be a critical factor in domestic violence. Merrill and Wolfe (2000), in their study of 52 gay male victims of domestic violence, found that a significant number of their respondents reported that HIV-related fears, such as a "fear of becoming sick and dying," "not wanting to abandon an HIV-positive partner," or a "fear of dating in the context of the HIV epidemic" played a major part in their decisions not to leave an abusive partner (p. 18). Gay batterers may also threaten to infect their partner with HIV, to withhold medication, or to reveal the HIV/AIDS status of their partners (Letellier, 1996). Alarmingly, approximately three-quarters of Merrill a\nd Wolfe's sample reported having been sexually abused by their partner, and 13% of their "respondents reported that their partners sometimes or frequently 'tried to infect or infected' them with HIV" (p. 11).

Issues Specific to Lesbian Couples

In contrast to boys, girls are socialized to define themselves in relation to others (Chodorow, 1978). On the one hand, this may enhance women's capacity for intimate relating and identification with others; on the other, it may also intensify the potential for merger (Burch, 1986; Elise, 1986). Much of the early writings focused on merger as a pathological construct in lesbian relationships (Elise, 1986; Krestan & Bepko, 1980), and merger in lesbian relationships has been identified as one factor that may contribute to domestic violence (Krestan & Bepko, 1980; Miller, Greene, Causby, White, & Lockhart, 2001). More recently, researchers have begun to redefine the concept of fusion in lesbian relationships and identify ways that fusion adaptively reinforces the bond between two women in a hostile and devaluing society (Miller et al., 2001). Given women's propensity toward intimate bonding, it is not surprising that in contrast to gay men, most lesbian relationships are monogamous, and nonmonogamy is the exception rather than the norm.

I suggest that merger be thought of dynamically and conceptualized as a continuum. Fusion and cohesion can indeed be healthy and adaptive elements of a lesbian relationship; however, rigidity can lead to destructive levels of fusion. Although the insular nature of the lesbian community, because of its small size and minority status, offers a great deal of support and protection for many lesbians, unhealthy merger can develop. For example, it is not uncommon for lesbian batterers to see all their female friends as potential rivals—leading to increased isolation, particularly for the battered partner.

Interestingly, in their examination of the functional and interpersonal style of 15 lesbians who had abused their partners, Poorman and Seelau (2001) found that the women were "more likely to be uncomfortable with both contact and closeness than the norm" (p. 97). Thus, normative levels of high cohesion in lesbian relationships may be quite threatening and disorganizing for some women. They suggest that underlying these women's preference for independence and self-sufficiency are "feelings of loneliness and isolation, as well as anger and hostility about being excluded or abandoned" (p. 97). They also found that in comparison to those lesbians identified as abused, the abusers were significantly more likely to want to dominate in a relationship as opposed to subordinating themselves. The personality characteristics described by Poorman and Seelau are consistent with insecure attachment and poor regulatory function—which may lead to abuse and violence as a way of regulating unmanageable internal affective states and interpersonal dynamics.

ASSESSMENT

Since I am in a private practice setting, the majority of couples I see present as needing "help with communication skills." For those couples *who do not identify* as having a problem with violence, I am careful to ask about how things go when they argue—starting with milder forms of conflict and including more severe forms of conflict in a matter-of-fact, noninflammatory manner. For instance, I may say, "All couples get into bad fights at one time or another. What is it like when the two of you argue or fight? Do you tend to yell and scream, throw things . . . physically fight with each other?" I evaluate how each responds and what the dynamics are between them as they talk about how they deal with conflict. If I have identified potential abuse or on those occasions when a couple's presenting problem is domestic violence, I will assess the following to get a sense of their relational dynamics. Who initiated treatment, and who starts talking first? Are they talking openly in front of one another? Is there an atmosphere of fear and anxiety and/or a high degree of hostility in the room? Who takes responsibility for the violence? How much are they blaming each other?

I then assess them individually, both orally and through the use of questionnaires[3]—such as the Revised Conflict Tactics Scales (Straus, Hamby, Boney-McCoy, & Sugarman, 1996). In the clinical interview, I ask about recent and past arguments in a detailed fashion. I am interested in the frequency, severity, and dynamics of abuse (who did what do whom and in what order) as well as the climate of the relationship. Who tends to initiate the violence and under what circumstances? Is violence used in self-defense? Have weapons been used, and/or are there weapons in the home? Is one partner controlling the other through the use and abuse of power and control in the relationship? Are both engaging in emotionally and physically abusive behavior? I want to get a sense of how much responsibility both take for their own behavior versus blaming others and/or defending themselves and their actions. I also want to get a sense of their level of pathology—is she or he operating at a psychotic, borderline, or neurotic level? Does she or he present with a personality disorder, mood disorder, substance abuse, and so on? Are children in the home, and, if so, how they have been affected—are they in danger?

I am also interested in their attachment styles. In general, it has been my experience that either one or both of the partners in a high-conflict couple have an insecure attachment. I attempt to identify the nature of their attachment topology and the ways in which this plays out in the couple relationship. For more information on the role of attachment in domestic violence, see Coleman (2003), Dutton (1998), Sonkin and Dutton (2003), and Vetere and Cooper (chapter 17 in this volume).

TREATMENT

In many cases, couple therapy is a viable and effective method for treating domestic violence and reducing/eliminating abusive couple dynamics. Because domestic violence occurs on a continuum (from low frequency, mild, mutual aggression/conflict to high aggression, severe unilateral battering), it is essential to assess the type and frequency of abuse that has occurred over time and in what ways, if any, it has changed over time. In "severe battering," violence is intentionally used to dominate and control, and there is frequent, significantly abusive and injurious behavior (Hamel, 2005). In such cases, couple therapy is not a safe or effective mode of treatment, and referrals are made for group and/or individual treatment. Other factors that preclude couple therapy as an appropriate treatment option are an atmosphere of fear and/or intimidation, lack of responsibility, high blame, personality disorders, and lack of motivation. For an in-depth discussion on the safety and efficacy of conjoint therapy in the treatment of domestic violence cases, see O'Leary and Cohen (chapter 16 in this volume).

The first tasks of the couple treatment are setting the frame and ensuring safety. A verbal contract is made regarding the parameters of treatment, and I may require that treatment occur more than once a week. I clarify limits of confidentiality and let the couple know that I do not necessarily hold confidentiality between partners; rather, I will use my clinical judgment about any information disclosed to me without the other partner present—for instance, in a phone call or if individual sessions are necessary. I will then go over the use of time-outs[4] and establish a verbal safety plan and "no violence" contract.

The first phase of the couple therapy, which may last several weeks or months, is educational and cognitive-behavioral in focus. My goal is to help them develop an observing ego regarding cycles of violence, destructive and abusive behaviors, emotional reactivity, and their attachment styles. Time is spent identifying the abusive behaviors in which they engage and confronting any minimization or denial around such behaviors. In discussing time-outs, I have found it crucial to identify the buildup of intrapersonal (physical cues, self-talk, and so on) and interpersonal (verbal and nonverbal expression, tone, and so on) tension, highlighting the cues each can use to increase awareness of when to call a time-out. It is important to clarify that this means calling a time-out for oneself versus further inflaming an argument by telling one's partner, "You need to take a time-out!" Windows of optimal communication and the need to decrease neurophysiological arousal during a time-out are discussed, and techniques for deescalating themselves during the time-out, such as journaling, walking, deep breathing, and meditating, are identified and implemented. In addition, worksheets or workbooks are used both in and between sessions to help identify key triggers of conflict and abuse—for example, anger and control logs, abusive behavior checklists, and the iceberg exercise (which labels feelings underneath their anger and separates thoughts from feelings; Fogelman, 1996).[5] It is essential that a differentiation be made between being "triggered" and how one handles being triggered. While providing empathy and understanding regarding triggers, the therapist reinforces that each individual must take responsibility and be accountable for her or his behavioral choices.

In the second phase of treatment, psychodynamic exploration and understanding moves into the forefront and is interwoven with cognitive-behavioral techniques. During this time, I gather more detailed information about family and relational history. This enables me to help them identify the ways in which their family and cultural backgrounds have contributed to their choice of partner, their coping styles, and the defensive tactics they use in the relationship. It is also important to explore how factors such as each individual's support system, level of being out about their sexual orientation, and impact of homophobia and hetero-sexism influence the relational dynamics.

As therapist, I am able to be attuned to each partner and empathi-cally resonate with her or his experience as we track the couple's emo-tional, physiological, and cognitive states of affect and arousal. My goal is to provide a level of attunement, through supportive understanding and constructive confrontation, that will decrease levels of shame and enable them to increase their capacity for empathy with themselves and each other. Shame is inextricably linked to insecure attachment and the need to disavow aspects of self, which in battering are easily projected onto and then attacked in one's partner (Coleman, 2003). Processing conflict as it happens in the sessions and discussing the details of arguments that happen in between help to identify their projections and illuminate how frequently they are engaged in "shadowboxing" with each other (i.e., fighting the shadows of internal objects cast on each other). Untangling the destructive dances in which the couple has been immersed necessitates that each develops the ability to self-soothe. Although the capacity to self-soothe can be expanded through couple therapy, it may be necessary for one or both partners to utilize individual or group therapy to further address areas of trauma and improve self-regulation. As the therapist illuminates the ways in which their respective insecure attachments are exacerbated by their relational dance, it is essential that she or he clarify that this does not mean that one person is "responsible" for the other's insecurities. Such elucidation and differentiation is especially critical in cases of unilateral battering where the battered partner has typically been made to feel responsible for the batterer's feelings and behavior.

When violence and other abusive behaviors have consistently stopped and there is evidence that both partners have sufficient self-regulation, the work can be deepened to allow for more vulnerability—enabling key moments of emotional connection (Johnson, 2004). The enhancement of moments of deep emotional understanding and connectivity facilitates a secure attachment that reinforces nonabusive, healthy communication and conflict resolution, which further reinforces secure attachment and so on. At this level of treatment, continued couple work consolidates new intrapsychic capacities and interpersonal skills that enable the partners to handle high levels of conflict and potentially dysregulating states in nonabusive, loving ways.

CASE EXAMPLE: JOEL AND MARTIN

Initial Assessment

In his initial phone call, Joel was warm and straight to the point: "Dr. S. referred us to you for couple therapy. We need to work on our relationship and I need help dealing with my anger." When I asked him about his anger, Joel responded that on a couple of occasions he had lost his temper and hit Martin, his live-in partner of three years—"It doesn't happen very often, but I know it's not right, and I don't want him to leave me because of it." They agreed to come in for an extended assessment session the following Tuesday.

My first impression was that Joel (29 years old, White) was charming and gregarious, whereas Martin (26 years old, Honduran American) appeared angry and rather sullen. I began the session by informing them that first we would all meet together, and then I would spend some time with each of them individually while the other filled out some paperwork and questionnaires. We would then all come back together, and I'd give them my initial recommendations. Joel was very talkative and started by saying that Martin didn't want to come and didn't believe in therapy. He went on: "But, I know it's been really helpful for me, so finally I was able to talk him into coming. I think we need to communicate better, and I know I need to work on how angry I get." Martin responded that he'd never been in therapy and didn't really see how it could help, "but I said I'd come, and I agree he needs to deal with his anger, but I'm not sure I even want to work on this."

Exploration of the fight that prompted Joel's call revealed that Joel's jealousy and Martin's indifference precipitated many arguments. The previous weekend they had gone out to a nightclub with friends. After a few hours, Joel wanted to leave, but Martin was not ready to go. When Martin went to the bar to get another drink and didn't come back for 30 minutes, Joel went to look for him. On finding him talking to another man at the bar, Joel angrily approached Martin and said, "Let's go!" When Martin didn't respond, Joel grabbed him by the arm. Martin pushed Joel away and told him to "lay off . . . stop getting your panties all in a knot!" Hurt and angry, Joel left the bar and went home without saying good-bye. A few hours later, Martin got a ride home from friends and came in angry at having been left by Joel. Joel stated that he was still awake and stewing when Martin got home— imagining he'd gone home with the guy from the bar. Joel started to get more upset:

JOEL: He's flirting with this guy, totally dissing me, and then he expects me to just wait around for him? Bullshit. Then he has the balls to come in yelling and cussing at me about leaving him there?!

MARTIN: Damn right—why don't you tell her about how you accused me of whoring around? [Turning toward me] So, of course I was yelling at him, he is so insecure and possessive, [rolls his eyes] and then he leaves me there—no way, I'm sick and tired of being treated like shit!!

I interrupted and stated that it was clear there were still a lot of "hot" feelings about what had happened and that clearly this seemed to be a pattern that was hurtful and enraging to both of them. I asked each to take a deep breath and see if they could finish telling me about what happened next:

MARTIN: I told him I expected an apology and that I wasn't going to take his shit anymore. I started to leave to go stay at my friends, and he got up and grabbed me, so I pushed him down and . . .

JOEL: You mean you slammed me into the wall.

MARTIN: I was just pushing you away; it's not my fault you slammed into the wall! [Turns to look at me] Then he gets up and punches me in the stomach. Then he looked crazy, like he was going to punch me in the face; instead he just walked out into the living room . . . so I let him go, and I stayed in the bedroom.

JOEL: I tried to get him to talk to me instead of leaving—that's what he does, he doesn't deal, he's a cold asshole. I didn't even really grab him, but then when he pushed me I lost it—plus you called me a "jealous faggot"—you're such a fucking jerk sometimes.

MARTIN: [hopeless voice] I don't even know why I bothered to come home that night. I shoulda just stayed out. I come home, and you think I'm fucking around anyway—I don't know why the hell I've stayed in this relationship.

Joel started to speak again, and I stopped him—redirecting them by asking them how often these kinds of fights happened. Both agreed that the violence had occurred only a handful of times, but they tended to get into big arguments about once a month. Further exploration revealed that their fights had increased over the past year and that the violence had escalated from pushing and shoving to hitting.

In the individual interviews, neither one of them expressed any fear, nor was there any evidence of intimidation in the relationship. Although Joel acknowledged that he needed to deal with his anger, he also tended to minimize the impact of his rage and aggression. And he vacillated between taking responsibility for his own actions and blaming Martin for making him "lose it." Martin was detached and angry, and I found myself struggling to find a way to connect with him. He again expressed his doubts about therapy and his uncertainty about whether he wanted to continue in the relationship. Martin denied that he had been having an affair but stated that he had been thinking about it and frequently found himself attracted to other men. When I asked him about how things were when they first met and what had attracted him to Joel, he began to soften a bit and stated that he missed the Joel he fell in love with and how things used to be between them. He described that when they first met, Joel was confident and successful and had a good sense of humor—"we used to have a lot of fun together."

The initial assessment revealed that both had engaged in emotionally abusive behaviors and perpetrated minor physical abuse. In general, Joel tended to initiate the physical abuse, and on a couple of occasions, he had verbally badgered Martin into having sex. Although Martin would fight back in self-defense, he acknowledged that he had intentionally slammed Joel against the wall on two occasions that were not in self-defense. I decided that they were good candidates for conjoint therapy for the following reasons: They did not exhibit frequent, severe physical abuse; neither expressed fear of the other or of speaking up in couple therapy; Joel acknowledged responsibility for his actions and was motivated for treatment; and they were able to deescalate in my office when I intervened. Furthermore, addressing their relationship dysfunction would likely result in improved, nonabusive conflict resolution. They agreed to take responsibility for their behavior, contracted for safety, and agreed to follow my treatment recommendations. Four more sessions were scheduled with the understanding that we would then reassess the treatment plan.

Safety

The next four sessions focused primarily on safety planning and implementing new ways of handling conflict. I worked with them to identify the precipitants of conflict and indicators of escalation. We went over the destructive and abusive tactics that both used in order to be heard, right a wrong, or feel in control. The guidelines for time-outs were agreed on with each learning to identify and take responsibility for creating safety and deescalating conflict. I worked with each of them on recognizing their own cues (bodily sensations, self-talk, tone of voice, and so on) for calling a time-out. They began to take in and acknowledge the ways in which they triggered each other and would "up the ante" during their arguments. The importance of practicing time-outs and "building emotional muscle" was stressed. I had them take mini time-outs in session, and they practiced at home by starting with minor irritations and disagreements. They were instructed to check in with each other after an hour to let the other know whether they could resume their conversation or if they needed to table it for later. In the initial phase of treatment, I encouraged them to table hot topics until our next session. Most challenging for them was how Joel's abandonment issues got triggered and made it difficult for him to respect time-outs when Martin called them. Joel also had trouble calling them himself, although he would get fed up and walk away at times in order to punish Martin. Over the next few weeks, both demonstrated a commitment to following time-outs. Despite the fact that they didn't always succeed in effectively using them, each failure served as a learning experience, and with each success, Joel's capacity to tolerate the separations increased. Because they were able to make use of and implement the work done in sessions and since neither of them evidenced severe psychopathology, I recommended that we proceed with conjoint treatment. Martin told Joel that he wasn't sure he wanted to continue the relationship, but he was willing to commit to working on it and seeing what happened as a result of the couple therapy.

The beginning phase of treatment continued to focus primarily on safety and building the treatment alliance. I actively and gently confronted Joel's tendency to minimize the impact of his abuse. Much of what I provided in the sessions was containment and regulation. Through their being "heard" by me, they slowly began to increase their ability to hear each other. The safety of the couple session also served as a container for the painful, angry, and shameful feelings that they were slowly able to reveal in front of each other.

Family Background

Having established a consistent sense of physical safety, I began to inquire about their families of origin, working to identify their internal models of self and other.

Joel grew up in what he described as a typical midwestern, blue-collar family. His father was a factory foreman who terrorized and controlled the family through rage and physical abuse. Being the older of two boys, Joel got the worst of it. When asked about his father, he stated, "I don't remember a whole lot; for the most part he wasn't around much, but when he was drunk, all hell would break loose." When his father sobered up, he would apologize, and things would be "okay" for a while. Joel's mother was a homemaker, and Joel recalled her spending lots of time with him until the age of five, when his brother was born. He described his mother as an anxious, depressed, and passive woman who was loving and warm when his father wasn't around. There were a few times when his mother left and took the children to her sister's house. Joel's relationship with his brother was mixed. On one hand, he remembered being really angry and upset when his mother told him he had a brother on the way; on the other, he loved his brother and would try to protect him during his father's rages.

Over the course of time, Joel revealed that he had been labeled a "sissy" and a "momma's boy" by both his peers in elementary school and his father, who would taunt him. After being beaten up at school in the fifth grade, Joel decided to take karate. He didn't stick with it very long, but he "toughened up" and began to fight back. As a teenager, he would fight back against his father—resulting in serious physical altercations. Through our work, Joel was able to identify the "little boy feelings" that he'd had to split off or repress in order to survive his childhood. When asked about his experience coming out as gay, Joel described that high school was "hell" because he was sure someone would find out he was attracted to other guys. He expressed feeling extreme shame and guilt about disappointing his mother and being a "sissy boy." He tried dating women in college but always found himself thinking about guys. He began to go out to bars and had numerous one-night stands with various men. After college, Joel relocated to Los Angeles and came out to his family. Although they were initially judgmental and unsupportive, his mother and brother are now more accepting, and his father does not talk about it. Prior to meeting Martin through mutual friends, Joel had a series of short-term, nonmonogamous relationships.

Born and raised in Los Angeles, Martin is the middle son in a large Catholic family (two older sisters and two younger brothers). Both of Martin's parents are Honduran, and he often felt conflicted between their culture and American culture. His father worked in construction, and his mother took care of the home and children. Martin described his family as a good, traditional Catholic family and characterized his parents and siblings as outgoing, loving people. However, he reported that he never felt very close to either his bothers or his sisters and noted that he spent a fair amount of time playing alone. He said that he was not comfortable coming out to his family because he could not bear to disappoint his parents by telling them their oldest son was gay. Thus, he went to great lengths to hide his relationship with Joel (his first serious gay relationship); this was a significant source of contention between Martin and Joel. Only later in the treatment was Martin able to identify that his mother's criticism and his father's unavailability and depressive nature had contributed to his feelings of shame and his fear of coming out to them.

In addition, he felt very conflicted about being Catholic and carried a great deal of guilt about his sexuality. Martin was bilingual; he spoke Spanish with his family and English outside the home. Exploration revealed that being gay and bicultural left Martin feeling that he did not really "fit in" or "belong" anywhere. I wondered aloud about how the fact that neither Joel nor I spoke Spanish impacted Martin's ability to fully communicate his feelings and experiences to us. Although he assured me that this was not a problem, I have found that there are some early experiences that may be more easily accessed and communicated in one's native tongue. During college, Martin had some sexual relationships with other men; however, he always hid them from his peers. After college, Martin worked as a bank teller, but he quickly tired of this and decided to pursue his MBA. His return to school, the previous year, had exacerbated Joel's feelings of insecurity and intensified his jealous behavior.

Aspects of Treatment

Building on our exploration of their family histories, I addressed the ways in which their cultural and religious differences had been difficult to navigate. For instance, Joel was frequently hurt and angry that Martin hid their relationship:

JOEL: He doesn't love me enough to come out to his parents . . . he's always hiding me; we have two bedrooms, and he pretends I'm just his roommate. He never takes me to family functions. It's bullshit; he's taken other guys he's slept with.

MARTIN: That's because they were mostly just friends, and no one would know by looking at them either.

JOEL: What the hell does that mean? What are you saying . . .

VC: [firmly] I'm going to stop you guys here because you are escalating and jabbing each other. It seems to me there are many levels to what is going on, and I want you both to try to stay with what you are feeling so we can sort this out. Joel, clearly it feels hurtful for you that Martin has not come out to his family and that he hides your relationship. However, I think you expect that if he loved you enough he would . . . which I'm not convinced is true. I want to hear more from Martin so that I can understand—and we can understand together—what this is like for him. [Looking at Joel] Can you take a couple deep breaths and recenter yourself? [making use of relaxation exercises we had practiced before]

JOEL: [angrily] I'm really triggered here . . . I don't know.

VC: Yes, I know this is really hard. I think it stirs up all those little boy feelings of not being good enough, not feeling lovable . . . and how much you got teased. Those are really painful, awful places, and when you can't feel Martin, when you don't experience his love and care, it leaves you feeling so much pain and shame that you automatically go to rage—that feels better, more powerful. [Here I was drawing on previous discussions of how he had identified with his father's aggression and power.] [Joel nodded, and I could see that he was beginning to calm down.] It makes complete sense to me that it feels hurtful to you to be hidden from Martin's family, but I have a feeling Martin hasn't come out to them for other reasons, and when you get angry and demanding with him, there is no way for him to hear you and know how much this is hurting you.

JOEL: Okay . . . I'll try to listen.

By mirroring Joel's experience, I was attempting to provide a soothing, regulating, and validating function while at the same time creating space for understanding how his rejecting and persecutory internal objects got projected onto Martin. I was also providing a similar function for Martin, creating analytic space in which he could then explore his feelings and make room to hear Joel's feelings—hopefully increasing their empathic connection and leading them to an experience of mutual regulation.

I then turned to Martin and encouraged him to share more about his fears of coming out to his family and his terror that they would disown him. This opened up a discussion around cultural and religious issues and the differences between he and Joel. In addition, it led to our being able to talk about Martin's internalized homophobia and the stereotypes he had about "fags." He was indeed afraid that his family would pick up on Joel's more effeminate style. This was really hard for Joel to hear—he became angry and verbally attacking in the session. I intervened and tried to calm him down, but I was quickly overridden. They began to fight and verbally attack each other. I finally managed to stop the escalation and had them take a time-out. We were near the end of our session time, and I was aware of feeling anxious. Had I made a mistake in encouraging them to enter this vulnerable territory? Would Joel initiate a physical assault after they left? Was I mistaken in thinking that couple therapy was an appropriate mode of treatment for them? I was glad for the short time-out, which allowed me to reduce my anxiety and return to as much of a mindful, assertive state as I could muster at the time. Later, I was able to consider the intensity of the projected anxiety with which I was identifying. It seemed that as they were becoming more vulnerable with each other, their intensifying anxiety played out through projection and enactment—Martin was defending against his fear of being deeply shamed and disowned by his family by shaming Joel, and Joel was managing his shame and terror by verbally attacking Martin. As a couple, their escalating shame and anxiety was projected onto, and identified with, by me.

I brought them back together and shared my concerns about how they might continue to escalate after leaving the session. I acknowledged how difficult this territory was and how it was triggering raw, painful places in each of them. I suggested that this all made sense given the negative societal and cultural attitudes about homosexuality that we all internalize. I then interpreted that this hatred and hurt was now being taken out on each other. In addition, I pointed out that as painful as this all was, it was also really courageous for them to be addressing these underlying issues. Rather than continuing the destructive dance they had been engaged in, they now had an opportunity to deal with this differently. We made a safety plan for how they would interact after leaving session, and at my encouragement they agreed to come back two days later.

In the next session, they shared that the past two days had been extremely difficult and that there had been one time when Joel tried to verbally "pin Martin down" and make him talk through the issue. Martin shared that he'd had the impulse to shove Joel, but instead he insisted on a time-out. Working through Joel's pain and how Martin's stereotypes and homophobia touched off his own pain, shame, and rage was a difficult process that continued, off and on, for several months. We cycled back and forth addressing the "kid places" that got touched off for both of them and how these dovetailed with their individual attachment styles/defenses. The treatment also addressed their use of alcohol as a defense and how it exacerbated their problems. They began to drink less and were able to become more attuned to the ways their respective insecure attachment styles activated insecurity in the other. For instance, Martin tended to withdraw, becoming emotionally cold and disconnected, which triggered Joel's demanding, jealous, and clingy behavior, which furthered Martin's shutting down and so on. We also addressed the ways in which Martin's flirtatious behavior served as a defense against his feelings of inferiority and conflict about being gay. Flirting made Martin feel powerful and gave him a kind of "high" that distracted him from his internal turmoil.

Gradually, they began to generate preventive strategies to interrupt their destructive cycles of engagement. We discussed various ways that Joel could feel secure in his connection to Martin when they went out with friends or out to clubs. For example, they were able to agree on ways Joel could check in and connect with Martin without Martin feeling smothered and taken over by Joel. Similarly, we worked on reducing/eliminating the ways in which Joel tried to force Martin into relating—for instance, pressuring him to have sex or trying to make Martin talk to him when Martin wanted to sleep. Synergistically, when Martin made efforts to stay present with Joel, Joel did not feel the internal pressure and anxiety that previously had fueled his attempts to forcibly elicit Martin's interest and affection. Although Martin's refusal to come out to his family continues to be a painful and difficult issue, the treatment has enabled them to struggle with their hurt, anxious, and angry feelings without escalating into abusive fights.

SUMMARY

The issues faced by Joel and Martin highlight how clinicians must be knowledgeable about same-sex relationships and attuned to the impact of heterosexism and homophobia. Providing ethical and effective treatment with lesbians and gay men requires an affirmative stance toward differing sexual orientations and same-sex relationships (American Psychological Association, 2006). Thus, it is essential that clinicians are conscious of their own beliefs and biases regarding same-sex relationships and aware of how their own internalized homophobia may play out in their countertransference.

Naturally, my work with Joel and Martin was more complex than can be conveyed in this chapter. Nonetheless, I have tried to exemplify how, under certain circumstances, couple therapy can be a powerful and effective multilevel treatment for domestic violence. Through the integration of cognitive-behavioral interventions and interpretive psychodynamic understanding, couple work can hold abusive individuals accountable for their behavior while helping both partners take responsibility for their steps of the relational dance. As abusive behaviors and destructive cycles of interaction are reduced/eliminated, opportunities for the couple to repair attachment wounds become available—enabling the development of deeper emotional connection and healthy relating.

NOTES

1. Heterosexism is the ideological denial, denigrating, and stigmatization of any non-heterosexual form of identity, relationship, behavior, or community (Herek, 1993). Homophobia is an irrational fear of, hatred for, or aversion to anyone who is lesbian/gay or to aspects of the lesbian/gay lifestyle.
2. The film *Brokeback Mountain* is an excellent portrayal of the hardships faced by gay men and the use of domestic violence to manage unbearable internal conflict and self-hatred.
3. Hamel's (2005) book *Gender Inclusive Treatment of Intimate Partner Abuse* is a wonderful resource and provides clinicians with several different assessment tools.
4. For a detailed explanation of time-out, see Sonkin and Durphy (1997).
5. For a more detailed description, see Coleman (2003, p. 195).

REFERENCES

Alonzo, D. (2005). Working with same-sex couples. In M. Harway (Ed.), *Handbook of couples therapy* (pp. 370–385). Hoboken, NJ: John Wiley & Sons.

American Psychological Association. (2006). *Guidelines for psychotherapy with lesbian, gay and bisexual clients.* Retrieved January 1, 2006, from http://www.apa.org/pi/lgbc/guidelines.html

Burch, B. (1986). Psychotherapy and the dynamics of merger in lesbian couples. In T. S. Stein & C. J. Cohen (Eds.), *Contemporary perspectives on psychotherapy with lesbians and gay men* (pp. 57–72). New York: Plenum Medical Book.

Burke, L. K., & Follingstad, E. R. (1999). Violence in lesbian and gay relationships: Theory, prevalence, and correlational factors. *Clinical Psychology Review, 19*(5), 487–512.

Chodorow, N. (1978). *The reproduction of mothering: Psychoanalysis and the sociology of gender.* Berkeley: University of California Press.

Coleman, V. E. (1991). Violence in lesbian couples: A between groups comparison (Doctoral dissertation, California School of Professional Psychology—Los Angeles, 1990). *Dissertation Abstracts International, 51,* 5634B.

Coleman, V. E. (2003). Treating the lesbian batterer: Theoretical and clinical considerations— A contemporary psychoanalytic perspective. *Journal of Aggression, Maltreatment and Trauma, 7*(1/2), 159–205.

Dutton, D. G. (1998). *The abusive personality: Violence and control in intimate relationships.* New York: Guilford Press.

Elise, D. (1986). Lesbian couples: The implications of sex differences in separation and individuation. *Psychotherapy, 23,* 305–310.

Fogelman, J. (1996). *Stop the violence: An introductory treatment program for gay male batterers.* Unpublished facilitators' manual.

Gardner, R. (1989). Method of conflict resolution and characteristics of abuse and victimization in heterosexual, lesbian, and gay male couples (Doctoral dissertation, University of Georgia, 1988). *Dissertation Abstracts International, 50,* 746B.

Gottman, J. (2004). *12-year study of gay and lesbian couples.* Retrieved December 20, 2005, from http://www.gottman.com/research/projects/gaylesbian.

Hamel, J. (2005). *Gender inclusive treatment of intimate partner abuse: A comprehensive approach.* New York: Springer.

Herek, G. M. (1993). The context of antigay violence: Notes on cultural and psychological heterosexism. In L. D. Garnets & D.C. Kimmel (Eds.), *Psychological perspectives on lesbian and gay male experiences* (pp. 89–108). New York: Colombia University Press.

Johnson, S. (2004). *The practice of emotionally focused couple therapy* (2nd ed.). New York: Brunner-Routledge.

Krestan, J., & Bepko, C. (1980). The problem of fusion in the lesbian relationship. *Family Process, 19,* 277–289.

Kurdek, L. (1994). The nature and correlates of relationship quality in gay, lesbian, and heterosexual cohabiting couples: A test of the individual difference, interdependence, and discrepancy models. In B. Greene & G. M. Herek (Eds.), *Lesbian and gay psychology: Theory, research, and clinical applications* (pp. 133–155). Thousand Oaks, CA: Sage.

Letellier, P. (1994). Gay and bisexual male domestic violence victimization: Challenges to feminist theory and responses to violence. *Violence and Victims, 9*(2), 1–22.

Letellier, P. (1996). Twin epidemics: Domestic violence and HIV infection among gay and bisexual men. In C. M. Renzetti & C. H. Miley (Eds.), *Violence in gay and lesbian domestic partnerships* (pp. 69–82). Binghamton, NY: Harrington Park Press.

Lie, G., Schilit, R., Bush, J., Montagne, M., & Reyes, L. (1991). Lesbians in currently aggressive relationships: How frequently do they report aggressive past relationships? *Violence and Victims, 6,* 121–135.

McLaughlin, E. M., & Rozee, P. D. (1996). Knowledge about heterosexual versus lesbian battering among lesbians. In E. Kaschak (Ed.), *Intimate betrayal: Domestic violence in lesbian relationships* (pp. 39–58). New York: Haworth Press.

Merrill, G. S., & Wolf, V. A. (2000). Battered gay men: An exploration of abuse, help seeking, and why they stay. *Journal of Homosexuality, 39*(2), 1–30.

Meyer, I. H., & Dean, L. (1998). Internalized homophobia, intimacy and sexual behavior among gay and bisexual men. In G. M. Herek (Ed.), *Stigma and sexual orientation: Understanding prejudice against lesbians, gay men, and bisexuals* (pp. 160–186). Thousand Oaks, CA: Sage.

Miller, D. H., Greene, K., Causby, V., White, B. W., & Lockhart, L. L. (2001). Domestic violence in lesbian relationships. In E. Kaschak (Ed.), *Intimate betrayal: Domestic violence in lesbian relationships* (pp. 107–128). New York: Haworth Press.

Poorman, P. B., & Seelau, S. M. (2001). Lesbians who abuse their partners: Using the FIRO-B to assess interpersonal characteristics. In Ellyn Kaschak (Ed.), *Intimate betrayal: Domestic violence in lesbian relationships* (pp. 87–106). New York: Haworth Press.

Renzetti, C. M. (1988). Violence in lesbian relationships: A preliminary analysis of causal factors. *Journal of Interpersonal Violence, 3,* 381–399.

Sonkin, S., & Durphy, M. (1997). *Learning to live without violence: A handbook for men.* Volcano, CA: Volcano Press.

Sonkin, D., & Dutton, D. (2003). Treating assaultive men from an attachment perspective. *Journal of Aggression, Maltreatment and Trauma, 7*(1/2), 105–133.

Straus, M. A., Hamby, S. L., Boney-McCoy, S., & Sugarman, D. B. (1996). The revised Conflict Tactics Scales (CTS2): Development and preliminary psychometric data. *Journal of Family Issues, 17,* 283–316.

Waldner-Haugrud, L. D., Gratch, L. V., & Magruder, B. (1997). Victimization and perpetration rates of violence in gay and lesbian relationships: Gender issues explored. *Violence and Victims, 12*(2) 173–184.

Waldron, C. M. (1996). Lesbians of color and the domestic violence movement. In C. M. Renzetti & C. H. Miley (Eds.), *Violence in gay and lesbian domestic partnerships* (pp. 43–52). Binghamton, NY: Harrington Park Press.

CHAPTER 19

Treatment of Family Violence: A Systemic Perspective

Michael Thomas

WHY WE COMMIT VIOLENCE AGAINST THE PEOPLE WE LOVE

Exploring family violence brings up profound questions that challenge the way we see ourselves and others. Our response to this problem reveals as much about us as it does the perpetrators and victims. Do we minimize the violence, believing that parents (especially mothers) always know and do what's best for their children? Do we justify frequent use of corporal punishment as a necessary response to "bad" kids? Are we so overwhelmed by the tragedy of family violence that we avoid the topic? Do we get so angry at the perpetrators of this violence that we just want to punish them? Are we so anxious about safety that we just want the victim to leave the perpetrator and get angry at them when they don't? Do we project our own dark side onto these perpetrators or our own fears onto the victims? The issue may be so complex that we seek out simplistic answers and solutions.

Family violence has a profound impact on everyone in the family system, whether they are the target of this violence or a witness:

✓ Early childhood abuse and neglect has a measurable impact on the neurophysiology of the infant, especially the orbitofrontal region. This is the region of the brain that is "experience dependent," where we form our attachment relationships. Early

417

childhood abuse or neglect by the primary parent can cause permanent damage to this region of the brain, leading to "a lifelong limited ability, especially under stress, to regulate the intensity, frequency, and duration of primitive negative states such as rage, terror, and shame" (Karr-Morse & Wiley, 1997, p. 38).

✓ Researchers have found numerous mental health problems correlated with family violence, such as increased depression, substance abuse, personality disorders, antisocial behaviors, and increased aggression and violence.

✓ The family, especially the quality of attachment with our parents, is the basis for our developing sense of self, the template for our relationships with others, and our core beliefs about the kind of world we live in.

✓ Family violence can affect the way family members treat each other. Abused children could abuse siblings or other children. Parents who are abused by their spouse could then abuse their children or abuse both their spouse and their children. Adults who are being abused by their spouse may not protect their children from abuse.

✓ Family violence can be learned and transmitted to the next generation if the abused grows up to abuse his or her family or marry an abuser.

✓ Family violence also changes our society. Cultures that endorse abusive child-rearing tactics or discipline are more likely to be violent, totalitarian, and warlike (DeMause, 1982; Miller, 1983).

Josh is a 15-year-old boy who was brought into a psychiatric unit by his mother, who reported serious discipline problems. She described her son as being out of control and angry, hitting her and his younger brother. The hospital staff chose to hospitalize Josh and based their decision solely on the mother's word. No one explored the family dynamics that might have precipitated this boy's anger and violence.

At the time, I had been treating the boys' father and stepmother for his sexual compulsivity (multiple affairs) and her posttraumatic stress disorder from severe physical abuse by her own stepfather. She did a good job of parenting her stepsons, but she became increasingly alarmed at evidence that they were being verbally abused by their mother. She described an incident where they were helping her carry groceries from the car into the house. When one of the boys dropped a bag of groceries, they looked at her in terror as though she was going to punish them. She didn't, but she began to talk to her husband about her concerns, trying to get him to protect his sons. Shortly after this, they began divorce proceedings.

Not long after, the mother then moved with her sons to another state. The stepmother stayed in contact with the boys and asked me for help when she discovered that Josh had been committed to a psychiatric unit for violence against his mother. I was able to discuss this with Josh's case manager and informed him about this mother's long history of verbal and emotional abuse. The case manager (and his clinic medical director) refused to consider this information or perform a more complete evaluation for treatment.

I never met Josh's mother, but she and the stepmother shared the experience of being married to a man having multiple affairs during their marriage. Perhaps some of the mother's rage may have been projected from her ex-husband onto her sons. This mother was also abused as a child by her father and mother and had witnessed her mother regularly browbeat her father. Yet the stepmother had the same problems of an unfaithful husband, parenting two teenage boys, and having previously experienced severe physical abuse at the hands of her stepfather. Both women experienced difficult relationships that affected their own attachment patterns as adults. One woman healed enough to nurture and protect her stepsons. The other acted out her rage, damaging her son's attachment to her and passing this on to the next generation.

We cannot offer effective treatment without a thorough evaluation. Family violence is hidden by shame, fear, projection, and rigid boundaries. So when we suspect abuse, we have to explore the family's conflict dynamics. Even when we ask, we rarely get the complete picture. We then have to begin therapy on the basis of limited or incomplete information. Early-stage therapy requires combining assessment and treatment if we want to be effective. Consider the difference in the previous case if a complete, unbiased assessment had been done and family therapy provided in addition to individual therapy for Josh. This case manager's refusal to consider contradictory information is a symptom of a much deeper problem in the family violence field.

OUR SPLINTERED RESPONSE TO FAMILY VIOLENCE

Unfortunately, our response to family violence has split into three arenas based on separate social advocacy movements: child physical abuse and neglect, child sexual abuse, and domestic violence. These different movements have created three separate arenas, each with its own theories, trained professionals, laws, research, and government agencies:

✓ Child Physical Abuse and Neglect

The child protection movement began in the United States after a famous court case ruled that the laws protecting animals from cruelty could also be applied to children:

> In 1873, 9-year-old Mary Ellen McCormack was an orphan living in New York City with Francis and Mary Connolly. Mrs. Connolly physically abused Mary Ellen almost daily, often using a rawhide whip. Mary Ellen had few clothes and no bed and was not allowed to leave the house. After learning of Mary Ellen's plight, Etta Wheeler, a Methodist social worker, went to the Connolly's apartment to see the conditions under which the child lived. Ms. Wheeler saw an undernourished and uncared-for child whose body bore the marks of repeated beatings. For the next 3 months, Etta Wheeler tried in vain to get someone to intervene on behalf of this beaten child. The police said they could do nothing; charitable institutions said much the same. The law seemed to provide no means for any public agency or private society to protect Mary Ellen. Unable to help this little girl through orthodox channels, Ms. Wheeler finally asked the Society for the Prevention of Cruelty to Animals (the "Society") to protect Mary Ellen as an abused member of the animal kingdom. Henry Bergh, the president of the Society, agreed to act. On April 9, 1874, as the result of efforts initiated by Etta Wheeler and Henry Bergh, a bruised and battered Mary Ellen McCormack was brought into a New York courtroom to tell her story to Judge Abraham Lawrence. Her face bore a fresh gash which would leave a lifelong scar. Jacob Riis, then a newspaper reporter, wrote that when Mary Ellen was brought before the Court, "the first chapter of children's rights was being written."[1]

Although child protection efforts continued for the next few decades, public attention to the problems of child abuse diminished over time. The social activists shifted their attention to other causes, such as mandatory education and child labor, and our national attention to child abuse disappeared. This issue of child abuse reemerged in 1962 when Kempe and his colleagues published their famous article "Battered Child Syndrome"(Kempe, Silverman, Steele, Droegemueller, & Silver, 1962). This is how these physicians described our professional denial of child abuse 40 years ago:

> Physicians have great difficulty both in believing that parents could have attacked their children and in undertaking the essential questioning of parents. . . . Many physicians attempt to obliterate such suspicions from their minds, even in the face of obvious circumstantial evidence. (Kempe et al., 1962, cited in Firstman & Talan, 1997, p. 413)

✓ Child Sexual Abuse

Our awareness of and response to child sexual abuse followed a different course. Our first modern awareness of this issue came from

Sigmund Freud's seduction theory presented to the Vienna Medical Society in 1896. In this address, Freud suggested that hysteria was caused by suppressed memories of real childhood sexual abuse. He was able to treat 18 cases of hysteria by uncovering this prior sexual trauma. Unfortunately, only 18 months later, he replaced the seduction theory with his "oedipal theory," which postulated that allegations of child sexual abuse were only childhood fantasies (wish fulfillment) toward the opposite-sex parent (Masson, 1984). Jeffrey Masson suggested that Freud abandoned his seduction theory because the patriarchal medical community was threatened by questions about men's sexual abuse of children. I would argue that the issue is much broader, functioning on an unconscious level. The culture wasn't ready to accept *both* male and female offending and the sex abuse of *both* girls and boys.[2]

The issue of child sexual abuse wasn't revived until the 1970s when the feminist rape crisis movement linked child sexual abuse (of girls) with the rape of women. This theoretical construct reinforced gender sexual stereotypes, attributed sexual abuse of children to patriarchy, increased our denial of female sex offending, and minimized the sexual victimization of boys.

✓ The Domestic Violence Movement

The first domestic violence shelters were created in London by Erin Pizzey beginning in the early 1970s. She also wrote the first book on domestic violence (Pizzey, 1974). Her shelters used approaches that would now be considered leading edge: the women themselves, not professional staff, ran their shelters; she advocated that shelters also be established for men; she insisted that child abuse and domestic violence were linked; and she regularly spoke out about women's violence (e.g., Pizzey observed that "62 of the first 100 women who came into her shelters were as violent as, or more violent than, their husbands or boyfriends" [Pizzey, personal communication, 1995]).

Unfortunately, the domestic violence movement was quickly co-opted by feminists in the mid-1970s and 1980s. The focus was changed from a gender-inclusive, family treatment model to a gender-specific focus based solely on feminist theories about male violence against women. The response to this family violence also shifted to punishing and reeducating the (male) perpetrators and protecting and advocating for the (female) victim to leave the relationship.

Although researchers found clear evidence of the complexity and mutuality of domestic violence (e.g., Straus, 1993; see also chapters 1, 2, 3, and 6 in this volume), the feminist model continues to dominate our understanding of and response to domestic violence. Fortunately, this gender-exclusive focus is finally beginning to change.

A FAMILY-SYSTEMS APPROACH

We will never have a chance to end the tragic cycle of family violence unless we reintegrate our responses to it. The child abuse movement gives us a different approach. More than 100 years ago, the child abuse and neglect field evolved from the New York Society's emphasis on arrest and punishment to the Massachusetts model of family support services and treatment. We need to do the same with all forms of family violence, whether it's violence between adults or all forms of child abuse, including sexual abuse. Over the past three decades, an increasing body of research has shown that our current models for both domestic violence (Dutton & Nicholls, 2005; Graham-Kevan & Archer, 2005) and sex abuse treatment are seriously flawed and that treatment based on these models is not effective. Attachment theory is increasingly gaining influence as a way to understand both domestic violence (Dutton & Sonkin, 2003; Hamel, 2005; Potter-Efron, 2005) and sex abuse (Madanes, 1990; Maddock & Larson, 1995), and there is a growing body of research on the neurobiology of attachment (Siegel, 1999). Why not, then, apply this research and clinical experience to modify our assessment of and response to family violence?

HOW DOES ATTACHMENT THEORY HELP US TREAT FAMILY VIOLENCE?

In the late 1950s and 1960s, Harry Harlow performed a number of famous experiments on attachment using rhesus monkeys. Lauren Slater (2004) described Harlow's experiments with the "iron maiden," a terry cloth–wrapped wire mannequin. Despite a cold, unemotional, and at many times even abusive response, the baby monkeys clung to their surrogate mothers:

> No matter what the torture, Harlow observed that the babies would not let go. They would not be deterred; they would not be thwarted. My God, love is strong. You are mauled and you come crawling back. You are frozen, and yet still you seek heat from the wrong source. There is no partial reinforcement to explain this behavior; there is only the dark side of touch, the reality of primate relationships, which is that they can kill us while they hold us—that's sad. But again, I find

some beauty. The beauty is this: We are creatures of great faith. We will build bridges, against all odds we will build them—from here to there. From me to you. Come closer. (p. 142)

We can't choose whether to attach. We are social beings. Humans, indeed most mammals, *require* an attachment to a primary caregiver. This caregiver can be loving and nurturing or abusive, but attach we must:

> Attachment is an enduring emotional bond that involves a tendency to seek and maintain proximity to a specific person, particularly when under stress. It is a mutual regulatory system that provides safety, protection, and a sense of security for the infant. Attachment is "an intense and enduring bond biologically rooted in the function of protection from danger." (Potter-Efron, 2005, p. 113)

Our job as clinicians is to help people improve the quality of these connections.

For adults, attachment exists both in the past and in the present. Our childhood experience of attachment with our parent(s) can be categorized according to four "styles" (internalized models) of attachment: secure, anxious/avoidant, anxious/ambivalent, or disorganized/disoriented. The adult counterparts of these are secure, dismissive, preoccupied, and fearful. Adults with a dismissive attachment style protect themselves emotionally by avoiding relationship intimacy, largely because their caregivers were not responsive to their needs as they grew up. Preoccupied attachment has its roots in inconsistent parenting and is characterized by a tendency to cling to one's adult partner and to fear abandonment. Children who experienced trauma and abuse are likely to develop a fearful attachment style as adults, characterized by a fear of both intimacy and abandonment. Securely attached adults neither fear emotional closeness nor have unreasonable fears of abandonment.

These attachment styles affect our sense of self and how we see the world and relate to others. They provide us with internalized models that are particularly powerful at moments of danger or significant change and in personal relationships, especially in our most intense relationships with a spouse (or lover) and with our child. In the emotional crucible of new family relationships, we inevitably re-create our family-of-origin attachment issues. This is both a danger and an opportunity.

We consciously and unconsciously choose and relate to a spouse on the basis of these internalized attachment models. So when conflict arises, we will inevitably view it through the lens of attachment: Will he listen to me? Will she accept me? Can I trust him? Why is she always critical of me? Why does he always hurt me? Will he/she be like my father/mother? Will I become my father/mother?

For children, this process is ongoing. Even though the fundamentals of attachment are laid down by age 2, this experience is constantly being modified or reinforced as children face the experience of growing up (see chapter 9 in this volume). Any intervention in family violence has the potential to modify these trauma bonds. And prevention or early intervention within the family unit is far more influential than years of individual therapy later in life.

A nine-year-old boy, Jesse, was referred to me for trauma treatment. Over a period of several years, he had watched his father and girlfriend scream at each other and had been subjected to emotional and physical abuse by the girlfriend, who routinely called him "stupid," slapped him across the face, and once punched him hard enough to break his nose. Jesse had just been returned to his mother's custody. He could certainly have evidenced a disorganized attachment style because of this severe abuse, but he was amazingly resilient. The fact that the abuser wasn't his parent reduced the damage.

Our second session started 10 minutes late. Jesse came in crying. His mother was very angry because he had forgotten about our session and got his good clothes dirty while playing with friends. When he began crying she hollered, "Stop crying, or I'll give you something to cry about." This only made things worse for both of them. This mother was afraid that I would consider her a bad parent. She originally lost her son because of her immaturity and drug use. Her own mother considered her unfit and had turned Jesse over to his father. Now that she finally had her son back, she was afraid of failing again. I simply commented that boys and girls were different at this age, normalizing his actions. This was a big relief for both of them: He wasn't a bad boy, and she wasn't a bad mother.

My treatment continued for about six months. In his individual sessions, we dealt with terrifying memories of abuse by his father's girlfriend. In the family sessions, we explored the normal day-to-day connections and problems with his mother and younger sister, who often pestered him. His mother encouraged him to be kind to his sister. Despite his frustrations, Jesse was able to do this and to take pride in being a good big brother. His mother lavished him with praise for his positive efforts, and mother and son developed a loving and secure attachment. In our last session, mother was coaching Jesse about his basketball play, reminding him to pass to his teammates. Therapy was finished.

Early in my career, I worked at Luther Child Center, a treatment center for child sexual abuse. Our consulting psychiatrist (Allen Leiter, MD) described these children as "living in a minefield." We couldn't rescue them or undo the abuse, and many times we couldn't significantly change their families. Allen would remind us, "They know this minefield better than us. Sometimes all we can hope to do is to walk them through the woods next to the minefield." We can't stop these tragedies from being recreated. It is the nature of intimate relationships to bring out the best (and worst) in us. All we can do is recognize these patterns, reduce our intense emotional reactivity, take responsibility for our part in these patterns, and work to create a different response to our conflict and distress. We can't change the past, but we can certainly change our response to the past, in the present.

WHAT ABOUT THE CHILDREN?

One of the primary flaws of the domestic violence movement is the assumption that "domestic" violence and child abuse are somehow separate phenomena. The reality is quite different. Domestic violence advocates have acknowledged child abuse but only in terms of children *witnessing* the domestic violence between their parents. While witnessing violence can certainly be traumatic, affecting children's emotional, behavioral, and social development, a false distinction is maintained that adult, heterosexual domestic violence, typically defined as the man battering the woman, must remain our primary concern. There are two problems with this position. First, it is contradicted by more than 130 studies of domestic violence that show that women perpetrate as much violence as men (Fiebert, 1997).Wouldn't these children also be traumatized witnessing their mother's violence against their father? Second, domestic violence is directly correlated with child physical abuse.

"Marital violence," according to one researcher, "is a statistically significant predictor of physical child abuse. The greater the amount of violence against a spouse, the greater the probability of physical child abuse by the physically aggressive spouse" (Ross, 1996, p. 589). An analysis of the National Family Violence Surveys reveal that the highest rates of child abuse were correlated with the most severe domestic violence, and that even "minor" domestic violence (i.e., pushing and shoving or slaps) resulted in twice the frequency of severe assaults on a child by the parent *being abused* (Straus & Smith, 1990, table 14.2, p. 253). Research by Appel and Holden (1998) found a 40% co-occurrence rate between domestic violence and child abuse; and according to a longitudinal study of 2,544 "at-risk" new mothers (McGuigan & Pratt, 2001), domestic violence during first six months of a child's life tripled the likelihood of child physical abuse during first five years of life and more than doubled the likelihood of emotional abuse and neglect.

Children are far more likely to be directly abused, not just witnesses to violence. They become *participants* in this tragedy, and they are far more likely to grow up and be abusive with their family or to marry an abuser. This is the *context* of violence that we must address. For these reasons I would argue that any reports of domestic violence must involve an assessment for the full spectrum of family violence, including child abuse.

BALANCING SAFETY AND FAMILY THERAPY

The primary argument against family and couples therapy is that we are putting the victims at risk of further abuse by either allowing the perpetrator to rationalize his or her violence or further escalating the violence after the session is over. If there is ongoing serious violence, the first priority is always to set up safeguards to create an environment of safety (Potter-Efron, 2005). But partner blaming and increased conflict are always possible risks in couples and family therapy. Any competent therapist has to learn to deal with this.

I want to comment here on the balance between safety and attachment. The only sure safety is never to get close to another human being. While there are a few people who choose this route, the vast majority of us need and seek out relationships. This is especially true for children. When we rigidly follow a victim's advocacy approach, the best answer to family violence is to leave, divorce, and cut off from the perpetrator. This rarely works. Either family members don't want to leave or leaving creates further trauma. If the violence is ongoing and the perpetrator won't stop, we still carry the wounds of this abuse to our graves, even if we find the courage to leave. No matter how far away we move, we'll carry these wounds with us. The best option is to change this pattern of violence within our family, or else take the longer road of healing the damage on our own.

Lynn and Shawn are a professional couple with two young sons. She had quit her management job to raise her sons full time, and he was a mid-level manager in a high-stress but well-paid job. They were referred to me following her psychiatric hospitalization for major depression and a suicide attempt. Shawn had a dismissive attachment style, was emotionally withholding and uncomfortable with relationship intimacy, but was dutifully obliged to take care of his wife through her depression and suicide attempts. He was a workaholic, ignoring his own distress and needs while isolating himself from friends. Lynn had a preoccupied attachment style, focusing on raising her sons and trying to get her husband to pay attention to her. These conflicting attachment styles, combined with very high levels of external stress, led to chronic marital problems. They finally had an argument that escalated to mutual violence after Lynn screamed at him that she felt ignored. Both of them had been drinking. She punched him, and then he put his hands around her neck to stop her. She began hitting him more, then he left the house to walk their dog. After he left, she got increasingly angry at him for putting his hand around her neck. When he returned, Lynn asked him to leave the house. Shawn refused. Lynn then called the police (later admitting this was out of anger and "wanting help"). When the police arrived, both of them were arrested and put in jail for 72 hours.

This is a classic case of mutual violence that escalated out of control. Neither of them used violence regularly or to control each other. Lynn and Shawn were decent people caught up in relationship patterns that amplified their distress. They recognized that their conflicts had an impact on their sons. Unfortunately, they had stopped conjoint therapy nine months before. All Lynn wanted was help, but the police were mandated to arrest both of them. If they had been charged, he could have lost his job, and their sons could have ended up in foster care. In our desire to "protect" this family, our response could have made their problems much worse.

THE ADVANTAGES OF FAMILY THERAPY

I'm still troubled by a case that I mishandled from early in my career when I was contacted by a mother to treat her 10-year-old son, Jack, for anger and acting out at home and school. In the first session, I met with Jack, his mother, her lesbian partner, and his father (his parents were divorced). His mother had a fearful attachment style. Having grown up in a chaotic family with an angry, alcoholic mother and a schizophrenic father who shot himself when she was six, she had difficulty maintaining healthy relationships as an adult and was almost totally dissociated from her son other than occasionally to scream at him. Jack's father loved Jack but was passive-avoidant with a dismissing attachment style. Neither parent engaged sufficiently with their son either to set limits or to provide love. The only adult in Jack's life who seemed concerned was his mother's partner. In this first session, as she related an incident in which Jack threw a bowl of cereal at her, she described him as "evil." I became concerned over the impact of this psychological abuse on Jack and had him leave the room while I talked with the adults. My supervisor later advised me to work only with Jack and his biological parents in the future.

Later I recognized that I had made a serious clinical error with this family. In a case consultation presentation, the clinical director, Dr. Verhulst, asked me the key question: "Why did I have Jack leave the room?" He pointed out that Jack lived with this abuse every day and that he would need help from me to change this family dynamic. By having Jack leave the room, I was saying that I (an adult) couldn't deal with the abuse either. I later discovered that his mother's partner was the only adult who seemed to be concerned about Jack and willing to take action. Her reaction to Jack's violence came out of her own childhood abuse from her brothers. My anxiety got in the way of demonstrating to Jack a healthy response to abuse. It also removed the one adult who both loved Jack and took action on his behalf. Family therapy with this woman would have also offered her a chance to heal from her own childhood abuse.

Family violence is complex and systemic. Treatment for each family member must be matched with the particular type of domestic violence: the classic man battering his wife, the wife battering her husband, mutual severe battering, or what has been termed "common couple's violence" (Johnson & Leone, 2005). Within each of these subcategories, treatment will vary, depending on each case. Some cases of common couples violence may be intractable, while cases of severe battering by one spouse may be very treatable.

The children may be totally sheltered from this violence, witnesses to the violence, or the targets of violence. Child abuse can exist without domestic violence, a child can be battered/abused by one or both parents, and there can be mutual abuse between an adolescent and a parent and between siblings. This child abuse can be caused primarily by external stressors (e.g., addiction, financial distress, or simply being overwhelmed), the parent may simply lack discipline skills, and the parent could be depressed, personality disordered, or psychotic.

In short, family treatment is complex. Assessment and treatment are intertwined. We can't treat what we don't see or deny because our theories won't allow it. And we have to reassess as we're treating to make sure that what we are doing is effective. Work with these families can be a very humbling experience.

THE THERAPIST'S STANCE

Family therapy is not simply a matter of technique; it's also largely a function of the therapist's stance. This is based on our sense of ourselves as therapists and the attitude we have toward the people we work with. Noel

Larson describes treatment with perpetrators and victims as counterintuitive (Noel Larson, personal communication, April 19, 1999). She suggests "going for the heart" (vs. confrontation) with perpetrators and "standing back" with victims (i.e., reinforcing their strength by not rescuing or caretaking). This work sometimes requires that clients reframe the way they describe their experiences.

A couple in their mid-40s came to see me to help them change a chronic pattern of emotional abuse. She was pregnant with their first child, although she had two teenage children from her first marriage. She complained of several years of increasingly angry interactions with her husband, who yelled and often spoke harshly to her. The more she complained of his abuse, the more he argued and withdrew. I suggested that she stop using the term "abuse" and instead talk about how his behavior hurt her. This shifted the focus from her description of his intent (to abuse) to her personal experience (certain words and behaviors hurt her). He loved his wife and agreed that his image of a good husband didn't include deliberately hurting her. He was able to begin listening to her experience instead of trying to argue that he wasn't trying to harm or control her. Once this destructive cycle stopped, we could change the focus to their underlying fears and concerns about the pregnancy. He was worried about her health, and she was afraid that he would be emotionally (and physically) absent after the baby was born.

> ✓ If we expect family members to respect each other and not resort to violence, we have to model this by being respectful with them. In order to do therapy, we need our clients to be honest with us, but they won't be open and honest unless we create a climate of therapeutic safety. This also requires that we separate therapy from control functions. If possible, have a caseworker or probation officer enforce rules. If court-ordered into therapy, we need to discuss this dilemma with our clients. In my experience, intense confrontation and "breaking down denial" is more likely to lead to compliance than to real change.

Look for family strengths and exceptions to patterns. No family is only violent or dysfunctional. Look for and reinforce any exceptions (e.g., "*How* were you able to stop from losing control of your anger Tuesday night?"). These contain the clues to solutions. Build on these strengths.

Steve is a 15-year-old who had serious problems with anger, fighting, and alcoholism. He had been suspended from school and kicked out of his aftercare addiction program after getting into fights. He was intensely oppositional with his parents and other authority figures. He had trashed his rooms many times, hurled lamps and other objects around the house, and once shoved a big-screen television to the floor. Prior therapy had not been effective. By the time he came to see me, Steve recognized that, despite his young age, he was already an alcoholic and could never drink again. He acknowledged that his anger was hurting himself and the people he loved, but he still saw fighting as necessary in some circumstances. In his early childhood, he witnessed his mother hitting his father as well as his father's binge drinking, and he had developed an ambivalent attachment to his parents. Hypersensitive to criticism and shame, he responded with violence or alcohol when hurt.

My treatment began with individual and family sessions, at first with his mother and then with his father. His father is also a recovered alcoholic, but he never had problems with anger and had grown enormously as a result of his involvement in 12-step programs. Increasing the connection with his father gave Steve a chance to see himself in the mirror of his father's eyes and to internalize male values of sobriety and peaceful responses to fear and conflict.

Recently, Steve got into another fight at school, confronting a boy who had made fun of another kid. The school suspended Steve and transferred him to an alternative program where kids could be protected from other kids and themselves. Given his initial progress, both parents were hurt and disappointed. I encouraged them to express these feelings and to praise Steve for the positive intention behind his actions—his concern for an underdog. I also helped his parents set firm but fair limits on his behavior with reasonable expectations. Their patience paid off because Steve finally began to look at his own "punk" behaviors, recognizing that this pattern of violence (going back to early elementary school) was destructive to his parents and himself, as he unwittingly pushed away the people whose love he valued the most. In therapy, the parents had in effect succeeded in reestablishing secure attachment bonds with their son, and he was able to acquire the emotional stability to overcome his problems.

✓ All of us need hope. Take a stance of "respectful inquiry" to understand why and how clients behave in violent patterns. This also helps them to open up instead of being guarded and defensive. Even if they can't answer our questions, this shifts the focus from shame and blame to an exploration of self and the seeking of alternatives.

✓ We have to contain our own anxiety and anger if we want to help the family face their violence and pain. My anxiety got in the way of helping Jack, thereby missing an opportunity for real change. Many therapists also worry so much about future abuse or being sued that they take the simplistic, traditional course of treating the perpetrators and victims separately without ever addressing family issues directly. And if we get hung up in our anger at the perpetrator for his or her violence or even at the victim for not leaving, we miss the underlying complexity of family systems. We have to begin by soothing ourselves so that we meet the family on their field of battle. From that position, we can make real change, even while individual family members do their own therapy.

Family therapy provides for the possibility of corrective emotional experiences:

I had been working with a young couple, Bob and Lila, for several years to help them manage their intense marital conflicts and differentiate from Bob's narcissistic family of origin. When Lila disclosed Bob's problem of marijuana abuse to his parents during a recent Mother's Day visit, her mother-in-law physically attacked her. This escalated the family triangulation, with his family blaming the argument on Lila. She was afraid that Bob wouldn't protect her or their daughter because of her own family-of-origin abuse experiences. As I was helping them reduce her triangulation with his family and her anxiety about his loyalty to his family over her, I used their parenting experiences with their two-year-old daughter to teach them differentiation. I challenged him to become a more active disciplinarian with his daughter to learn to face his daughter's (and his own) anger while experiencing that she would still love him. And I suggested that Lila learn from her daughter that it's okay to state your needs, even if others might get angry at you. Her two-year-old daughter would regularly say "Self" whenever she wanted to do something herself or do it her way. I jokingly suggested that Lila practice saying "Self" to Bob whenever she needed to stand up for herself.

- ✓ If family therapy isn't working, consider widening the system. For example, include grandparents, aunts and uncles, friends, a minister, or church members in the sessions. A widened system is more stable and can provide respite care at times of high stress and support the family in changing violent patterns. A wider system can better "contain" the intensity of family conflict and violence, offering support as well as boundaries to the family.
- ✓ Healing rituals: Given the emotional intensity and attachment of families, healing rituals around violence can be very powerful.

Cloe Madanes (1990) describes a healing ritual with a family where the older brother committed incest with his sister. The key to this ritual was that everyone in the family (beginning with the parents) gets on their knees and apologizes to the sister for not protecting her. Then her offender has to do the same. With the parents taking the lead, the family makes reparations to the victim and holding the perpetrator responsible in a nonjudgmental way.

I regularly discuss making amends with couples and families where someone has harmed a loved one. The four components of this are *acknowledging the truth* that someone has been harmed, *taking full responsibility* for the abuse, *demonstrating empathy* by describing how their behavior has harmed the family member (with affect), and *reparation* for the harm in a way that specifically addresses how the victim has been harmed (e.g., if there has been verbal abuse in front of family members, then the abuser has to acknowledge and be respectful of their spouse in front of these same family members).

Attachment bonds are strong and lasting. The next example illustrates the healing that can occur when once-abusive parents take responsibility for their behavior:

I was working with a 15-year-old boy, Ted, who had been placed in a therapeutic foster home. The presenting problems were violence toward an older sister, disorganized attachment, and a serious hearing/speech disability. He grew up in a violent family, witnessing his father's severe physical and emotional abuse of his mother. The foster parents were excellent and participated in all our family sessions. Ted was making good progress: connecting with his foster parents and other kids and getting passing grades at school. The last phase of his treatment consisted of reconciliation with his father, Carl, who had recently gotten out of prison. Carl was now sober and took responsibility for his past violence. His honest, direct statements about his previous behavior reinforced the foster father's efforts to model positive ways of controlling anger and nonviolence. Carl had also grown up in a family with severe violence. As an adult, he had developed a fearful attachment style, tending to become rageful both when feeling emotionally suffocated and when his wife showed any signs of anger, which he perceived as abandonment.

Ted began visiting with Carl. During the sessions with his father and foster parents, Ted became increasingly verbal, sharing with his father his experiences in his foster home and with us the visits with his father. He was planning to move out of his foster home after graduation and live with Carl. At our last session, Ted gave his father a handmade birthday card and gift, openly expressing his love for him.

TREATING "PERPETRATORS" AND "VICTIMS"

The victim–perpetrator dyad is overstated. Perpetrators commit abuse for many reasons, including external stressors such as financial problems, unemployment, extended family pressures, community violence, racism, personal addictions, insecurity, fear of abandonment, or jealousy. Pregnancy and the birth of a new child raises multiple issues for new couples. Or there can be escalating conflict prior to and just after separation. One of the primary reasons for violence is multigenerational abuse:

Dominic was sent to me for treatment after abusing his son, Jacob. He was resistant to treatment, minimizing his abuse as merely "kicking him during their horseplay." He also didn't recognize the impact on his children of witnessing him abuse their mother, such as the time he grabbed her by the neck and shoved her up against the wall. I was able to break through his denial by asking Dominic to remember this incident of "horseplay" and to imagine "looking into your son's eyes." He could finally admit seeing fear in his those eyes. "Is this how you want Jacob to see you?" I asked him. He could finally admit that his kicking had terrified his son. Over the following sessions, we continued to break through his emotional barriers, alternating between building empathy for Jacob (the breakthrough occurred while discussing an incident in which his son nearly drowned) and working through his own traumas resulting from combat in Vietnam and severe abuse at the hands of his mother.

This man couldn't see the impact of his own behavior on his son because his own trauma had been buried. He felt that he couldn't possibly be abusive because he loved his son and was so much less violent than his mother had been with him.

Victims are not just beaten down, terrified, and helpless; many can become perpetrators themselves, switching back and forth in these roles: There can be mutual battering, hitting back in moments of rage and revenge, or acting out their anger on someone else (a child or pet).

In addition, victims can be resilient and have great courage. Any time I begin therapy with someone who has suffered abuse, I want to know how they got to where they are now. How did they survive? What kept them from going crazy or perpetrating against others? If they did perpetrate, what kept them from being as abusive as their abuser? The tragedy of the victim advocacy approach is that these strengths may be overlooked out of the desire to protect and save the victims from further abuse. But their own goals are rarely considered. The abused woman or child is assumed to be unable to make good decisions for him- or herself. Linda Mills's excellent *Insult to Injury* (2003) argues that professionals and victim's advocates who follow these conventional approaches paradoxically undercut the control and personal power these women need to recover and protect themselves from future violence.

In short, whether working with victims or perpetrators, we need to seek out the best in them. Reinforce that. That's the basis of real change.

Why do people drop out of treatment? Unfortunately, we tend to blame our clients for their intransigence, denial, or lack of responsibility when they don't follow our recommendations or drop out of treatment. Many of these individuals are very difficult to treat. They can have personality disorders, addictions, and even an "addiction" to these unhealthy relationships. But the problem can be ours. Don't blame the client if therapy doesn't work. Perhaps our treatment model is flawed or ineffective for this client. Maybe we've missed something in our assessment. Perhaps we haven't engaged them or are moving too quickly toward our goals instead of their goals.

I heard a fascinating research paper presented at a national conference (Carney, Buttell, & Muldoon, 2004). The authors were trying to determine why so many men dropped out of batterer's treatment. They cited intake testing from a South Carolina program and did a complicated multivariate analysis comparing the men who dropped out of treatment to the men who stayed in treatment. The most interesting piece of data was what the researchers and the batterer's program ignored. Part of their testing involved administering the revised Conflict Tactics Scales (CTS2). This testing showed a great deal more physical, sexual, and psychological abuse by these men's wives and girlfriends. The one difference I could see was that the men who completed treatment were more likely to cause injury with their abuse, while the men who dropped out were more likely to have been injured. Yet this key piece of data was ignored by the researchers in their analysis and by the program in their treatment.

A young man came to see me after charges of having abused his wife. He had torn her blouse during a fight. I asked him to describe what happened. During a dispute over money, she kicked and punched him, and he was attempting to push her away. During another recent fight, she began attacking him with a knife. He stopped this attack by holding up a chair to keep her from cutting him. Both her father and her uncle had been killed with knives. I worked with him on deescalating the violence and trying to leave if their conflicts escalated. Soon after our treatment, he moved with her to another state. There she reported him for domestic violence after another fight. He was sent to batterer's treatment, and she was sent to a shelter for "victim" treatment.

CALMING OUR OWN ANXIETY

Working with family violence can be very difficult. We have to learn to soothe our own anxiety and anger. Our own experiences of family violence can lead to countertransference. We have to accept the limits of what we can accomplish and not try to rescue or fix these families. Sometimes, the best we can do is sit in the middle of the chaos of these families and maintain our calm and our boundaries. We have to deal with our own gender stereotypes so that we can help men face their own vulnerability and wounds and women face their own dark side. We have to be willing to let go of our theories and assumptions. This kind of therapy requires that we do our own therapy and healing.

Yet work with family violence can be very powerful and healing as we help individuals break these cycles of violence.

NOTES

1. Adapted from the report "Secrets That Can Kill: Child Abuse Investigations in New York State" by the Temporary Commission of Investigation of the State of New York.
2. Six of Freud's 18 cases were males, and his case examples cite sex offending by *both* women and men.

REFERENCES

Appel, A. E., & Holden, G. W. (1998). The co-occurrence of spouse and physical child abuse: A review and appraisal. *Journal of Family Psychology, 12*(4), 578–599.

Carney, M., Buttell, F., & Muldoon, J. (2004, September 21). *Predictors of batterer intervention program attrition: Developing and implementing logistic regression models in practitioner-researcher partnerships.* Paper presented at the International Conference on Family Violence, San Diego, California.

DeMause, L. (1982). The evolution of childhood. In L. DeMause (Ed.), *Foundations of psychohistory* (pp. 1–83). New York: Creative Roots, Inc.

Dutton, D., & Nicholls, T. (2005). A critical review of the gender paradigm in domestic violence research and theory: Part I—Theory and data. *Aggression and Violent Behavior, 10*, 680–714.

Dutton, D. G., & Sonkin, D. (2003). Treating assaultive men from an attachment perspective. In D. G. Dutton & D. Sonkin (Eds.), *Intimate violence: Contemporary treatment innovations* (pp. 105–133). New York: Haworth Maltreatment & Trauma Press.

Fiebert, M. S. (1997). References examining assaults by women on their spouses/partners. *Sexual Harassment and Sexual Consent, 1*, 273–286.

Firstman, R., & Talan, J. (1997). *The death of innocents: A true story of murder, medicine, and high-stakes science.* New York: Bantam Books.

Graham-Kevan, N., & Archer, J. (2005, July 10–13). *Using Johnson's domestic violence typology to classify men and women in a non-selected sample.* 9th International Family Violence Research Conference, Portsmouth, New Hampshire.

Hamel, J. (2005). *Gender inclusive treatment of intimate partner abuse: A comprehensive approach.* New York: Springer.

Johnson, M., & Leone, J. (2005). The differential effects of intimate terrorism and situational couple violence: Findings from the national violence against women survey. *Journal of Family Issues, 26*(3), 322–349.

Karr-Morse, R., & Wiley, M. S. (1997). *Ghosts from the nursery: Tracing the roots of violence.* New York: Atlantic Monthly Press.

Kempe, C. H., Silverman, F., Steele, B., Droegemueller, W., & Silver, H. (1962). The battered-child syndrome. *Journal of the American Medical Association, 181*(1), 17–24.

Madanes, C. (1990). *Sex, love, and violence: Strategies for transformation.* New York: Norton.

Maddock, J. W., & Larson, N. R. (1995). *Incestuous families: An ecological approach to understanding and treatment.* New York: Norton.

Masson, J. (1984). *The assault on truth.* New York: Farrar, Straus and Giroux.

McGuigan, W. M., & Pratt, C. C. (2001). The predictive impact of domestic violence on three types of child maltreatment. *Child Abuse and Neglect, 23,* 869–883.

Miller, A. (1983). *For your own good: Hidden cruelty in child-rearing and the roots of violence* (H. H. Hannum, Trans.). New York: Farrar, Straus and Giroux.

Mills, L. G. (2003). *Insult to injury.* Princeton, NJ: Princeton University Press.

Pizzey, E. (1974). *Scream quietly or the neighbors will hear.* London: Penguin.

Potter-Efron, R. T. (2005). *Handbook of anger management: Individual, couple, family, and group approaches.* New York: Haworth Clinical Practice Press.

Ross, S. (1996). Risk of physical abuse to children of spouse abusing parents. *Child Abuse and Neglect, 20*(7), 589–598.

Siegel, D. J. (1999). *The developing mind: How relationships and the brain interact to shape who we are.* New York: Guilford Press.

Slater, L. (2004). *Opening Skinner's box: Great psychological experiments of the twentieth century.* New York: Norton.

Straus, M. (1993). Physical assaults by wives: A major social problem. In R. Gelles & D. Loseke (Eds.), *Current controversies on family violence* (pp. 67–87). Newbury Park, CA: Sage.

Straus, M., & Gelles, R. (Eds.). (1990). *Physical violence in American families: Risk factors and adaptations to violence in 8,145 families.* New Brunswick, NJ: Transaction Publishers.

Straus, M., & Smith, C. (1990). Family patterns and child abuse. In M. Straus & R. Gelles (Eds.), *Physical violence in American families* (pp. 245–262). New Brunswick, NJ: Transaction Publishers.

CHAPTER 20

Anger, Aggression, Domestic Violence, and Substance Abuse

Ronald T. Potter-Efron

Perhaps the best single word that describes the relationship between anger/aggression/domestic abuse and substance abuse/chemical dependency/addiction is "complicated." As is noted later, there are at least seven basic general possibilities that range from there being absolutely no connection between the two variables for some people to there being a perfect causal relationship for others.

That is why an individualized assessment is required whenever therapists attempt to ascertain this relationship for any actual client. Furthermore, treatment plans should be made carefully and cautiously, never assuming, for instance, that treatment for either concern will have a positive effect on the other. Careful consideration must be given to all details, especially to deciding whether a client should be treated first for either condition or simultaneously for both.

At the same time, it should be recognized that appropriate treatment for both conditions almost certainly improves the likelihood that clients will have better, happier, more pro-social and productive lives than if either problem is left untreated. The remainder of this chapter provides assessment and treatment ideas that will enable therapists to help their doubly affected clients confront these two interactive problems.

COMMON THEMES, SITUATIONS, AND MESSAGES FOR FAMILIES IN WHICH BOTH FAMILY VIOLENCE AND SUBSTANCE ABUSE ARE CO-OCCURRING PROBLEMS

While families are strongly affected by the presence of either substance abuse or domestic violence, the presence of both factors together promotes the likelihood that individual family members will be more damaged and the family as a whole will be even more disrupted. It is quite possible that while a family might be capable of containing either singular issue, the crush of both problems might overwhelm the family's coping capacity to the point of chaos or disintegration.

The interconnections between substance abuse and domestic violence are abetted by several commonalities: (a) Family violence and chemical dependency both tend to be intergenerational problems, getting passed along by modeling, genetics, or both; (b) similar personality dynamics, such as symbiotic dependency on others, low self-esteem, misplaced responsibility, and impulsivity affect many members of the family; (c) both concerns are characterized by at least apparent loss of control on some occasions by certain family members; and (d) both problems increase family tension and so increase the possibility for further family problems.

Here are examples of situations that demonstrate a few of the multiple ways in which substance abuse and family violence might co-occur:

✓ *Family violence may be strongly intertwined with an aggressor's immediate assaultiveness.* For instance, the children keep a lookout for Dad on Friday nights because that's when he goes to the tavern, gets drunk, and comes home to beat up them and their mom.

✓ *A situation that might normally be handled without violence becomes violent after one or more members become intoxicated.* Granted, some people do consciously get drunk in order to have an excuse to become violent (and later to blame their behavior on the alcohol). Still, it is far more common that incidents of family violence will be more common and more severe because of the poor judgment, impulsivity, and disinhibition of aggressive urges that occurs when people are under the influence of a mood-altering substance. Thus, a verbal dispute is more likely to morph into a physical altercation whenever any party to the argument is intoxicated, including perpetrator or mutual perpetrators, victims, and even bystanders.

✓ *One family member may turn to alcohol or drugs to escape the pain of family violence.* This person could be an adolescent who quietly gets stoned just about every night while turning on her stereo as loud as she can so she doesn't have to hear her parents arguing.

✓ *Some family members may become increasingly violent in reaction against other members' substance abuse problems.* Several years ago, I worked at an adolescent inpatient chemical dependency treatment center. One day, a mother and father brought in their 16-year-old daughter for treatment. She had a black eye that was inflicted when her father held her and her mother struck her in the face. These parents, normally nonviolent, became assaultive after catching their daughter sniffing paint. However, they admitted that they had become increasingly angry and aggressive toward her over the past two years as her obvious substance abuse pattern worsened.

✓ *Each incident of either problem triggers increases in the other in a disastrous feedback loop.* Thus, an incident of family violence increases the overall prevalence of substance abuse, while an incident of drunken or drug-affected deportment triggers family violence. The end result is likely to be that family members feel helpless and hopeless to change things.

There is a set of common messages that may help families with this double problem address their issues: (a) Violence is never an acceptable solution for family problems, including substance abuse, and only increases problems; (b) the misuse of alcohol or drugs or other addictive behaviors promotes family violence and cannot be accepted; (c) secrets keep a family sick so that denial or minimization of either problem will only perpetuate family pain; (d) each member of a family has a right to a decent life, free from daily fear, pain, dishonesty, and shame; (e) the entire family has been affected by the substance abuse and family violence problems within the family; everyone hurts together, and all need to work together to get well; and (f) change is possible both individually and for the entire family.

THE CHALLENGE TO CORE PARADIGMS IN BOTH FIELDS

Before continuing, I would like to mention that the two fields of substance abuse and domestic violence treatment have an interesting parallel that has significantly affected how clients with these concerns are treated. This interesting similarity in the two fields of domestic violence and substance abuse is that both developed as "maverick" fields originally shunned by mainstream mental health workers. It should be remembered that when Alcoholics Anonymous was being created in the mid-1900s, alcoholics were frequently looked on with such contempt that many were not even allowed into hospitals for treatment. Similarly, and until much more recently, women who had been battered by their husbands were told by their churches, law enforcement agencies, and even counselors that their husbands had a right to hit them and that it was probably their own fault for any marital problems in the relationship. Given that mainstream help was unavailable, both fields were initially developed by people who themselves were "recovering" or "surviving" members of each group. These individuals, gathering their ideas from their own experiences, developed models that both explained the problem and freed them from moral judgment. These models, the "alcoholism is a disease" perspective in addiction treatment and the "domestic abuse as caused by male privilege" perspective in the field of domestic abuse, became so popular that they dominated each field to the point of excluding competitive models for decades. They morphed from initial exploratory models that could explain some but not all relevant problems into paradigms that ruled their respective fields. These paradigms have allowed each field to grow exponentially in terms of the number of people served. They have saved many lives. They even have made each discipline profitable enough to ensure that mainstream counselors, psychologists, and physicians were attracted to these areas. Thus, "addictionolgy" is now a certified medical specialty, while domestic violence classes are taught regularly in university sociology, psychology, and counseling programs.

However, as Thomas S. Kuhn (1996) argued so elegantly, paradigms represent a mixed blessing to any developing field. Most critically, practitioners who accept the paradigm tend to do so unconditionally, truly believing it is the best and only way to interpret reality. This is particularly true when a field is brand new, when its first practitioners are outsiders, and when these individuals must fight to oust a previous paradigm (in this case the previously mentioned moral failure model). Furthermore, paradigms tend to create their own crises as practitioners attempt to apply the original model to increasingly distant situations. For example, the concept of alcoholism as a disease and abstinence as the only goal makes pretty good sense when applied to a middle-aged, middle-class White male with more than 30 years of drinking experience, a gradual buildup of tolerance for the drug, and a history of failed attempts at social drinking. That model is less effective, though, when applied to a 14-year-old girl who just got caught at a teen party where alcohol and marijuana were consumed by everybody there and who has never had trouble before with alcohol or drug consumption. The same reasoning says that the patriarchal dominance model generally fits a mentally healthy middle-aged man who lives in a small community that still emphasizes men's right to control women.

That paradigm works less well in many situations, however, including ones in which the man is clearly mentally unwell (especially if that man suffers from borderline or antisocial personality disorders), when the violence occurs between gay or lesbian couples, when the couples engage in truly mutual aggression, or when the woman is the only or primary aggressor.

At the time of this writing, both fields are undergoing challenges to their previously dominant paradigms. The process is farther along in the field of alcohol and drug treatment, where cognitive therapy and evidence-based models have gradually infiltrated the field at the same time many of the original "amateur" healers have been replaced by bachelors- and masters-level counselors. The challenge is relatively recent in the field of domestic abuse, a field in which the dominant model is so powerful that state law in several states requires that all domestic abuse programs be organized along the power and control theory consistent with the male privilege paradigm. However, it too is developing along predictable lines: Treatment personnel with less than total allegiance to the primary paradigm first raise subtle questions about it among themselves and then dare to state them aloud. Hamel's (2005) book on gender-inclusive treatment for batterers is an example of this development.

The outcome of these paradigmatic challenges is also fairly predictable. Eventually, some core concepts from the original model will be retained but probably incorporated as special cases into a more wide-ranging paradigm that better explains more situations than the original paradigm. Of course, the fate of that paradigm may be also be supplanted over time as this process repeats itself.

POSSIBLE RELATIONSHIPS BETWEEN ALCOHOLISM/ SUBSTANCE ABUSE AND ANGER/AGGRESSION/ DOMESTIC ABUSE

There are many possible linkages between anger/aggression and substance abuse. That is because the relationships between these two areas are complex and convoluted. Therefore, the specific relationship between substance abuse and anger or aggression must be carefully analyzed with each client, preferably from an initially neutral position. Here are some guidelines to help assess the situation with clients who have been affected by both conditions:

✓ *Any mood-altering substance is capable of promoting anger and/or aggression, but no such substance inevitably does so.*

✓ *Many individuals with anger and aggression problems also have substance abuse problems.*

✓ *There may be no intrinsic connection between the two conditions.* In other words, they are functionally independent variables so that treatment for one will have no impact on the other.

✓ *There may be an apparently causal relationship between the two variables that goes in either direction.* Certain individuals seemingly only have anger or aggression problems after they consume mood-altering substances. Others consume such substances only after they become angry. However, the apparent causal connection must be scrutinized carefully since what appear to be one-way relationships often turn out to be mutually interactive.

✓ *Both problems may be apparently caused by or linked with a third condition, such as major depressive disorder.*

✓ *Short- and long-term reactions to substances of abuse create many different types of problems with regard to anger and aggression.* Miller (in Potter-Efron, 2005) notes that aggression may become associated with the following substance-induced conditions: intoxication, intoxication delirium, withdrawal, withdrawal delirium, idiosyncratic/paradoxical responses, substance-induced dementia, chronic substance-induced paranoia, and drug-procuring violence. Particular drugs are associated with particular conditions. Two examples are the regular association between aggression and alcohol withdrawal and the common association of aggression with immediate methamphetamine intoxication.

✓ *White (2004) notes that the general relationship between violence and substance abuse can be written with the formula P(Person) + D(Drug) + E (Environment) = V(Violence).* This formula depicts the multiple relationships factors that can interact to increase the risk for violence. He describes seven separate possible interactive effects between substance abuse and violence:

   ✓ *Independence*—Acts of violence by an instigator have no causal relationship to that individual's substance use pattern.

   ✓ *Rationalizing Effect*—A person excuses his or her acts of aggression by claiming they were caused by the effects of a mood-altering substance when in reality the substances had no causal effect.

   ✓ *Causative Effect*—Here violence is elicited by the direct effects of a drug with little or no contribution from the person or environment. One example occurs when acute or chronic substance use creates toxic organic psychoses that subsequently impair the individual's ability to perceive their environment.

✓ *Additive Effect*—The substance use contributes to but does not independently cause acts of violence. This could occur when an individual's threshold for violence is more easily reached when intoxicated because of increased disinhibition and impairment of judgment.

✓ *Synergistic Effect*—This exceptionally dangerous interaction happens when persons with extremely high risk for serious violence also make high-risk drug choices, dosages, and methods of ingestion. This combination may produce acts of aggression far exceeding a simple additive effect. These individuals often have histories indicative of neurological trauma, neurological impairments, violent coaching, abandonment, and so on. They are violent even without drugs, but drug use greatly increases the risk for especially violent acts.

✓ *Neutralizing Effect*—Certain illicit drugs, such as marijuana, have long been claimed to reduce some people's tendency toward aggression. Drugs that lower anxiety, lower one's sense of sensory overload, blunt emotional experiences, or lower psychomotor activity could produce such an effect.

✓ *Contextual Effect*—In this situation, violence occurs when an act of aggression is a learned way to achieve status and power and/or to resolve problems.

Tables 20.1 and 20.2 summarize, first, some specific relationships between particular drug groups and aggression risk, and second, therapeutic approaches that are helpful when treating clients with both concerns.

RESEARCH CORRELATIONS BETWEEN SUBSTANCE ABUSE AND DOMESTIC VIOLENCE

There is little question that domestic violence correlates well with substance abuse patterns. For example, Kantor and Straus (1987) found that 22% of males and 10% of females reported consuming alcohol prior to their most recent or severe incident of abuse. Similarly, Roizen (1997) reports that use of alcohol during domestic violence incidents is associated with more severe injuries to the victim. In addition, Leonard and Quigley (1999) discovered that husbands were more likely to be drinking in physically violent interactions with their partners than during verbal disputes. Furthermore, Tolman and Bennett (1990) found that chronic alcohol

TABLE 20.1   Anger/Aggression Relationship to Alcohol/Drugs

Drug Group	Overall Risks	Why?
Alcohol	High	Societal permission/ expectation; disinhibition; withdrawal; irritability; pervasiveness within society
Sedatives and barbiturates	High	Promotes irritability; assaultiveness; self-destructive attacks
Crystal methamphetamine	High	Amphetamine use (long term) can produce both immediate aggression and long-term personality changes
Cocaine and stimulants	High	Highly associated with irritability and impulsive attacks
PCP	High	Produces angry/assaultive tendencies
Steroids	Medium-high	Seems to encourage anger and aggression, especially in already prone individuals
Inhalants	Medium	Generally incapacitates users but associated with aggressive lifestyles
Opiates	Medium-low	Generally diminishes all emotions during use; aggression to procure drug money main problem
Cannabis	Medium-low	Mistakenly assumed to diminish anger/aggression; can exacerbate underlying paranoia
Hallucinogens	Low	May exacerbate underlying psychotic delusions.

abuse is a better predictor of intimate partner violence than acute intoxication. Moreover, males entering programs for domestic abuse consistently report relatively high rates of alcohol usage (Barnett and Fagan, 1993). Thus, substance abuse appears to be associated with both the increased likelihood for and greater intensity of domestic aggression incidents.

TABLE 20.2   Therapeutic Approaches When Dealing With Simultaneous Substance Abuse and Anger/Aggression Concerns

Primary Concern	Suggested Approach
No apparent connection between the two	Treat as independent problems; Make referral for anger work
Excessive anger/aggression episodes *always* linked with intoxication/addictive patterns	Focus on need for abstinence; "Keep the plug in the jug"
Excessive anger/aggression episodes *frequently* linked with intoxication/addictive patterns	Map out the connections; phase 2 recovery (vs. "dry drunk"); may need to learn how to express anger in moderation when sober
Uses substances/addictive patterns to submerge feelings of anger and/or expression of anger	Warn clients that anger may emerge; Assertiveness training
Anger/aggression and substance abuse patterns both used to increase internal stimulation	Possible neuropsychological testing and medication trial; need for alternative lifestyle
Getting angry used as a justification for immediate intoxication or being resentful for long-term addiction	Acknowledge the anger but question the user's claim that "I have to drink as a justification (use drugs etc.) when I feel angry"
Becoming angry or resentful as part of a relapse pattern	Fully detail the relapse chain of predictable events and feelings and then plan ways to intervene on that sequence
Denial of either problem affects total treatment	Ask client how he or she plans to address primary problem if the secondary one is not addressed honestly
Dual denial system minimizes motivation	Provide fact-based challenges to denial systems; enlist family and workplace support for intervention
Substance abuse triggers or increases paranoia	Cognitive interventions: "If you hadn't been using, how might you have interpreted that situation?"

(Continued)

TABLE 20.2 **Therapeutic Approaches When Dealing With Simultaneous Substance Abuse and Anger/Aggression Concerns**

Primary Concern	Suggested Approach
Substance abuse and anger/ aggression appear to be unthinking, "automatic" activities	Treat both as learned patterns of behavior that can be altered
Use of mood-altering substances allows user to feel stronger, more powerful (which then leads to aggression)	Need for self-esteem work
Substances as a substitute for potentially conflictual interpersonal relationships	Social skills training; AA as a bridge to relationships with both recovering and other persons
Client utilizes both substance abuse and anger/aggression to defy authority	Counter "You can't make me" stance with "No, but you have choices" observation
Family members' immediate anger at active substance abusing and/or excessively angry parent, sibling, or child	Refer to Al-Anon, Al-Ateen; "What could you do with your anger?" as main theme; empathy versus moral repudiation; disease model reframe
Adult children's resentments toward angry and/or substance-abusing parent	Refer to adult/child groups; forgiveness work

Victims of domestic violence are also likely to suffer increased risk of both acute and chronic substance abuse problems. For instance, Bergman, Larsson, Brismar, and Klang (1987) note that 51% of battered women were high alcohol consumers as against 28% of the control population, while Covington (1997) indicates that women entering treatment for substance abuse report high rates of physical and sexual abuse experiences. Jordan, Nietzel, Walker, and Logan (2004) write that the significant correlation between victimization and substance abuse should be comprehensively addressed in treatment. They suggest that women victims of domestic violence who also have substance abuse problems will be more vulnerable to aggression for several reasons, including impaired ability to detect developing problems, risky lifestyles associated with substance abuse, poor judgment while intoxicated, poor impulse control, and the targeting of intoxicated women for abuse. There is no reason to believe that these comments would not be equally applicable to male victims of domestic abuse.

Real questions arise, however, when the exact relationship between substance abuse and domestic violence is discussed. Fazzone, Holton, and Reed (1997) write that substance abuse is only one of many factors that influence a batterer's violent behavior. Other significant factors might include depression, psychopathology, violence in the family of origin, social norms approving of violence, high levels of marital and relationship conflict, and low income. Jordan et al. (2004) conclude that there are

> very complex relationships between violence, substance abuse, personality disorder or traits, depression, cognitive functioning (particularly frontal-lobe activity), and situational context. Substance abuse adds considerable complexity to the understanding of aggression in intimate partner violence offenders. While it is tempting to see the specific drug or alcohol as a cause of violence, this interpretation is not supported by the evidence. . . . Even when substance abuse is very evident in a case, it is unlikely to be the cause of the violence; other factors such as personality or executive functioning of the frontal lobes may be more explanatory. (p. 54)

This conclusion may be excessively conservative, however. It might be better to suggest that the specific relationship, including causality, between any one person's pattern of substance use/abuse and that individual's pattern of domestic aggression as perpetrator, coperpetrator, or victim must be assessed carefully and cautiously. In theory, either variable could be causal of the other, so it is possible to find certain people whose domestic violence ceases entirely once they quit abusing substances and others whose substance abuse ends immediately on their ceasing domestic abusiveness. However, it is more likely that each factor contributes to the other in far more complex patterns while interacting with many other immediate and long-term sources of stress. It seems quite likely, though, that failure to address either problem while attempting to address the other will lessen the chances of successful treatment for either substance abuse or domestic violence.

TYPES OF DOMESTIC ABUSERS AND SUBSTANCE ABUSE

Many authors have recognized that not all male domestic abusers are alike. Hence, they have developed typologies of abusers that attempt to differentiate between these men so as to allow for more appropriate treatment approaches (Dutton, 1998; Groetsch, 1996; Jacobsen and Gottman, 1998; Potter-Efron, 2005; Saunders, 1992). Although the specific labels differ, at least four types of male domestic abusers are frequently identified in the relevant literature: (a) relatively "normal" men whose aggression is fairly low level and who appear to suffer from no severe pathologies, (b) excessively needy men whose aggression is maintained by severe ego deficits and who often fit the criteria for a diagnosis of borderline personality disorder, (c) particularly oppositional men with widespread antisocial personality structures, and (d) men whose domestic abuse patterns can best be explained as deriving from a more primary physical or psychological condition such as dementia, paranoid schizophrenia, and so on. Female domestic aggressors may fit this model as well. At least one study (Babcock, Miller, & Siard, 2003) distinguishes between generally violent women and those whose violence is demonstrated only with their partners, noting that generally violent women tended to use instrumental violence in many situations. While it is yet to be determined how well the four types of abusers noted here fit the populations of female heterosexual, gay, and lesbian domestic abusers, still they prepare the ground for different treatment approaches. Specifically, the first group should do best in standard batterer educational group settings or structured couples or family counseling, whereas the borderline batterers will need much more individualized psychologically oriented treatment focused on attachment themes. Antisocial batterers will probably need their education augmented with immediate and effective monitoring through criminal justice auspices. The fourth group, a diverse lot, will need to have their primary physical and mental health issues treated (such as by prescribing antipsychotic medications for paranoid schizophrenics) before effective domestic abuse treatment can commence.

It must be recognized that substance abuse problems may predictably differ among these groups. One would expect, for instance, that the first group of batterers will have only an average number of substance abuse difficulties comparable to the general population. Furthermore, the effect of their use of alcohol or other mood-altering substances on their pattern of violence will vary greatly, ranging from having no perceptible impact to increasing the likelihood and severity of aggression to always being associated with violence. Those batterers of this type who are indeed chemically dependent will need to be confronted in order to break through a "double-denial" pattern in which they deny, minimize, and justify both their physical aggression and their substance abuse.

Needy abusers may present another pattern. These individuals feel chronically empty. Their violence usually occurs as they experience or anticipate experiencing emotional or physical abandonment. Unable to self-soothe, they rely on external sources of comfort for their very emotional survival. The theme of their domestic violence centers on the idea that "I can't live without you, so I can't let you go."

External sources of comfort, however, are not limited to relationship partners. What better source to meet this need could there be than alcohol or drugs, utterly reliable old friends that can be counted on to fill any momentary or lingering feeling of anxiety with a burst of dopamine and/or serotonin, a warm sense of contentment, and a secure (for the moment) sense of belonging? Treatment for these persons, whether centered on domestic violence or substance abuse, will eventually fail if this overwhelming need for external succor is not fully addressed.

Oppositional domestic abusers often display high levels of aggression and antisocial behavior both inside and outside their primary relationships. Their frequent pattern of rampant alcohol and drug use is consistent with their "I'll do whatever I can get away with" attitude toward life. They also have generally low levels of empathy toward others so that they tend not to get much from group settings, especially self-help groups such as AA, where mutual caring and understanding are key ingredients. Unfettered by empathy, their violence against partners tends to be more extreme than the other types of batterers. Just as treatment for domestic abuse should be augmented with criminal justice monitoring, chemical dependency treatment should be augmented by careful monitoring with random urine screening, collateral reports, home visits, and so on.

Finally, the residual group, because of their significant other problems, may both become violent and utilize substances in unusual patterns. For example, one client of mine, a victim of brain injury from an automobile accident, would seemingly almost randomly lash out at his wife as well as consuming strange combinations of foodstuffs in the belief they would get him high. Again, primary treatment for these individuals needs to focus on the underlying conditions that cause or exacerbate their violence and addictive patterns.

ASSESSMENT QUESTIONS

Table 20.3 contains a set of six questions designed to help gain information from clients while lessening their tendencies to deny or minimize the links between their aggressive behavior and their alcohol or drug use.

The first question simply gets clients talking about their alcohol and drug history. The next four questions, though, ask clients to seriously consider the exact nature of how these two variables interact. Many individuals have never taken the time to think about these relationships, while others are acutely aware of them. In either case, merely asking these questions informs clients that the interviewer recognizes the possibility that

TABLE 20.3   Questions That Help Clients Understand the Linkages Between Their Anger/Aggression and Their Use of Alcohol

1. What is your experience with alcohol and other mood-altering substances?

Substance	Current or Recent Use	Past Use	Frequency
a. Alcohol			
b. Amphetamines			
c. Barbiturates			
d. Cocaine			
e. Inhalants			
f. Marijuana			
g. Prescribed medications			
h. Opiates			
i. Other (designer drugs etc.). Which?			
j. Drug combinations? Which?			

2. What connections could there be between your use of these substances and your anger or aggression?

    a. When I use _____ I often become more angry than usual.

    b. When I use _____ I can become violent (making threats, pushing, shoving, hitting, etc.).

    c. When I use _____ I get argumentative.

    d. When I use _____ I become controlling or demanding.

    e. When I use _____ I sometimes have poor judgment.

    f. When I use _____ I get jealous or paranoid.

    g. I only get in trouble with my anger when I use _____.

    h. Others tell me I get angrier or more violent when I use _____.

    i. Mixing _____ and _____ makes me more aggressive.

    j. I often use _____ to try to cool down.

    k. Another connection between my using and my anger is _____
    _____.

    l. ____ I don't see any connection between my use of alcohol or drugs and my anger or aggression.

(Continued)

TABLE 20.3   (Continued)

3.   How does your use of alcohol or drugs affect:

  a. How often you get angry (frequency)?_____

  b. How strongly you get angry (intensity)?_____

  c. How likely you are to be violent?

  ✓ Against yourself?_____

  ✓ Against others? _____

  ✓ Against objects, pets, etc. ? _____

4.   How does getting angry affect your drinking or drug use?

  a. Does it give you an excuse to use? _____

  b. Does it affect your choice of drugs? _____

  c. Is your anger a regular part of the way you relapse? _____

5.   Are there times you want both to get angry and get high? _____

  When does this happen (e.g., shame episodes, depression, etc.)?

6.   How do you plan to stop or control your anger if you don't deal with your alcohol/drug use? _____

How do you plan to stop or control your drinking/drugs if you don't deal with your anger? _____

both issues will need to be addressed during treatment. Finally, the last question is designed both to gather information and to motivate clients to work on both concerns.

CASE STUDY: AN ANGRY MAN WHO BECOMES DANGEROUS TO HIS WIFE WHEN HE DRINKS

Larry came into my office with a broken hand that he had injured when, drunk, he had tried to hit his wife and punched the wall instead. He had succeeded in terrifying her, however, and her 911 call quickly got him a free ride in a police car, an overnight stay in jail, a restraining order, and an anger/domestic abuse assessment. Today, Larry was seeing me for the assessment.

  Larry quickly admitted that he had a serious drinking problem. In fact, he argued that his drinking was the cause for his violent behavior that evening. "Now I'm not gonna say it was only the alcohol that made me do it. I won't use that for an excuse. But I never go after my wife when I'm not drinking."

As part of the assessment process, I administered Spielberger's (1999) State-Trait Anger Expression Inventory-2 (STAXI-2) to Larry. The results were clear. This man had a significant anger problem whether or not he was intoxicated. In fact, he scored at the 95th percentile on the STAXI-2, indicative of people whose anger plays a significant and negative role in their lives.

With the help of the questions in Table 20.3 and the STAXI-2, Larry's statement about his drinking could be put into better perspective. True, he might become violent only when he drank (pending confirmation of this claim from collateral resources), but he still frequently became angry with his wife and children. On these occasions, he yelled and screamed at them loudly and threateningly.

Larry's drinking would fit what White (2004) calls an additive pattern. The combination of anger and alcohol send him over the edge from verbal aggression and barely contained physical urges to full-fledged assaultive behavior.

The result of the assessment: Larry needed immediate treatment for alcohol addiction in which he would be given special assignments to help him begin dealing with his deeply seated anger problems. His aftercare plan would include individual therapy with a counselor experienced with both addiction and anger concerns.

CASE STUDY OF AN ANGRY AND VIOLENT "NEEDY" WOMAN

Helene, age 35, attends an intake session with her boyfriend of five years named Charlie. Charlie speaks up first, saying that he has become quite afraid of Helene since she threatened him with a gun a couple weeks before. Helene, though, dismisses his concern by saying, "I don't know why you are still so bothered by that gun thing. After all, I did put it down. And you deserved it. You said you were going to move out." "Besides," Helene adds, "it would never have happened if we weren't drinking."

Helene is an insecurely attached professional actress who cannot stand the thought of Charlie leaving her. She is both fearful and preoccupied, constantly needing evidence that Charlie will stay forever no matter how severely she tests him. Those tests so far have included having sex with another man, running up huge bills on the home they are building together, and regular physical threats and attacks when she believes Charlie may be thinking about leaving. Helene states it succinctly: "When he says he's gonna leave me, I get angry quick." Helene describes herself as an "all or nothing person" in relationships. Leaving, for her, "is not an option." Actually, Helene's statement that she gets angry quickly is a tremendous understatement. Sober or drunk, she experiences blind rages during which she fails to remember her actions, totally loses control, and destroys objects as well as attacks people.

Helene's basic attachment insecurity is a given in her life. But her alcohol consumption is the randomizing element, making every drinking bout a crap shoot with regard to whether she will become violent. Some nights, Helene will stay sweet and loving and sexual when they drink. Indeed, that is one reason Charlie hesitates about asking Helene to quit drinking. He says that she permits sexual intercourse only after she's had several drinks. But on other occasions, Helene's insecurities emerge unabridged and uncontrolled when she's intoxicated. That's when she attacks Charlie, one time breaking two of his fingers and, most recently, threatening him with that gun.

Treatment for this couple was difficult. Helene did accept a referral to a psychiatrist who placed her on an anticonvulsant that relieved some of her extreme rage reactions. Unfortunately, Charlie also was a heavy drinker and wanted Helene to keep drinking both to support his alcoholic tendencies and for sexual gratification mentioned previously. They subsequently dropped out of therapy rather than accept the need to curtail their drinking.

CASE STUDY OF A FAMILY WITH VIOLENCE AND SUBSTANCE ABUSE ISSUES: "WHO GETS TO THROW THE TURKEY THIS YEAR?"

Paul was an angry adolescent who had the habit of punching holes in his basement bedroom when he got fed up with his family. Although I was seeing the entire family, there was no doubt in their minds that Paul was the problem.

But why Paul? Dad was himself an angry man a lot of the time, very demanding and continually wanting attention. Mom was the silent type who might not speak to you for days when she became upset. Sue, the 18-year-old daughter, was openly defiant and told us that "I'm mad, I like being mad, and I'm never going to change." Little Alan, the baby, was already in training and could throw tantrums that would exhaust any parent. There was even an oldest son, Marty, who had been expelled from the home for drug use and hadn't been heard from for three years.

Not that substance abuse had been eliminated when Marty left. Indeed, the family scene was so impacted by Dad's drinking and Mom's abuse of prescription medication for alleged chronic pain that holidays became fiascos. Thanksgiving was particularly interesting because for the last three years in a row, someone had gotten so mad that he or she had literally thrown the Thanksgiving turkey on the floor. First it was Mom in a prescription medication paranoid fog, then Dad in a drunken uproar, and then Paul just last year because he was so angry with both Mom and Dad for getting into a substance-abetted argument and shoving match just when relatives were arriving.

So why Paul? When asked, Mom said because he would never change, and the others all agreed. Besides, Dad said Paul was so loud, he couldn't sleep. Sue called him a whiner and tattletale.

And so family therapy began. All of them were given instructions on fair fighting. *Only Paul listened.* Each was given ideas on what to do to be less angry. *Only Paul changed.* No more holes in the walls. No more endless screaming. Polite requests for food at the table.

"So how's Paul doing?' I would ask at each session. "Terrible," the others agreed. "He's just the same as always." The family was absolutely convinced that Paul would remain the family scapegoat. His real behavior was apparently irrelevant.

Paul needed an ally, and so therapeutic neutrality was temporarily abandoned. As family therapist, I insisted that others acknowledge Paul's changes. Paul was lavishly praised for his efforts, and his parents were challenged to do the same. Only then did the total family picture emerge. Paul's "problem behavior" was just about the only thing the parents discussed together without clawing at each other's throats. Without his sacrifice, the family faced dissolution. Besides, as long as the family maintained its focus on Paul, neither parent would have to address their substance abuse problems.

Paul's parents were challenged to make two intertwined commitments: (a) to deal effectively with their alcohol and medication addictions and (b) to get the anger and aggression out of their home. I explained to them that it was unrealistic and unfair to expect Paul to take all the blame for the family's pain or to do all the work to make the family better. Besides, from a practical standpoint, unless at least one parent emerged as a leader in a movement toward peace, the family would almost certainly remain indefinitely angry (Potter-Efron, 2005).

Fortunately, both of Paul's parents agreed to these goals. Although neither parent quit all use of mood-altering substances, they did greatly curtail their use. That gave them the strength to confront Sue, informing her that she would have to move away if she would not agree to quit being so angry. Sue would have none of that nonsense, though. She did actually move out, only to ask to be allowed to return six months later as she realized the world would not tolerate very long her habitual anger.

The family worked together on anger management themes, not without difficulty and numerous setbacks.

Thanksgiving rolled around as we were nearing the end of therapy. This time, Dad stayed sober, and Mom took only her prescribed single pain pill even though she got nervous when company came. This Thanksgiving, nobody threw the turkey.

SUMMARY

Domestic violence is a complicated problem in and of itself. When substance abuse accompanies domestic violence, treatment often goes from complicated to convoluted. The substance-abusing tendencies of at least four types of domestic aggressors must be considered as well as at least seven possible relationships between substance abuse and anger/aggression. It is therefore incumbent on assessment and treatment personnel to make every effort fully to comprehend the specific relationship between these two variables as they play out uniquely with each client.

REFERENCES

Babcock, J., Miller, S., & Siard, C. (2003). Toward a typology of abusive women: Differences between partner-only and generally violent women in the use of violence. *Psychology of Women Quarterly, 27,* 153–171.

Barnett, O., & Fagan, R. (1993). Alcohol abuse in male spouse abusers and their female partners. *Journal of Family Violence, 8,* 1–25.

Bergman, B., Larsson, B., Brismar, B., & Klang, M. (1987). Psychiatric morbidity and personality characteristics of battered women. *Acta Psychiatrica Scandinavica, 76,* 678–683.

Covington, S. (1997). Women, addiction and sexuality. In L. Straussner & E. Zelvin (Eds.), *Gender and addictions: Men and women in treatment* (pp. 79–95). Northvale, NJ: Jason Aronson.

Dutton, D. (1998). *The abusive personality.* New York: Guilford Press.

Fazzone, P., Holton, J., & Reed, B. (1997). *Substance abuse treatment and domestic violence: Treatment Improvement Protocol (TIP) Series, 25.* Rockville, MD: U.S. Department of Health and Human Services.

Groetsch, M. (1996). *The battering syndrome.* Brookfield, WI: CPI Publishing.

Hamel, J. (2005). *Gender inclusive treatment of intimate family abuse.* New York: Springer.

Jacobsen, N., & Gottman, J. (1998). *When men batter women.* New York: Simon & Schuster.

Jordan, C., Nietzel, M., Walker, R., & Logan, T. K. (2004). *Intimate partner violence.* New York: Springer.

Kantor, G., & Straus, M. (1987). The drunken bum theory of wife beating. *Social Problems, 34,* 213–231.

Kuhn, T. (1996). *The structure of scientific revolutions* (3rd ed.). Chicago: University of Chicago Press.

Leonard, K., & Quigley, B. (1999). Drinking and marital aggression in newlyweds: An event-based analysis of drinking and the occurrence of husband marital aggression. *Journal of Studies on Alcohol, 60,* 537–545.

Potter-Efron, R. (2005). *Handbook of anger management: Individual, couple, family and group approaches.* New York: Haworth Press.

Roizen, J. (1997). Epidemiological issues in alcohol-related violence. In M. Galanter (Ed.), *Recent developments in alcoholism: Vol. 13. Alcoholism and violence* (pp. 7–41). New York: Plenum Press.

Saunders, D. (1992). A typology of men who batter: three types derived from cluster analysis. *American Journal of Orthopsychiatry, 62*(2), 264–275.

Spielberger, C. (1999). *Manual for the State-Trait Anger Expression Inventory-2.* Odessa, FL: Psychological Assessment Resources.

Tolman, R., & Bennett, W. (1990), A review of quantitative research on men who batter. *Journal of Interpersonal Violence, 5*(1), 87–118.

White, W. (2004, January). Substance use and violence: Understanding the nuances of the relationship. *The Addiction Professional,* 13–19.

CHAPTER 21

Therapy With Clients Accused of Domestic Violence in Disputed Child Custody Cases

Michael Carolla

Within the family court system, there appears to have been an increase in the number of domestic violence allegations by one partner toward the other. Several factors may be contributing to this phenomenon, the most significant of which is the paradigm shift from the "tender years" doctrine (children should spend more significant time with the "nurturing" mother), toward the "best interests of the child" standard (children benefit most from full inclusion of both parents in their lives). Mothers can no longer assume that the father's custody time will be limited to occasional visits or every other weekend. Because of legislation in most states limiting a parent's custodial time in cases when there is a history of domestic violence (Jaffe & Geffner, 1998), litigants of both genders are motivated to employ more aggressive strategies in pursuit of custody.

These court battles are often referred to qualified custody evaluators who employ a complex system of clinical interview, psychological evaluations, and collateral interviews (Austin, 2001; Gould, 1998). In the initial interviews, parties are often asked about their perceptions of the other parent and their parenting skills, time spent with the children, and other factors that could affect percentage of custody granted. Three major conditions that can affect a parent's custody share in these cases are mental instability, substance abuse, and family abuse (intimate partner as well as child abuse or neglect). There are many methods available to assess for mental instability and drug use; however, family abuse accusations are much harder to assess for and often get caught up in "he said/she said" allegations.

The family court mediator is often the first to grapple with such accusations. Because of the prevailing patriarchal research paradigm (Dutton, 2005), most of the domestic violence training these mediators receive, whether from the local women's shelter or from someone else who has worked with victims of domestic violence, tends to focus on women as victims and minimizes their role as perpetrators. The abuse that victim advocates see is quite real and frightening; however, it cannot be extrapolated to the general population. It is understandable that family court mediators would respond to domestic abuse allegations by limiting custody time with the accused for the safety of the children. Unfortunately, this leaves the accused the burden of proof to clear him or her of the accusations. Furthermore, once the accusation is made, true or not, a cloud of suspicion remains throughout the whole process. As I heard one judge say, "Where there is smoke, there is fire." Knowing this, many litigants are tempted to produce some smoke to create the illusion of fire. Mediators and judges usually do not have the resources to investigate fully the accusations and consequently choose to "err on the side of the children's safety." Given this, it is easy to see how parents in child custody disputes might be motivated to exaggerate or minimize the abuse history.

When interviewing a client for a domestic violence group or coparenting mediation, I often hear such statements as "I have never had problems like this with anyone else, ever in my life." Because of the particular dynamics involved, such as the pairing of individuals with highly incompatible attachment styles (Roberts & Noller, 1998), the conflict in one relationship may more readily escalate and abuse be limited to that couple. In addition, it can be difficult for mediators and judges to separate a parent's difficulty in managing conflict with their spouse from their ability to parent adequately when they are not together. So this begs the question, "Does couple conflict or violence necessarily indicate a reduced ability to parent adequately?" In most states, the current assumption is that it does. The problem here is that domestic abuse is more complex than that. In high-conflict families, partner abuse may or may not be accompanied by child abuse, and physical assaults may be perpetrated by a number of family members, including the children (Potter-Efron, 2005; chapter 8 in this volume). As mental health clinicians, we must be prepared to work with a variety of situations—those involving unfounded allegations, those involving exaggerated but somewhat substantiated allegations, and those in which there is serious violence that threatens the physical and emotional well-being of parents and children.

ONE SIZE DOESN'T FIT ALL

It is important to get away from the "one size fits all" type of categorization of an accused perpetrator. As discussed elsewhere in this book (e.g., chapters 1, 2, 3 and 6), the notion that all male perpetrators commit their crime because of a learned patriarchal sense of entitlement has not been supported by research. Rather, we can better treat this problem by looking at it honestly and openly, without the prejudice that comes from political dogma. There are different types of domestic abuse, with varying causal explanations, that may be broken down broadly according to the following categories:

✓ Psychopathology

Includes antisocial, borderline, narcissistic, and histrionic personality disorders as well as bipolar and other mood disorders. Causes of violence are often due to a person's inability to regulate his or her emotions. Although these make up a smaller percentage of overall domestic abuse cases, they usually involve the most violence, so these are the ones that become newsworthy. Without proper training in assessment and differential diagnosis of family violence, family court professionals may mistakenly assume that such highly visible cases are more representative than they actually are.

✓ Substance Abuse

Substance abuse is involved in a large number of domestic violence cases. Many who argue for the "patriarchy is the cause" approach state that the violence would occur whether or not the man was under the influence because he assumes the right to engage in this behavior. While few would disagree with the idea that one should be held accountable for one's actions, even under the influence of mind-altering substances, anyone who has had a substance abuse problem will tell you that they have done things under the influence that they would never have done sober. To not include substance abuse as a possible contributing factor in domestic abuse is irresponsible and potentially contributes to further abuse (see chapter 20 in this volume).

✓ Ongoing Couples Conflict

Couples conflict is not necessarily pathological; in the absence of abuse and contempt, it may be of relatively minor concern (Gottman, 1999). The danger, of course, is that it may quickly escalate, and many couples have difficulty in breaking free from their conflict dynamics. One couple told me they kept a spare supply of telephones and bedroom doors in the garage because they would break one on the average of once a week. Both had acknowledged being equally responsible for the ongoing violence.

✓ Situational Abuse

Abuse may happen only once or may have been a rare event throughout the course of a relationship. A major study by Johnston and Campbell (1993) found that in nearly half the cases of disputed child custody involving domestic violence, there had been little or no violence prior to the separation. It is not rare to hear in a batter's treatment group intake that before the violent incident, the primary wage earner was unemployed. The stress this puts on a relationship cannot be overstated. The men often feel very vulnerable. As the stress builds, many of these men react uncharacteristically to the continued pleas of their partner's to "just find something to bring in some money." These men come to group shocked at what they had done and very committed to learning how to not do it again. Other one-time situations include discovery of infidelity and economic dishonesty by the partner (hiding purchases; going on spending sprees after credit debts were paid off; lending money they don't have to relatives; and so on). One client had refinanced his home twice because of his wife's shopaholic spending sprees, only to discover a secret credit card account, his signature forged, with a $30,000 balance.

There are a number of treatment options for child custody cases involving allegations of domestic violence. The most relevant of these options are discussed in the following sections.

Batterer Intervention Programs

When one parent has a history of perpetrating high levels of physical and emotional abuse as well as controlling behaviors or when that parent has engaged in lesser levels of such abuse but either justifies, minimizes, or denies that abuse, a batterer intervention treatment group would be the treatment modality of choice.

Anger Management Groups/Classes

When it is clear that one or both parties have been having difficulty managing their emotions, especially their anger, but their aggression has been limited to verbal abuse and infrequent displays of lower-level violence and controlling behaviors, an anger management class is a reasonable referral. Anger management classes, typically of shorter duration than batterer intervention groups, can help individuals learn tools for better managing as well as expressing their anger in appropriate ways. These classes can also help with learning positive assertiveness skills.

High-Conflict /Family Violence Parent Groups

When the children have been the victims of abuse, as a result of having observed interparental violence or as a result of having been directly abused, there are parenting groups modeled on the batterer treatment programs that address the treatment needs of the parents (see chapter 24 in this volume).

Therapeutic Supervised Visitation

When accusations of abuse or questionable parenting practices have been made or indeed have occurred, an initial step toward normal parental visits may be therapeutic supervised visitation. The parent in question meets with the children and therapist for an initial half an hour session, during which the visit, where to go, what to eat, boundaries, and acceptable behavior are discussed. The family members then leave for a 3- to 4-hour outing to a public place (dinner and a movie, the beach, a picnic at the park). Immediately afterwards, the parent returns with the children to the therapist, who meets first with the children alone to assess for any improper behavior and to document the children's comments, positive or critical. This can help protect both the children and the parent who may fear that false accusations will be made afterwards.

When there has been a history of abuse and the children and parent need help in healing the relationship breach, the therapist can help coach the parent and children to be proactive in having a good and productive visit as well as help deal with any issues that may have arisen during the visit. These supervised visits may, in time, be a bridge to short-term or ongoing family therapy sessions in which lingering issues can be more thoroughly addressed.

Coparenting Mediation

It should not be surprising that a great deal of couple conflict, even violence, occurs during the process of divorce. The parties often continue to participate by the rules of the past relationship. Abuse, as well as accusations of abuse, can occur as a result of ongoing power struggles when parents refuse to consider each others' views on how to raise the children and/or actively seek to undermine each other's parental role through sabotaging and alienating behaviors. Coparenting mediation can help the parties establish a new relationship as coparents rather than divorce litigants. Unlike conjoint counseling for intact couples, the therapist must maintain rigid limits on what is discussed, and the parties are discouraged from rehashing old issues and resentments. With a focus on what is in the best interests of the children, both parties are encouraged to acknowledge one another's strengths and are helped to figure out how to cooperate and compromise so that the children can get the most from each parent.

Family Therapy

The types and uses of family therapy can be quite varied and structured to fit the situation. Where there is general conflict and the children feel caught in the middle, the whole family can be brought in so that everyone has a part in redefining the new family relationships.

There can be many different reasons that children feel alienated from a particular parent. These can include actual domestic abuse as well as accusations of abuse where the child feels compelled to defend the "abused" parent. Sometimes, children find reasons to alienate from a parent who has actually done little wrong. They desire to be part of the new family unit but can't emotionally handle the loyalty split. In addition, in cases of infidelity children see the offending parent as the cause of the family breakup, especially where there have been incidences of violence around the affair. Family therapy can be useful in helping the children come to terms with their feelings, needs, and relationship with the alienated parent. And where there has been a real history of domestic abuse, family therapy can be an incredibly useful way for the abuser to take responsibility for his or her behavior, to apologize, and to make amends.

In their book *Impasses of Divorce,* Janet Johnston and Linda Campbell (1988) describe how friends, family, and others can be influenced to take sides or, as they put it, form "tribes" during ongoing custody disputes. Children very often get swept up in this process. This can be further influenced by one or both parents telling the children how the other is trying to hurt them in court. One 12-year-old told me during a family therapy session that she didn't want to talk to her mother because the mother cared only about hurting her father in court. The father in question refused to allow either child to see their mother more than four hours per week even though a court mediator recommended weekends. Court was the mother's only option. Family therapy can help the family members focus on the parent-child relationship rather than the court battle.

It can also help heal breaches in parent–child relationships brought on by the stresses and conflicts inherent in family court conflicts. Typically, the alienated parent and the child in question enter into therapy to clear out misunderstandings, make amends for inappropriate behavior, and learn how to focus on the future changing relationship.

When substance abuse has been identified as a key factor, it is usually addressed before other interventions are suggested. A client may find it very difficult when dealing with substance abuse issues to acquire the insight necessary to take responsibility for healing any breaches in the parent–child relationship. Once the substance abuse has been addressed and is being monitored, other options can then be considered.

Should mental health be an issue, having played a large part in the abuse, regular individual therapy as well as medication evaluations are called for. Anxiety disorders, bipolar disorders, depression with anxiety, obsessive-compulsive disorders, borderline personality disorder, and other mental health–related issues can significantly contribute to ongoing as well as single-incident abuse. It is not unusual for a therapist to discover that a client with a history of cyclical emotional and/or violent outbursts has been going through an anxiety buildup/explosive release cycle. This does not excuse or minimize the abuse; it just gives the therapist a better focus for treatment. Often the disorder has gone undiagnosed most of the perpetrator's life, and proper treatment can be quite effective in limiting future reoffenses.

Situational abuse can also be adequately addressed with individual therapy. The majority of situational perpetrators are shocked about what they did and are highly remorseful, so helping them come to terms with and atone for their behavior is usually quite effective. This population has the lowest rate of reoffense. When it is clear that the couple has engaged in ongoing mutual combat, coparenting mediation therapy, combined with an anger management treatment group, can yield very positive results. Even though each person can usually attest that he or she has had abuse issues only with the other party, emotional regulation can still be an ongoing challenge with these clients. When it is, individual therapy may be required.

Each individual has different needs and therefore requires different treatment to best help him or her parent his or her children. This is especially true when allegations of domestic abuse have been made. Continuing assessment for substance abuse, mental and emotional stability, parenting attitudes, and abuse history is a vital part of the treatment process. Many mental health professionals have had good training and experience in assessment. However, I am continually bewildered by the many clinicians who lack the level of assessment skills needed to do this kind of work.

Learning adequate assessment skills is one of the frontline skills needed before engaging in this kind of work.

I often work with clients referred because of accusations of some form of abuse. Reasons for the referral range from helping the client change behaviors that could possibly be interfering with his or her ability to parent to helping the client deal with the emotional results of dealing with the consequences of unfounded accusations. Very often the client has a combination of the two needs.

CASE EXAMPLES

EXAMPLE 1: BOB

Bob was referred by the custody evaluator and his son's attorney because of emotional outbursts when he felt that his wife, Suzanne, was not following court orders or was lying about him to the evaluator, mediator, or judge. Suzanne had been diagnosed by her previous therapist with borderline personality disorder and depression, and she had made suicide attempts during their marriage. She had tricked Bob into moving to another state to find a home in a more peaceful, rural area. When Bob had relocated expecting her to move with him, Suzanne then notified him that the marriage was over and that she had moved in with someone else. Bob moved back and insisted on being an equal parent in their four-year-old son's life. The custody battle was on. Unfortunately, the evaluator chose to ignore Suzanne's past hospitalizations and believed without question her accusations of past emotional and physical abuse by Bob. Bob admitted to having sometimes yelled at her in response to her own frequent rage outbursts when she would scream and throw things around the house (e.g., dishes, books), but he denied ever hitting her, and Suzanne could not provide any corroborating evidence. Because of the alleged abuse, the evaluator nevertheless recommended that she have full legal and physical custody. Bob was emotionally distraught about this and quite outspoken to the judge, mediator, and custody evaluator. Although the wife was ordered to keep him informed of their son's events, health, school progress, and so forth, by all accounts she failed to do so. Bob would call and e-mail her demanding she follow the court order. She filed a restraining order to get Bob to "stop harassing her."

On one occasion, Bob went to a festival at a local park and was soon dancing with some friends and their children. Bob's son walked up and wanted to dance too. Bob was overjoyed to see his son and danced with him. When his son said he had to go because "mommy would be mad," Bob told him he had better go. A short while later as Bob was leaving, he saw his ex yelling at their son. Bob walked over and pleaded with her, in front of friends, not to punish their son for dancing with him. Bob was jailed and denied visitation for violation of the restraining order.

On another occasion, Bob went to his son's school, court order in hand, saying he had a right to be informed of his son's progress and asked to talk to his teacher. Bob was informed that his ex had told them not to give the information to him, and they refused his request. Bob yelled at the school officials demanding they follow the court order. The police were called, and the incident was reported to the custody evaluator. The child's attorney could see that there was a close bond between father and son but disclosed to me that she was not able to see the things Bob claimed about his ex because of his behavior, and she was concerned that if Bob couldn't control himself in the previously mentioned situations, he might not be able to control himself around his son.

Clearly Bob could have benefited from learning some effective tools in managing his emotions because at this point he was his own worst enemy. He also needed help in learning how to better present to the evaluator as well as child's counsel that he was being systematically closed out of his son's life. Bob, however, was unclear on the concept of legal process and kept confusing what he thought was right and just with what the law allowed. For example, being at a parade that he knew his ex and son would be attending is considered a violation of a restraining order. Talking to his son when he knew his wife had to be close by was also a violation. Bob was unable to see how his actions could be interpreted as controlling and abusive.

Most of Bob's "unacceptable" behavior was motivated by his feelings of being underpowered as a father and the belief, shared by many fathers in this situation, that he must constantly fight for his parental rights. Therapy with Bob was tricky because, as he saw it, he was not the problem; he didn't need to be "fixed." An analogy I have found effective with this population is to imagine you are on a football field. While playing ball, you are constantly getting knocked around and hit. You keep asking the refs to do something about it, but they just roll their eyes and tell you to play on. You don't get it! Why isn't everyone playing fair? It's then that someone taps you on the shoulder and tells you that "this is a rugby game." I then tell the person, "You need to learn the rules of this game, not the one you thought you were playing." Learning new rules can be empowering. Learning how the system works and doesn't work can help clients settle down and become less emotionally wounded when something doesn't go their way.

Bob felt that every legal decision that went against him was a condemnation of his parenting. It was important to help him see that the recommendations of the parenting coordinator (special master in some states) were based mainly on the court order, not on his "rational" reasoning. This helped him reorganize his approach toward coparenting and the legal conflict. Bob also needed to understand that others saw him as "taking up a lot of space." In other words, his physical size and demeanor alone were often intimidating to others regardless of his intent. He learned to rephrase his requests in a less intimidating way and over time found that people listened to him more.

His ex continued to use the abuse issue to avoid revisiting the custody arrangement. While this continued to frustrate Bob, he found some empowerment in focusing much of his energy on being the best father he could during his every other weekend with his son. Bob also started to refocus his off parenting time on his personal life. He quickly realized that while the custody issue was very frustrating, he was quite empowered in other areas of his life, both professionally and personally. As part of my initial evaluation of the case, I had Bob send me his recent job performance review. It showed him to be respected and highly valued, especially in high-stress and emergency situations. This was used later in therapy to help him reorganize around the empowered parts of his life rather than the one underpowered part. Bob continues to work on accepting that this area of his life is just not going to be fair as he sees it but has ceased being his own worst enemy in the continuing conflict.

I believe the most acting-out behavior is motivated by feelings of being unempowered in one's life. So often, the goals of therapy with this population are to help the clients find appropriate and healthy empowerment.

EXAMPLE 2: TRACY AND JOHN

Tracy had been brought up to believe that her mission in life was to take care of her man and in turn to be taken care of by him. After surviving a relationship with a boyfriend who demeaned her on a regular basis and once spat in her face, she met John. She felt she was unable to take care of herself in this world and saw John as her knight in shining armor. John felt great being looked up to like this as well as being able to provide for her and their two children. Over time, Tracy matured and found that she was quite intelligent and able. She was hired at a local business and soon worked herself up to a well-paying management position. She started asserting herself and depending less on John. Unable to handle the new her, John belittled Tracy, pushed her around and yelled at her in front of the children. This precipitated a relapse in her emotional stability, and she soon decided she needed to leave to maintain her newfound sense of self. Because of limited resources, Tracy left the children with John until she felt financially able to take them. She had always believed John to be a good and caring father. John was very angry at Tracy for abandoning him. He refused to let her see the girls, and continued to belittle and verbally abuse her over the phone when she called to talk to them.

Tracy remarried. Because of her frequent emotional deregulation and drinking on the part of her new husband, Mike, an incident occurred in which Mike grabbed Tracy and was arrested. Tracy then turned to her children for emotional support, sharing with them in inappropriate ways details of her married life, which the children shared with their father. Even before charges were filed against him, Mike voluntarily agreed to enroll in a batterer intervention program. When Tracy reconciled with Mike, the children felt betrayed. How could their mother return to this person she had previously portrayed as a monster? When it came time for the custody evaluation, John fought with everything he had, including accusations of questionable behavior on the part of Mike toward the girls as well as the domestic violence incident. John went all out in portraying Tracy and Mike as abusive and controlling and Mike as a possible pedophile. The children were eager to portray Mike in a bad light. One incident reported by the 13-year-old was that she went in to use the shower in the master bath and was "freaked out" that her stepdad "just lay in bed in his underwear." It was also reported that the eight-year-old had said that Mike had tried to "peek under the door" when she took a shower. The custody evaluator took all this as fact and recommended that the mom have limited visits and that under no circumstances could the children be around the stepdad.

Later interviews with the children during reunification therapy showed that the accusations had been greatly exaggerated; the younger daughter said she never said the stepdad was looking under the door. And the older daughter had decided to use the master bath shower while her stepfather was still sleeping, without asking her mother for permission. However, at this point the damage had been done. The children had quickly bonded with their father's new wife and saw their mom's efforts to see them as a way to undermine their happy family.

Initial coparenting therapy was unproductive because of the ongoing breach in the relationship between Tracy and her daughters. Tracy had not dealt with the effects that the domestic violence incident had on the girls. She had also yet to accept her own responsibility in her children's opinion of her husband. Because John had been so controlling in their marriage, she assumed he was controlling the girls' actions and statements. Given Tracy's emotional state and her tendency to blame John, the custody evaluator assumed that Tracy was a typical battered spouse and unable to protect herself and children from further domestic abuse.

Family therapy started with Tracy. Her children felt "guilted" by their mother's emotional breakdowns and didn't trust her to manage herself let alone them. Tracy needed to take control of her emotional outbursts and take responsibility both for her own lapses in parenting judgment and her part in the children's perception of Mike. Tracy learned how to separate the parataxic distortions from her past abuse and from feelings about situations in the present. When John was being controlling and refused to let her see the children, therapy helped her manage her fears of further physical abuse from him and to be more assertive around coparenting issues as well as in family court. Tracy learned to be more appropriate in her role as a parent, to confidently assert parental authority rather than cry and plead when the children were acting out.

Family therapy with John was focused on his narcissistic splitting of Tracy and himself. He could not see any positive contributions that Tracy had to offer as a mother and often told the children so. With narcissists, therapy is often a process of trying to find a chink in the armor and then working on opening up that chink. Unfortunately, as things started getting better with Tracy and the children, John became increasingly angry about being forced to share time with her. Because of his rigidity about visits and his refusal to consider expanding mother's time with the children, court orders were needed to force the issue. As Tracy secured an increased amount of custody time, therapy with John focused on adopting a more balanced view of Tracy as a mother. John continues to magnify every questionable incident between Tracy and the children, making accusation after accusation. However, because Tracy is better regulated emotionally, the focus in on John and his outbursts, and his past abusive behaviors are coming to light.

EXAMPLE 3: MITCH AND SHERYL

Mitch and Sheryl had a long on-again, off-again relationship before marrying in their mid-40s. Sheryl would often become violent with Mitch—punching, kicking, and throwing objects—when she felt emotionally unsupported by him. She often yelled and someti mes hit their three-year-old son when he "wasn't cooperating." On one occasion, their son was jumping on the bed after being warned not to. She yelled and started to hit him. Mitch grabbed the boy and ran into the bathroom, followed closely by Sheryl. She began to punch Mitch on the back as he shielded their son from her attack. Finally, Mitch had had enough and pushed her into the door, causing a bruise on her arm. Neighbors heard her yelling and called the police. After interviewing both parties, the police determined that Mitch was not the aggressor. Fight/flight responses are varied and can be misleading. A deer, cornered and in danger, will kick and bite to get away from the danger. While this is an aggressive act, it is still a "flight" response to danger. A victim of abuse will often lash out in a self-protective way. Mitch, cornered in the bathroom, son in his arms, did roughly push Sheryl so that he could get away from her attack.

The police asked if he wanted Sheryl arrested. Mitch declined. However, the next day Mitch was served with a restraining order and wouldn't see his son for another two months. Sheryl, who had enlisted the services of an aggressive attorney, insisted that Mitch not see his son until he enrolled in a domestic violence class. Mitch complied so that he would be able to secure visitations.

There had been a long history of conflict between them. Mitch didn't view himself as superior to women, and his struggles with his wife were not of a "patriarchal" nature. While Mitch insisted that he was always on the defense with Sheryl because of her verbal and physical assaults, her version was that he would suddenly become angry at her and that it was she who would have to strike out to defend herself. Further clinical assessment made it clear that Mitch maintained a passive role in the relationship and that Sheryl initiated the violence. However, he tended to let his anger build up rather than set limits and take care of himself. Inevitably, when the attacks became too much for him, he would start yelling and hitting back. Treatment for Mitch, aside from the domestic violence program, included individual therapy to address his passivity and poor self-esteem as well as referral to an assertiveness skills workshop. No longer in an intimate relationship, Mitch had also lost his base for emotional support. It was important to address this problem because he ran the risk of using his son to get the emotional support he so badly needed and thus compromising the youngster's emotional development.

On several visitations, Mitch noticed bruises on his son's arm and asked about them. "I wasn't cooperating" was the three-year-old's reply. The allegations of child abuse against Sheryl have not been investigated by the custody evaluator. Mitch continues to have limited visitation because of Sheryl's allegations of domestic violence.

EXAMPLE 4: FRED

Fred was a large middle-aged man from the Bronx, an old-school patriarchal type of guy who believed that "all women are crazy." A perfectionist, he subjected his wife and children to frequent barrages of criticism. Although he never hit his wife, he was uncomfortable with displays of emotion and on two occasions shook his wife to "shut her up." He had a need to be in control and would harass and sometimes bully others to get his way, taking advantage of his booming voice and intimidating physical presence. Fed up with the abuse, his wife finally left him. The divorce was financially costly, and the judge's decision to award his wife sole custody only reaffirmed his belief that "men always get screwed in court." Because of his harsh discipline of the children, his wife was very reluctant to set any limits on them at all. After the divorce, the children, both in their early teens, started to act out at their mother's house. Reluctantly, his ex called on him to coparent and provide some of the structure that was missing in the children's lives.

Therapy started with a 52-week high-conflict family violence parent group. Over the course of the year, Fred came to trust the group facilitator and his coparticipants. Ridden with guilt about having failed his children and no longer willing to be the "bad guy," he was motivated to find ways to tone down his language and voice as well as learn to speak to his children and ex-wife in a more appropriate manner. Once he began to participate in family and coparenting therapy, Fred was much better prepared to assume his role as father with his ex and children and, in time, to address the family-of-origin issues that contributed to his abusive behavior. Fred came from a family in which yelling at children was a common occurrence and family members regularly insulted one another. He honestly felt his behavior was no big deal, clinging to the belief that "you just get over it." Over time, Fred began to acknowledge the effects his behavior had on his wife and children. He learned how to manage his anger and distinguish between being aggressive and being assertive. It was important for him to see that *what* he found wanting in his children's behavior was less important than *how* he was addressing the misbehavior.

EXAMPLE 5: JOHN AND JASMINE

Both John and his wife Jasmine immigrated from Iran. A long-standing custody and divorce battle with accusations of abuse and infidelity had left their 10-year-old son Michael taking his mother's side and rejecting his father. Michael told his therapist that his father had hit him on several occasions and that he had witnessed his father beat his mother. John strongly denied this. The only physical altercation, he insisted, took place when Michael had reported that he helped his mother steal from a department store. John became furious and grabbed Jasmine's purse and started to rip up her credit cards. A struggle ensued over the purse, and the police were called. According to the investigating officer, Michael indicated that this was the only time he had heard his parents fight and that he witnessed the struggle over the purse but saw no hitting. Listening only to Michael's therapist and rejecting the custody evaluator's recommendations of joint custody, the judge allowed John only supervised visits with Michael, two hours per month.

These meetings were counterproductive because the supervisor, who had gotten an earful from Jasmine about John's abusiveness, treated him as an abusive man and limited his comments and input regarding the visit. Every time John protested about the supervisor's intrusiveness, she reported that he had been hostile and threatening, which John adamantly denied. At one point, I had suggested to John some topics to talk to his son about and to ask such questions as "How is school going?" or "What sports are you playing?" John was told by the supervisor that he was not allowed to ask those questions. His complaints to the supervisor were regarded as belligerent.

John was similar to many of the Middle Eastern men I have worked with. His delivery, expression, and body language, while normal for his culture, was often interpreted by court mediators and evaluators as threatening. Phrases like "you have to understand . . . " came off as a demand rather than the plea for understanding he intended. John also had the issue of his ex playing the domestic abuse card to the hilt. His son had become alienated from him because of the mother's frequent show of emotional reaction to any mention of his father. It was beneficial for John to learn some cultural adaptations to his speech and delivery. In reunification therapy, I modeled for Michael how to talk to his father about his feelings without being afraid, and modeled for his father how to express himself in a less threatening way. Another intervention was to insist on a different supervisor for the visits, one that would stick to the court order and not be swayed by either parent's efforts to win her over. This change made a huge difference in the success of visitation.

Michael, however, insisted that his father had beaten him and his mother. I have found that what often distinguishes between parental alienation and true abuse are the details in the story. Someone who has experienced abuse and trauma usually has very clear and vivid memories of the events and can tell in detail what happened to them. Allegations of abuse stemming from parental alienation are often vague. When asked for details, reporters give short answers, are rarely able to come up with more than a few details, and wind up repeating word for word what has been previously reported while becoming frustrated at having to tell the story. Another clue is a refusal to see any good in the alienated parent. Most truly abused children hold a secret wish for the offending parent to "make it all better." Michael continued to maintain that there was nothing good about his father. However, when confronted with his rigid stance, as well as his self-contradictory statements, Michael began to relent. Accusations of "you beat my mother" changed to "you were yelling at her," which then further changed to "I couldn't stand it, you guys were so quiet around each other, it was like you were yelling, it was so tense all the time." At this point, John was able to grasp how terrible the marriage problems must have been for his son and apologized for what he had put him through. Visits progressed to "wraparound supervision" (parent and child check in before and after the visit; child is interviewed separately to check for appropriate behavior during the visit) and eventually to unsupervised visits.

CONCLUSION

The previously discussed cases illustrate the dire need for improving assessment for abuse in child custody cases. What has been problematic is the tendency of some in the field to fit accusations of abuse into gender stereotypes. Too often if a man is accused of abuse, it's believed because he is a man. If a woman is accused of being unstable and to be living with an abusive man, it's believed because of the assumption that women are helpless to repeat abusive relationships. What seems to be missing from many of the cases I have dealt with are assessment procedures grounded in empirical principles. Evaluators and therapists often rely on cultural and gender paradigms to help make custody decisions rather than follow up on the evidence trail, and their conclusions and recommendations are made without any substantial evidence to back them up, leading to recommendations of a "one size fits all" type of treatment or structure.

In the first vignette, Bob was constantly accused by his ex of being emotionally unstable. My first step in working with him was to assess to what degree this was true. People with long-standing emotional problems tend to leave a trail, which can be found in their job history, past relationships, police records, and current relationships with family.

Bob readily agreed to have his most recent job performance evaluation sent to me. Bob worked in a high-stress, inner-city emergency room. His performance evaluation stated that one of his strengths was "keeps rational and calm during stressful situations" and that he "always communicated positively with others even during high-stress situations." He had kept the same job for many years and was given his job back when he returned from out of state. He maintained close relationships with siblings and his parents, seeing family on a regular basis, and reported no past violence or conflict with past girlfriends. He also had no police contact before the conflict started with his ex. (It is important to note that when asking for history, I tell the client that anything he or she leaves out or are less than truthful about will be exposed by the ex, so it's best to discuss openly, in a friendly setting, any past conflicts or issues. I have rarely found these disclosures to be less than honest.) The evidence here did not support the type of behavior claimed by Bob's ex. More to the point, there was no evidence to suggest that his son was in any danger being with his father. However, Bob was having difficulty managing his feelings of righteous betrayal by his ex as well as the legal system. He was not so much in need of psychological change as he was in need of behavioral change. In therapy, Bob learned to disengage emotionally from the consistent character attacks and blunt refusal by his ex to cooperate in coparenting. This helped him be less emotionally reactive to her actions and eventually led to a new custody evaluation and a more favorable custody arrangement.

Tracy had some issues to work on, too. However, it was important to separate out the possibility that her oldest daughter was suffering from MAM (mad at mom) syndrome, from her father's effort to maintain custody by exaggerating every conflict between mother and daughter. The evidence trail started with the two girls. When individually interviewed, it became clear that the incidents as reported by their father had been greatly exaggerated. In addition, an interview with the stepfather as well as a follow-up interview with his 52-week domestic violence facilitator confirmed that his physical aggression was limited to a one-time incident and that he had made great progress in class. Moreover, the stepfather, at my request, did a psychological evaluation performed by a separate psychologist. The psychological evaluation suggested that while he was a bit narcissistic, he was more likely to retreat from rather than enter into conflict with others. There was no suggestion of danger to others. Furthermore, it was important to determine if Tracy might benefit from individual therapy to better manage her being emotionally overwhelmed at losing custody of her children because of what she felt were unfounded allegations. The children had reported in family therapy that Tracy "guilted" them for not stating that they wanted to live with her. It was important for Tracy to learn more appropriate skills in carrying out her role as parent. Before we could move on to coparenting mediation, each member of the family needed to accept their part in the continuing conflict. This was addressed by individual therapy for each member of the family.

Mitch was an emotional shipwreck after receiving the restraining order. He was devastated by not being able to see his son for so long. When finally able to visit with his son for a few hours, he met for pickup at a local pizza parlor. When it came time to return him, his son was crying. Mitch tried to comfort his son by taking him to his mom's car and trying to put him in the child's seat. Sheryl started screaming in the parking lot for him to get away from her. Later, she filed a harassment complaint, and Mitch was forced to pay for local safe exchange services. Mitch benefited from individual therapy, which provided emotional support and helped him to mourn the loss of his marriage. By separating its idealized form of how he dreamed it should have been from how it actually was, Mitch was able to more clearly see the dysfunctional aspects of the relationship while holding onto the hope of a better one in the future. There were also depression and anxiety issues to deal with. Mitch found an assertiveness skills class helpful in learning how to calmly express his needs to his lawyers and his ex. But what he needed most was to let go of his resentments about not being considered an equal legal parent and accept that he needed to better manage his behavior around his ex-wife and child. Part of the therapy consisted of helping him understand how the courts viewed things and how he was to conduct himself if he wanted to have a chance at securing his parenting rights.

Insight into Fred's behavior came during the family history part of the initial assessment. He reported a "crazy family, my mom is still nuts, drives us all crazy." He also reported little or no contact with his two siblings. Further questions revealed a history of constant conflict between all family members. Fred tended to minimize this, regarding it as "no big deal." Interviews with Fred's ex-wife were also helpful. While there were no reports of police contact outside the domestic violence complaint, there were several Children and Family Services investigations because of allegations of abuse. When asked about the several incidents his wife reported, he again attempted to minimize his behavior. This, of course, was helpful in assessing what kind of treatment would be most appropriate to enhance Fred's relationship with his children.

There are different skill sets involved in working with this population. While "joining" with a client can be useful in individual therapies dealing with depression, anxieties, family-of-origin issues, and the like, treatment of clients referred through the family court system, especially those where accusations of domestic abuse exist, require a different skill set. Working with these families requires the therapist to be able to handle feelings of ambiguity, tolerate conflict in the therapy session, and have the confidence that the work can help children have the healthiest relationship possible with both parents.

REFERENCES

Austin, W. (2001). Partner violence and risk assessment in child custody evaluations. *Family Court Review, 39*(4), 483–496.

Dutton, D. (2005). The domestic abuse paradigm in child custody assessments. *Journal of Child Custody, 2*(4), 23–42.

Gottman, J. (1999). *The marriage clinic.* New York: Norton.

Gould, J. (1998). *Conducting scientifically-crafted child custody evaluations.* Thousand Oaks, CA: Sage.

Jaffe, P., & Geffner, R. (1998). Child custody disputes and domestic violence: Critical issues for mental health, social service, and legal professionals. In G. Holden, R. Geffner, &

E. Jouriles (Eds.), *Children exposed to marital violence: Theory, research and applied issues* (pp. 371–408). Washington, DC: American Psychological Association.

Johnston, J., & Campbell, L. (1988). *Impasses of divorce: The dynamics and resolution of family conflict*. New York: Simon & Schuster.

Johnston, J., & Campbell, L. (1993). A clinical typology of interpersonal violence in disputed-custody divorces. *American Journal of Orthopsychiatry, 63*(2), 190–199.

Potter-Efron, R. (2005). *Handbook of anger management: Individual, couple, family, and group approaches*. New York: Haworth Press.

Roberts, N., & Noller, P. (1998). The association between adult attachment and couple violence. In J. Simpson & W. Rholes (Eds.), *Attachment theory and close relationships* (pp. 317–350). New York: Guilford Press.

CHAPTER 22

Family Therapy and Interpersonal Violence: Targeting At-Risk Adolescent Mothers

Jennifer Langhinrichsen-Rohling, Lisa A. Turner, and
Marilyn McGowan

Both intimate partner violence and child maltreatment are types of interpersonal violence that have been identified as public health problems (U.S. Department of Health and Human Services, 2000). With regard to intimate partner violence, national surveys estimate that a romantic partner has physically victimized approximately 11.6% of women during the past year. About one-third of these women reported experiencing severe violence from their partner (Straus & Gelles, 1990). Women, however, are not the only victims of interpersonal violence, as accumulated evidence indicates that women use relationship violence at rates equivalent to or greater than men (Archer, 2000). Women also engage in power and control tactics that are similar to men and describe similar motives for engaging in their partner-directed violence (e.g., Babcock, Miller, & Siard, 2003; chapters 3, 4, and 7 in this volume), although they are less likely than men to inflict physical injury as a result of their abuse (Cascardi, Langhinrichsen, & Vivian, 1992).

These findings have led researchers to consider adoption of a gender-inclusive term for relationship abuse, namely, "intimate partner violence."

Grant No. 2001-SI-FX-0006 awarded by the Office of Juvenile Justice and Delinquency Prevention, Office of Justice Programs, U.S. Department of Justice, supported this project. Points of view or opinions in this document are those of the authors and do not necessarily represent the official position or policies of the U.S. Department of Justice.

The financial and emotional consequences due to intimate partner violence are substantial. Evidence shows that approximately 15% of the 1992 U.S. homicides were committed by an intimate partner (Bachman & Saltzman, 1995). Injury at the hands of an intimate partner is also common. About one-fourth of all intentional injuries examined in hospital emergency rooms were sustained as a result of intimate partner violence (Greenfeld et al., 1998).

A number of risk factors for intimate partner violence have been identified, although researchers primarily have considered what women's risk factors are for receiving abuse from men's violence and what men's risk factors are for intimate violence perpetration against women. These risk factors include reduced levels of education, partner unemployment, living in poverty, and a history of experiencing emotional and verbal abuse in childhood, a condition known as the intergenerational transmission of violence (Schumacher, Feldbau-Kohn, Slep, & Heyman, 2001).

Poverty, in particular, may be an important risk factor for both women's and men's perpetration of intimate partner violence and child maltreatment. For example, in a review article, Cunradi, Caetano, and Schafer (2002) reported that annual household income had the greatest relative influence on the probability of partner violence occurring. Similarly, Aldarondo and Sugarman (1996) conducted a risk marker analysis of the cessation and persistence of wife assault. They reported that low socioeconomic status was associated with both the occurrence and the continuity of wife assault across time. Considering this risk factor from a systemic perspective, Brown (2002) wrote how poverty provides a culture of hopelessness, invisibility, shame, and disenfranchisement from power that significantly increases both the risk of intimate partner violence and child maltreatment. Raver and Leadbeater (1999) also described how poverty and its associated hardships could work to reduce feelings of competence about both maternal and familial roles. They then related lower maternal self-efficacy both to increased interparental conflict and to decreased child outcomes.

Consistent with this relational or dynamic perspective, other interpersonal or dyadic factors have been shown to increase the risk of intimate partner violence (e.g., high levels of belligerence in conflictual communications, poor communication and conflict management skills, problems with emotional regulation and stress management; e.g., Babcock, Waltz, Jacobson, & Gottman, 1993; Follingstad, Bradley, Helff, & Laughlin, 2002). Emotional and interactional deficits have been noted for both men and women in violent relationships. Violent and distressed couples have been shown to have a greater tendency to engage in patterns of negative reciprocity during conflict, more than nonviolent/distressed or happily married couples (Cordova, Jacobson, Gottman, Rushe, & Cox, 1993).

Taken as a whole, these findings highlight that intimate partner violence can be conceptualized as occurring within a dynamic system in which each person's actions influence and provide feedback for the behaviors that occur in the relationship. This conceptualization is consistent with evidence showing that intimate partner violence is more likely to be mutual or bidirectional than perpetrated by only one spouse (Vivian & Langhinrichsen-Rohling, 1994). These findings also lend credence to the position that family- or relationship-oriented therapy, which is gender-inclusive rather than gender-specific, may be an appropriate treatment for some couples who are experiencing intimate partner violence (e.g., Greene & Bogo, 2002; O'Leary, Heyman, & Neidig, 1999). A further benefit of this type of approach is that it may simultaneously reduce the incidence of other types of violence that frequently co-occur within the family system, such as child maltreatment and psychological abuse and neglect. Systemic interventions may hold particular promise as a means to intervene in the intergenerational cycle of violence.

In this chapter, we describe both parenting and relationship-oriented interventions that have been directed toward undereducated teen mothers. We have identified adolescent mothers as an important target for gender-inclusive violence interventions because they are more likely to live in poverty than adult mothers (Bissell, 2000), they tend to have lower educational and occupational attainment than older mothers (Furstenburg, 1991; Hockaday, Crase, Shelley, & Stockdale, 2000; Monahan, 2002; Moore & Brooks-Gunn, 2002), and they are also more likely to be financially dependent on welfare programs (Furstenburg, 1991). Thus, they demonstrate many risk factors for intimate partner violence. In fact, researchers have already documented a high rate of victimization from intimate partner violence among these women (Silverman, Raj, Mucci, & Hathaway, 2001; Sussex & Corcoran, 2005). However, few investigators have considered the degree to which pregnant adolescent women or teenage mothers might be perpetrators of abuse in their intimate relationships in addition to being victims.

Specifically, as shown in Figure 22.1, we assert that high-risk, low-income adolescent mothers are an important focus for family-based in interventions because they often form a central element in the intergenerational transmission of interpersonal violence as well as in the intergenerational transmission of pregnancy and poverty. Our contention is consistent with evidence demonstrating that teenage mothers are more likely than nonpregnant adolescent women to have experienced childhood sexual abuse as well as other types of violence or neglect in their family-of-origin (De Paul & Domenech, 2000; Herrenkohl, Herrenkohl, Egolf, & Russo, 1998). Adolescent mothers are also more likely to have been raised by a mother who experienced a pregnancy in

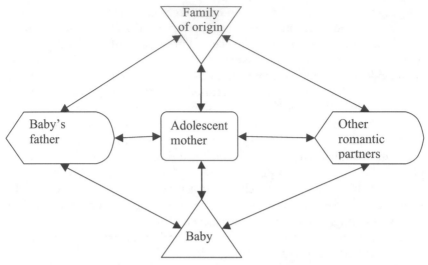

FIGURE 22.1   A model of the intergenerational dynamics occurring with adolescent pregnancy

her own adolescence, raising the question, What aspect of these experiences is transmitted through the generations? (Langhinrichsen-Rohling, Hankla, & Stormberg, 2004).

However, even adolescents who did not experience family-of-origin violence may face a variety of intrapersonal challenges with the advent of a teen pregnancy that may be mollified with exposure to a family therapy–based intervention. Both wanted and unwanted sexual experiences in adolescence have been broadly related to family dysfunction (Kellogg, Burge, & Taylor, 2000). For example, age at first pregnancy has been related both to the experience of physical violence in the family-of-origin and to having a family member with a drug or alcohol problem (Kellogg & Hoffman, 1999).

Additional developmental and family-of-origin issues often get raised as the adolescent mother simultaneously attempts to meet her own needs and the needs of her child, perhaps while she is still residing in her parent's residence and continues to feel the tension between separation and individuation (Coren, Barlow, & Stewart-Brown, 2003). Difficulties occur because the adolescent mother is being asked to provide a secure base of attachment for her child, typically before her own adult identity is established and perhaps while she is concurrently struggling with a less-than-secure attachment to her own mother, with whom she may be sharing baby caregiving responsibilities (Hess, Papas, & Black, 2002).

It may also be useful to target pregnant adolescents because these women may provide a point of contact with men who are at high risk for intimate partner violence and child abuse, yet historically these men have not willingly sought treatment for their abusive behavior. Research suggests that men who father babies with high-risk adolescent women are, on average, significantly older than the mothers, are frequently undereducated, and often have financial stressors that increase the risk for relationship conflict and violence (Bolton, 1987). However, relatively little focus has been placed on understanding the father–child dyad or the surrogate father–child dyad and how it may be related to increased chances of family violence occurring in families containing an adolescent mother (Osofsky & Thompson, 2000).

Family therapy or therapy that focuses on the interactional patterns between family members is also warranted for many high-risk adolescent mothers because the co-occurrence of intimate partner abuse and physical child abuse within families has been well documented (see review of 42 studies by Appel & Holden, 1998). While Appel and Holden (1998) reported a wide range of co-occurrence estimates (6% in community samples to 100% in some clinical samples), they suggested that a median co-occurrence rate of 40% could be anticipated. Several different models for co-occurrence were proposed; however, bidirectional violence models have received the most recent empirical support (e.g., Moore & Pepler, 1998). For example, McGuigan, Vuchinich, and Pratt (2000) recently argued that preexisting domestic abuse increases the likelihood that parents of a newborn will perceive that child negatively. These negative perceptions will then increase the likelihood of co-occurring child abuse. Furthermore, recent evidence indicates that young maternal age, low education, low income, and lack of involvement in a religious community all significantly increase the risk for child maltreatment in the context of a domestically violent intimate partner relationship (Cox, Kotch, & Everson, 2003). These risk factors are relevant for adolescent mothers.

There are several pathways to establishing a negative parent–child relationship. Researchers have demonstrated that adolescent mothers are likely to have less appropriate developmental expectations and less knowledge of child development (Brooks-Gunn & Furstenberg, 1986; Vukelich & Kliman, 1985), and this may contribute to a greater level of frustration for these mothers and place them at a higher risk for abusing or neglecting their children (Garbarino, 1976; Stern & Alvarez, 1992). Adolescent mothers may have also fewer emotional resources to offer their children. For example, Osofsky and Thompson (2000) found that interactions between teen mothers and their children were characterized by either an overemphasis on negative affect or on misread affective cues between mother and baby.

In summary, adolescent parents are an important group to target for family-oriented prevention and intervention activities because of their high numbers, as well as the intergenerational family dynamics that have been shown to be associated with the occurrence of teenage pregnancy. Evidence shows the greater likelihood that the adolescent mother will have had unmet developmental needs, the increased risk that adolescent mothers will experience negative and/or violent events in either this or future interpersonal relationships, the increased likelihood that adolescent mothers will perpetrate child abuse, and the greater likelihood of a variety of adverse consequences for adolescent mothers and the children they parent. These factors have been related, in part, to interactional patterns between these mothers and their children, these mothers and their partners, and these mothers and their own family-of-origin caregivers (e.g., Turner, Grindstaff, & Phillips, 1990).

To address these concerns, two main types of family interventions have historically been directed toward adolescent mothers: parenting interventions and relationship-oriented interventions. In the next section, we review parenting interventions that have been designed to support the personal development and parenting skills of adolescent mothers, and a case example is described. In the section following that, relationship-oriented interventions directed toward adolescent mothers are briefly reviewed. We then describe a newly developed relationship-oriented intervention that has been created by these authors in order to intervene in the intergenerational cycle of family violence that frequently co-occurs with adolescent pregnancy. Finally, a case example is offered that demonstrates issues related to administering this intervention with undereducated, high-risk adolescent mothers who are living in poverty.

PARENTING INTERVENTIONS WITH ADOLESCENT MOTHERS

Adolescent parenting interventions vary significantly in their focus, particularly in terms of whether the goal is to improve the woman's chances of economic self-sufficiency by continuing her education or delaying future pregnancy, or whether the intervention is designed to enhance and improve her parenting practices. Across studies, there seems to be a consistent finding of improvements in these goals while adolescent mothers are enrolled in the study, but the evidence for long-term impact on either of these foci is mixed (Granger & Cytron, 1999).

For example, intervention programs aimed at supporting and improving parenting practices have reported improvements in parenting attitudes and knowledge (e.g., Fulton, Murphy, & Anderson, 1991; Unger & Wandersman, 1985) and behaviors (e.g., Heinicke et al., 1999). In addition, several parenting interventions have resulted in improvement in the child's development (e.g., Fewell & Wheedon, 1998; Field, Widmayer, Stringer, & Ignatoff, 1980). Similarly, programs aimed at improving economic self-sufficiency have resulted in larger numbers of participants completing the general equivalency diploma, and often improvements have been noted in employment and earnings (Granger & Cytron, 1999).

Consistent with the premise that relational or systemic factors may be an important component of the negative outcomes sometimes experienced by adolescent mothers and their children, parenting interventions that include a relationship-based component have been shown to have promise with this population. Specifically, a growing number of researchers and practitioners believe that the positive outcomes reported in home visitation parenting programs are due to the nurturing relationship established and maintained between the parent and the home visitor (Heinicke et al., 1999; Musick & Stott, 1990; Robinson, Emde, & Korfmacher, 1997). Korfmacher and Marchi (2002) theorize that a positive relationship is essential in interventions because the adolescent parent may be differentially responsive to information and guidance offered within the context of a trusting relationship. Heinicke et al. (1999) found that mothers participating in a relationship-based parenting intervention were more responsive to their infant's needs and expressed more positive affect toward their children than mothers in the control group. The researchers theorized that the support and understanding offered by the home visitors allowed the first-time mothers to express their feelings related to the challenges of parenthood. Adolescent mothers may have more emotional resources to offer their children once their own personal and developmentally appropriate needs have been supported.

Similarly, Olds and colleagues report positive results from the Nurse Home Visitation Program Trials implemented in Elmira, New York, and Memphis, Tennessee (Olds, Kitzman, Cole, & Robinson, 1997; Olds et al., 1999). They indicate that the formation of a therapeutic alliance between the mother and the intervener served as a "corrective experience" for the mothers, most of whom reported that they had never received such consistent care and encouragement in their family-of-origin. It is possible that these interveners demonstrated the benefits of a securely attached and nurturing relationship, which then translated to better child outcomes and reduced levels of child maltreatment by the adolescent mothers. Thus, the research on parenting interventions has shown significant reductions in state-verified incidents of child abuse and neglect by supplying home-based, relationship-oriented interventions to high-risk women (e.g., low income, young age, high stress) during their pregnancy and continuing afterward for two years (Olds, Henderson, & Kitzman, 1998).

The authors of this chapter, in conjunction with Borkowski et al. (2005), employed a parenting intervention that focused on adolescent mothers and used volunteer mentors as an integral part of the program. Each participant in the intervention was paired with her own volunteer mentor, each of whom had received extensive training and support for the duration of the 11-month intervention. The goal was for the mentor to form a supportive relationship with the adolescent mother, to model positive relationship skills, to provide child development and child-care information, and to provide emotional support for the adolescent mother's own concerns. Our findings indicate that throughout the parenting intervention program, mentors supported and encouraged the adolescent mothers both during and between sessions. Support provided by mentors varied from giving advice; providing food in emergencies; helping mothers access available resources for housing, utilities, and food; socializing; and teaching a mom to drive. A specific case example is described next.

Case 1: Parenting Intervention

Latonya, a 17-year-old African American female, enrolled in the parenting intervention when her son, Jerome, was three months old. At the time of delivery, she was an 11th-grade student, unmarried and residing with her mother and stepfather. She reported to the intervention staff and to her mentor that she felt her pregnancy was a result of sexually coercive behavior perpetrated by her boyfriend. She was, however, still involved with this boyfriend, and he did acknowledge Jerome as his son. The father's involvement in the baby's life consisted of providing limited financial support to Latonya and visiting Jerome on a weekly basis.

During the initial interview, Latonya appeared to project an outward demeanor of confidence and efficacy in her role as a parent. She had a tendency to talk more than the other participants and often would dominate the group discussions and interrupt while others were speaking. Both her mentor and project staff noted that Latonya appeared to overestimate her parenting skills and knowledge. She often seemed to be resistant to learning new concepts presented during the group sessions. This negativity particularly concerned her mentor, who directly encouraged Latonya to be open to receiving new information and different opinions regarding child-care and child development issues.

The approach the mentor used was to share with Latonya some of her own struggles with being a teenage mother. Through these interactions, the pair appeared to develop a trusting and reciprocal relationship, although the mentor continued to initiate the majority of both the telephone and the in-person contacts that occurred both in and out of the parenting group format. The outside group contacts included eating out, attending church, and going to high school football games. Additionally, getting a driver's license was a top priority for Latonya. Near the end of the formal intervention, Latonya sought out her mentor's assistance and asked her to teach her how to drive. The pair met on several occasions to work on Latonya's driving skills. One week prior to the culmination of the intervention, Latonya received her driving license.

Moreover, over the course of the program, both her mentor and the intervention staff observed that Latonya began interacting with her baby in a fundamentally different way. There was also evidence that she was implementing some of the strategies she had learned in the group sessions. In a self-report measure at the end of the intervention, Latonya reported that she placed great value on the importance of reading to, talking with, and verbally and emotionally interacting with Jerome. Reciprocity in the relationship was evident as well. Posttest measures of Jerome's language and cognitive development indicated that, by the end of the intervention, he was functioning at least at the norm for his age and about one-half a standard deviation above his performance at pretest. Additionally, although the intervention program formally ended, Latonya continued her contact with her mentor and with the intervention staff. For example, she routinely called with updates about herself and Jerome, and, with considerable pride, she invited her mentor and the intervention staff to her high school graduation. This occurred more than one year after her initial involvement with the program.

INTIMATE PARTNER RELATIONSHIP INTERVENTIONS WITH ADOLESCENT MOTHERS

As stated previously, although intimate partner violence can occur in any relationship, it has consistently been shown to be more likely to occur in young, distressed, stressed, and low-income relationships (e.g., Straus & Gelles, 1990). Violent couples also have higher levels of expressed hostility, poorer methods of anger expression, and more rigid patterns of conflict management, such as demand/withdrawal, than do nonviolent couples (e.g., Babcock et al., 1993; Follingstad et al., 2002). Preventing relationship violence may thus be enhanced by preventing relationship distress and stress (such as that associated with the transition to parenthood; Langhinrichsen-Rohling, Heyman, Schlee, & O'Leary, 1997). Injury prevention and positive health outcomes can also be expected with improvements in relationship satisfaction, as researchers have demonstrated declines in immune functioning after relationship conflicts (Kiecolt-Glaser, Malarkey, & Chee, 1993).

There is evidence that relatively brief couples-based skill-building interventions can be used successfully to prevent marital distress (e.g., EPL in Germany; PREP in the United States; Alexander, Holtzworth-Munroe, & Jameson, 1994; Hahlweg, Markman, Thurmaier, Engl, & Eckert, 1998; Markman, Floyd, Stanley, & Storaasli, 1988). The major premise of these programs is that relationship partners can, relatively quickly, learn the communication and conflict management skills that are necessary to handle their issues safely and productively (Hahlweg et al., 1998). These communication skills should then lessen the probability of violence, as violence has been shown to be a tactic that partners use when they are in conflict with one another.

To date, however, there is little research on the effectiveness of these types of interventions with adolescent mothers. Typically, interventions directed at adolescent mothers have focused on changing risky sexual behavior rather than explicitly targeting relationship behaviors and the potential for family violence in this population. Yet the need to construct and implement a family systems approach to adolescent sexuality and teenage pregnancy has been called for repeatedly, as has the need to consider issues related to the father of the baby (Chilman, 1989; Pistole, 1999; Robinson & Frank, 1994; Tuten, Jones, Tran, & Svikis, 2004). The family therapy interventions that have been tried in this population have often targeted the adolescent mother and both her parents or the teenage mother and just her mother (McFarland, 1997; Owens, Scofield, & Taylor, 2003). Evidence has accumulated that there are many barriers toward involving the families of pregnant adolescents in treatment (Hanson, 1992). In contrast, relatively few interventions have been designed to target the intimate partner relationship dynamics of adolescent mothers (e.g., Caring for My Family, Michigan State University Extension, 2003). Even fewer, if any, researchers have used systemic interventions that are gender-inclusive to tackle the intergenerational transmission of violence that often occurs in the families of adolescent mothers. To fill this gap, Langhinrichsen-Rohling, McGowan, and Turner (2004) developed the Building a Lasting Love relationship intervention.

THE BUILDING A LASTING LOVE RELATIONSHIP INTERVENTION

We designed the Building a Lasting Love intervention to include individual and dyadic goals in a brief four-session format. Theoretically, this program reflects an integration of a number of existing curriculum including Spouse Abuse: A Treatment Program for Couples (Neidig & Friedman, 1984), Communication and Conflict Management Skills in

Intimate Relationships (Brown & Brown, 2002), Premarital Interpersonal Choices (Van Epp, 1999), PREP (Markman, Blumberg, & Stanley, 1989; Markman, Jamieson, & Floyd, 1980; Markman, Renick, Floyd, Stanley, & Clements, 1993; Markman, Stanley, & Blumberg, 1994), Caring for My Family (Michigan State University Extension, 2003), Family Preservation (Mantooth, Geffner, Franks, & Patrick, 1987), and *Skills Training Manual for Treating Borderline Personality Disorder* (Linehan, 1993). The resulting B.A.L.L. curriculum draws extensively from the literature on evidence-based interventions to enhance couple functioning and communication strategies as well as from the literature on domestic violence interventions for couples.

Gender-inclusive couple-related strategies to reduce violence are aware that both male and female partners can engage in violence in a relationship. Therefore, it is important to help each partner recognize and take responsibility for his or her own behavior in the relationship. It is also important to teach each partner the skills he or she needs to manage anger, reduce stress, increase the ability to communicate effectively, and resolve conflicts with others to his or her satisfaction. Consequently, teaching teen mothers skills that will help prevent conflict escalation and enhance the likelihood of successful conflict resolution should provide some protection against the occurrence of violence both within that specific intimate relationship and in their other dyadic contexts (e.g., in conflicts between the teen mother and her parents/relatives or in conflicts between the teen mother and her child). These skills should enhance communication and emotional regulation. Thus, the B.A.L.L. intervention, while conducted individually with teen mothers, is expected to have an impact on a variety of intergenerational relationships and to be systemic and family oriented in its focus.

The four sessions of the intervention are briefly described here. Session 1 includes activities to help the adolescent mothers identify characteristics of healthy versus unhealthy, distressed, or violent relationships. Discussion centers on what is experienced after the baby is born when there is a shift from a romantic relationship to a relationship that includes both an intimate partner/romantic and a coparenting/child-rearing component. Characteristics of healthy and unhealthy relationships are identified and debated. Emphasis is placed on the choices that are available to each participant. Actions that can be taken to nurture important relationships are delineated, as are ways to avoid unhealthy relationship patterns. The participants are educated about what constitutes intimate violence and how the program espouses violence-free relationships. The women discuss their beliefs about violence and the violent or abusive behaviors that they believe are considered acceptable or unacceptable within their particular subculture. Efforts are made to help the women consider how their babies might interpret or respond to witnessing or experiencing violent or abusive behaviors within the dyadic relationship. Mothers are encouraged to make a safety plan for themselves and their babies, and they consider when or if they would need to implement this type of plan. At the end of session 1, each mother chooses a specific family-focused or relationship-focused goal to work on for the remainder of the group.

In session 2, we present the SCOPE model, in which each participant is encouraged to evaluate themselves and their partners in terms of their relationship Skills, Choices, Old baggage, interaction Patterns, and ability to handle difficult Emotions, such as anger, jealousy, and hurt. We begin to practice important interactional skills, including how to manage anger, jealousy, hurt, and lack of trust (with baby, money, drug use). Skills that facilitate emotional regulation are emphasized. A frequently mentioned concern by the adolescent mother is her relationship with her mother "in-law," who often initially denies that her son fathered the baby. Discussion also often centers on how the woman's romantic relationship with the baby's father is negatively affected by his friends.

The focus in session 3 is on learning what it takes to build L.A.S.T.ing and loving intimate relationships. In this session, the adolescent mothers learn that the building blocks of a healthy relationship include continuing to Learn about each other and grow, as opposed to mind reading and stagnation, and practicing good communication techniques, particularly with regard to "hot" topics that generate Anger and violence rather than Acceptance. They also learn that long-lasting relationships ensue partly when both partners make a commitment to Stick together and work things out regardless of the difficulties they will encounter. We talk about ways to foster Trust and Teamwork rather than engaging in win-lose strategies with their partners. Finally, we discuss the importance of Sexual connection and intimacy in intimate relationships and how that might vary over time. The teen mothers often talk about how their sexuality has changed since they became pregnant. Much of this session centers on the verbal and nonverbal skills that are needed for productive communication (e.g., speaker/listener, "I" statements, congruence between verbal and nonverbal messages, ratio of positives to negatives, choose your battles). Interactive activities occur during which participants practice assertive requests and describe the differences among passive, assertive, and aggressive communication styles. They consider the pros and cons of using each type of communication.

The final session is focused on helping the participants identify methods to reduce their stress or increase their ability to cope with the stressors in their lives while they are finding more ways to have fun with themselves, their families, their partners, and their babies. Discussion focuses how a high level of stress increases the risk of intense, violent, or dysfunctional conflict or poor communication with their partners. They evaluate how they currently handle stress and learn some new coping strategies. Particular focus is given to time management techniques and activities that are fun but not expensive. The session ends with participants reviewing what they have accomplished in the group and how they will continue to support themselves to have the kind of intimate relationships they want with their partners, their parents, their "in-laws," and their children.

The Building a Lasting Love program is noteworthy for its brevity, its interpersonal focus, and its stance that all violence in relationships is detrimental regardless of the gender of the perpetrator. There were several reasons we felt it was important to develop a brief intervention in spite of the gravity of the problems to be addressed by these high-risk teenage mothers and the number of issues that we wanted to consider. First, we knew that attendance to long-lasting interventions is inconsistent in this population. Second, we felt that the brevity of the intervention would be well suited to a population who struggles with transportation, child-care, and time constraint issues. These factors continued to be concerns for the women in the group, although the intervention staff provided child-care and transportation for the mothers as needed. Third, participants who have a positive experience with a brief intervention are more likely to consider engaging in another intervention in the future. Fourth, the intervention was designed to include the main and overlapping elements of existing marital and domestic violence interventions that have been demonstrated to be effective, allowing us, it is hoped, to demonstrate more change with less intervention effort.

Finally, according to Prochaska's model of change, the most effective interventions are suited to participants' readiness to change (Prochaska, Norcross, & DiClemente, 1994). Prochaska describes readiness to change as fitting along a continuum from precontemplation (unaware of behavior that needs changing; individual is not convinced that change is needed now or later), through contemplation (have considered making a change, but that is all), preparation (need help to change, plans are being made to change), to action (change process is begun), and then developing maintenance strategies for the new behavior.

A priori, we expected that a significant number of high-risk adolescent mothers would be in the precontemplation stage with regard to their perceptions of their risk for experiencing or perpetrating relationship violence or child maltreatment as well as for their need to enhance their intergenerational relationship skills. Consequently, our intervention was designed with the goal of helping participants move toward a greater readiness to change by including exercises that should foster moving from precontemplation to contemplation (i.e., what are the pros and cons associated with engaging in these behaviors) as well as from contemplation to preparation to action (i.e., making plans, discussing specific strategies for change). While these mothers may not engage in many different actions at the end of the brief intervention, they might be more ready to consider the part that they play in their intimate relationships and environments, in essence recognizing their role in the systemic interactions of their families.

Case 2: Relationship Intervention With Teenage Mothers With a High-Risk of Child Abuse: Breaking the Cycle of Family Violence

Tonya is a 19-year-old high school senior. She is raising her 2-year-old son Cory, who was conceived with "Zack" when Tonya was 16 years old. Zack is a boy whom Tonya had dated for only a few months prior to the conception. Tonya describes Zack as a wild, drug-using guy with a bad group of friends. In the first session, she indicated that she always "went for" the troublemakers and wondered if that was because she liked excitement and got "bored" easily.

Zack was three years older than Tonya, although he was only one grade ahead of her in school. He had repeated several grades and reportedly had difficulty reading. Shortly after their child was born, Zack dropped out of school for good. Since that time, he has had a difficult time keeping a job. According to Tonya, Zack had been fired for attendance problems, drug use on the job, and inappropriate displays of anger. Consequently, Zack provides only sporadic financial support for Cory. Tonya has gone back to court several times for financial assistance. This occurs after Tonya learns, typically through mutual friends, that Zack is working again. Financial issues are a frequent point of conflict between the couple as Tonya is living independently from her family-of-origin. She was kicked out of her family home when she became pregnant and has little contact with her biological family. Tonya expressed a lot of anger over their treatment of her and her baby. Zack does have contact with Cory. He lives with his mother (his parents are divorced), and Zack and his mother keep Cory every other weekend.

Although they are no longer romantically involved, Tonya and Zack continue to have a conflict-ridden and tumultuous relationship with one another. They see each other twice a month when they are exchanging Cory. These interactions included aggression several times in the six months before the relationship intervention group began. In one incident, Tonya kicked Zack and deliberately ran over some items in his driveway. Tonya and Zack are also in phone contact with one another. These calls can occur on an almost daily basis and usually end with one or both of them yelling, swearing, and hanging up without saying good-bye. Cory has overhead these verbal altercations on numerous occasions. He now uses swear words regularly in his play. In fact, the most recent fight between Tonya and Zack ensued when Cory called his father a swear word that he had heard Tonya use toward him on the phone. At the start of the intervention, Tonya reported that she found this "funny." She also indicated that Zack was a jerk (and worse) and believed he was to blame for many of the negative behaviors she was seeing in Cory (i.e., hitting other children, refusing to share, biting, going to bed at midnight, waking up in the middle of the night and destroying his room, being kicked out of a playgroup, and so on). Tonya also indicated that Cory was a constant ball of energy and that no one she knew would babysit him for her.

Tonya was an active participant in group. In the first session, her comments were designed to illustrate how difficult it was for her to deal with Zack. She spoke with pride about how she had told Zack off on the phone and hung up on him. She also indicated that she thought violence, in the form of spanking repeatedly, was needed in order to discipline her son, who was out of control. When the group generated the pros and cons of using violence in relationships, she indicated that she hadn't really thought about what these actions were conveying to her son about what was acceptable. She also acknowledged that she perpetrated the majority of the violence in her relationship with Zack but believed it was justified.

In contrast, by the end of the intervention, Tonya acknowledged that she had a problem controlling her quick temper and that it was interfering with all of her important relationships. She told the group that she was using strategies that she had learned in session 2 to help herself regulate her emotions and to stop and consider the situation from different vantage points. While assessment data did not show a change in her level of satisfaction with her relationship with Zack, there was a significant change in the amount of stress she was experiencing in that relationship (preintervention = 5 on a scale of 1 to 5; posttreatment = 1 on a scale of 1 to 5). Furthermore, Tonya reported that her romantic relationship with a new romantic partner was impacted such that both of them were using fewer insults and swear words with one another during conflicts. Assessment data also demonstrated that Tonya was considerably less irritable after the intervention and that she felt more confident that she could handle her anger in a positive manner and express herself clearly and without fear. She gave the intervention high marks and indicated that the changes she had made in herself had resulted in more compliance and less aggression from her child (a behavioral observation that was shared by the intervention child-care staff) and more respect and hopefulness for their relationship from her new boyfriend. Most important, postassessment data indicated that Tonya had not perpetrated any violence or engaged in any aggressive outbursts for the duration of the intervention.

FUTURE DIRECTIONS

As was typified by the case examples described previously, it is likely that there is considerable heterogeneity among adolescent mothers with regard to their risk factors for interpersonal violence and their potential responsiveness to a family-based intervention. This contention is consistent with work conducted by Larson (2004) that indicated about 30% of a sample of adolescent mothers experienced an episode of severe parenting stress at least one point across a two to three year period. The experience of stress was found to be associated both with receiving criticism about their parenting from their own parent and with the experience of intimate partner violence. Additional research is needed to identify adolescent mothers who are at relatively higher risk for relationship difficulties (as we did with mothers at risk for child abuse). Specific barriers to interventions and particular motivations for participation within this subgroup also need to be determined.

Furthermore, as the literature clearly indicates, parenting and relationship issues co-occur in this population. Future research should focus on the development of a unified family intervention that specifically helps adolescent mothers generalize their relationship skills to different contexts (e.g., interactions with their mothers, the baby's father, a new relationship partner, their baby). An example of this type of intervention would be the CARRI program (Children at Risk: Resources and Intervention), which was developed in New Jersey. This program utilizes a home-based, multigenerational, family therapy model with high-risk adolescent mothers (Carver & Herzog, 1993). While this program represents advances by (a) the inclusion of the grandmother in the intervention process, (b) the explicit acknowledgment of the need to address communication processes between individuals, and (c) the inclusion of a developmental focus for the family as well as for the baby; we assert that future interventions may also require a direct focus on the adolescent mothers' romantic relationship patterns and their own potential for intimate partner violence.

Clearly, other family members have important contributions to the interpersonal processes that these mothers are describing. To date, our intervention, while systemic in conceptualization, is individual in implementation. Our preliminary efforts to engage adolescent fathers in treatment were largely unsuccessful, as has been found by others. Consequently, there is a need to understand the best way to motivate these men to become involved in a family-oriented intervention. It is our contention that maintaining a gender-inclusive focus in our intervention rather than a blaming stance will be a vital element of the engagement process with these men.

Finally, intimate partner violence is associated with poverty. Individuals living in poverty have additional barriers to service delivery, including difficulties with transportation, child-care, and scheduling conflicts. Successful interventions with poor individuals are likely to need to incorporate use of paraprofessionals as well as other interveners that can have long-term supportive relationships with high-risk individuals (Calzada et al., 2005). These new relationships should also be conceptualized in a systemic multigenerational fashion.

REFERENCES

Aldarondo, E., & Sugarman, D. B. (1996). Risk marker analysis of the cessation and persistence of wife assault. *Journal of Consulting and Clinical Psychology, 64,* 1010–1019.

Alexander, J. F., Holtzworth-Munroe, A., & Jameson, P. B. (1994). The process and outcome of marital and family therapy. In A. E. Bergin & S. L Garfield (Eds.), *Handbook of psychotherapy and behavior change* (4th ed., pp. 595–630). Oxford, England: John Wiley & Sons.

Appel, A. E., & Holden, G. W. (1998). The co-occurrence of spouse and physical child abuse: A review and appraisal. *Journal of Family Psychology, 12,* 578–599.

Archer, J. (2000). Sex differences in aggression between heterosexual partners: A meta-analytic review. *Psychological Bulletin, 126,* 651–680.

Babcock, J., Miller, S. A., & Siard, C. (2003). Toward a typology of abusive women: Differences between partner-only and generally violent women in the use of violence. *Psychology of Women Quarterly, 27,* 153–161.

Babcock, J., Waltz, J., Jacobson, N., & Gottman, J. (1993). Power and violence: The relation between communication patterns, power discrepancies, and domestic violence. *Journal of Consulting and Clinical Psychology, 61,* 40–50.

Bachman, R., & Saltzman, L. (1995). *Violence against women: Estimates from the redesigned National Crime Victimization Study.* Washington, DC: U.S. Department of Justice, Bureau of Justice Statistics.

Bissell, M. (2000). Socio-economic outcomes of teen pregnancy and parenthood: A review of the literature. *Canadian Journal of Human Sexuality, 9*(3), 191–204.

Bolton, F. G., Jr. (1987). The father in the adolescent pregnancy at risk for child maltreatment. I. Helpmate or hindrance? *Journal of Family Therapy, 2,* 67–80.

Borkowski, J. G., Noria, C. W., Langhinrichsen-Rohling, J., Turner, L. A., McGowan, M., & Blackwell, P. (2005). *Intervening with adolescent mothers.* Unpublished manuscript.

Brooks-Gunn, J. M., & Furstenberg, F. F. (1986). The children of adolescent mothers: Physical, academic, and psychological outcomes. *Developmental Review, 6,* 224–251.

Brown, J. H., & Brown, C. S. (2002). *Marital therapy concepts and skills for effective practice.* Pacific Grove, CA: Brooks/Cole.

Brown, R. M. (2002). The development of family violence as a field of study and contributors to family and community violence among low-income fathers. *Aggression and Violent Behavior, 7,* 499–511.

Calzada, E. J., Caldwell, M. B., Brotman, L. M., Brown, E. J., Wallace, S. A., McQuaid, J. H., et al. (2005). Training community members to serve as paraprofessionals in an evidence-based, prevention, program for parents of preschoolers. *Journal of Child and Family Studies, 14,* 387–402.

Carver, P. N., & Herzog, E. P. (1993). *Intergenerational family therapy in home-based work with adolescent parents*. Unpublished manuscript.

Cascardi, M., Langhinrichsen, J., & Vivian, D. (1992). Marital aggression: Impact, injury, and health correlates for husbands and wives. *Archives of Internal Medicine, 152,* 1178–1184.

Chilman, C. S. (1989). Some major issues regarding adolescent sexuality and childbearing in the United States. *Journal of Social Work and Human Sexuality, 8,* 3–25.

Cordova, J. V., Jacobson, N. S., Gottman, J. M., Rushe, R., & Cox, G. (1993). Negative reciprocity and communication in couples with a violent husband. *Journal of Abnormal Psychology, 102,* 559–564.

Coren, E., Barlow, J., & Stewart-Brown, S. (2003). The effectiveness of individual and group-based parenting programmes in improving outcomes for teenage mothers and their children: A systematic review. *Journal of Adolescence, 26,* 79–103.

Cox, C. E., Kotch, J. B., & Everson, M. D. (2003). A longitudinal study of modifying influences in the relationship between domestic violence and child maltreatment. *Journal of Family Violence, 18,* 5–17.

Cunradi, C. B., Caetano, R., & Shafer, J. (2002). Socioeconomic predictors of intimate partner violence among white, black, and Hispanic couples in the United States. *Journal of Family Violence, 17,* 377–389.

De Paul, J., & Domenech, L. (2000). Childhood history of abuse and child abused potential in adolescent mothers: A longitudinal study. *Child Abuse and Neglect, 24,* 701–713.

Fewell, R. R., & Wheedon, C. A. (1998). A pilot study of intervention with adolescent mothers and their children: A preliminary examination of child outcomes. *Topics in Early Childhood Special Education, 18,* 18–25.

Field, T. M., Widmayer, S. M., Stringer, S., & Ignatoff, E. (1980). Teenage, lower-class, black mothers and their preterm infants: An intervention and developmental follow-up. *Child Development, 51,* 426–436.

Follingstad, D., Bradley, R., Helff, C., & Laughlin, J. (2002). A model of predicting dating violence: Anxious attachment, angry temperament and a need for relationship control. *Violence and Victims, 17,* 35–47.

Fulton, A. M., Murphy, K. R., & Anderson, S. L. (1991). Increasing adolescent mothers' knowledge of child development: An intervention program. *Adolescent, 26,* 73–81.

Furstenberg, F. (1991). As the pendulum swings: Teenage childbearing and social concern. *Family Relations, 40,* 127–138.

Garbarino, J. (1976). A preliminary study of some ecological correlates of child abuse: The impact of socioeconomic stress on mothers. *Child Development, 47,* 178–185.

Granger, R. C., & Cytron, R. (1999). Teenage parent programs: A synthesis of the long-term effects of the new chance demonstration, Ohio's learning, earning, and parenting program, and the teenage parent demonstration. *Evaluation Review, 23,* 107–145.

Greene, K., & Bogo, M. (2002). The different faces of intimate violence: Implications for assessment and treatment. *Journal of Marital and Family Therapy, 28,* 455–466.

Greenfeld, L., Rand, M. R., Craven, D., Klaus, P. A., Perkins, C. A., Ringel, C., et al. (1998). *Violence by intimates: Analysis of data on crimes by current or former spouses, boyfriends, and girlfriends* (NCJ-167237). Washington, DC: U.S. Department of Justice, Bureau of Statistics.

Hahlweg, K., Markman, H. J., Thurmaier, F., Engl, J., & Eckert, V. (1998). Prevention of marital distress: Results of a German prospective longitudinal study. *Journal of Family Psychology, 12,* 543–556.

Hanson, S. L. (1992). Involving families in programs for pregnant adolescents: Practices and obstacles. *Families in Society: The Journal of Contemporary Human Services, 73,* 274–281.

Heinicke, C. M., Fineman, N. R., Ruth, G., Recchia, S. L., Guthrie, D., & Rodning, C. (1999). Relationship-based intervention with at-risk mothers: Outcomes in the first year of life. *Infant Mental Health Journal, 20,* 349–374.

Herrenkohl, E. C., Herrenkohl, R. C., Egolf, B. P., & Russo, M. J. (1998). The relationship between early maltreatment and teenage parenthood. *Journal of Adolescence, 21,* 291–303.

Hess, C. R., Papas, M. A., & Black, M. M. (2002). Resilience among African American adolescent mothers: Predictors of positive parenting in early infancy. *Journal of Pediatric Psychology, 27,* 691–629.

Hockaday, C., Crase, S. J., Shelley, M. C., & Stockdale, D. F. (2000). A prospective study of adolescent pregnancy. *Journal of Adolescence, 23,* 423–438.

Kellogg, N. D., Burge, S., & Taylor, E. R. (2000). Wanted and unwanted sexual experiences and family dysfunction during adolescence. *Journal of Family Violence, 15,* 55–68.

Kellogg, N. D., & Hoffman, T. J. (1999). Early sexual experiences among pregnant and parenting adolescents. *Adolescence, 34,* 293–304.

Kiecolt-Glaser, J. K., Malarkey, W. B., & Chee, M. (1993). Negative behavior during marital conflict is associated with immunological down-regulation. *Psychosomatic Medicine, 55,* 395–409.

Korfmacher, J., & Marchi, I. (2002). The helping relationship in a teen parenting program. *Zero to Three, 21,* 21–26.

Langhinrichsen-Rohling, J., Hankla, M., & Stormberg, C. D. (2004). The relationship behavior networks of young adults: A test of the intergenerational transmission of violence hypothesis. *Journal of Family Violence, 19,* 139–151.

Langhinrichsen-Rohling, J., Heyman, R. E., Schlee, K., & O'Leary, K. D. (1997). Before children: Preparenthood cognitions of distressed and husband-to-wife aggressive couples. *Journal of Family Psychology, 11,* 176–187.

Langhinrichsen-Rohling, J., McGowan, M., & Turner, L. A. (2004). *Building a lasting love.* Unpublished treatment manual.

Larson, N. C. (2004). Parenting stress among adolescent mothers in the transition to parenthood. *Child and Adolescent Social Work Journal, 21,* 457–475.

Linehan, M. M. (1993). *Skills training manual for treating borderline personality disorder.* New York: Guilford Press.

Mantooth, C. M., Geffner, R., Franks, D., & Patrick, J. (1987). *Family preservation: A treatment manual for reducing couple violence.* Tyler: University of Texas at Tyler Print Shop.

Markman, H. J., Blumberg, S. L., & Stanley, S. M. (1989). *Prevention and Relationship Enhancement Program, PREP: Leader's manual.* Denver, CO: Prevention and Relationship Enhancement Program.

Markman, H. J., Floyd, F. J., Stanley, S. M., & Storaasli, R. D. (1988). Prevention of marital distress: A longitudinal investigation. *Journal of Consulting and Clinical Psychology, 56,* 210–217.

Markman, H. J., Jamieson, K., & Floyd, F. (1980). The assessment and modification of premarital relationships: Implication for the etiology and prevention of marital distress. In G. Vincent (Ed.), *Advances in family intervention: Assessment and theory* (pp. 41–90). Greenwich, CT: JAI Press.

Markman, H. J., Renick, M. J., Floyd, F., Stanley, S. M., & Clements, M. (1993). Preventing marital distress through communication and conflict management training: A 4- and 5-year follow-up. *Journal of Consulting and Clinical Psychology, 61,* 70–77.

Markman, H. J., Stanley, S., & Blumberg, S. L. (1994). *Fighting for your marriage: Positive steps for preventing divorce and preserving a lasting love.* San Francisco: Jossey-Bass.

McFarland, J. A. (1997). Effects of family interventions on adolescent mother's self-differentiation, personal authority, and health risks. *Dissertation Abstracts International: B. The Sciences and Engineering, 58*(1-B), 136.

McGuigan, W. M., Vuchinich, S., & Pratt, C. C. (2000). Domestic violence, parents' view of their infant, and risk for child abuse. *Journal of Family Psychology, 14,* 613–624.

Michigan State University Extension. (2003). *Caring for my family.* Retrieved August 28, 2005, from http://www.fcs.msue.msu.edu/cfmf/cfmf-resources.html.

Monahan, D. (2002). Teen pregnancy prevention outcomes: Implications for social work practice. *Families in Society, 83,* 431–440.

Moore, M. R., & Brooks-Gunn, J. (2002). Adolescent parenthood. In M. H. Borstein (Ed.), *Handbook of parenting* (pp. 173–190). Mahwah, NJ: Lawrence Erlbaum Associates.

Moore, T. E., & Pepler, D. J. (1998). Correlates of adjustment in children at risk. In G. W. Holden, R. Geffner, & E. N. Jouriles (Eds.), *Children exposed to marital violence: Theory, research, and applied issues* (pp. 157–221). Washington, DC: American Psychological Association.

Musick , J. S., & Stott, F. M. (1990). Paraprofessionals, parenting, and child development: Understanding the problems and seeking solutions. In S. J. Miesels & J. P. Shonkoff (Eds.), *Handbook of early childhood intervention* (pp. 651–667). Cambridge, England: Cambridge University Press.

Neidig, P. H., & Friedman, D. H. (1984). *Spouse abuse: A treatment program for couples.* Champaign, IL: Research Press.

Olds, D. L., Henderson, C. R., & Kitzman, H. J. (1998). The promise of home visitation: Results of two randomized trials. *Journal of Community Psychology, 26,* 5–21.

Olds, D. L., Henderson, C. R., Kitzman, H. J., Eckenrode, J. J., Cole, R. E., & Tatelbaum, R. C. (1999). Prenatal and infancy home visitation by nurses: Recent findings. *The Future of Children, 9,* 44–65.

Olds, D., Kitzman, H., Cole, R., & Robinson, J. (1997). Theoretical foundations of a program of home visitation for pregnant women and parents of young children. *Journal of Community Psychology, 25,* 9–25.

O'Leary, D. K., Heyman, R. A., & Neidig, P. H. (1999). Treatment of wife abuse: A comparison of gender-specific and conjoint approaches. *Behavior Therapy, 30,* 475–505.

Osofsky, J. D., & Thompson, M. D. (2000). Adaptive and maladaptive parenting: Perspectives on risk and protective factors. In J. P. Shonkoff & S. J. Meisels (Eds.), *Handbook of early childhood intervention* (2nd ed., pp. 54–75). New York: Cambridge University Press.

Owens, M. D., Scofield, B. E., & Taylor, C. E. (2003). Incorporating mother-daughter groups within clinical settings to increase adolescent females' self-esteem. *Journal of Family Issues, 24,* 895–907.

Pistole, M. C. (1999). Preventing teenage pregnancy: Contributions from attachment theory. *Journal of Mental Health Counseling, 21,* 93–113.

Prochaska, J. O., Norcross, J. C., & DiClemente, C. C. (1994). *Changing for good.* New York: William Morrow.

Raver, C. C., & Leadbeater, B. J. (1999). Mothering under pressure: Environmental, child, and dyadic correlates of maternal self-efficacy among low-income women. *Journal of Family Psychology, 13,* 523–534.

Robinson, J. L., Emde, R. N., & Korfmacher, J. (1997). Integrating an emotional regulation perspective in a program of prenatal and early childhood home visitation. *Journal of Community Psychology, 25,* 59–75.

Robinson, R. B., & Frank, D. I. (1994). The relation between self-esteem, sexual activity, and pregnancy. *Adolescence, 29,* 113–140.

Schumacher, J. A., Feldbau-Kohn, S., Smith Slep, A. M., & Heyman, R. E. (2001). Risk factors for male-to-female partner physical abuse. *Aggression and Violent Behavior,* 6, 281–352.

Silverman, J., Raj, A., Mucci, L., & Hathaway, J. (2001). Dating violence against adolescent girls and associated substance abuse, unhealthy weight control, sexual risk behavior, pregnancy, and suicidality. *Journal of the American Medical Association,* 286, 572–579.

Stern, M., & Alvarez, A. (1992) Knowledge of child development and caretaking attitudes: A comparison of pregnant, parenting, and nonpregnant adolescents. *Family Relations, 41,* 297–302.

Straus, M. A., & Gelles, R. J. (1990). How violent are American families? Estimates from the National Family Violence Resurvey and other studies. In M. A. Straus & R. J. Gelles (Eds.), *Physical violence in American families* (pp. 95–112). New Brunswick, NJ: Transaction Publishers.

Sussex, B., & Corcoran, K. (2005). The impact of domestic violence on depression in teen mothers: Is the fear or threat of violence sufficient? *Brief Treatment and Crisis Intervention, 5,* 109–120.

Turner, R. J., Grindstaff, C. F., & Phillips, N. (1990). Social support and outcome in teenage pregnancy. *Journal of Health and Social Behavior, 31,* 43–57.

Tuten, M., Jones, H. E., Tran, G., & Svikis, D. S. (2004). Partner violence impacts the psychosocial and psychiatric status of pregnant, drug-dependent women. *Addictive Behaviors, 29,* 1029–1034.

Unger, D. G., & Wandersman, L. P. (1985). Action research contributions to theory and application. *Journal of Social Issues, 41,* 29–45.

U.S. Department of Health and Human Services. (2000, November). *Healthy people 2010* (2nd ed.). Washington, DC: U.S. Government Printing Office.

Van Epp, J. (1999). *Everything that parents should teach, and singles should know about: How to avoid marrying a jerk: The way to follow your heart without losing your mind.* Premarital Interpersonal Training Choices Training Program. Retrieved May 18, 2006, from http://no jerks.com.

Vivian, D., & Langhinrichsen-Rohling, J. (1994). Are bi-directionally violent couples mutually victimized? A gender-sensitive comparison. *Violence and Victims, 9,* 107–124.

Vukelich, C., & Kliman, D. S. (1985). Mature and teenage mothers' infant growth expectations and use of child development information sources. *Family Relations, 34,* 189–196.

CHAPTER 23

Family Group Therapy: A Domestic Violence Program for Youth and Parents

Nancy Carole Rybski

The literature on aggressive youth tends to associate violent behavior with parenting deficits (Doumas, Margolin, & John, 1994; Zastowney & Lewis, 1990) and/or the youth's intrapersonal characteristics (Carlson, 1990; Lochman & Dodge, 1994). Juvenile aggression toward parents and other individuals, both inside and outside the family, may be driven by certain parenting deficits defined by inconsistent authority and discipline by the parent, indifference, rejection or physical abuse of the child, lack of positive support for the growth of the child's self-esteem (Lowry, Sleet, Duncan, Powell, & Kolbe, 1995), and the modeling of aggression by perpetrating abuse towards intimate partners (Mahoney, Donelly, Boxer, & Lewis, 2003; chapter 9 in this volume).

Paulson, Coombs, and Landsverk (1990) posited that violent youth are clinically marked by general unhappiness and low self-esteem that derive from inadequate social reinforcement by parents. Herrenkohl, Herrenkohl, and Toedter (1983) suggested that the major contributory condition for abusive behavior by adolescents is an "inner deficit" (p. 130) resulting from parental rejection and lack of nurturance. That "inner deficit"—the intrapersonal characteristics that support aggressive behavior—may be comprised of attributional biases, problem-solving deficiencies, and inadequate coping mechanisms, all of which sum to favor aggression as a situational outcome (Lochman & Dodge, 1994). As aggressiveness develops in childhood, it

499

remains fairly stable over time and through life stages of adolescence into adulthood (Ehrensaft, Moffitt, & Caspi, 2004; Sampson & Laub, 1993). The literature is largely in agreement that youthful violence is multifaceted, comprised of cognitive, behavioral, and emotional components (Kiselica, Baker, Thomas, & Reedy, 1994; Lochman & Dodge, 1994). It follows, then, that a program designed to address juvenile violence would incorporate cognitive, behavioral, and affective components into treatment (Valliant, Jensen, & Raven-Brook, 1995; Veenstra & Scott, 1993).

For families of violent youth, the cognitive component can be approached by teaching members to communicate more effectively (Infante, Sabourin, Rudd, & Shannon, 1990), to identify angering stimuli and each person's reactions (Neidig & Friedman, 1984), and to discern personal stressors and learn coping strategies to reduce stress (Garbarino, Sebes, & Schellenbach, 1984). Behaviorally, the family members can be trained to change communication patterns, respond to angering stimuli less aggressively, and manage stress by physical relaxation or other means. Finally, members also learn to express affect more appropriately in communication, identify and reduce anger aroused by situations, and manage the frustration of stress more effectively. Few treatment programs incorporate all these aspects into a family-focused treatment program.

In 1984, Neidig and Friedman published a manual for the treatment of spousal abuse. Originally developed for the military and then routinely applied to a civilian population, the program has undergone repeated empirical tests for efficacy, with consistently demonstrated success in the elimination of domestic violence within couples. The treatment addresses the behavioral, cognitive, and affective aspects within modules of anger management, stress reduction, and communication skill building—three areas of personal competence consistently lacking in violent offenders (Infante et al., 1990; Tremblay, Kurtz, Masse, Vitaro, & Phil, 1995). While the language of Neidig and Friedman's (1984) program is framed for couple interaction, the underlying concepts address the basic personal and relationship dynamics listed previously. It seemed reasonable that this multimodal program could be tailored to adolescent–parent interactions, redirecting the focus of interactions from interspousal to adolescent-mother, provided that all the essential ingredients of treatment were included.

BACKGROUND AND JUSTIFICATION

Adolescent–parent violence is a serious social problem not only because of its immediate effects but also because it implicates family problems that exist prior and subsequent to the violence. Antecedent conditions may include interparental abuse that serves as a template for the child's aggression (Kitzmann, Gaylord, Holt, & Kenny, 2003;

see also chapter 9 in this volume), dysfunctional personality character-istics that arise from the observation of violence (Kempton, Thomas, & Forehand, 1989), and truncated social and relational skills due to an overall dysfunctional home with inadequate parenting (Repetti, Taylor, & Seeman, 2002; Straus & Donnelly, 2001). Children who witness their parents assault one another or are subjected to direct physical abuse by them are at risk for developing symptoms of internal distress (e.g., anxiety and depression) as well as conduct disorders (Margolin & Gordis, 2000), including retributional violence directed against the parents (Ulman & Straus, 2003). Subsequent conditions involve the continuance of violence into adulthood (Patterson & Yoerger, 1993), with violent behaviors against one's partners and children (Simons, Wu, Johnson, & Conger, 1995), and the maintenance of inade-quate social and interpersonal skills (Lochman & Dodge, 1994). It is clear that adolescent–parent violence is a complex problem with far-reaching implications.

Social Learning Theory

Social learning theory suggests that aggression and violence are learned behaviors for violent youth (Bandura, 1973; Tolan, Guerra, & Kendall, 1995) based on the premise that observers cognitively note behavioral activity by others along with the outcome of those behaviors. The observed interactions may be modeled by different sources: by media, within peer interactions, or by family-of-origin members. In order to be learned, a specific behavior is modeled by a party and observed by an actor. The actor replicates the behavior and, based on the rewards associated with the behavior, retains or abandons the activity (Bandura, 1977, 1986).

Beyond positive or negative reactions from others, mediating cogni-tions and attitudes help the actor decide whether to continue an aggressive behavior. Bandura (1977) suggested that a number of cognitive apprais-als determine the degree of acceptability of the behavior. Justification of behaviors and projection of responsibility to external factors decrease personal culpability. However, a juvenile's ability to thoroughly assess the social desirability of a behavior is frequently inadequate. Aggressive youth, especially, may be unable to use the appraisal review objectively because of information-processing deficiencies. These deficiencies may pre-dispose youth to leap to abusive conclusions based on simple behavioral repetition of observed violence rather than reasoned logic (Lochman & Dodge, 1994).

Stress Theory

The second theory reviewed in this chapter is stress theory. Family stress theory (Hill, 1958) suggests that how families—and the individuals within them—react to stressful situations are dependent on three variables: (a) the type of provoking event, (b) the family's resources and strengths at the time of the stressful event, and (c) the meaning attached to the event by the family, both collectively and individually (Boss, 1988). Provoking events can encompass a universe of stressful situations, from the everyday challenges of living in society to any type of acute or chronic stress. The juvenile's lack of sophistication in gathering personal resources or correctly evaluating the stressor impairs his or her ability to cope with stress (Ebata, Petersen, & Conger, 1990; Licitra-Kleckler & Waas, 1993). Without this ability to successfully diminish stress, maladaptive outcomes, such as either internalizing or externalizing problems, can develop. The accumulation of stress, then, spirals with each maladaptive outcome, creating more stress and frustration.

Family support has emerged as the single most important type of social support for adolescents (Cauce, Felner, & Primavera, 1982). Conversely, negative or underdeveloped parent–child relationships may negatively impair the child's ability to develop coping skills. A poor relationship between the parent and child can be highly indicative of the youth's feelings of incompetence with difficult or provocative situations (Paulson et al., 1990). Without perceived family support acting as a "powerful buffer" (Cauce et al., 1982, p. 427), the adolescents tend to be more vulnerable to physical and psychological symptoms of stress.

Family Systems Theory

The third theory that addresses adolescent–other domestic violence is family systems theory. A family system is a concept that identifies the family as a collection of interdependent individuals with assigned roles, tasks, and identities (Zastowney & Lewis, 1990).

Two areas within family systems that warrant detailed discussion are boundaries and hierarchies. Boundaries are the degree of "connectedness" among family members—"who participates and how" (Minuchin, 1974, p. 12). Variability describes how boundaries may differ between subsystems or as perceived by individuals. Permeability, then, indicates how much—and how clearly defined—information or emotional impact passes among family members. Diffuse boundaries, on the other hand, obfuscate role definition, confusing relational paths and information sharing. Problems arise when boundaries are "either too permeable or too rigid, or when people are either too involved (enmeshed) or not involved enough (disengaged)" (Tavantzis, Tavantzis, Brown, & Rohrbaugh, 1985, p. 73). These problematic situations are called "boundary breaches" (Haley, 1976). Boundaries among subsystems may be breached in a number of ways—through intrafamily triangulations or a collapse of parent–child roles.

Another major concept in family systems theory is hierarchy, associated with rules that dictate varying degrees of decision-making power for various individuals and subsystems. The family's structure can be stratified into vertical levels (Haley, 1976; Minuchin, 1974). Within the vertical strata, the higher the placement, the greater that person or dyad's decision-making authority and power. Typically, a functional hierarchy is one where the parental subsystem and the marital dyad serve as the foundation of the family, overseeing its functioning with the greatest amount of power and control among the members. Ambiguity about role—that is, who is in control within the family—leads to unclear boundaries between family members, increasing stress in an already stressed environment (Zastowney & Lewis, 1990), and can bring the family to crisis. Families with confused organizations of hierarchy most frequently present with clinical problems (Haley, 1976). When the parents' subsystem is not appropriately elevated within the family structure and the children's subsystem is in control, the family will experience chaos and children become at risk for developing symptomology.

Haley (1976) suggested that children who act as authority in the family cannot keep it from descending into chaos. Unable to keep control, they act out behaviorally in order to focus attention on the family in crisis. It is assumed that the attention directed on the family will help the family in reasserting appropriate hierarchy and will assist the parents in taking authority out of the hands of the children and back into the rightful hands of the parents (Haley, 1976).

NEIDIG AND FRIEDMAN'S DOMESTIC VIOLENCE PROGRAM

Neidig and Friedman's (1984) conflict containment program presented a "primary goal of immediate and complete cessation of violence" (p. 1). The original core curriculum was multifunctional and directed participants in a number of exercises that included accepting personal responsibility for violent behavior and contracting for a commitment to change. Having made this commitment, clients were then directed in developing and utilizing time-outs and other security mechanisms and understanding the factors (such as stress) involved in the violence sequence. In a structured group context, the clients were assisted in mastering anger control and stress reduction skills and developing more effective communication. Program components included instruction, behavioral rehearsal, and feedback.

Instruction was accomplished by use of brief lectures and demonstrations. Lessons were condensed modules and were well structured, with clearly defined goals and sequentially ordered steps. Each module had group exercises and homework assignments to facilitate learning. Behavioral rehearsal encouraged couples to apply what they had learned from instruction and took place during group exercises or homework assignments. Rehearsal allowed the clinician to observe participants' levels of mastery and compliance with treatment overall. If, for example, behavioral rehearsal had not been attempted, then the module was reviewed again with the couple and the homework reassigned. Obviously, the couples needed to stay fairly contemporary with the group format or risk falling out of treatment.

Feedback was a critical component in the process of social learning. Care was taken that feedback always be positive, specific, and focused on the performance of group participants. Treatment compliance was continually monitored, but positive achievement and expectations were noted and reflected often.

While Neidig and Friedman's original program (1984) focused on spousal interaction, as mentioned, a careful review of the program suggested that the modules were amenable to revision into parent–child interactional sequences. The revision was tailored to fit into a current southwestern U.S. superior court allowance for juvenile therapeutic treatment, fixed at 10 hours of service per youth. Within those 10 hours of treatment, the three main identified maladaptations were addressed: anger management, stress reduction, and communication skills deficits. The four weekly group sessions focused on achieving those goals.

RESEARCH DESIGN

Subjects

With approval by a southwestern U.S. juvenile probation supervisor, subjects were referred to the program by probation officers under specified criteria. The criteria were that the referrals must be adolescent males or females, between the ages of 13 and 18, who have a recent arrest on domestic violence charges against their single-parenting mothers and whose listed guardian is female—in all cases, this female guardian was the youth's birth mother. Criminal charges for violence were any of three types: physical assault, wherein the youth physically harmed another person; property damage, without physical harm to another; or disorderly conduct, which constitutes antisocial or disruptive behavior. A fourth category of criminal charge was entered for this project: combination, which was physical assault plus another domestic violence offense at the same arrest.

After arrest, each of the youth was processed through criminal intake at a county juvenile correctional center and then released to his or her parents. As a first offense, each case was referred to the Family Violence Prevention Program (FVPP). The FVPP receives domestic violence referrals from an intake center, then places those eligible referrals into a diversion program for first-time criminal offenders that permits an arrested youth to remain uninvolved from the judicial system. In order to be eligible for the diversion program, the youth must admit to the charges against him or her, the youth and his or her parent must agree to participate in therapeutic treatment, and the youth must not be arrested for any further illegal activity while in the program. This program received all its referrals from FVPP's diversion rosters.

A nonprofit mental health agency in the Southwest underwrote the costs of the pilot program in order to produce and evaluate a marketable program for the juvenile justice system.

Between August and December 1996, 57 families were referred to the agency for inclusion in the research project. Of the 57 families, four families refused treatment as described to them at the first telephone contact, and their referral information was sent back to probation. The remainder of families were randomly assigned to the two types of group: 27 families were assigned to the experimental group, and 26 families were originally assigned to the waiting list control group. An interesting phenomenon occurred, however. Twelve of the families assigned to waiting list control groups contacted the research, requesting immediate therapeutic services. Thus, after initial assignment, those 12 families were reassigned to the experimental groups, resulting in 14 families remaining in the waiting list control and 35 families in the experimental groups.

The repeated-measures, pretest–posttest design was selected because of the ability to control for threats to internal validity and for ease in statistical analysis. The data collected were quantitative. The experimental groups participated in a modified family version of Neidig and Friedman's (1984) group therapy focusing on development of anger management skills, communication skills, and stress reduction skills. The waiting list control subjects were evaluated at the same times as the experimental subjects but were not given therapy until the matched time period had passed.

Variables

Independent Variables—As described previously, the independent variable was group, divided into treatment and waiting list control groups. Treatment was Neidig and Friedman's (1984) domestic violence program, modified to treat families with domestically violent youth. A waiting list control group constituted a "no treatment" group.

Dependent Variables

Abusive Behavior—The Abusive Behavior Inventory (ABI; Shepard & Campbell, 1992) is an expansion of the Conflict Tactics Scales (Straus, 1990), which is the most widely used assessment measure for relational violence. This instrument was originally created to measure the psychological and physical abuse persons in relationships use against their partners. Verbal and psychological abuse was defined as nonphysical tactics used to gain control and guarantee submission. Physical abuse was assault used in order to keep or gain dominance. The ABI contains 30 items, using a 5-point Likert-type scale to measure frequency of abusive behaviors over a six-month period. The six items in the categories of emotional abuse and intimidation were selected to represent psychological abuse in this study. The category of assaultive behavior was the sole category for 10 items of physical abuse.

Multidimensional Functioning—Observation of interparental violence can result in the formation of either internalizing or externalizing behavioral symptoms (Licitra-Kleckler & Waas, 1993; Margolin & Gordis, 2000). Those symptoms can significantly influence the child's functioning in a number of areas: school, home, and community role performances; the child's social or antisocial behaviors; moods and general affect; the child's propensity to abuse substances; and, in some cases, the organization of thought processes.

The Child and Adolescent Functional Assessment Scale (CAFAS; Hodges, 1995) is a clinician-completed assessment of the youth's functioning on five subscales, with an assessment of caregiver functioning on an additional scale. This instrument assesses the degree of impairment in children and adolescents secondary to emotional, behavioral, or substance abuse problems. The CAFAS is scaled on (a) role performance, with subscales of school/work, home, and community; (b) behavior toward others; (c) moods/self-harm, with subscales of moods/emotions and self-harmful behaviors; (d) substance abuse; and (e) thinking. There is an additional scale of caregiver resources that evaluated material needs and family/social support. The child's household composition is assessed on the basis of the defined caregiver (primary family, noncustodial family, or surrogate family). In general, the higher the score, the poorer the degree of functioning. Youth with higher CAFAS scores are much more likely to display high-risk behaviors of harming self or others, have poor social relationships, display difficulties in school, and have more involvement with the juvenile justice system than youth with lower scores (Hodges & Wong, 1996).

Anger—The Siegel Multidimensional Anger Inventory (MAI; Siegel, 1986) is a 38-item self-report instrument that measures the following dimensions of anger: frequency, duration, magnitude, range of anger-arousing situations, mode of expression, and hostile outlook. Each of the statements is rated in terms of how self-descriptive they are, with responses ranging from completely undescriptive (1) to completely descriptive (5).

Intake Session

At the intake session, the youth and his or her single mother completed formal intake documents as well as the research instruments (the ABI and the MAI). The subject's consent form was reviewed and completed. An in-depth clinical interview was also performed by this researcher.

Group Sessions

As sufficient numbers of families completed their intake sessions, they were placed in groups consisting of four to six families (8 to 12 individual group members), which commenced within two weeks of intake. Groups met at different days of the week and at different times—the families were typically able to choose between a couple of different two-hour sessions.

The following is a brief synopsis of the curriculum for each week.

Week 1—Handouts were given for this session were Program Principles (including the program's primary goal: to stop violence in the home—see Table 23.1), Anger Lessons Worksheet, Violence Cycle Worksheet, Time-Out Contract, and Anger Log I, in which participants were asked to record recent aggressive incidents, along with their anger levels, their cognitions, and their subsequent behavior (the outcome).

Introduction of members of the group and the therapist took place. The reason for all families being present was reviewed—all juvenile members have arrests for domestic violence. Confidentiality of sessions was stressed. The therapist went over the program principles in detail, emphasizing that violence was a crime, and that whether or not youths admit it, the people they hurt really are among the most important people in the world to them. The premises of social control, social learning, and family systems theories were briefly discussed. Members of the group completed the Anger Lessons Worksheet, and the mothers then talked about intergenerational patterns they saw—or failed to see—between their families of origin and the present nuclear families. All members were encouraged to review their own behaviors and to begin taking responsibility for their part in increasing family conflict and family violence. The premise of cyclical violence was discussed—if the cycle is not broken, it will be repeated.

Each person completed the Violence Cycle Worksheet, listing at least three examples of a cycle, including the stressors and cues of phase 1 (tension building), triggers for phase 2 (violent episode), and evidences of remorse (phase 3). The "corkscrew" spiral of violence was described, with each repetition becoming more frequent and more intense, with less of a "honeymoon period" occurring between violent outbreaks. Positive communication and problem-solving skills were introduced.

Each family completed two copies of the Time-Out Contract—one copy for them to keep and one to be handed in to the therapist. The importance of honoring the contract between mother and child was greatly stressed. The therapist then reviewed Anger Log I, describing a sample incident and completing it on the log. All families were requested to describe a minimum of anger-provoking three incidents over the next week on Anger Log I.

Week 2—Handouts of Anger Log II and the Anger Control Self-Analysis Worksheet were given out to all group members.

Time-Out Contracts from the past week were collected. General discussion of family conflict behaviors over the past week ensued. Each member then selected the more intense, higher-point-value episode from Anger Log I to use in completing the Anger Control Self-Analysis Worksheet. Anger Log II, which expands on the first by asking participants to distinguish between automatic (hot) thoughts and rational (cool) thoughts, was assigned for next session. As in week 1, a minimum of

TABLE 23.1   Program Principles of the Family Violence Treatment Program

1. The primary goal of this program is to stop violence in the home.

2. Although anger and conflict are part of family life, violence has no place in the family and is never okay.

3. Abusiveness is a learned behavior.

4. Abusive behavior happens when people are in a relationship, but it is the responsibility of the violent person to control his or her violent behavior.

5. Abusiveness is a desperate but unhealthy way to make things change in a family.

6. Abusiveness tends to get worse, both in terms of severity and how often it occurs, if it is not stopped.

7. Children who are abusive to their family members very often grow up and continue to be abusive to their spouses and children.

Source: Neidig and Friedman (1984).

three incidents were required. Focus on positive communication and problem solving was continued.

Week 3—The following handouts were given: Stress Symptoms, Anger Management Self-Statements (for use in the four sequential steps of "preparing for provocation," "impact and confrontation," "coping with arousal," and "subsequent reflection"), and Nonassertive, Assertive, and Aggressive Behaviors (Table 23.2).

TABLE 23.2 Table of Nonaggressive, Assertive, and Aggressive Behaviors

	Nonaggressive Behavior	Assertive Behavior	Aggressive Behavior
Character-istics of the behavior	Ignores, does not express own rights, needs, or desires; permits others to infringe on rights	Expresses and asserts own rights and needs; stands up for legitimate rights in a way that does not violate the rights of others	Expresses own rights at expense of others; inappropriate outburst or hostile over reaction
Your feelings when you engage in this behavior	Weak, hurt, anxious; disappointed in self at the time and possibly angry later	Confident, self-respecting; feels good about self at the time and later	Angry, self-righteous, indignant; feels superior, possibly guilty later
Nonverbal behavior	Avoidant, slumped body; nervous gestures and mannerisms, weak voice	Open, direct; good eye contact; standing comfortable, does not appear nervous; clear, steady tone of voice	Glaring, narrowed eyes; leaning forward, stiff, rigid posture; clenched fists; raised, haughty tone of voice
Verbal behavior	Rambling statements; qualifiers (maybe/I wonder if you would/only); negatives (Don't bother/It's not important)	Concise "I" statements, cooperative words; empathic statements of interest	Clipped, interrupting statements; threats; name calling, putdowns, accusations; sarcasm
Outcome	Does not achieve desired goals	May achieve desired goals	Achieves desired goals by hurting others

Source: Neidig and Friedman (1984, p. 54).

Anger Log II and personal progress was reviewed. The sheet of behaviors was discussed, defining both nonassertive and aggressive behaviors' cost in terms of lost personal benefits and increased stress. Each person described a brief situation of each type of behavior and evaluated his or her experiential outcomes.

The Stress Symptoms handout was reviewed, noting common etiology in frustration due to nonassertive or aggressive behaviors. Current and past symptomology of group members was discussed, along with the "snowball" effect of stress-induced symptomology and interactional effect with nonassertive or aggressive behaviors. Progressive relaxation directives were given, incorporating positive self-directive statements into calming statements during the relaxation segment. Following this, Anger Log II was again assigned, describing a minimum of three angering situations. Three 10-minute sessions of self-directive relaxation exercises were assigned as well, reinforcing both cool thoughts and self-actualization statements.

Week 4—The handouts given were Feelings List, Feeling Talk (e.g., using "I" statements), Making Positive Requests (e.g., being prompt, positive, and specific), and Positive Expressions, consisting of demonstrations of affection and caring, praise and compliments, and verbalization of appreciation.

Assignments from the previous week were reviewed, as was the handout Making Positive Requests, tying the same into last week's discussion of nonassertive, passive, and aggressive behaviors. Members role-played feelings talks within each family dyad. At the end of this session, feedback—both positive and negative—was encouraged by all group members regarding this therapy program, and remaining areas of need were identified and discussed for each of the participating families. The assessment and closure sessions were held at the agency within one week after the termination of group.

Closure Session

The families were debriefed on the group therapies, with feedback on performance, current levels of functioning, and the like. This clinician's perception of each family's level of accomplishment was discussed, and if the family was perceived to be in need of additional treatment, that perception was shared with them. The mothers were given the agency's Consumer Satisfaction Survey. Each woman was asked to complete the evaluation of the program. The results of each Consumer Satisfaction Survey would not be reviewed by this writer until after each subject's termination summary had been forwarded to his or her probation officer and, therefore, could not influence this clinician's perception of program completion.

Instruments completed by the family at closure were the ABI and the MAI. This researcher completed the CAFAS within one week of the last session. A termination summary outlining the youth's participation in treatment was sent to the referring probation officer.

RESULTS

The assessments completed by both the youth and his or her mother were the MAI and the ABI, divided into two subscales: verbal abuse and physical abuse. This clinician assessed the youths' multidimensional functioning and assigned scores on the CAFAS. Statistical analysis of the participants' and clinician's responses are described next.

Dependent Variables by Group—Simple 2 × 2 factorial analyses of variance were conducted on each of the seven dependent variables by group. Differences were present between the waiting list control group and the experimental group.

Statistical analysis of the dependent variables of anger, abuse, and functioning between the treatment and no-treatment groups seems to suggest that the treatment had effects on certain behaviors of parents and youth in assaultive families. The Consumer Satisfaction Survey suggests, further, that the treatment was well received by the families.

DISCUSSION

The results of this study suggest three conclusions. First, because the control condition was empirically demonstrated, the differences between the waiting list control and the experimental groups were likely a result of the treatment itself rather than nonspecific effects. Second, this program had a significantly positive impact on self-reported psychological and physical abuse behaviors by both the youths and their mothers. Third, the youths' overall multidimensional functioning improved.

To examine those conclusions more closely, the hypotheses derived from the three main theories associated with this program are reviewed. Accordingly, each of the hypotheses is restated in a null form, and each null hypothesis is either rejected or failed to be rejected.

Hypothesis 1: Since these youth have been arrested for violence, it is presumed that they have observed violence between their mothers and an adult partner.

Null Hypothesis 1: Domestic violence was not an antecedent condition in the families of domestic violence.

We can reject this null hypothesis. In the initial intake session, families were asked if the mother had been involved in any interparental domestic violence; 84.4% of mothers of sons and 82.4% of mothers of daughters reported that domestic violence had been present in the home during the life of the child. While a clear causal link cannot be established between observed parental violence and a youth's own violent activity, observed adult domestic violence is the most consistent marker for violent reenactment (Carlson, 1990).

Hypothesis 2: Alternative behaviors to violence can be taught, extinguishing the aggressive response to anger. Therefore, the teaching of anger management and communication skills will reduce the number of verbal and physical abusive acts the youth perpetrates against others. Likewise, these skills will reduce the number of psychological and physical abusive acts the parents commit against the youths.

Null Hypothesis 2: Treatment will not change the number and frequency of psychological and physical abusive acts between offspring and mothers.

We can reject this null hypothesis. Analyses of variance of the three groups displayed different levels of change in the areas of youthful and parental violence (see Table 23.3). The experimental group revealed that both the parents and the youth used fewer psychological and physical violence acts after treatment than before.

Hypothesis 3: Violent youth report that they have high levels of stressors in their lives and, therefore, will have high levels of anger and frustration from unresolved stress. Teaching anger and stress management will increase subjects' abilities to cope effectively with stress, decreasing the overall levels of frustration and anger reported by youth and their parents.

Null Hypothesis 3: Treatment will not decrease the level of anger for parents and youth.

We cannot reject this null hypothesis. However, no one group of youth reported a reduction in anger. Waiting list and experimental parents also failed to report reduced anger.

Hypothesis 4: More effective coping strategies and reduced stress will result in higher functioning of the youth in psychosocial and emotional areas of home, school, and community.

Null Hypothesis 4: Treatment will not change the youths' psychosocial and emotional functioning in school, home, and community.

TABLE 23.3 Means and Standard Deviations of Dependent Variables at Pre- and Posttest Assessment by Group

Variable	Waiting List Control			Experimental		
	n	Pre	Post	n	Pre	Post
Multidimensional functioning (CAFAS)	14	109.29(36.68)	103.57(34.78)	39	109.13(41.66)	79.56***(43.95)
Youth anger (MAI)	14	60.50(8.76)	57.29(11.15)	39	59.91(20.59)	56.91(15.83)
Youth psychological abuse (ABI)	14	30.86(21.45)	22.71*(22.74)	39	27.35(26.73)	10.35***(13.47)
Youth physical abuse (ABI)	14	13.43(12.66)	11.21(10.83)	39	17.78(29.68)	6.91**(18.26)
Parent anger (MAI)	12	48.17(17.07)	53.21(19.09)	21	51.39(13.66)	48.90(15.03)
Parent psychological abuse (ABI)	14	14.28(11.87)	16.00(13.90)	28	21.16(20.88)	5.17***(8.79)
Parent physical abuse (ABI)	14	9.29(11.89)	9.29(13.90)	28	8.70(11.99)	0.96**(2.34)

Note. Standard deviations are in parentheses. *$p < .05$. **$p < .01$. ***$p < .001$.

We can reject this null hypothesis. The CAFAS scores reflecting the youth's level of functioning decreased for both the original and the reassigned experimental groups, indicating higher levels of functioning and reduced symptomology. Interestingly, the waiting list control group's p value approached significance for this variable. When a t test for paired samples was run on the waiting list control group, the two-tailed significance for the CAFAS comparison was .071. This may suggest that, across groups, the act of being arrested may indeed inhibit the youth's antisocial behavior to some degree.

Hypothesis 5: Parents who learn to communicate with their offspring effectively will learn to use authority appropriately and regain control within their home. Youth who are relegated to the appropriate offspring subsystem will not compete as actively for control within the family system. Therefore, levels of psychological and physical abuse will decrease for both parent and offspring.

Null Hypothesis 5: Treatment will not change the levels of psychological and physical abuse displayed by either parents or offspring.

As discussed previously, we can reject this null hypothesis. The reduction in psychological and physical violence as a result of treatment seems to be clear; what is confounded is the identification of the causal relationship in reference to the specific theories. As mentioned earlier, the three theories are used as an integrative framework by which to view youth-instigated domestic violence. That integration being the case, a clear separation of theory and relevant change mechanism is not possible. Rather, a good deal of overlap occurs among the theories and the causal factors presumed to be associated with each. Therefore, it is not clear whether the decrease in violence on the parts of the parents and offspring is due to the participants' attaining alternative learned behaviors, improved coping skills, or strengthened family hierarchies.

DISCUSSION OF DIFFERENCES

In summary, this program can be considered successful, although the results were not as strong as predicted. Measures (ABI and CAFAS) that assessed specific behaviors reflected change, but an attitudinal measure did not (MAI). This could have implications for only short-term compliance as opposed to long-term substantive change. If compliance is the change mechanism here in treatment, then it must be considered that treatment itself may not be a causal factor in the reported differences in the measures. The very acts of being arrested and having treatment assigned can be powerful acts of social control that can serve temporarily, to at least, dampen antisocial behaviors. It was not within the scope of this evaluation, however, to determine if either external social control or perhaps the participants themselves effected change.

More specifically, three areas of change—or lack thereof—can be examined. The first area of change was demonstrated by the psychological and physical activity of parents and youth. These dependent variables showed a decrease from intake through the completion of the program. According to all three theories, this result was anticipated. Social learning theory suggested that alternative responses to violence as a learned behavior could be taught. In this treatment, those alternatives included positive communication and anger management skills development. Stress theory also suggested that violence was a maladaptive response to anger and frustrations. Violence erupted as overaccumulation of stress swamped each individual's inadequate coping abilities. By enhancing participants' stress management skills, maladaptive responses such as violence would be reduced.

Finally, family systems theory suggested one important avenue of violence. Youth-to-parent violence is viewed as a direct power struggle for control within the parent–child dyad, with the parent and child occupying competing roles. In this program, communication skills were demonstrated and taught to family members, ostensibly reducing conflict and positioning the parent back into the authority role within the parental subsystem. That realignment of family vertical structure strengthens the parental role for the mother, reducing conflict primarily and psychological and physical abuse secondarily.

The second area of change is that, overall, youth achieved higher functioning in home, school, and community. Again, these findings were expected under the three theories. The third area of change is in reported anger. According to the three theories, anger should have decreased for the experimental groups. Under social learning theory, conflict behaviors without anger were modeled in order to be retained and used by youth and parents. Positive coping mechanisms, based on stress theory, were taught to help participants reduce anger and frustration and avoid unwieldy accumulations of stress. The realignment of hierarchies, per family systems theory, should have reduced role confusion and the power struggle for authority, along with the anger generated by that struggle. However, in spite of such expectations, anger did not decrease. It is possible that a deep-seated anger arose from early observation of domestic violence, too complex or profound for easy remediation. Family conflict, likewise, for most of these families was a long-standing interactional pattern. It could be that treatment was too brief to address such an accumulation of relational anger.

DIRECTIONS FOR FUTURE RESEARCH

This program was a compacted and more tightly focused version of Neidig and Friedman's (1984) couples treatment. Given the constraints of superior court funding for juvenile treatment, this writer attempted to provide treatment that could be performed within the allocated 10 hours of service. It could be that this amount of time is simply too brief to make substantive changes in attitudes and belief systems but is sufficient to allow for immediate behavioral changes. The brevity of the revised program, condensed to four weekly sessions of two hours each, with family interview sessions pre- and posttreatment, was a concern of two mothers who completed the Consumer Satisfaction Survey. One woman suggested that the program "needs to be longer. Make it 12 weeks." Another mother concurred: "Make it longer. Problems are just getting reached at three to four weeks." On a similar track, another parent suggested having "groups more often so that the chance of other problems happening would be minimized." Having groups twice weekly instead of weekly could also allow for closer monitoring of family participation and completion of homework assignments for sharing within the group.

In summary, the study reached a positive conclusion. The treatment program was successful in reducing psychological and physical violence within families. This family-focused intervention was also intended to elevate multidimensional functioning of the youth in home, school, and the community. That change occurred as well. The last goal—to reduce anger in youth and parents—was not achieved. It would be appropriate to replicate this study in the future to determine if high, stable anger is a function of either treatment or measurement. Overall, however, it appears that this treatment program was a success in treating youth-to-parent violence.

REFERENCES

Bandura, A. (1973). *Aggression: A social learning analysis.* Englewood Cliffs, NJ: Prentice-Hall.

Bandura, A. (1977). *Social learning theory.* Englewood Cliffs, NJ: Prentice Hall.

Bandura, A. (1986). *Social foundations of thought and action: A social cognitive analysis.* Englewood Cliffs, NJ: Prentice Hall.

Boss, P. (1988). *Family stress management.* Newbury Park, NJ: Sage.

Carlson, B. E. (1990). Adolescent observers of marital violence. *Journal of Family Violence, 5,* 285–299.

Cauce, A. M., Felner, R. D., & Primavera, J. (1982). Social support in high-risk adolescents: Structural components and adaptive impact. *American Journal of Community Psychology, 10,* 417–428.

Doumas, D., Margolin, G., & John, R. S. (1994). The intergenerational transmission across three generations. *Journal of Family Violence, 9,* 157–175.

Ebata, A. T., Petersen, A. C., & Conger, J. J. (1990). The development of psychopathology in adolescence. In J. Rolf, A. S. Masten, D. Cicchetti, K. H. Nuechterlein, & S. Weintraub (Eds.), *Risk and protective factors in the development of psychopathology* (pp. 308–333). New York: Cambridge University Press.

Ehrensaft, M., Moffitt, T., & Caspi, A. (2004). Clinically abusive relationships in an unselected birth cohort: Men's and women's participation and developmental antecedents. *Journal of Abnormal Psychology, 113*(2), 258–270.

Garbarino, J., Sebes, J., & Schellenbach, C. (1984). Families at risk for destructive-parent-child relations in adolescence. *Child Development, 55,* 174–183.

Haley, J. (1976). Development of a theory: A history of a research project. In C. E. Sluzki & D. C. Ransom (Eds.), *Double-bind: The foundation of the communication approach to the family.* New York: Grune & Stratton.

Herrenkohl, E., Herrenkohl, R., & Toedter, L. (1983). Perspectives on the intergenerational transmission of abuse. In D. Finklehor (Ed.), *The dark side of families: Current family violence research* (pp. 305–316). Beverly Hills, CA: Sage.

Hill, R. (1958). Generic features of families under stress. *Social Casework, 49,* 139–150.

Hodges, K. (1995). *Manual for the Child and Adolescent Functional Assessment Scale.* Ann Arbor: University of Michigan Press.

Hodges, K., & Wong, M. M. (1996). Psychometric characteristics of a multidimensional measure to assess impairment: The Child and Adolescent Functional Assessment Scale. *Journal of Child and Family Studies, 5*(4), 445–468.

Infante, D. A., Sabourin, T. C., Rudd, J. E., & Shannon, E. A. (1990). Verbal aggression in violent and nonviolent marital disputes. *Communication Quarterly, 4,* 361–371.

Kempton, T., Thomas, A. M., & Forehand, R. (1989). Dimensions of interparental conflict and adolescent functioning. *Journal of Family Violence, 4,* 297–307.

Kiselica, M. S., Baker, S. B., Thomas, R. N., & Reedy, S. (1994). Effects of stress inoculation training on anxiety, stress, and academic performance among adolescents. *Journal of Counseling Psychology, 41,* 335–342.

Kitzmann, K., Gaylord, N., Holt, A., & Kenny, E. (2003). Child witnesses to domestic violence: A meta-analytic review. *Journal of Consulting and Clinical Psychology, 71,* 339–352.

Licitra-Kleckler, D. M., & Waas, G. A. (1993). Perceived social support among high-stress adolescents: The role of peers and family. *Journal of Adolescent Research, 8,* 381–402.

Lochman, J. E., & Dodge, K. A. (1994). Social-cognitive processes of severely violent, moderately aggressive, and nonaggressive boys. *Journal of Consulting and Clinical Psychology, 62,* 366–374.

Lowry, R., Sleet, D., Duncan, C., Powell, K., & Kolbe, L. (1995). Adolescents at risk for violence. *Educational Psychology Review, 7,* 7–39.

Mahoney, A., Donnelly, W., Boxer, P., & Lewis, T. (2003). Marital and severe parent-to-adolescent physical aggression in clinic-referred families: Mother and adolescent reports on co-occurrence and links to child behavior problems. *Journal of Family Psychology, 17*(1), 3–19.

Margolin, G., & Gordis, E. (2000). The effects of family and community violence on children. *Annual Review of Psychology, 51,* 445–479.

Minuchin, S. (1974). *Families and family therapy.* Cambridge, MA: Harvard University Press.

Neidig, P. H., & Friedman, D. H. (1984). *Spouse abuse: A treatment program for couples.* Champaign, IL: Research Press.

Patterson, G. R., & Yoerger, K. (1993). Development models for delinquent behavior. In S. Hodgins (Ed.), *Mental disorder and crime.* Newbury Park, CA: Sage.

Paulson, J. M., Coombs, R. H., & Landsverk, J. (1990). Youth who physically assault their parents. *Journal of Family Violence, 5,* 121–133.

Repetti, R., Taylor, S., & Seeman, T. (2002). Risky families: Family social environments and the mental and physical health of offspring. *Psychological Bulletin, 128*(2), 330–366.

Sampson, R. J., & Laub, J. H. (1993). *Crime in the making: Pathways and turning points through life.* Cambridge, MA: Harvard University Press.

Shepard, M., & Campbell, J. A. (1992). The Abusive Behavior Inventory: A measure of psychological and physical abuse. *Journal of Interpersonal Violence, 7,* 291–305.

Siegel, J. M. (1986). The Multidimensional Anger Inventory. *Journal of Personality and Social Psychology, 51,* 191–200.

Simons, R. L. Wu, C., Johnson, C., & Conger, R. D. (1995). A test of various perspectives on the intergenerational transmission of domestic violence. *Criminology, 33,* 141–172.

Straus, M. (1990). The Conflict Tactics Scales and its critics: An evaluation and new data on validity and reliability. In M. A. Straus & R..J. Gelles (Eds.), *Physical violence in American Families: Risk factors and adaptations to violence in 8,145 families* (pp. 49–73). New Brunswick, NJ: Transaction Publishers.

Straus, M., & Donnelly, D. (2001). *Beating the devil out of them.* New Brunswick, NJ: Transaction Publishers.

Tavantzis, T., Tavantzis, M., Brown, L., & Rohrbaugh, M. (1985). Home-based structural family therapy for delinquents at risk of placement. In M. Mirkin and S. L. Koman (Eds.), *Handbook of adolescents and family therapy* (pp. 69–88). New York: Gardner Press.

Tolan, P. H., Guerra, N. G., & Kendall, P. C. (1995). A developmental-ecological perspective on antisocial behavior in children and adolescents: Toward a unified risk and intervention framework. *Journal of Consulting and Clinical Psychology, 63,* 579–584.

Tremblay, R. E., Kurtz, L., Masse, L. C., Vitaro, F., & Phil, R. O. (1995). A bimodal preventive intervention for disruptive kindergarten boys: Its impact through adolescence. *Journal of Consulting and Clinical Psychology, 63,* 560–568.

Ulman, A., & Straus, M. (2003). Violence by children against mothers in relation to violence between parents and corporal punishment by parents. *Journal of Comparative Family Studies, 34,* 41–60.

Valliant, P. M., Jensen, B., & Raven-Brook, L. (1995). Brief cognitive behavioral therapy with male adolescent offenders in open custody or on probation: An evaluation of management of anger. *Psychological Reports, 76,* 1056–1058.

Veenstra, G. J., & Scott, C. G. (1993). A model for using time out as an intervention technique with families. *Journal of Family Violence, 8,* 71–87.

Zastowney, T. R., & Lewis, J. L. (1990). Family interaction patterns and social support systems in single-parent families. *Journal of Consulting and Clinical Psychology, 65,* 235–251.

CHAPTER 24

Family Violence Parent Groups

L. Darlene Pratt and Tom Chapman

A review of the literature provides ample evidence of the adverse effects on children who are raised in families in which they experience child abuse and/or witness parental violence (Kitzmann, Gaylord, Holt, & Kenny, 2003), including anxiety, depression, posttraumatic stress, conduct disorder, school-related problems, substance abuse, and risky sexual behavior. Davies and Sturge-Apple (chapter 8 in this volume) write that children from "domestically violent homes may draw on their affective and sensory analogues (e.g., high vigilance, negative representations, avoidance or intervention) as 'scripts' or alarm systems for scanning new or stressful social settings for old threats that originally stemmed from exposure to interparental conflict" (p. 174). This can set the stage for poor conflict resolution, discord, and aggression in interpersonal relationships—both in childhood and in adulthood.

Indeed, there is also a correlation between witnessing violence in one's childhood of origin and perpetration of intimate abuse as an adult for men as well as women (e.g., Langhinrichsen-Rohling, Neidig, & Thorn, 1995; Straus, 1992). Violence in the family of origin is one of the warning signs when assessing for partner violence (Hamel, 2005; chapter 12 in this volume). The relationship between intimate partner abuse and child abuse is well documented. Based on data from the 1975 and 1985 National Family Violence Surveys, Straus and Smith (1990) determined that husbands who are verbally aggressive to their partners physically abuse their children at a rate of 11.2 incidents per year compared to 4.9 for other husbands. Wives who are verbally aggressive to their spouses physically abuse their children at a rate of 12.3 per year compared to 5.3 for other wives. A more recent study with 177 families in a large metropolitan area (Margolin and Gordis, 2003) echo these findings, having found significant correlations between the perpetration of partner abuse and child abuse for both men and women. In the study by Mahoney, Donnelly, Boxer, and Lewis (2003), two-thirds of adolescents who had been exposed to marital aggression in the past year had also been subjected to parental aggression. Both mothers and fathers who perpetrated or were victims of partner aggression were more likely to be aggressive with their adolescent children.

According to Wolak and Finkelhor (1998), children may experience internalizing and externalizing symptoms and learn to become aggressive when they merely witness parental conflict and verbal abuse rather than physical violence. Research by Repetti, Taylor, and Seeman (2002) delineates the relationship between poor mental and physical health and early childhood experiences in "risky" families. They characterized risky families as those with overt family conflict and aggression as well as deficient nurturing—cold, unsupportive, and neglectful. They postulate that these "family characteristics create vulnerabilities and/or interact with genetically based vulnerabilities in offspring that produce disruptions in psychosocial functioning" (p. 330). The researchers focus on threats over the life span, from the immediate threats posed by abuse and neglect to the continuing threats posed by the stresses on the child's developing physiological and neuroendocrine systems, the lack of self-regulatory skills, and vulnerability to behavior problems and substance abuse. They also touch on the relationship between early childhood attachment styles, serotonin levels, and adverse outcomes, such as aggression and depression. Behavioral regulation and social competence are needed in high-stress environments, yet, according to these authors, these skills are deficient in risky families. Citing the importance of the social context in which these families exist, the authors recommend several types of family interventions—including individual, couples, and group therapy as well as parent training and home visits.

Gutierrez (2000), Schore (1994), and Siegel (1999) have shed light on the relationship between disturbed childhood attachment and the release of stress chemicals and hormones, which can lead to physical changes in the frontal occipital lobe and the limbic system. When children are abused, witnesses to domestic violence, or harshly criticized, rejected, or abandoned, they experience elevated levels of anxiety and an attendant loss of a healthy sense of self and an inability to regulate their emotions and to interact appropriately with others. According to Gutierrez, male batterers raised in such environments have an anxiety-based style of relating to others. Relationships often trigger their feelings of shame, loss, and self-doubt. Their violence may be an external, aggressive way to meet an unconscious need to acquire an internal physiological balance. Violent homes do not provide children with a secure base for exploration or a haven of safety when facing other challenges. This can lead to insecure attachment styles and may set the stage for future aggression.

Much like the studies cited earlier, research examining the role of stress in family violence (Salzinger et al., 2002) found a significant relationship between partner abuse and child abuse. The authors identified two important casual pathways: One pathway was family stress, which increased the risk for partner aggression, thus increasing the risk for child abuse; the other pathway was the link between family stress, caregiver distress, and resulting child abuse. Their hypothesis is that family stress is the most significant variable for negative impacts on child functioning in its tendency to exacerbate other conditions. In the study by Margolin and Gordis (2003), both mothers and fathers who experienced high levels of financial and parenting stress were found to be at high risk for perpetrating child abuse, although the correlation between the perpetration of child abuse and having been a victim of partner abuse was higher for the women. The risk for child abuse therefore increases for both perpetrators and victims of domestic violence.

As we await findings from a "second generation" of research on the processes that mediate the association between domestic violence and children's adjustment (chapter 8 in this volume), help for distressed families can't wait. Family interventions, including group therapy and parent training, have been shown to be both necessary and effective (Repetti et al., 2002). One treatment option is the High Conflict Family Violence Parent Group or Anger Management Parenting Program. In the remainder of this chapter, program features are presented, including case examples, for programs offered at two agencies in the Greater San Francisco Bay Area.

JOHN HAMEL & ASSOCIATES

The High Conflict Family Violence Parent Group, offered at offices in Pleasant Hill and Greenbrae in the San Francisco Bay Area, is intended for parents who have been verbally or physically abusive to their children or who have been verbally or physically abusive to their partner around their children. The group is appropriate for self-referred clients, Child Protective Services (CPS) cases, individuals involved in a child custody dispute, and those referred per California PC 273-1 following a conviction of physical child abuse. Clients undergo a one- or two-session psychosocial assessment prior to entering the group with an emphasis on current family functioning, including parenting capacities; family structure; the use of verbal, emotional, and physical abuse; and previous abuse in their adult relationships and in their families of origin. Unlike batterer intervention programs, which under California law must segregate clients into same-gender groups, this group is open to both men and women and comprised of individuals from a variety of economic and cultural backgrounds. Couples are encouraged to participate together, but only when there is a minimum risk for further violence between them. When the risk for further violence is high, we recommend separate groups and typically refer one or both partners to a batterer intervention program. In addition, because the group is primarily psychoeducational rather than therapeutic, it is not appropriate for couples wishing to explore couples issues in depth (see chapter 17 in this volume).

At the end of the assessment process, parents are given a workbook with (a) introductory information, including a definition of child abuse and a basic outline of anger management skills; (b) log sheets to help them understand their abuse patterns and gauge their progress (Figure 24.1); and (c) a section containing informational/exercise sheets to help clients more thoroughly incorporate the new skills into their day-to-day relations. The exercises included in this latter section include meditation and relaxation techniques; ways for participants to identify and challenge distorted cognitions and irrational beliefs and improve parenting, listening, and assertiveness skills; and ways of identifying and overcoming both their current family cycle of violence and the patterns they acquired in their families of origin. Several sessions are devoted to a review and discussion of children's development and needs throughout each stage of the life span. The topics for each session, many similar to those used in our 52-week batterers' intervention program, can be found in Table 24.1. The entire course material is included in the book by Hamel (2005).

Sessions are 90 minutes in duration, meet each week for a period of 26 to 52 weeks depending on client needs, and are limited to no more than eight or nine participants to encourage greater group cohesion and participation. Each session consists of an open discussion period, followed by a didactic presentation, using material from the leader's guide, as well as a workbook that the clients are required to complete. Group norms, which encourage support, empathy, and respectful feedback among the participants, can be helpful in resolving many of the issues that plague parents and children in aggressive families. Learning, sharing, and disclosing with other parents who are struggling with problems of poor functioning and abuse provides an environment conducive to

FIGURE 24.1 Progress log

Month_____ Year_____ Complete on a weekly basis:

A. At the end of each week, enter the number of times you engaged in the behaviors listed below, then enter the total at the end of the month.

	name(s)						name(s)				
Week#:	1	2	3	4	Total	Week#:	1	2	3	4	Total
No. days contact						8. Listing injustices					
No. conflicts						9. Mind reading					
Discuss without aggression						10. Fortune-telling					
Aggression						11. Being sarcastic					
Yell, shout						12. Rejecting compromise					
Swear at, put down						13. Playing the martyr					
Threaten to hurt						14. Giving advice					
Throw, hit things						15. Using terminal language					
Grab, push						16. Lecturing					
Slap											
Punch, kick						**Abusive/ Control Tactics**					
Bite/choke/pull hair						1. Threats/intimidation					
Other						2. Isolation and jealousy					
Dirty Fighting						3. Economic abuse					
1. Timing						4. Diminish self-esteem					
2. Brown bagging						5. General control					
3. Overgeneralizing						6. Obsessive rel.intrusion					
4. Cross complaints						7. Passive aggressive/withdraw					
5. Blaming						8. Using children					
6. Pulling rank						9. Legal system abuse					
7. Not listening						10. Sexual coercion					

B.   What I need to work on:

(Continued)

FIGURE 24.1   Progress log.

C. Record times when you got aggressive/angry in the past month. Include situations outside home.

Date: Situation: Anger temperature (1–10):   Other emotions: Thoughts: What I did wrong/right:
Date: Situation: Anger temperature (1–10):   Other emotions: Thoughts: What I did wrong/right:
Date: Situation: Anger temperature (1–10):   Other emotions: Thoughts: What I did wrong/right:
Date: Situation: Anger temperature (1–10):   Other emotions: Thoughts: What I did wrong/right:

D.   Indicate how you applied each parenting skill outlined below on a scale of 1 to 5.
       (1 = "very poor," 2 = "poor," 3 = "satisfactory," 4 = "good," and 5 = "excellent")

	Week 1	Week 2	Week 3	Week 4
Showed acceptance and warmth	_____	_____	_____	_____
Set firm limits	_____	_____	_____	_____
Held child accountable (for his or her age)	_____	_____	_____	_____
Responded to child's needs	_____	_____	_____	_____
Was positively involved in his or her life	_____	_____	_____	_____
Gave choices instead of commands	_____	_____	_____	_____
Communicated "do" rather than "don't"	_____	_____	_____	_____
Followed through with consequences	_____	_____	_____	_____
Did not argue when enforcing rules	_____	_____	_____	_____
Presented "united front" with spouse	_____	_____	_____	_____

TABLE 24.1   Group Curriculum

1. Characteristics of healthy families
2. Anger management
3. Anger management
4. Anger management
5. Child abuse laws; physical child abuse facts; 10 myths about corporal punishment
6. Coping with stress
7. Coping with stress
8. Goals of misbehavior; how children learn: modeling, reinforcement
9. Discipline; alternatives to punishment; behavior plans
10. Identifying distorted thinking
11. Challenging and replacing distorted thinking
12. Stages of child development: infancy to age 3
13. Stages of child development: age 3 through middle childhood
14. Stages of child development: preadolescence to young adulthood
15. Basic principles of communication; metacommunication
16. Active listening
17. Anger management review
18. Effects of parental and partner violence on children
19. Positive communication
20. Identifying feelings beneath anger
21. Identifying and expressing needs and wants; assertiveness
22. Assertiveness
23. Family violence cycle
24. Family conflict and conflict escalation
25. Resolving conflict
26. Responding to tantrums; helping children manage their own anger
27. Characteristics of healthy families
28. Anger management
29. Anger management
30. Anger management
31. Child abuse laws; 10 myths about corporal punishment; parenting styles
32. Coping with stress; preparing for provocations
33. Coping with stress

(Continued)

TABLE 24.1   Group Curriculum

34. Goals of misbehavior; how children learn: modeling, reinforcement

35. Discipline; alternatives to punishment; behavior plans

36. Irrational beliefs

37. Irrational beliefs

38. Child development review

39. Child development review

40. Child development review

41. Basic principles of communication; metacommunication

42. Active listening; listening to criticism

43. Anger management review

44. Marital violence and child abuse

45. Positive communication

46. Developing empathy

47. Identifying and expressing needs and wants; assertiveness

48. Assertiveness

49. Overcoming resistance to change

50. Family conflict and conflict escalation

51. Resolving conflict

52. Coping with angry people; helping children manage their own anger; family meetings

Source. Adapted from Dinkmeyer and McKay (1983), *Step Teen Parent's Guide.*

self-disclosure and learning of crucial skills and leads to understanding and appropriate remorse, social competence, improved bonding and attachment with family members, self-regulation, better communication and listening skills, and a reduction in toxic shame. As clients gain new skills and inner resources, their self-esteem and confidence is enhanced. They become better equipped to shape functional behavioral and self-regulatory skills in their children.

The ongoing nature of the group allows for continued assessment, evaluation, and feedback for the participants. In CPS cases, we work diligently with caseworkers, after assessing thoroughly for victim safety, to begin the reunification process while participants are still in the group so that they can receive support as well as corrective feedback as they apply their new skills. Through facilitated group interactions and the curriculum, members learn anger and stress management skills and more effective ways to communicate and resolve conflicts with their partners and children and become educated about healthy parenting/partner norms, the importance of cognitive appraisals/distortions, co-occurrence of partner and child abuse, and the intergenerational transmission of violence. Taking a whole-system approach to family violence, the program addresses child abuse, intimate partner violence, sibling violence, and the problem of child-on-parent violence, which becomes more significant (and dangerous) with adolescents.

CASE EXAMPLE: RUNEL

Runel, a soft-spoken 62-year-old short-order cook and grandfather of two boys, was referred for an anger management assessment and treatment during the course of a contentious child custody evaluation. His son-in-law accused him of child abuse and made it clear that he did not want him to have contact with the children. Prior to his daughter's divorce, Runel had been a part-time caretaker of the children as both parents worked. As immigrants, Runel and his wife had a strong sense of family and were dedicated to their children and grandchildren, providing financial resources and a great deal of child care. Runel had been physically punished as a child. Being hit with sticks or household objects, he said, was normal in his country of origin. He had also been physically and emotionally abusive to his wife until he was arrested about 10 years ago for repeatedly punching her on her arms and head. He was not referred for treatment at that time, but her threats to leave the marriage caused him to discontinue his physical assaults. Runel's daughter stated that her father had disciplined her and her siblings harshly and yelled at them when upset. Carrying the legacy of physical abuse into her own family, she had become overly punitive and was hitting her own children. She also shared that, like her father, her husband had been possessively jealous—berating her for wanting to play cards with her girlfriends, whom he accused of being "tramps."

Runel's family is a clear example of the intergenerational transmission of family violence as well as the co-occurrence of partner abuse and child abuse. Since entering the family court system, his daughter has completed a parenting class and says she no longer physically disciplines the boys. She and her ex-husband have been ordered to undergo coparenting counseling (see chapter 21 in this volume), and the boys are seeing a therapist familiar with family violence dynamics. Runel has been participating in our High Conflict/Family Violence Parent Program. As he learns about the destructive nature of violence and the value of effective parenting and positive conflict resolution skills, the court may grant him the right to spend time with his grandchildren. A positive reunification would

TABLE 24.2   Goals of Misbehavior

1. The Four basic goals and the unhelpful ways parents can respond:

Child's Goal	Behavior	Unhelpful Parental Response	Helpful Parental Response
Attention	Clowning around, engaging in minor mischief, unique dress, forgetting, neglecting chores	Become annoyed; remind, nag	Refuse to give attention on demand; ignore inappropriate bids for attention; wait for the child to do something right and give them proper attention
Power	Aggressive, disobedient, defiant, hostile, resistant, stubborn	Feel angry and provoked; either fight power with power or else give in	Withdraw from conflict and enforce consequences for misbehavior; Help child use his or her power constructively by asking him or her to help work things out
Revenge	Rude, hurtful, destructive, violent, glaring	Feel deeply hurt, retaliate	Try to empathize with the child; build a trusting relationship through understanding/acceptance
Prove their inadequacy	Avoid trying, quit easily; school truancy, escape through alcohol, drugs	Feel hopeless, discouraged; agree with child that nothing can be done; give up	Avoid criticism or pity; arrange for child to have successful experiences and praise positive efforts

2. Other goals of misbehavior, common with adolescents: excitement, peer acceptance, superiority
3. Questions for discussion:

   ✓ Based on the previous list, why do you think *your* child misbehaves?
   ✓ What are some of the negative and positive ways you tend to respond?

alleviate stress across the family system, reattach functional bonds, and increase the children's emotional security and psychological adjustment.

Right away, Runel benefited greatly from the workbook information, especially the introductory information on anger management and the "10 Myths About Corporal Punishment" (Straus & Donelly, 2001); however, he was initially quiet during sessions and seemed intimidated by the other group members, some of whom were far more extroverted. Runel eventually warmed up and began to fully participate after a new member was added—a young woman, much like his own daughter, who was struggling to raise three young children. Runel paid particular attention to the discussions on behavior plans and on "goals of misbehavior" (Table 24.2). In the past, he tended to interpret everything the boys did personally either as defiance of his authority or as evidence of being "spoiled." The material helped him gain a better understanding of the children's misbehavior, thus increasing his frustration tolerance around them. Over time, Runel became more aware of the association between family stress and aggression—how his yelling caused the boys to act out (e.g., by aggressively wrestling, sometimes leading to injury) and how his inability to effectively set limits on this behavior simply added to the existing levels of family stress. With the understanding that corporal punishment can teach violence through both observational learning and the association between violence and love, he looks forward to utilizing a privilege/reward system when he is reunited with his grandchildren. He will also be able to help his grandsons deal with their own anger from tools he acquired in the program.

CASE EXAMPLE: LYDIA

Lydia, a 35-year-old nurse and mother of two, was referred to our High Conflict/Family Violence Parent Program by the Contra Costa County court because of her verbal and physical aggression toward both her husband and her children. There had been many instances of partner abuse prior to her arrest, but her husband, David, had been reluctant to call the police, fearing the embarrassment that this would bring on him and his family. In addition, because Lydia would typically offer seemingly heartfelt apologies following her violent outbursts, he was inclined to believe that things would get better.

As his wife's outbursts grew more intense and more frequent, David sought individual psychotherapy to help him cope. He came to understand how destructive his wife's behavior was to the children. Even while Lydia temporarily cycled into her contrition stage and controlled herself, their elder daughter, Annie—the most frequent target of the mother's screaming, criticisms, and slaps—was becoming increasingly silent and withdrawn, blaming herself for the chaos. The three-year-old, Jake, was clingy, fretful, and highly insecure, unwilling to sleep in his own bed. Finally, after an especially explosive episode in which Lydia repeatedly punched her husband and scratched him while ripping his eyeglasses off his face, he decided to call the police. Although he minimized the danger to himself, knowing that the unresolved, contentious conflict was escalating the family stress levels and was detrimental to the children gave him the courage to let his wife be arrested, thus compelling her into treatment.

Lydia had been raised with a father who was verbally and at times physically abusive to her and her mother. She continued to spend a great deal of time with her family of origin. Although he had mellowed somewhat over the years, her father was still prone to engage in the occasional verbal tirade, and these reawakened all her childhood fears and insecurities. She continued both to love him and resent him and had remained powerless to change her own behavior or to understand the resentment and fear her own daughters were experiencing. The group process and exercises increased her understanding of the family violence cycle, giving her the motivation to make changes. She came to understand the psychological problems she was creating by targeting her children and partner, making it difficult for the girls to navigate their normal developmental tasks.

Lydia took the program quite seriously. Using the progress logs and list of dirty fighting/other control tactics (Figure 24.1) helped her to take responsibility for her violence and to identify the various ways she would emotionally abuse David, such as belittling him in front of the children. She also benefited from the workbook handouts on conflict containment as well as the exercise "Misuses of Anger" (Table 24.3). Because of her professional training as a nurse, Lydia sometimes tried to dominate discussions with her mental health knowledge, and for some time the group facilitator had to gently guide her back to a discussion of her *own* family and her *own* feelings. After temporarily dropping out in protest, Lydia came back to the group, willing to learn and grow. Although she found the exercise "Abuse in Family of Origin" (Table 24.4) humbling, it was a powerful experience. Following that session, she was better able to identify with some of the other group members, both male and female, who had experienced similar abuse in their families of origin and to draw on their support for developing empathy for and understanding herself as a victim of her father's abuse. Consequently, she was then able to empathize with her daughters' feelings and work toward becoming a secure support figure.

Lydia joined with her husband to improve their conflict resolution skills, thus further alleviating the children's distress. They periodically use the "Healthy Families Checklist" (Table 24.5) to gauge their progress. At the conclusion of her 52-week program, Lydia reported a reduction in family stress along with a marked decrease in unresolved conflict.

TABLE 24.3   Misuses of Anger

A. Anger can be a negative or a positive emotion, depending on what you do with it. Because it is such a strong emotion, it can easily be misused. For each of the misuses listed here, give one or two recent examples from your own life.
   1. Intimidate:
   2. Control:
   3. Punish:
   4. Protect self from hurt:
   5. Feel morally superior:
   6. Maintain a connection with partner:
   7. Get a rush or "high":

B. Now go back to each misuse of anger and ask yourself:
   1. Did my aggression work in the short run? Do people comply out of respect—or fear?
   2. Did my aggression work in the long run? Did my aggression have negative consequences, such as hurt feelings and resentments in the other person or guilt and shame in myself?

TABLE 24.4   Abuse in Family of Origin

Taking responsibility for your *current* behavior is crucial in learning to overcome problems with anger and aggression. It is ultimately self-defeating to wallow in the past or to use it as a way to avoid changing the present. However, it is equally crucial that you have a thorough *understanding* of your aggression and how you got that way. An awareness of the past will remind you of how you *don't* want to act so that you don't pass on to your own children the dysfunction you may have experienced growing up. Such an awareness is also necessary in order to work through the feelings of resentment, guilt, and shame that prevent you from healing. Answer the following questions as honestly as you can. Share with the group what you are willing to share. You may want to discuss the rest with a trusted confidant or therapist.

1. How did your parents/stepparents settle their differences? Did they yell or swear at one another or throw things? Ever fight physically? Give some examples. Try to remember the worst fight. What happened? How did you feel about it at the time?
2. Did your parents/stepparents ever spank you? What about other forms of physical punishment, such as hitting you with a belt or some other object? What was the worst episode? How did you feel about it at the time? What about now?
3. Overall, how good of a job did you parents do of caring for you? Were they there for you when you needed them? Did they provide for your needs—food, shelter, love, a sense of safety? Or did you resent them in any way? If so, why?
4. Did your parents ever swear at you, call you names, or put you down in front of other people? Give some examples. How did you feel?
5. Were there any other times when they did something that made you feel bad, like there was something terribly wrong with you?

TABLE 24.5   Healthy Families Checklist

	Great	Fair	Bad
1. Maintain clear boundaries between children and parents—I have the responsibility to raise my children, and therefore, have authority over them. I can be their friend, but I am a parent first and do not use them to get my emotional needs met. I take care of my needs, and my spouse and I have a relationship apart from the children. We do not side with any child or encourage "alliances." My children are individuals, even if they remind me of people I'm angry with, and I don't take my frustrations out on them.			
2. Use an "authoritative" style of parenting—My style of parenting is neither permissive nor authoritarian, and my rules are reasonable. My spouse and I act like "benevolent dictators" with our children. We are willing to hear them out but reserve the right to have the final say. Our decisions are made out of love and to meet the best interests of the family.			
3. Communication is respectful—With my spouse and children, communication is always respectful. I am an attentive listener and talk in a nonaggressive manner, careful to avoid putdowns and comments that shame my children. I am secure enough to allow my children to express strong feelings and opinions.			
4. Discussion and negotiation preferred—My partner and I never try to impose our will on each other but are open to hearing each other's points of view. When appropriate, I engage in discussion and negotiation with my children, allowing them to contribute to the problem-solving process. I am open to changing the rules if necessary.			
5. Autonomy encouraged—I give my children as much responsibility as they can handle. Although I am responsible for			

(Continued)

TABLE 24.5   (Continued)

	Great	Fair	Bad
their welfare and seek to keep them safe, I avoid overprotecting or overcontrolling them. I teach them in such as way that they *internalize* my rules and lessons, and they behave because they think it is the right thing to do rather than out of fear.			
6. Marital relationship healthy and secure— I actively nurture my relationship with my partner. We help each other, are flexible in our roles, and show mutual respect. We set aside time to talk, but we also go out on dates and have fun together so that our home is not simply a "child rearing business."			

She seldom resorts to yelling and no longer physically assaults her husband or children.

PEACE CREATIONS

Peace Creations also offers a 26- to 52-week program for parents who have been verbally physically or aggressive to their children or who have been aggressive with their partner in front of the child. It is the program's philosophy that the very nature of family violence and treatment precludes the treatment of violent partners in the same group. Only when our assessment determines that couple violence is at a low level and when neither partner has been charged with and convicted of domestic violence will we allow the couple to participate in the parenting program together. Most of the clients are referred to our 26- to 52-week Anger Management Parenting Program by Child Protective Services (CPS) or family court. We also get one parent or the other referred to our short-term anger management group or else the 52-week domestic violence batterer intervention program, both by criminal court and CPS.

The thread that runs through these cases has been well documented— partners who are violent with each other are at risk for also being violent with their children and often experienced abuse in their pasts. Through the normal course of treatment, the client(s) will spend a substantial number of sessions exploring not only basic prosocial skills such as anger management, effective communication, and conflict resolution but also the intergenerational aspects of family violence and the effects of violent relationship, directly and indirectly, on children. The course material for the Anger Management Parenting Program, some of which is described later in this chapter, can be found in Chapman (2005).

CASE EXAMPLE: MAURICE AND SHIELA

This working-class couple (he operated a forklift, she tended bar part time) were referred to our Domestic Violence Program as well as to our Anger Management Parenting Program by CPS because of violence in the home. The neighbor's complaints stemmed from constant yelling at and pushing and slapping of their children at their apartment complex. When their 12-year-old son, Travis, arrived at school with a bruise under his eye, CPS was brought in to investigate. It was determined that Shiela, a methamphetamine user, perpetrated most of the verbal and physical abuse in the family. In her rampages, she attacked everyone whom she perceived to be in her way—primarily Maurice, her main target, whom she would routinely punch, scratch, and kick (sometimes to the groin area). When the children attempted to stop their parents, everyone became embroiled in the battle. The social workers removed Shiela from the home, left the children with Maurice, and ordered treatment. Shiela was required to enter a substance abuse program, and the children received individual counseling. Although Shiela was determined to be the most aggressive partner, she was never charged with domestic violence. The question of Shiela returning to the home has not yet been resolved. Her addiction is still a problem, and her last visit with the children ended in her attacking Maurice—stomping on the cast over his broken leg he suffered at work.

In group, Maurice had a lot to learn about the most basic parenting principles, such as the proper use of time-outs, giving praise rather than criticizing, and "catching them being good." Maurice admitted that his home of origin looked much the same as his current household. Both parents were crack addicted and violent with each other and their children. His epiphany came in the group with an exercise in the chapter "Getting Anger Out" called "I AM" (Box 24.1). With the facilitator's assistance and the encouragement of the other group members, Maurice was able to get past the embarrassment he felt around his poor writing skills and to compose a letter to his parents. Writing this letter allowed him to identify and work through the anger he had been repressing over his parents' abandonment of him. Shiela has been remanded to a residential treatment program for six months and will return to the completion of anger management on release. Although family stress levels have

BOX 24.1

MANAGING ANGER

There are several methods of getting anger out of your body. (Remember that (stuffing) anger is not healthy—we have to move it out of us). Let's look at them now.

BREATHING: When we get angry, we tend to alter or maybe even stop our breathing patterns. Lack of oxygen actually increases the stress our body is undergoing at the moment. When you are in stress, take a deep breath as a way of keeping yourself focused on the argument at hand and what is actually being said. As you feel the feelings that come up for you, keep breathing. You will find that keeping your breath going:

✓ Defends us against other people's expression of feelings while communicating to them that they are free to feel their feelings.
✓ Increases our energy to get us out of a bad mood and get us moving.
✓ Enables us to stay in our feelings and feel them.

TALKING is a fine way to express and release present anger. One thing is clear: Many anger experiences are too strong to be talked out right away with the person who caused them or apparently caused them. Talking can express present anger, but it usually can't handle deeply suppressed anger. Talking about your anger with a safe person is helpful, that is, only if the person you talk with will not be hurt by whatever you say or try to hurt you for saying it. Someone who is not involved, like a therapist, can listen and be objective and supportive of the process you are undertaking.

WRITING is an excellent way to get at the feelings you may have about a given angry scenario or life. The following are six methods that may help. First, let yourself sit quietly and breathe. As you write, concentrate on what you're writing about; try to feel it, remembering that the way to get in touch with your feelings is to keep breathing.

✓ LIST OF DYSFUNCTIONS: Make a list of all the dysfunctional things you do. Make it as long as you can. Next to each item put an M if your mother did the same thing and put an F if your father did the same or different thing. This can give you an idea of pattern development in your life.

(continued)

✓ "I AM" : Complete the sentences:

When Dad got angry, he . . .
When Mom got angry, she . . .
When I got angry as a child, I . . .

- ✓ DESCRIPTION OF WHEN YOU WERE ABANDONED, that is, when you were not supported as a child. Write about that event with your nondominant hand. If you are right handed, write with your left hand. If you are left handed, write with your right hand. Do not worry about penmanship. Let your hand do the work and hear the story our child tells.
- ✓ LIST OF PEOPLE YOU ARE ANGRY AT: That's it, put them all down and put down why you are angry at them. Put down the littlest things as well as the big things. You need to know what really matters to you. When you have made the list, add to it as things come to mind. Let the feelings you are writing about come up.
- ✓ LETTER WRITING: With your opposite hand, write a letter to someone you are really angry at: your parents, the judge, the prosecutor, your lawyer, your partner, your ex-partner, your children, and the yard cop. It doesn't matter if they are living or dead; what matters is that you are writing the letter for yourself, not them. Let it all hang out, dump as much on them as you wish, feel the feelings, and keep breathing. If you are still angry, write another letter. You may not release everything, but you may get it out for now and get rid of some of the stored anger.
- ✓ JOURNAL KEEPING is one way to keep track of where you are in life. Tell the truth and feel the feelings. So review your day in your journal on a daily basis as a way of releasing ill feelings.

GET PHYSICAL, not with the person you are angry at, but get a good workout to relieve the stress and physical emotion of anger. Run the track, go to the gym, play a hard game of handball—do all of these in a safe way, don't take it out on others.

Responses

- ✓ Have you ever let your anger out in a safe, nonviolent way? What did you do and how did it feel?
- ✓ Have you ever held your anger in only to notice it seeping out or blowing out all at once? What happened the last time you did that? How did it feel?

(continued)

✓ What prevents you from letting your anger out safely? (Be honest—if not with yourself, then with whom?)

✓ Has your anger separated you from someone? Who abandoned that relationship and how?

✓ What is the event that most brings up your anger? How does that event repeat itself in your life? How does that feel?

✓ Anytime you think of the things of the past that get you "fired up," practice breathing your way through it. How does that feel? Describe what, if anything, happens.

---

lessened considerably during her absence, Maurice has had his hands full handling his children, who constantly test him, sometimes hitting each other. While final solutions have not been found, Maurice continues to work on establishing functional boundaries around his children and improving his parenting skills. He is still, despite everything, committed to reunification with Shiela.

CASE EXAMPLE: RAKEESH AND ROSLYN

Rakeesh, a 45-year-old software engineer, and his wife Roslyn have been referred to the Anger Management Parenting Program at Peace Creations by CPS for charges of physical child abuse under California PC 273-1. Their joint participation in the same group fit with our assessment and the social worker's case plan. Rakeesh is also attending AA three times per week as a condition of remaining in the house. Although court mandated, he quickly took to the program, developed a network of supportive friends, and obtained a "sponsor" to guide him.

While presenting as very meek in class, has admitted to engaging domineering behavior at home and has slapped not only his wife Roslyn but also the two children. His behavior comes out in a negative way only, according to him, when he has something to drink; however, the cultural aspects of their case bring in elements of male dominance, which conflicts with the freedom Roslyn found when they immigrated to the United States. Both of them report that their upbringing in India was in a very male-dominated family system where the elder male ruled everything, even their own arranged marriage. For both of them, the establishment of a family system where everyone is safe and not subject to violence is a struggle. Although Rakeesh has the more serious anger problem, both he and Roslyn tend to let disagreements between them escalate out of control. Their conversation level improved markedly when we presented the chapter "Say It With Feeling," including

BOX 24.2

HANDLING CRITICISM

Criticism—Can You Take It Without Anger?

Criticism is rarely given in the proper way. When we criticize another person we are forgetting that they are the only one who can change themselves and will not do so no matter how much pressure you put on them—unless they want to. The only way that we can do this at all is to come from our own feelings about what is going on. If we have a friend who drinks too much, we have to come from our feelings about that. "John, when you drink as much as you do, I feel scared. I'm afraid that you will say or do something to people who do not care about you. At the club, that could start a fight or worse! The thought of that gets me sick to my stomach."

When the shoe is on the other foot, we sometimes blow up because of the words of others that degrade us, put us down, somehow intimate that we are defective. I maintain that we must set boundaries when someone comes at us with "You sure did a lousy job last week when we played that ball game against the guys from the other town." The answer could be, "You know that game is over, I learned a lot about the position, and I refuse to hear about it now. I'm ready for the next game; how about you?" In this way you have set your boundary, taken better care of yourself, and do not have to beat yourself up about how you played.

Responses

✓ Part of dealing with criticism is being able to express yourself without starting conflict. The use of "I" statements and feelings that you are having is one way to work with unwanted criticism. What are the feelings you have about criticism? How have you used "I" statements to talk to one another?
✓ In case you forgot: "I" statements are used in four parts:

A. "When you . . ."
B. " I feel . . ."
C. "Because . . ."
D. "What I prefer is . . ."

✓ Take different scenarios in your life and rephrase what you said into this format using the list of feeling words.

the exercise on how to respond constructively to criticism (Box 24.2). Both Rakeesh and Roslyn report that they now have a more balanced relationship with fewer arguments and no violent outbursts on his part. He continues to be substance free and to be more interested in compromise than domination. Court involvement, while embarrassing and financially costly for both of them, has been a "wake-up call," and his continued participation in the group provides positive reinforcement for peaceful behavior.

Other Programs

Peace Creations reaches parents at many levels through both community-based programs and those for incarcerated parents. The QUEST© program we developed has just been certified by the Ohio Department of Rehabilitation and Corrections as a "prerelease" program. It is also the main component for parenting groups at Santa Rita County Jail in California and halfway houses and faith-based programs in Florida, Oklahoma, Ohio, and Texas.

The facilitator-led process is designed to address issues of life choices, responsibility, family violence, anger and reduction of anger, communication skills, relationships, and parenting. Through group interaction and individual workbooks, the participants can identify and track their personal progress toward becoming a better partner, parent, and individual. The process leads to *recognition* of behaviors that are detrimental to the individual, their relationships, or others around them; *response* to the many choices that can make positive change for their lives; *replacement* of old behaviors with new skills for meeting life's challenges; *reinforcement* of behaviors that are good for the participants by practicing with other group members; and *reproduction* of the newfound way of being in the "world," where positive behavior becomes an integral part of life and positive change begins to happen. The QUEST© program (Chapman, 2005) has been developed for domestic violence groups, parenting groups, and anger management groups both in and out of custody.

REFERENCES

Chapman, T. (2005). *Quest workbook*. Available from the author at peacecreations@yahoo.com

Cummings, E. M., & Davies, P. (2002). Effects of marital conflict on children: recent advances and emerging themes in process-oriented research. *Journal of Child Psychology and Psychiatry, 43*(1), 31–63.

Dinkmeyer, D., & McKay, M. (1983). The parent guide: STEP teen, systematic training for effective parenting of teens. Circle Pines, MN: American Guidance Service.

Gutierrez, K. (2000). *Male batterers and their children: Transmission of narcissistic wounding and violent coping*. Unpublished doctoral dissertation.

Hamel, J. (2005). *Gender inclusive treatment of intimate partner abuse: A comprehensive approach*. New York: Springer.

Kitzmann, K., Gaylord, N., Holt, A., & Kenny E. (2003). Child witnesses to domestic violence: A meta-analytic review. *Journal of Consulting and Clinical Psychology, 71*(2), 339–352.

Langhinrichsen-Rohling, J., Neidig, P., & Thorn, G. (1995). Violent marriages: Gender differences in levels of current violence and past abuse. *Journal of Family Violence, 10*(2), 159–175.

Mahoney, A., Donnelly, W. O., Boxer, P., & Lewis, T. (2003). Marital and severe parent-to-adolescent physical aggression in clinic-referred families: Mother and adolescent reports on co-occurrence and links to child behavior problems. *Journal of Family Psychology, 17*(1), 3–19.

Margolin, G., & Gordis, E. B. (2003). Co-occurrence between marital aggression and parents' child abuse potential: The impact of cumulative stress. *Violence and Victims, 18*(3), 243–258.

Repetti, R., Taylor, S. E., & Seeman, T. E. (2002). Risky families: Family social environments and the mental and physical health of offspring. *Psychological Bulletin, 128*(2), 330–366.

Salzinger, S., Feldman, R., Ing-mak, D., Majica, E., Stockhammer, T., & Rosario, M. (2002). Effects of partner violence and physical child abuse on child behavior: A study of abused and comparison children. *Journal of Family Violence, 17*(1), 23–52.

Schore, A. (1994). *Affect regulation and the origin of the self: The neurobiology of emotional development*. Hillsdale, NJ: Lawrence Erlbaum Associates.

Seigel, D. (1999). *The developing mind: How relationships and the brain interact to shape who we are*. New York: Guilford Press.

Straus, M. (1992, September). *Children as witnesses to marital violence: A risk factor for lifelong problems among a nationally representative sample of American men and women*. Report of the Twenty-Third Ross Roundtable: On Critical Approaches to Common Pediatric Problems, M5796, Columbus, OH.

Straus, M., & Donelly, D. (2001). *Beating the devil out of them*. New Brunswick, NJ: Transaction Publishers.

Straus, M., & Smith, C. (1990). Family patterns and child abuse. In M. Strauss & R. Gelles (Eds.), *Physical violence in American families* (pp. 245–261). New Brunswick, NJ: Transaction Publishers.

Wolak, J., & Finkelhor, D. (1998). Children exposed to partner violence. In J. Jasinski & L. Williams (Eds.), *Partner violence: A comprehensive review of 20 years of research* (pp. 73–112). Thousand Oaks, CA: Sage.

CHAPTER 25

Healing Child Victims and Their Parents in the Aftermath of Family Violence

Christina M. Dalpiaz

The dynamics of parenting in the aftermath of traumatic events such as family violence are unlike any other. In previous years, children's behaviors and emotional development were rarely correlated with their exposure to partner violence, so this problem was seldom addressed. Now, however, victims fleeing violence are reaching out for resources to protect and help their children through the trauma they experienced. The increased demands for services have led many researchers and child experts into new, uncharted territories. The rise in behavioral problems from abused children has increased substantially, and the system is scrambling to find prevention and intervention strategies to aid these families. It seems no matter how diligently the community works to find solutions and generate programs, more victims are surfacing. We are experiencing an epidemic where the needs of these families often exceed the resources.

At this point, research is still sparse regarding the dynamics of family violence, and what little is available is often misunderstood. For example, many people suppose that domestic violence refers to a physical altercation between two adults. By doing so, they gravely underestimate the impact that other forms of abuse (e.g., emotional or financial) have on families. Because these less conspicuous abuses produce no physical scars, they are often ignored or discounted. The reality, however, is that the emotional assaults often become predictors for future physical violence, and they need to be taken more seriously. Thus, the answer to eliminating later physical assaults is to interrupt the nonphysical precursors in the earlier stages. In addition to changing how abuse is perceived, the system must respond differently so that the possibility of physical violence may be lessened.

This begins with redefining domestic violence and then reevaluating its players. Until recently, little attention was given to its impact on child development. The definition of and the response to family violence for the most part excluded children. Unfortunately, professionals are now finding a correlation between witnessing violence and subsequent behavioral problems, suggesting that the severe conflict between parents significantly impacts children's physical, emotional, and social development (see chapter 8, this volume). Some researchers now believe that witnessing physical and other forms of abuse against a parent may in some cases be more devastating than experiencing the violence firsthand. It seems reasonable to conclude that children should be recognized as primary victims. My intent is to alert families and professionals to the problem of all forms of interparental abuse, to demonstrate the lasting impact it has on child development, and then to provide strategies that change outcomes not only for children but for society as well. But first we must evaluate how the psychological dynamics contribute to the physical violence.

POPULAR TERMINOLOGY: THE BUZZWORDS

Power and *control* are the two buzzwords most often expressed when describing the dynamics of family violence. Usually, these two words have a negative connotation. Professionals would agree that many batterers seek to manipulate their families through power and control. Although this is so, it might be helpful to understand why manipulative behavior is necessary in the first place. Rather than believing that power and control are always the problem, we can instead acknowledge that everyone, on some level, needs a sense of power and control over their lives and thus see these as possible solutions. The key is teaching abusive parents and partners how to manage, express, and meet their needs more positively and appropriately so that the strong-armed approach is no longer necessary. It is my opinion that most people do not intentionally want to hurt their families—but because of generational learning and social tolerance, it is what they know. When new positive skills are introduced, it gives abusive parents new tools and choices that were not previously available.

Because so little is known about how to handle family violence cases, abusers and their victims are rarely provided with effective replacement skills. Consequently, the pendulum swings from aggression (severe punishment) to passivity (no punishment), which is equally as dysfunctional. One father professed that he could no longer control his teenage daughter (i.e., hitting her) anymore because he feared going back to jail. Although he had attended a batterers' treatment program twice, he had not been given replacement tools to guide his child. He admittedly felt helpless (loss of power and control), and his daughter saw it as "payback time." Without the necessary replacement skills, the family dynamics simply shifted the abusive behavior from one family member to another, and nothing was resolved.

EXAMPLE 1

An abusive wife who exercised power and control over her battered husband forced him to "discipline" the children, or she would do it for him. Ironically, to keep the kids "safer" (his power and control), he would inflict the spankings so that their punishment wasn't so harsh. She eventually turned him in for abusing the kids, and he was court-ordered into treatment. This man had no self-confidence. Fearful of everyone, he maintained no eye contact, and his body language suggested that he was terrified of social interactions. Almost every sentence out of his mouth was "I am sorry." After the relationship ended, his ex-wife wanted to maintain the status quo, so she coerced their three sons into abusing their father—using the same threatening tactics that she used earlier against them.

To help boost his confidence, he was taught how to change his bodily stance. He would be gently reminded to look toward the treatment provider when addressing her. Over time, as he began to believe that he would not be judged or punished, he was able to interact more socially with others. Unfortunately, however, he was forced to give up his parental rights because the court saw the children's violence against their father as a "clear sign" that they had been abused by him and were merely retaliating.

There are several reasons why people use power and control to get their needs met. The first is that they have learned (mostly through modeling) that physical or emotional abuse are the *only* ways to be heard and that coercion is the most effective and immediate way to meet their *requests*. The second is that abusers may not trust their environment enough to meet their needs, so they feel compelled to be in control of everything and everyone. Finally, batterers may not consciously recognize that they can and do deserve to get their needs met the right way. These concepts apply to victims as well. Teaching victims how to get their needs met appropriately can also help interrupt the cycle of violence. When both parents become healthy, they can provide a secure and positive environment for the entire family.

CHANGING THE IMPACT ABUSE HAS ON PARENT–CHILD RELATIONSHIPS

In this section, I discuss how to assist parents with changing the relationship they have with their children. Because parenting children is a skill, techniques are provided to modify the parent–child interaction for both violent and victimized parents.

Violent Parents

The first step is to help offending parents understand that positive alternatives are available to them. Batterers typically have well-defended egos, making them resistant to new ideas and impeding progress, so trust needs to be established between the treatment provider and the offender. Many clients report feeling defensive, and most admit that they personalize any outside criticism. The answer, then, lies in finding ways to redirect bad behavior without offending the perpetrator personally. Instead of changing who the abusers are, the strategy should be to change what they do or how they behave (see chapter 24 in this volume). When the behavior is separated from the person, a client seems more receptive to change and less resistant to treatment.

No matter how dysfunctional the parent–child relationship might seem to outsiders, it is no less a lasting connection. Without intervention strategies, the impact the abusers have on their children can be psychologically detrimental with permanent consequences. It is widely accepted that the closer the bond is between batterers and their children, the more traumatic the experience becomes. Kids deeply personalize abuse by a "loved" one and struggle with the conflicting emotions generated by their polarized feelings (fear and love). The objective, then, should be to assist abusers with changing the bond they share with their children. Even in the most severe cases of abuse, children are willing to forgive their batterers because they want their parents' love and validation. When parents acknowledge their mistakes and work toward learning more effective methods of parenting, their children tend to recover more easily.

Victimized Parents

Effective parenting skills for victimized parents require a reorganization of roles and expectations. When they were living with the abusers, victimized parents had little power to make decisions or choices for their families. Children may adopt an abusive style and rationalize to themselves that victims deserve what they get. Altering this mentality is challenging but not futile. Victims should be warned that children might initially be resistant to new limitations or rules but that with persistence they will adjust. Kids are looking for boundaries, consistency, and fairness. When these needs are provided, over time, children become more receptive to the adjustments. Victimized parents have to take back their position in their families before established dysfunctional patterns and mind-sets can be modified.

The children's natural presumption might be that their victimized parents were unable to keep them out of harm's way, so the kids distrust them. As the new heads of households, the victimized parents must see to it that trust is rebuilt. The twofold challenge for treatment providers is to convince the children that the victimized parents can now be their protectors, and to assist the parents in acquiring the skills to be alert, engaged, and protective. Parents should be warned that their children might feel safe enough in their new environment to emote more freely and that they need to be adequately prepared for the meltdowns that come in the aftermath of family violence.

When parenting abused children alone, especially when burdened with guilt, the tendency is for the victimized parent to let children slip into adult roles, which ultimately confuses everyone in the family. Although mutual respect is essential in any relationship, victims must remember that parent-child relationships are not equal. Ultimately, the goal should be to transfer responsibility back to the victimized parents by providing instruction on how to build self esteem so that they will feel empowered and make choices that feel right for them. Most victims express self-doubt due to the conditioning they experienced during their abusive relationship. As a result, some victims may rely too heavily on what others think, and this can impede progress toward self-reliance. The caution here should be that when victims are overdependent on others for decisions, it places them back in their past role. They need to be encouraged to hear what others think without giving up their opinions entirely.

Since victimized parents often suffer from lowered self-esteem and other emotional issues, their progress may be hindered. Therefore, it is important that they identify the characteristics that could limit their ability to be successful parents and that they receive help to overcome them.

Characteristics of Victims

To help victimized parents be more effective, the treatment provider must first recognize the character attributes that develop as a result of persistent emotional and physical assault. Next, the treatment provider needs to address these traits individually to change the parent–child dynamic. A checklist of victims' attributes from *Mental Disorders of the New Millennium* (Dalpiaz, in press), as well as definitions and possible intervention strategies, are outlined next.

✓ *Depression—manifests through a sense of helplessness and/or hopelessness*

Helplessness is generated by the victim's past environment. To help clients combat helplessness and depression and acquire a greater sense of purpose, treatment providers must encourage them to build stronger support systems and develop well-thought-out plans of action. Depressive symptoms are alleviated when individuals become empowered. Direct them to enroll in supportive counseling and interactive classes, listen to motivational talks, and read inspirational books. In severe cases a referal for intensive psychotherapy or a medication evaluation may also be necessary.

✓ *Anxiety/hypervigilant reactions—mimic hyperactivity or learning difficulties*

Anxiety causes individuals to have racing thoughts that make focusing difficult and sometimes can lead to panic attacks. Anxiety can be overcome by practicing relaxation techniques, such as yoga and meditation, or through other physical activities, such as exercise and running. Breathing normally and rhythmically is essential in reducing anxiety and gives the mind the opportunity to slow down and redirect its focus.

✓ *Poor self-image—victims behave the way they feel; unwilling to excel or be self-reliant*

Poor self-image is a result of negative external input, such as put-downs, constant criticism, and statements intended to shame and invalidate. The old information must be discounted and replaced. An obvious first step in improving one's self-image would be for the individual to remove him- or herself from such abuse and to find more healthy relationships. In addition, victims can benefit from techniques that encourage internal input and assistance with verbally acknowledging any positive attributes they already have. Provide them with exercises that promote positive affirmations and help them value themselves.

✓ *Incompetence— inadequacy created through constant berating or emotional browbeatings*

Feelings of incompetence can be debilitating. Teach clients strategies to change these feelings through programs such as wilderness training, assertiveness classes, or team-building exercises. Initially, any strategies used should be fun and easily mastered so that victims can experience success. Accomplishing short-term goals first builds competencies for the more difficult long-term challenges.

✓ *Fear of failure—victims learn that making mistakes has grave consequences, so they either avoid trying or strive for perfection, believing they can manage the violence*

Fear on any level is paralyzing, but fear of failure tops the list. Many victims learn that even the simplest mistakes can jeopardize their safety. Introducing fear reduction exercises that encourage mistakes should help. For example, families can participate in games or activities where the goal is to have fun and not worry about who wins or loses. Rather than concentrating on "why" the individuals did something wrong, a strategy-building exercise that focuses on "what" they can do next time to change the outcome might be better. Asking the question "what" versus "why" sets clients up to focus on future problem solving rather than past blaming. Teach them to laugh at themselves and incorporate the old adage "We are laughing with you, not at you." They have personalized the severe criticism inflicted on them and need help lightening up.

✓ *Poor social skills—leads to inadequate relationship skills*

Poor social skills, a direct consequence of being isolated from external interaction, can be enhanced when adult and child victims are educated on how to select friends and establish healthy relationships. Because the violent interaction was so ingrained in them, they now perceive abusive relationships as normal and may feel some discomfort with relating to the new style of interaction. Teach them how to verbalize their needs and include themselves in the relationship — this will be key to changing how they relate to others.

✓ *Poor eye contact—generates detachment issues and potential pathologies*

Poor eye contact is due, in part, to the fear that connecting emotionally to anyone can provoke violence and subsequently pain. Therefore, individuals must learn how to trust that their environment is safe enough for them to interact with others. Because animals are nonjudgmental and are most often submissive, treatment providers should start by introducing exercises where victims look into the eyes of nonthreatening animals (e.g., a bunny). Once they feel comfortable, the next step is for victims to connect with their children. If the kids have poor eye contact, they might need to follow the same protocol as their victimized parents by also beginning with something less threatening. The inability to connect with others can result in later pathologies; therefore, making eye contact is a must for these traumatized families.

✓ *Overreactive startle response—victims fear severe repercussions because of relentless abuse; body is held in a high state of arousal*

An overreactive startle response usually means that victims are always ready for an attack. They live in constant fear because their environment is so unpredictable and explosive. The only way to overcome this response is for them to stop being afraid. This occurs when the victims are assured that they are genuinely safe. To help them reduce the intense fear, direct clients to stress management classes or, if appropriate, to self-defense training.

✓ *Inadequate protective factors—victims believe that they cannot protect their children or themselves or minimize danger*

Inadequate protective factors occur when victims have bought into their batterers' mind-set and have rationalized that the situation "isn't that bad." Or—for whatever reason—they feel that they can somehow control the violent environment, so they lack the protective instincts needed to keep their kids safe. Because of the mounting dysfunction that occurs with the escalation of violence, the boundaries between healthy and unhealthy interaction may become blurred and children may be unwittingly placed in harm's way to the point of severe neglect or abuse. Victims should learn how to protect their children against any scarring—whether visible or not—that could potentially cause lasting damage. An example might be when a victim permits a perpetrator to watch the children even though a restraining order restricts contact. The victim may feel that the abuser is doing better and may choose to ignore the potential danger. Building verbal, emotional, and physical protective factors that ensure children's future safety is a must.

✓ *Poor impulse control—forms when internal needs are met through external sources that can never be satiated*

Poor impulse control is developed over time and usually starts in childhood. The body learns to regulate itself by searching for means to fulfill the empty emotional needs within it (e.g., food or shopping). Curbing these feelings for clients means teaching them skills that promote internal satisfaction. With children, start by giving them opportunities to earn privileges over an extended period of time rather than instantly. This forces them to wait and teaches them to depend on their internal value for reward because the external reward is not immediately accessible. The goal is to get the victims to meet their internal needs with internal resources (e.g., pride and confidence).

✓   *Meltdowns—victims react inappropriately because of an inability to cope with stress*

Meltdowns occur as a direct result of not being able to manage emotions. Usually, frustration levels run high and coping skills low. Take, for example, a child who fails a test or is teased by a classmate for making a mistake. This experience might be a painful reminder of how his batterer relentlessly called him a stupid loser. His reaction might be exaggerated to the point that he cusses at someone or hits his desk. Providing this child with replacement skills (e.g., communication or conflict management skills) for his inappropriate behaviors should help him deal with his emotions and reduce the frequency and intensity of these overwhelming episodes.

✓   *Regressive behavior—reversion to a younger age that may be inappropriate (e.g., bed-wetting or thumb sucking)*

Regressive behavior is most evident in child victims but can also occur with adults. Unable to cope with their current violent situation, victims will often use emotional avoidance by reverting to a stage in their lives when they felt protected or cared for. For example, children may begin bed-wetting, thumb sucking, or baby babbling, whereas adults may become shy and withdrawn like an awkward teenager. In either case, the victims are attempting to preclude their situation through an unhealthy emotional escape because they might genuinely believe that the earlier stages were a safer time. Essentially, people behave the way they feel; therefore, if they feel incompetent or helpless, then they act those feelings out. The emotional deprivation that caused them to regress requires certain needs to be met again before they can feel safe enough to return to their chronological age. For example, when children have experienced traumatic events, the parents may need to rock their kids to sleep or hold them more often for comfort. When they feel safe enough, they will want to move forward. Victims cannot be forced back into their chronological age; therefore, patience and compassion are needed until they are emotionally ready.

✓ *Passive or passive-aggressive behavior—victims express self-defeating or improper behavior because of low self-esteem and self-worth; believe they do not deserve to have needs met appropriately*

Passive or passive-aggressive behavior indicates that an individual does not feel deserving. Motivating clients to get their needs more effectively requires that they are provided with communication and conflict management skills. When victims believe that they have the right to speak out without severe repercussions, they can move toward assertive behaviors. The treatment provider's job is a daunting one, and helping clients identify self-defeating traits and develop strategies to combat them takes some ingenuity.

Because victims often feel so badly about themselves, they do not believe they are worthy of love or praise. Penetrating these embedded emotional filters might be challenging. To protect what little ego they have left, victims may withdraw from or reject others before they can be rejected. Having drawn the conclusion that they simply cannot trust their environment and anticipating problems, they tend to disengage and avoid social opportunities. Victims need to recognize that those who were abusive, negative, and cruel were unjust. They will need encouragement to recognize that their requests were not unreasonable and that loved ones should want to meet their needs. That's what relationships are all about.

Survivors of family violence build walls around their lives to protect themselves from being revictimized. They unwittingly shut the world out in order to protect themselves against vulnerabilities. A victim once proclaimed, "I will never let another man take me to a fancy dinner . . . I am not giving him a chance to trick me." Comments such as this one say, "I was weak for believing that this was real." These strong emotions are impacting not only the choices victims make but also their behaviors.

Characteristics of Children Who Have Witnessed/ Experienced Family Violence

Children in the aftermath of family violence have emotional issues that impede their ability to process and react effectively to the world around them. The severity and duration of the trauma and the amount of support they get will determine how children cope with their experience. Initially, these children are mistrustful, apprehensive, and fearful. How they react to those feelings, however, varies from one child to the next. Some act out aggressively and defiantly question the most insignificantly minute requests. Take, for instance, a teacher who announces to the class that they have 10 pages of reading for homework. The mistrusting child does not want anyone to control her, so she blurts out, "Why do we have to do that?" or "That's stupid, I am not going to do it." Over time, this persistent reaction compounds existing problems in the adult–child relationship and generates negative assumptions regarding the child's disposition that are then reflected in the adult's interaction with the child. As the child internalizes how the adult feels, her sense of efficacy decreases, oppositional behavior persists, and negative self-concepts are negatively reinforced. Eventually, the dynamics of this relationship spread to other facets of her life. Without different input, she will ultimately stop caring about everything, make poor choices, and continue on a destructive course.

On the other hand, some children become passive, making them target practice by malicious others so that the abuse is not only occurring at home but happening in other social settings as well. These children become viewed as unimportant, and their trauma usually goes unnoticed because they are not acting out. Whether children are aggressive or passive, the bottom line is that they are wearing their emotions on their sleeves for the whole world to see. They require help in changing their responses and interactions to others.

Treatment providers need to understand the children's cognitive processing *before* they can change any behaviors. Children from violence have cluttered and busy minds that run a mile a minute. Their thoughts race with anxiety and fear, and their focus scatters in every direction. Their minds are cluttered, and so are their rooms. The way they live is the way they feel. They may therefore need assistance with organizing their lives, cleaning up the chaos, and creating a sense of serenity.

Peaceful surroundings are not so familiar to children living in violence. They struggle with their emotions, and their inability to cope with the trauma often leads to inappropriate behavior. Therefore, skills must be introduced that can help them learn better coping mechanisms and increase their chances of being successful. Although we can take children out of a violent environment, it takes years to take the violent environment out of them (Dalpiaz, 2004). Tolerance for their poor coping abilities is necessary to see them survive this devastation; using an authoritarian or hard-nosed approach with them simply does not work. Punishing these emotionally bruised children only reinforces how they already feel (bad), and serves to reinforce negative self-perceptions and acting-out behavior. Alternatives such as reward and praise should be considered, as well as substituting punishments, such as having children earn their privileges in lieu of taking them away. Adults need to be patient during any new changes and remember that behavior can be learned—or unlearned. Parents should be reminded that children are apt to make good things better rather than make bad things good.

Modifying child behaviors requires adults to see the situations through the eyes of the children and respect their perception. While disciplining, adults may not think that they are scary or intimidating, to battered children they are. As a result, many children expect conflict and prepare for the worse. They are walking around with their fists raised, ready to take on anything or anyone. They see any confrontations as dangerous. Their reactions to others can be compared to a pot of water near its boiling point. The treatment provider's job is to reduce the heat. Otherwise, the argument increases the emotional boiling point where everything spills over and makes a mess, and someone ultimately gets burned.

Children in this high state of arousal have soaring stress levels along with an overwhelming sense of helplessness that make it difficult for them to manage their emotions. To help them be more receptive to criticism or correction, they will need a calm, nonthreatening environment. Assisting them with learning how to trust and have regard for themselves requires an authoritative and lovingly firm approach. Using negotiation and compromise works best for most kids, but children from family violence especially benefit from this approach because it give them back some of the control they lost while exposed to the abuse.

GENERATING PLANS TO MEET CHILDREN'S GOALS

Every child affected by family violence has some degree of lowered self-regard. The emotional abuse has taken its toll on them and eroded their confidence and their self-image. Many experience a deep fear of failure, and they give up more easily when they anticipate making mistakes. The stories that some children have disclosed about their experiences are so outrageous that people not familiar with their situation would find them incomprehensible. Consider the following case.

EXAMPLE 2

A child reported that his mother's boyfriend severely beat his puppy because he forgot to let her out to go to the bathroom. The batterer felt the child should learn a lesson about responsibility and how it affects others. The message the abuser gave to this young boy was that when a person makes mistakes, someone else suffers the consequences. For abused children, the punishments are far more severe than they need to be.

Experiences such as this contribute exponentially to children's self-images. Their fear of failure is often overpersonalized when they make mistakes. These children have a strong sense of inadequacy and may avoid trying anything that could potentially set them up for criticism or failure. They will need to be encouraged to fail and be okay with it. This starts by raising their self-esteem so they don't associate their mistakes with who they are.

Esteem-Building Exercises

High self-esteem is important to developmental growth. To assist those who lack good esteem, therapists should use exercises that promote positive feelings.

EXAMPLE 3

A young man in counseling grew anxious when asked verbally to acknowledge some of his positive attributes in exchange for monetary rewards. Although he could gain a coin for each item he could list, he struggled with this exercise because throughout his entire life he had heard only criticism. He could define himself only as bad, yet, when asked, he could not verbalize why he felt that way. The treatment provider initiated the exercise by provoking the child, declaring traits that were blatantly untrue about the boy, such as "I know why you're bad . . . you're bad because you steal cars and you beat people up." As the incited child emphatically denied each allegation, he was rewarded with a coin. As negative traits were discounted and positive attributes acknowledged, the pile of coins mounted. The treatment provider's outrageous examples continued until the child was able to note the positive traits without assistance. When the exercise was complete, he was asked to look at the two piles and pretend that the traits belong to someone else. Then he was asked whether he thought this person was a good or a bad person. His response was, "I would have to say that he's good."

EXAMPLE 4

The treatment provider can use symbols to serve as esteem builders. In one case, a young boy was removed from his parents, both of whom had been violent towards each other and towards him, and placed in foster care. He felt scared, rejected, and unwanted. These feeling became so embedded within him that he felt unworthy of attention or love. The treatment provider decided that this boy needed to be recognized for the strides that he had made in treatment, so she purchased a trophy and inscribed it, "To the bravest guy I know." Obviously, this token piece of metal could not remove all the pain he had, but it did serve as a visual reminder that he was much more than he had ever imagined.

Children believe in symbols like lucky rocks, charm bracelets, and certificates of achievements. In a world that has punished and admonished them for so long, they need something tangible to hold on to—something that can serve as a constant reminder that they are something great.

EXAMPLE 5

To promote healthier self-images, a safe place to start is with the written word rather than through verbal praise. When children are not accustomed to praise, it will seem foreign and uncomfortable. An abused mother asked for help with changing her communication with her son. The relationship had been rocky, and any positive interaction between the two was rare. The mother was asked to purchase a notebook and place it in plain sight where she could record her son's personal achievements. She worked on this list for 1 week and then reported happily that not only did her son appreciate the list, but the boy reciprocated by making a list of her positive attributes. This exercise served two functions: to raise esteem and to show just how powerful role modeling can be.

Some children, when given praise, withdraw and become uncomfortable. The emotional conflict they feel is likely based on being told that they are good when they have been conditioned, for so long, to think otherwise. Therefore, children recovering from abuse may not always be ready to hear verbal praise, so using the previously mentioned exercise might be safer for them because it is less direct and confrontational. When children are not placed in a situation where they have to respond to the accolades, they may be able to embrace the acclaims by viewing the compliments when others are not present. Although the ultimate goal is verbal praise, some children need to address their emotional safety first.

Competency Building

Building competence and confidence requires children to move beyond their current set of emotions and work toward acquiring more positive feelings. It takes many adults to raise a child—not just the parents. Because many victimized parents were isolated and the few role models available to their children were often unhealthy and unsafe, it is essential that these children be introduced to others who can help redirect their lives. Find neutral adults who are not currently familiar with the children's background. Athletic coaches or adult mentors, such as those from the Big Brothers and Big Sisters program, are among the unbiased strangers who can be helpful in allowing children greater opportunities to create new self-images. The old proverb "This project needs a new set of eyes" fits nicely here. We all know that children act better for other people than they do for their parents. They need a chance to participate in activities where their parents are not involved and allowed to associate with others who have no preconceived ideas about who they are or who they "should" be. This provides them with opportunities to practice a different way of living. It also frees them to be who they really want to be.

As mentioned earlier, taking the violent environment out of children takes time. Because a great deal of damage has been inflicted on their psyches, they will need to develop coping mechanisms, boundaries, and emotional safety nets. The residual effects of violence last long after the family has left their abuser and follow the victims wherever they go. Victims and their children will feel suspicious and fearful of others until they can let go of the past. Teaching them to be interactive with others after violence can prove challenging. Most have experienced severe emotional deprivation, which dampens their sense of worth. They will need assistance in learning how to combat these emotions.

To enhance a child's self-confidence, have him or her do role-playing exercises in a darkened room or with a blindfold. This exercise requires caution and should be done under safe conditions and only when the child feels comfortable enough to participate. The premise behind eliminating visual connection is that, by preventing the child from seeing the reactions of others, he or she can work toward overcoming his fear of them. For victimized children, even positive social situations can be intimidating because they feel unworthy of being treated nicely. Teach them to interact more appropriately by introducing exercises where they are asked to greet others by looking them straight in the eye, smiling, and returning the salutation. Again, preparing them for the anticipated anxiety is important—if they know it is coming, they can brace themselves. So warn them that this exercise might be scary the first few times they try it and that their new, positive interaction might feel somewhat funny. But also let them know that once they master this exercise, they can overcome some of their bad feelings.

Another exercise that promotes a better self-image is to have them watch themselves, privately, in a mirror for five minutes twice a day for several days. Initially, children will struggle with this exercise and feel extremely uncomfortable because they have been conditioned to loathe themselves. But it is imperative that these feelings change. Once the children have mastered looking at themselves privately, the next step is to have them go to a public restroom and repeat the exercise. In the beginning, perhaps they could look at themselves only when no one is around them, but eventually they will need to be able to accomplish looking at themselves while in the company of others.

Cognitive Processing: Arranging Thoughts

The challenges of working with victimized children are obviously greater the longer they remain in their volatile environment. According to Johnson (1998), children produce a negative internal dialogue that matches with and that is a result of the negative input. Consequently, victimized children are much more apt to acknowledge criticism than to accept praise. Positive integration exercises should be provided to allow new affirmative information to replace the negative embedded input.

EXAMPLE 6

An adolescent girl, diagnosed with bipolar disorder and failing academically and socially in school, was ordered into treatment. She had been exposed to family violence her entire life. She had seen her mother punch and slap her father on several occasions, and both parents had abused her verbally. Their harsh criticisms and put downs reinforced her low self-image. She reported having been taunted and berated, both at home and in school where her peers called her derogatory names because of her diagnosis. Initially, her negative dialogue focused exclusively on her disorder and her weight (one side effect of lithium). The therapeutic strategy was to identify other positive qualities that she possessed and work toward overcoming the diagnosis. The girl was asked to generate a list of positive attributes that could redefine her, then to write the disorder in the middle of a piece of paper in small print and circle it. Next, the treatment provider drew extending lines from the circle and added the positive traits (purposely making the positive qualities larger in print). Seeing how the diagnosis was overpowered by the other characteristics, the young girl became excited. The schematic was copied and strategically placed throughout the house to serve as visual reminders that she was so much more than her diagnosis.

During the next session, she made a beaded bracelet where each bead represented an attribute listed on the schematic. After two months, her mother reported that the young girl was excelling in school both academically and socially and that her behavior at home improved immensely.

The previously mentioned technique illustrates just how much children need adult guidance to discern and process external input. Prior to treatment, this young girl readily believed any unwarranted criticism inflicted on her. She needed an adult to help her recognize her true internal value. Emotional growth is progressive, and often children, especially from abusive homes, lack the maturity to discern truths from untruths, making them susceptible to developing poor self-images. Intervention strategies, such as the one previously mentioned, can assist with these vulnerabilities and help children understand their own value. Acquiring an adequate level of coping skills permits children to reject any negative input thrown at them. The following case explains how to promote positive coping skills.

EXAMPLE 7

A young girl recently removed from her home after being physically assaulted by her alcoholic mother, was threatened with expulsion from school because of fighting. When asked why she hit other children, she responded, "They call me names, so I have to hit them." This young girl's internal dialogue was negative. To change the belief system, a role-playing exercise was designed to teach her that she did not have to accept what the others were saying. The treatment provider warned the girl that she would be calling her names and that each time she heard the names, the girl needed to repeat the following silently in her mind: "I don't have to believe that." After several minutes of name-calling, the girl began to smile. At that point, the treatment provider told her to say the phrase as loud as she could in her head so that no names being said out loud could get in. The exercise continued for several more minutes. Weeks later, the mother reported that while her daughter was playing with play dough, her cousin called her a loser. The young girl ignored the usual negative internal dialogue, looked up from her activity, and retorted out loud, "I don't have to believe that." The coping strategy appeared to be successful. In addition, the girl's behavior in school improved.

This exercise, which helped the young girl determine whether others really deserved credibility, can also be used to help children with difficult adults. Many children referred to treatment have problems with their teachers because of "inappropriate" behavior. Because teachers are authority figures, these children must learn to react in a balanced way. They should be instructed to sit quietly during the negative criticism and be respectful but be encouraged to understand that, although they may have to *take it,* they do not have to *take it in* and personalize what the adults are saying (Dalpiaz, 2004). Children should be able to present their concerns to their parents so their issues can be dealt with on a more even playing field.

Big Picture Concepts

Abused children do not have the ability to process information globally, and they see every situation as distinct and separate. Consequently, they react to each circumstance independently and, often, inappropriately. Teaching children how to recognize the big picture requires that parents help them obtain an overall view of their situation. For example, when an abused child scores badly on a test, the likelihood is that he or she might focus only on the grade. The adults must break down the day to find something positive for this child to concentrate on that would give him a sense of accomplishment. For instance, by praising a child for having kept his room clean or playing quietly with his brother, the adults are reminding him that there was more to the day than just a bad grade. With patience and effort, adults can help children change their negative perspectives and see the "brighter" side of things.

Teaching the big-picture concept to abusers is also important and can be very effective. The majority of abusers were also abused children who never adopted a global outlook.

EXAMPLE 8

A father recommended for treatment for throwing objects and violently screaming while his son cowered in a corner was introduced to the big-picture concept. During treatment, it was disclosed that he was impulsively moody and reacted badly even when the day seemed to be going well. When he practiced utilizing the big-picture concept, he was able to learn how to view unexpected situations differently. This father wanted to stop his abusive behavior and was willing to hear his wife say, "Honey, remember the big picture." This man reported that the technique allowed him to slow down, reevaluate what he was reacting to, and redirect his focus on the positive events of the day.

Overcoming Fear of Disclosure and Building Trust

Abused and mistreated children fear the outside world's response, and they are often unwilling to share the degree of violation that they had experienced with their peers, other adults, or even their parents.

EXAMPLE 9

In one violent home, an adolescent girl who went out drinking was tied and gang-raped by a group of young men. She was fortunate enough to escape, but she never told her parents because she was more afraid of their response than of being raped. In treatment, she explained that the fear of telling her parents was so great that the traumatic violation seemed the lesser of two evils. The goal should be to help such children learn not only how to cope with the victimization but also how to develop healthy relationships with others so that they won't become isolated and further traumatized.

Traumatized children are often withdrawn emotionally and physically, and do not trust others. Because at least one parent in the family dyad lacked nurturing skills, touching, such as hugging, was absent. In fact, physical contact in violent homes often resulted in pain, so children learned to avoid contact with others to protect themselves. But the fact is that humans are social creatures by nature, and avoidance is detrimental to these children's mental health. Physical interaction is essential to increasing children's feelings of trust and safety. The unconditional affection that animals provide can often facilitate trust and help children recognize that they can share their secrets without judgment. When possible, encourage children to be responsible for animals because they can develop competency and self-esteem through contribution while at the same time developing empathy. It forces them to think about something other than their circumstances.

Happiness, Purpose and Well-Being

After the violence, victims don't immediately feel better. To reestablish a sense of well-being, they first need to find ways to be happy. As simplistic as this may seem, they have to learn how to have fun. Recently, during a court-ordered parenting class, I had the students list attributes that described what effective parenting looked like. One of the characteristics listed was fun. The class was then asked to determine whether fun was an attitude or a skill. The entire group declared that fun was a skill. With this mind-set, no wonder life after violence seems like drudgery.

With all the sadness these families have experienced, it makes sense that they might overlook happiness. To change this mind-set, the treatment provider should introduce fun activities that would make the family feel good (e.g., have parents run through sprinklers with their kids). Have parents start by randomly selecting one day each week when they imagine that this is the last day they ever get to be with their children. This exercise gives parents permission to disregard the extraneous demands that currently consume them. Clients who have consciously used this technique report that they feel better about themselves as parents.

Often, family members are not immediately aware of what makes them happy. Have them generate a list of activities that would feel good for them to do. Start with events or projects that are realistic and achievable. Initially, the daily goal should be to do a minimum of two activities (e.g., go to the zoo and ride bikes.) Most times, unhappiness is due to feeling helpless or out of control and is usually self-imposed. For instance, a father once reported resenting his children because he could no longer participate in the things he enjoyed. When he was given permission to make time for these activities, his feelings toward his children changed drastically. One way to ensure that fun happens is to get a calendar to schedule these activities. It makes sense that if people can use a planner to get obligations done, then they can get fun done as well.

Well-being can also be accomplished by getting involved in activities that make one feel useful and provide a sense of purpose, such as volunteering for a worthy cause. Doing a fund-raising walk for children, animals, or cancer patients can take some of the focus off the family's misery, allow them to contribute to society, and generate positive feelings. Mahatma Gandhi once said, "The best way to find yourself is to lose yourself in the service of others." Those who give to others gain self-value if they allow themselves to embrace their gifts.

This chapter has covered a wide range of material. It is my hope that the information provided has shed light on the devastating impact that family violence has, not only on the individuals involved, but on society as well, and that treatment providers will use the techniques suggested to help move victimized children and parents toward healing in the aftermath of the trauma they have suffered.

REFERENCES

Dalpiaz, C. (2004). *Breaking free, starting over: Parenting in the aftermath of family violence*. Westport, CT: Praeger.

Dalpiaz, C. (in press). Family violence and its degrees of deviance: Understanding the truth or paying the consequences. In T. Plante (Ed.), *Mental disorders of the new millennium* (Vol. 2). Westport, CT: Praeger.

Johnson, K. (1998). *Trauma in the lives of children*. Alameda, CA: Hunter House.

CHAPTER 26

Gender-Inclusive Work With Victims and Their Children in a Coed Shelter

Carol Ensign and Patricia Jones

Imagine being too afraid to return to your home. Imagine leaving your home in the dead of night with only the clothes on your back. Imagine sitting in your car with your children not knowing where to go or who to call. Every year, thousands of women, men, and children face these struggles, fearing the very place they live and the loved one they once trusted. The only refuge for many of these families is one of the more than 2,000 domestic violence shelters operating in the United States today, and while that number seems large, it is far from the number needed to assist the millions of victims in this country each year. Relatively speaking, animal shelters have outnumbered (and continue to outnumber) domestic violence shelters at a rate of two to one, an alarming comparison given the number of children fleeing violent homes every day.

The decision to enter a shelter is far from an easy one, and many people would find every sense of comfort challenged by the accommodations, as most exist on limited budgets and the generosity of the communities in which they operate. Shelters average in capacity anywhere from five to more than 100 beds, with some offering residential and emergency food services exclusively and others operating multifaceted programs providing services such as counseling, job development, and advocacy.

The number of shelters currently operating worldwide is undetermined; however, shelters continue to develop and have even become evident in many countries with extreme patriarchal social systems. The overall development of such a large network is impressive given the relatively "young" age of the movements that gave birth to the concept.

THE SHELTER MOVEMENT

While organized and compensated police departments have operated for well over a 100 years in the United States (e.g., New York's began in 1845), their focus has been on apprehending lawbreakers, and only relatively recently would they regard victims as anything more that an evidentiary part of a criminal act. The domestic violence shelter movement was an offspring of the larger victim advocacy movement that gained strength from the determination of the victims themselves. The idea of "victimology" was an increasing area of interest in the United States as concern for the rising crime rate was considered; subsequently, the President's Commission on Law Enforcement and the Administration of Justice were established in the 1960s. This alone, however, was not enough to illuminate the needs of domestic violence victims; indeed, it would be the women's movement that would focus attention on the victimization of women—in particular, domestic abuse and sexual assault.

Rural England was the setting for the first "victory" for the domestic violence movement with the opening of the first shelter dedicated to victims of domestic violence by Chiswick Women's Aid in 1971 under the guidance of Erin Pizzey, who would later publish the first recognized book on domestic violence from the perspective of a battered woman, *Scream Quietly or the Neighbors Will Hear* (Pizzey, 1974). The following year, the United States would follow with the opening of Haven House in Pasadena, California, and the establishment of the nation's first domestic violence hotline by the Women's Advocates in St. Paul, Minnesota.

The next decade would see a multitude of advancements addressing the issue of domestic violence: the formation of the first dedicated task force by the National Organization for Women, the first national conference hosted by the Milwaukee Task Force on Battered Women in 1976, the organization of the National Coalition Against Domestic Violence in 1978, and the dedication in October 1980 of the First Day of Unity, which would later develop into Domestic Violence Awareness Month.

Throughout these years, individual states would begin to address the variables of domestic abuse, including Oregon's 1977 legislation mandating arrest in domestic violence cases; the Minnesota law, passed in 1978, allowing probable cause arrests, regardless of whether a protection order has been issued against the offender; and the 1976 groundbreaking legislation in Nebraska abolishing the marital rape exemption (1976). Nationally, the U.S. attorney general convened the first Task Force on Family Violence in 1984, the same year the Family Violence Prevention and Services Act passed, earmarking federal funding for domestic violence programs. The following year, the U.S. surgeon general identified domestic violence as a major health problem. These efforts ultimately culminated in the passage of the Violence Against Women's Act of 1994, which enacted laws and promoted interventions for domestic violence while also emphasizing the need for continued research and program development.

The effort and findings of the multitude of pioneers working for the abolishment of domestic violence have laid the foundation for modern-day strategies that recognize the need to not only shelter victims and their children but also help them identify and develop the skills necessary to exist independent of their abusers. This is accomplished through a wide variety of programs offering emotional, psychological and financial support, job training and education, living skills development, and community education and advocacy.

THE VALLEY OASIS SHELTER: ORIGINS

The Antelope Valley Domestic Violence Council (AVDVC) was organized in 1980 at the request of the Los Angeles County Board of Supervisors. The Antelope Valley is located in the Northern High Desert area of the county and, during the 1980s, was experiencing an inordinate amount of family violence. Spearheaded by supervisor Michael Antonovich, the AVDVC was formed to address this important social problem. Through his efforts, a lifelong, free-lease on an area of county property was obtained.

Subsequent to approval of the free lease, renovation of the property, and granting of the nonprofit status, the Valley Oasis Shelter opened its doors on September 21, 1981. Since that time, the shelter has served approximately 25,000 victims of domestic violence with 24 hours of shelter services, around-the-clock crisis intervention, and meals that are prepared by the residents in their cottages. In its early years, Valley Oasis was the largest shelter in the state of California with a bed capacity of 102. The capacity has been reduced over the years to accommodate space for service programs; however, the shelter still remains one of the largest in the state. The current shelter configuration allows emergency space for 65 men, women, and children. The reputation of the shelter is nationally known, and victims from Ohio, Wisconsin, Colorado, and as far away as Florida have sought shelter with Valley Oasis.

As the domestic violence movement progressed, it became apparent that shelter was far from the only service needed by victims and their children. Counseling, peer support, education, and child care were only a few of the additional services in demand. Responding to the growing needs of victims, the AVDVC developed a variety of support programs designed to address the personal and communal challenges facing its clients. Current services include crisis intervention, transitional housing, child care, school readiness programming, peer counseling, case management, social service advocacy, legal advocacy, domestic violence education, living skills and parenting education, individual and group therapy for both adults and children, and community awareness and education.

The AVDVC has grown from its modest beginning with a start-up grant for $50,000 to its current budget of more than $3,000,000, employing an average of 45 employees and operating seven program locations. While the AVDVC is far more than a shelter, the Valley Oasis Shelter remains the agency's core program, the beginning of each victim's long journey to well-being.

THE COED MODEL

The agency's decision to accept male victims of family violence and offer them the same residential and support services offered nationwide to female victims seemed not only a practical one but also, essentially, a *necessary one*. Nowhere in the definition of violence, "the act or an instance of violent action or behavior; abusive or unjust exercise of power" (*American Heritage Dictionary*), does it state that violence is a gender-specific issue. In other words, a particular act should not be deemed violent only when perpetrated by a male. Yet, because of the feminist roots of the victims' movement, efforts to help female victims have somehow overshadowed the reality that men can be and are abused by female intimate partners. Depending on whose research you accept, the percentage of domestic violence perpetrated by women on their male partners is anywhere between 15% of the total, according to crime reports (Rennison, 2003), and 50% or more, according to most random sample surveys (Archer, 2000). The AVDVC, however, has never been compelled to pinpoint the exact percentage; the program has always been based on the belief that even one male victim in need of services is sufficient. In addition, because domestic violence perpetrated by either parent is detrimental to children (see the introduction and chapter 8 in this volume), the absence of services for victimized fathers and their children seemed to us a problem in dire need of remediation.

It cannot be overlooked that the decision of Valley Oasis to accept men was rooted in its unique configuration. While many shelters began and still remain single-unit, "dormitory" settings, the agency has been fortunate to operate in a location offering multiple housing units, thus allowing for the residential separation of male and female clients; however, it should be noted that, on occasion, capacity has forced the coed housing of clients, and no problems or objections have arisen.

COOPERATION WITH LAW ENFORCEMENT AND BATTERER INTERVENTION PROGRAMS

The Antelope Valley is in the jurisdiction of only one law enforcement agency: the Los Angeles County Sheriff. There are two stations, one in the city of Palmdale and the other in the city of Lancaster. The administrative staff of Valley Oasis has worked diligently to develop a positive relationship with law enforcement. For five years, the sheriff's department had a domestic violence response team. The team was comprised of two officers, one sergeant and one lieutenant, who were highly trained in the field of domestic violence. The agency had two domestic violence advocates who actually responded with the deputies to domestic violence calls. Over the five years the team was in operation, successful filing and prosecution of domestic violence cases rose 40%. This team was dissolved in 2003 because of state and county fiscal cutbacks. The agency continues to have advocates go to the sheriff's stations to pick up reports for follow-up calls and services. The agency staff go to monthly roll calls at both stations to answer questions the deputies may have and to provide ongoing domestic violence training. The agency has two officers from the sheriff's department on its board of directors. The trust that has been groomed over the years has been a key factor in the agency staff educating sheriff deputies to the issues, dynamics and behaviors of domestic violence victims, especially male victims. The deputies have been open to learning about male victimization and as a result have been able to identify male victims and make referrals to the agency as well as to encourage these men to go to the shelter. In addition to being given resources and referrals by law enforcement, male victims in the Antelope Valley receive more understanding and compassion from law enforcement officers. A positive result from the relationship between Valley Oasis and the sheriff's department is that deputies from other stations in Los Angeles County are aware of the services that Valley Oasis provides and not only make referrals for male victims but also, on numerous occasions, have driven them up to the shelter.

The Antelope Valley has one district attorney's office. This office has a designated domestic violence attorney who works with the agency very closely. Up until the cutbacks of 2003, the agency had a district attorney on its board of directors. The agency provides training to the district attorneys on domestic violence and male victim issues. As a result, they are accepting more cases involving male victims.

The agency has developed a close working relationship with the judges and commissioners at the courthouse. At the request of several judges, the agency has advocates at the courthouse to provide support and resources to victims. The advocates work out of an office that is shared with local attorneys. This arrangement was solicited by the attorneys and has proven successful. It has provided the advocates an opportunity to educate attorneys about issues concerning male victims. In addition, the agency has been able to meet with local judges and discuss male victim concerns and issues. This relationship has resulted in judges having an increased awareness of the dynamics and behaviors of couples in domestic violence relationships where the male is the victim, and male victims are being treated with compassion and understanding in more courtrooms.

Valley Oasis is the only domestic violence shelter in the Antelope Valley, and there are five or six batterer intervention programs. Staff members attend monthly batterer service provider meetings to discuss treatment issues of domestic violence victims and perpetrators, including male victims and female batterers, and the impact this dynamic has on children, family members, and society. Present at these meetings are also judges and attorneys.

RESPONSES FROM THE DOMESTIC VIOLENCE COMMUNITY

Valley Oasis has provided services to male victims for more than 17 years. The agency has provided these services quietly and steadily during this time, focusing on how to improve the services it provides and advocating for male victims in the local area. As this issue has risen to the forefront, the agency has been thrown into a spotlight that was not desired but from which it will not be backed down. Valley Oasis maintains the philosophy that all victims of domestic violence have the right to services and to be treated with respect and dignity. The agency also believes that domestic violence is a societal issue, not a gender issue. These beliefs challenge the original concepts and models of domestic violence. In addition, the agency's philosophy challenges the myth that only women can be victims and also challenges traditional societal gender stereotypes and roles.

Initial responses from most domestic violence advocates were those of anger and defensiveness. Comments included that men could not be victims, that domestic violence is a woman's issue, and that acknowledging that males can be victims minimized the degree of suffering and pain that women experience at the hands of men. As time has passed, the agency has had mostly positive responses to the services that are provided to men. The staff have been applauded for its work with male victims and has been asked to provide training to other domestic violence agency staff and consultation on how to run a program for male victims. We receive compliments on our courage and conviction to treat all victims of domestic violence and have earned the respect of many domestic violence programs both nationally and internationally.

RESPONSES FROM VICTIMS AND THEIR FAMILIES

Overall, victims and their families who have obtained shelter services have had a very favorable response. The coed environment of the Valley Oasis Shelter extends beyond the residents, as the agency has always employed male staff members in all capacities, including as advocates, case managers, and shelter supervisor. It is not unusual for a client who has previously resided in a different shelter program to alert staff to the presence of a "man" on grounds, often identifying a member of the maintenance staff. It is rare, however, that a client requests a transfer when assigned to a male advocate, with most welcoming feedback from a positive member of the gender. When such a transfer is requested, it is granted, as the program priority is the provision of services to clients, not gender education.

The single most important factor of the success of Valley Oasis in operating a coed shelter is without a doubt the overall agency approach, which creates a respectful environment in which all victims of domestic violence are welcome and equally served. Individual staff members who cannot reconcile stereotypical responses to male victims often resign their positions early in their employment, as it has been made clearly evident to all that bias and discrimination are unacceptable and that, essentially, "a victim is a victim is a victim."

Clients are obviously surprised to find that there is no separation in the provision of group services, with male and female victims attending group together, along with gay, lesbian, bisexual, and transgendered clients. This approach is based on the fact that battering, at its core, involves the struggle for power and control by one partner over another. Regardless of the batterer's gender, his or her objectives are all the same—to control his or her victim. We believe that gender differences can be found primarily in the particular tactics used. With this clarification, group members have welcomed the feedback received from victims of the other gender, often commenting on the benefit of being reminded that all men or all women are not approving of the violent actions of their peers.

In the residential setting, those clients with children often cite the benefit of their children being exposed to mothers and fathers who are not abusive to their family members. The playgroup often serves as place of recovery as the parents and children begin to discover moments of enjoyment while also being exposed to the positive parenting of members of the other gender.

A final benefit related by victims who have completed the Valley Oasis program is that of unbiased services. Many female victims who, encouraged by friends, family, and sometimes previous service providers, had previously expressed sentiments of "male bashing" later comment on the positive impact the discouragement of these feelings had on their ultimate healing. This was particularly important to the mothers of sons, who stated that they were often conflicted by the message of the abusive male and its impact on their sons; hence, the program's focus on the behaviors of the batterer, backed up by the presence of men during their stay, had helped them and their children correctly focus blame on the abuser, whether male or female.

SERVICES

The Valley Oasis Shelter provides a variety of services designed to provide residents with a safe environment in which to heal—emotionally, psychologically, and physically—as well as review options for themselves and their children. The shelter and Children's Services programs employ approximately 14 staff members as advocates, child care specialists, and therapists, while the agency as a whole employs an average of 45 staff members throughout the various programs. The number of clients served each year by the shelter varies in accordance with space availability (i.e., space closure due to renovation or damage as well as family size); however, the average residents per year range from 300 to 400.

Our shelter serves all victims of domestic violence regardless of age, race, ethnicity, religion, gender, sexual orientation, or socioeconomic status and has historically provided shelter to victims as old as 90 and others born during residency. While the majority of the residents originate from a 3,600-square-mile service area immediately around the shelter, residents have been received from nearly every state in search of safety or program-specific services. Unlike many other shelters, ours does not restrict the gender or ages of children residing with the parent and accepts families with adolescent boys as well as adult children residing in the violent home (adult children are registered as individual residents), with potentially at-risk situations abated by careful placement of families within the residential units and attention given to the age, gender, and history of the children in each residence. In addition, victims who have previously stayed at the shelter are welcome to return, provided that there have been no reports of violence or abuse on their part. This allowance is fairly unusual in the shelter movement because of the safety issues surrounding shelter locations; however, research indicates that a victim will most likely leave his or her abuser seven to nine times before leaving permanently. With this in mind, it seems counterproductive to limit the amount of service a resident receives from the program. As a result of the shelter's broad eligibility criteria, it is often the first call in another agency's search for a safety move location, and the shelter regularly receives residents from other shelters.

A victim wishing to enter the program must first make contact through the agency's hotline, where they will respond to a series of intake questions designed to identify their eligibility for the shelter as well as the appropriateness of the program for their specific needs. A client's acceptance is based on space availability (assistance in locating other shelters will be given in cases of full capacity), willingness and ability to participate fully in shelter programs, and ability to care for themselves and their minor children.

On arrival at the shelter, residents are assigned to a room, provided with the immediate essentials (i.e., food, hygiene items, clothing, and bedding), and placed on a 48-hour "quiet time." This time is allowed for the resident to acclimate to his or her new environment, rest, provide for the immediate needs of children, and establish a sense of safety. In addition, the resident is assigned to an advocate who will be responsible for completing a comprehensive needs assessment with the victim in order to develop a service plan to best utilize the 60-day stay at the shelter.

At the end of the 48-hour quiet period, the resident will begin to attend scheduled groups, including domestic violence education, career and job development, living skills, and group therapy. All groups, with the exception of the therapy groups, are divided on the basis of the length of time a resident has been at the shelter, with those residing one to four weeks and those residing five to eight weeks attending different groups. This schedule is designed to address the unique issues facing the two groups, as the first group is in the early stages of the program, learning the basics, and identifying resources, while the latter group is preparing for their eventual departure and coping with the anxiety related to the move.

Individually, residents will work with their assigned advocate to identify community resources for which they are eligible, complete individual safety plans for themselves and their children, and identify and monitor weekly goals. The primary goals for clients during their shelter stay are the identification of financial resources, location of affordable and safe housing, and initiation or continuation of legal action.

Children's Services, a companion program to the shelter, provides child care for the resident children in a safe and supportive environment while also offering school readiness curriculum for preschool-age children and educational tutoring for schoolchildren. Advocates also assist the parent in the enrollment of the children in the appropriate school program or the application for independent study for those whose safety issues prevent school attendance.

ADDRESSING SAFETY CONCERNS

The most common question posed to staff members of the agency is, How can you have men and women living together—doesn't that threaten the women? In reality, this has not been the case, and, as previously discussed, the women often find the presence of male victims to be a benefit. Operating a coed facility is not without concern; however, staff have found that the establishment of universal policies and procedures prevents any accusation of gender bias or favoritism, such as the one stating that "no resident shall be in a residential unit other than his or her own." Furthermore, rather than having a rule preventing romantic or sexual contact between male and female residents, the policy states that "there shall be no romantic or sexual contact between residents" period.

An honest review of shelter operations anywhere will reveal that safety issues exist regardless of the gender of the clients. Female clients can be and often are abusive to other female residents; it is not easy to live with someone you don't know and even harder when you are experiencing the uncertainty of leaving an abusive relationship. Still, Valley Oasis has been fortunate that, in its 24 years of operation, it has never experienced a serious incident of violence from either residents or an abuser. Staff and clients work well together to identify potential dangers and alert one another so that proper action may be taken. Clients are encouraged to report violations that may compromise the safety of a resident or the facility in general; in addition, staff are trained to identify the early signs of conflict and implement preventative action wherever possible.

CLINICAL SERVICES

The Valley Oasis shelter provides a full range of clinical services to adults and children staying at the shelter. These services are provided by a licensed marriage family therapist, a licensed clinical social worker, and master's-level interns. The interns are supervised by the licensed clinical social worker.

The clinical services offered at the shelter include individual and group counseling, crisis intervention, forensic interviews, and family therapy. Within these modalities, the therapist will complete assessments, make a thorough diagnosis on all five axes according to the *Diagnostic and Statistical Manual of Mental Disorders,* and develop a treatment plan and an individual service plan that includes short- and long-term goals. Additional services include case management, advocacy, and referrals.

When a person enters the shelter, an intake and needs assessment is completed within the first 48 hours they are there. All individuals entering the program will have an appointment with a therapist within the first 24 hours. The focus of this session is to assess the emotional stability of the individual.

The shelter is a 60-day program. All therapeutic interventions are crisis oriented with the focus being on stabilizing the individual so they can make necessary immediate plans for their future and overall safety and that of their children. Therapeutic modalities used for short-term crisis intervention by the therapist include brief solution-focused therapy, cognitive-behavioral therapy, and EMDR.

Individual one-hour therapy sessions are held on the basis of the individual client's needs. Although all clients come to the shelter to escape domestic violence, each client's situation and coping skills are different. Not all clients want to attend individual therapy, nor do they require short-term crisis intervention. The therapist refers approximately 82% of all shelter clients to therapy at the time they exit the program to deal with long-term psychological/emotional issues. Clients who are seen in individual therapy are seen for one hour sessions on a weekly basis. Although the therapy is focused on the immediate crisis of homelessness, trauma, and abuse, the therapist will use traditional psychotherapy modalities, such as Rogerian theory, psychoanalysis, Bowenian theory, Ericksonian theory, and grief and loss work. Other services include psychological testing and psychoeducation.

Group therapy occurs twice a week. Each group is an hour and a half long. One group focuses on specific topics, such as self-esteem, self-confidence, support building, and insight work. The second therapy group is quite controversial. A licensed therapist cofacilitates this group with an ex-batterer. The focus of this group was originally to educate the clients about batterer behavior and dynamics. It has evolved into a therapeutic group where the focus is on role playing and gestalt. This group has been used to train law enforcement interns and was highlighted on an award-winning documentary called *Hidden Victims: Children of Domestic Violence* (Lifetime Television, 2002).

In many homes where domestic violence occurs, the victim has to focus all his or her attention on the batterer. The children have experienced inconsistent parenting, abusive and harsh discipline, and/or emotional neglect. They may also have been forced to take part in the battering. In one case at the shelter, a young woman of 27 had five children. The children's ages were between one and eight. The father would come home drunk and wake the children up. They would have to sit on the couch and watch him beat up their mother. Then, before they could go back to bed, each one would have to get off the couch and kick their mother. If they did not, they would get hit. Other children would try to rescue their mothers from the batterer or would identify with the batterer, and once they were at the shelter, the child would become abusive to the mother. Many children are confused and angry and do not know how to talk to their parents, and the parents do not know how to parent their children.

Family therapy is available to all clients who request it. Staff may also make referrals to the therapist for a family either by completing a referral form or by discussing the case in case review. When a family is referred to therapy by a staff member, it is usually due to an observation the staff has made of poor parenting, abusive behavior by the parent toward the child, or abusive behavior toward the parent by the child. On receiving the referral, the therapist will schedule an appointment for a family assessment. Because of the time limitations at the shelter (it is a 60-day shelter), the focus of the therapy is on short-term interventions that will improve parenting and communication, empower the parent, and set limits.

CASE EXAMPLES

YOKO

Yoko is a 37-year-old Japanese female. She has no children. Yoko reported that her parents had a violent and abusive relationship. She also stated that she was both physically and verbally abused by her mother. She met her husband in Japan when he was stationed there in the military. The verbal abuse began early in the marriage, and she was later subjected to physical assaults that included slapping, punching, and hair pulling. But there was nothing she could do; her culture did not allow her to leave the marriage or to challenge her husband's authority over her. In addition, the military would do nothing to protect her. Within two years, he was transferred to the United States, and she was then totally isolated. They lived on the military base, and she had no transportation. He would not allow her to go anywhere. He allowed her to work, but he controlled all the money. His violence was increasing, and Yoko felt that she had to escape, or he would kill her. She spoke with a counselor on the base who referred her to Valley Oasis.

Yoko came to Valley Oasis in 2001, her face and arms still swollen with bruises from the last beating. She felt very isolated and focused all her attention on school and completing the program. Yoko had a strong desire to please and attended all required groups. While at the shelter, she received group and individual therapy, job development and living skills, and domestic violence education and participated in peer support groups. Yoko's self-esteem quickly rose, and she was soon able to face her abusive husband and demand a divorce. It took longer for her to deal with the abuse she had suffered from her mother. Yoko applied for one of the transitional housing programs operated by the shelter. She was accepted and quickly began working toward achieving her goals of going to graduate school and getting her own apartment. During the two years she was in the transitional housing program, she went to school, worked part time, and attended therapy. After one year of being in the transitional housing program, an opening became available in the Scattered Site transitional housing program. Yoko applied for the opening. She was accepted and moved to an apartment. After two years in this program, Yoko has completed and graduated from the transitional housing program. After six months out of the program, she contacted the executive director and asked if she could do her clinical internship at the shelter. She was accepted. After two months of her clinical internship, an opportunity came up in the agency, and Yoko was hired full time. She has completed therapy and is currently living in her own apartment, has a full-time job, and lives without violence in her life.

FRANK

Frank is a 38-year-old White gay male. He was referred to Valley Oasis by an LGBT (lesbian, gay, bisexual, transgender) counselor after being severely beaten by his partner of 14 months. This was Frank's second abusive relationship. The first one he left after three and a half years. Frank had a long history of drug and alcohol abuse beginning when he was a teenager and after coming out to his family, who could not accept his lifestyle. Frank had a history of mental illness. He had been hospitalized on two occasions because of suicide attempts and was diagnosed with depression.

The abuse Frank suffered in this relationship included being hit, punched, kicked, and bit and having his hair pulled out. His abuser was very verbally abusive and was emotionally abusive as well. Frank endured threats, social isolation, and deprivation of food and shelter, and his partner constantly followed Frank wherever he went. During the last episode of abuse, Frank had his collarbone broken. Frank's abuser would not let him work, and he did not allow Frank to have any money.

When Frank came to the shelter, he did not have a job, he had no money, and he had only an 11th-grade education. Frank entered Valley Oasis in 2003. During his stay, Frank complied with the shelter rules, regulations, and program requirements. He attended group and individual therapy, domestic violence education, and job development, living skills, and peer support groups. Frank received legal advocacy and secured a temporary restraining order and ultimately a permanent restraining order. Although he was uncomfortable initially, Frank quickly adapted to the shelter and developed friendships with other residents and got along well with staff. Just before his two months were up, he applied for one of the transitional housing programs run by the agency. At this time, the agency had not had a male request transitional housing, and the program was designed for families. We contacted the funding agency and asked if we could accept Frank into the program. The funding agency stated they would allow Frank into the program if we, the agency, accepted him. Frank was accepted and became our first male victim in our transitional housing program.

Frank's established goals were to complete his education, get a job, and get permanent housing. While he was in the transitional housing program, Frank received job development training, case management, counseling, and living skills.

Frank initially applied for and received General Assistance. He enrolled in school to finish his high school course work. He also enrolled in a temporary employment agency after receiving job development training in the transitional housing program. Eventually, Frank graduated from the two-year program, having accomplished all his goals. He has a full-time job that he has had for two years. He completed his adult education and received his high school diploma. He currently lives in his own apartment. Frank has remained single and has dated but has not been in an abusive relationship in more than three years.

Frank has stayed connected to the agency in many ways, initially by attending ongoing counseling through the outreach program. He also was offered and accepted a position on the Client Advisory Committee, where he was an active member and was instrumental in reviewing and developing policies regarding clients. Frank is currently an active member on the board of directors for the agency and sits on the Program Development Committee. Frank also is active on the agency's Speakers Bureau.

EDDIE

Eddie was a 30-year-old White male who arrived at the shelter with his three children: Michael (8), Mary (5), and Nancy (2). His wife, Rhonda, a 29-year-old of Hispanic origin, had verbally and physically assaulted him for years, demeaning him in front of the children, punching and kicking him, and once scratching his face so badly that he nearly lost an eye. Eddie had no prior history of drug or alcohol usage and no criminal convictions and had been previously employed. The couple had been married approximately nine years. Eddie had limited experience with the "system" and had not previously attempted to leave the relationship. The area in which the family resided was fairly remote in relation to the nearest "metropolitan" community, and local resources were limited primarily to county services (i.e., Child Protective Services, social services, and so on). Visually, this couple presented the very paradox that promotes the stereotypical response to male victimization: "How could she abuse him?" At 5 feet, 10 inches, and a little over 200 pounds, Eddie almost doubled Rhonda's 5-foot, 7-inch, 125-pound frame. Eddie's nonviolent beliefs and concern for the welfare of his children presented a dilemma, as he would not fight back against Rhonda's physical and emotional abuse, yet he refused to leave without his children. Eventually, after reaching out to an advocacy group for fathers' rights, Eddie realized that it was critical to the welfare of himself and his children that he leave home and begin divorce and custody proceedings.

Eddie and his children adapted well to the shelter environment, and he actively participated in all the programs. He was able to secure housing for himself and the children in a community whose proximity allowed him to continue to participate in the agency's outreach programs. Eddie was eventually awarded custody of his children, and they have established the safe and nurturing environment they all sought.

POSTDISCHARGE SERVICES

Residents who complete the 60-day program at the shelter typically transfer to a transitional program (possibly within the agency), relocate with friends or family, or, on occasion, return home to the batterer. The latter is the most difficult for staff to address; however, the agency has established a policy of offering a supportive exit. It is vitally important that residents returning to their abuser know that the staff respect their right to decide for themselves and, while fearful for their safety, that they will provide them with the support necessary to make the transition as smooth as possible. Essentially, the staff will begin the process of "safety planning the client home." Safe exist procedures, code words, and safe resources will be established. In addition, the resident may secure copies of important documents with the shelter staff to eliminate one more concern in the event that the client must flee the home again.

Wherever residents exit the program to, whether it is home or another program, they are encouraged to maintain contact as necessary, and, in the cases where they are remaining in the community, clients are encouraged to continue support services with the agency's outreach facility. It is not certain that each client's new location will be the safe place he or she seeks; however, those who have completed the program carry with them an increased awareness of the behaviors that their batterer exhibits that should indicate impending danger as well as their own behaviors that place them in danger. It is hoped that in the event of an abusive incident in the future, the client will remember what he or she learned about safety and escape as well as the support offered by the program and leave before more violence occurs.

A follow-up survey is sent to any shelter client who provides a forwarding address and permission to contact them. This survey is designed to identify the current living situation of clients, those services that they have continued to utilize, and the program practices that ultimately provided the most preparation for their move into the community.

THE FUTURE

The agency is currently in a planning and developing period and will have celebrated its 25th anniversary in September 2006. This is a time for reflection and planning. To look at how the agency began, what it has accomplished, what we need to do in the future, and the direction we want to take, the board of directors, the administration, and the staff are working together to establish the goals for the agency for the next 25 years. There is, however, an immediate plan of action.

The first part of the plan is to continue to assess and evaluate the effectiveness and quality of care of the existing programs. The agency has identified tools and will be implementing them at this time. The second part of the plan is to evaluate the performance and attitudes of existing staff. The agency will continue to identify areas of need and will provide ongoing training to staff to improve quality and effectiveness of care.

The agency never set out to become the single light at the end of the tunnel facing male victims. It had, in fact, hoped to begin a movement that would lead to the development of full-service agencies and shelters for male victims nationwide. And, while the agency is proud to have been the first agency in the United States to open its doors to men, we are saddened to remain one of less than a handful operating today. As the request for services for male victims continues to grow, the agency will be evaluating existing programs and looking for ways to improve services.

REFERENCES

Archer, J. (2000). Sex differences in aggression between heterosexual partners: A meta-analytic review. *Psychological Bulletin, 126*(5), 651–680.

Fiebert, M. (1997). References examining assaults by women on their spouses or male partners: An annotated bibliography. Retrieved January 10, 2006, from http://www.csulb.edu~mfiebert/assault.htm.

Lifetime Television. (2002). *Hidden victims: Children of domestic violence.*

Pizzey, E. (1974). *Scream quietly or the neighbors will hear.* New York: Penguin.

Rennison, C. (2003, February). *Intimate partner violence* (NXJ 197838). Washington, DC: U.S. Department of Justice, Office of Justice Programs. Retrieved January 12, 2005, from http://www.ojp.usdoj.gov/bjs/pub/pdf/ipv01.pdf.

CHAPTER 27

Justice Is in the Design: Creating a Restorative Justice Treatment Model for Domestic Violence

Peggy Grauwiler, Nicole Pezold, and Linda G. Mills

The battered women's movement was the first group to bring public attention to the prevalence of intimate abuse in American homes. Early on, this movement developed an educational approach, specifically tailored to male perpetrators who were victimizing female partners, that strove to change patriarchal attitudes and beliefs, which they held to be the root cause of violence against women. While these educational approaches addressed heterosexual male perpetrators of intimate abuse, they overlooked entirely the prevalence and dynamics of abuse in same-sex relationships or by heterosexual female perpetrators. This resulted in a political ideology that has subsequently influenced major federal legislation while blocking experimentation with any treatments for intimate abuse that brought together the victim and the offender, such as couples counseling and restorative justice–based interventions. Generally, it was believed that because of the perceived power imbalance, female victims could not safely participate in any treatment with their abusive partner. This chapter reviews the arguments for and against using restorative justice in intimate abuse cases and outlines how important issues like safety may be enfolded into restorative treatment models. To properly place restorative approaches in context, we briefly review the history of and research on intimate abuse treatment, particularly batterer intervention programs, as well as the existing literature on the use of restorative justice in family violence cases. Finally, we discuss the development of a new restorative treatment now being tested in Nogales, Arizona, that has taken the lessons learned from batterer interventions and restorative justice approaches in family violence to provide a safe, flexible, and egalitarian treatment program for couples and families affected by intimate abuse.

AN ALTERNATIVE THEORY OF JUSTICE[1]

Restorative justice (hereafter RJ) programs bring together professional and concerned citizens to restore victims, offenders, and communities through participation of a plurality of stakeholders in the process of recovering from crime (Braithwaite, 1999). At its core, RJ emphasizes interdependence between citizens and families and assumes that all cultures will find this approach more emotionally satisfying than retribution (Braithwaite, 1999). Those who have something at stake in the events that occurred define what restoration means in a specific context; however, it generally encompasses what matters to the stakeholders, including restoration from injury or lost property, restoration of dignity, social support, security, and a sense of empowerment (Braithwaite, 1999; Zehr, 2002). While the modern RJ movement began in the 1970s, restorative practices were the dominant model of justice in many cultures until the modern era (Braithwaite, 1999). Many indigenous peoples have never stopped using it (Mirsky, 2004; Walker & Hayashi, 2004).

A major principle underlying restorative approaches generally is that all cultures must adapt their restorative traditions in ways that are meaningful to them (Braithwaite, 1999). This allows great flexibility to address the needs of each offender, victim, or crime. In addition, all participants are regarded as having equal voices in the justice process and equal opportunities to air their concerns and participate in the discussion and, possibly, resolution of an offense (Burford & Pennell, 1995; Mills, 2006 Pranis; 2002; Sherman, 2000). A final idea that has emerged from such approaches is that restoring the parties to one crime can have a ripple effect in the family and community that surrounds them and may potentially expose and mitigate past offenses or prevent new ones (Mills, 2006; Robinson; 2003). In other words, the driving presumption of RJ is that justice can be personal, interactive, egalitarian, and transformative.

RJ models include victim–offender dialogue, community reparative boards, family group conferencing (FGC), and peacemaking circles, among others; all are united in theory but vary in approach. The focus of this chapter is FGC, which gathers family and supportive friends of the offender and the victim, together with a facilitator and relevant child welfare and criminal justice professionals, in a structured setting to hold the offender accountable for the harm done, ensure victim safety, facilitate open dialogue about the violence, and develop a plan to rectify the problem. The underpinning theory of FGC is that family and social networks are in a strategic position to encourage the offender's reform, to oversee the family's plan to stop abuse, and to monitor safety, thus preventing future violence (Burford & Pennell, 1998; Zehr, 2002). While some offenders may be moved to compliance with domestic violence laws and by the intervention of police and courts (Sherman & Berk, 1984), RJ proponents argue that the most potent force in changing behavior lies with the family and friends the offender trusts and loves (Braithwaite, 2002; Mills, 2003, 2006).

While feminist academics and victim advocates continue to debate the utility of RJ practices in intimate abuse cases, they agree that more interventions are needed to address the complexities of this problem (Curtis-Fawley & Daly, 2005; Mills, 2003; Pennell & Francis, 2005). In addition, advocates recognize that whether or not a couple separates following a violent incident, they may remain connected through their children and that interventions must address this reality and enhance the safety of both partners and their children (Mills, 2003; Pennell & Francis, 2005). The growing use of family decision-making conferences in child welfare settings and the well-documented co-occurrence of child maltreatment and intimate abuse (Edleson, 1999) have sparked a new discussion on how to safely apply RJ practices in intimate partner abuse cases (Curtis-Fawley & Daly, 2005; Mills, 2003; Pennell & Francis, 2005; Strang & Braithwaite, 2002).

THE PROBLEM OF SAFETY IN TREATING INTIMATE ABUSE

Over the past 30 years, safety has been the driving concern in developing treatments for domestic violence and has significantly shaped systematic responses to this problem. One approach has been to develop coordinated community response models that encourage close collaboration among system and service providers to offer comprehensive, wraparound services to better guarantee safety (Pennell & Francis, 2005). Proarrest policies, introduced in the 1980s (Maxwell, Garner, & Fagan, 2001), and restraining, or no-contact, orders were also designed to legally separate batterers from victims, while the shelter system sought to provide women victims a safe place away from home should they need it. In time, women victims expressed their desire for treatment programs for their partners rather than arrest and incarceration, and in response, courts began referring offenders to batterer intervention programs (BIPs), such as the Duluth model, a feminist, psychoeducational approach whereby men are taught in isolation from their victims that battering is part of a range of male behaviors used to control women (Feder & Wilson, 2005; Jackson et al., 2003; Pence, Paymar, Ritmeester, & Shepard, 1993). This coordinated community response continues to be the dominant approach to domestic violence, with an estimated 300 judicial systems nationwide using special domestic violence courts, court-ordered BIPs, judicial monitoring of defendants and probationers, and no-contact orders (Keilitz, Guerrero, Jones, & Rubio, 2001).

Such strategies have reinforced the trend to separate abusive partners to address each party's legal and treatment needs individually—and have been almost exclusively designed to address male violence perpetrated against females while ignoring the fact that intimate violence afflicts both women *and* men (Mills, 2003; Straus, 1999). Furthermore, this approach presumes that all abusive men are equally socialized and that their partners, parents, and even a violent community are secondary to the central causes of abusive behavior (Gondolf & Williams, 2001). As a result, much of the relevant theory and research has been similarly focused on a gendered conception of intimate violence and treatment.

Indeed, many advocates have argued that diverting the batterer's attention toward family history, cultural identity, and dysfunctional behaviors excuses male privilege and violence (Adams, 1988; Kelly, 2003). Empirical studies, however, have shown a strong correlation between a childhood history of domestic violence, sexual abuse, and other familial neglect and an increased risk of adult offending and victimization (Ehrensaft et al., 2003; Straus & Gelles, 1986). Alcohol abuse has been found to be a consistent risk marker for repeat assault (Gondolf, 2001). Although substance abuse or a history of childhood abuse does not relinquish domestic violence offenders from accountability, the research suggests that effective interventions must consider these factors (Mills, 1998, 2003; Cavanaugh & Gelles, 2005).

It is also important to acknowledge that criminal justice strategies often overlook the fact that many couples remain inextricably bound for a variety of reasons regardless of intervention or divorce (Mills, 2003; Straus, 1999). Despite no-contact orders or the threat of future violence, offenders and victims often have continued contact during or after state interventions (Mills, 2003; Peled, Eisikovits, Enosh, & Winstok, 2000). Many other victims, even if they have left the relationship, remain connected to their abusers through children in common or other family and community attachments.

In practice, most BIPs and probation services have inconsistent contact with victims and often rely on a one-time contact. Practitioners have advocated for ongoing risk assessment and case management support from BIPs for the batterer as well as the victim, whose appraisal of safety has been shown to be a significant predictor of additional violence (Davies, Lyon, & Monti-Catania, 1998; Gondolf, 2001; Pennell & Francis, 2005; Goodman, Dutton, & Bennett, 2000). Those closest to the victim and offender may also be important resources in predicting and possibly preventing future violence (Pennell & Francis, 2005).

Initially, studies of BIPs indicated high rates of success in reducing the frequency and severity of violence among offenders; however, methodological issues, such as small sample size and a lack of appropriate comparison/control groups, rather than actual program success, have since been shown to be important factors in determining the reliability of this evidence (Feder & Wilson, 2005; Jackson et al., 2003). Recent evaluations using more rigorous designs have found little or no reduction in battering (Jackson et al., 2003). Low response rates and a failure to determine model fidelity also continue to hinder this research (Feder & Wilson, 2005; Jackson et al., 2003). This chapter aims to answer the concerns of this literature and underscore how more inclusive treatments, such as RJ, may be applied to the complex range of intimate violence cases.

Restorative Justice and Why This May Be a Better Approach

Given safety concerns and, at the same time, the propensity of many couples to reunite after a violent incident, communities must recognize the importance of engaging those closest to the violence and their social supports in order to enhance safety and treatment. Treatments must also move away from one explanation for intimate abuse—patriarchy—and acknowledge the range of factors that may contribute to violence between partners, including substance abuse, financial problems, or family history of abuse. Interventions with a restorative approach are promising because they place the problem at the center—not the person or the gender.

Proponents of RJ contend that this approach facilitates conversations between willing victims, offenders, their families, and support networks and increases the chance of condemning the violence while permitting victims to express their needs and concerns (Curtis-Fawley & Daly, 2005). They contend that RJ encourages admissions of offending rather than denial, validates the victim's experience, and provides assurances that the victim is not to blame for the abuser's violent behavior. It also gives victims a meaningful role in legal and treatment processes (Mills, 2006; Pranis 2002). In addition, RJ may offer more options to victims who believe that prosecution does not meet their needs (Mills, 2006). They argue that RJ attends to the lay rather than the legal perspectives of crime and encourages a holistic understanding of the offense (Curtis-Fawley & Daly, 2005). Finally, some who promote RJ believe that it can better attend to the complexities of intimate violence, including when the victim is male or the violence is bidirectional (Mills, 2003).

Both proponents and critics of RJ recognize that attention to victim safety and offender accountability must remain a priority. Central to this debate is whether standards can be developed to make RJ models satisfactory and safe for domestic violence victims while also considering just outcomes for offenders (Braithwaite, 2002; Carter, 2003; Frederick & Lizdas, 2003; Koss, Bachar, & Hopkins, 2003; Pranis, 2002). By all accounts, the successful activism of some feminist advocates and academics who believe that RJ is too "soft" on male offenders or may quiet female victims has restricted application of RJ in domestic violence cases thus far; one consequence is the current dearth of scientific evidence to confirm or discount these claims (Curtis-Fawley & Daly, 2005).

However, strong support for using RJ in domestic violence cases comes from Burford and Pennell's (1998) study of an FGC-based approach to family violence in Canada. This study found a marked reduction in indicators of both child abuse/neglect and abuse of mothers/ partners after the intervention, advancement in children's development, and an extension of social supports (Pennell & Burford, 2002). One year after the conferences, the incidents of abuse/neglect were 50% less compared to the year before, while incidents increased significantly for 31 families in the control group, who did not participate in an RJ intervention (Strang & Braithwaite, 2002).

Critics and proponents have expressed concern for victim safety and empowerment in RJ models where both the victim and the offender are present (Umbreit & Zehr, 1996). Pennell and Francis (2005) conducted a series of focus groups with women survivors, shelter staff, and academics to discuss the use of "safety conferences," which are drawn from the FGC model and gather together the victim and her social support network to make decisions regarding safety. Focus group participants viewed the safety conferences as an opportunity to eliminate the secrecy about the abuse while also offering a comprehensive approach to plan for women's safety using family support. Shelter staff pointed out that safety conferences have the potential to educate the family group about domestic violence, gather support for both parties to address the violence, and help remove the stigma of returning to or failing to leave an abusive relationship. All focus group members agreed that it might be too risky for some women, such as those residing in shelters or who lacked familial or emotional support, to participate in conferences; however, one survivor welcomed input from her abuser's family, particularly from her abuser's mother, who was also abused. She felt the grandmother's presence and experience would be helpful for herself as much as for her children. Finally, survivors agreed that, when possible, children should participate in conferences because they were aware of the violence and needed to be part of the deliberations (Pennell & Francis, 2005). While this study focused on women victims, the lessons learned could be applied to enhance the safety of all intimate abuse victims generally.

Recent studies of FGC in Minnesota, Pennsylvania, Australia, and Canada have found higher rates of victim participation and satisfaction when compared to traditional approaches to crime (Bazemore & Umbreit, 2001; Braithwaite, 2002; Burford & Pennell, 1998; Strang & Sherman, 2003). While critics of FGC have often expressed concern over power and control dynamics during and after the conferences (Busch, 2002), FGC partnership building has been found to foster collaboration between family and service providers and enhance safety and empowerment (Pennell & Burford, 2002). Pennell and Burford (2002) found that despite concerns that the offender's presence at the FGC would silence victims, female victims took leadership roles in deliberations and in developing plans to address offender accountability and problem solving.

Admittedly, FGC research is still in its infancy—especially in domestic violence, where many programs exclude such cases in their referral criteria (Chandler & Giovannucci, 2004; Pennsylvania Department of Child Welfare, 2005). Several communities, however, are experimenting with RJ in intimate abuse crimes in Arizona, Hawaii, Canada, and Minnesota (Koss et al., 2003; Mills, 2006; Mirsky, 2004). In Nogales, Arizona, the community, together with the Santa Cruz County Court, has implemented an RJ-based domestic violence intervention called *Construyendo Circulos de Paz* (CCP), or Constructing Circles of Peace. This program is a hybrid of the FGC and peacemaking circle models and draws on the lessons learned from FGCs and batterer treatment, such as the need to improve standards and approaches to safety for all and enhance the availability of supplemental services (substance abuse treatment, job training) to address related problems. Although CCPs are offender focused and administered through the criminal justice system in Santa Cruz County, they are driven by the Nogales community, who adapted the model to their needs and have made this process their own.

CONSTRUYENDO CIRCULOS DE PAZ: A NEW RESTORATIVE MODEL

The CCP model began as a vague notion in Linda Mills's (2003) book *Insult to Injury* and was refined by a roundtable of experts in RJ and domestic and family violence practice in 2004 (Aymer, Brown, Cavanaugh, Friend, & Grauwiler, et al., 2004). The CCP preparation process was heavily influenced by Gale Burford, Joan Pennell, and Susan MacLeod's (1995) FGC model developed for three communities in Newfoundland, Canada. One major distinction of CCPs, however, is that it requires multiple contacts with participants rather than a single conference and follow-up conference. In fact, Arizona law requires that domestic violence treatments provide clients with 26 sessions. While other communities may adjust the number of sessions according to their needs or local law, we believe that maintaining multiple contacts with the client and participants is a key feature of this model because it increases the likelihood of safety for all involved. It is important to note that in defining the CCP approach and practice, we drew considerably from the experience of those who had used restorative practices for intimate abuse. For example, the family preparation section was informed by the work of Judy Brown and the Tubman Family Alliance as set out in the *Community Circles of Washington County—Cottage Grove Manual,* while the art of leading a safe and just circle was drawn directly from the work of Kay Pranis, Barry Stuart, and Mark Wedge (2003).

Overall Approach

The CCPs approach violence as a possible element in any relationship dynamic, intimate or otherwise. While gender identity and patriarchy may play a part, CCPs are expansive enough to allow for the consideration of other factors that may cause or aggravate violence, including substance abuse, financial strain or disagreement, and family or personal history of abuse. The CCPs are designed to provide a safe place to address all these issues, so that those traditionally not afforded a voice may find one and that all may experience personal growth or healing. Everyone, regardless of title or role, has an equal voice in the circle and may offer observations or points of view. This process upholds the integrity and dignity of all participants by allowing them to take a leadership role in resolving the violence in their relationships and other identified issues through joint problem solving and consensus building. In addition, certain labels, such as victim and perpetrator, that commonly define family and domestic violence work are modified on acceptance into CCPs. The offender becomes known as the *applicant* and the victim and all other support people as *participants*. These changes are meant to move the treatment away from judgmental and hierarchical language and are integral to maintaining the spirit of the peacemaking process.

There are four phases to this process: referral, preparation, circles, and maintenance, which may be modified according to community or participant needs.

Referral

In Nogales, an offender is referred to the CCP program by a presiding judge after a careful review of information on the offender/applicant, including criminal charges and history and his or her relevant psychosocial history (prepared by the probation department). Once an applicant is accepted into the program, the circle coordinator begins the preparation process.[2] Over a four-week period, the coordinator conducts individual intake interviews with the applicant and all potential participants. In the Nogales program, the coordinator is a professional with knowledge and experience in the areas of family or domestic violence, mental health, and substance abuse and familiar with the criminal justice and child welfare systems. Circles are cofacilitated by the coordinator and a trained community member, known as the cocircle keeper. Community members participate in a five-day initial training and thereafter attend additional quarterly trainings on relevant topics (e.g., safety planning, substance abuse). In addition, a community panel, called the Restorative Justice Advisory Team (RJAT), acts as a sounding board for the circle coordinator. The panel is intended to support the coordinator in balancing the risks of further abuse to family members with the goal of empowering the applicant and care community to take constructive action. The panel is made up of professionals who may offer additional mental health or other clinical support to the program as well as laypeople from the community. They help the coordinator make judgments about whom to include or not include in the circle.

Preparing for Circles

Once a case has been referred to the CCP program, a comprehensive intake and preparation process is conducted with all participants, including the offender, the victim (if they choose), family members, friends and other support people, and any professionals who might attend the circle conferences to provide information to the group. We believe that an intensive circle preparation process is the integral first step to the safety and success of circle meetings. Individual intake meetings take place with each participant to him or her them fully about the CCP process and answer questions, to discuss safety and develop a safety plan (both emotional and physical safety is addressed), and to review each person's role in the circle proceedings. Intake interviews also give individuals a safe space and time to think through and process any emotional reactions that might hinder their positive participation in the circle process. In this way, each potential participant has an adequate opportunity to consider the invitation and to determine his or her interest in participating.

Preparing the Applicant—During the initial intake meeting between the circle coordinator and the offender/applicant, some of the following elements should be apparent in order to determine the applicant's desire and capacity to participate: The applicant takes responsibility for the incident(s) in question, the applicant indicates a desire and/or willingness to change his or her harmful behaviors, the applicant may have passed through the criminal justice system in the past without successfully making necessary life changes and may benefit from community members' mentoring and supervision, and the victim/participant indicates that the applicant may benefit from an extended care community's support. If the circle coordinator, in consultation with RJAT, seriously believes that circles would be unhelpful for the applicant or victim/participant, he or she may refer the case back to the judge for another disposition.

As part of the CCP safety preparation process, the circle coordinator completes a psychosocial assessment (mental status, substance abuse history, social support, educational and vocational history, risk assessment, and criminal history) to evaluate how the applicant can/will meaningfully participate in CCPs. The mental status assessment covers current and past suicidal and homicidal behaviors, including attempts, plans, and current or past history of psychosis. If an applicant is currently suicidal, homicidal, or psychotic, the applicant is deemed ineligible for CCPs, and the case will be referred back to court.

During the intake interview(s), the circle coordinator also helps the applicant identify a *care community*, including a designated support person and safety monitor. A care community may include family, the victim/participant, or friends who seek to help this applicant address his or her violence in constructive ways. Participation by care community members, including the victim/participant, is voluntary. In order to facilitate contact between the circle coordinator and the applicant's care community, the applicant must provide contact information to the circle coordinator. All care community members should have the right to attend unless they have been formally excluded by the circle coordinator (see the exclusion criteria discussed later). If members of the care community choose not to attend, their views about how to stop the violence in the family may be communicated through the circle coordinator or through a special representative who participates in CCPs. The circle coordinator holds the final say about who will be invited, but this must be done in consultation with the applicant, the victim/participant, and the care community.

From this care community, the applicant chooses a *safety monitor,* with the circle coordinator's input. A safety monitor is a person designated by participants to maintain constant contact with the applicant and victim/participant in order to monitor safety on an ongoing basis. A safety monitor must (a) maintain close contact with the parties involved, (b) have direct or indirect experience with the parties and their history of violence, (c) be able to judge changes in the behavior of the applicant and victim/participant in order to interrupt potential violence, (d) have the trust of the parties involved, and (e) show a capacity to share sensitive safety information with the appropriate parties, including the authorities, if threats are made.

In addition, the applicant identifies a *support person*. This person may be a family member, friend, or other supportive person whom the applicant respects and who will be able to help resolve any anger that may emerge during or after circles and can comfort the applicant if he or she is apprehensive about the process. The circle coordinator may veto the applicant's selection. Some applicants may resist having a "support" person; however, it's critical that they have someone on whom they can count when the conversation gets tough. This person could "help them cool off if things get tense" or "take them for a break if they get angry."

BOX 27.1

Strategies for Applicant Participation

✓ Inform the applicant of the details of the abuse to be presented in the circle so that he or she is prepared for what will be discussed.
✓ Suggest that the applicant prepare a statement to read during the circle (if one wants to publicly take responsibility for one's actions or finds it hard to talk about one's feelings).
✓ Remind the applicant that the focus of the circles is to develop a plan for the future care and safety of all family members, not to lay blame or determine guilt or innocence. The safety monitor will play a role in ensuring that these goals are met.

Finally, the circle coordinator assists the applicant in preparing an Initial Social Compact (ISC). This document commits to writing the applicant's goals for change and restoration, including pre-CCP treatment and a commitment to nonviolence. The ISC is modified in the circles with input from participants and as change occurs throughout the CCP process.

Preparing the Victim/Participant—A victim's participation is absolutely voluntary. If a victim decides to participate in CCPs, he or she must also go through a rigorous preparation process with the circle coordinator (see the previous section on applicant preparation) that includes filling out a danger assessment tool, such as Campbell's *Danger Assessment Instrument* (Campbell, 1985), and exploring the benefits and risks of taking part in the circle process. The victim/participant must also choose a care community, including a support person. It is crucial for the circle coordinator to develop strategies to ensure that the views of the victim/participant(s) of abuse in the family are heard, especially if they are still at risk for further abuse. A victim advocate can assist in this process and should be contacted if the victim/participant requests one.

BOX 27.2

Strategies for Victim Participation

✓ Give him or her as much information as possible about available social services.

✓ Help identify a support person for *all persons* attending circles who are known to have been abused by the applicant in question.

✓ Have the victim/participant(s) write down his or her views to be read by his or her support person during the circle. This strategy can help silence critics since the support person can tell the family what life has been like for the victim/participant and what help he or she would like. This can also increase the level of support for the abused person among circle participants.

✓ Identify members of the family who are familiar with the abuse (e.g., someone who has witnessed the abuse or walked in just after an incident occurred) and who can play a role as safety monitor. Prepare them to raise these concerns so that the abused person does not have to offer information that may put him or her at risk of further abuse.

✓ Ensure that all issues are presented in a manner that does not jeopardize the future safety of any family member, especially those most at risk of abuse.

A victim/participant may choose to participate in CCPs directly or may designate one or more friends, family members, or community volunteers to attend the circles as his or her representative and to advocate for their concerns, provide his or her concerns in writing to the circle coordinator or to a community member to be read aloud at the circle, or discuss the victim/participant's concerns with the circle coordinator or co–circle keeper and/or the applicant's support persons in advance of the circle.

Preparing the Care Community—Finally, the circle coordinator individually prepares each care community member identified by the applicant and victim/participant by assessing him or her for safety, offering a detailed overview of the CCP process, assessing the individual's ability to participate productively in CCPs, and explaining the role of the safety monitor and support persons. The circle coordinator should stress that the best solutions for the long-term needs of the victim/participant will be those developed and supported by the care community. Care community members are also informed of any legal undertakings or agreements made by the public/court authorities pertaining to the circle (e.g., applicant's guilty plea and noncompliance conditions set by the referring judge).

The circle coordinator will provide ample opportunity for care community members to discuss their feelings about each family member whom the circle coordinator will be contacting, including the applicant and the victim (if participating). Potential care community members' concerns should be expressed directly to the circle coordinator. If a care community member asks the circle coordinator not to contact another potential care community member, the circle coordinator must explore the reasons for concern and negotiate these requests with each member. Sometimes the very person the member does not wish to invite has the most information about what has been happening in the family.

There may be serious, legitimate concerns expressed about inviting certain members who have been abusive, aggressive, or otherwise destructive in the past. The circle coordinator should explore these concerns fully and, with the care community identified so far, decide on a safety plan and a strategy for contacting that potential member (if the group decides to reach out to this person). One strategy commonly used is for the circle coordinator first to interview the person without offering an invitation and then to consult further with the group about whether this person should be involved.

Including a Child or Young Person—Children or young people who participate in CCPs require special consideration. In the case of minors, their view of the problem should be given weight, depending on age, maturity, and culture. The circle coordinator should interview each child and assess his or her capacity for meaningful participation. A parent or guardian *must* provide written consent for a minor to be interviewed and/or to participate in CCPs. It is preferable—but not necessary—to have the consent of both parents.

When a child or young person plans to attend circles, it is important that the circle coordinator prepare him or her completely for what to expect and how he or she can make his or her voice and views heard. Before the circles are held, the circle coordinator should meet several times with the child or young person and his or her support person to ensure that both the circle keeper(s) and the support person understand the child or young person's views and to discuss the best strategy for presenting his or her concerns or wishes.

BOX 27.3

To prepare a child participant, the circle coordinator should do the following:

✓ Get signed release forms for children under 16 who are considered mature enough to participate.

✓ Secure the verbal consent of children ages 12 to 16 who either will be interviewed or wish to participate in CCPs.

✓ Allow each parent the opportunity to participate with his or her child. (In cases where the parent and child have maintained little or no contact, the circle coordinator must extensively prepare both parties.)

✓ Contact extended family of a parent who has had little or no contact with their children or relatives.

✓ Include caregivers. (In cases where caregivers have a significant psychological attachment to a child or young person, they should attend as full participants. In cases where they are not deeply involved with the family, such as short-term or emergency caregivers, have them attend as information or advice givers.)

✓ Assess the child or young person for safety and develop safety plan.

✓ Offer a detailed overview of the CCP process helping the child or young person understand his or her role and preparing him or her for participation.

✓ Identify a support person to attend with the child or young person.

Anyone under 16 years of age who plans to attend circles must choose a support person to attend with them. The selection of the person is subject to veto by the circle coordinator, who must determine that the support person is not "aligned" in some negative way with any other participant and that he or she is capable of fulfilling this role (e.g., a trusted adult or relative rather than a school friend). The circle coordinator cannot act as the support person for the child or young person. In addition, social workers, Child Protective Services workers, and other persons representing the referring agency are generally not appropriate support people for children. The chosen support person should be an adult free to concentrate on care and protection issues for this child or young person.

BOX 27.4

Strategies for Presenting a Child or Young Person's View:

✓ Help the child or young person write down what he or she would like to say at the circle. This helps the young person to think about his or her feelings and concerns in advance.

✓ Identify a person to read these views at the circle. This is often a very powerful way to present a child or young person's view and can lend credibility to his or her words in the eyes of adult family members.

✓ There may be some issues the child or young person would like to see addressed but that he or she does not feel can be raised safely. Identify a support person or a neutral family member to raise these issues.

✓ Ensure that the safety monitor is aware of safety issues related to the child and any attending threats and has knowledge of the safety plan.

✓ Someone should be available to a child or young person after each circle to deal with any leftover emotions or concerns.

In cases where a child or young person will not attend CCPs, the circle coordinator interviews him or her to determine the best way to ensure that his or her views will be presented at the circles. The child or young person's view may be included via a written statement, picture, or audio- or video-tape. A trusted adult or relative (support person) may also present the child or young person's view. In these situations, it is useful to have reminders of the child present at the circles (e.g., a photograph, an empty chair).

Reasons for Exclusion—When the circle coordinator, in consultation with RJAT, seriously believes that proceeding to circles would be unhelpful for the victim/participant or the applicant, he or she has the right to halt the process at any time and refer the case back to the court. The circle coordinator may exclude a care community member from CCPs if his or her attendance is adverse to the interests of the applicant or the victim/participant or would be undesirable for other reasons. The circle coordinator may exclude a child or young person for the same reason or because the child's age or maturity level indicates an inability to understand the proceedings. The circle coordinator may exclude a participant if there is a serious threat of harm, a substantiated risk is posed to others, or a person exhibits serious mental disturbance, including unremitting substance abuse, that may interrupt the circles. The circle coordinator may exclude a participant if that person will be significantly distressed by what is discussed or when full participation may cause significant stress to the abused person in question.

Circles[3]

Constructing Peace—The stages outlined here should be described in the first formal circle. After this initial meeting, the phases are modified to fit the goals of each successive circle over the 26-week period of treatment.

Opening the Dialogue—The opening should *not* deal directly with issues related to the crime but should provide participants with a space in which to feel comfortable connecting and sharing. This phase plants the seeds of community *before* participants delve into more difficult, highly charged issues.

- ✓ *Set the Tone on Arrival*—Give participants a chance to interact and connect.
- ✓ *Welcome Circle Participants*—Circle keepers provide a brief description of the opening ceremony and explain how to use the talking piece (a symbolic object, such as a feather or leaf, chosen by the family to indicate that someone is speaking).
- ✓ *Opening Ceremony*—Circle keepers offer a reading, meditation, or any activity of special meaning to the community.
- ✓ *Introductions and Check-In*—Passing the talking piece, participants may share who they are, how they feel, and what they hope to achieve.
- ✓ *Limits of Confidentiality*—Circle keepers explain that they are required to report threats of suicide, homicide, child abuse, or other acts of violence to appropriate authorities or agencies.
- ✓ *Values and Guidelines*—Circle keepers review basic values and guidelines, such as respecting each member's right to speak uninterrupted in the circle, making decisions by consensus, and agreeing to ensure that no more violence will occur in this family.
- ✓ *Storytelling*—Participants are invited to share a personal life experience to create deeper understanding and connections.
- ✓ *Summary*—Circle keepers affirm everyone's participation and clarify the purpose of the circle.

Other Considerations for Circles:

- ✓ *Legal Information*—It is important for everyone to know the facts of the crime. If a judge or investigating authority is present, he or she may lead this part. Other things may be shared, including brief opening statements by the probation officer or child welfare worker.
- ✓ *Information or Social Service Providers Presentations*—Information or social service providers inform participants about certain relevant issues (e.g., dynamic of abuse) and treatment resources available (e.g., AA or job training). Participants are given a chance to ask questions and address concerns about the information provided.
- ✓ *Update on Applicant and Victim/Participant*—An informed person updates the circle on the victim and applicant, relying on information from support persons and others.

✓ *Safety Monitor*—The circle coordinator reiterates the safety monitor's role to the participants and addresses any new concerns.

✓ *The ISC*—The ISC is presented to the circle and described as the applicant's first steps toward recovery. (See "Preparing the Applicant" earlier in this chapter for a more complete description of the ISC.)

✓ *Initial Discussion*—Initial discussion focuses on the purpose of the ISC and the Social Compact that participants create each time they meet. Next, the discussion should focus on issues that lead to outbreaks of violence, underlying problems and dynamics, and intergenerational matters.

✓ *Resources and Needs*—The circle coordinator identifies what needs to take place in order to move forward, including whether all interests and concerns have been addressed, necessary funds are available, all people and agencies needed are on board, commitments have been spelled out, and the circle's goals and expectations are realistic and feasible. Participants should be aware of what happens if commitments are violated.

✓ *Safety Net*—Provisions should be made for delays, violations, or unforeseen interferences. It is important to set up "safety nets" in case some arrangements fall through (e.g., select backup support persons for the applicant or victim/participant).

✓ *Summary*—The circle must ensure that participants' commitments and expectations are clearly articulated, that what qualifies as success or as failure is defined, and that a policy for handling violations of the social compact is created.

Building consensus is critical to moving the CCP process forward but may take days, weeks, or even months. Sometimes the circle will convene only for the purpose of supporting the applicant as he or she makes changes in his or her life. It isn't necessary that every circle involve the discussion of "heavy" issues; what is important is that the work continues on a weekly basis. If consensus cannot be reached on critical issues, even with this support, the case may be referred back to the judge.

BOX 27.5

Strategies for Building Consensus:

✓ *Address the Issues*—Focus on repairing harm done to the victim/participant, healing the applicant, making amends with the community, and addressing the underlying causes of the violence or abuse to prevent further incidents. Circle members respond, identify challenges, and express feelings, concerns, or hopes for change. All participants come up with a diverse range of options for addressing the problems that build off the ISC.

✓ *Move Forward Issues for Action*—A circle keeper summarizes points of agreement, highlights remaining issues, and stresses the emerging potential of participants to revise and enhance the Social Compact or to affirm the ISC.

✓ *Manage Consensus*—Circle keepers acknowledge all participants' responses, restating their concerns and thanking everyone for contributing.

Closing and Honoring the Good Achieved—Circle keepers review points of agreement and disagreement. Circle participants share their final thoughts and review what each person has agreed to do. Circle keepers then summarize what has emerged from the circle, thank everyone for their participation, and introduce the closing ceremony, where participants may celebrate what has been accomplished and transition from the circle space back into their everyday lives.

Ongoing circles meet weekly during the initial six-month period and are essential to ensure that people are accountable to the agreements they make in CCPs, that old patterns do not reemerge (or, if they do, that they are promptly addressed), and that those who need support receive it. In each ongoing circle, the Social Compact is revised and updated as necessary. If the applicant, support persons, or agency professionals are not meeting their commitments, additional circles evaluate and determine the next steps. Each new circle follows a similar format to that laid out for the initial circle, depending on the needs of the participants.

Maintenance

Follow-up circles, which run beyond the initial six months, extend the community's ability to be self-reliant in dealing with crime and preventing further harms. The CCPs celebrate progress and successes made by offenders, victims, and the care community. Participants, along with the circle keepers, develop a plan for maintenance that meets the needs of each individual applicant, each victim/participant, and their families.

As this overview of CCPs makes apparent, the restorative treatment of intimate abuse requires considerable resources and investment by all members of a community. However, the potential of this model to address intimate abuse in a more inclusive, safe, and productive manner should energize those concerned by this social problem. The CCPs and a BIP, also offered in Nogales, are being compared in a randomized study, funded by the National Science Foundation, currently under way at New York University. (See New York University's Center on Violence and Recovery at http://www.nyu.edu/cvr.[4]) While this program and study signal an important new direction in domestic violence practice and research, the need to rigorously test restorative and other treatments still remains. We hope this chapter inspires such endeavors.

NOTES

1. This section was originally published as part of an article titled "Enhancing Safety and Rehabilitation in Intimate Violence Treatments: New Perspectives" in the July/August 2006 issue of *Public Health Reports.*
2. The circle coordinator's responsibilities of preparing participants and facilitating circles may be divided among several staff members depending on a community's size and needs.
3. This summary is drawn directly from *Peacemaking Circles* (2003) by Kay Pranis, Barry Stuart, and Mark Wedge. Pranis trained the Nogales community in this method in June and September 2004 and January 2005.
4. This material is based on work supported by the National Science Foundation (NSF) grant no. 0452933-0027854000. Any opinions, findings and conclusions or recommendations expressed in this material are those of the author and do not necessarily reflect the views of NSF. For the period of the study, offenders are randomized into either CCPs or BIPs upon sentencing.

REFERENCES

Adams, D. (1988). Treatment models of men who batter: A pro-feminist analysis. In K. A. Yllo & M. Bograd (Eds.), *Feminist perspectives on wife abuse* (pp. 177–199). Newbury Park, CA: Sage.

Aymer, S., Brown, J. A., Cavanaugh, M., Friend, C., Grauwiler, P., Longtin, K. M., et al. (2004). *Roundtable on restorative justice treatments for intimate abuse conducted at New York University, New York, New York.* Retrieved from http://www.nyu.edu/cvr/intimate/index.html#restorative

Bazemore, G., & Umbreit, M. (2001, February). A comparison of four restorative conferencing models. *Juvenile Justice Bulletin.* Retrieved from http://www.ncjrs.org/html/ojjdp/2001_2_1/contents.html.

Braithwaite, J. (1999). Restorative justice: Assessing optimistic and pessimistic accounts. *Crime and Justice, 25,* 1–127.

Braithwaite, J. (2002). *Restorative justice and responsive regulation.* Oxford, England: Oxford University Press.

Burford, G., & Pennell, J. (1995). *Family group decision making: New roles for "old" partners in resolving family violence: Implementation report summary.* St. John's, Newfoundland, Canada: Memorial University of Newfoundland.

Burford, G., & Pennell, J. (1998). *Family group decision making project: Outcome report* (Vol. I). St. John's, Newfoundland, Canada: Memorial University of Newfoundland.

Burford G., Pennell, J., & MacLeod, S. (1995). *Manual for coordinators and communities: The organization and practice of family group decision making.* Retrieved from http://social.chass.ncsu.edu/~jpennell/fgdm/Manual/TOC.htm.

Busch, R. (2002). Domestic violence and restorative justice initiatives. In H. Strang & J. Braithwaite (Eds.), *Restorative justice and family violence* (pp. 223–248). Cambridge, England: Cambridge University Press.

Campbell, J. C. (1985). *Danger Assessment Instrument*. Retrieved from http://www.musc.edu/vawprevention/research/instrument.shtml.

Carter, L. S. (2003). Family team conferences in domestic violence cases: Guidelines for practice. Family Violence Prevention Fund. Retrieved from http://endabuse.org/programs/display.php3?DocID=79.

Cavanaugh, M. M., & Gelles, R. J. (2005). New directions for research, policy, and practice, *Journal of Interpersonal Violence, 20*(2), 155–166.

Chandler, S. M., & Giovannucci, M. (2004). Family group conferences: Transforming traditional child welfare policy and practice. *Family Court Review, 42*(2), 216–231.

Curtis-Fawley, S., & Daly, K. (2005). Gendered violence and restorative justice: The views of victim advocates. *Violence Against Women, 11*(5), 603–638.

Davies, J., Lyon, E. & Monti-Catania, D. (1998). *Safety planning with battered women: Complex lives/difficult choices*. Thousand Oaks, CA: Sage Publications.

Edleson, J. (1999). The overlap between child maltreatment and woman battering. *Violence Against Women, 5*, 134–154.

Ehrensaft, M. K., Cohen, P., Brown, J., Smailes, E., Chen, H., & Johnson, J. G. (2003). Intergenerational transmission of partner violence: A 20-year prospective study. *Journal of Consulting and Clinical Psychology, 71*, 741–753.

Feder, L., & Wilson, D. B. (2005). A meta-analytic review of court-mandated batterer intervention programs: Can courts affect abusers' behavior? *Journal of Experimental Criminology, 1*(2), 239–262.

Frederick, L., & Lizdas, K. C. (2003, September). *The role of restorative justice in the battered women's movement*. Battered Women's Justice Project. Retrived from http://www.bwjp.org/documents/finalrj.pdf.

Gondolf, E. W. (2001). *Batterer intervention systems: Issues, outcomes and recommendations*. Thousand Oaks, CA: Sage.

Gondolf E. W., & Williams, O. (2001). Culturally-focused batterer counseling for African American men. *Trauma, Violence, and Abuse, 2*(4), 283–295.

Goodman, L. A., Dutton, M. A., & Bennett, L. (2000). Predicting repeat abuse among arrested batterers: Use of the Danger Assessment Scale in the criminal justice system. *Journal of Interpersonal Violence, 15*(1), 63–74.

Jackson, S., Feder, L., Forde, R. D., Davis, C. R., Maxwell, D. C., & Taylor, B. G. (2003). *Batterer intervention programs: Where do we go from here?* (NCJ 195079). Washington, DC: National Institute of Justice, U.S. Department of Justice.

Keilitz, S., Guerrero, R., Jones, A. M., & Rubio, D. M. (2001). *Specialization of domestic violence case management in the courts: A national survey*. (NCJ 186192). Washington, DC: National Center for State Courts, National Institute of Justice.

Kelly, L. (2003). Disabusing the definition of domestic abuse: How women batter men and the role of the feminist state. *Florida State University Law Review, 30*, 791–855.

Koss, M., Bachar, K., & Hopkins, Q. (2003). Restorative justice for sexual violence: Repairing victims, building community, and holding offenders accountable. *Annuals of the New York Academy of Science, 989*, 384–396.

Maxwell, C. D., Garner, J. H., & Fagan, J. A. (2001). *The effects of arrest on intimate partner violence: New evidence from spouse assault replication program*. Washington, DC: National Institute of Justice, U.S. Department of Justice.

Mills, L. G. (1998). *The heart of intimate abuse: New interventions in child welfare, criminal justice, and health settings*. New York: Springer.

Mills, L. G. (2003). *Insult to injury: Rethinking our responses to intimate abuse*. Princeton, NJ: Princeton University Press.

Mills, L. G. (2006). The justice of recovery: How the state can heal the violence of crime. *Hastings Law Journal, 57*(3), 457–508.

Mirsky, L. (2004, May). *Restorative justice practices of Native American, first nation and other indigenous people of North America.* Retrieved from http://www.realjustice. org/library/natjust2.html.

Peled, E., Eisikovits, Z., Enosh, G., & Winstok, Z. (2000). Choice and empowerment for battered women who stay: Toward a constructivist model. *Social Work, 45,* 9–24.

Pence, E., Paymar, M., Ritmeester, T., & Shepard, M. (1993). *Education groups for men who batter: The Duluth model.* New York: Springer.

Pennell, J., & Burford, G. (2002). Feminist praxis: Making family group conferencing work. In H. Strang & J. Braithwaite (Eds.), *Restorative justice and family violence* (pp. 108–127). Cambridge, England: Cambridge University Press.

Pennell, J., & Francis, S. (2005). Safety conferencing: Toward a coordinated and inclusive response to safeguard women and children. *Violence Against Women, 11*(5), 666–692.

Pennsylvania Department of Child Welfare, Office of Children, Youth, and Families & Pennsylvania Child Welfare Training Program. (2005). Family group conferencing/decision making as a practice with families experiencing sexual abuse and domestic violence. Child Welfare League of America. Retrieved from http://www.pacwcbt.pitt. edu/Organizational%20Effectiveness/Practice%20Reviews/FGCdv-sa.doc.

Pranis, K., Stuart, B., & Wedge, M. (2003) *Peacemaking circles: From crime to community.* St. Paul, MN: Living Justice Press.

Pranis, K. (2002). Restorative values and confronting family violence. In H. Strang & J. Braithwaite (Eds.), *Restorative justice and family violence* (pp. 23–41). Cambridge, England: Cambridge University Press.

Robinson, P. H. (2003). The practice of restorative justice: The virtues of restorative processes, the vices of restorative justice. *Utah Law Review, 2003,* 375–388.

Sherman, L. W. (2000). Violence in the family: Domestic violence and restorative justice: Answering key questions. *Virginia Journal of Social Policy and Law, 8, 263–267.*

Sherman, L. W., & Berk, R. A. (1984). The specific deterrent effects of arrest for domestic assault. *American Sociological Review, 49,* 261–272.

Strang, H., & Braithwaite, J. (2002). *Restorative justice and family violence.* Cambridge, England: Cambridge University Press.

Strang, H., & Sherman, L. S. (2003). Repairing the harm: Victims and restorative justice. *Utah Law Review, 2003,* 15–42.

Straus, M. (1999). The controversy over domestic violence by women: A methodological, theoretical, and sociology of science analysis. In X. B. Arriaga & S. Oskamp (Eds.), *Violence in intimate relationships* (pp. 17–44). Thousand Oaks, CA: Sage.

Straus, M., & Gelles, R. (1986). Societal change and change in family violence from 1975 to 1985 as revealed by two national surveys. *Journal of Marriage and Family, 48,* 465–479.

Umbreit, M., & Zehr, H. (1996). Restorative family group conferences: Differing models and guidelines for practice. *Federal Probation, 60*(3), 24–29.

Walker, L., & Hayashi, L. A. (2004, May). *Pono Kaulike:* A pilot restorative justice program. *Hawaii Bar Journal,* pp. 4, 6–7, 9–15.

Zehr, H. (2002). *The little book of restorative justice.* Intercourse, PA: Good Books Press.

CHAPTER 28

Domestic Violence: New Visions, New Solutions

Cathy Young, Philip Cook, Sheila Smith, Jack Turteltaub,
and Lonnie Hazlewood

Our intent in this chapter is to focus on public policy recommendations for domestic violence, with implications for those involved in implementing public policy, as well as clinicians providing intervention services.

Domestic violence remains a serious and tragic problem, and more can and should be done to help women who are abused by their partners. However, a major criticism of current policy is that legal and public policy response to domestic violence has focused almost exclusively on the male batterer and female victim to the detriment of male victims and victims in same-sex relationships, at the same time overlooking needed treatment for female abusers. This does not preclude "conventional" legal interventions, but any one-size-fits-all policy in an area as complex and fraught with unintended consequences as family violence is bound to fail some of its intended beneficiaries. There is no single factor that accounts for domestic violence:

Family Violence and Socioeconomic Status—While it is true that domestic abuse occurs in every social class, it is not equally prevalent in all social groups. Low income and low educational levels are major risk factors for domestic abuse (Straus & Gelles, 1990).

Portions of this chapter previously appeared as a position paper, "Domestic Violence: An In-Depth Analysis," September 2005, written by Cathy Young and published by The Independent Women's Forum, http://www.IWF.org (used by permission).

Domestic Violence and Substance Abuse—Numerous studies demonstrate a strong correlation between domestic violence and alcohol or drug abuse (Anderson, 2002; Magdol, Moffitt, Caspi, Fagan, & Silva, 1997; chapter 20 in this volume).

Female Violence—A growing body of research documents the role of female aggression in intimate violence (Archer, 2000; see also the introduction and chapters 2 and 3 in this volume). All available evidence suggests that women are in greater danger of injury and death from domestic violence, but a large minority of those injured or killed are men.

Mutual Abuse—Maybe one reason for the lack of greater progress is that mainstream discourse on domestic violence does not recognize another major aspect of the problem—the possibility of mutual abuse when violence is not in self-defense.

Without consideration of these factors in program design, intervention, and treatment, policies dealing with domestic violence are bound to remain woefully inadequate.

ARREST AND PROSECUTION

At present, mandatory or presumptive arrest, when there is probable cause to believe that domestic violence has occurred, is the law in more than half of all states (Mills, 2003). This policy remains the subject of some controversy. Although further research is needed, men who were the subject of a domestic violence complaint were somewhat less likely to reoffend if they were arrested; however, chronically aggressive batterers did not seem to be deterred by arrest. Some studies indicate that a majority of suspects discontinued aggressive behaviors even without an arrest (Maxwell, Garner, & Fagan, 2001). This suggests that policies requiring arrest for all suspects may unnecessarily dilute community resources by mandating arrest for all suspects and thus fail to provide specialized and targeted intervention strategies for the worst offenders and those victims most at risk.

Gender-biased application of mandatory arrest law raises serious civil rights issues. According to known prevalence rates in the population, men are arrested and mandated to batterer intervention programs in alarmingly greater numbers compared to women (Homel, 2005). This sends dangerous signals to both men and women in mutually violent relationships. Women may feel exonerated, absolved of any accountability for aggressive or violent behavior, escaping necessary interventions or counseling. Men may become alienated and hostile to a system they believe is stacked against them and unjustly favorable to women.

Paradoxically, mandatory arrests may disempower victims by taking the decision-making power out of their hands. The same criticism has been made of no-drop prosecution policies in which domestic assault cases are prosecuted even if the victim does not want to press charges (Mills, 2003).

According to Mills's (2003) research, female victims are less likely to report further violence if the original arrest led to prosecution of their male partner, the justice system failed to enact a "more therapeutic" approach with the offender; and the victim felt she had no rights or input in the criminal justice system.

RESTRAINING ORDERS

Restraining orders or orders of protection, which typically prohibit not only harassment or abuse against the victim/plaintiff but also any contact (including by mail, e-mail, telephone, or through a third party), are another common tool used to decrease domestic violence. Most recently, many states have streamlined the process of obtaining an order, extended eligibility to people who had been in a relationship but had not lived together, and introduced harsh measures against violators, such as warrantless arrest, pretrial detention, and stiff jail sentences.

A number of legal professionals and civil libertarians have argued that the current restraining order system can often result in serious violations of defendants' civil rights. In an article pointedly titled "Speaking the Unspeakable," Elaine Epstein (1993), past president of the Massachusetts Bar Association and the Massachusetts Women's Bar Association, wrote that the pendulum had swung too far: "The facts have become irrelevant. Everyone knows that restraining orders and orders to vacate are granted to virtually all who apply, lest anyone be blamed for an unfortunate result. . . . In many [divorce] cases, allegations of abuse are now used for tactical advantage" (p.1).

A temporary (emergency) restraining order can be issued ex parte, that is, without the defendant being present or even notified, much less informed of the specific allegations against him or her. Usually within less than 30 days, a hearing must be held on issuing a permanent restraining order that typically remains in place for a year. At the hearing, the defendant can present his or her side of the story.

Boston attorney Miriam Altman, however, has written that in practice, the deck is stacked heavily against the accused: Cross-examination may be limited, normally inadmissible evidence such as hearsay may be allowed, and "the mere allegation of domestic abuse . . . may shift the burden of proof to the defendant" (Altman, 1995, p. B6). In September 2004, the Massachusetts Supreme Judicial Court struck down a restraining order partly on the grounds that the defendant was not allowed to cross-examine the complainant or to call witnesses on his behalf (*C.O. v. M.M.,* 2004). It is noteworthy that, according to an official study, fewer than half the restraining orders issued in the state every year involve even an *allegation* of physical abuse, and in many cases there were no accusations of verbal threats but only of verbal abuse (Adams & Powell, 1995).

Once the restraining order is in place, a vast range of ordinarily legal behavior, such as all contact with a former spouse or children, is criminalized. A defendant can be prosecuted even if the complainant agreed to meet with the accused or had initiated the contact. It is difficult to determine the percentage of restraining orders that are based on frivolous charges or manipulation of the system.

The typical response to complaints about restraining order abuse is that protecting women must be a top priority. Balancing the rights of the accused against the safety of potential victims is always a difficult task in a free society. Yet, do restraining orders actually protect women from domestic homicide? A man who prepares to kill a woman and face a murder charge or take his own life, which often happens in such cases, is unlikely to be deterred by a charge of violating a court order. Tragically, in case after case, women have been slain after filing a restraining order.

A study published in 1984 by Janice Grau, Jeffrey Fagan, and Sandra Wexler sought to evaluate the effectiveness of restraining orders in Pennsylvania. According to the study abstract, "Interviews with recipients of restraining orders suggest that the orders are generally ineffective in reducing the rate of abuse of violence. However, they were effective in reducing abuse for women with less serious histories of family violence or where the assailant was less violent in general. They were *ineffective* in stopping physical violence" (Grau, Fagan & Wexler, 1984, p. 13).

One particularly troublesome finding is contained in a 2001 report by Laura Dugan, Daniel Nagin, and Richard Rosenfeld prepared for the National Institute for Justice under a Violence Against Women Act grant, "Exposure Reduction or Backlash? The Effect of Domestic Violence Resources on Intimate Partner Homicide." After examining domestic violence policies and homicide trends in various jurisdictions, the authors note, "Increases in the willingness of prosecutors' offices to take cases of protection order violation are associated with *increases* in the homicide of white married intimates, black unmarried intimates, and white unmarried females (Dugan, Nagin, & Rosenfeld, 2001, p. 35). In some cases, abusive men have obtained restraining orders against their victims as a form of harassment.

BATTERER INTERVENTION AND VICTIM COUNSELING

In addition to a punitive response to domestic violence, recent proactive policies have emphasized batterer treatment. Such treatment programs first appeared in the 1970s; a model program, the Duluth Domestic Abuse Intervention Project (DAIP), established in Duluth, Minnesota, in 1980, served as a model for many subsequent programs that proliferated in the 1980s (Van Wormer & Bednar, 2002). In a large percentage of domestic violence cases (whether assaults or restraining order violations), batterer treatment is offered as an alternative to incarceration and mandated as a condition of probation.

At least in theory, this policy is commendable. Researchers, advocates, and professionals who work with abuse victims typically note that the majority of women do not want the relationship to end; rather, they want the abuse to stop. Thus, effective treatment for batterers, preferably coupled with counseling for the victims, would seem like a salutary approach. Yet the efficacy of these programs has been repeatedly called into question.

Some of the findings on the subject are reviewed by Katherine van Wormer and Susan G. Bednar in a 2002 article in *Families in Society: The Journal of Contemporary Human Services*. Van Wormer and Bednar report that a 1987 evaluation found significant reductions in abuse in the first three months of the abuser's participation in the program and some reductions over a one-year period. But a later study that reviewed the records of 100 former program participants over a five-year period found a 40% recidivism rate. It is worth noting that at least one of the studies above reported that 60% to 70% of domestic violence offenders did not reoffend *regardless* of criminal justice intervention (Van Wormer & Bednar, 2002).

Van Wormer and Bednar also cite a 1991 survey of 76 shelters for battered women on the effects of batterers' programs. Only 12% of the respondents reported a decrease in emotional abuse toward women following the men's participation in batterers' programs, while 46% saw no impact in this area, and 42% reported an *increase* in such behavior.

Another criticism is that batterer treatment programs are often rooted in feminist ideology, having strong ties with battered women's advocacy groups. Typically, these programs embrace a model that regards battering as a pattern of coercive control and male domination of women. Other factors that contribute to violence (i.e., psychological, mental and emotional disorders, drug and alcohol abuse, violent family dynamics involving one or both partners) are at best considered of minor importance or, worse, ignored. While the focus on "power and control" may be the right approach for some abusive offenders, it does not fit most men or women. The reality of domestic violence is far more varied and complex. Indeed, in recent years, some who have worked within Duluth-style programs for years—and even those who participated in the design of the model—have candidly admitted the limitations of this approach.

Ellen Pence (1999), one of the creators of the Duluth program, wrote,

> By determining that the need or desire for power was the motivating force behind battering, we created a conceptual framework that, in fact, did not fit the lived experience of many of the men and women we were working with. The DAIP staff . . . remained undaunted by the difference in our theory and the actual experiences of those we were working with. . . . It was the cases themselves that created the chink in each of our theoretical suits of armor. Speaking for myself, I found that many of the men I interviewed did not seem to articulate a desire for power over their partner. Although I relentlessly took every opportunity to point out to men in the groups that they were so motivated and merely in denial, the fact that few men ever articulated such a desire went unnoticed by me and many of my coworkers. Eventually, we realized that we were finding what we had already predetermined to find. . . . We had to start explaining women's violence toward their partners, lesbian violence, and the violence of men who did not like what they were doing. (p. 29)

The majority of states today establish guidelines for the certification of programs into which the courts may direct domestic violence offenders. In many states, the certification requirements explicitly and specifically require compliance with a restrictive model of domestic violence. A 1998 review of 31 sets of batterer intervention standards currently in use in the United States found that "patriarchy is often cited as causing and/or maintaining men's violence against women" (Austin & Dankwort, 1998, p. 4). Often, the guidelines also require that programs be monitored and evaluated by battered women's advocates. Methods considered ideologically suspect by the advocates, such as joint counseling for couples in violent relationships or counseling involving other family members, are rejected outright, while other approaches, such as substance abuse treatment, are deemphasized.

For instance, the Massachusetts guidelines state, "While the following methods may, from time to time, be incorporated into an intervention model that focuses on power and control in relationships, they are inadequate and inappropriate for batterer intervention if they stand alone as the focus of intervention:

A. Psychodynamic individual or group therapy, which centers causality of the violence in the past;

B. Communication enhancement or anger management techniques, which lay primary causality on anger;

C. Systems theory approaches, which treat the violence as a mutually circular process, blaming the victim;

D. Addiction counseling models, which identify the violence as an addiction and the victim and children as enabling or co-dependent in the violent drama;

E. Family therapy or counseling which places the responsibility for adult behavior on the children;

F. Gradual containment and de-escalation of violence;

G. Theories or techniques, which identify poor impulse control as the primary cause of the violence;

H. Methods, which identify psychopathology on either parties' part as a primary cause of violence;

I. Fair fighting techniques, getting in touch with emotions or alternatives to violence" (Commonwealth of Massachusetts Executive Office of Health and Human Service, 1995, p. 10).

The guidelines also reject outright the option of couples counseling as a component of batterers' intervention and state that joint counseling should not be permitted until there has been no violence for a minimum of nine months.

Ellen Pence of the DAIP concedes that in their zeal to counter negative stereotypes of women, many battered women's advocates have fallen into the trap of a "women are saints" mentality: "In many ways, we turned a blind eye to many women's use of violence, their drug use and alcoholism, and their often harsh and violent treatment of their children" (Pence, 1999, p. 30). Abused lesbians have been the most obvious victims of the battered women's movement's reluctance to confront female violence, which has begun to change only in the past few years. Among heterosexual women, women who are abusive toward spouses or children, or those involved in mutually violent relationships, are unlikely to benefit from interventions that encourage them to see themselves solely as victims.

In recent years, the domestic violence advocacy community has somewhat broadened its perspective to include "nontraditional" victims and perpetrators. Partly, this has happened because of the efforts of a few organizations that have promoted a better understanding of male victimization, female violence, and gay and lesbian abuse without using antifeminist rhetoric (as many "men's rights" groups have done) or by attacking the positive gains of the battered women's movement.

Foremost among these is SAFE (Stop Abuse for Everyone; http://www.safe4all.org), a national group comprised of social workers, psychologists, attorneys, academics, and victim services advocates. The organization's mission is to assist all underserved victim populations. The National Crime Prevention Council now lists SAFE as a victim resource, and the nationally syndicated advice columnist "Dear Abby" has supported the SAFE brochure for abused men. The Battered Men's Helpline in Maine has also received positive attention from the press (Routhier, 2002).

In some regions of the United States in 2005, male victims were included in Silent Witness vigils for domestic violence victims. On a more practical level, some domestic violence agencies have begun to provide services to male victims, such as support groups, legal assistance, and vouchers for hotels in lieu of shelter space.

Stanley Green, a victim services advocate who works to bring public attention to the plight of male victims, asserts that, compared to a few years ago, "battered women's advocates are *much* more receptive to considering males as victims" (personal communication, October 19, 2004). In addition to a shift toward more gender-neutral agency names, Green notes, "Major conferences, including that of the Family Violence and Sexual Assault Institute (which rejected proposals for papers addressing female aggression and male victimization as recently as 2001) are including more sessions on non-mainstream views on intimate partner violence" (personal communication, October 19, 2004). Harry Crouch, an activist with the Los Angeles chapter of the National Coalition of Free Men who joined the San Diego Domestic Violence Council in 2002, reports that he has been very successful in promoting gender-inclusive materials such as public service announcements, posters, and brochures.

Along with change, however, there has been resistance. Speaking to the *Boston Globe*, Nancy Scannell, legislative director of the domestic violence coalition Jane Doe Inc., cautioned that the recognition that men are sometimes victims did not change the organization's basic outlook on the causes and nature of domestic violence. She maintains that domestic violence "happens because of sexism and power, and control of men over women in our society" (cited in Stockman, 2002, p. B1).

Greater acceptance and inclusion of male victims, gay and lesbian victims, and other "nontraditional" victims of domestic violence addresses only some of the limitations of the current approach to intimate partner violence. Other needed changes include the recognition of mutual abuse as a part of the domestic violence problem, a better understanding of the role of substance abuse and psychopathology as contributing factors, and more alternatives to law enforcement–oriented solutions.

FAMILY VIOLENCE: NEW VISIONS, NEW SOLUTIONS

A great deal has been accomplished over the past 30 years in making domestic violence a national issue and bringing it to the forefront of America's attention. This might well have been impossible without the feminist zeal of the battered women's movement, whose militancy helped shatter the wall of secrecy and neglect that too often surrounded violence in the home. Given women's greater risk for domestic violence victimization and the sexist attitudes that were still prevalent when the battered women's movement began, it was understandable that the initial focus of the effort to combat domestic violence would be on women as victims.

The greatest triumph of battered women's advocates came in 1994 with the passage of the Violence Against Women Act (VAWA). Cosponsored by Senator Joseph Biden (D-DE) and Senator Orrin Hatch (R-UT), the bill had broad bipartisan support when it passed, and most of its backers undoubtedly viewed it as a practical measure and a moral imperative rather than an ideological crusade. VAWA and its successor, the Violence Against Women Act of 2000, contained many positive practical measures in the area of victim services and criminal justice, such as making restraining orders issued in one state enforceable in another. It also encouraged some solid research on domestic violence, sexual assault, victim services, and related issues.

However, VAWA has also enshrined a dogmatic and one-sided approach to domestic violence: the unrealistic assumption that in every domestic violence situation there is a clear-cut and usually gender-based distinction between abuser and victim, the almost exclusive reliance on criminal justice measures, and the substitution of dogmatic, feminist "reeducation" for interventions that fail to address the specific problems of individuals and families. Another troubling aspect of VAWA is that it creates a symbiotic relationship between the federal government and the battered women's advocacy movement, which is dominated or at least heavily influenced by radical feminist ideology. Such a nexus also exists on the state level. The state coalitions against domestic violence, which formally require their member organizations to embrace the feminist analysis of abuse as sexist coercion, play a decisive role in the allocation of VAWA grants and in overseeing the implementation of VAWA-based programs and policies.

The evolving understanding of domestic violence, based on 30 years of research and policy experiments, should incorporate aspects of the feminist analysis but also needs to include a broader and more nuanced view of the realities of family violence.

Recommendations

1. Arrest and prosecution.

Appropriately, our society currently views domestic violence as a crime, not a private matter. However, if in the past battering was often treated as a family squabble, current law frequently treats every family squabble as battering. Instead of a sweeping, one-size-fits-all approach, there should be more differentiation between serious and potentially dangerous cases. More studies are needed on the enforcement and the consequences of mandatory or presumptive arrest policies. Anti–dual arrest clauses, which often serve as vehicles for gender bias, should be repealed and left to the discretion of the police officers to decide whether there is one primary aggressor, as in stranger assaults, or whether one or both parties are at fault. Unless the victim is in danger or has suffered serious injury or children are involved, the victim's desire not to prosecute should at least be considered.

Initial Response Assessment Team

There is considerable debate over the effectiveness of mandatory arrest laws, the lack of or type of training law enforcement receives in determining primary aggressors, whether dual arrest is warranted or should be used as a tool, and whether the wishes of a victim who does not seek an arrest of a perpetrator should be honored (Mills, 2003). It may be an unrealistic expectation that law enforcement officers have the time or the training to make effective assessments when initially responding to a domestic dispute. In addition, law enforcement officers in many localities do not have access to a database on prior child abuse reports from the domicile.

One way to overcome these obstacles is to have a member of a local initial response assessment team also respond to the scene. Team members should not be associated with or part of a victim advocacy group or organization. Those associated with local batterer intervention programs (BIPs), however, could be part of this team if they have adequate training in gender-neutral rapid assessment and testing, which should be a requirement of BIP professionals in any case. Community professionals with adequate assessment training, psychologists, and certified counselors, could also be a part of this team. The cost of such a team should be relatively minimal for most areas, provided that the costs are shared across multiagency lines, such as sheriff, city police, state police, county/city/state government, district attorney office, judicial district, and so on. Team members should also have access to child abuse reporting agency databases as well as other databases more commonly available to on-scene law enforcement, such as whether a restraining order has been issued, prior arrest records, and whether there have been prior complaints. Team members could be on call via pager or other device for rotating assignment for 24-hour coverage.

In many areas, a relatively small team can be on call to respond as needed, be paid less for on-call duties, and compensated at a higher rate when actually responding. Liability insurance, waivers, and other needs would be necessary for such a team to be assembled, but these conditions can be met at minimal cost. Team members would receive training by law enforcement in how to proceed without interfering in officer duties, making the assessment process a joint effort with the officer(s) on scene.

Physical danger to the assessment team member should be relatively minimal for two reasons: (a) The team member always allows the officer(s) to secure the scene, and (b) the team member begins the assessment process only when the officer determines it is safe and appropriate for an assessment. Given the research indicating that 50% of domestic disputes involve mutual non–self-defense combat and that the majority of cases involve relatively minor physical attacks (see in this volume) and victim resistance to arrest and ultimate prosecution, there is a clear need for more effective and appropriate assessments and recommendations for the on-scene officer.

Such recommendations may include arrest or no arrest, involving or not involving Child Protective Services and dual- or single-party arrest when warranted. With more fully trained assessment personnel on scene, alternatives to arrest and prosecution can be contemplated. For example, the officer could issue a citation in a relatively minor family conflict scenario that would mandate that the couple attend and complete an assessment of the couple at a later date.

With the current availability of family conflict and aggression testing tools and consensual dual polygraph testing, citations for mandatory assessment can result in recommendations to district attorneys and courts with much greater reliability regarding whether prosecution should move forward, on what basis a restraining order should or should not be issued, and whether Child Protective Services should be involved.

In cases where no further official action is warranted, couples would have much improved access to counseling and information regarding preventing similar conflicts in the future. Accurate identification of victims and perpetrators would be more likely, and victims would have improved access to information about available resources. Under the further *assessment citation method,* victims would be more likely to assist in prosecution. Each state and locality would have to examine the legal basis for citation mandating assessments. However, in many areas, legislation may not be needed, as mandatory assessment could be an added component of existing disturbing-the-peace statutes.

2.   Restraining orders/orders of protection.

Restraining orders seem to be of value in protecting people from non-violent harassment. However, the issuance and enforcement has troubling implications for civil liberties, and greater steps need to be taken to ensure that restraining orders are not used merely as a legal tactic to gain an advantage in divorce/child custody cases.

One solution would be an expedited evidentiary hearing soon after a restraining order is issued. Furthermore, domestic violence victims must be educated about the fact that a restraining order is unlikely to stop a truly dangerous batterer. In extreme cases, criminologist Lawrence Sherman (1992) has suggested the equivalent of the "witness protection program"—state-subsidized relocation and resettlement under a new name—for victims who fear for their lives once the abuser is released from jail. Another possibility for consideration is civil detention for particular abusers after they have served a jail or prison sentence, if a review determines that they pose a danger to their victims, akin to the current practice in some jurisdictions of civil detention for dangerous sex offenders. However, such a remedy should be used very cautiously because of obvious potential civil rights problems.

Courts have little difficulty in issuing protective orders in cases in which there is forensic evidence, medical records, witnesses, obvious injuries, and other evidence. As noted previously, when there is no such evidence and only the two parties' veracity to determine, courts must err on the side of safety but should also be mindful of the very real possibility that an order may simply be a tactic to gain custody of children and possession of a domicile.

Mandatory Assessment

In cases where child abuse is not alleged, where allegations of abuse are disputed (and the court has some doubt as to whether abuse has actually occurred), or where the accuser may be the actual perpetrator or in the case of mutual abuse, the court can follow a policy of ordering temporary mutual shared physical custody of minor children. The couple is then mandated to an assessment. If both parties fail to attend and comply with the assessment, the order is vacated. If only the complainant complies, the order stands. It is not our purpose here to go into great detail about the nature of such an assessment (for details on practical repeatable assessment tools, see Hamel, 2005a; chapter 12 in this volume). With the advent of such tools, trained assessors, and consensual dual polygraph testing, the court would have an unbiased, knowledge-based report in which to order a continuance of a restraining/protective order or to issue a mutual restraining/protective order and to decide whether one or both parties would retain temporary custody of minor children or whether only one party should have temporary custody pending the outcome of further litigation.

In less populated areas, the cost of the proposed program could be shared by multiple court jurisdictions, and the assessment team could secure grants by establishing a nonprofit corporation. While it is desirable that licensed psychologists or other licensed mental health practitioners conduct assessments, they could play a supervisory role once the program is up and running. Highly trained and lower-cost personnel could conduct the majority of the assessments, preferably individuals with additional experience in the field of criminology.

3. Treatment options.

In order to move toward a gender-inclusive model of domestic violence treatment, communities and the stakeholders that guide interventions must move away from an ideological view of domestic violence. A patriarchal model of domestic violence must be reexamined in the light of past and current research that indicates little support for a patriarchal view of causation. It is equally important to examine the full context and complexities of family violence: to seriously recognize members of either gender as primary abusers and violent perpetrators, the existence of mutual couples violence, sequential intimate violence where current abusers were past victims of abuse in the same relationship, violence by children toward parents, sibling violence, parental abuse of children, and violence in general within the kinship family system. A sincere and concerted effort must be made to avoid simplistic yet appealing dichotomies of victim–perpetrator.

Research indicates that victim–perpetrator labels can readily shift in a person's lifetime, depending on the point at which an individual's behavior is observed. Current stakeholders must allow inclusive community dialogue and hear the voices of those advocating, including *all victims,* for a reconciliation and restorative approach to keep families intact (Mills, 2003). This can be accomplished with due consideration for the safety of the most vulnerable family members.

A major review and overhaul of state guidelines for batterer treatment programs is in order and should contain these essential features:

Court-certified abusers' programs should incorporate additional appropriate victim-safety-first options that might include anger management, substance abuse and mental health assessments, and couples/family and individual counseling. It is also critical that advocacy groups do not play a central role in determining and enforcing the standards for batterers' programs. Instead, states should draw on a diverse community of scholars, mental health professionals, police and probation officers, judges, family counselors, and criminologists.

From the beginning of the intake process, BIPs must have a risk assessment protocol that has as its goal a determination of the level of risk for serious reassault and lethality (chapter 15 in this volume). In addition, significant attention needs to be paid to the role of alcohol and other substances in violent offenses. The risk assessment is then used, in conjunction with a couple's/family assessment, in order to place individuals and couples/families within a range of treatment and intervention options or for referral to a threat management team. This function can be assumed by a centralized referring agency, a multidisciplinary team, or a single comprehensive program structure.

A couples/family assessment would identify couple/family dynamics that contribute to abuse and violence with the goal of recommending individual/systems interventions and treatment with attention to the motivation and wishes of the couple or family (chapter 11 in this volume).

A multidimensional and multitracked treatment system that includes but is not limited to same-sex group treatment for men and women, individual psychotherapy, medication evaluations and treatment, group and single couple conjoint counseling, family therapy, inpatient and outpatient substance abuse treatment, and foreign-language cultural-specific interventions that can be mixed or matched with individual, couple, and family needs.

Ongoing, short-term, and long-term follow-up is necessary to identify the continuing intervention needs of couples and families, for outcome and evaluation studies to be conducted on the efficacy of different interventions, and to develop a pool of mentoring professionals for those providing treatment. Ongoing monitoring should be given priority to those couples or families that have the highest risk of serious violence.

4. The relationship between government and advocacy groups.

The close relationship between federal (and state) government and state domestic violence coalitions and other politically militant advocacy groups raises troubling questions about government-subsidized ideologies and interest groups. The advocacy groups should have input in shaping domestic violence policy, but not an exclusive one. The next version of the Violence Against Women Act should direct each state (or states should create their own) to develop domestic violence boards on which members of battered women's advocacy groups can fill no more than a third of the seats. Scholars, mental health professionals, criminologists, etc., should hold the remaining positions. These boards would replace the present ideologically driven state domestic violence coalitions in determining domestic violence policy, programs and funding. VAWA re-authorization language in 2005 did include a statement that funds could be used for male as well as female victims. A request by the Men's Health Network to include language changing the structure of the state advisory boards, however, was not included.

5. Research.

Same-Sex Partners—We know very little about same-sex domestic violence. The few studies that meet minimal experimental design and statistical analysis requirements suggest that the frequency is similar or possibly higher for heterosexual couples. Some metropolitan programs and shelters might be excellent sources of data for further studies. Many more surveys and research in this regard are critical.

BIP Research—As has been noted by other authors in this volume, studies by the National Institute of Justice and others have determined that traditional BIPs have minimal or no effect on recidivism. A representative sample of states that have adopted standards indicates that very few have included treatment outcome measurements as a requirement. We support the recommendations of the California Attorney General Task Force calling for *outcome measurements:* "The court and probation department in each county should immediately develop standards and procedures for collecting, measuring, and evaluating BIP enrollment rates, completion rates, and recidivism rates; the reasons for noncompletion; and judicial responses to noncompliance" (Report to California Attorney General from the Task Force on Local Criminal Justice Response to Domestic Violence, 2005, p. 79). The authors of this article suggest that measurements of victim satisfaction be added to this list of requirements.

There is also a need for research that would *compare and contrast different types of programs.* With outcome measurements in place, jurisdictions have a means to compare the efficacy of different types of programs. Research should be conducted over at least a two-year period in similar localities and should compare and contrast a traditional Duluth model type of program to an alternative program, such as the one outlined by John Hamel of the Family Violence Treatment and Education Association (Hamel, 2005a) or other alternative approach programs, such as the innovative Core Value Workshop approach developed by Stosny (2004). Standard research protocols should be developed in these studies to compare similar populations. Critical in research of BIP comparisons and treatment outcome would be a research design that differentiated levels of violence and types of offenders within BIPs.

Alternative Treatment Research—Research has already begun comparing the effectiveness of new treatment models, such as structured couples counseling, with BIP's (see Chapters 1 and 16 in this volume). Preliminary research has also been conducted comparing dyadic couples counseling with structured multicouples group (Stith, Rosen, & McCollum, 2004). More comparative studies are urgently needed to examine the effectiveness of couples counseling, family therapy, individual counseling, and restorative justice interventions.

6. Services for all.

Whether one accepts the results of the National Crime Victimization Survey (15%), the Violence Against Women Survey (36%), or the National Family Violence Survey (50%), it is clear that heterosexual men represent a significant percentage of intimate partner assault victims. It is also clear that these men are underserved in terms of services in nearly all regions of the United States with respect to outreach (public service ads, brochures), support groups, crisis lines, victim advocacy, and shelters. Lack of services for homosexual men is even more apparent. Lesbian victims also suffer from a lack of public acknowledgment of abuse, outreach services, and access to educational literature. Victims of violence within the elderly and teen populations are also underserved. Flying under the radar of most agencies, private or government, are the victims of severe sibling violence.

Moving toward a more realistic and holistic view of family conflict and violence recognizes that human beings of any race, culture, age, gender, or sexual orientation can be either the perpetrator or the victim of intimate partner violence. Such an approach does not presuppose a predilection toward violence or assume victimology based on gender, age, or race.

It is often assumed that expanding services to the underserved reduces funding for existing services to heterosexual women. There is no evidence supporting this belief simply because services for *all victims* have not been available in most regions. Agencies such as the Valley Oasis Shelter in Lancaster, California (shelter/crisis line/victim advocacy/ support groups), Peace for All in Illinois (crisis line/victim advocacy), and SAFE of New Hampshire (crisis line/victim advocacy) report no reduction in services to heterosexual women by offering services to all victims.

To accommodate and provide for underserved victims, relatively minor changes can be made within existing service agencies at very low cost. Rather than establishing agencies that serve only men, minor expansion of existing agencies could provide needed services for all victims. Support groups for male victims, teens, or the elderly can be facilitated by volunteers at no cost. Outreach brochure literature is already available at very low cost for heterosexual men, gay men, and lesbian, sibling, teen dating, and elderly family violence victims. The fact that very few agencies have availed themselves of the material is a curious tragedy and certainly not due to a lack of funds.

An official change of agency name might be necessary in order to alert all victims of the services and encourage universal access. The expense of new phone directory listings, letterheads, business cards, and so forth is minor. For example, the Women's Crisis Line in a particular locality could easily change its name to the Family Crisis Line. Additional training in areas of gender, race, ethnicity, and sexual orientation would be needed, but again costs are minimal.

Shelters—The overwhelming majority of heterosexual female victims of intimate partner violence do not seek on-site shelter even when it is available. Shelters in most areas act as a nexus for the provision of other services such as information and referral, support groups, counseling, crisis line, hotel vouchers, and victim advocacy within legal and social service systems. To raise the awareness of victims and the community at large that services are available to all victims, a change in service provider name is essential. Gender, race, ethnicity, and sexual-orientation training of staff and volunteers; purchase or creation of outreach literature; and support groups for the underserved are minimal cost expansions of existing services, with little or no reduction in services to heterosexual women. When a man needs emergency shelter, for example, hotel vouchers can be offered in partnerships with existing homeless shelters that offer other vital services for men.

Serving men who are accompanied by children is more challenging, but the hotel voucher system is still available. Coordination and cooperation with existing homeless shelters should improve the availability of accommodation for men with children. Shelters that currently serve only women can apply for additional funding to accommodate men in separate nearby facilities—as Valley Oasis currently does (chapter 26 in this volume). If this is impossible, other shelter services can be accessed at minimal shelter cost. Prescreened and qualified volunteer homes in the community could serve as temporary foster families for abused men and their children.

CONCLUSION

Although domestic violence cannot be eradicated, good policy can reduce occurrence and mitigate harm. Addressing the plight of battered women was a critical first step. A realistic and balanced view of the full scope of domestic violence, current strategies, interventions, and current remedies to meet expanding needs is the next challenge.

REFERENCES

Adams, S., & Powell, A. (1995, October 12). *The tragedies of domestic violence: A qualitative analysis of civil restraining orders in Massachusetts*. Office of the Commissioner of Probation Massachusetts Trial Court.

Altman, M. G. (1995, October 23). Litigating domestic abuse cases under Ch. 209A. *Massachusetts Lawyers Weekly*, p. B6.

Anderson, K. (2002). Perpetrator or victim? Relationships between intimate partner violence and well-being. *Journal of Marriage and the Family, 64*, 851–863.

Archer, J. (2000). Sex differences in aggression between heterosexual partners: A meta-analytic review. *Psychological Bulletin, 126*(5), 651–680.

Austin, J., & Dankwort, J. (1998, August). A review of standards for batterer intervention programs. Violence Against Women Online Resources. Retrieved August 3, 2002, from htp://www.vaw.umn.edu/Vawnet/standard.htm.

C.O. v. M. M., Supreme Judicial Court Case No. 09271 (September 8, 2004–October 6, 2004). Retrieved from http://www.fathersandfamilies.org/NEWS/C.O.V.M.M.2004-10–06.htm.

Commonwealth of Massachusetts Executive Office of Health and Human Service, Department of Public Health. (1995, March). *Massachusetts Guidelines and Standards for the Certification of Batterers' Intervention Programs*. Retrieved from http://www.biscmi.org/other_resources/docs/massachusetts.html.

Dugan, L., Nagin, D., & Rosenfeld, R. (2001). *Exposure reduction or backlash? The effect of domestic violence resources on intimate partner homicide* (NCJRS 186194 35). Retriered from http://www.ncjrs.org/pdffiles1/nij/grants/186194.pdf.

Epstein, E. (1993, June–July). Speaking the unspeakable. *Massachusetts Bar Association Newsletter, 33*, 1.

Grau, J., Fagan, J., & Wexler, S. (1984). Restraining orders for battered women: Issues of access and efficacy. *Women and Politics, 4*, 13–28.

Hamel, J. (2005a). *Gender-inclusive treatment of intimate partner abuse: A comprehensive approach*. New York: Springer.

Hamel, J. (2005b). Fixing only part of the problem: Public policy and batterer intervention. *Family Violence and Sexual Assault Bulletin, 21* (2/3), 18–27.

Magdol, L., Moffitt, T., Caspi, A., Fagan, J., & Silva, P. (1997). Gender differences in partner violence in a birth cohort of 21 year olds: Bridging the gap between clinical and epidemiological approaches. *Journal of Consulting and Clinical Psychology, 65*, 68–78.

Maxwell, C., Garner, J., & Fagan, J. (2001, July). *The effects of arrest on intimate partner violence: New evidence from the Spouse Assault Replication Program* (National Institute of Justice, NIJ 188199). Retrieved from http://www.ncjrs.org/pdffiles1/nij/188199.pdf.

Mills, L. (2003). *Insult to injury: Rethinking our responses to intimate abuse*. Princeton, NJ: Princeton University Press.

Pence, E. (1999). Some thoughts on philosophy. In M. Shepard & E. Pence (Eds.), *Coordinating community responses to domestic violence: Lessons from Duluth and beyond* (pp. 25–40). Thousand Oaks, CA: Sage.

Report to the California Attorney General from the Task Force on Local Criminal Justice Response to Domestic Violence. (2005, June). Batterer accountability, victim safety and keeping the promise. Retrieved from http://safestate.org/documents/DV_Report_AG.pdf.

Routhier, R. (2002, October 20). Hidden victims: A conference and exhibit in Portland are among events shedding light on the often taboo topic of male victims of domestic violence. *Portland (Maine) Press Herald*, p. 1G.

Sherman, L. (1992). *Policing domestic violence: Experiments and dilemmas.* New York: Free Press.

Stith, S., Rosen, K., & McCollum, E. (2004, July). Treating intimate partner violence within intact couple relationships: Outcomes of multi-couple versus individual couple therapy. *Journal of Marital and Family Therapy, 30*(6), 305–315.

Stockman, F. (2002, October 28). A search of equality: Domestic abuse groups dispute status of claims made by men. *Boston Globe,* p. B1.

Stosny, S. (2004). *Manual of the Core Value Workshop.* North Charleston, NC: Book Surge Publishing.

Straus, M., & Gelles, R. (1990). *Physical violence in American families.* New Brunswick, NJ: Transaction Publishers.

Van Wormer, K., & Bednar, S. (2002). Working with male batterers: A restorative-strengths perspective. *Families in Society: The Journal of Contemporary Human Services, Families in Society, 83*(5), 557–565.

Index

AA. *See* Alcoholics Anonymous
Abandonment, 8, 33, 38–39, 92, 131, 423
ABI. *See* Abusive Behavior Inventory
Abused Men (Cook), 314
Abuse Index Questionnaire, Revised (AI-2), 352–353
Abusive Behavior Inventory (ABI), 94, 506, 511, 514
The Abusive Personality (Dutton), 347
Ackerman Institute for the Family, Gender and Violence Project, 253, 254, 255
Adjustment and anchoring, 277
Administration of Justice, 562
Adolescent adjustment, and interparental violence, 191–192
   aggression in, 192–197, 499
   anxious-ambivalent/preoccupied attachment, 199–200
   bullying behavior in, 193

family support, importance of, 502
inner deficit, and abusive behavior, 499
insecure attachment in, 198–200, 202
internal working model, 198–199
lessons learned from, 197–203
maternal IPV *vs.* paternal IPV, 203–206
physical IPV *vs.* verbal IPV, 196–197
prevention and intervention, 207–208
research implications, future, 206–207
romantic relationships, 201–202, 206, 207
social learning theory, 194, 198
Adolescent mothers, at-risk
   future directions, 492–493

intergenerational dynamics of, 479–480

men who father babies with, 480–481

negative parent-child relationship, establishing, 481

risk factors, 477–479

therapy for, 481

See also Intervention, for adolescent mothers

Adolescent-parent violence
background and justification, 500–501

dynamics of, 541–544

family systems theory, 502–503

family therapy, 499–500

power and control in, 542–544

research, future directions of, 516

social learning theory, 501

stress theory, 501–502

See also Domestic Violence Program (Neidig and Friedman)

Advocacy movements, social, 419–422

African Americans, and DV
men, intervention for, 235–236

prevalence studies, 323–324

prevention/intervention programs, 325–327

racial oppression, 323, 324–325

SES, 324

whipping post legislation, 27

Aggression, 6
aggressors, dominant and primary, 9, 264–265

anxious-ambivalent/preoccupied attachment, and link between, 200

behaviors of, table, 509

biological sex, 146–147

bullying behavior, 193

in childhood development, 192–195

in conflict behaviors, 135–136

conjoint intervention, 364–365, 366–368

in controlling behaviors, 94–96

head injuries linked to, 150

sexual, 99–100, 101, 148, 149, 325, 326, 367, 369

substance abuse, 441–443, 444, 445–446, 450–451

typology of, 151–154

verbal, 88–89, 99

in women in shelters, research on, 152–155

See also Controlling behaviors

Aggressive-sadistic personality disorder, 34, 48, 131

AI-2. See Abuse Index Questionnaire Revised

AIDS, 312, 399, 400

Alcohol abuse. See Substance abuse

Alcoholics Anonymous (AA), 359, 440, 449, 537

Altman, Miriam, 603

Anger
attachment theory, 33

intimacy, and frustration of attachment, 38–39

personality disorders, 33–34

substance abuse, and DV, 441–446, 450–451

violence and, in physically assaultive males, 33–34

See also Anger management

Anger management
Anger Management Parenting Program (CPS), 533, 534

in child custody cases, 460–461

in interventions, evolution of, 226–227

in interventions, family, 535–537

Anger Styles Questionnaire, 262

Antelope Valley Domestic Violence Council (AVDVC), 563–566
Antisocial personality disorder, 7, 33–34, 48, 148, 234–235, 441
Antonovich, Michael, 563
Anxiety, 39, 136
    abandonment, 39, 131, 158
    attachment theory, 199–200, 202
    calming, in family therapy, 435
    in children from violence, 520–521, 551, 555
    in dating violence, 129, 131
    overcoming, 435, 546
    in therapists, 411–412, 428, 430–431, 435
    victim characteristics, 546
    withdrawal in conflict, 136
Area under the curve (AUC), 286, 289
Arrest and prosecution. See Law enforcement
Asian Americans, and DV, 331–332
    immigrants vs. refugees, 332
    prevention/intervention programs, 333–334
    rates of DV in, 332–333
Attachment theory
    abusiveness, 38–39
    anxiety, 199–200, 202
    anxious-ambivalent/preoccupied, 199–200
    in CCV, 131
    in conjoint intervention, 386–388
    in DAIP, 33, 34, 35
    disorganized, 201, 202, 206, 261, 326, 423, 424, 432
    in family violence treatment, 422–425
    fearful, 34, 38–39, 131, 158, 423, 427
    Harlow's "iron maiden" experiments, 422–423
    insecure, 199–200

preoccupied, 35, 39, 131, 158, 200, 423, 427
    rejection sensitivity, 39
Availability heuristic, 276–277
AVDVC. See Antelope Valley Domestic Violence Council

The Backlash Book: A Media and Political Guide for Battered Women's Advocates (Family Violence Prevention Fund), 310–311
B.A.L.L., 487
"Battered Child Syndrome" (Kemp, Silverman, Steele, & Silver), 420
Battered Men's Helpline (Maine), 608
Battered women's movement, 28, 349, 579, 607, 609
Batterer intervention programs (BIPs), 269, 581–583, 610, 613–614, 615
Battering, 11–12
Behaviors, table of, 509
Bent-Goodley, Tricia, 326
Bias, 277–279
Biden, Joseph, 609
BIPs. See Batterer intervention programs
Bisexuals, 94, 397, 567
Blackburn, Wayne, 137
Borderline personality disorder, 7, 33, 38, 39, 234
Boston Globe, 608
Brief Spousal Assault Form for the Evaluation of Risk (B-SAFER), 286–287
British Columbia Institute Against Family Violence, 286
Brown, Judy, 586
B-SAFER. See Brief Spousal Assault Form for the Evaluation of Risk

Building a Lasting Love intervention, 486–490
Bullying behavior, 193
Burford, Gale, 586

CAFAS. *See* Child and Adolescent Functional Assessment Scale
California Attorney General Task Force, 615
Caring for My Family, 487
CARRI. *See* Children at Risk: Resources and Intervention
CAT. *See* Controlling and Abusive Tactics Questionnaire
CBS. *See* Controlling Behaviors Scale
CBS-R. *See* Controlling Behaviors Scale-Revised
CCP. *See Construyendo Circulos de Paz*
CCV. *See* Common couple violence
Center for Social Research Abuse Index, 342, 351, 354
Characterological violence, 228, 230, 233–235, 237
Child abuse
    abusers as victims of, 7, 9
    "Battered Child Syndrome," 420
    child protection movement, 420
    DV as predictor of, 175
    emotional, defined, 87
    marital abuse as predictor of, 425–426
    movement, 422
    neurophysiological impact of, 417–418
    PTSD, 39–40
    sexual, 419, 420–421, 422, 425, 479, 582
    shaming, 39–40
    See also Family intervention, for child abuse

Child and Adolescent Functional Assessment Scale (CAFAS), 506, 511, 514
Child custody cases, disputed, 457–458
    abuse accusations, 458
    anger management groups/ classes, 460–461
    assessment, 458
    batterer intervention programs, 460
    case examples, 464–472
    categorization, of accused perpetrator, 459–460
    conditions affecting, 457
    co-parenting mediation, 461–462
    family therapy, 462–464
    high-conflict/family violence parent groups, 461
    mediators, 458
    partner violence typologies in, 156
    situational abuse, 460, 463
    substance abuse, 459, 463
    visitation, supervised therapeutic, 461
Child development, and interparental violence, 165–168
    adaptation to DV, 168–171
    age and developmental period, 181–182
    behaviors, modifying, 551–552
    bidirectional processes, underlying risks, 182–184
    big picture concepts, 558
    characteristics of children who have witnessed/experienced family violence, 550–552
    cognitive contextual framework, 172–174
    cognitive processing, and arranging thoughts, 556–558
    competency building, 554–556

disclosure, overcoming fear of, 558–559
emotional security theory, 172, 173–175, 177, 182, 183
esteem-building exercises, 553–554
family systems theory, 178–179, 182–183
gender, and risk factors, 179–181
goal planning, 552–553
interparental process models, 171–175
neurophysiological impact of, 417–418
parenting process models, 175–179
social learning theory, 172–173, 194, 198, 349, 501, 515
stress, physiological responses to, 174
trust-building, 558–559
well-being, 559–560
See also Adolescent adjustment, and interparental violence
Child Protective Services (CPS), 260, 304, 521, 533, 592, 611
Anger Management Parenting Program, 533, 534
Children at Risk: Resources and Intervention (CARRI), 492
Christians, 311
Clinical fallacy, 79, 127
Cognitive-behavioral therapy (CBT)
DAIP, 29, 30, 33, 224
marital, 366
for personality disorders, 234–235
vs. psychoeducational, 224
vs. psychotherapy, 224
for same-sex group therapy, 37, 403
Colorado Department of Probation Services, 288–289

Common couple violence (CCV), 151–152
anger, in physically assaultive males, 33–34
child custody cases, 459–460
common, 151
counseling for, 4
female potential for abuse in, 125–126
heart rate responses to, 150
individual contributing factors of, 139
injury in, 128–129
interactional studies on, 43–49
intimate terrorism in, 127–128
male potential for abuse in, 137–138
male views of, surveys on, 91
mutual, 8
New Zealand longitudinal study on, 139–140
vs. patriarchal terrorism, 43
PTSD, 39–40
situationally violent couples, 127, 228, 229, 230–233
stalking, 111
therapy/treatment for, 43, 49–52
types of, 43–45, 127–128
women in shelters, research on, 152–155
See also Intervention, for couples (conjoint); Levels-of-analysis issue, in couple violence
Communication and Conflict Management Skills in Intimate Relationships, 486–487
Communication Apprehension Inventory, 43
Community Circles of Washington County—Cottage Grove Manual, 586
Confirmatory or confirmation bias, 277–278

Conflict behaviors, 135–136
Conflict resolution, 7
Conflict Tactics Scale: Parent-Child
    Version (CTS-PC), 262, 270
Conflict Tactics Scale (CTS)
    ABI, 94, 506
    aggression, measures of, 368, 369
    CCV, interactional studies on,
        43, 44
    Dominance-Isolation subscale
        (DI), 99
    Emotional-Verbal subscale (EV),
        99
    family violence assessment, 262,
        267, 270
    Hispanic wife abuse, 328
    for male DV assessment, 313
    physical aggression scale of, 99,
        100, 369
    physical assault scale of, 68, 73
    rejection sensitivity, 133
    seriously violent items on, 129
    verbal aggression scale of, 99
Conflict Tactics Scale—Revised
    (CTS2), 5, 68, 73, 97, 262, 369,
    434
Constructing Circles of Peace. See
    Construyendo Circulos de Paz
Construyendo Circulos de Paz
    (CCP)
    applicant participation, strategies
        for, 589
    approach phases of, 586
    care communities in, 588, 590
    child or young person's view,
        presentation strategies for,
        592–593
    child participation, preparations
        for, 591, 592
    circles, 587–593
    circles, preparing for, 593–596
    consensus building, strategies for,
        595–596

danger assessment instrument,
    589–590
exclusion, reasons for, 593
family preparation section, 586
implementation of, 585
Initial Social Compact (ISC), 589
intake procedures, 587–588
maintenance, 596–597
overview of, 585–586
psychosocial assessment, 588
referral, 587
Restorative Justice Advisory
    Team (RJAT), 587, 588 593
safety monitors, 588–589, 591
support person, 589, 591, 592
victim participation, 589, 590
Controlling and Abusive Tactics
    Questionnaire (CAT), 101–102,
    262, 267, 268, 270
Controlling behaviors
    vs. abusive, 90
    acts of, 89
    in bisexuals, 94
    clinical intervention, 103
    conflict theories of, 92–93
    consequences of, 90
    degrees of, 89
    developmental theories of, 91–92
    evolutionary theories of, 93–94
    feminist theories of, 90–91
    isolation in, 94, 95, 96, 97,
        99–101
    mate guarding, 93
    of patriarchal terrorist, 152
    physical aggression, research on,
        94–98
    protest behavior, 92
    research, future, 102
    scales that measure, 98–102
    terminology of, 87–90
Controlling Behaviors Scale (CBS),
    101
Core Value Workshop, 615

CPS. *See* Child Protective Services
Criticism, handling, 538
Crouch, Harry, 608
CTS. *See* Conflict Tactics Scale
CTS-PC. *See* Conflict Tactics Scale:
    Parent-Child Version
CTS2S. *See* Conflict Tactics Scale—
    Revised

DA. *See* Danger Assessment
DAIP. *See* Duluth Domestic Abuse
    Intervention Project
Danger Assessment (DA), 284,
    287–288, 347
DAS. *See* Dyadic Adjustment Scale
Dating violence
    conclusions, from previous stud-
        ies, 64–65, 79–80
    data analysis, 69–70
    data collection, 65–67
    Dominance scale, 79, 80
    information on, relevance of, 62
    limitations of, 78–79
    marginally significant interac-
        tions, 77
    minor assaults, 70–71, 73–74,
        77–78
    policy and practice, implications
        of, 80–82
    Posttraumatic Stress Symptoms,
        77, 78
    prevalence rates, 70, 73
    Relationship Conflict, 77, 78
    respondents, characteristics and
        relationships of, 66–68
    risk factor variables, measures of,
        68–69
    sample, 65
    scarcity of previous studies,
        62–63
    SES, measurement of, 69
    severe assaults, 72–73, 74–75, 78
    Sexual Abuse History, 76, 78

significant interactions, 76
similar findings in, 63–64
Social Desirability scale, 69
specific gender differences and
    similarities, 64
Substance Abuse, 76, 78
Violence Approval, 76, 78
See also Personal and
    Relationships Profile (PRP)
"Dear Abby," 608
Decision Making in Abusive
    Relationships Interview (DIARI),
    295
Decision theory, 278–279
Demand/withdraw communication,
    134–135
Dependency, 7, 42, 131
Depression, 118, 546
Deschner, Fran, 249
*Diagnostic and Statistical Manual of
    Mental Disorders*, 218, 259, 571
Diagnostic overshadowing, 278
DIARI. *See* Decision Making in
    Abusive Relationships Interview
Domestic Abuse Helpline for Men
    and Women, 314
Domestic Abuse Intervention
    Project, 101
Domestic Conflict Containment
    Program, 49
Domestic Violence Awareness
    Month, 562
Domestic violence (DV)
    causes of, and similarities across
        genders, 5–7
    characterological form of, 228,
        230, 233–235
    communication skills, 229
    criminal justice response to,
        344–346
    emotional consequences for, 478
    emotions in, role of, 226–227
    financial consequences of, 478

gender-inclusive approach,
256–258
hotline, first, 562
incidence and prevalence rates,
215
intimate partner violence, as gender inclusive term for, 477
labeling, 9
as major health problem (U.S.
surgeon general), 563
mutual nature of, 479
policy, and relationship between
government and advocacy
groups, 614–615
recidivism rates, 36–37, 51, 216
research, future, 615–616
risk factors for, 7–8, 478
services for all, 616–617
situational, 228, 229, 230–233,
460, 463
treatment approaches to,
346–349
See also Partner violence typologies
Domestic Violence Movement, 312,
317, 421–422, 425, 564
Domestic Violence Program (Neidig
and Friedman), 503–504
areas of change, discussion on,
514–515
behaviors, table of, 509
closure session, 510–511
conclusions, discussion on,
511–512, 514
Consumer Satisfaction Survey,
510, 516
group sessions, 507–510
intake procedures, 507
principles of, 508
results of, 511
subjects of, criteria for, 504–505
variables, dependent, 506–507
variables, independent, 505–506

Domestic Violence Screening
Inventory (DVSI), 286, 288–289,
347
Domestic Violence Threat
Containment Intensive Treatment
Program, 351, 354
Dual perpetrator model, 267–269
Duluth Domestic Abuse Intervention
Project (DAIP), 27–28, 605, 606,
607
anger and violence, 33–34
attachment theory in, 33, 34, 35
CBT, 29, 30, 33
vs. cognitive-behavioral interventions, 224
failure of, empirical reasons for,
220–222
failure of, theoretical reasons for,
219–220
vs. feminist psychoeducational
model, 219
objective of, 28
perpetrator subtypes, 34–35
power and control wheel of,
218
psychological problems, perspective on, 29
recidivism, impact on, 219
theoretical problem with, 30–33
therapeutic problem with, 28–30
treatment goals of, 218
treatment outcome studies of,
35–37, 219
treatment providers, and lack of
training, 32–33
DV. See Domestic violence
DVSI. See Domestic Violence
Screening Inventory
Dyadic Adjustment Scale (DAS), 43,
44, 370

EAP. See Employee Assistance
Program

EARL-20B. *See* Early Assessment
    Risk List for Boys, Version 2
Early Assessment Risk List for Boys,
    Version 2 (EARL-20B), 282
East Texas Crisis Center, 256
Emotional abuse, 9, 10–11, 12, 100,
    262, 264, 329, 369–370
Emotional security theory, 172,
    173–175, 177, 182, 183
Employee Assistance Program
    (EAP), 303, 359
"Exposure Reduction or Backlash?
    The Effect of Domestic Violence
    Resources on Intimate Partner
    Homicide" (NIJ report), 604
Eye contact, 547–548

*Families in Society: The Journal of
    Contemporary Human Services*
    (Van Wormer & Bednar), 605
Family dysfunction, 269–271
Family group counseling (FGC),
    580–581, 584, 585, 586
Family interventions, for child abuse
    anger management, 535–537
    case example, 534, 537
    criticism, handling, 538–539
    High Conflict Family Violence
        Parent Group, 521–533
    Peace Creations, 533–534, 537,
        539
    QUEST©, 539
Family Preservation, 487
Family Research Laboratory, Univer-
    sity of New Hampshire, 313
Family systems theory
    in adolescent-parent violence,
        502–503
    boundaries, 502–503
    boundary breaches, 502
    child development, and inter-
        parental violence, 165–168,
        178–179, 182–183

couples therapy, 49
    effects of marital violence on, 17
    exploring, for family violence
        assessment, 260–262
    gender-inclusive family interven-
        tions, 260–262
    hierarchy, 503
    objections to, 251–252
    power struggle, 515
    variability, 502
    violence, impact on, 417–419
Family therapy, 4, 256–257
    for adolescent mothers, at-risk,
        479, 481
    for adolescent-parent violence,
        499–500
    advantages of, 427–428
    anxiety, calming, 435
    attachment bonds, healing of,
        432
    attachment theory, 422–425, 426
    for child custody cases, 462–464
    conducting, preconditions for,
        256–257
    emotional experiences, provisions
        for corrective, 431–432
    family-systems approach to, 422
    FGC, 580–581, 584, 585, 586
    gender-inclusive approach,
        256–258
    high conflict, and child custody
        cases, 461
    making amends, components of,
        432
    safety, balancing, 426–427
    therapist's stance in, 428–432
    at Valley Oasis shelter, 572
    victim-perpetrator dyad, 433–434
Family violence
    anger management, 535–537
    case example, 537, 539
    child abuse, 425–426, 519–521
    criticism, handling, 538

drop outs, from treatment, 434
family system, impact on,
    417–419
multigenerational abuse, 433
recognition and understanding of,
    evolving, 608–609
response to, social advocacy
    movements, 419–422
SES, 601
stress, 521
See also High Conflict Family
    Violence Parent Group
Family Violence and Sexual Assault
    Institute, 608
Family Violence Diversion Network,
    342
Family Violence Prevention and
    Services Act, 563
Family Violence Prevention Fund,
    310–311
Family Violence Prevention Program
    (FVPP), 505
Family Violence Treatment and
    Education Association, 615
Farrell, Warren, 310
Fear, 547
Female privilege, 13, 308
Female victims
    battered woman syndrome, 47,
        147
    battered women's movement, 28,
        349, 579, 607, 609
    concepts surrounding, 145
    victim blaming, 35, 41, 145, 147,
        236
Female violence, 602
    as dominant aggressors, 9
    personality disorders in, 42
    risk factors for, 7
    treatment of, 41–43
    typology of, 133–134,
        148–149
    violence in, 28, 41, 125–126

Femicide, 284, 285, 287, 291
    See also Intimate partner homi-
        cide
Feminist theory, 37, 93, 137–138
FGC. See Family group counseling
First Day of Unity, 162
Fluoxetine, 235
Freud, Sigmund, 421
Friedman, D.H., 249–250, 503–504
FVPP. See Family Violence
    Prevention Program

Gallup Survey, 91
Gay and lesbian couples, and DV, 5
    controlling behaviors in, 91, 94
    gay male couples, issues specific
        to, 399–400
    homophobia, 398–399
    lesbian couples, issues specific to,
        400–401
    vs. male patriarchy, 137
    monogamy in vs. heterosexual
        couples, 400
    overview of, 397–399
    rates of, compared to hetero-
        sexual, 30
    research, 615
    studies on, 397–398
    support resources available to,
        paucity of, 398
    treatment of, 5, 402–404,
        410–412
Geffner, Robert, 256
Gender and Violence Project,
    Ackerman Institute for the
    Family, 253, 254, 255
Gender feminist, 310, 311, 312,
    313
Gender-Inclusive Treatment of
    Intimate Partner Abuse (Hamel),
    257
Gender politics, 311–313
General practitioner (GP), 388–389

General Social Survey on
Victimization, 195
Goldner, Virginia, 254
Goodwill Toward Men (Kammer),
316
Government, and advocacy groups,
614–615
GP. *See* General practitioner
Green, Stanley, 608
Group therapy, 349–359
Abuse Index Questionnaire,
Revised, 352–353
assessment, 351–254
case examples, 356–359
complaints about intimate partners, handling, 356
court-ordered, resentment
against, 355
models for, 349
reassault rates, 350
responsibility, promoting,
354–355
same-sex, 349, 350
substance abuse, 350–351
therapeutic alliance in, 354
at Valley Oasis shelter, 572

Hamel, John, 308–309, 521–522, 615
Handbook of Anger Management
(Potter-Efron), 257
Hare Psychopathy Checklist—
Revised (PCL-R), 291–292
Harlow, Harry, 422
Hatch, Orin, 609
Haven House (Pasadena,
California), 562
HCR-20: Assessing Risk for
Violence, 282, 283, 290–291
Helplessness, 546
Heuristics, 276–277, 278–279
*Hidden Victims: Children of
Domestic Violence* (Lifetime
Television), 572

High Conflict Family Violence
Parent Group, 521–533
abuse in childhood of origin, 531
anger, misuse of, 531
assessment process of, 522,
523–524
candidates for, 521–522
case example, 527, 529–530, 533
CPS cases, 521, 526
curriculum, 525–526
healthy families checklist,
532–534
misbehavior goals, 528
sessions of, 522, 526
whole-system approach of, 527
Hindsight bias, 278
Hispanics/Latinos, and DV,
327–331
Catholics, 328, 331
cultural values, 327–328
DV rates, 328–329
husband abuse, 329
interventions, 330–331
spousal abuse, predictors of,
329–330
The Hitting Habit (Deschner), 249
HIV, 399, 400
Hoff-Sommers, Christina, 310, 311
Homicide. *See* Intimate partner
homicide

Immigration and Naturalization
Service, 330
Impass of Divorce (Johnston &
Campbell), 462
Impulse control, 548–549
Incompetence, feelings of, 547
Index of Spouse Abuse, 101
Insecure attachment, 199–200
Institute for Teaching and Research
on Women, 351
Integrative behavior couples therapy,
366

Interparental violence (IPV). *See* Adolescent adjustment, and interparental violence; Child development, and interparental violence

Interpersonal partner violence (IPV), 29, 32, 42

Intervention
advocacy approach to, 252–253
for African Americans, 325–327
for Asian Americans, 333–334
assessment for, unbiased basis of, 3–4
BIPs, 581–583
Building a Lasting Love, 486–490
certification guidelines for, 606–607
in child custody cases, 460
counseling, 605–608
culturally focused, 235–236
effectiveness of, studies on, 225–226
family dysfunction, gender-inclusive, 269–271
for Hispanics/Latinos, 330–331
for male violence and victims, 607–608
"Mending the Sacred Hoops," 323
for Native American Indians, 322–323
nested ecological model of, 30, 130
for personality disorders, 234–235
political obstacles, 221–222
psychoeducational, 27, 32, 36, 218–219, 581, 582 (*see also* Duluth Domestic Abuse Intervention Project)
psychotherapeutic models of, 29
sociopolitical/pro-feminist, 156
systemic, 9–10
in U.K., 382

for victim-perpetrator dyad, 433–435
See also Intervention, court-ordered; Intervention, evolution of; Intervention, for adolescent mothers; Intervention, for couples (conjoint); Intervention, gender-inclusive family

Intervention, court-ordered
approaches to, 606–607, 613–614
clinical perspective, developing, 341–344
corollary, 345–346
criminal justice response to, 344–346
Family Violence Diversion Network Abuse Reports, 343
group treatment, 349–359
mediation and crisis intervention, 345
for prisoner rehabilitation, 216–217
psychotherapy, court mandated *vs.* nonmandated, 223

Intervention, evolution of, 215–217
anger management, 226–227
for characterological violence, 233–235
client motivation, and effective psychotherapy, 223–224
in couples therapy, 228–230
for cultural groups, 235–236
feminist psychoeducational model *vs.* Duluth model, 219
grassroots movement, 217–219
group *vs.* individualized, 224–225
motivational interviewing techniques, 225
psychoeducational *vs.* cognitive-behavioral, 224

relationship enhancement,
    225–226
shame, and other primary emo-
    tions, 227
for situational violence, 231–233
therapeutic alliance, and effective
    psychotherapy, 222–223
for women arrested for DV,
    236–237
Intervention, for adolescent mothers
Building a Lasting Love, 486–490
CARRI program, 492
couples-based skill-building, 486
effectiveness of, 486, 489
future directions, 492–493
for high-risk of child abuse,
    490–491
intimate partner relationship,
    485–486, 490–491
parenting, 482–485
readiness to change, 489
sessions of, four, 487–489
Intervention, for couples (conjoint)
aggression, 364–365, 366–368
arguments for use of, 366–368
attachment theory, 386–388
bias against, 228
candidates for, 363–365,
    369–370
caring days in, 376
case study, 388–395
collaboration, 385–386
communication exercises, 237,
    376–377
effectiveness, outcome studies on,
    365–366
family backgrounds, 408–409
follow-up, 377
goals and methods of, 373–374
guidelines for, 254–255
hope, establishing, 374–375
interacting styles of partners,
    origin of, 372–373

intimacy and fear, 386–388
maintaining change, 377
model for, 370
no-violence contract, 383, 384
overview of, 370–371
positive interchanges, increasing,
    376
Reading Safer Families project,
    381–383
recidivism rates, 365–366
responsibility, assessing, 384–385
risk management and assessment,
    383–384
safety issues, 267, 402, 403,
    407–408
same-sex, 37, 402–404, 410–412
shadowboxing, 404
skill-building, 486
stable third in, 383
therapeutic bond, establishing,
    371–372
time-outs, teaching, 375–376
Intervention, gender-inclusive family
for adolescent mothers, 479
advocacy approach to, 252–253
assessments, family violence,
    258–260
dual perpetrator model, 267–269
engagement and joining process,
    263
family dysfunction, 269–271
family system, exploring,
    260–262
hybrid approaches to, 253–256
models of co-occurring spousal
    and child abuse, 264
patriarchal paradigm, 247–248
perpetrator and victim, distinc-
    tions between, 265
primary aggressor assessment,
    responsibility, empowerment,
    262–265
research on, 256–258

systems theories, objections to, 251–252
theorists, of early systems theories, 248–251
Intimate partner homicide, 10, 284, 319, 604
See also Femicide
Intimate partner violence (IPV). *See* Domestic violence
Intimate terrorism, 11–12, 113, 127–128, 154–155
IPV. *See* Interparental violence; Interpersonal partner violence; Intimate partner violence
Isolation, in controlling behaviors, 94, 95, 96, 97, 99–101
IT. *See* Intimate terrorism

Jane Doe, Inc., 608
Jealousy, 7
Johnson, Michael, 257

Kammer, Jack, 316
Kuhn, Thomas S., 341, 440

Lane, G., 249
L.A.S.T.ing and loving intimate relationships, 488
Latinos. *See* Hispanics/Latinos
Law enforcement, 609–610
    arrest and prosecution recommendations, 609–610
    assessment, mandatory, 612–613
    civil rights issues, 602
    DV intervention, 344–346
    initial response assessment team, 610–611
    for male victims of violence, 314–315
    mandatory arrest law, gender-biased application of, 602–603

Native American Indians, 322–323
no-drop prosecution policies, 603
policy implementation, 294
restraining orders/orders of protection, 603–604, 611–612
sex role stereotyping by, 399
state legislation in domestic violence cases, 562–563
treatment, court ordered, 606–607, 613–614
in U.K., 382
Valley Oasis referrals, 565
See also Intervention, court-ordered; Restorative justice
Lesbian couples. *See* Gay and lesbian couples, and DV
Level of Service Inventory—Revised (LSI-R), 290
Levels-of-analysis issue, in couple violence, 129–130
    conflict behavior, 135–136
    demand/withdraw communication, 134–135
    dyadic factors, 134
    individual-level issues, 130
    men, 130–133
    societal level issues, 137
    women, 133–134
Lithium, 235, 556
Los Angeles County Board of Supervisors, 563
Los Angeles Gay and Lesbian STOP Partner Abuse Program, 612
LSI-R. *See* Level of Service Inventory—Revised
Luther Child Center, 425

MacLeod, Susan, 586
Madanes, Chloe, 250–251
Mad at mom syndrome (MAM), 473

MAI. *See* Siegel Multidimensional Anger Inventory

Male dominance, 5–6, 80–81, 137
  patriarchal dominance theory, 62, 81

Male privilege, 28–29, 34, 35, 95, 130, 308, 342, 440, 441, 582

Male victims, 303–304
  addressing the problem of, 304–306
  emotions, expressing and suppressing, 307, 315
  feminism, 308–311
  gender politics, 311–313
  patriarchy, 306–308
  statistics, 304–305
  treatments for, 313–317
  wimp factor, 306, 307, 308, 313–314, 315

Male violence
  abuse potential of, 137–138
  as dominant aggressors, 9
  male privilege, social beliefs of, 28, 29
  rejection hypersensitivity of, 131–133
  survey rates on, and inhibition of respondents, 4–5
  typologies of violent men, 130–133, 147–148, 448

MAM. *See* Mad at mom syndrome

Manual for the Structured Assessment of Violence Risk in Youth (SAVRY), 282

Margolin, Gayla, 43

Marital Interaction Coding Scheme (MICS), 46

Marital rape exemption (Nebraska), 563

Marlowe-Crowne Social Desirability Scale, 69

Masson, Jeffrey, 42

Mate guarding, 93

Mate value, 93–94

MATTERS program, 255, 262

MCMI. *See* Millon Clinical Multiaxial Inventory

Measure of Wife Abuse, 100

Meltdowns, 549

"Mending the Sacred Hoops," 323

Men Don't Tell (CBS movie), 306

Mental Disorders of the New Millennium (Dalpiaz), 546

Mexican Americans, 91, 97, 328–329

Michigan Governor's Task Force, 32

MICS. *See* Marital Interaction Coding Scheme

Millon Clinical Multiaxial Inventory (MCMI), 42, 48

Mills, Linda, 585

Milwaukee Task Force on Battered Women, 562

Minority groups, and DV
  African Americans, 323–327
  Asian Americans, 331–335
  Hispanics/Latinos, 327–331
  Native American Indians, 320–323
  statistics on, 319–320
  See also individual group listings

Mormons, 101

Multi Health Systems, 286

Mutual abuse, 159, 275, 315, 602, 608, 612

Mutual violent control (MVC), 154, 155

MVC. *See* Mutual violent control

Narcissistic personality disorder, 7

National Alcohol and Family Violence Survey, 91

National Coalition Against Domestic Violence, 562

National Coalition of Free Men, 608

National Crime Prevention Council, 607

National Crime Victimization Survey (NCVS), 248, 305, 616

National Domestic Violence hotlines, 119

National Family Violence Resurvey (NFVR), 321

National Family Violence Survey (NFVS), 8, 80, 91, 152–153, 248, 306, 329, 342, 368, 425, 519

National Institute of Justice (NIJ), 109, 350, 604

National Institute of Mental Health, 234

National Organization for Women, 310, 562

National Science Foundation, 596

National Study of Couples, 329

National Survey of Families and Households, 324

National Violence Against Women Survey (NVAW), 10, 42, 111, 116, 119, 154, 320, 321, 328, 332, 616

Native American Indians, and DV, 320–323
alcohol abuse, 322
European settlers, effect on, 321
interventions and treatments, 322–323
rates of DV, 321–322

NCVS. See National Crime Victimization Survey

Nebraska, marital rape exemption, 563

Negative Intentions Questionnaire, 133

Neidig, P. H., 249–250, 503–504

New York Society, 422

NFVR. See National Family Violence Resurvey

NFVS. See National Family Violence Survey

NIJ. See National Institute of Justice

Nurse Home Visitation Program Trials, 483

NVAW. See National Violence Against Women (NVAW) Survey

ODARA. See Ontario Domestic Assault Risk Assessment

Oedipal theory (Freud), 421

Ohio Department of Rehabilitation and Corrections, 539

Ontario Domestic Assault Risk Assessment (ODARA), 287

Orders of protection, 603–604, 611–612

PACT. See Physical Aggression Couples Treatment

Partner violence typologies
behavioral typologies, 150–157
biological factors, 150
biological sex, 146–147
child custody disputes, 156
clinical implications, 157–159
psychopathology, 147–149
unitary theory and research, 145–146
women in shelters, research on, 152–155

Passive-aggressive personality disorder, 34, 550

PCL-R. See Hare Psychopathy Checklist—Revised

PCL:SV. See Psychopathy Checklist: Screening Version

PCW. See Power and control wheel

Peace Creations, 533–534, 537, 539

Peace for All, 616

Pennell, Joan, 586

Pennsylvania Coalition Against Domestic Violence, 347

Perilla, Julia, 331
Personal and Relationships Profile (PRP)
dating violence, risk factor research data collection, 68–69
minor violence probabilities, variables of, 74
personal characteristic scales of, 69
relationship characteristic scales of, 69
severe violence probabilities, variables of, 74–75
Social Desirability scale of, 69
variables measured by, 69
Personality disorders
abusiveness, 38
aggressive-sadistic, 34, 48, 131
anger, 33–34
antisocial, 7, 33–34, 48, 148, 234–235, 441
borderline personality disorder, 7, 33
CBT for, 234–235
fearful attachment, 39
in female violence, 42
intervention, 234–235
narcissistic, 7
passive-aggressive, 34, 550
Physical Aggression Couples Treatment (PACT), 49
Pizzey, Erin, 421, 562
PMWI. See Psychological Maltreatment of Women Inventory
Politics, gender, 311–313
Posttraumatic stress disorder (PTSD), 39–40, 118–119
Power and control wheel (PCW), 28, 95, 101, 218, 308, 349
Premarital Interpersonal Choices, 487

PREP. See Prevention and Relationship Enhancement Program
President's Commission on Law Enforcement, 562
Prevention and Relationship Enhancement Program (PREP), 486, 487
Protest behavior, 92
PRP. See Personal and Relationships Profile
Psychological abuse, 87–88, 98–99
Psychological Maltreatment of Women Inventory (PMWI), 94, 95–96, 98–100
Psychopathology, 147–149, 459
Psychopathy Checklist: Screening Version (PCL:SV), 291–292
Psychotherapy, 216
client motivation, and success of, 223
vs. cognitive-behavioral interventions, 224
confrontational stance of therapist in, 224
court mandated vs. nonmandated, 223
evolution of, 217
flight into process, 222
group, and efficacy of, 224–225
individual, motivation interventions in, 225
PTSD. See Posttraumatic stress disorder

Quality of Marriage Index, 370
QUEST©, 539

Rape, 11
Reading Safer Families project, 381–383
Regressive behavior, 549
Rejection sensitivity, 39, 131–133

Rejection Sensitivity Questionnaire, 133

Relationship Attribution Measure, 133

Representativeness heuristic, 277

Representative sample fallacy, 79, 127, 152

Response biases, 278

Restorative justice (RJ), 4, 579–580
  BIPs, 581–583
  empowerment, 580, 584, 585
  FGC, 580–581, 584, 585, 586
  models of, 580–581
  principle of, 580
  proponents and critics of, 581, 583–585
  safety issues, 581–583, 584
  satisfaction/participation rates, of victims, 585
  See also Construyendo Circulos de Paz

Restraining orders, 603–604, 611–612

Risk assessments, 275–276
  actuarial vs. clinical approach, 279–281
  adjustment and anchoring, 277
  for adolescent mothers, 477–479
  assessment citation method, 611
  clinical implications, 292–294
  in conjoint intervention, 383–384
  decision-making process of, 276–280
  defined, 347
  initial response assessment team, 610–611
  instruments for, 285–292, 347, 348
  mandatory, proposed, 612–613
  monitoring of intimate partner, 348
  no-violence contract, 383, 384
  policy implications, 294–295

poverty, 478, 479, 482, 493
  responsibility, assessing, 384–385
  in same-sex couples, 402
  SPJ model, 281–283
  substance abuse, 446
  for treatment paths, 347–349
  validity/reliability of, 348
  victims' perception of abusers' risk, accuracy of, 284–285

Risk for Sexual Violence Protocol, 282–283

RJ. See Restorative justice

Russell, T., 249

SAFE. See Stop Abuse for Everyone

Sally Jessie Raphael (television show), 314–315

San Diego Domestic Violence Council, 608

Santa Rita County Jail (California), 539

SARA. See Spousal Assault Risk Assessment Guide

SAVRY. See Manual for the Structured Assessment of Violence Risk in Youth

Scannell, Nancy, 608

SCOPE model (Skills, Choices, Old Baggage, interaction patterns), 488

Scream Quietly or the Neighbors Will Hear (Pizzey), 562

Seduction theory (Freud), 421

Self-defense, 8–9

Self-image, 546

Self-report questionnaires, 43

Separation assault. See Stalking

SES. See Socioeconomic status

Sexual abuse
  child, 419, 420–421, 422, 425, 479, 582
  in dating violence, 69, 76, 78, 101
  posttraumatic, 133

Sexual Violence Risk—20 (SVR-20), 282
Shadowboxing, 404
Shaming, 39–40, 227
Shelters, 561–562, 617
    creation of, 421
    hotel voucher system, 617
    research on CCV, and women in, 152–155
    shelter movement, 14, 217, 221, 236, 247, 312, 342, 562–563, 569
    See also Valley Oasis shelter
Short-Term Assessment of Risk and Treatability (START), 283
Siegel Multidimensional Anger Inventory (MAI), 507, 511, 514
Silent Witness vigils, 608
Situational violence, 228, 229, 230–233, 460, 463
Skills Training Manual for Treating Borderline Personality Disorder (Linehan), 487
Social learning theory, 172–173, 194, 198, 349, 501, 515
Social skills, 547
Socioeconomic status (SES), 69, 70, 320, 324, 328, 601
SPJ model. *See* Structured professional judgment
Spousal Assault Risk Assessment Guide (SARA), 283, 285–287, 347
Spouse Abuse: A Treatment Program for Couples, 486
Spouse Abuse (Neidig & Friedman), 249–250
Spouse Specific Assertiveness Scale, 43
Stages-of-change model, 223
Stalking
    breakup stalking, 110–113
    clinical implications of, 118–120

courtship stalking, in relation to breakup stalking, 110, 113–116
    defined, 109–111
    gender in, and partner violence, 116–118
    intimate terrorism, 113
    motivating factors for, 111–112
    predictability of, 113, 114–115
    separation assault, 112
    types of, 110–111
    violent forms of, 111
START. *See* Short-Term Assessment of Risk and Treatability
Startle response, 548
State-Trait Anger Expression Inventory-2 (STAXI-2), 452
STAXI-2. *See* State-Trait Anger Expression Inventory-2
Stony Brook Treatment Project, 49
Stop Abuse for Everyone (SAFE), 607–608
STOP Violence Against Women, 322, 616
Straus, Murray, 313
Stressors, situational, 7
Stress theory, 520–521
Structured professional judgment (SPJ), 282–283, 285, 290, 292, 295
The Structure of Scientific Revolutions (Kuhn), 341
Studies, interactional, 43–49
Substance abuse, and DV, 7, 437, 602
    abusers, and types of, 447–449
    addressing the issue, common messages, 439
    anger/ aggression, 441–446, 450–451
    assessment, 441–443, 449–451
    binge drinking, and violence, 80
    case studies, 451–455

child custody cases, 459, 463
co-occurrence, examples of,
    438–439
dating violence, gender interac-
    tions, 76
group treatment, 350–351
in Hispanic/Latinos, 330
increased risks of, 446
interactive effects, 442–443
interconnections, 438–439
in Native American Indians, 322
negativity levels, 48
paradigms, 439–441
research correlations, 443–444,
    445–447
therapeutic approaches, 445–446
Suicide, 42, 288, 325, 348, 426,
    464, 574
Surveys, credibility of, 4–5
Survivors of Stalking Web site, 119
SVR-20. See Sexual Violence Risk-
    20
Systems theory
    family, 178–179, 182–183, 349,
        502–503, 515
    feedback, 249, 252
    in intervention guidelines, 607
    language of, 251, 252
    objections to, 251–252
    theorists, early, 250–251

Task Force on Family Violence, 563
Terrorism
    intimate, 11–12, 113, 127–128,
        154
    patriarchal, 43, 96, 151–152, 154
Therapeutic alliances, 31–32
    in conjoint therapy, 371–372
    defined, 31
    developing, 31–32
    in group therapy, 354
    triangulation, 372
    types of, 31

Therapists
    anxiety in, 411–412, 428,
        430–431, 435
    supervised visitation, and court
        custody cases, 461
    See also Therapeutic alliances
Therapy
    for adolescent mothers, at-risk,
        481
    blended behavioral, 40
    for CCV, 49–52
    conjoint, 49–52, 237, 254–255,
        267, 363–365, 402, 407, 427
    gender inclusive, 479
    individual, evolution of, 227–228
    integrative behavior couples,
        366
    reconstructive, 253–254
    See also Group therapy;
        Psychotherapy
Trauma
    childhood, 39–40
    symptomology of, 9, 15, 38, 40,
        133
    See also Posttraumatic stress
        disorder
Treatment, for same-sex couples,
    402–404
    aspects of, 410–412
    assessment, 401–402, 404–407
    case example, 404–413
    family background, 408–409
    safety planning, 407–408
Treatment approaches, 43, 157–159,
    346–349
    alternative treatment research,
        615–616
    for CCV, 43
    court-ordered, 216, 346–349,
        613–614
    determining, through risk assess-
        ment, 347–349
    for female batterers, 41–43

for gay and lesbian couples of
DV, 5, 402–404, 410–412
gender-inclusive family, 265–268
individualized, 4
for male victims, 159, 313–317
options, recommended, 613–614
See also Treatment, for same-sex
couples
Triangulation, 372
Tribal Court Bench Book, 322
Tubman Family Alliance, 586

Unemployment (as risk factor), 7
United Kingdom, zero-tolerance
campaign, 382
University of Massachusetts, treat-
ment program for women, 42
University of New Hampshire,
Family Research Laboratory,
313
University of Washington, 45, 46
U.S. Census, 324
U.S. Department of Justice, 319,
321, 322, 329
U.S. Navy recruits, controlling
behaviors of, 97
U.S. 1985 National Survey, 34

Valley Oasis shelter
advocates of domestic violence,
and responses from, 566–567
Children's Services programs,
568, 570
clinical services, and case
examples of, 571–575
coed model of, and acceptance of
men, 564–565
family therapy, 572
48-hour "quiet time," 569
future of, 576–577
goals of clients, 570
group therapy in, 569, 571
intake procedures, 569, 571

law enforcement cooperation
with, 565–566
origins of, 563–564
postdischarge services of,
575–576
reputation of, 563
safety concerns, 570
safety planning the client home,
576
success of, and agency's coed
approach, 567–568
victims and families, responses
from, 567–568
VAWA. *See* Violence Against Women
Act
Verbal abuse, 17, 100, 134, 264
Victim blaming, 35, 41, 145, 147,
236
Victimization, disclosing, 4–5
Victims, characteristics of, 545–546
anxiety, 546
in children, 550–552
eye contact, poor, 547–548
fear, 547
helplessness, 546
impulse control, 548–549
incompetence, feelings of, 547
meltdowns, 549
passive or passive-aggressive
behavior, 550
poor self-image, 546
protective factors, inadequate,
548
regressive behavior, 549
social skills, poor, 547
startle response, overactive, 548
Vienna Medical Society, 421
Violence, common couple. *See*
Common couple violence
Violence, defined, 564
Violence Against Indian Women, 322
Violence Against Women Act
(VAWA), 81, 563, 604

Violence Risk Appraisal Guide
(VRAG), 280, 291
The Violent Couple (Stacey,
Hazlewood, & Shupe), 341
Violent resistance (VR), 154,
155
"Violent Touch: Breaking Through
the Stereotype" (Fontes), 305
VR. *See* Violent resistance
VRAG. *See* Violence Risk Appraisal
Guide

Whipping post legislation, 27
Who Stole Feminism (Hoff-
Sommers), 310
Women's Advocates (St. Paul,
Minnesota), 562
Women's Experience with Battering
Scale, 100

Young, Cathy, 310, 311

Zero-tolerance campaign (U.K.), 382